Beginning iPhone Development with Swift 3

Exploring the iOS SDK

Third Edition

Molly Maskrey

Kim Topley

David Mark

Fredrik Olsson

Jeff Lamarche

Apress®

Beginning iPhone Development with Swift 3: Exploring the iOS SDK

Molly Maskrey
Parker, Colorado, USA

Kim Topley
New York, USA

David Mark
Arlington, Virginia, USA

Fredrik Olsson
Stockholm, Sweden

Jeff Lamarche
New Hartford, New York, USA

ISBN-13 (pbk): 978-1-4842-2222-5   ISBN-13 (electronic): 978-1-4842-2223-2
DOI 10.1007/978-1-4842-2223-2

Library of Congress Control Number: 2016959268

Managing Director: Welmoed Spahr
Lead Editor: Aaron Black
Technical Reviewer: Bruce Wade
Editorial Board: Steve Anglin, Pramila Balen, Louise Corrigan, James DeWolf, Jonathan Gennick,
     Robert Hutchinson, Celestin Suresh John, Nikhil Karkal, Michelle Lowman, James Markham,
     Susan McDermott, Matthew Moodie, Jeffrey Pepper, Douglas Pundick, Ben Renow-Clarke,
     Gwenan Spearing
Coordinating Editor: Jessica Vakili
Copy Editor: Kim Burton-Weisman
Compositor: SPi Global
Indexer: SPi Global

Distributed to the book trade worldwide by Springer Science+Business Media New York, 233 Spring Street, 6th Floor, New York, NY 10013. Phone 1-800-SPRINGER, fax (201) 348-4505, e-mail orders-ny@springer-sbm.com, or visit www.springer.com. Apress Media, LLC is a California LLC and the sole member (owner) is Springer Science + Business Media Finance Inc (SSBM Finance Inc). SSBM Finance Inc is a Delaware corporation.

For information on translations, please e-mail rights@apress.com, or visit www.apress.com.

Apress and friends of ED books may be purchased in bulk for academic, corporate, or promotional use. eBook versions and licenses are also available for most titles. For more information, reference our Special Bulk Sales–eBook Licensing web page at www.apress.com/bulk-sales.

Any source code or other supplementary materials referenced by the author in this text is available to readers at www.apress.com. For detailed information about how to locate your book's source code, go to www.apress.com/source-code/.

Printed on acid-free paper

I feel incredibly fortunate to have been given the chance to write this revision. It was the very first version, years ago, that launched me toward developing for iOS. To that end, I want to thank the special people in my life that deserve much credit to bringing this to fruition.

First, to Chana, who was there with me for probably 95% of the writing, keeping my spirits up—especially on those days when I didn't think I could go on. She went from someone I met at "work" to one of the closest friends I've ever had. Every day I feel like she was a gift to raise my quality of life. I will be there for her whenever she needs me.

To my BFF Jessica (Goldi) for nearly two years now. She stood with me as my maid of honor and knows when I need her and is always there for me as I have been and will be for her. We drink together, dance together, crash company parties together, laugh together, and cry together.... She won't let me get away with anything, especially feeling sorry for myself. While on her seven-week South American wine journey, we communicated nearly every day. And though we were a continent apart, it brought us closer.

Ashley, I promised you I'd put you in here. Ash relates to me in a way unlike my other friends. A tech geek, we'll sit at her kitchen table drinking wine and talking about rebuilding computers. She's smart, pretty, and one of the sweetest and most fun people I know.

Finally, to my new bride, Jennifer. My friend, business partner, boss, "sometimes" dance partner, and the person beside me at night when I go to sleep and when I wake up. She read every word of this book and made sure it was great.

In my personal struggles over the preceding months, these friends kept me from falling into an abyss so deep I might never have returned. Writing can be a lonely thing and having a support system such as these beautiful, wonderful women are the only reason this endeavor was a success. A special friend told me just a couple weeks ago that some friends are only in your life for a season. I pray that these women are friends for a lifetime.

—MM, September 2016

Contents at a Glance

Contents

About the Author

Molly Maskrey started as an electrical engineer in her 20s at various large aerospace companies, including IBM Federal Systems, TRW (now Northrup Grumman), Loral Systems, Lockheed Martin, and Boeing. After successfully navigating the first dot-com boom, she realized that a break was in order and so she took several years off—moving to Maui and teaching windsurfing at the beautiful Kanaha Beach Park.

Never one to stay still, Molly moved to Denver, Colorado, and opened several businesses with her friend and partner Jennifer, including Global Tek Labs, an iOS development and accessory design services company that is now one of the leading consulting services for new designers looking to create smart attachments to Apple devices.

That same year, Molly, under her previous persona, published her first book through Apress. It was on how to create accessories for the iPhone operating system; to this day it remains the only major description of the process.

In 2014, Molly and Jennifer formed Quantitative Bioanalytics Laboratories—a wholly owned subsidiary of Global Tek—to bring high-resolution mobile sensor technology to physical therapy, elder balance and fall prevention, sports performance quantification, and instrumented gait analysis (IGA).

Molly recently began the Galvanize Data Science Immersive program in Denver, learning everything from Python, SQL, R, web scraping, big data analytics, Bayesian analysis, and many other skills in order to help with her next business adventure: a scalable, real-time analytics platform for IoT (the Internet of Things).

Molly lives in Parker, Colorado, with Jennifer and their two Labradors.

About the Technical Reviewer

Bruce Wade is a software engineer from British Columbia, Canada. He started software development when he was 16 years old by coding his first web site. He went on to study computer information systems at the DeVry Institute of Technology in Calgary, and then to further enhance his skills, he studied visual and game programming at The Art Institute of Vancouver. Over the years, he has worked for large corporations and several start-ups. His software experience has led him to utilize many different technologies, including C/C++, Python, Objective-C, Swift, Postgres, and JavaScript. In 2012, he started the company Warply Designed to focus on mobile 2D/3D and OS X development. Aside from hacking out new ideas, he enjoys spending time hiking with his Boxer, Rasco, working out, and exploring new adventures.

Acknowledgments

First, I want to acknowledge all my friends who gave me the support to persevere and go through with writing when it would have been so easy to just give up. To Sam, Brittany, Amanda, Kristie, Pyper, Peter, the Mikes, Kelly, and the whole team at Galvanize-Platte in Denver who I came to know and love, thank you.

To Children's Hospital Colorado and the Center for Gait and Movement Analysis who have been so generous with letting me be a part of understanding the significance of what they do for young adults with cerebral palsy and other gait disorders: the understanding I've gained drives me to focus efforts to help the many who truly need it.

To the clients and friends of Global Tek Labs who so generously allowed me to include some of their projects in this book for illustrative purposes. To the hundreds of people who have attended my talks over the past year and have given me ideas for what to include, such as John Haley who told me of his personal woes in understanding Auto Layout in Xcode. Those actual experiences helped drive the subject matter I chose to include.

Finally, I want to acknowledge all the authors before me that set the stage for my own little work to fit in to a much broader landscape.

CHAPTER 1

■ ■ ■

Getting to Know the iOS Landscape

Coding for Apple mobile devices provides developers a rewarding and lucrative career path where you might not only change people's lives with your app (see Figure 1-1), but you'll also have a great time being with bright, like-minded women and men such as yourself. Though you're bound to find some difficulty in learning the language, tools, and processes, these new associates will not only help you through the landscape of this new world, but will also challenge you to be your best and to stand out from the mediocre.

Figure 1-1. *One of the greatest feelings you can experience as an iOS developer is seeing other people using your creation out in the real world*

Electronic supplementary material The online version of this chapter (doi:10.1007/978-1-4842-2223-2_1) contains supplementary material, which is available to authorized users.

And for now, think of me as one of those friends along your journey of iOS discovery. I'm so proud to be able to help you by providing this initiation into the world of iOS development, whether it is for iPhone, iPod Touch or the iPad. iOS provides an exciting platform that has been seeing explosive growth since it first came out in 2007. The proliferation of mobile devices means that people are using software everywhere they go, whether it is a phone or a wearable, such as the Apple Watch. With the release of iOS 10, Xcode 8, Swift 3, and the latest version of the iOS software development kit (SDK), things continue to be exciting and generally become easier for the new developer.

About the Book

This book guides you down the path to creating your own iOS applications. I want to get you past the initial difficulties to help you understand the way that iOS applications work and how they are built.

As you work your way through this book, you will create a number of small applications, each designed to highlight specific iOS features and to show you how to control or interact with those features. If you combine the foundation you'll gain through this book with your own creativity and determination, and then add in the extensive and well-written documentation provided by Apple, you'll have everything you need to build your own professional iPhone and iPad applications.

■ **Note** Throughout most of this book, I tend to refer to the iPhone and iPad, as they are the devices that we'll most commonly use. This does not preclude the iPod Touch by any means; it is just a matter of convenience.

■ **Tip** The authors of the previous revisions of this book have set up a forum for this book. It's a great place to meet like-minded folks, get your questions answered, and even answer other people's questions. The forum is at http://forum.learncocoa.org. Be sure to check it out!

Things You'll Need

Before you can begin writing software for iOS, you'll need a few items. For starters, you'll need an Intel-based Macintosh running Yosemite (OS X 10.10), El Capitan (OS X 10.11), Sierra (macOS 10.12) or later. Any recent Intel-based Macintosh computer—laptop or desktop—should work just fine. Of course, as well as the hardware, you'll need the software. You can learn how to develop iOS applications and get the software tools that you'll need as long as you have an Apple ID; if you own an iPhone, iPad, or iPod, then you've almost certainly already have an Apple ID, but if you don't, then just visit https://appleid.apple.com/account to create one. Once you've done that, navigate to https://developer.apple.com/develop. That will bring you to a page similar to the one shown in Figure 1-2.

Figure 1-2. *Apple's Development Center resources site*

Click on **Downloads** across the top bar to go to the main resources page (see Figure 1-3) for the current production release and (if there is one) the current beta release of iOS. Here, you'll find links to a wealth of documentation, videos, sample code, and the like—all dedicated to teaching you the finer points of iOS application development. Be sure to scroll to the bottom of the page and check out the links to the Documentation and Videos sections of the web site. You'll also find a link to the Apple Developer Forums, where you can follow discussions on a wide variety of topics covering the whole iOS platform, as well as macOS, watchOS, and tvOS. To post to the forums, you'll need to be a registered Apple developer.

Figure 1-3. *You can download all the production and beta releases of the development tools from the Downloads page. You will need to sign in with your Apple ID*

> ■ **Note**   At the 2016 developer conference, WWDC 2016, Apple changed the name of OS X back to the previously used *macOS* to become more in line with the other naming conventions used throughout the four major system platforms.

The most important tool you'll be using to develop iOS applications is called Xcode, Apple's integrated development environment (IDE). Xcode includes tools for creating and debugging source code, compiling applications, and performance tuning the applications you've written.

You can download the current beta release of Xcode by following the Xcode link from the developer Download page shown in Figure 1-3. If you prefer to use the latest production release, you'll find it in the Mac App Store, which you can access from your Mac's Apple menu.

SDK VERSIONS AND SOURCE CODE FOR THE EXAMPLES

As the versions of the SDK and Xcode evolve, the mechanism for downloading them changed over the past few years. Apple now publishes the current production version of Xcode and the iOS SDK on the Mac App Store, while simultaneously providing developers the ability to download preview versions of upcoming releases from its developer site. Bottom line: unless you really want to work with the most recent development tools and platform SDK, you usually want to download the latest released (non-beta) version of Xcode and the iOS SDK, so use the Mac App Store.

This book is written to work with the latest versions of Xcode and the SDK. In some places, new functions or methods are introduced with iOS 10 that are not available in earlier versions of the SDK.

Be sure to download the latest and greatest source code archive for examples from this book's page at www.apress.com. The code is updated as new versions of the SDK are released, so be sure to check the site periodically.

Your Options as a Developer

The free Xcode download includes a simulator that will allow you to build and run iPhone and iPad apps on your Mac, providing the perfect environment for learning how to program for iOS. However, the simulator does *not* support many hardware-dependent features, such as the accelerometer and camera. To test applications that use those features, you'll need an iPhone, iPod touch, or iPad. While much of your code can be tested using the iOS simulator, not all programs can be. And even those that can run on the simulator really need to be thoroughly tested on an actual device before you ever consider releasing your application to the public.

Previous versions of Xcode required you to register for the Apple Developer Program (which is not free) to install your applications on a real iPhone or other device. Fortunately, this has changed. Xcode 7 started allowing developers to test applications on real hardware, albeit with some limitations that we'll cover as we go along, without purchasing an Apple Developer Program membership. That means you can run most of the examples in this book on your iPhone or iPad for free! However, the free option does not give you the ability to distribute your applications on Apple's App Store. For those capabilities, you'll need to sign up for one of the other options, which aren't free:

- **The Standard program** costs $99/year. It provides a host of development tools and resources, technical support, distribution of your applications via Apple's iOS and Mac App Stores. Your membership lets you develop and distribute applications for iOS, watchOS, tvOS, and macOS.

- **The Enterprise program** costs $299/year. It is designed for companies developing proprietary, in-house iOS applications.

For more details on these programs, visit `https://developer.apple.com/programs` (see Figure 1-4). If you are an independent developer, you can definitely get away with just buying the standard program membership. You don't have to do that until you need to run an application that uses a feature such as iCloud that requires a paid membership, or you want to post a question to the Apple Developer Forums, or you are ready to deploy your application to the App Store.

Apple Developer Program

What's Included   **How It Works**

Program Membership Details

Software and Tools

Download and install the latest beta OS releases for development and distribution. Access your account to configure resources required for the development and distribution process.

Beta OS Releases

Download the latest beta OS releases and install them on your development Apple devices.

- iOS 10
- macOS Sierra
- watchOS
- tvOS

Developer Account Tools

Access the resources you need to configure app services, manage your devices and development teams, and to submit new apps and updates.

Figure 1-4. *Signing up for a paid membership gives you access to Beta and OS tools releases*

Because iOS supports an always-connected mobile device that uses other companies' wireless infrastructures, Apple has needed to place far more restrictions on iOS developers than it ever has on Mac developers (who are able—at the moment, anyway—to write and distribute programs with absolutely no oversight or approval from Apple). Even though the iPod touch and the Wi-Fi-only versions of the iPad don't use anyone else's infrastructure, they're still subject to these same restrictions.

Apple has not added restrictions to be mean, but rather as an attempt to minimize the chances of malicious or poorly written programs being distributed and degrading performance on the shared network. Developing for iOS may appear to present a lot of hoops to jump through, but Apple has expended quite an effort to make the process as painless as possible. And also consider that $99 is still much less expensive than buying, for example, any of the paid versions of Visual Studio, which is Microsoft's software development IDE.

Things You Should Know

In this book, I'm going to assume that you already have some programming knowledge in general and object-oriented programming in particular (you know what classes, objects, loops, and variables are, for example). But of course, I don't assume that you are already familiar with Swift. There's an Appendix at the end of the book that introduces you to both Swift and the Playground feature in Xcode that makes it easy to try out the features. If you'd like to learn more about Swift after reading the material in the Appendix, the best way to do so is to go directly to the source and read *The Swift Programming Language*, which is Apple's own guide and reference to the language. You can get it from the iBooks store or from the iOS developer site at https://developer.apple.com/library/ios/documentation/Swift/Conceptual/Swift_Programming_Language/index.html.

You also need to be familiar with iOS itself, as a user. Just as you would with any platform for which you wanted to write an application, get to know the nuances and quirks of the iPhone, iPad, or iPod touch. Take the time to get familiar with the iOS interface and with the way Apple's iPhone and/or iPad applications look and feel.

Because the different terms can be a little confusing at first, Table 1-1 shows the relationships of IDE, APIs, and language to the platform operating system for which you are developing.

Table 1-1. Platform, Tools, Language Relationships

DEVELOP FOR	IDE	API	LANGUAGE
macOS	Xcode	Cocoa	Objective-C, Swift
iOS	Xcode	Cocoa Touch	Objective-C, Swift

Some Unique Aspects About Working in iOS

If you have never programmed for the Mac using Cocoa, you may find Cocoa Touch—the application framework you'll be using to write iOS applications—a little alien. It has some fundamental differences from other common application frameworks, such as those used when building .NET or Java applications. Don't worry too much if you feel a little lost at first. Just keep plugging away at the exercises and it will all start to fall into place after a while.

■ **Note**   You'll see a lot of reference to "frameworks" in this book. Although the term is a little vague and used in a few different ways depending on the context, a framework is a collection of "stuff," which may include a library, or several libraries, scripts, UI elements, and anything else in a single collection. A framework's stuff is generally associated with some specific function such as location services using the CoreLocation framework.

If you have written programs using Cocoa, a lot of what you'll find in the iOS SDK will be familiar to you. A great many classes are unchanged from the versions that are used to develop for macOS. Even those that are different tend to follow the same basic principles and similar design patterns. However, several differences exist between Cocoa and Cocoa Touch.

Regardless of your background, you need to keep in mind some key differences between iOS development and desktop application development. These differences are discussed in the following sections.

iOS Supports One Single Application at a Time—Mostly

On iOS, it's usually the case that only one application can be active and displayed on the screen at any given time. Since iOS 4, applications have been able to run in the background after the user presses the Home button; but even that is limited to a narrow set of situations and you must code for it specifically (you'll see exactly how to do it in Chapter 15). In iOS 9, Apple added the ability for two applications to run in the foreground and share the screen, but for that, the user needs to have one of the more recent iPads. We'll talk about that feature, which Apple calls Multitasking, in Chapter 11.

When your application isn't active or running in the background, it doesn't receive any attention whatsoever from the CPU. iOS allows background processing, but making your apps play nicely in this situation will require some effort on your part.

There's Only a Single Window

Desktop and laptop operating systems allow many running programs to coexist, each with the ability to create and control multiple windows. However, unless you attach an external screen or use AirPlay, and your application is coded to handle more than one screen, iOS gives your application just one "window" to work with. All of your application's interaction with the user takes place inside this one window and its size is fixed at the size of the screen, unless your user has activated the Multitasking feature, in which case your application may have to give up some of the screen to another application.

For Security, Access to Device Resources Are Limited

Programs on a desktop or a laptop computer pretty much have access to everything that the user who launched it does. However, iOS seriously restricts which parts of the device your program can use.

You can read and write files only from the part of iOS's file system that was created for your application. This area is called your application's **sandbox**. Your sandbox is where your application will store documents, preferences, and every other kind of data it may need to retain.

Your application is also constrained in some other ways. You will not be able to access low-number network ports on iOS, for example, or do anything else that would typically require root or administrative access on a desktop computer.

Apps Need to Respond Quickly

Because of the way it is used, iOS needs to be snappy, and it expects the same of your application. When your program is launched, you need to get your application open, the preferences and data loaded, and the main view shown on the screen as fast as possible—in no more than a few seconds. Your app should have low latency.

■ **Note** By latency, we do not mean speed. Speed and latency are commonly interchanged but that is not really true. Latency refers to the time between an action is taken and a result happens. If the user presses the Home button, iOS goes home, and you must quickly save everything before iOS suspends your application in the background. If you take longer than five seconds to save and give up control, your application process will be killed, regardless of whether you finished saving. There is an API that allows your app to ask for additional time to work when it's about to go dark, but you've got to know how to use it. So, in general, you want to get things done quickly which might mean dumping and losing unnecessary information.

Limited Screen Size

The iPhone's screen is really nice. When introduced, it was the highest resolution screen available on a handheld consumer device, by far. But even today, the iPhone display isn't all that big, and as a result, you have a lot less room to work with than on modern computers. The screen was just 320 × 480 on the first few iPhone generations and it was later doubled in both directions to 640 × 960 with the introduction of the iPhone 4's Retina display. Today, the screen of the largest iPhone (the iPhone 6/6s Plus) measures 1080 × 1920 pixels. That sounds like a decent number of pixels, but keep in mind that these high-density displays (for which Apple uses the term **Retina**) are crammed into pretty small form factors, which has a big impact on the kinds of applications and interactivity you can offer on an iPhone and even an iPad. Table 1-2 lists the sizes of the screens of all of the current commonly available Apple devices that are supported by iOS 10 at the time of writing.

Table 1-2. *iOS Device Screen Sizes*

DEVICE	HARDWARE SIZE	SOFTWARE SIZE	SCALING
iPhone 5 and 5s	640 x 1136	320 x 568	2x
iPhone 6/6s	750 x 1334	375 x 667	2x
iPhone 6/6s Plus	1080 x 1920	414 x 736	3x
iPhone SE	640 x 1136	320 x 568	2x
iPad 2 and iPad mini	768 x 1024	768 x 1024	1x
iPad Air, iPad Air 2, iPad Retina, and iPad mini Retina	1536 x 2048	768 x 1024	2x
iPad Pro	2732 × 2048	1366 × 1024	2x

The hardware size is the actual physical size of the screen in pixels. However, when writing software, the size that really matters is the one in the Software Size column. As you can see, in most cases, the software size reflects only half that of the actual hardware. This situation came about when Apple introduced the first Retina device, which had twice as many pixels in each direction as its predecessor. If Apple had done nothing special, all existing applications would have been drawn at half-scale on the new Retina screen, which would have made them unusable. So Apple chose to internally scale everything that applications draw by a factor of 2, so that they would fill the new screen without any code changes. This internal scaling by a factor of 2 applies to all devices with a Retina display, apart from the iPhone 6/6s Plus, which has a higher-density screen that requires a scaling factor of 3. For the most part, though, you don't need to worry too much about the fact that your application is being scaled—all you need to do is work within the software screen size and iOS will do the rest.

The only exceptions to this rule center on bitmap images. Since bitmap images are, by their nature, fixed in size, for best results you can't really use the same image on a Retina screen as you would on a non-Retina screen. If you try to do that, you'll see that iOS scales your image up for a device that has a Retina screen, which has the effect of introducing blur. You can fix this by including separate copies of each image for the 2x and 3x Retina screens. iOS will pick the version that matches the screen of the device on which your application is running.

■ **Note**   If you look back at Table 1-1, you'll see that it appears that the scale factor in the fourth column is the same as the ratio of the hardware size to the software size. For example, on the iPhone 6/6s, the hardware width is 750 and software width is 375, a ratio of 2:1. Look carefully, though, and you'll see that there's something different about the iPhone 6/6s Plus. The ratio of the hardware width to the software width is 1080/414, which is 2.608:1, and the same applies to the height ratio. So in terms of the hardware, the iPhone 6/6s Plus does not have a truly 3x Retina display. However, as far as the software is concerned, a 3x scale is used, which means that an application written to use the software screen size of 414 × 736 is first logically mapped to a virtual screen size of 1242 × 2208 and the result is then scaled down a little to match the actual hardware size of 1080 × 1920. Fortunately, this doesn't require you to do anything special because iOS takes care of all the details.

Limited Device Resources

Software developers from just a decade or two ago laugh at the idea of a machine with at least 512MB of RAM and 16GB of storage being in any way resource-constrained, but it's true. Developing for iOS doesn't reside in the same league as trying to write a complex spreadsheet application on a machine with 48KB of memory. But given the graphical nature of iOS and all it is capable of doing, running out of memory happens from time to time.

The iOS devices available right now have either 512MB (iPhone 4S, iPad 2, the original iPad mini, the latest iPod touch), or 1024MB of physical RAM (iPhone 5c, iPhone 5s, iPhone 6/6s, iPhone 6/6s Plus, iPad Air, iPad Air 2, iPad mini Retina), though this will likely increase over time. Some of that memory is used for the screen buffer and by other system processes. Usually, no more than half of that memory is left for your application to use, and the amount can be considerably less, especially now that other apps can be running in the background.

Although that may sound like it leaves a pretty decent amount of memory for such a small computer, there is another factor to consider when it comes to memory on iOS. Modern computer operating systems like macOS take chunks of memory that aren't being used and write them to disk in something called a **swap file**. The swap file allows applications to keep running, even when they have requested more memory than is actually available on the computer. iOS, however, will not write volatile memory, such as application data, out to a swap file. As a result, the amount of memory available to your application is constrained by the amount of unused physical memory in the iOS device.

Cocoa Touch has built-in mechanisms for letting your application know that memory is getting low. When that happens, your application must free up unneeded memory or risk being forced to quit.

Features Unique to iOS Devices

Since we've mentioned that Cocoa Touch is missing some features that Cocoa has, it seems only fair to mention that the iOS SDK contains some functionality that is not currently present in Cocoa—or, at least, is not available on every Mac:

- The iOS SDK provides a way for your application to determine the iOS device's current geographic coordinates using Core Location.

- Most iOS devices have built-in cameras and photo libraries, and the SDK provides mechanisms that allow your application to access both.

- iOS devices have built-in motion sensors that let you detect how your device is being held and moved.

User Input and Display

Since iOS devices do not have a physical keyboard or a mouse, you interact differently with your user than you do when programming for a general-purpose computer. Fortunately, most of that interaction is handled for you. For example, if you add a text field to your application, iOS knows to bring up a keyboard when the user touches that field, without you needing to write any extra code.

■ **Note**　All iOS devices allow you to connect an external keyboard via Bluetooth or the Lightning connector, which provides a nice keyboard experience and saves you some screen real estate. Currently, iOS does not support connecting a mouse.

What's in this Book

When I first started programming applications for iOS, then called iPhone OS, I picked up the original version of this book based on Objective-C. I became, at least in my mind, a capable and productive app developer, even making some money with my products. So, I want to return the favor by providing the latest and greatest version to help you achieve that same level of success and more. So, here's what I'm going to be covering:

- In Chapter 2, you'll learn how to use Xcode's user interface (UI) developer tool, Interface Builder, to create a simple visual result, placing some text on the screen.

- In Chapter 3, I'll show you how to start interacting with the user, building an application that dynamically updates displayed text at runtime based on buttons the user presses.

- Chapter 4 follows on Chapter 3 by introducing you to several more of iOS's standard user-interface controls. I'll also demonstrate how to use alerts and action sheets to prompt users to make a decision or to inform them that something out of the ordinary has occurred.

- In Chapter 5, we'll look at handling rotation and Auto Layout, the mechanisms that allow iOS applications to be used in both portrait and landscape modes.

- In Chapter 6, I'll start discussing more advanced user interfaces and explore creating applications that support multiple views. I'll show you how to change which view is shown to the user at runtime, which will greatly enhance the potential of your apps.

- iOS supports Tab bars and pickers as part of the standard iOS user interface. In Chapter 7, we'll look at how to implement these interface elements.

- In Chapter 8, we'll cover table views, the primary way of providing lists of data to the user and the foundation of hierarchical navigation–based applications. You'll also see how to let the user search your application data.

- One of the most common iOS application interfaces, the hierarchical list, lets you drill down to see more data or more details. In Chapter 9, you'll learn what's involved in implementing this standard type of interface.

- From the beginning, iOS applications have used table views to display dynamic, vertically scrolling lists of components. A few years ago, Apple introduced a new class called `UICollectionView` that takes this concept a few steps further, giving developers lots of new flexibility in laying out visual components. Chapter 10 introduces you to Collection Views.

- Chapter 11 shows how to build master-detail applications and present a list of items (such as the emails in a mailbox) allowing the user to view the details of each individual item, one at a time. You'll also work with iOS controls that support this concept, originally developed for the iPad and now also available on the iPhone.

- In Chapter 12, we'll look at implementing application settings, which is iOS's mechanism for letting users set their application-level preferences.

- Chapter 13 covers data management on iOS. We'll talk about creating objects to hold application data and see how that data can be persisted to iOS's file system. I'll present the basics of using Core Data, allowing you to save and retrieve data easily; however, for an in-depth discussion of Core Data, you'll want to check out *Pro iOS Persistence Using Core Data*, by Michael Privat and Robert Warner (Apress, 2014).

- In iOS 5, Apple introduced iCloud, which allows your document to store data online and sync it between different instances of the application. Chapter 14 shows you how to get started with iCloud.

- iOS developers have access to a powerful library that simplifies multithreaded development called Grand Central Dispatch, or GCD for short. In Chapter 15, I'll introduce you to Grand Central Dispatch and also show you how to use the iOS features that allow you, under certain circumstances, to run your application in the background.

- Everyone loves to draw, so we'll look at doing some custom drawing in Chapter 16, where we'll introduce you to the Core Graphics system.

- In iOS 7, Apple has introduced a new framework called Sprite Kit for creating 2D games. It includes a physics engine and animation systems, and works for making macOS games, too. You'll see how to make a simple game with Sprite Kit in Chapter 17.

- The multitouch screen common to all iOS devices can accept a wide variety of gestural inputs from the user. In Chapter 18, you'll learn all about detecting basic gestures, such as the pinch and swipe.

- Your iPhone easily tells you latitude and longitude thanks to its Core Location functionality. In Chapter 19, we'll write some code that uses Core Location to figure out your current position.

- In Chapter 20, we'll look at interfacing with iOS's accelerometer and gyroscope, which is how your device knows which way it's being held, the speed and direction it is moving, and where in the world it's located.

- Nearly every iOS device includes a camera and a library of pictures, both of which are available to your application, Chapter 21 discusses the use of camera and access to the photo library.

- Apple currently ships iOS devices to more than 90 countries. In Chapter 22, I'll show you how to write your applications in such a way that all parts can be easily translated into other languages. This helps expand the potential audience for your applications.

- Finally, there's an Appendix that introduces the Swift programming language in its current state and covers all of the features that you'll need to know to understand the example code in this book.

What's New in this Update?

After the first edition of this book hit the bookstores, the iOS development community grew at a phenomenal rate. The SDK continually evolved, with Apple releasing a steady stream of SDK updates. iOS 10 and Xcode 8 contain a lot of new enhancements. I've been hard at work updating the book to cover the new technologies that you'll need to be aware of to start writing iOS applications.

Swift and Xcode Versions

Though having been out for over two years now, Swift is still in a state of flux and likely to remain so for some time to come. Interestingly, Apple promised that the compiled binaries for applications written now will work on later versions of iOS, but it is *not* guaranteed that the source code for those same applications will continue to compile. As a result, it is possible that example code that compiled and worked with the version of Xcode that was current when this book was published no longer works by the time you read it. Xcode 6.0 shipped with Swift version 1, Xcode 6.3 had Swift version 1.2 and Xcode 7 introduced Swift 2. The code in this book was written for and tested with the Beta release of Xcode 8 and Swift 3.

If you find that some of the example source code no longer compiles with the release of Xcode that you are using, please visit the book's page at www.apress.com and download the latest version. If after doing this you are still having problems, please bring it to our attention by submitting an Erratum on the Apress web site.

Let's Get Started

iOS provides an incredible computing platform and an exciting new frontier for your development career. You'll likely find programming for iOS to be a new experience—different from working on any other platform. For everything that looks familiar, there will be something alien—but as you work through the book's code, the concepts should all come together and start to make sense.

Keep in mind that the examples in this book are not simply a checklist that, when completed, magically grant you iOS developer expert status. Make sure that you understand what you did and why before moving on to the next project. Don't be afraid to make changes to the code. By observing the results of your experimentation you can wrap your head around the complexities of coding in an environment like Cocoa Touch.

That said, if you've already downloaded and installed Xcode, turn the page and take your next steps to becoming a real iOS app developer.

CHAPTER 2

■ ■ ■

Writing Our First App

I want to get you started right away with a feel for what this is all about and to motivate your continued progress toward being a great developer, so let's get to it and do something with our iPhone (see Figure 2-1). In this chapter, using Xcode, let's create a small iOS application that will display **Hello, World!**. We'll look at what's involved in creating the project in Xcode, work through the specifics of using Xcode's Interface Builder to design our application's user interface, and then execute our application on the iOS simulator and an actual device. We'll finish up by giving our application an icon to make it feel more like a real iOS application.

Figure 2-1. *The results of the app we create in this chapter might seem simple, but our work will start us down the road to potential iOS greatness*

Creating the Hello World Project

By now, you should have installed Xcode 8 and the iOS SDK onto your Mac. You can also download the book's source code archive from the Apress web site (`www.apress.com`). While you're at it, take a look at the book forums at `http://forum.learncocoa.org`. The book forums are a great place to discuss iOS development, get your questions answered, and meet up with like-minded people.

© Molly Maskrey, Kim Topley, David Mark, Fredrik Olsson and Jeff Lamarche 2016
M. Maskrey et al., *Beginning iPhone Development with Swift 3*, DOI 10.1007/978-1-4842-2223-2_2

■ **Note**   Even though you have the complete set of project files at your disposal in this book's source code archive, you'll get more out of the book if you create each project by hand, rather than simply running the version you downloaded. By doing that, you'll gain familiarity and expertise working with the various application development tools.

The project we're going to build in this chapter is contained in the 02 - Hello World folder of the source code archive.

Before we can start, we need to launch Xcode, the tool that we'll use to do most of what we do in this book. After downloading it from the Mac App Store or the Apple Developer site, you'll find it installed in the /Applications folder, as with most Mac applications. You'll be using Xcode a lot, so you might want to consider dragging it to your dock so you'll have ready access to it.

If this is your first time using Xcode, don't worry; we'll walk you through every step involved in creating a new project. If you're already an old hand but haven't worked with Xcode 7, you may find that some things have changed (mostly for the better, I think).

When you first launch Xcode, you'll be presented with a welcome window like the one shown in Figure 2-2. From here, you can choose to create a new project, connect to a version-control system to check out an existing project, or select from a list of recently opened projects. The welcome window gives you a nice starting point, covering some of the most common tasks you might do after starting Xcode. All of these actions can be accessed through the menu as well, so close the window and we'll proceed. If you would rather not see this window in the future, just uncheck the Show this window when Xcode launches check box at the bottom of the window before closing it.

Figure 2-2. The Xcode welcome window

Create a new project by selecting New ➤ Project... from the File menu (or by pressing Shift-Command-N). A new project window will open, showing you the project template selection sheet (see Figure 2-3). From this sheet, you'll choose a project template to use as a starting point for building your application. The bar at the top is divided into five sections: iOS, watchOS, tvOS, macOS, and Cross-platform. Since we're building an iOS application, select the iOS button to reveal the application templates.

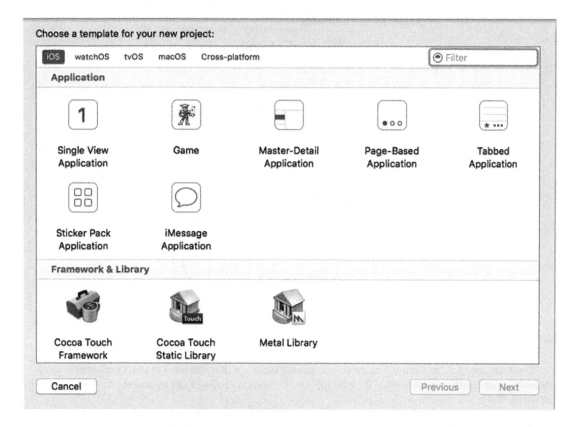

Figure 2-3. The project template selection sheet lets you select from various templates when creating a new project

Each of the icons shown in the upper-right pane in Figure 2-3 represents a separate project template that can be used as a starting point for your iOS applications. The icon labeled Single View Application contains the simplest template and the one we'll be using for the first several chapters. The other templates provide additional code and/or resources needed to create common iPhone and iPad application interfaces, as you'll see in later chapters.

Click the Single View Application (see Figure 2-3), and then click the Next button. You'll see the project options sheet, which should look like Figure 2-4. On this sheet, you need to specify the Product Name and Company Identifier for your project. Xcode will combine these to generate a unique bundle identifier for your app. You'll also see a field that lets you enter an Organization Name, which Xcode will use to automatically insert a copyright notice into every source code file you create. Name your product Hello World and enter an organization name and identifier in the Organization Name and Organization Identifier fields, as shown in Figure 2-4. Don't use the same name and identifier as the ones shown in Figure 2-4—for reasons that you'll see when we try to run this application on a real device at the end of the chapter, you'll need to choose an identifier that's unique to you (or your company).

Figure 2-4. *Selecting a product name and organization identifier for your project*

The Language field lets you select the programming language that you want to use, choosing between Objective-C and Swift, but since all of the examples in the book are in Swift, the appropriate choice here is, of course, Swift.

We also need to specify the devices. In other words, Xcode wants to know if we're building an app for the iPhone and iPod touch, if we're building an app for the iPad, or if we're building a universal application that will run on all iOS devices. Select iPhone in the Devices drop-down menu if it's not already selected. This tells Xcode that we'll be targeting this particular app at the iPhone and iPod touch, which have roughly the same screen size and form factor. For the first few chapters of the book, we'll be using the iPhone device, but don't worry—we'll cover the iPad also.

Leave the Core Data check box unchecked—we'll make use of it in Chapter 13. We'll also leave the Include Unit Tests and Include UI Tests check boxes unchecked. Xcode has very good support for testing of your applications, but that's outside the scope of this book, so we don't need Xcode to include support for them in our project. Click Next again and you'll be asked where to save your new project using a standard save sheet (see Figure 2-5). If you haven't already done so, use the New Folder button to create a new master directory for these book projects, and then return to Xcode and navigate into that directory. Before you click the Create button, take note of the Source Control check box. Git isn't covered in this book, but Xcode includes some support for using Git and other kinds of source control management (SCM) tools. If you are already familiar with Git and want to use it, enable this check box; otherwise, feel free to turn it off.

Figure 2-5. *Saving your project in a project folder on your hard drive*

The Xcode Project Window

After you dismiss the save sheet, Xcode will create and then open your project. You will see a new project window, as shown in Figure 2-6. There's a lot of information in this window; it's where we'll spend a lot of iOS development time.

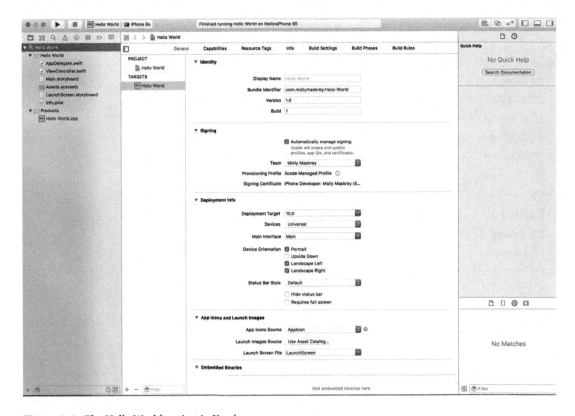

Figure 2-6. *The Hello World project in Xcode*

The Toolbar

The top of the Xcode project window is called the **toolbar** (see Figure 2-7). On the left side of the toolbar you'll see controls to start and stop running your project, as well as a pop-up menu to select the scheme you want to run. A scheme brings together target and build settings, and the toolbar pop-up menus let you select a specific setup quickly and easily.

Figure 2-7. *The Xcode toolbar*

The big box in the middle of the toolbar is the **Activity View**. As its name implies, the activity view displays any actions or processes that are currently happening. For example, when you run your project, the activity view gives you a running commentary on the various steps it's taking to build your application. If you encounter any errors or warnings, that information is displayed here, as well. If you click the warning or error, you'll go directly to the **Issue Navigator**, which provides more information about the warning or error, as described in the next section.

On the right side of the toolbar are two sets of buttons. The left set lets you switch between three different editor configurations:

- The **Editor Area** gives you a single pane dedicated to editing a file or project-specific configuration values.

- The powerful **Assistant Editor** splits the Editor Area into multiple panes, left, right, top, and bottom. The pane on the right is generally used to display a file that relates to the file on the left, or that you might need to refer to while editing the file on the left. You can manually specify what goes into each pane, or you can let Xcode decide what's most appropriate for the task at hand. For example, if you're designing your user interface on the left, Xcode will show you the code that the user interface is able to interact with on the right. You'll see the Assistant Editor at work throughout the book.

- The **Version Editor** button converts the editor pane into a time machine–like comparison view that works with version control systems like Git. You can compare the current version of a source file with a previously committed version or compare any two earlier versions with each other.

To the right of the editor buttons is a set of toggle buttons that show and hide large panes on the left and right sides of the editor view, as well as the debug area at the bottom of the window. Click each of those buttons a few times to see these panes in action. We'll explore how these are used soon.

The Navigator

Just below the toolbar on the left side of the project window is the Navigator. The Navigator offers eight views that show you different aspects of your project. Click each of the icons at the top of the navigator to switch among the following navigators, going from left to right:

- **Project Navigator**: This view contains a list of files in your project, as shown in Figure 2-8. You can store references to everything you expect—from source code files to artwork, data models, property list (or .plist) files (discussed in the "A Closer Look at the Hello World Project" section later in this chapter), and even other project files. By storing multiple projects in a single workspace, those projects can easily share resources. If you click any file in the navigator view, that file will display in the Editor Area. In addition to viewing the file, you can also edit it, if it's a file that Xcode knows how to edit.

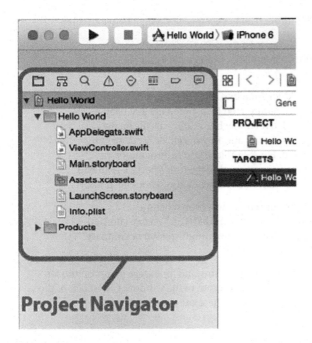

Figure 2-8. *The Xcode Project Navigator. Click one of the eight icons at the top of the view to switch navigators*

- **Symbol Navigator**: As its name implies, this navigator focuses on the **symbols** defined in the workspace (see Figure 2-9). Symbols are basically the items that the compiler recognizes, such as classes, enumerations, structs, and global variables.

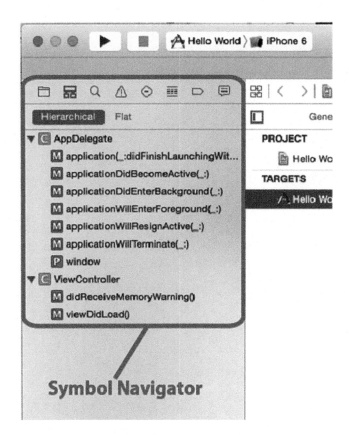

Figure 2-9. *The Xcode Symbol Navigator. Open the disclosure triangle to explore the classes, methods, and other symbols defined within each group*

- **Find Navigator**: You'll use this navigator to perform searches on all the files in your workspace (see Figure 2-10). At the top of this pane is a multileveled pop-up control letting you select Replace instead of Find, along with other options for applying search criteria to the text you enter. Below the text field, other controls let you choose to search in the entire project or just a portion of it, and specify whether searching should be case-sensitive.

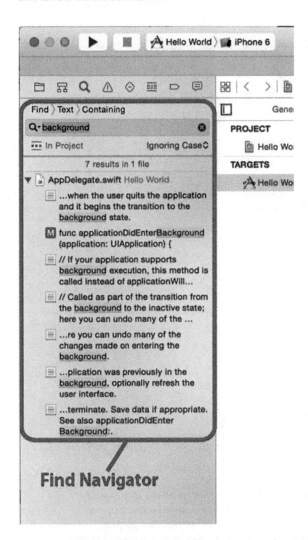

Figure 2-10. *The Xcode Find Navigator. Be sure to check out the pop-up menus hidden under the word Find and under the buttons that are below the search field*

- **Issue Navigator:** When you build your project, any errors or warnings will appear in this navigator, and a message detailing the number of errors will appear in the activity view at the top of the window (see Figure 2-11). When you click an error in the issue navigator, you'll jump to the appropriate line of code in the editor.

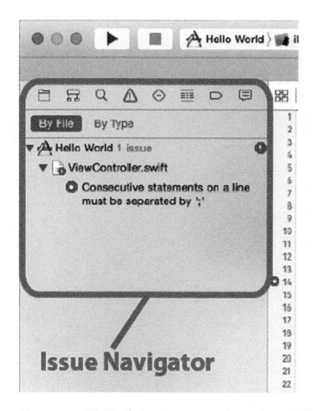

Figure 2-11. *The Xcode Issue Navigator. This is where you'll find your compiler errors and warnings*

- **Test Navigator**: If you're using Xcode's integrated unit testing capabilities (a topic that isn't covered in this book), this is where you'll see the results of your unit tests. Since we didn't include unit tests in the project, this navigator is empty (see Figure 2-12).

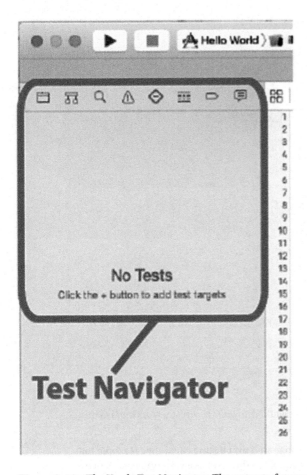

Figure 2-12. *The Xcode Test Navigator. The output of your unit tests will appear here*

- **Debug Navigator:** This navigator provides your main view into the debugging process (see Figure 2-13). If you are new to debugging, you might check out this part of the Xcode Overview (`https://developer.apple.com/library/prerelease/ content/documentation/ToolsLanguages/Conceptual/Xcode_Overview/ UsingtheDebugger.html`). The Debug Navigator lists the stack frame for each active thread. A **stack frame** is a list of the functions or methods that have been called previously, in the order they were called. Click a method, and the associated code appears in the editor pane. In the editor, there will be a second pane that lets you control the debugging process, display and modify data values, and access the low-level debugger. A button at the bottom of the debug navigator allows you to control which stack frames are visible. Another button lets you choose whether to show all threads or just the threads that have crashed or stopped on a breakpoint. Hover your mouse over each of these buttons in turn to see which is which.

Figure 2-13. *The Xcode Debug Navigator. Controls at the bottom of the navigator let you control the level of detail you want to see*

- **Breakpoint Navigator**: The breakpoint navigator lets you see all the breakpoints that you've set, as shown in Figure 2-14. Breakpoints are, as the name suggests, points in your code where the application will stop running (or **break**), so that you can look at the values in variables and do other tasks needed to debug your application. The list of breakpoints in this navigator is organized by file. Click a breakpoint in the list and that line will appear in the editor pane. Be sure to check out the plus sign (+) button at the lower-left corner of the project window when in the breakpoint navigator. This button opens a pop-up that lets you add four different types of breakpoints, including symbolic breakpoints, which are the ones that you will use most often.

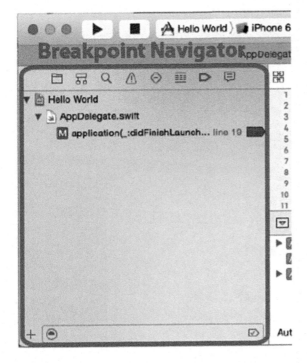

Figure 2-14. *The Xcode Breakpoint Navigator. The list of breakpoints is organized by file*

- **Report Navigator**: This navigator keeps a history of your recent build results and run logs, as shown in Figure 2-15. Click a specific log, and the build command and any build issues are displayed in the edit pane.

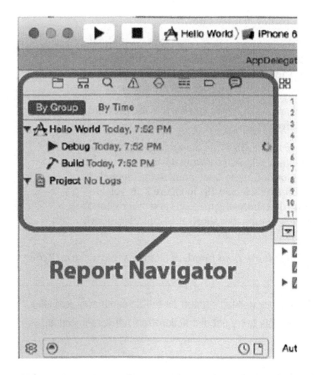

Figure 2-15. *The Xcode Report Navigator. The Report Navigator displays a list of builds, with the details associated with a selected view displayed in the editor pane*

The Jump Bar

Across the top of the editor, you'll find a control called the **jump bar**. With a single click, the jump bar allows you to jump to a specific element in the hierarchy you are currently navigating. For example, Figure 2-16 shows a source file being edited in the editor pane.

Figure 2-16. *The Xcode editor pane showing the jump bar, with a source code file selected. The submenu shows the list of methods in the selected file*

The jump bar sits just above the source code. Here's how it breaks down:

- The funky-looking icon at the left end of the jump bar is actually a pop-up menu that displays submenus listing recent files, counterparts, superclasses, and subclasses, siblings, categories, includes, and more. The submenus shown here will take you to just about any other code that touches the code currently open in the editor.

- To the right of the menu are left and right arrows that take you back to the previous file and return you to the next file, respectively.

- The jump bar includes a segmented pop-up that displays the hierarchical path to reach the selected file in the project. You can click any segment showing the name of a group or a file to see all the other files and groups located at the same point in the hierarchy. The final segment shows a list of items within the selected file. In Figure 2-16, you see that the tail end of the jump bar is a pop-up that shows the methods and other symbols contained within the currently selected file. The jump bar shows the AppDelegate.swift file with a submenu listing the symbols defined in that file.

Look for the jump bar as you make your way through the various interface elements that make up Xcode.

■ **Tip**   Like most of Apple's macOS applications, Xcode includes full support for full-screen mode. Just click the full-screen button in the upper right of the project window to try out distraction-free, full-screen coding!

XCODE KEYBOARD SHORTCUTS

If you prefer navigating with keyboard shortcuts instead of mousing to on-screen controls, you'll like what Xcode has to offer. Most actions that you will do regularly in Xcode have keyboard shortcuts assigned to them, such as ⌘B to build your application or ⌘N to create a new file.

You can change all of Xcode's keyboard shortcuts, as well as assign shortcuts to commands that don't already have one using Xcode's preferences, under the Key Bindings tab.

A really handy keyboard shortcut is ⇧⌘O, which is Xcode's Open Quickly feature. After pressing it, start typing the name of a file, setting, or symbol, and Xcode will present you with a list of options. When you narrow down the list to the file you want, hitting the Return key will open it in the editing pane, allowing you to switch files in just a few keystrokes.

The Utilities Area

As mentioned earlier, the second-to-last button on the right side of the Xcode toolbar opens and closes the utilities area. The upper part of the utilities area is a context-sensitive inspector panel, with contents that change depending on what is being displayed in the editor pane. The lower part of the utility area contains a few different kinds of resources that you can drag into your project. We'll see examples of this throughout the book.

Interface Builder

Earlier versions of Xcode included a separate interface design application called **Interface Builder** **(IB)**, which allowed you to build and customize your project's user interface. One of the major changes introduced in later versions of Xcode integrated Interface Builder into the workspace itself. Interface Builder is no longer a separate stand-alone application, which means you don't need to jump back and forth between Xcode and Interface Builder as your code and interface evolve.

We'll be working extensively with Xcode's interface-building functionality throughout the book, digging into all the various details. In fact, we'll start working with Interface Builder later in this chapter.

Integrated Compiler and Debugger

Among the most important changes that were brought in by Xcode 4 lies under the hood: a brand-new compiler and a low-level debugger. Both are significantly faster and smarter than their predecessors, and each release since then has added improvements.

For many years, Apple used GCC (the GNU Compiler Collection) as the basis for its compiler technology. But over the course of the past few years, it has shifted over completely to the LLVM (Low Level Virtual Machine) compiler. LLVM generates code that is faster by far than that generated by the traditional GCC. In addition to creating faster code, LLVM also knows more about your code, so it can generate smarter, more precise error messages and warnings.

Xcode is also tightly integrated with LLVM, which gives it some new superpowers. Xcode can offer more precise code completion and it can make educated guesses as to the actual intent of a piece of code when it produces a warning and offers a pop-up menu of likely fixes. This makes errors like misspelled symbol names and mismatched parentheses a breeze to find and fix.

LLVM brings to the table a sophisticated **static analyzer** that can scan your code for a wide variety of potential problems, including problems with memory management. In fact, LLVM is so smart about this that it can handle most memory management tasks for you, as long as you abide by a few simple rules when writing your code. We'll begin looking at the new feature called **Automatic Reference Counting** (ARC) in the next chapter.

A Closer Look at the Hello World Project

Now that we've explored the Xcode project window, let's take a look at the files that make up our new Hello World project. Switch to the Project Navigator by clicking the leftmost of the eight navigator icons on the left side of your workspace (as discussed in the "The Navigator" section earlier in the chapter) or by pressing ⌘1.

■ **Note**   The eight navigator configurations can be accessed using the keyboard shortcuts ⌘**1** to ⌘**8**. The numbers correspond to the icons starting on the left, so ⌘**1** is the Project Navigator, ⌘**2** is the Symbol Navigator, and so on up to ⌘**8**, which takes you to the Report Navigator.

The first item in the Project Navigator list bears the same name as your project—in this case, Hello World. This item represents your entire project and it's also where project-specific configuration can be done. If you single-click it, you'll be able to edit a number of project configuration settings in Xcode's editor. You don't need to worry about those project-specific settings now, however. At the moment, the defaults will work fine.

Flip back to Figure 2-8. Notice that the disclosure triangle to the left of Hello World is open, showing a number of subfolders (which are called **groups** in Xcode):

- **Hello World**: The first group, which is always named after your project, is where you will spend the bulk of your time. This is where most of the code that you write will go, as will the files that make up your application's user interface. You are free to create subgroups under the Hello World group to help organize your code. You're even allowed to add groups of your own if you prefer a different organizational approach. While we won't touch most of the files in this folder until the next chapter, there is one file we will explore when we use Interface Builder in the next section. That file is called **Main.storyboard** and it contains the user interface elements specific to your project's main view controller. The Hello World group also contains files and resources that aren't Swift source files, but that are necessary to your project. Among these files is one called Info.plist, which contains important information about the application, such as its name, whether it requires any specific features to be present on the devices on which it is run, and so on. In earlier versions of Xcode, these files were placed into a separate group called Supporting Files.

- **Hello WorldTests**: This group is created if you enable unit testing for the project (we didn't, so it's not there for our project) and it contains the initial files you'll need if you want to write some unit tests for your application code. We're not going to talk about unit testing in this book, but it's nice that Xcode can set up some of these things for you in each new project you create if you want it to. Like the Hello World folder, this one contains its own Info.plist file.

- **Products**: This group contains the application that this project produces when it is built. If you expand Products, you'll see an item called Hello World.app, which is the application that this particular project creates. If the project had been created with unit testing enabled, it would also contain an item called Hello WorldTests.xctest, which represents the testing code. Both of these items are called **build targets**. Because we have never built either of these, they're both red, which is Xcode's way of telling you that a file reference points to something that is not there.

■ **Note**   The "folders" in the navigator area do not necessarily correspond to folders in your Mac's file system. They are just logical groupings within Xcode that help you keep everything organized and make it faster and easier to find what you're looking for while working on your application. Often, the items contained in those groups are stored directly in the project's directory, but you can store them anywhere—even outside your project folder if you want. The hierarchy inside Xcode is completely independent of the file system hierarchy, so moving a file out of the Hello World group in Xcode, for example, will not change the file's location on your hard drive.

Introducing Xcode's Interface Builder

In your project window's Project Navigator, expand the Hello World group, if it's not already open, and then select the Main.storyboard file. As soon as you do, the file will open in the editor pane, as shown in Figure 2-17. You should see something resembling an all-white iOS device centered on a plain white background, which makes a nice backdrop for editing interfaces. This is Xcode's Interface Builder, which is where we'll design our application's user interface.

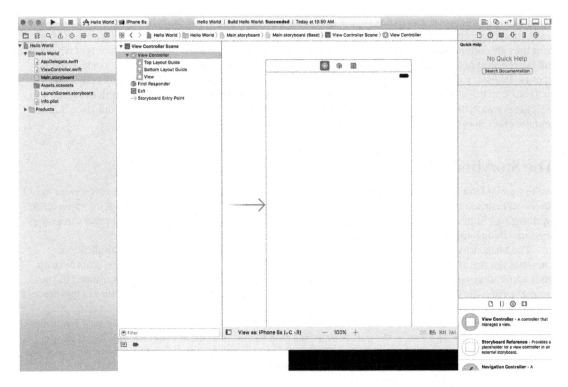

Figure 2-17. *Selecting Main.storyboard in the Project Navigator opens the file in Interface Builder*

Interface Builder has a long history. It has been around since 1988 and has been used to develop applications for NeXTSTEP, OpenStep, OS X, macOS, and now iOS devices such as the iPhone, iPad, Apple TV, and also for the Apple Watch.

File Formats

Interface Builder supports a few different file types. The oldest is a binary format that uses the extension .nib, now an XML-based format using the .xib extension. Both of these formats contain exactly the same sort of document, but the .xib version, being a text-based format, has many advantages, especially when you're using any sort of source control software. For the first 20 years of Interface Builder's life, all of its files had the .nib extension. As a result, most developers took to calling Interface Builder files **nib files**. Interface Builder files are often called nib files, regardless of whether the extension actually used for the file is .xib or .nib. In fact, Apple sometimes uses the terms **nib** and **nib file** interspersed through its documentation.

Each nib file can contain any number of objects, but when working on iOS projects, each one will usually contain a single view (often a full-screen view) and the controllers or other objects to which it connects. This lets us compartmentalize our applications, only loading the nib file for a view when it's needed for display. The end result: we save memory when our app is running on a memory-constrained iOS device. A newly-created iOS project contains a nib file called LaunchScreen.xib that contains a screen layout that will be shown, by default, when your application launches. We'll talk more about this file at the end of the chapter.

The other file format that IB has supported for the past few years is the **storyboard**. You can think of a storyboard as a "meta-nib file" since it can contain several view controllers, as well as information about how they are connected to each other when the application runs. Unlike a nib file, the contents of which are loaded all at once, a storyboard cannot contain freestanding views and it never loads all of its contents at once. Instead, you ask it to load particular controllers when you need them. The iOS project templates in Xcode 8 all use storyboards, so all of the examples in this book will start with a storyboard. Although you only get one storyboard for free, you can add more if you need them. Now let's go back to Interface Builder and the Main.storyboard file for our Hello World application (see Figure 2-17).

The Storyboard

We're now looking at the primary tool for building user interfaces for iOS apps. Let's say that you want to create an instance of a button. You could create that button by writing code, but creating an interface object by dragging a button out of a library and specifying its attributes is so much simpler, and it results in exactly the same thing happening at runtime.

The Main.storyboard file we are looking at right now loads automatically when your application launches (for the moment, don't worry about how), so it is the right place to add the objects that make up your application's user interface. When you create objects in Interface Builder, they're instantiated in your program when the storyboard or nib file that you added them loads. We'll see many examples of this process throughout the book.

Every storyboard gets compartmentalized into one or more **view controllers** and each view controller has at least one **view**. The view is the part you can see graphically and edit in Interface Builder, while the controller is application code you will write to make things happen when a user interacts with your app. The controllers are where the real action of your application happens.

In IB, you often see a view represented by a rectangle representing the screen of an iOS device (actually, it represents a view controller, a concept that you'll be introduced to in the next chapter, but this particular view controller covers the whole screen of the device, so it's pretty much the same thing). Near the bottom of the IB window you'll see a drop-down control that begins with **View as:** with a default device type. Click the device type. You can choose which device that we'll be creating the layout for, as shown in Figure 2-18.

Figure 2-18. *In Xcode 8, IB lets you select the device type and orientation that you work in*

Returning to our storyboard, click anywhere in the outline and you'll see a row of three icons at the top of it, like those shown in Figure 2-17. Move your mouse over each of them and you'll see tooltips pop up with their names: View Controller, First Responder, and Exit. Forget about Exit for now and focus instead on the other two.

- **View Controller** represents a controller object that is loaded from file storage along with its associated view. The task of the view controller is to manage what the user sees on the screen. A typical application has several view controllers, one for each of its screens. It is perfectly possible to write an application with just one screen, and hence one view controller, and many of the examples in this book have only one view controller.

- **First Responder** is, in very basic terms, the object with which the user is currently interacting. If, for example, the user is currently entering data into a text field, that field is the current first responder. The first responder changes as the user interacts with the user interface, and the First Responder icon gives you a convenient way to communicate with whatever control or other object is the current first responder, without needing to write code to determine which control or view that might be.

We'll talk more about these objects starting in the next chapter, so don't worry if it's a bit confusing right now determining when you would use **First Responder** or how a **View Controller** gets loaded.

Apart from those icons, the rest of what you see in the editing area is the space where you can place graphical objects. But before we get to that, there's one more thing you should see about IB's editor area: its hierarchy view—or the **Document Outline** to give it its correct name. The Document Outline is shown in Figure 2-19.

Figure 2-19. *The Document Outline contains a useful hierarchical representation of the storyboard contents*

If the Document Outline is not visible, click the little button in the lower-left corner of the editing area and you'll see it slide in from the left. It shows everything in the storyboard, split up into **scenes** containing chunks of related content. In our case, we have just one scene, called the **View Controller Scene**. We see that it contains an item called View Controller, which in turn contains an item called the View (along with some other things you'll learn about later). This provides a good way to get an overview of the content where everything you see in the main editing area is mirrored here.

The View icon represents an instance of the UIView class. A UIView object is an area that a user can see and interact with. In this application, we currently have only one view, so this icon represents everything that the user can see in our application. Later, we'll build more complex applications that have several views. For now, just think of this view as an object that the user can see when using your application.

If you click the View icon, Xcode will automatically highlight the square screen outline that we were talking about earlier. This is where you can design your user interface graphically.

The Utilities Area

The Utilities area makes up the right side of the workspace. If it's not currently selected, click the rightmost of the three View buttons in the toolbar, select View ➤ Utilities ➤ Show Utilities, or press ⌥⌘0 (Option-Command-Zero). The bottom half of the Utilities area, shown in Figure 2-20, is called the **Library pane**, or just plain **Library**.

Figure 2-20. *In the Library you'll find stock objects from the UIKit that are available for use in Interface Builder. Everything above the Library but below the toolbar is known collectively as the Inspector*

The Library provides a collection of reusable items for use in your own programs. The four icons in the bar at the top of the library pane divide it into four sections. Click each icon in turn to see what's in each section:

- **File Template Library**: This section contains a collection of file templates you can use when you need to add a new file to your project. For example, if you want to add a new Swift source file to your project, one way to do it is to drag one type from the file template library and drop it onto the Project Navigator.

- **Code Snippet Library**: This section features a collection of code snippets you can drag into your source code files. If you've written something you think you'll want to use again later, select it in your text editor and drag it to the Code Snippet Library.

- **Object Library**: This section contains reusable objects, such as text fields, labels, sliders, buttons, and just about any object you would ever need to design your iOS interface. We'll use the Object Library extensively in this book to build the interfaces for our sample programs.

- **Media Library**: As its name implies, this section is for all your media, including pictures, sounds, and movies. It's empty until you add something to it.

■ **Note**   The items in the Object Library come from the iOS UIKit, which is a framework of objects used to create an app's user interface. UIKit fulfills the same role in Cocoa Touch and as AppKit does in Cocoa on macOS. The two frameworks are similar conceptually; however, because of differences in the platforms, there are obviously many differences between them. On the other hand, the Foundation framework classes, such as NSString and NSArray, are shared between Cocoa and Cocoa Touch.

Note the search field at the bottom of the library. If you want to find a button, type **button** in the search field; the current library will show only items with "button" in the name. Don't forget to clear the search field when you are finished searching, otherwise not all the available items will be shown.

Adding a Label to the View

Let's start working with IB. Click the Object Library icon (it looks like a circle with a square in the center—you can see it in Figure 2-20) at the top of the library area to bring up the Object Library. Just for fun, scroll through the library to find a **Table View**. That's it—keep scrolling and you'll find it. But, there's a better way: just type the words **Table View** in the search field and you'll see it appear.

■ **Tip**   Here's a useful shortcut: press ^⌥⌘3 to jump to the search field and highlight its contents. Next, you can just type the name for the item you wish to search.

Now find a **Label** in the library. Next, drag the label onto the view we saw earlier. (If you don't see the view in your editor pane, click the View icon in the Interface Builder Document Outline). As your cursor appears over the view, it will turn into the standard, "I'm making a copy of something" green plus sign you know from the Finder. Drag the label to the center of the view. A pair of blue guidelines—one vertical and one horizontal—will appear when your label is centered. It's not vital that the label be centered, but it's good to know that those guidelines are there, when you drop the label it should appear, as shown in Figure 2-21.

Figure 2-21. *We've found a label in our library and dragged it onto our view*

User interface items are stored in a hierarchy. Most views can contain subviews; however, there are some, like buttons and most other controls, that can't. Interface Builder is smart. If an object does not accept subviews, you will not be able to drag other objects onto it.

By dragging a label directly to the view we're editing, we add it as a subview of that main view (the view named View), which will cause it to show up automatically when that view is displayed to the user. Dragging a label from the library to the view called View adds an instance of UILabel as a subview of our application's main view.

Let's edit the label so it says something profound. Double-click the label that you just created, and then type **Hello, World!**. Next, click off the label, and then reselect it and drag the label to re-center it or position it wherever you want it to appear on the screen.

We've completed this part, now let's save it to finish up. Select File ➤ Save, or press ⌘S. Now check out the pop-up menu at the upper left of the Xcode project window, the one that says **Hello World**. This is actually a multi-segment pop-up control. The left side lets you choose a different compilation target and do a few other things, but we're interested in the right side, which lets you pick which device you want to run on. Click the right side and you'll see a list of available devices. At the top, if you have any iOS device plugged in and ready to go, you'll see it listed. Otherwise, you'll just see a generic iOS Device entry. Below that, you'll see a whole section, headed by iOS Simulator, listing all the kinds of devices that can be used with the iOS simulator. From that lower section, choose iPhone 6/6s, so that our app will run in the simulator, configured as if it were an iPhone 6/6s.

There are several ways to launch your application: you can select Product ➤ Run, press ⌘R, or press the Run button that's just to the left of the simulator pop-up menu. Xcode will compile your app and launch it in the iOS simulator (see Figure 2-22).

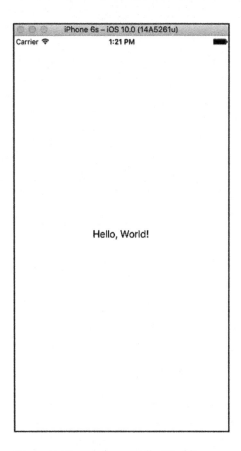

Figure 2-22. *Here's our Hello, World! program running in the iPhone 6s simulator*

■ **Note**   Prior to the added features of Xcode 8, the text would not automatically center and you would need to work with Auto Layout to add in things called constraints to make sure that it was centered on any device.

That's really all there is to our first app at its most basic level—and notice that we wrote no Swift code at all.

Changing Attributes

Back in Xcode single-click the Hello World label to select it and notice the area above the library pane. This part of the utility pane is called the Inspector. The Inspector pane is topped by a series of icons, each of which changes the Inspector to view a specific type of data. To change the attributes of the label, we'll need the fourth icon from the left, which brings up the Attributes Inspector (see Figure 2-23).

Attributes Inspector

***Figure 2-23.** The Attributes Inspector showing our label's attributes*

■ **Tip** The Inspector, like the Project Navigator, has keyboard shortcuts corresponding to each of its icons. The Inspector's keyboard shortcuts start with ||⌘1 for the leftmost icon, ||⌘2 for the next icon, and so on. Unlike the Project Navigator, the number of icons in the Inspector is context-sensitive, and it changes depending on which object is selected in the navigator and/or editor. Note that your keyboard may not have a key that's marked ||. If it doesn't, use the **Option** key instead.

Change the label's appearance any way you like, feeling free to play around with the font, size, and color of the text. Note that if you change the font size, you'll need to add an auto layout constraint to make sure that it has the correct size at run time. To do that, select the label, and then choose Editor ➤ Size to Fit Content from the Xcode menu (see Figure 2-24). Once you've finished playing, save the file and select Run again. The changes you made should show up in your application, once again without writing any code.

Figure 2-24. *Changing the font size larger will force you to change the layout constraints by selecting Size to Fit Content from the Editor drop-down menu*

■ **Note** Don't worry too much about what all of the fields in the Attributes Inspector mean because as you make your way through the book, you'll learn a lot about the Attributes Inspector and what most of the fields do.

By letting us design our interface graphically, Interface Builder frees us to spend time writing the code that is specific to your application, instead of writing tedious code to construct your user interface.

Most modern application development environments have some tool that lets you build your user interface graphically. One distinction between Interface Builder and many of these other tools is that Interface Builder does not generate any code that must be maintained. Instead, Interface Builder creates user interface objects, just as you would in your own code, and then serializes those objects into the storyboard or nib file so that they can be loaded directly into memory at runtime. This avoids many of the problems associated with code generation and is, overall, a more powerful approach.

Finishing Touches

Now let's refine our application making it feel more like an authentic iPhone app. First, run your project again. When the simulator window appears, press ⇧⌘H. That will bring you back to the iPhone home screen, as shown in Figure 2-25. Notice that the app icon now shows as a plain, default image.

Figure 2-25. *The Hello World application shown on the home screen*

Take a look at the Hello World icon at the top of the screen. To change from this boring, default image, we need to create an icon and save it as a portable network graphic (.png) file. Actually, for best results you should create five icons for the iPhone in the following: sizes 180 × 180 pixels, 120 × 120 pixels, 87 × 87 pixels, 80 × 80 pixels, and 58 × 58 pixels. There's another set of four icons that are required if you plan to release your application for the iPad. You'll also need an image that is 187 × 187 pixels for the iPad Pro. The reason for so many icons is because they are used on the home screen, in the Settings app and in the results list for a Spotlight search. That accounts for three of them, but that's not the end of the story—the iPhone 6/6s Plus, with its larger screen, requires higher resolution icons, adding another three to the list. Fortunately, one of these is the same size as an icon from the other set, so you actually only need to create five versions of your application icon for the iPhone. If you don't supply some of the smaller ones, a larger one will be scaled down appropriately; but for best results, you (or a graphic artist on your team) should probably scale it in advance.

■ **Note**   The issue of icon sizes is even more complex than this. Before iOS 7, the side dimension of an icon for all modern iPhones was 114 × 114 pixels. But if you wanted to support older, non-Retina iPhones, you needed to include an icon at half that resolution, or 57 × 57. Then there's the issue of the iPad, which has other icons sizes, both Retina and non-Retina, for both iOS 10 and for earlier versions of iOS.

Do not try to match the style of the buttons that are already on the device when you create the icons; your iPhone or iPad automatically rounds the edges. Just create normal, square images. You'll find a set of suitable icon images in the project archive 02 - Hello World - icons folder.

■ **Note**   For your application's icon, you must use .png images; in fact, you should actually use that format for all images in your iOS projects. Xcode automatically optimizes .png images at build time, which makes them the fastest and most efficient image type for use in iOS apps. Even though most common image formats will display correctly, use .png files unless you have a compelling reason to use another format.

Press ⌘1 to open the Project Navigator, and look inside the Hello World group for an item called **Assets. xcassets**. This is something called an **asset catalog**. By default, each new Xcode project is created with an asset catalog, ready to hold your app icons and other resource files. Select Assets.xcassets and turn your attention to the editor pane.

On the left side of the editor pane, you'll see a column with an entry labeled AppIcon. Select this item and to the right you'll see an area with the text AppIcon in the upper-left corner, as well as dashed-line squares for the icons we just talked about (see Figure 2-26). This is where we'll drag all of our app icons.

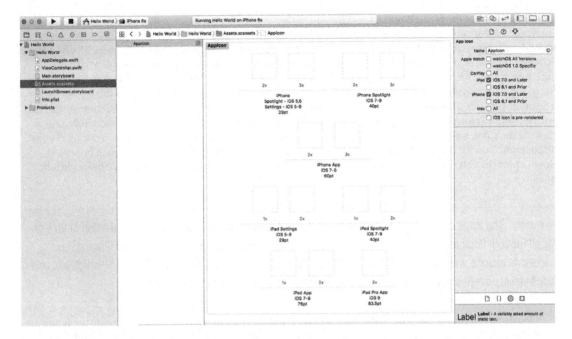

Figure 2-26. *The AppIcon boxes on your project's assets catalog. This is where you set your application's icon*

In the Finder, open the 02 - Hello World - icons folder, select all the files, and drag the bunch of them to IB. Most of the icons should automatically fill with the correct name. You'll likely have a few empty squares left over where you'll find the right file and drag them individually to make sure that there are no empty squares. You do this by comparing the file size as part of the name to the number of points on the square. Note that you'll need to find the double or triple size file if a square has 2x or 3x below it. For example, note in Figure 2-27 that the icon for iPhone Spotlight iOS 7-9 is empty and also says t. Also see that the square has a 3x label. This means that you'll need to find the file that corresponds to 120pts; that is, 3 × 40pts.

Figure 2-27. *Be sure to match .png files to the proper size requirement for the icon*

Now compile and run your app. When the simulator has finished launching, press ⇧⌘P to go to the home screen, and check out your icon (see Figure 2-28). To see one of the smaller icons in use, swipe down inside the home screen to bring up the spotlight search field, and start typing the word Hello—you'll see your new app's icon appear immediately.

Figure 2-28. *The new app icon for our Hello World app*

■ **Note** As we work through this book, our simulator's home screen will get cluttered with the icons for the example applications that we'll be running. If you want to clear out old applications from the home screen, choose iOS Simulator ➤ Reset Content and Settings… from the iOS simulator's application menu.

The Launch Screen

When you launched your application, you may have noticed the white launch screen that appeared while the application was being loaded. iOS applications have always had a launch screen. Since the process of loading an application into memory takes time (and the larger the application, the longer it takes), the purpose of this screen is to let the user see as quickly as possible that something is happening. Prior to iOS 8, you could supply an image (in fact, several images of different sizes) to act as your app's launch screen. iOS would load the correct image and immediately display it before loading the rest of your application. Starting with iOS 8, you still have that option, but Apple now strongly recommends that you use a launch file instead of a launch image, or as well as a launch image if your application still needs to support earlier releases.

A launch file is a storyboard that contains the user interface for your launch screen. On devices running iOS 8 and later, if a launch file is found, it is used in preference to a launch image. Look in the Project Navigator and you'll see that you already have a launch file in your project—it's called **LaunchScreen. storyboard**. If you open it in Interface Builder, you'll see that it just contains a blank view, as shown in Figure 2-29.

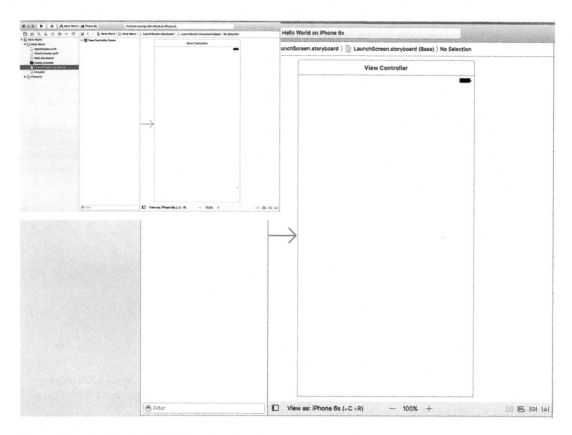

Figure 2-29. *Our application's default launch file*

Apple expects you to build your own launch screen using Interface Builder, in the same way as you would construct any other part of your application's user interface. Apple recommends that you don't try to create a complex or visually impressive launch screen, so we'll follow those guidelines. Instead, we're just going to add a label to the storyboard and change the background color of the main view, so that you can distinguish the launch screen from the application itself. As before, drag a label onto the storyboard, change its text to **Hello World**, and then use the Attributes Inspector (see Figure 2-23) to change its font to System Bold 32. Making sure that the label is selected, click Editor ➤ Size to Fit Content in the Xcode menu. Now center the label in the view and click Editor ➤Resolve Auto Layout Issues ➤Add Missing Constraints to add layout constraints that make sure that it stays there. Next, select the main view by clicking on it in the storyboard or in the Document Outline and use the Attributes Inspector to change its background color. To do that, locate the control labeled **Background** and choose any color you like—since this is an Apress book, I chose yellow. Now just run the application again. You'll see the launch screen appear and then fade away as the application itself appears, as shown in Figure 2-30.

Figure 2-30. *A yellow launch screen for the Hello World application*

You can read more about the launch file, launch images and application icons in Apple's *iOS Human Interface Guidelines* document, which you'll find online at https://developer.apple.com/library/ios/documentation/UserExperience/Conceptual/MobileHIG/LaunchImages.html.

Running the Application on a Device

Before we bring this chapter to a close, there's one more thing we should do. Let's load our app and run it on an actual device. The first step is to connect an iOS device to your Mac using its charging cable. When you do that, Xcode should recognize it and will spend some time reading symbol information from it. You may also see security prompts on both your Mac and your device asking whether you want one to trust the other. Wait until Xcode finishes processing symbol files from the device (check the Activity View to see that), and then open the device selector in the toolbar. You should see your device listed there, as shown in Figure 2-31.

Figure 2-31. *The list of devices and simulators now includes the author's iPhone 6s*

Select the device and click the Run button on the toolbar to start the process of installing and running the application on it. Xcode will rebuild the application and run it on your device. However, because I'm using an early Beta release of Xcode 8, you may see a prompt like the one shown in Figure 2-32.

Figure 2-32. *If the automated provision features fail, you may see this message*

■ **Note**   Apple has made improvements to the provisioning system in Xcode 8 and many of these "fix issue" features have become obsolete, and the process more seamless and successful. Here, we address the topic in a way to make sure that we complete the provisioning to get the app to run on our actual device.

Before you can install an application on an iOS device, it has to have a provisioning profile and it needs to be signed. Signing the application allows the device to identify the author of the application and to check that the binary has not been tampered with since it was created. The provisioning profile contains information that tells iOS which capabilities, such as iCloud access, your application needs to have and which individual devices it can run on. To sign the application, Xcode needs a certificate and a private key.

■ **Tip**   You can read about code signing, provisioning profiles, certificates, and private keys in Apple's App Distribution Workflows in the *App Distribution Guide* at `https://developer.apple.com/library/ios/documentation/IDEs/Conceptual/AppDistributionGuide`.

In the early days of iOS development, you had to sign in to your developer program account and manually create both of these items, and then register the test devices on which you want to install the application. This was a non-trivial and frustrating process. Xcode 7 was improved to be smart enough to do this for you, and Xcode 8 has improved things even more so this should all just work when all you need do is to put an app on a device for testing. In some cases, for different specialized builds to be distributed to particular users, we'll want to customize our provisioning process, but for our learning process, the default, easy-to-use mechanisms work just fine.

There are a couple of things that can go wrong. First, if you see a message saying that your App ID is not available, you'll need to choose a different one. The App ID is based on the project name and the Organization Identifier that you chose when you created the project (see Figure 2-4). You'll see this message if you used com.beginningiphone or another identifier that somebody else has already registered. To fix it, open the Project Navigator and select the Hello World node at the top of the project tree. Then click the Hello World node under the TARGETS section in the Document Outline. Finally, click the General button at the top of the editor area (see Figure 2-33).

Figure 2-33. *Changing your application's bundle identifier*

The App ID that Xcode uses for signing is taken from the Bundle Identifier field in the editor. You'll see that it contains the Organization Identifier that you selected when you created the project—it's the part of the field that's highlighted in Figure 2-33. Choose another value and try building again. Eventually, you should find an identifier that hasn't already been used. When you've done that, make a note of it and be sure to use it to fill in the Organization Identifier field whenever you create a new project. Once you've done that correctly once, Xcode will remember it so you shouldn't have to do it again.

The other thing that can go wrong is shown in Figure 2-34.

Figure 2-34. *Failure to launch in iOS 9 or 10*

You'll see this message only if you are not enrolled in the developer program. It means that your iOS device does not trust you to run applications signed with your Apple ID. To fix this, open the Settings application on the device, and then go to General ➤ Profile. You'll reach a page with a table that contains your Apple ID. Tap the table row to open another page that looks like Figure 2-35.

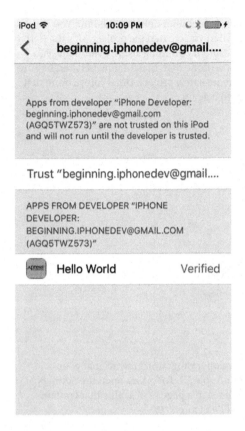

Figure 2-35. *On iOS 9 and above, developers without a developer program membership are not trusted by default*

Chapter Summary

We should be pleased with the progress we've made in this chapter. Although it may not seem like we accomplished all that much, we actually covered a lot of ground. You learned about the iOS project templates, created an application, learned key knowledge about Xcode8, started using Interface Builder, learned how to set your application icon and how to run your application on the simulator and on a real device.

The Hello World program, however, is a strictly one-way application. We show some information to the users, but we never get any input from them. In the next chapter, we'll look at how to go about getting input from the user of an iOS device and taking actions based on that input.

CHAPTER 3

■ ■ ■

Basic User Interactions

Our Hello World app provided a good introduction to iOS development using Xcode and Cocoa Touch, but it lacked a crucial capability—the ability to interact with the user. Without the ability to accept user input, we severely limit the usefulness of our efforts.

In this chapter, we'll write a slightly more complex application—one that will feature two buttons and a label (see Figure 3-1). When the user taps either of the buttons, the label's text changes. This demonstrates the key concepts involved in creating interactive iOS apps. We'll also learn about the `NSAttributedString` class, which lets you use styled text with many Cocoa Touch visual elements.

Figure 3-1. *In this chapter, we'll develop this simple two-button app*

© Molly Maskrey, Kim Topley, David Mark, Fredrik Olsson and Jeff Lamarche 2016
M. Maskrey et al., *Beginning iPhone Development with Swift 3*, DOI 10.1007/978-1-4842-2223-2_3

The MVC Paradigm

If you don't know of MVC, you will. It stands for model-view-controller (MVC) and represents a very logical way of dividing the code that makes up a GUI-based application. These days, almost all object-oriented frameworks build upon MVC, but few adhere to the MVC model as much as Cocoa Touch.

The MVC pattern divides all functionality into three distinct categories:

- **Model**: The classes that hold your application's data.

- **View**: Made up of the windows, controls, and other elements that the user can see and interact with.

- **Controller**: The code that binds together the model and view. It contains the application logic that decides how to handle the user's inputs.

MVC makes certain that the objects implementing these three types of code are as distinct from one another as possible. Any object you create should be readily identifiable as belonging in one of the three categories, with little or no functionality that could be classified as being either of the other two. An object that implements a button, for example, shouldn't contain code to process data when that button is tapped, and an implementation of a bank account shouldn't contain code to draw a table to display its transactions.

MVC helps ensure maximum reusability. A class that implements a generic button can be used in any application. A class that implements a button that does some particular calculation when it is clicked can be used only in the application for which it was originally written.

When you write Cocoa Touch applications, you primarily create your view components using Interface Builder, although you will sometimes modify, and sometimes even create, parts of your user interface in code.

You create your model by writing Swift classes to hold your application's data. We won't be creating any model objects in this chapter's application because we do not need to store or preserve data. We will introduce model objects as our applications get more complex in future chapters.

Your controller component contains classes that you create and that are specific to your application. Controllers are completely custom classes, but more often they exist as subclasses of one of several existing generic controller classes from the UIKit framework, such as `UIViewController`. By subclassing one of these existing classes, you get a lot of functionality for free and won't need to spend time recoding the wheel, so to speak.

As we get deeper into Cocoa Touch, we quickly start to see how the classes of the UIKit framework follow the principles of MVC. Keeping this concept in the back of your mind as you develop and you will end up creating cleaner, more easily maintained Swift code.

Creating the ButtonFun App

It's time to create our next Xcode project. We'll use the same template that we used in the previous chapter: Single View Application. By starting with this simple template again, it's easier to see how the view and controller objects work together in an iOS application. We'll use some of the other templates in later chapters.

Launch Xcode and select File ➤ New ➤ Project... or press ⌘N. Select the Single View Application template, and then click Next.

You'll be presented with the same options sheet that you saw in the previous chapter. In the Product Name field, type the name of our new application, **Button Fun**. The Organization Name, Company Identifier, and Language fields should still have the values you used in the previous chapter, so you can leave those alone. Once again, we are going to use Auto Layout to create an application that works on all iOS devices, so in the Devices field, select Universal. Figure 3-2 shows the completed options sheet.

Choose options for your new project:

Product Name:	ButtonFun
Team:	Molly Maskrey
Organization Name:	MollyMaskrey
Organization Identifier:	com.mollymaskrey
Bundle Identifier:	com.mollymaskrey.ButtonFun
Language:	Swift
Devices:	Universal

◯ Use Core Data
◯ Include Unit Tests
◯ Include UI Tests

Cancel　　　　　　　　　　　　　　　　　　　　Previous　　Next

Figure 3-2. *Naming our project and selecting options*

Hit Next. You'll be prompted for a location for your project. You can leave the Create Git repository check box checked or unchecked, whichever you prefer. Press Create and save the project with the rest of your book projects.

The ViewController

A little later in this chapter, we'll design a view (or user interface) for our application using Interface Builder, just as we did in the previous chapter. Before we do that, we're going to look at and make some changes to the source code files that were created for us. Before we make any changes, let's look at the files that were created for us. In the Project Navigator, the Button Fun group should already be expanded; but if it's not, click the disclosure triangle next to it (see Figure 3-3).

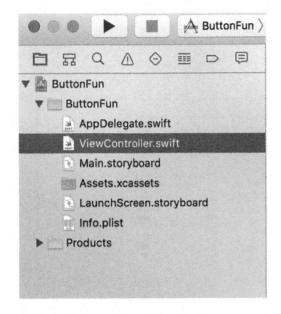

Figure 3-3. *The Project Navigator shows the class files created for us by the project template*

The Button Fun group should contain two source code files along with the main storyboard file, the launch screen storyboard file, an asset catalog for containing any images our app needs and an Info.plist file, which we'll discuss in later chapters. The two source code files implement the classes our application needs: our application delegate and the view controller for our application's only view. We'll look at the application delegate a little later in the chapter. First, we'll work with the view controller class that was created for us.

The controller class called ViewController manages our application's view. The name identifies that this class is, well, a view controller. Click ViewController.swift in the Project Navigator and take a look at the contents of the view controller file (see Listing 3-1).

Listing 3-1. ViewController Code Generated by Our Template

```swift
import UIKit

class ViewController: UIViewController {

    override func viewDidLoad() {
        super.viewDidLoad()
        // Do any additional setup after loading the view, typically from a nib.
    }

    override func didReceiveMemoryWarning() {
        super.didReceiveMemoryWarning()
        // Dispose of any resources that can be recreated.
    }
}
```

Because it was generated by the template, clearly there's not much there yet. ViewController exists as a subclass of UIViewController, which is one of those generic controller classes mentioned earlier. It is part of the UIKit framework, and by subclassing this class, we get a bunch of functionality included. Xcode doesn't know what our application-specific functionality is going to be, but it does know that we're going to have some, so it has created this class for us to write that specific functionality ourselves.

Outlets and Actions

In Chapter 2 we used Xcode's Interface Builder to design a simple user interface and in listing 3-1 we saw the shell of a view controller class. We'll now discuss how the code in this view controller class can interact with the objects (buttons, labels, etc.) in the storyboard. A controller class can refer to objects in a storyboard or nib file by using a special kind of property called an **outlet**. Think of an outlet as a pointer that points to an object within the user interface. For example, suppose you created a text label in Interface Builder (as we did in Chapter 2) and wanted to change the label's text from within your code. By declaring an outlet and connecting that outlet to the label object, you would then be able to use the outlet from within your code to change the text displayed by the label. We'll do that later in this chapter.

Going in the opposite direction, interface objects in our storyboard or nib file can be set up to trigger special methods in our controller class. These special methods are known as **action methods** (or just **actions**). For example, you can tell Interface Builder that when the user taps a button, a specific action method within your code should be called. You could even tell Interface Builder that when the user first touches a button, it should call one action method; and then later, when the finger is lifted off the button, it should call a different action method.

Xcode supports multiple ways of creating outlets and actions. One way is to specify them in our source code before using Interface Builder to connect them with our code, but Xcode's Assistant View gives us a much faster and more intuitive approach that lets us create and connect outlets and actions in a single step, a process we're going to look at shortly. Before we start making connections, let's talk about outlets and actions in a little more detail. Outlets and actions are two of the most basic building blocks you'll use to create iOS apps, so it's important that you understand what they are and how they work.

Outlets

Outlets are ordinary Swift properties that are tagged with the decoration @IBOutlet. An outlet looks something like this:

```
@IBOutlet weak var myButton: UIButton!
```

This example depicts an outlet called myButton, which can be set to point to any button in the user interface.

The Swift compiler doesn't do anything special when it sees the @IBOutlet decoration. Its sole purpose is to act as a hint to tell Xcode that this is a property that we're going to want to connect to an object in a storyboard or nib file. Any property that you create and want to connect to an object in a storyboard or nib file must be preceded by @IBOutlet. Fortunately, as you'll see, you can create outlets in Xcode just by dragging from the object to the property that you want to link it to, or even just by dragging to the class in which you'd like to have a new outlet created.

You may be wondering why the declaration of the myButton property ends with an !. Swift requires all properties to be fully initialized before the completion of every initializer, unless the property is declared to be optional. When a view controller loads from a storyboard, the values of its outlet properties get set from information saved in the storyboard, but this happens *after* the view controller's initializer has been run. As a result, unless you explicitly give them dummy values (which is not desirable), outlet properties have to be declared as optional. That gives you two ways to declare them, using either ! or ?, as shown in Listing 3-2.

Listing 3-2. Two Ways to Declare Optional Variables

```
@IBOutlet weak var myButton1: UIButton?
@IBOutlet weak var myButton2: UIButton!
```

Generally, you'll find the second one easier to use, because there is no need to explicitly unwrap the optional later when it's used in the view controller's code (see Listing 3-3). Be aware that if you do use the second version, you must make sure that it gets set and does not become nil later.

Listing 3-3. Eliminating the Need to Explicitly Unwrap an Optional

```
let button1 = myButton1!    // Optional needs to be unwrapped
let button2 = myButton2     // myButton2 is implicitly unwrapped
```

■ **Note**   The weak specifier attached to the declaration of the outlet property means that the property does not need to create a strong reference to the button. Objects are automatically deallocated as soon as there are no more strong references to them. In this case, there is no risk that the button will be deallocated because there will be a strong reference to it as long as it remains part of the user interface. Making the property reference weak allows deallocation to happen if the view is no longer required and is removed from the user interface at some point. If this happens, the property reference is set to nil.

Actions

In a nutshell, actions are methods that are tagged with the decoration @IBAction, which tells Interface Builder that this method can be triggered by a control in a storyboard or nib file. The declaration for an action method will usually look like this:

```
@IBAction func doSomething(sender: UIButton) {}
```

It might also look like this:

```
@IBAction func doSomething() {}
```

The actual name of the method can be anything you want and it must either take no arguments or take a single argument, usually called sender. When the action method is called, sender will contain a pointer to the object that called it. For example, if this action method was triggered when the user tapped a button, sender would point to the button that was tapped. The sender argument exists so that you can respond to multiple controls using a single action method giving you a way to identify which control called the action method.

■ **Tip**   There's actually a third, less frequently used way to declare an action method that looks like this:

@IBAction func doSomething(sender: UIButton,

                forEvent event: UIEvent) {}

You would use this form if you need more information about the event that caused the method to be called. We'll talk more about control events in the next chapter.

It won't hurt anything to declare an action method with a sender argument and then ignore it. You'll likely see a lot of code that does just that. Action methods in Cocoa and NeXTSTEP needed to accept sender whether they used it or not, so a lot of iOS code, especially early iOS code, was written that way.

Now that you understand what actions and outlets are, we'll see how they work as we design our user interface. But first, let's take care of a little bit of housekeeping.

Simplifying the View Controller

Single-click ViewController.swift in the Project Navigator to open the implementation file. As you can see, there's a small amount of boilerplate code in the form of viewDidLoad() and didReceiveMemoryWarning() methods that were provided for us by the project template we chose. These methods are commonly used in UIViewController subclasses, so Xcode gave us stub implementations of them. If we need to use them, we can just add our code there. However, we don't need either of these stub implementations for this project, so all they're doing is taking up space and making our code harder to read. We're going to do ourselves a favor and clear away methods that we don't need, so go ahead and delete both of them. When you've done that, your file should look like Listing 3-4.

Listing 3-4. Our Simplified ViewController.swift File

```
import UIKit

class ViewController: UIViewController {

}
```

Designing the User Interface

Make sure that you save the changes you just made, and then single-click Main.storyboard to open your application's view using Interface Builder (see Figure 3-4). As you'll remember from the previous chapter, the white window that shows up in the editor represents your application's one and only view. If you look back at Figure 3-1, you can see that we need to add two buttons and a label to this view.

Figure 3-4. *Main.storyboard open for editing in Xcode's Interface Builder*

Let's take a second to think about our application. We're going to add two buttons and a label to our user interface, and that process is very similar to what we did to add a label to the application that we built in the previous chapter. However, we're also going to need outlets and actions to make our application interactive.

The buttons will each need to trigger an action method on our controller. We could choose to make each button call a different action method; but since they're going to do essentially the same task (update the label's text), we will need to call the same action method. We'll differentiate between the two buttons using that sender argument discussed earlier. In addition to the action method, we'll also need an outlet connected to the label so that we can change the text that the label displays.

We'll add the buttons first and then place the label, creating the corresponding actions and outlets as we design our interface. We could also manually declare our actions and outlets, and then connect our user interface items to them, but Xcode can handle this for us.

Adding the Buttons and Action Method

First, we'll add two buttons to our user interface. We'll then have Xcode create an empty action method for us and we will connect both buttons to it. Any code we place in that method will be executed when the user taps the button.

Select View ➤ Utilities ➤ Show Object Library or press ^⌥⌘3 to open the object library. Type **UIButton** in the object library's search box. (You actually need to type only the first four characters, **uibu**, to narrow down the list. You can use all lowercase letters to save yourself the trouble of pressing the Shift key.) Once you're finished typing, only one item should appear in the object library: Button (see Figure 3-5).

Figure 3-5. *The Button as it appears in the object library*

Drag the button from the library and drop it on the white window inside the editing area to add the button to your application's view. Place the button along the left side of the view the appropriate distance from the left edge by using the vertical blue guideline that appears as you move the button toward the left edge of the view. For vertical placement, use the horizontal blue guideline to place the button halfway down in the view. You can use Figure 3-1 as a placement guide, if that helps.

■ **Note**   The little blue guidelines that appear as you move objects around in Interface Builder are there to help you stick to the *iOS Human Interface Guidelines* (HIG). Apple provides the HIG for people designing iPhone and iPad applications. The HIG tells you how you should—and shouldn't—design your user interface. You really should read it because it contains valuable information that every iOS developer needs to know. You'll find it at `https://developer.apple.com/library/ios/documentation/UserExperience/Conceptual/MobileHIG/`.

Double-click the newly added button. This will allow you to edit the button's title. Give this button the title **Left**.

Select View ➤ Assistant Editor ➤ Show Assistant Editor, or press ⌥⌘↩ to open the Assistant Editor. You can also show and hide the Assistant Editor by clicking the middle editor button in the collection of seven buttons on the upper-right side of the project window (see Figure 3-6).

Figure 3-6. *The Show the Assistant Editor toggle button (double circles)*

The Assistant Editor appears to the right of the editing pane, which continues to show Interface Builder. The Assistant Editor should automatically display ViewController.swift, which is the implementation file for the view controller that "owns" the view you're looking at.

■ **Tip**   After opening the Assistant Editor, you may need to resize your window to have enough room to work. If you're on a smaller screen, like the one on a MacBook Air, you might need to close the Utility View and/or Project Navigator to give yourself enough room to use the Assistant Editor effectively (see Figure 3-7). You can do this easily using the three view buttons in the upper right of the project window (see Figure 3-6).

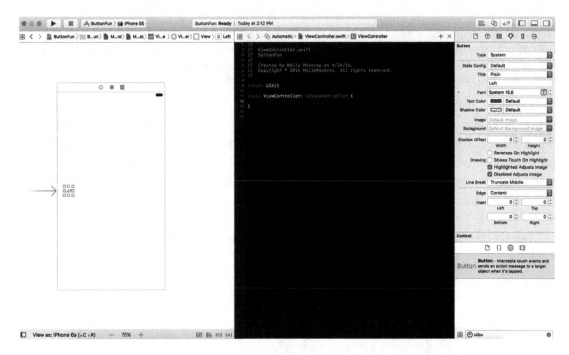

Figure 3-7. *You may have to close other views to see both editing windows on smaller displays*

Xcode knows that our view controller class is responsible for displaying the view in the storyboard, and so the Assistant Editor knows to show us the implementation of the view controller class, which is the most likely place we'll want to connect actions and outlets. However, if it is not displaying the file that you want to see, you can use the jump bar at the top of the Assistant Editor to fix that. First, locate the segment of the jump bar that says Automatic and click it. In the pop-up menu that appears, select Manual ➤ Button Fun ➤ Button Fun ➤ ViewController.swift. You should now be looking at the correct file.

We'll now let Xcode automatically create a new action method for us and associate that action with the button we just created. We're going to add these definitions to the view controller's class extension. To do this, begin by clicking the button that you added to the storyboard so that it is selected. Now, hold down the Control key on your keyboard, and then click-and-drag from the button over to the source code in the Assistant Editor. You should see a blue line running from the button to your cursor, as shown in Figure 3-8. This blue line allows us to connect objects in IB to code or other objects. Moving your cursor so it's inside the class definition, as shown in Figure 3-8, a pop-up appears, letting you know that releasing the mouse button will insert an outlet, an action, or an outlet collection for you.

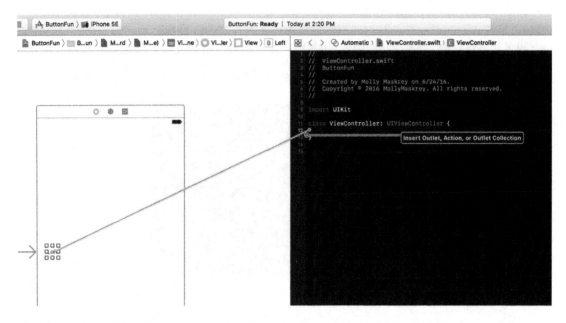

Figure 3-8. *Control-dragging to source code will give you the option to create an outlet, action, or outlet collection*

■ **Note**   We use actions and outlets in this chapter and we'll use outlet collections later in the book. Outlet collections allow you to connect multiple objects of the same kind to a single array property, rather than creating a separate property for each object.

To finish this connection, release your mouse button, and a floating pop-up will appear, like the one shown in Figure 3-9.

Figure 3-9. *The floating pop-up that appears after you Control-drag to source code*

This window lets you customize your new action. In the window, click the pop-up menu labeled Connection and change the selection from Outlet to **Action**. This tells Xcode that we want to create an action instead of an outlet (see Figure 3-10). In the Name field, type **buttonPressed**. When you're finished, do *not* hit the Return key. Pressing Return would finalize our outlet; we're not quite ready to do that. Instead, press the Tab key to move to the Type field and type **UIButton**, replacing the default value of AnyObject.

Figure 3-10. *Changing from Outlet to Action*

There are two fields below Type, which we will leave at their default values. The Event field lets you specify when the method is called. The default value of Touch Up Inside fires when the user lifts a finger off the screen if–and only if–the finger is still on the button. This is the standard event to use for buttons. This gives the user a chance to reconsider. If the user moves a finger off the button before lifting it off the screen, the method won't fire.

The Arguments field lets you choose between the three different method signatures that can be used for action methods. We want the sender argument, so that we can tell which button called the method. That's the default, so we just leave it as is.

Hit the Return key or click the Connect button, and Xcode will insert the action method for you. The ViewController.swift file in the Assistant Editor should now look like Listing 3-5. We'll come back here to write the code that needs to execute when the user taps either this button or the one we'll add shortly.

Listing 3-5. Our ViewController.swift File with the Added IBAction

```swift
import UIKit

class ViewController: UIViewController {

    @IBAction func buttonPressed(_ sender: UIButton) {
    }
}
```

In addition to creating the method code segment, Xcode also connected that button to that method and stored that information in the storyboard. That means we don't need to do anything else to make that button call this method when our application runs.

Go back to Main.storyboard and drag out another button, this time placing the button on the right side of the screen. The blue guidelines will appear to help you align it with the right margin, as you saw before, and they will also help you align the button vertically with the other button. After placing the button, double-click it and change its name to **Right**.

■ **Tip** Instead of dragging out a new object from the library, you could hold down the ⌥ key (the Option key) drag out a copy of the original object (the Left button in this example) over. Holding down the ⌥ key tells Interface Builder to make a copy of the object you drag.

This time, we don't want to create a new action method. Instead, we want to connect this button to the existing one that Xcode created for us a moment ago. After changing the name of the button, Control-click it and drag toward the declaration of the `buttonPressed()` method code in the Assistant Editor. This time, as your cursor gets near `buttonPressed()`, that method should highlight and you'll get a gray pop-up saying Connect Action (see Figure 3-11). If you don't see it straightaway, move the mouse around until it appears. When you see the pop-up, release the mouse button, and Xcode will connect the button to the action method. That will cause the button, when tapped, to trigger the same action method as the other button.

Figure 3-11. *Dragging to an existing action will connect the button to that action*

Adding the Label and Outlet

In the object library, type **lab** into the search field to find the Label user interface item (see Figure 3-12). Drag the Label to your user interface, somewhere above the two buttons you placed earlier. After placing it, use the resize handles to stretch the label from the left margin (as indicated by the blue guideline) to the right margin. That should give it plenty of room for the text we'll be displaying to the user.

Figure 3-12. The label as it appears in the object library

The text in a label, by default, is left-aligned, but we want the text in this one to be centered. Select View ➤ Utilities ➤ Show Attributes Inspector (or press ⌥⌘4) to bring up the Attributes Inspector (see Figure 3-13). Make sure that the label is selected, and then look in the Attributes Inspector for the Alignment buttons. Select the middle Alignment button to center the label's text.

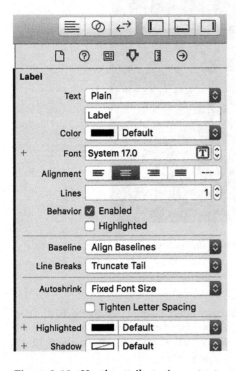

Figure 3-13. Use the attributes inspector to center the label's text

Before the user taps a button, we want the label blank, so double-click the label (so the text is selected) and press the Delete button on your keyboard. That will delete the text currently assigned to the label. Hit Return to commit your changes. Even though you won't be able to see the label when it's not selected, it's still there.

■ **Tip**   If you have invisible user interface elements, like empty labels, and want to be able to see where they are, select Canvas from the Editor menu. Next, from the submenu that pops up, turn on Show Bounds Rectangles. If you just want to select an element that you can't see, just click its icon in the Document Outline.

Finally, let's create an outlet for the label. We do this exactly the way we created and connected actions earlier. Make sure that the Assistant Editor is open and displaying ViewController.swift. If you need to switch files, use the pop-up in the jump bar above the Assistant Editor.

Next, select the label in Interface Builder and Control-drag from the label to the header file. Drag until your cursor is right above the existing action method. When you see something like Figure 3-14, let go of the mouse button and you'll see the pop-up window again (shown in Figure 3-9).

Figure 3-14. *Connecting the UILabel outlet*

Leave the Connection at the default type of Outlet. We want to choose a descriptive name for this outlet so we'll remember what it is used for when we're working on our code. Type **statusLabel** into the Name field. Leave the Type field set to UILabel. The final field, labeled Storage, can be left at the default value.

Hit Return to commit your changes, and Xcode will insert the outlet property into your code. Your code should now look like Listing 3-6.

Listing 3-6. Adding Our Label Outlet to the View Controller

```
import UIKit

class ViewController: UIViewController {

    @IBOutlet weak var statusLabel: UILabel!
```

```
@IBAction func buttonPressed(_ sender: UIButton) {
}
}
```

Now we have an outlet where Xcode has automagically connected the label to our outlet. This means that if we make any changes to statusLabel in code, those changes affect the label in our user interface. Setting the text property on statusLabel, for example, changes the text that is displayed to the user.

AUTOMATIC REFERENCE COUNTING

If you're familiar with languages like C or C++ where you have to be careful to release memory that you allocate when you no longer need it, you might be somewhat concerned that we seem to be creating objects but not destroying them.

The LLVM compiler that Apple includes with Xcode these days is smart enough to release objects for us, using a feature called **Automatic Reference Counting**, or ARC.

ARC applies only to Swift objects and structures, not to Core Foundation objects or to memory allocated with C-language library functions like malloc(), and there are some caveats and gotchas that can trip you up. But for the most part, worrying about memory management is a thing of the past.

To learn more about ARC, check out the ARC release notes at this URL:

http://developer.apple.com/library/ios/#releasenotes/ObjectiveC/RN-TransitioningToARC/

ARC is very helpful, but it's not magic. You should still understand the basic rules of memory management in iOS to avoid getting in trouble with ARC. To learn about the iOS (and macOS) memory management contract, read Apple's *Memory Management Programming Guide* at this URL:

https://developer.apple.com/library/ios/documentation/Cocoa/Conceptual/MemoryMgmt/Articles/MemoryMgmt.html

---

Writing the Action Method

So far, we've designed our user interface and wired up both outlets and actions. All that's left to do is to use those actions and outlets to set the text of the label when a button is pressed. Single-click ViewController. swift in the Project Navigator to open it in the editor. Find the empty buttonPressed() method that Xcode created for us earlier.

To differentiate between the two buttons, we'll use the sender parameter. We'll retrieve the title of the button that was pressed using sender, and then create a new string based on that title and assign that as the label's text. Change the buttonPressed() method to that shown in Listing 3-7.

Listing 3-7. Completing the Action Method

```
@IBAction func buttonPressed(sender: UIButton) {
    let title = sender.title(for: .selected)!
    let text = "\(title) button pressed"
    statusLabel.text = text
}
```

This is pretty straightforward. The first line retrieves the tapped button's title using `sender`. Since buttons can have different titles depending on their current state (although not in this example), we use the `UIControlState.selected` parameter to specify that we want the title when the button is in its selected state since the user selected it by tapping it. We'll look at control states in more detail in Chapter 4.

■ **Tip** You probably noticed that the argument we used to call the `title(for: )` method was `.selected`, not `UIControlState.selected`. Swift already understands that the argument must be one of the values of the `UIControlState` enumeration, so we can omit the enumeration name to save typing.

The next line creates a new string by appending this text to the title we retrieved in the previous line: **button pressed**. So, if the left button, which has a title of Left, is tapped, this line will create a string that reads: **Left button pressed**. The final line assigns the new string to the label's text property, which is how we change the text that the label is displaying.

Testing the ButtonFun App

Select Product ➤ Run. If you run into any compile or link errors, go back and compare your code changes to those shown in this chapter. Once your code builds properly, Xcode will launch the iOS simulator and run your application. If you run with an iPhone simulator and tap the Left button, you'll see something like Figure 3-15.

Figure 3-15. Running the application on our iPhone 6s

While everything seems to be good with this, the layout of everything needs some work. To see why, change the active scheme, as shown in Figure 3-16 to an iPhone SE and run the application again.

Figure 3-16. *Changing the scheme, and thus the target of execution, to a different size and shape*

The result, shown in Figure 3-17, shows the problems. Note that while the left button still works, the label itself is off to the right a bit and the right button has completely vanished.

Figure 3-17. *Our layout is a little off using a different simulated device*

To start to see why, in Xcode underneath our Interface Builder window, tap the right button to select it and see the outline, and then below select the View As for iPhone SE, as shown in Figure 3-18. You can see that because we set up our layout to work on a device with a larger screen size, when we move to a smaller device, some of the controls have moved within our new display.

Figure 3-18. *When viewing our layout on a device with a smaller screen area, our right button shifted so that it is no longer visible*

Fixing Issues Using Auto Layout

The left button is in the right place, but the label and the other button are not. In Chapter 2, we fixed a similar problem by using Auto Layout. The idea behind Auto Layout is that you use constraints to specify how you want your controls to be placed. In this case, here's what we want to happen:

- The Left button should be vertically centered and close to the left margin of the screen.

- The Right button should be vertically centered and close to the right margin of the screen.

- The label should be horizontally centered, a little down from the top of the screen.

Each of the preceding statements contains two constraints—one of them a horizontal constraint, the other a vertical constraint. If we apply these constraints to our three views, Auto Layout will take care of positioning them correctly on any screen. So how do we do that? You can add Auto Layout constraints to views in code by creating instances of the NSLayoutConstraint class. In some cases, that's the only way to create a correct layout, but in this case (and in all of the examples in this book), you can get the layout that you want by using Interface Builder. Interface Builder lets you add constraints visually by dragging and clicking. First, in the View As under the IB window, reselect 6s as our device so that we see all our controls as we had them. Set the scale to where you can see the whole screen; I'm using 75%. We'll use Auto Layout to fix the other device configurations as well (see Figure 3-19).

Figure 3-19. *We'll use Auto Layout with the same device we started with to configure for all other device types*

We'll start by positioning the label. Select Main.storyboard in the Project Navigator and open the Document Outline to show the view hierarchy. Find the icon labeled View. This represents the view controller's main view and it's the one relative to which we need to position the other views. Click the disclosure triangle to open the View icon if it's not already open, and reveal the two buttons (labeled Left and Right) and the label. Hold down the Control key and drag the mouse from the label to its parent view, as shown on the left in Figure 3-20.

Figure 3-20. *Positioning the label with Auto Layout constraints*

By dragging from one view to another, you are telling Interface Builder that you want to apply an Auto Layout constraint between them. Release the mouse and a gray pop-up with various choices will appear, as shown on the right in Figure 3-20. Each choice in this pop-up is a single constraint. Clicking any of them will apply that constraint, but we know that we need to apply two constraints to the label and both of them are available in the pop-up. To apply more than one constraint at a time, you need to hold down the Shift key while selecting them. So hold down the Shift key and click **Center Horizontally in Container** and **Vertical Spacing to Top Layout Guide**. To actually apply the constraints, click the mouse anywhere outside the pop-up or press the return key. When you do this, the constraints that you have created appear under the heading Constraints in the Document Outline and are also represented visually in the storyboard, as shown in Figure 3-21.

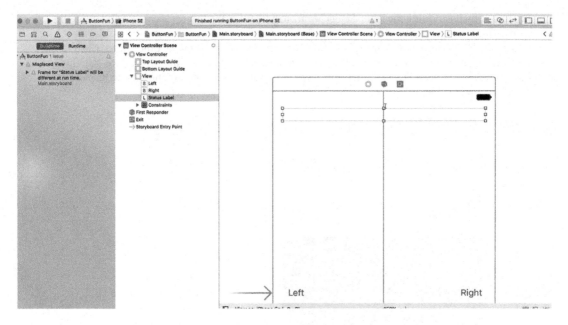

Figure 3-21. *Two Auto Layout constraints have been applied to the label*

■ **Tip** If you make a mistake when adding a constraint, you can remove it by clicking its representation in the Document Outline, or in the storyboard, and pressing Delete.

You'll probably also see that the label has an orange outline. Interface Builder uses orange to indicate an Auto Layout problem. There are three typical problems that Interface Builder highlights in this way:

- You don't have enough constraints to fully specify a view's position or size.

- The view has constraints that are ambiguous—that is, they don't uniquely pin down its size or position.

- The constraints are correct, but the position and/or size of the view at runtime will not be the same as it is in Interface Builder.

You can find out more about the problem by clicking the yellow warning triangle in the Activity View to see an explanation in the Issue Navigator (see Figure 3-21, far left). If you do that, you'll see that it says **Frame for "Status Label" will be different at run time**—the third of the problems listed. You can clear this warning by having Interface Builder move the label to its correct runtime position and give it its configured size. To do that, look at the bottom-right side of the storyboard editor. You'll see four buttons, as shown in Figure 3-22.

Figure 3-22. Auto Layout buttons at the bottom right of the storyboard editor

You can find out what each of these buttons does by hovering your mouse over them. The left button relates to the UIStackView control, which we'll talk about in Chapter 10. Working from left to right, here's what the other three buttons are:

1. The Align button lets you align the selected view relative to another view. If you click this button now, you'll see a pop-up that contains various alignment options. One of them is Horizontal Center in Container, a constraint that you have already applied to the label from the Document Outline. There is often more than one way to achieve Auto Layout-related things in Interface Builder. As you progress through this book, you'll see alternate ways to do the most common Auto Layout tasks.

2. The pop-up for the Pin button contains controls that let you set the position of a view relative to other views, and to apply size constraints. For example, you can set a constraint that constrains the height of one view to be the same as that of another.

3. The Resolve Auto Layout Issues button lets you correct layout problems. You can use menu items in its pop-up to have Interface Builder remove all constraints for a view (or the entire storyboard), guess which constraints might be missing, add them, and adjust the frames of one or more views to what they will be at runtime.

You can fix the label's frame by selecting it in the Document Outline or the storyboard and clicking the Resolve Auto Layout Issues button. The pop-up for this button has two identical groups of operations (see Figure 3-23).

Figure 3-23. *The pop-up for the Resolve Auto Layout Issues button*

■ **Tip**   If none of the items in the pop-up is enabled, click the label in the Document Outline to ensure that it's selected and try again.

If you select an operation from the top group, it's applied only to the currently selected view, whereas operations from the bottom group are applied to all of the views in the view controller. In this case, we just need to fix the frame for one label, so click Update Frames in the top part of the pop-up. When you do this, both the orange outline and the warning triangle in the Activity View disappear, because the label now has the position and size that it will have at runtime. In fact, the label has shrunk to zero width and it's represented in the storyboard by a small, empty square, as shown in Figure 3-24.

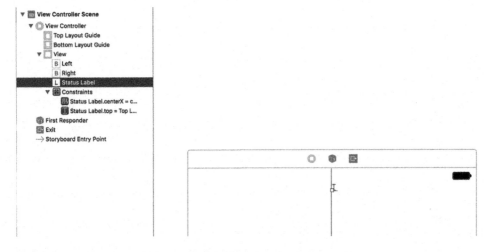

Figure 3-24. *After fixing its frame, the label has shrunk to zero size*

It turns out that this is actually what we want to see. Many of the views that UIKit provides, including UILabel, are capable of having Auto Layout set their size based on their actual content. They do this by calculating their natural or intrinsic content size. At its intrinsic size, the label is just wide enough and tall enough to completely surround the text that it contains. At the moment, this label has no content, so its intrinsic content size really should be zero along both axes. When we run the application and click one of the buttons, the label's text is set and its intrinsic content size changes. When that happens, Auto Layout will resize the label automatically so that you can see all of the text.

Now that we've taken care of the label, we'll fix the positions of the two buttons. Select the Left button on the storyboard and click the Align button at the bottom right of the storyboard editor (the second button in Figure 3-22, counting from the left). We want the button to be vertically centered, so select Vertical Center in Container in the pop-up, and then click Add 1 Constraint (see Figure 3-25).

Figure 3-25. *Using the Align pop-up to vertically center a view*

We need to apply the same constraint to the Right button, so select it and repeat the process. While you were doing this, Interface Builder found a couple of new issues, indicated by the orange outlines in the storyboard and the warning triangle in the Activity View. Click the triangle to see the reasons for the warnings in the Issue Navigator, as shown in Figure 3-26.

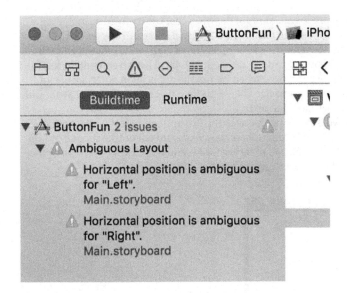

Figure 3-26. *Interface Builder warnings for missing constraints*

Interface Builder warns us that the horizontal positions of both buttons are ambiguous. In fact, since we haven't yet set any constraint to control the buttons' horizontal positions, this should not be a surprise.

■ **Note**   While setting Auto Layout constraints, it is normal for warnings like this to appear. You should use them to help you set a complete set of constraints. You should have no warnings once you have completed the layout process. Most of the examples in this book have instructions for setting layout constraints. While you are adding those constraints, you will usually encounter warnings, but don't be concerned unless you still have warnings when you have completed all of the steps. In that case, you missed a step, you performed a step incorrectly, or possibly there is an error in the book. In the latter case, please let us know by submitting an erratum on the book's page at www.apress.com.

We want the Left button to be a fixed distance from the left side of its parent view and the Right button to be the same distance from the right side of that view. We can set those constraints from the pop-up for the Pin button (the one to the right of the Align button in Figure 3-22). Select the Left button and click the Pin button to open its pop-up. At the top of the pop-up, you'll find four input fields connected to a small square by orange dashed lines, as shown on the left in Figure 3-27. The small square represents the button that we are constraining. The four input fields let you set the distances between the button and its nearest neighbors above it, below it, to its left and to its right. A dashed line indicates that no constraint yet exists. In the case of the Left button, we want to set a fixed distance between it and the left side of its parent view, so click the dashed orange line to the left of the square. When you do this, it becomes a solid orange line indicating that there is now a constraint to apply. Next, enter **32** in the left input field to set the distance from the Left button to its parent view.

Figure 3-27. *Using the Pin pop-up to set the horizontal position of a view*

To fix the position of the Right button, select it, press the Pin button, click the orange dashed line to the right of the square (since we are pinning this button to the right side of its parent view), enter 32 in the input field, and press Add 1 Constraint.

We have now applied all of the constraints that we need, but there may still be warnings in the Activity View. If you investigate, you'll see that the warnings are because the buttons are not in their correct runtime locations. To fix that, we'll use the Resolve Auto Layout Issues button again. Click the button (it's the rightmost one) to open its pop-up, and then click Update Frames from the bottom group of options. We use the option from the bottom group because we need the frames of all of the views in the view controller to be adjusted.

■ **Tip**   You may find that none of the options in the top group is available. If this is the case, select the View Controller icon in the Document Outline and try again.

The warnings should now go away and our layout is finally complete. Run the application on an iPhone simulator. You'll see a result that's almost like Figure 3-1 at the beginning of this chapter. When you tap the right button, this text should appear: **Right button pressed**. If you then tap the left button, the label will change to **Left button pressed**. Run the example on an iPad simulator and you'll find that the layout still works, although the buttons are further apart because of the wider screen. That's the power of auto layout.

■ **Tip**   When running the application on simulated devices with large screens, you may find that you can't see the whole screen at once. You can fix this by selecting Window ➤ Scale in the iOS Simulator menu and choosing a scale that's appropriate for the screen you're using.

If you look back at Figure 3-1, you'll see that one thing is missing. The screenshot we showed you for our end result displays the name of the chosen button in bold text; however, what we've made just shows a plain string. We'll bring on the boldness using the NSAttributedString class in just a second. Let's look at another useful feature of Xcode—layout previews.

Previewing Layout

Return to Xcode and select Main.storyboard, and then open the Assistant Editor if it's not already showing (refer back to Figure 3-6 if you need a reminder of how to do this). At the left of the jump bar at the top of the Assistant Editor, you'll see that the current selection is Automatic (unless you changed it to Manual to select the file for the Assistant Editor to display). Click to open the pop-up for this segment of the jump bar and you'll see several options, the last of which is Preview. When you hover the cursor over Preview, a menu containing the name of the application's storyboard will appear. Click it to open the storyboard in the Preview Editor.

When the Preview Editor opens, you'll see the application as it appears on an iPhone in portrait mode. This is just a preview, so it won't respond to button clicks and, as a result, you won't see the label. If you move your mouse over the area just below the preview, where it says iPhone 6s, a control will appear that will let you rotate the phone into landscape mode. You can see the control on the left of Figure 3-28, and the result of clicking it to rotate the phone.

Figure 3-28. *Previewing the layout of the iPhone in landscape mode*

Using Auto Layout, when we rotate the phone, the buttons move so that they remain vertically centered and the same distance away from the sides of the device, as in portrait orientation. If the label were visible, you would see that it is in the correct position as well.

We can also use the Preview Assistant to see what happens when we run the application on a different device. At the bottom left of the Preview Assistant (and in Figure 3-28), you'll see a + icon. Click this to open a list of devices, and then select iPhone SE to add the new preview to the Preview Assistant. If you still can't see everything, you can zoom the Preview Assistant in a couple of different ways. The easiest is to double-click the Preview Assistant pane—this toggles between a full size view and a much smaller view. If you'd like more control over the zoom level you can use a pinch gesture on your trackpad (unfortunately, this is not supported on the magic mouse, at least not at the time of writing). Figure 3-29 shows the two iPhone previews, zoomed out to fit in the space available on my screen. Once again, Auto Layout has arranged for the buttons to be in the correct locations. Rotate the iPhone SE preview to see that the layout also works in landscape mode.

Figure 3-29. *Previewing layouts on two devices at the same time*

■ **Note**   At the time of writing, Preview Assistant did not correctly show iPad 9.7-inch and 12.9-inch preview layouts correctly. This was likely due to bugs in the beta release of Xcode 8. However, running them in the simulator showed them working correctly.

Changing the Text Style

The NSAttributedString class lets you attach formatting information, such as fonts and paragraph alignment, to a string. This metadata can be applied to an entire string, or different attributes can be applied to different parts. If you think about the ways that formatting can be applied to pieces of text in a word processor, that's basically the model for how NSAttributedString works. Most of the main UIKit controls let you use attributed strings. In the case of a UILabel like the one we have here, it's as simple as creating an attributed string, and then passing it to the label via its attributedText property.

So, select ViewController.swift and update the buttonPressed() method, as shown in Listing 3-8.

Listing 3-8. Updated buttonPressed() Method to Add Bold Font Characteristic

```
import UIKit

class ViewController: UIViewController {

    @IBOutlet weak var statusLabel: UILabel!

    @IBAction func buttonPressed(_ sender: UIButton) {
        let title = sender.title(for: .selected)!
        let text = "\(title) button pressed"
        let styledText = NSMutableAttributedString(string: text)
        let attributes = [
            NSFontAttributeName:
                UIFont.boldSystemFont(ofSize: statusLabel.font.pointSize)
        ]
        let nameRange = (text as NSString).range(of: title)
        styledText.setAttributes(attributes, range: nameRange)

        statusLabel.attributedText = styledText
    }
}
```

The first thing the new code does is create an attributed string—specifically, an NSMutableAttributedString instance—based on the string we are going to display. We need a mutable attributed string here because we want to change its attributes.

Next, we create a dictionary to hold the attributes we want to apply to our string. We have just one attribute right now, so this dictionary contains a single key-value pair. The key, NSFontAttributeName, lets us specify a font for a portion of an attributed string. The value we pass in is the bold system font of the same size as the font currently used by the label. Specifying the font this way is more flexible in the long run than specifying a font by name, since we know that the system will always have a reasonable idea of what to use for a bold font.

Next, we ask our text string to give us the range (consisting of a start index and a length) of the substring where our title is found. We use the range to apply the attributes to the part of the attributed string that corresponds to the title and pass it off to the label. Let's take a closer look at the line that locates the title string:

```
let nameRange = (text as NSString).range(of: title)
```

Notice that the text variable is cast from the Swift type String to the Core Foundation type NSString. That's necessary because both String and NSString have methods called range(of: String). We need to call the NSString method to get the range as an NSRange object, since that's what the setAttributes() method on the next line expects.

Now you can hit the Run button. You'll see that the app shows the name of the clicked button in bold text, as shown in Figure 3-1.

Examining the Application Delegate

Now that our application works, before we move on to our next topic, let's take a minute to look through the source code file we have not yet examined—**AppDelegate.swift**. This file implements our **application delegate.**

Cocoa Touch makes extensive use of **delegates**, which are objects that take responsibility for doing certain tasks on behalf of another object. The application delegate lets us do things at certain predefined times on behalf of the UIApplication class. Every iOS application has exactly one instance of UIApplication, which is responsible for the application's run loop and handles application-level functionality, such as routing input to the appropriate controller class. UIApplication is a standard part of the UIKit; it does its job mostly behind the scenes, so you generally don't need to worry about it.

At certain well-defined times during an application's execution, UIApplication calls specific methods on its delegate, if the delegate exists and implements the method. For example, if you have code that needs to be executed just before your program quits, you would implement the method applicationWillTerminate() in your application delegate and put your termination code there. This type of delegation allows your application to implement behavior without needing to subclass UIApplication or, indeed, without needing to know anything about the inner workings of UIApplication. All of the Xcode templates create an application delegate for you and arrange for it to be linked to the UIApplication object when the application launches.

Click AppDelegate.swift in the Project Navigator to see the stub application delegate that the project template provides. The first couple of lines should look like that shown in Listing 3-9.

Listing 3-9. Application Delegate Initial Code

```
import UIKit

@UIApplicationMain
class AppDelegate: UIResponder, UIApplicationDelegate {

    var window: UIWindow?
```

The code highlighted in bold indicates that this class conforms to a protocol called UIApplicationDelegate. Hold down the ⌥ key. Your cursor should turn into crosshairs. Move your cursor so that it is over the word UIApplicationDelegate. Your cursor will turn into a question mark, and the word UIApplicationDelegate will be highlighted, as if it were a link in a browser (see Figure 3-30).

```
 9  import UIKit
10
11  @UIApplicationMain
12  class AppDelegate: UIResponder, UIApplicationDelegate {
13
14      var window: UIWindow?
15
```

Figure 3-30. When you hold down the ⌥ key (the Option key) in Xcode and point at a symbol in your code, the symbol is highlighted and your cursor changes into a pointing hand with a question mark

With the ⌥ key still held down, click this link. A small pop-up window will open, showing a brief overview of the UIApplicationDelegate protocol (see Figure 3-31).

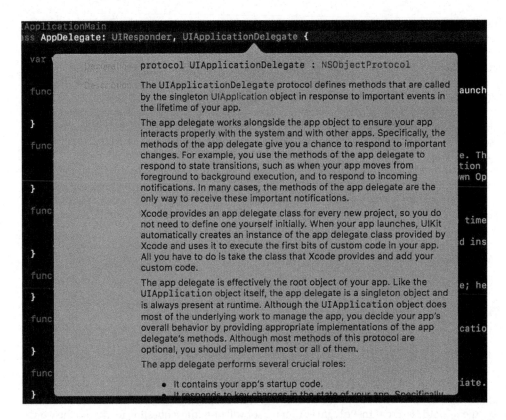

Figure 3-31. *When we Option-clicked UIApplicationDelegate from within our source code, Xcode popped up this window, called the Quick Help panel, which describes the protocol*

Scrolling the pop-up to the bottom, you'll find two links (see Figure 3-32).

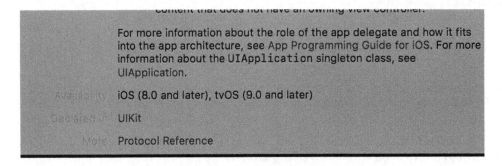

Figure 3-32. *Links to additional information about the selected item*

Notice the two links at the bottom of this new pop-up documentation window; click the More link to view the full documentation for this symbol or click the Declared In link to view the symbol's definition in a header file. This same trick works with class and protocol names, as well as method names displayed in the editor pane. Just Option-click a word, and Xcode searches for that word in the documentation browser.

Knowing how to look up things quickly in the documentation is definitely worthwhile, but looking at the definition of this protocol is perhaps more important. Here's where you'll find which methods the application delegate can implement and when those methods will be called. It's probably worth your time to read over the descriptions of these methods.

Back in the Project Navigator, return to AppDelegate.swift to see the implementation of the application delegate. It should look something like Listing 3-10.

Listing 3-10. Our AppDelegate.swift File

```swift
import UIKit

@UIApplicationMain
class AppDelegate: UIResponder, UIApplicationDelegate {

    var window: UIWindow?

    func application(_ application: UIApplication, didFinishLaunchingWithOptions
    launchOptions: [NSObject: AnyObject]?) -> Bool {
        // Override point for customization after application launch.
        return true
    }

    func applicationWillResignActive(_ application: UIApplication) {
        // Sent when the application is about to move from active to inactive state. This
        // can occur for certain types of temporary interruptions (such as an incoming phone
        // call or SMS message) or when the user quits the application and it begins the
        // transition to the background state.
        // Use this method to pause ongoing tasks, disable timers, and throttle down OpenGL
        // ES frame rates. Games should use this method to pause the game.
    }

    func applicationDidEnterBackground(_ application: UIApplication) {
        // Use this method to release shared resources, save user data, invalidate timers,
        // and store enough application state information to restore your application to its
        // current state in case it is terminated later.
        // If your application supports background execution, this method is called instead
        // of applicationWillTerminate: when the user quits.
    }

    func applicationWillEnterForeground(_ application: UIApplication) {
        // Called as part of the transition from the background to the active state; here
        // you can undo many of the changes made on entering the background.
    }

    func applicationDidBecomeActive(_ application: UIApplication) {
        // Restart any tasks that were paused (or not yet started) while the application was
        // inactive. If the application was previously in the background, optionally refresh
        // the user interface.
    }
```

```
func applicationWillTerminate(_ application: UIApplication) {
    // Called when the application is about to terminate. Save data if appropriate. See
    also applicationDidEnterBackground:.
}

}
```

At the top of the file, you can see that our application delegate has implemented one of those protocol methods covered in the documentation, called `application(_: didFinishLaunchingWithOptions:)`. As you can probably guess, this method fires as soon as the application has finished all the setup work and is ready to start interacting with the user. It is often used to create any objects that need to exist for the entire lifetime of the running app.

You'll see more of this later in the book, especially in Chapter 15 where we'll say a lot more about the role that the delegate plays in the application life cycle. We just wanted to give you a bit of background on application delegates and show how this all ties together before closing this chapter.

Summary

This chapter's simple application introduced you to MVC, creating and connecting outlets and actions, implementing view controllers, and using application delegates. You learned how to trigger action methods when a button is tapped. And you saw how to change the text of a label at runtime. Although we built a very simple application, the basic concepts used are the same as those that underlie the use of all controls under iOS, not just buttons. In fact, the way we used buttons and labels in this chapter is pretty much the way that we will implement and interact with most of the standard controls under iOS.

It's critical to understand everything we did in this chapter and why we did it. If you don't, make sure to review the parts that you don't fully understand. If things are not completely clear, you will only get more confused as we get into creating more complex interfaces later in this book.

In the next chapter, we'll take a look at some of the other standard iOS controls. You'll also learn how to use alerts to notify the user of important happenings and how to use action sheets to indicate that the user needs to make a choice before proceeding.

CHAPTER 4

Adding Intermediate Level User Interactions

In Chapter 3, we discussed MVC and built an application using it. You learned about outlets and actions, and you used them to tie a button control to a text label. In this chapter, we'll build an application with a broader set of controls to increase your familiarity with developing a user interface, like the one shown in Figure 4-1.

Figure 4-1. *This chapter's project increases your UI skills by adding several new controls to the mix*

© Molly Maskrey, Kim Topley, David Mark, Fredrik Olsson and Jeff Lamarche 2016
M. Maskrey et al., *Beginning iPhone Development with Swift 3*, DOI 10.1007/978-1-4842-2223-2_4

We'll implement an image view, a slider, two different text fields, a segmented control, a couple of switches, and an iOS button that looks like buttons did before iOS 7. You'll see how to set and retrieve the values of various controls. You'll learn how to use action sheets to force the user to make a choice, and how to use alerts to give the user important feedback. You'll also learn about control states and the use of stretchable images to change the appearance of buttons.

Because this chapter's application uses so many different user interface items, we're going to work a little differently than we did in the previous two chapters. We'll break our application into pieces, implementing one piece at a time. Bouncing back and forth between Xcode and the iOS simulator, we'll test each piece before we move on to the next. Dividing the process of building a complex interface into smaller components makes it much less intimidating, as well as more like the actual process you'll go through when building your own applications. This **code-compile-debug** cycle makes up a large part of a software developer's typical day.

Our app uses only a single view and controller; but as you can see in Figure 4-1, there's a lot more complexity in this one view.

The logo at the top of the screen exists in an image view, which, in this app, does nothing more than display a static image. I placed two text fields below the logo: one allowing the entry of alphanumeric text and the other permitting only numbers. A slider sits just below the text fields. As the user moves the slider, the value of the label next to it changes so that it always reflects the slider's current value.

Below the slider are a segmented control and two switches. The segmented control toggles between two different types of controls in the space underneath it. When the application first launches, two switches appear below the segmented control. Changing the value of either switch causes the other one to change its value to match. While this isn't something you would likely do in a real application, it demonstrates how to change the value of a control programmatically and how Cocoa Touch animates certain actions without you needing to do any work.

Figure 4-2 shows what happens when the user taps the segmented control. The switches disappear and are replaced by a button.

Figure 4-2. *Tapping the segmented controller on the left side causes a pair of switches to be displayed. Tapping the right side causes a button to be displayed, as shown here*

Pressing Do Something causes an action sheet to pop up, asking if the user really meant to tap the button (see Figure 4-3). Notice how the action sheet is now highlighted and in the foreground, while the other controls become dimmed.

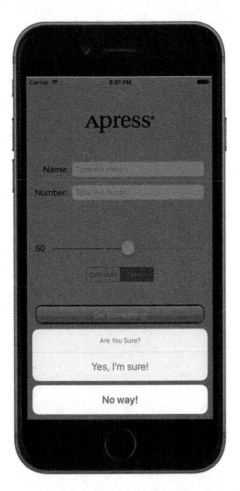

Figure 4-3. *An action sheet requests a response from the user*

This provides a standard way of responding to input that is potentially dangerous or that could have significant repercussions, and it gives the user a chance to stop potential problems from happening. If Yes, I'm Sure! is selected, the application displays an alert, letting the user know that everything is OK (see Figure 4-4).

Figure 4-4. *Alerts notify the user when important things happen. Our app uses one to confirm that everything went OK*

Active, Static, and Passive Controls

Interface controls operate in three basic modes: active, static (or inactive), and passive. The buttons that we used in the previous chapter provide classic examples of active controls. You push them, and something happens—usually, a piece of Swift code you've written executes.

Although many of the controls you use directly trigger action methods, not all controls work this way. The image view that we'll be implementing in this does nothing other than show an image in our application; though it can be configured to trigger action methods—here, the user doesn't do anything with it. Labels and image controls often work in this manner.

Some controls operate in a passive mode, simply holding on to a value that the user has entered until you're ready for it. These controls don't trigger action methods, but the user can interact with them and change their values. A classic example of a passive control is a text field on a web page. Although it's possible to create validation code that fires when the user tabs out of a field, the vast majority of web page text fields simply contain data that's submitted to the server when the user clicks the submit button. The text fields themselves usually don't cause any code to fire, but when the submit button is clicked, the text field's data gets passed to the associated Swift code.

On an iOS device, most of the available controls function in all three modes, and nearly all of them can function in more than one mode, depending on your needs. All iOS controls exist as subclasses of UIControl, which makes them capable of triggering action methods. Many controls can be used passively, and all of them can be made inactive or invisible. For example, using one control might trigger another inactive control to become active. However, some controls, such as buttons, really don't serve much purpose unless they are used in an active manner to trigger code.

Some behavioral differences exist between controls on iOS and those on your Mac. Here are a few examples:

- Because of the multitouch interface, all iOS controls can trigger multiple actions, depending on how they are touched. The user might trigger a different action with a finger swipe across the control than with just a tap.

- You could have one action fire when the user presses down on a button and a separate action fire when the finger is lifted off the button.

- You could have a single control call multiple action methods on a single event. For example, you could have two different action methods fire on the Touch Up Inside event when the user's finger is lifted after touching that button.

■ **Note** Although controls can trigger multiple methods on iOS, the vast majority of the time, you're better off implementing a single action method that does what you need for a particular use of a control. You won't usually need this capability, but it's good to keep it in mind when working in Interface Builder. Connecting an event to an action in Interface Builder does not disconnect a previously connected action from the same control! This can lead to surprising misbehaviors in your app, where a control will trigger multiple action methods. Keep an eye open when retargeting an event in Interface Builder, and make sure you remove old actions before connecting to new ones.

Another major difference between iOS and the Mac stems from the fact that, normally, iOS devices do not have a physical keyboard. The standard iOS software keyboard is actually just a view filled with a series of button controls that are managed for you by the system. Your code will likely never directly interact with the iOS keyboard.

Creating the Control Fun Application

Open Xcode and create a new project called **Control Fun**. We'll use the Single View Application template again, so create the project just as we did in the previous two chapters.

Now that we've created our project, let's get the image we'll use in our image view. The image must be imported into Xcode before it will be available for use inside Interface Builder, so let's do that now. You'll find three files in the 04 - Logos folder in the example source code archive, named apress_logo.png, apress_logo@2x. png, and apress_logo@3x.png, which are a standard version and two Retina versions of the same image. We're going to add all three of these to the new project's asset catalog and let the app decide which of them to use at runtime. If you'd rather use a set of images of your own choosing, make sure that they are .png images sized correctly for the space available. The small version should be less than 100 pixels tall and a maximum of 300 pixels wide, so that it can fit comfortably at the top of the view on the narrowest iPhone screen without being resized. The larger ones should be twice and three times the size of the small version, respectively.

In Xcode, select Assets.xcassets in the Project Navigator, and then go to the 04 - Logos folder in the Finder and select all three images. Now drag the images onto the editor area in Xcode and release the mouse. Xcode uses the image names to figure out that you are adding three versions of an image called apress_logo and does the rest of the work for you (see Figure 4-5). You'll see that there is now an apress_logo entry in the left column of the editing area below the AppIcon entry that we started with. You can now use the name apress_logo in code or in Interface Builder to refer to this image set and the correct one will be loaded at runtime.

Figure 4-5. *Adding our apress_logo images into our Xcode project*

Implementing the Image View and Text Fields

With the image added to your project, your next step is to implement the five interface elements at the top of the application's screen: the image view, the two text fields, and the two labels, as shown in Figure 4-6.

Name: Type in a name

Number: Type in a number

Figure 4-6. *The image view, labels, and text fields we implement first*

Adding the Image View

In the Project Navigator, click Main.storyboard to open the main storyboard in Interface Builder. You'll see the familiar white background and a single square view where you can lay out your application's interface. As we did in the last chapter, beneath the IB window select iPhone 6s as our View As: choice.

■ **Note** This section below the canvas, new in Xcode 8 and known as the View Dimension, allows us to select how we view the scene we're working with in our IB canvas.

If the Object Library is not open, select View ➤ Utilities ➤ Show Object Library to open it. Scroll about one-fourth of the way through the list until you find ImageView (see Figure 4-7) or just type **image** in the search field. Remember that the Object Library corresponds to the third icon on top of the library pane.

Figure 4-7. *The Image View element in Interface Builder's Object Library*

Drag an image view onto the view in the storyboard editor and drop it somewhere near the top of the view, as shown in Figure 4-8. Don't worry about exactly positioning yet—we'll adjust that in the next section.

Figure 4-8. *Adding a UIImageView to our storyboard*

94

With the image view selected, bring up the Attributes Inspector by pressing ⌥⌘4. You should see the editable options of the UIImageView class. The most important setting for our image view is the topmost item in the inspector, labeled Image. Click the little arrow to the right of the field to see a pop-up menu that lists the available images. This list includes any images you added to your project's assets catalog. Select the apress_logo image you added earlier and it should appear in your image view, as shown in Figure 4-9.

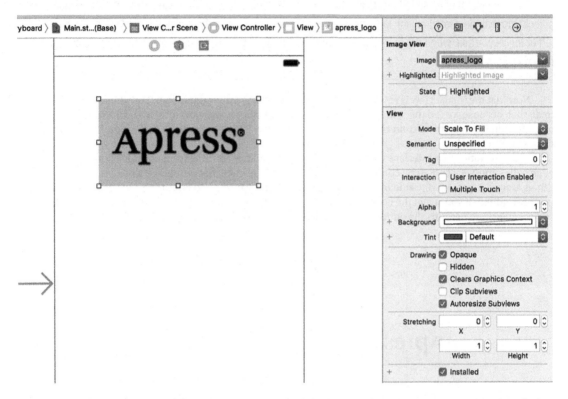

Figure 4-9. *The image view Attributes Inspector. We selected our image from the Image pop-up at the top of the inspector, and this populated the image view with our image*

Resizing the Image View

The image we used is not the same size as the image view in which it was placed. Xcode, by default, scales the image to completely fill its image view. A big clue that this is so is the Mode setting in the Attributes Inspector, which is set to Scale To Fill. Though we could keep our app this way, it's generally a good idea to do any image scaling that's needed before runtime, as image scaling takes time and processor cycles. In this case, we don't want any scaling at all, so let's resize our image view to the exact size of our image. Start by changing the Mode attribute to **Center**, which says that the image should not be scaled and should be centered in whatever space is assigned to the image view. Now let's fit the image view to the size of the image. To do that, make sure the image view is selected, so that you can see its outline and resize handles, and then press ⌘= or select Editor ➤ Size to Fit Content in Xcode's menu. If pressing ⌘= does not work, or Size to Fit Content is grayed out, reselect the image view, drag it a little way to the side, and try again.

■ **Tip**   If you encounter difficulty selecting an item in the editing area, you can open the Document Outline by clicking the small rectangular icon in the lower-left corner. Now, click the item you want selected in the Document Outline and, sure enough, that item will be selected in the editor.

To get at an object that is nested inside another object, click the disclosure triangle to the left of the enclosing object to reveal the nested object. In this case, to select the image view, first click the disclosure triangle to the left of the view. Then, when the image view appears in the Document Outline, click it, and it will be selected in the editing area.

Now that the image view is resized, let's move it back to its centered position. You already know how to do that, because we did the same thing in Chapter 3. Drag the image view until it's horizontally centered, click the Align icon at the bottom right of the editor area, check the Horizontally in Container check box, and click Add 1 Constraint.

You may notice that Interface Builder shows some solid lines running from an edge of one view to an edge of its superview (not to be confused with the dashed blue lines that are shown while you're dragging things around.), or from one side of the superview to another. These solid lines represent the constraints that you have added. If you select the constraint that you just added by clicking it, you'll see that it becomes a solid orange line that runs the entire height of the main view, as shown in Figure 4-10.

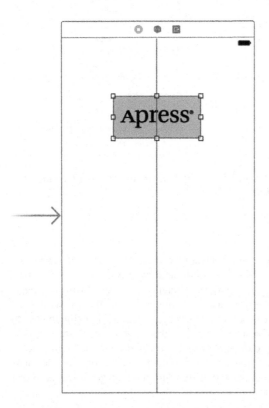

Figure 4-10. *Once we have resized our image view to fit the size of its image, we drag it into position using the view's blue guidelines, and create a constraint to keep it centered*

The solid line indicates that you have selected the constraint. The fact that it is orange means that the position and/or size of the image view are not yet fully specified and so you need to add more constraints. You can find out what the problem is by clicking on the orange triangle in the Activity View. In this case, Xcode is telling us is that we need to set a vertical constraint for the image view. You can either do so now, using the techniques you saw in Chapter 3, or wait until we fix all the constraints for our layout later in the chapter.

■ **Tip**   Dragging and resizing views in Interface Builder can be tricky. Don't forget about the Document Outline, which you can open by clicking the small rectangular icon at the bottom left of the editing area. When it comes to resizing, hold down the ➤ key, and Interface Builder will draw some helpful red lines on the screen that make it much easier to get a sense of the image view's position. This trick won't work with dragging, since the ➤ key will prompt Interface Builder to make a copy of the dragged object. However, if you select Editor ➤ Canvas ➤ Show Bounds Rectangles, Interface Builder will draw a line around all of your interface items, making them easier to see. You can turn off those lines by selecting Show Bounds Rectangles a second time.

Setting View Attributes

Select your image view and then switch your attention back over to the Attributes Inspector. Below the Image View section in the inspector is the View section. As you may have deduced, the pattern here is that the attributes that are specific to the selected object are shown at the top, followed by more general attributes that apply to the selected object's parent class. In this case, the parent class of UIImageView is UIView, so the next section is simply labeled View, and it contains attributes that any view class has.

The Mode Attribute

The first option in the view inspector is a pop-up menu labeled Mode. The Mode menu defines how the view will display its content. As you've already seen, in the case of the image view, this determines how the image will be aligned inside the view and whether it will be scaled to fit. Feel free to try various options for apress_logo, but remember to reset it to Center when you have finished.

As noted earlier, choosing any option that causes the image to scale will potentially add processing overhead at runtime, so it's best to avoid that whenever possible and size your images correctly before you import them. If you want to display the same image at multiple sizes, generally it's better to have multiple copies of the image at different sizes in your project, rather than force the iOS device to do scaling at runtime. Of course, there are times when scaling at runtime is appropriate and even unavoidable; this is a guideline, not a rule.

The Semantic Attribute

Immediately below Mode, you'll find the Semantic attribute. Added in iOS 9, this attribute lets you specify how the view should be rendered in a locale that uses a right-to-left reading order, such as Hebrew or Arabic. By default, the view is unspecified, but you can change this by selecting an appropriate value here. Refer to the description of the semanticContentAttribute property in the Xcode documentation for the UIView class for more details.

Tag

The next item, Tag, is worth mentioning, though we won't be using it in this chapter. All subclasses of UIView, including all views and controls, have a property called tag, which is just a numeric value that you can set here or in code. The tag is designed for your use—the system will never set or change its value. If you assign a tag value to a control or view, you can be sure that the tag will always have that value unless you change it.

Tags provide an easy, language-independent way of identifying objects in your interface. Let's say that you have five different buttons, each with a different label, and you want to use a single action method to handle all five buttons. In that case, you probably need some way to differentiate among the buttons when your action method is called. Unlike labels, tags will never change, so if you set a tag value here in Interface Builder, you can use it as a fast and reliable way to check which control was passed into an action method by using the sender argument.

Interaction Check Boxes

The two check boxes in the Interaction section have to do with user interaction. The first check box, User Interaction Enabled, specifies whether the user can do anything at all with this object. For most controls, this box will be checked because, if it's not, the control will never be able to trigger action methods. However, image views default to unchecked because they are often used just for the display of static information. Since all we're doing here is displaying a picture on the screen, there is no need to turn this on.

The second check box is Multiple Touch, and it determines whether this control is capable of receiving multitouch events. Multitouch events allow complex gestures like the pinch gesture used to zoom in in many iOS applications. We'll talk more about gestures and multitouch events in Chapter 18. Since this image view doesn't accept user interaction at all, there's no reason to turn on multitouch events, so leave this check box unchecked.

The Alpha Value

The next item in the inspector is Alpha. Be careful when using Alpha as it defines how transparent your view is—how much of what's beneath it shows through. It's defined as a floating-point number between 0.0 and 1.0, where 0.0 is fully transparent and 1.0 is completely opaque. If you use any value less than 1.0, your iOS device will draw this view with some amount of transparency so that any objects behind it show through. With a value of less than 1.0, even if there's nothing interesting behind your view, you will cause your application to spend processor cycles compositing your partially transparent view over the emptiness behind it. Therefore, don't set Alpha to anything other than 1.0 unless you have a very good reason for doing so.

Background

The next item down, Background, determines the color of the background for the view. For image views, this matters only when an image doesn't fill its view and is letterboxed, or when parts of the image are transparent. Since we've sized our view to perfectly match our image, this setting will have no visible effect, so we can leave it alone.

Tint

The next control lets you specify a tint color for the selected view. This is a color that some views use when drawing themselves. The segmented control that we'll use later in this chapter colors itself using its tint color, but the UIImageView does not.

Drawing Check Boxes

Below Tint you'll find a series of Drawing check boxes. The first one is labeled Opaque. That should be checked by default; if not, click to check that check box. This tells iOS that nothing behind your view needs to be drawn and allows iOS's drawing methods to do some optimizations that speed up drawing.

You might be wondering why we need to select the Opaque check box when we've already set the value of Alpha to 1.0 to indicate no transparency. The alpha value applies to the parts of the image to be drawn; but if an image doesn't completely fill the image view, or there are holes in the image thanks to an alpha channel, the objects below will still show through, regardless of the value set in Alpha. By selecting Opaque, we are telling iOS that nothing behind this view ever needs to be drawn, no matter what, so it does not need to waste processing time with anything behind our object. We can safely select the Opaque check box because we selected Size To Fit earlier, which caused the image view to match the size of the image it contains.

The Hidden check box does exactly what you think it does. If it's checked, the user can't see this object. Hiding an object can be useful at times, as you'll see later in this chapter when we hide our switches and button; however, the vast majority of the time—including now—you want this to remain unchecked.

The next check box, Clears Graphics Context, will rarely need to be checked. When it is checked, iOS will draw the entire area covered by the object in transparent black before it actually draws the object. Again, it should be turned off for the sake of performance and because it's rarely needed. Make sure this check box is unchecked (it is likely checked by default).

Clip Subviews is an interesting option. If your view contains subviews, and those subviews are not completely contained within the bounds of its parent view, this check box determines how the subviews will be drawn. If Clip Subviews is checked, only the portions of subviews that lie within the bounds of the parent will be drawn. If Clip Subviews is unchecked, subviews will be drawn completely, even if they lie outside the bounds of the parent.

Clip Subviews is unchecked by default. It might seem that the default behavior should be the opposite of what it actually is, so that child views won't be able to draw all over the place. However, calculating the clipping area and displaying only part of the subviews is a somewhat costly operation, mathematically speaking; most of the time, a subview won't lie outside the bounds of its superview. You can turn on Clip Subviews if you really need it for some reason, but it is off by default for the sake of performance.

The last check box in this section, Autoresize Subviews, tells iOS to resize any subviews if this view is resized. Leave this checked, but since we don't allow our view to be resized, it really does not matter whether it's checked or not.

Stretching

Next you'll see a section simply labeled Stretching, which refers to the form of rectangular views being redrawn as they're resized on the screen. The idea is that, rather than the entire content of a view being stretched uniformly, you can keep the outer edges of a view, such as the beveled edge of a button, looking the same even as the center portion stretches.

The four floating-point values set here let you declare which portion of the rectangle is stretchable by specifying a point at the upper-left corner of the view and the size of the stretchable area, all in the form of a number between 0.0 and 1.0 that represents a portion of the overall view size. For example, if you wanted to keep 10% of each edge not stretchable, you would specify 0.1 for both X and Y, and 0.8 for both Width and Height. In this case, we're going to leave the default values of 0.0 for X and Y, and 1.0 for Width and Height. Most of the time, you will not change these values.

Adding the Text Fields

With your image view finished, it's time to bring on the text fields. Grab a text field from the Object Library and drag it onto the storyboard. Use the blue guidelines to align it with the right margin and place it a little way below the image view, as shown in Figure 4-11.

Figure 4-11. *Drag a text field out of the library and drop it onto the view, just below the image view and touching the right-hand side's blue guideline*

Next, grab a label from the library, and then drag that over so it is aligned with the left margin of the view and vertically with the text field you placed earlier. Notice that multiple blue guidelines will pop up as you move the label around, making it easy to align the label to the text field using the top, bottom, or middle of the label. We're going to align the label and the text field using the baseline, which shows up as you're dragging around the middle of those guidelines (see Figure 4-12).

Figure 4-12. *Aligning the label and text field using the baseline guide*

Double-click the label you just dropped, change it to read **Name:** instead of Label (note the colon character at the end of the label), and press the Enter key to commit your changes.

Next, drag another text field from the library to the view and use the guidelines to place it below the first text field, as shown in Figure 4-13.

Figure 4-13. *Adding the second text field*

Once you've added the second text field, grab another label from the library and place it on the left side, below the existing label. Again, use the middle blue guideline to align your new label with the second text field. Double-click the new label and change it to read **Number:** (again, don't forget the colon).

Now, let's expand the size of the bottom text field to the left, so it is up against the right side of the label. Why start with the bottom text field? We want the two text fields to be the same size, and the bottom label is longer.

Single-click the bottom text field and drag the left resize dot to the left until a blue guideline appears to tell you that you are as close as you should ever be to the label, as shown in Figure 4-14. This particular guideline is somewhat subtle—it's only as tall as the text field itself, so be sure to look closely.

Figure 4-14. *Expand the width of the bottom text field*

Now, expand the top text field in the same way, so that it matches the bottom one in size. Once again, a blue guideline provides some help, and this one extends all the way down to the other text field, making it easier to spot.

We're basically finished with the text fields, except for one small detail. Look back at Figure 4-1. Do you see how the Name: and Number: are right-aligned? Right now, ours are both against the left margin. To align the right sides of the two labels, click the Name: label, hold down the ⇧(Shift) key, and click the Number: label, so both labels are selected. Next, press ⌥⌘4 to bring up the Attributes Inspector and make sure the Label section is expanded, so you can see the label-specific attributes. If it's not expanded, click the Show button on the right of the header to open it. Now use the Alignment control in the inspector to make the content of these labels right-justified, and then make a constraint to make sure that these two fields are always the same width by clicking the Pin icon at the bottom of the editing area, checking the Equal Widths check box in the pop-up that appears, and clicking Add 1 Constraint. At this point, you'll have an orange warning triangle in the Activity View and some layout warnings in the Issue Navigator. Ignore these for now—we'll fix them later.

When you are finished, this part of the interface should look very much like Figure 4-1. The only difference is the light-gray text in each text field. We'll add that now. Select the top text field (the one next to the Name: label) and press ⌥⌘4 to bring up the Attributes Inspector (see Figure 4-15). The text field is one of the most complex iOS controls, as well as one of the most commonly used. Let's look through the settings, beginning from the top of the inspector. *Make sure you've selected the text field and not the label or other elements.*

Figure 4-15. *The inspector for a text field showing the default values*

Text Field Inspector Settings

In the first section, the Text label is linked to two input field that give you some control over the text that will appear in the text field. The upper one is a pop-up button that lets you choose between plain text and attributed text, which can contain a variety of fonts and other attributes. We used attributed text to add bold to part of the text in our example in Chapter 3. Let's leave that pop-up button set to Plain for now. Immediately below that, you can set a default value for the text field. Whatever you type here will show up in the text field when your application launches, instead of just a blank space.

After that comes a couple of controls that let you set the font and font color. We'll leave the Color at the default value of black. Note that the Color pop-up is divided into two parts. The right side allows you to select from a set of preselected colors, and the left side gives you access to a color picker to more precisely specify your color.

The Font setting is divided into three parts. On the right side is a control that lets you increment or decrement the text size, one point at a time. The left side allows you to manually edit the font name or size. You can click the T-in-a-box icon to bring up a pop-up window that lets you set the various font attributes. We'll leave the Font at its default setting of System 14.0 or to whatever size your configuration may be set.

Below these fields are five buttons for controlling the alignment of the text displayed in the field. We'll leave this setting at the default value of left-aligned (the leftmost button).

Rounding out this first section, Placeholder allows you to specify a bit of text that will be displayed in gray inside the text field, but only when the field does not have a value. You can use a placeholder instead of adding a label to the layout (as we did) if space is tight, or you can use it to clarify what the user should type in this text field. Type the text **Type in a name** as the placeholder for our currently selected text field, and then hit Enter to commit the change.

The next two fields, Background and Disabled, are used only if you need to customize the appearance of your text field, which is unnecessary and actually ill-advised the vast majority of the time. Users expect text fields to look a certain way. We'll leave these set to their defaults.

Next are four buttons labeled Border Style. These allow you to change the way the text field's edge will be drawn. The default value (the rightmost button) creates the text field style that users are most accustomed to seeing for normal text fields in an iOS application. You may want to look at all four different styles, but when you're finished, put this setting back to the rightmost button.

Below the border setting is a Clear button pop-up button, which lets you choose when the Clear button should appear. The Clear button is the small X that can appear at the right end of a text field. Clear buttons are typically used with search fields and other fields where you would be likely to change the value frequently. They are not typically included on text fields used to persist data, so leave this at the default value of **Never appears**.

The Clear When Editing Begins check box specifies what happens when the user touches this field. If this box is checked, any value that was previously in this field will be deleted, and the user will start with an empty field. If this box is unchecked, the previous value will remain in the field, and the user will be able to edit it. Leave this unchecked.

The next section starts with a control that lets you set the minimum font size that the text field will use for displaying its text. Leave that at its default value for now. The Adjust to Fit check box specifies whether the size of the text should shrink if the text field is reduced in size. Adjusting to fit will keep the entire text visible in the view, even if the text would normally be too big to fit in the allotted space. This check box works in conjunction with the minimum font size setting. No matter the size of the field, the text will not be resized below that minimum size. Specifying a minimum size allows you to make sure that the text doesn't get too small to be readable.

The next section defines how the keyboard will look and behave when this text field is being used. Since we're expecting a name, let's change the Capitalization pop-up to **Words**. This causes the first letter of every word to be automatically capitalized, which is what you typically want with names.

The next four pop-ups—Correction, Spell Checking, Keyboard Type, and Appearance—can be left at their default values. Take a minute to look at each to get a sense of what these settings do.

Next is the Return Key pop-up. The Return key is on the lower right of the virtual keyboard, and its label changes based on what you're doing. If you are entering text in Safari's search field, for example, it says **Search**. In an application like ours, where the text fields share the screen with other controls, **Done** is the right choice. Make that change here.

If the Auto-enable Return Key check box is checked, the Return key is disabled until at least one character is typed into the text field. Leave this unchecked because we want to allow the text field to remain empty if the user prefers not to enter anything.

The Secure check box specifies whether the characters being typed are displayed in the text field. You would check this check box if the text field was being used as a password field. Leave it unchecked for our app.

The next section (which you will probably have to scroll down to see) allows you to set control attributes inherited from UIControl; however, these generally don't apply to text fields and, with the exception of the Enabled check box, won't affect the field's appearance. We want to leave these text fields enabled, so that the user can interact with them. Leave the default settings in this section.

The last section on the inspector, View, should look familiar. It's identical to the section of the same name on the image view inspector we looked at earlier. These are attributes inherited from the UIView class; since all controls are subclasses of UIView, they all share this section of attributes. As you did earlier for the image view, check the Opaque check box and uncheck Clears Graphics Context and Clip Subviews—for the reasons discussed earlier.

Setting the Attributes for the Second Text Field

Next, single-click the lower text field (the one next to the Number: label) in the storyboard and return to the Attributes Inspector. In the Placeholder field, type **Type in a number**, and make sure Clear When Editing Begins is unchecked. A little farther down, click the Keyboard Type pop-up menu. Since we want the user to enter only numbers, not letters, select Number Pad. On the iPhone, this ensures that the users will be presented with a keyboard containing only numbers, meaning they won't be able to enter alphabetical characters, symbols, or anything other than numbers. We don't need to set the Return Key value for the numeric keypad because that style of keyboard doesn't have a Return key; therefore, all of the other inspector settings can stay at the default values. As you did earlier, check the Opaque check box and uncheck Clears Graphics Context and Clip Subviews. On the iPad, selecting Number Pad has the effect of bringing up a full virtual keyboard in numeric mode when the user activates the text field, but the user can switch back to alphabetic input. This means that in a real application, you would have to verify that the user actually entered a valid number when processing the content of the Number field.

■ **Tip** If you really want to stop the user typing anything other than numbers into a text field, you can do so by creating a class that implements the textView(_ textView: shouldChangeTextInRange: replacementText text:) method of the UITextViewDelegate protocol and making it the text view's delegate. The details are not too complex, but beyond the scope of this book.

Adding Constraints

Before we continue, we need to adjust some layout constraints. When you drag a view into another view in Interface Builder (as we just did), Xcode doesn't create any constraints for it automatically. The layout system requires a complete set of constraints, so when it's time to compile your code, Xcode generates a set of default constraints describing the layout. The constraints depend on each object's position within its superview, whether it's nearer the left or right edge, it will be pinned to the left or right. Similarly, depending on whether it's nearer the top or the bottom edge, it will be pinned to the top or the bottom. If it's centered in either direction, it typically gets a constraint pinning it to the center.

To complicate matters further, Xcode may also apply automatic constraints pinning each new object to one or more of its "sibling" objects within the same superview. This automatic behavior may or may not be what you want, so normally you're better off creating a complete set of constraints within Interface Builder before your app is compiled and in the previous two chapters, we worked through some examples.

Let's again look at where we're at on this. To see all the constraints that are in play for any particular view, try selecting it and opening the Size Inspector. If you select either of the text fields, you'll see that the Size Inspector shows a message claiming that there are no constraints for the selected view. In fact, this GUI we've been building has only the constraints that we applied earlier, binding the horizontal centers of the image view and the container view and making the labels equally sized. Click the image view and the labels to see these constraints in the inspector.

What we really want is a full set of constraints to tell the layout system precisely how to handle all of our views and controls, just as it would get at compile time. Fortunately, this is pretty simple to accomplish. Select all the views and controls by click-dragging a box around them, from inside the upper-left corner of our container view down toward the lower right. If you start dragging and find that the view starts moving instead, just release the mouse, move it a little bit further inside the view, and try again. When all items are selected, use the menu to execute the Editor ➤ Resolve Auto Layout Issues ➤ Add Missing Constraints command from the All Views in View Controller section of the menu. After doing that, you'll see that all our views and controls now have some little blue sticks connecting them to one another and to the container view. Each of those sticks represents a constraint. The advantage of creating these now instead of letting Xcode create them at compile time is that we have a chance to modify each constraint if we need to. We'll explore more of what we can do with constraints throughout the book.

■ **Tip**   Another way to apply constraints to all the views owned by a view controller is to select the view controller in the Document Outline, and then choose Editor ➤ Resolve Auto Layout Issues ➤ Add Missing Constraints.

At this point, with all the necessary constraints in place, we can fix the layout warnings in the Issue Navigator. To do that, select the view controller in the Document Outline, and then click Editor ➤ Resolve Auto Layout Issues ➤ Update Frames in the Xcode menu. The layout warnings should be gone.

Creating and Connecting Outlets

For this first part of the interface, all that's left is creating and connecting our outlets. The image view and labels on our interface do not need outlets because we don't need to change them at runtime. The two text fields, however, will hold data we'll need to use in our code, so we need outlets pointing to each of them

As you probably remember from the previous chapter, Xcode allows us to create and connect outlets at the same time using the Assistant Editor, which should already be open (but if it's not, open it as described earlier).

Make sure your storyboard file is selected in the Project Navigator. If you don't have a large amount of screen real estate, you might also want to select View ➤ Utilities ➤ Hide Utilities to hide the utility pane during this step. In the Assistant Editor's jump bar, select Automatic. You should see the ViewController.swift file, as shown in Figure 4-16.

Figure 4-16. *The storyboard editing area with the Assistant Editor open. You can see the Assistant Editor on the right, showing the code from ViewController.swift*

Let's starting connecting things up. Control-drag from the top text field over to the ViewController.swift file, right below the ViewController line. You should see a gray pop-up that reads Insert Outlet, Action, or Outlet Collection (see Figure 4-17). Release the mouse button and you'll get the same pop-up you saw in the previous chapter. We want to create an outlet called nameField, so type **nameField** into the Name field, and then hit Return or click the Connect button.

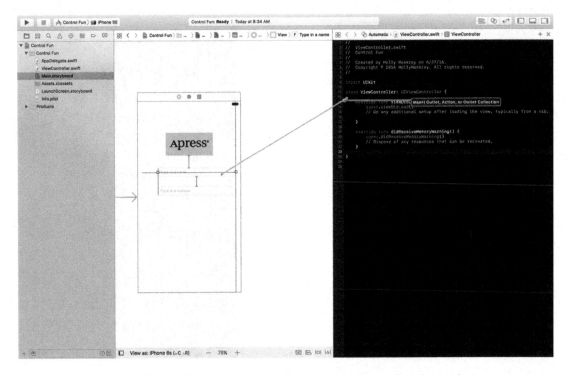

Figure 4-17. *With the Assistant Editor open, we Control-drag over to the source code in order to simultaneously create the nameField outlet and connect it to the appropriate text field*

You now have a property called nameField in ViewController, and it has been connected to the top text field. Do the same for the second text field, creating and connecting it to a property called numberField. When you've done that, your code should look like Listing 4-1.

Listing 4-1. Our Connected Text Fields

```
class ViewController: UIViewController {
    @IBOutlet weak var nameField: UITextField!
    @IBOutlet weak var numberField: UITextField!
```

Closing the Keyboard

Let's see how the app works so far, select Product ➤ Run. Our application should come up in the iOS simulator. Click the Name text field, and the traditional keyboard should appear.

■ **Tip** If the keyboard does not appear, the simulator may be configured to work as if a hardware keyboard had been connected. To fix that, uncheck Hardware ➤ Keyboard ➤ Connect Hardware Keyboard in the iOS simulator menu and try again.

Type a name and then tap the Number field. The numeric keypad should appear, as shown in Figure 4-18. Cocoa Touch gives us all this functionality for free just by adding text fields to our interface.

Figure 4-18. *The keyboard comes up automatically when you touch either the text field or the number field*

But there's a little problem. How do you get the keyboard to go away? Go ahead and try. You'll see that nothing happens.

Closing the Keyboard When Done Is Tapped

Because the keyboard is software-based rather than a physical keyboard, we need to take a few extra steps to make sure the keyboard goes away when the user is finished with it. When the user taps the Done button on the text keyboard, a Did End On Exit event will be generated. When that happens, we need to tell the text field to give up control so that the keyboard will go away. In order to do that, we need to add an action method to our controller class.

Select ViewController.swift in the Project Navigator and add the action method in Listing 4-2 at the bottom of the file, just before the closing brace.

Listing 4-2. Method to Close the Keyboard When Done

```
@IBAction func textFieldDoneEditing(sender: UITextField) {
    sender.resignFirstResponder()
}
```

109

As we saw in Chapter 2, the first responder acts as the control with which the user is currently interacting. In our new method, we tell our control to resign as a first responder, giving up that role to the previous control the user worked with. When a text field yields first responder status, the keyboard associated with it goes away.

Save the ViewController.swift file. Let's look back at the storyboard and arrange to trigger this action from both of our text fields.

Select Main.storyboard in the Project Navigator, single-click the Name text field, and press ⌥⌘6 to bring up the connections inspector. This time, we don't want the Touch Up Inside event that we used in the previous chapter. Instead, we want Did End On Exit since that event will fire when the user taps the Done button on the text keyboard.

Drag from the circle next to Did End On Exit to the yellow View Controller icon in the storyboard, in the bar that's just above the view you've been configuring, and let go. A small pop-up menu will appear containing the name of a single action, the one we just added. Click the textFieldDoneEditing action to select it. You can also do this by dragging from the circle in the Connections Inspector to the textFieldDoneEditing() method in the Assistant Editor, if you still have it open. Repeat this procedure with the other text field, save your changes, and then run the app again.

When the simulator appears, click the Name field, type something, and then tap the Done button. As expected, the keyboard drops away, but what about the Number field, since there is no Done button, as you can see back in Figure 4-18?

Not all keyboard layouts, including the numeric keypad, include a Done button. We could force the user to tap the Name field and then tap Done, but that's not very user-friendly. And we most definitely want our application to be user-friendly. Let's see how to handle this situation.

Touching the Background to Close the Keyboard

Apple's iPhone applications allow tapping in most text fields—anywhere in the view where there's no active control that causes the keyboard to go away. Let's implement that for our app.

The answer may surprise you because of its simplicity. Our view controller includes a property called view that it inherited from UIViewController. This view property corresponds to the main view in the storyboard. The view property points to an instance of UIView that acts as a container for all the items in our user interface. It is sometimes referred to as a **container view** because its main purpose is to simply hold other views and controls. Essentially, the container view provides the background to our user interface. All we need to do is detect when the user taps on it. As you'll see in Chapter 18, there are a couple of ways to do that. First, there are methods in the UIResponder class, from which UIView is derived, that are called whenever the user places one or more fingers onto a view, moves those fingers around, or lifts them up. We can override one of those methods (specifically the one that's called when the user lifts a finger from the screen) and add our code in there. The other way to do this is to add a **gesture recognizer** to the container view. Gesture recognizers listen to the events that are generated when the user interacts with a view and try to figure out what the user is doing. There are several different gesture recognizers that respond to different sequences of actions, as you'll see in Chapter 18. The one that we need to use is the **tap gesture recognizer**, which signals an event when the user puts a finger on the screen, and then lifts it up again within a reasonably short time.

To use a gesture recognizer, you create an instance, configure it, link it to the view that you want it to monitor for touch events and attach it to an action method in your view controller class. When the gesture is recognized, your action method is called. You can create and configure the recognizer in code, or you can do it in Interface Builder. Here, we'll use Interface Builder because it's easier. Return to the storyboard and make sure that the Object Library is showing, and then locate a tap gesture recognizer, drag it over the storyboard, and drop it onto the container view. The recognizer is not visible at runtime, so you can't see it in the storyboard, but it appears in the Document Outline, as shown in Figure 4-19.

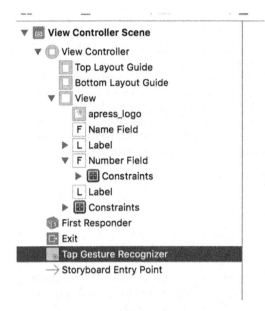

Figure 4-19. *Tap Gesture Recognizer in the Document Outline*

Selecting the gesture recognizer reveals its configurable attributes in the Attributes Inspector, as shown in Figure 4-20.

Figure 4-20. *The attributes of the tap gesture recognizer*

The Taps field specifies how many times the user needs to tap before the gesture is recognized and the Touches field controls how many fingers need to be tapped. The defaults of one tap with one finger are exactly what we need, so leave both fields unchanged. The other attributes are fine too, so all we need to do is link the recognizer to an action method. To do that, open ViewController.swift in the Assistant Editor and Control-drag from the recognizer in the Document Outline to the line just above the closing brace in ViewController.swift. Release the mouse when you see the usual gray pop-up like the one shown in Figure 4-16. In the pop-up that opens, change the connection type to Action and the method name to **onTapGestureRecognized** to have Xcode add the action method and link it to the gesture recognizer. This method will be called whenever the user taps on the main view. All we need to do is add the code to close the keyboard, if it's open. We already know how to do that, so change the code to that shown in Listing 4-3.

Listing 4-3. Our Gesture Recognizer Code to Remove the Keyboard

```
@IBAction func onTapGestureRecognized(sender: AnyObject) {
    nameField.resignFirstResponder()
    numberField.resignFirstResponder()
}
```

This code simply tells both text fields to yield first responder status if they have it. It is perfectly safe to call resignFirstResponder() on a control that is not the first responder, so we can call it on both text fields without needing to check whether either is the first responder. Build and run your application again and this time, the keyboard should disappear not only when the Done button is tapped, but also when you tap anywhere that's not an active control, which is the behavior that your users will expect.

Adding the Slider and Label

Let's add a slider and a label, the idea being that the value shown by the label will change as the slider is moved. Select Main.storyboard in the Project Navigator, so we can add more items to our application's user interface. From the Object Library, bring over a slider and arrange it below the Number text field, using the right-hand side's blue guideline as a stopping point, and leaving a little breathing room between the slider and the bottom text field. Single-click the newly added slider to select it, and then press ⌥⌘4 to go back to the Attributes Inspector if it's not already visible (see Figure 4-21).

Figure 4-21. *The inspector showing default attributes for a slider*

A slider lets you choose a number in a given range. Use the inspector to set the Minimum value to 1, the Maximum value to 100, and the Current value to 50. Leave the Events Continuous Update check box checked. This ensures a continuous flow of events as the slider's value changes.

Bring over a label and place it next to the slider, using the blue guidelines to align it vertically with the slider and to align its left edge with the left margin of the view (see Figure 4-22).

Figure 4-22. *Placing the slider's label*

Double-click the newly placed label, and change its text from Label to **100**. This is the largest value that the slider can hold, and we can use that to determine the correct width of the slider. Since 100 is shorter in length than Label, Interface Builder automatically makes the label smaller for you, as if you had dragged the right-middle resize dot to the edge. Despite this automatic behavior, you're still free to resize the label however you want, of course. If you later decide you want the tool to pick the optimum size for you again, just press ⌘= or select Editor ➤ Size to Fit Content.

Next, resize the slider by single-clicking the slider to select it and dragging the left resize handle to the left until the blue guidelines indicate that you're getting close to the label's right-side edge.

Now that we've added two more controls, we need to add the matching Auto Layout constraints. We'll do it the easy way again this time, so just select the View Controller icon in the Document Outline, and then click Editor ➤ Resolve Auto Layout Issues ➤ Add Missing Constraints. Xcode adjusts the constraints so that they match the positions of all of the controls on screen.

Creating and Connecting the Actions and Outlets

All that's left to do with these two controls is to connect them to an outlet and an action—we need an outlet that points to the label, so that we can update the label's value when the slider is used, and we are also going to need an action method for the slider to call as it's changed. Make sure the Assistant Editor is open and showing ViewController.swift, and then Control-drag from the slider to just below the onTapGestureRecognized() method in the Assistant Editor. When the pop-up window appears, change the Connection field to **Action**, type **onSliderChanged** in the Name field, set the Type to UISlider, and then hit Return to create and connect the action.

Next, Control-drag from the newly added label (the one showing 100) over to the Assistant Editor. This time, drag to just below the numberField property declaration at the top of the file. When the pop-up comes up, type **sliderLabel** in the Name text field, and then hit Return to create and connect the outlet.

Implementing the Action Method

Though Xcode has created and connected our action method, it's still up to us to actually write the code that makes up the action method so it does what it's supposed to do. Change the onSliderChanged() method to that shown in Listing 4-4.

Listing 4-4. Changing the Label Based on the Slider Position/Value

```
@IBAction func onSliderChanged(_ sender: UISlider) {
    sliderLabel.text = "\(lroundf(sender.value))"
}
```

The call to the lroundf() function (which is part of the standard C library) takes the current value of the slider and rounds it to the nearest integer. The rest of the line converts the value to a string containing that number and assigns it to the label.

That takes care of our controller's response to the movements of the slider; but in order to be really consistent, we need to make sure that the label shows the correct slider value before the user even touches it. To do that, add the following line of code to the viewDidLoad() method: **sliderLabel.text = "50"**.

This method executes immediately after the running app loads the view from the storyboard file, but before it's displayed on the screen. The line we added makes sure that the user sees the correct starting value right away.

Save the file. Next, press ⌘R to build and launch your app in the iOS simulator, and try out the slider. As you move it, you should see the label's text change in real time. Another piece falls into place. But if you drag the slider toward the left (bringing the value below 10) or all the way to the right (setting the value to 100), you'll see an odd thing happen. The label to the left will shrink horizontally when it drops down to showing a single digit, and will grow horizontally when showing three. Now, apart from the text it contains, you don't actually see the label itself, so you can't see its size changing, but what you will see is that the slider actually changes its size along with the label, getting smaller or larger. It's maintaining a size relationship with the label, making sure the gap between the two is always the same.

This is simply a side effect of the way Interface Builder works, helping you create GUIs that are responsive and fluid. We created some default constraints previously, and here you're seeing one in action. One of the constraints created by Interface Builder keeps the horizontal distance between these elements constant.

Let's override this behavior by making our own constraint. Back in Xcode, select the label in the storyboard and click the Pin icon at the bottom of the storyboard. In the pop-up, click the Width check box followed by Add 1 Constraint. This makes a new high-priority constraint that tells the layout system, "Don't mess with the width of this label." If you now press ⌘R to build and run again, you'll see that the label no longer expands and contracts as you drag back and forth across the slider.

We'll see more examples of constraints and their uses throughout the book. But for now, let's look at implementing the switches.

Implementing the Switches, Button, and Segmented Control

Let's go back to Xcode once again; this back and forth may seem a bit strange, but it's fairly common to bounce around between source code, storyboards, and nib files in Xcode, testing your app in the iOS simulator while you're developing.

Our application will have two switches, which are small controls that can have only two states: on and off. We'll also add a segmented control to hide and show the switches. Along with that control, we'll add a button that is revealed when the segmented control's right side is tapped.

In the storyboard, drag a segmented control from the Object Library (see Figure 4-23) and place it on the View window, a little below the slider and horizontally centered.

***Figure 4-23.** Placing a segmented control onto our storyboard*

Double-click the word **First** on the segmented control and change the title from First to **Switches**. After doing that, repeat the process with the other segment, renaming it **Button** (see Figure 4-24), and drag the control back into its centered position.

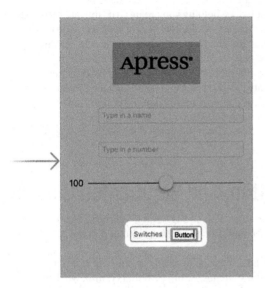

Figure 4-24. *Renaming the segments in the segmented control*

Adding Two Labeled Switches

Next, take a switch from the library and place it on the view, below the segmented control and against the left margin. Then drag a second switch and place it against the right margin, aligned vertically with the first switch, as shown in Figure 4-25.

Figure 4-25. *Adding switches to the view*

■ **Tip**   Holding down the ⌥ key and dragging an object in Interface Builder will create a copy of that item. When you have many instances of the same object to create, it can be faster to drag only one object from the library, and then Option-drag as many copies as you need.

The three new controls we've added need layout constraints. This time, we'll add the constraints manually. Start by selecting the segmented control and aligning it to the center of the view by clicking the Align icon, checking Horizontally in Container in the pop-up and clicking Add 1 Constraint. Next, select the segmented control again and Control-drag upward a little until the background of the main view turns blue. Release the mouse and select Vertical Spacing to Top Layout Guide in the pop-up menu to fix the distance from the segmented control to the top of the view.

Now let's adjust the switches. Control-drag from the left switch diagonally left and upward relative to the switch, and release the mouse. Hold down the Shift key and select Leading Space to Container Margin and Vertical Spacing to Top Layout Guide from the pop-up, release Shift and press the Return key or click anywhere outside the pop-up to apply the constraints. Do a similar thing with the other switch, but this time Control-drag to the upper right relative and select Trailing Space to Container Margin and Vertical Spacing to Top Layout Guide. When you apply constraints by dragging, Xcode offers you different options depending on the direction in which you drag. If you drag horizontally, you'll have options that let you attach the control to the left or right margins of its parent view, whereas if you drag vertically, Xcode assumes you want to set the position of the control relative to the top or bottom of its parent. Here, we needed one horizontal and one vertical constraint for each switch, so we dragged diagonally to indicate that to Xcode, and we got both horizontal and vertical options.

Connecting and Creating Outlets and Actions

Before we add the button, we'll create outlets for the two switches and connect them. The button that we'll be adding next will actually sit on top of the switches, making it harder to Control-drag to and from them, so we want to take care of the switch connections before we add the button. Since the button and the switches will never be visible at the same time, having them in the same physical location won't be a problem.

Using the Assistant Editor, Control-drag from the switch on the left to just below the last outlet in ViewController.swift. When the pop-up appears, name the outlet **leftSwitch** and hit Return. Repeat this process with the other switch, naming its outlet **rightSwitch**.

Now, select the left switch again by single-clicking it. Control-drag once more to the Assistant Editor. This time, drag to just above the brace at the end of the class declaration before letting go. When the pop-up appears, change the Connection field to **Action**, name the new action method onSwitchChanged(), and set the Type of its sender argument to UISwitch. Next, hit Return to create the new action. Now repeat this process with the right switch, with one change: instead of creating a new action, drag the mouse over the onSwitchChanged() method that was just created and connect to it instead. Just as we did in the previous chapter, we're going to use a single method to handle both switches.

Finally, Control-drag from the segmented control to the Assistant Editor, right below the onSwitchChanged() method. Insert a new action method called toggleControls(), just as you've done before. This time, set the Type of its sender parameter to UISegmentedControl.

Implementing the Switch Actions

Save the storyboard and let's add some more code to ViewController.swift, which is already open in the Assistant Editor. Look for the onSwitchChanged() method, changing it to that, as shown in Listing 4-5.

Listing 4-5. Our New onSwitchChanged() Method

```
@IBAction func onSwitchChanged(_ sender: UISwitch) {
    let setting = sender.isOn
    leftSwitch.setOn(setting, animated: true)
    rightSwitch.setOn(setting, animated: true)
}
```

The onSwitchChanged() method gets called whenever one of the two switches is tapped. In this method, we simply grab the value of the isOn property of sender (which represents the switch that was pressed) and use that value to set both switches. The idea here is that setting the value of one switch will change the other switch at the other time, keeping them in sync at all times.

Now, sender is always going to be either leftSwitch or rightSwitch, so you might be wondering why we're setting them both. We do it that way out of practicality since it's less work to set the value of both switches every time than to determine which switch made the call and set only the other one. Whichever switch called this method will already be set to the correct value, and setting it again to that same value won't have any effect.

Adding the Button

Next, go back to Interface Builder and drag a Button from the library to your view. Add this button directly on top of the leftmost switch, aligning it with the left margin and vertically aligning its top edge with the top edge of the two switches, as shown in Figure 4-26.

Figure 4-26. Adding a button on top of the existing switches

Now, grab the button's right-center resize handle and drag all the way to the right until you reach the blue guideline that indicates the right-side margin. The button should completely overlay the space occupied by the two switches, but because the default button is transparent, you will still see the switches (see Figure 4-27).

Figure 4-27. *The button, once placed and resized, fills the space occupied by the two switches*

Double-click the newly added button to give it the title **Do Something**.

The button needs Auto Layout constraints. We're going to pin it to the top and to both sides of the main view. Control-drag upward from the button until the view background turns blue, and then release the mouse and select Vertical Spacing to Top Layout Guide. Then Control-drag horizontally to the left until the main view background turns blue again and select Leading Space to Container Margin. You'll only get this option if you drag far enough to the left, so if you don't see it, try again by dragging left until the mouse is outside the bounds of the button. Finally, Control-drag to the right until the main view background turns blue, and then select Trailing Space to Container Margin. Now run the application to see what we've just done.

Adding an Image to the Button

If you compare your running application to Figure 4-2, you'll immediately notice a difference. Your Do Something button doesn't look like the one in the figure. That's because, starting with iOS 7, the default button displays a very simple appearance: it's just a piece of plain text with no outline, border, background color, or other decorative features. That conforms nicely to Apple's design guidelines for iOS 7 and later, but there are still cases where you'll want to use custom buttons, so we're going to show you how to do that.

Many of the buttons you see on your iOS device are drawn using images. We've provided images that you can use for this example in the 04 – Button Images folder of the source code archive for this book. In the Project Navigator in Xcode, select Assets.xcassets (the same assets catalog that we used earlier when we added images for the Apress logo), and then just drag both images from the 04 – Button Images folder in the Finder straight into the editing area in your Xcode window. The images are added to your project and will be immediately available to your app.

Stretchable Images

If you look at the two button images we just added, you'll see they're very small and seem much too narrow to fill out the button you added to the storyboard. That's because these graphics are meant to be stretchable. It so happens that UIKit can stretch graphics to nicely fill just about any size you want. Stretchable images are an interesting concept. A stretchable image is a resizable image that knows how to resize itself intelligently, so that it maintains the correct appearance. For these button templates, we don't want the edges to stretch evenly with the rest of the image. **Edge insets** are the parts of an image (measured in pixels) that should not be resized. We want the bevel around the edges to stay the same, no matter what size we make the button, so we need to specify how much non-stretchable space makes up each edge.

In the past, this could only be accomplished in code. You'd have to use a graphics program to measure pixel boundaries of your images, and then use those numbers to set edge insets in your code. Xcode 6 eliminated the need for this by letting you visually "slice" any image you have in an assets catalog! That's what we're going to do next.

Select the Assets.xcassets asset catalog in Xcode, and inside that select whiteButton. At the bottom right of the editing area, you'll see a button labeled Show Slicing. Click that to initiate the slicing process, which begins by simply putting a Start Slicing button right on top of your image. Click it. You'll see three new buttons that let you choose whether you want the image to be sliced (and therefore stretchable) vertically, horizontally, or both. Choose the button in the middle to slice both ways. Xcode does a quick analysis of your image, and then finds the sections that seem to have unique pixels around the edges, and vertical and horizontal slices in the middle that should be repeatable. You'll see these boundaries represented by dashed lines, as shown in Figure 4-28. If you have a tricky image, you may need to adjust these (it's easy to do, just drag them with the mouse); but for this image, the automatic edge insets will work fine.

whit...n - 1x

Figure 4-28. *Default slicing for the white button*

Next, select blueButton and do the same automatic slicing for it. Now it's time to put these graphics to use.

Go back to the storyboard you've been working on and single-click the Do Something button. With the button selected, press ⌥⌘4 to open the Attributes Inspector. In the inspector, use the Type pop-up menu to change the type from System to **Custom**. At the bottom of the Button section in the Inspector, you'll see that you can specify an image and a background for your button. We're going to use the Background to show our resizable graphic, so click in the Background pop-up and select whiteButton. You'll see that the button now shows the white graphic, perfectly stretched to cover the entire button frame.

We want to use the blue button to define the look of this button's highlighted state, which is what you see while the button is pressed. We'll talk more about control states in the next section of this chapter; but for now, just take a look at the second pop-up from the top, labeled State Config. A UIButton can have multiple states, each with its own text and images. Right now we've been configuring the default state, so switch this pop-up to Highlighted, so that we can configure that state. You'll see that the Background pop-up has been cleared; click it to select blueButton—and you're done.

Control States

Every iOS control has five possible control states and is always in one, and only one, of these states at any given moment:

- **Default**: The most common state is the default control state, which is the default state. It's the state that controls are in when not in any of the other states.

- **Focused**: In focus-based navigation systems, a control enters this state when it receives the focus. A focused control changes its appearance to indicate that it has focus, and this appearance differs from the appearance of the control when it is highlighted or selected. Further interactions with the control can result in it also becoming highlighted or selected.

- **Highlighted**: The highlighted state is the state a control is in when it's currently being used. For a button, this would be while the user has a finger on the button.

- **Selected**: Only some controls support the selected state. It is usually used to indicate that the control is turned on or selected. Selected is similar to highlighted, but a control can continue to be selected when the user is no longer directly using that control.

- **Disabled**: Controls are in the disabled state when they have been turned off, which can be done by unchecking the Enabled check box in Interface Builder or setting the control's isEnabled property to NO.

Certain iOS controls have attributes that can take on different values depending on their state. For example, by specifying one image for isDefault and a different image for isHighlighted, we are telling iOS to use one image when the user has a finger on the button and a different image the rest of the time. That's essentially what we did when we configured two different background states for the button in the storyboard.

■ **Note**   In previous versions of this book there were four states: Normal, Highlighted, Disabled, and Selected, with the enumerated values in Objective-C as UIControlStateNormal, UIControlStateHighlighted, UIControlStateEnabled, and UIControlStateSelected. You may see older, pre-Xcode 8 and Swift 3 reference these values.

Connecting and Creating the Button Outlets and Actions

Control-drag from the new button to the Assistant Editor, just below the last outlet already in the section at the top of the file. When the pop-up appears, create a new outlet called **doSomethingButton**. After you've done that, Control-drag from the button a second time to just above the closing brace at the bottom of the file. There, create an action method called onButtonPressed() and set the Type to UIButton.

If you save your work and try running the application, you'll see that the segmented control will be live, but it won't do anything particularly useful since we still need to add some logic to make the button and switches hide and unhide.

We also need to mark our button as hidden from the start. We didn't want to do that before because it would have made it harder to connect the outlets and actions. Now that we've done that, however, let's hide the button. We'll show the button when the user taps the right side of the segmented control; but when the application starts, we want the button hidden. In the storyboard, select the button and press ⌥⌘4 to bring up the Attributes Inspector. Scroll down to the View section and click the Hidden check box. The button will still be visible in Interface Builder.

Implementing the Segmented Control Action

Save the storyboard and focus once again on ViewController.swift. Look for the toggleControls() method that Xcode created for us and add the new code shown in Listing 4-6.

Listing 4-6. Hide or Unhide the Switches Depending on the Segmented Control

```
@IBAction func toggleControls(_ sender: UISegmentedControl) {
    if sender.selectedSegmentIndex == 0 {  // "Switches" is selected
        leftSwitch.isHidden = false
        rightSwitch.isHidden = false
        doSomethingButton.isHidden = true
    } else {
        leftSwitch.isHidden = true
        rightSwitch.isHidden = true
        doSomethingButton.isHidden = false
    }
}
```

This code looks at the selectedSegmentIndex property of sender, which tells us which of the sections is currently selected. The first section, called switches, has an index of 0. We've noted this fact in a comment, so that when we revisit the code later, we will know what's going on. Depending on which segment is selected, we hide or show the appropriate controls.

Before we run the application, let's apply a small tweak to make it look a little better. With iOS 7, Apple introduced some new GUI paradigms. One of these is that the status bar at the top of the screen is transparent, so that your content shines right through it. Right now, that yellow Apress icon really sticks out like a sore thumb against our app's white background, so let's extend that yellow color to cover our entire view. In Main.storyboard, select the main content view (it's labeled View in the Document Outline), and press ⌥⌘4 to bring up the Attributes Inspector. Click in the color swatch labeled Background (which currently contains a white rectangle) to open the standard OS X color picker. One feature of this color picker is that it lets you choose any color you see on the screen. With the color picker open, click the dropper icon at the bottom right to open a magnifying glass. Drag the magnifying glass over the Apress image view in the storyboard and click when it's over a yellow part of the image. You should now see the background color of the Apress image in the color picker next to the dropper icon in the color picker. To set it as the background color for the main content view, select the main view in the Document Outline, and then click the yellow color in the color picker. When you're done, close the color picker.

On the screen, you may find that the background and the Apress image seem to have slightly different colors, but when run in the simulator or on a device, they will be the same. These colors appear to be different in Interface Builder because macOS automatically adapts colors depending on the display you're using. On an iOS device and in the simulator, that doesn't happen.

Run the app. You'll see that the yellow color fills the entire screen, with no visible distinction between the status bar and your app's content. If you don't have full-screen scrolling content, or other content that requires the use of a navigation bar or other controls at the top of the screen, this can be a nice way to show full-screen content that isn't interrupted by the status bar quite as much.

If you've typed everything correctly, you should also be able to switch between the button and the pair of switches using the segmented control. And if you tap either switch, the other one will change its value as well. The button, however, still doesn't do anything. Before we implement it, we need to talk about action sheets and alerts.

Implementing the Action Sheet and Alert

Action sheets and **alerts** are both used to provide the user with feedback:

- Action sheets are used to force the user to make a choice between two or more items. On iPhones, the action sheet comes up from the bottom of the screen and displays a series of buttons (see Figure 4-3). On the iPad, you specify the position of the action sheet relative to another view, typically a button. Users are unable to continue using the application until they have tapped one of the buttons. Action sheets are often used to confirm a potentially dangerous or irreversible action, such as deleting an object.

- Alerts appear as a rounded rectangle in the middle of the screen (see Figure 4-4). Like action sheets, alerts force users to respond before they are allowed to continue using the application. Alerts are usually used to inform the user that something important or out of the ordinary has occurred. Like action sheets, alerts may be presented with only a single button, although you have the option of presenting multiple buttons if more than one response is appropriate.

■ **Note**   A view that forces users to make a choice before they are allowed to continue using their application is known as a **modal view**.

Displaying an Action Sheet

Switch to ViewController.swift and we'll implement the button's action method. Begin by looking for the empty onButtonPressed() method that Xcode created for you, and then add the code in Listing 4-7 to create and show the action sheet.

Listing 4-7. Displaying the Action Sheet

```
@IBAction func onButtonPressed(_ sender: UIButton) {
    let controller = UIAlertController(title: "Are You Sure?",
                             message:nil, preferredStyle: .actionSheet)

    let yesAction = UIAlertAction(title: "Yes, I'm sure!",
                         style: .destructive, handler: { action in
                             let msg = self.nameField.text!.isEmpty
                                 ? "You can breathe easy, everything went OK."
                                 : "You can breathe easy, \(self.nameField.text),"
                                 + "everything went OK."
                             let controller2 = UIAlertController(
                                 title:"Something Was Done",
                                 message: msg, preferredStyle: .alert)
                             let cancelAction = UIAlertAction(title: "Phew!",
                                                         style: .cancel,
                                                         handler: nil)
                         controller2.addAction(cancelAction)
                         self.present(controller2, animated: true,
                                                 completion: nil)
    })
```

```
let noAction = UIAlertAction(title: "No way!",
                                style: .cancel, handler: nil)

controller.addAction(yesAction)
controller.addAction(noAction)

if let ppc = controller.popoverPresentationController {
    ppc.sourceView = sender
    ppc.sourceRect = sender.bounds
}

present(controller, animated: true, completion: nil)

}
```

What exactly did we do there? Well, first, in the onButtonPressed() action method, we allocated and initialized a UIAlertController, which is a view controller subclass that can display either an action sheet or an alert:

```
let controller = UIAlertController(title: "Are You Sure?",
                                message:nil, preferredStyle: .actionSheet)
```

The first parameter is the title to be displayed. Refer back to Figure 4-3 to see how the title we're supplying will be displayed at the top of the action sheet. The second parameter is a message that will be displayed immediately below the title, in a smaller font. For this example, we're not using the message so we supply the value nil for this parameter. The final parameter specifies whether we want the controller to display an alert (value UIAlertControllerStyle.alert) or an action sheet (**UIAlertControllerStyle.actionSheet**). Since we need an action sheet, we supply the value **UIAlertControllerStyle.actionSheet** here.

The alert controller does not supply any buttons by default—you have to create a UIAlertAction object for each button that you want and add it to the controller. Listing 4-8 shows the part of the code that creates the two buttons for our action sheet.

Listing 4-8. Creating the Action Sheet Buttons

```
let yesAction = UIAlertAction(title: "Yes, I'm sure!",
                                style: .destructive, handler: { action in
        // Code omitted - see below.
    })

let noAction = UIAlertAction(title: "No way!",
                                style: .cancel, handler: nil)
```

For each button, you specify the title, the style, and a handler to be called when the button is pressed. There are three possible styles to choose from:

- UIAlertActionStyle.destructive should be used when the button triggers a destructive, dangerous, or irreversible action, such as deleting or overwriting a file. The title for a button with this style is drawn in red in a bold font.

- UIAlertActionStyle.default is used for a normal button, such as an OK button, when the action that will be triggered is not destructive. The title is drawn in a regular blue font.

- UIAlertStyle.cancel is used for the Cancel button. The title is drawn in a bold blue font.

Finally, you add the buttons to the controller:

```
[controller addAction:yesAction];
[controller addAction:noAction];
```

To make the alert or action sheet visible, you need to ask the current view controller to *present* the alert controller. Listing 4-9 shows how you present an action sheet.

Listing 4-9. Presenting an Action Sheet

```
if let ppc = controller.popoverPresentationController {
    ppc.sourceView = sender
    ppc.sourceRect = sender.bounds
}
present(controller, animated: true, completion: nil)
```

The first four lines configure where the action sheet will appear by getting the alert controller's popover presentation controller and setting its sourceView and sourceRect properties. We'll say more about these properties shortly. Finally, we make the action sheet visible by calling our view controller's present (_:animated:completion:) method, passing it the alert controller as the controller to be presented. When a view controller is presented, its view temporarily replaces that of the view controller that's presenting it. In the case of the alert view controller, the action sheet or alert partially covers the presenting view controller's view; the rest of the view is covered by a dark, translucent background that lets you see the underlying view but makes it clear that you can't interact with it until you dismiss the presented view controller.

Now let's revisit the popover presentation controller configuration. On the iPhone, the action sheet always pops up from the bottom of the screen, as shown in Figure 4-3, but on the iPad, it's displayed in a popover—a small, rounded rectangle with an arrow that points toward another view, usually the one that caused it to appear. Figure 4-29 shows how our action sheet looks on the iPad Air simulator.

Figure 4-29. *Action Sheet presented on an iPad Air*

As you can see, the popover's arrow points to the Do Something button. That's because we set the `sourceView` property of the alert controller's popover presentation controller to point to that button and its `sourceRect` property to the button's bounds, as shown in Listing 4-10.

Listing 4-10. Setting the sourceView and sourceRect Properties

```
if let ppc = controller.popoverPresentationController {
    ppc.sourceView = sender
    ppc.sourceRect = sender.bounds
}
```

Notice the `if let` construction—this is necessary because on the iPhone, the alert controller does not present the action sheet in a popover, so its `popoverPresentationController` property is `nil`.

In Figure 4-29, the popover appears below the source button, but you can change this, if you need to, by setting the popover presentation controller's `permittedArrowDirections` property, which is a mask of permitted directions for the popover's arrow. The following code moves the popover above the source button by setting this property to `UIPopoverArrowDirection.down`, as shown in Listing 4-11.

Listing 4-11. Setting the Direction of the Popover

```
if let ppc = controller.popoverPresentationController {
        ppc.sourceView = sender
        ppc.sourceRect = sender.bounds
        ppc.permittedArrowDirections = .down
}
```

If you compare Figure 4-29 and Figure 4-3, you'll see that the No Way! button is missing on the iPad. The alert controller does not use buttons with style `UIAlertStyle.cancel` on the iPad, because users are accustomed to dismissing a popover without taking any action by tapping anywhere outside of it.

Presenting an Alert

When the user presses the Yes, I'm Sure! button, we want to popup an alert with a message. When a button that was added to an alert controller is pressed, the action sheet (or alert) is dismissed and the button's handler block is called with a reference to the `UIAlertAction` from which the button was created. The code that's executed when the Yes, I'm Sure! button is pressed is shown in Listing 4-12.

Listing 4-12. Pop up the Alert Message

```
let yesAction = UIAlertAction(title: "Yes, I'm sure!",
                        style: .destructive, handler: { action in
                        let msg = self.nameField.text!.isEmpty
                                    ? "You can breathe easy, everything went OK."
                                    : "You can breathe easy, \(self.nameField.
                                    text),"
                                    + "everything went OK."
                        let controller2 = UIAlertController(
                                    title:"Something Was Done",
                                    message: msg, preferredStyle: .alert)
                            let cancelAction = UIAlertAction(title: "Phew!",
                                                            style: .cancel, handler: nil)
                        controller2.addAction(cancelAction)
```

```
                     self.present(controller2, animated: true,
                                        completion: nil)
})
```

The first thing we do in the handler block is create a new string that will be displayed to the user. In a real application, this is where you would do whatever processing the user requested. We're just going to pretend we did something, and notify the user by using an alert. If the user has entered a name in the top text field, we'll grab that, and we'll use it in the message that we'll display in the alert. Otherwise, we'll just craft a generic message to show:

```
let msg = self.nameField.text!.isEmpty
        ? "You can breathe easy, everything went OK."
        : "You can breathe easy, \(self.nameField.text),"
        + " everything went OK."
```

The next few lines of code are going to look kind of familiar. Alert views and action sheets are created and used in a very similar manner. We always start by creating a UIAlertController:

```
let controller2 = UIAlertController(
              title:"Something Was Done",
              message: msg, preferredStyle: .alert)
```

Again, we pass a title to be displayed. This time, we also pass a more detailed message, which is that string we just created. The final parameter is the style, which we set to UIAlertControllerStyle.alert because we want an alert, not an action sheet. Next, we create a UIAlertAction for the alert's cancel button and add it to the controller:

```
 let cancelAction = UIAlertAction(title: "Phew!",
                          style: .cancel, handler: nil)
 controller2.addAction(cancelAction)
```

Finally, we make the alert appear by present the alert view controller:

```
self.present(controller2, animated: true, completion: nil)
```

You can see the alert that's created by this code in Figure 4-4. You'll notice that our code does not attempt to get and configure the alert controller's popover presentation controller. That's because alerts appear in a small, rounded view in the center of the screen on both iPhone and iPad, so there is no popover presentation controller to configure.

Save ViewController.swift and then build, run, and try out the completed application.

Summary

In this lengthy chapter, hopefully we didn't hit you with too much new stuff, but we went through the use of a good number of controls and showed many different implementation details. We got more practice with outlets and actions, saw how to use the hierarchical nature of views to your advantage, and got some more practice adding Auto Layout constraints. You learned about control states and stretchable images. You also learned how to use both action sheets and alerts.

There's a lot going on in our Control Fun application. Feel free to go back and try things out. Change values, experiment by adding and modifying code, and see what different settings in Interface Builder do. There's no way we could take you through every permutation of every control available in iOS, but the application you just put together is a good starting point and covers a lot of the basics.

In the next chapter, we're going to look at what happens when the user rotates an iOS device from portrait to landscape orientation or vice versa. You're probably well aware that many apps change their displays based on the way the user is holding the device, and we're going to show you how to do that in your own applications.

CHAPTER 5

Working with Device Rotations

The iPhone and iPad exude amazing engineering in form, fit and function. Apple engineers found all kinds of ways to squeeze maximum functionality into a very small and elegant package. One example of this exists in the ability of these devices to be used in either portrait (tall and skinny) or landscape (short and wide) mode, and how that orientation can be changed at runtime simply by rotating the device. You see an example of this **autorotation** behavior in the iOS Safari browser, as shown in Figure 5-1. In this chapter, we'll cover rotation in detail, starting with an overview of the ins and outs of autorotation, and then move on to different ways of implementing that functionality in your apps.

Figure 5-1. *Like many iOS applications, Mobile Safari changes its display based on how it is held, making the most of the available screen space*

© Molly Maskrey, Kim Topley, David Mark, Fredrik Olsson and Jeff Lamarche 2016
M. Maskrey et al., *Beginning iPhone Development with Swift 3*, DOI 10.1007/978-1-4842-2223-2_5

Prior to iOS 8, if you wanted to design an application that would run on both iPhones and iPads, you created one storyboard with a layout for the iPhone and another one with your iPad layout. In iOS 8, that all changed when Apple added APIs to UIKit and tools in Xcode, making it possible to build an application that runs on (or, using their terminology, adapts to) any device with a single storyboard. You still must design carefully for the different form factor of each type of device, but now you do it all in one place. Even better, using the Preview feature that we introduced in Chapter 3, you see immediately how your application would look on any device without even having to start up the simulator. We'll take a look at how to build adaptive application layouts in the second part of this chapter.

The Mechanics of Rotation

The ability to run in both portrait and landscape orientations might not work for every application. Several of Apple's iPhone applications, such as the Weather app, support only a single orientation. However, iPad applications function differently with Apple recommending that most apps, with the exception of immersive apps like games, should support every orientation and most of Apple's own iPad apps work fine in both orientations. Many of them use the orientations to show different views of your data. For example, the Mail and Notes apps use landscape orientation to display a list of items (folders, messages, or notes) on the left and the selected item on the right. In portrait orientation, however, these apps let you focus on the details of just the selected item.

For iPhone apps, the base rule is that, if autorotation enhances the user experience, you should add it to your application. For iPad apps, the rule is you should add autorotation unless you have a compelling reason not to. Fortunately, Apple did a great job of hiding the complexities of handling orientation changes in iOS and in UIKit, so implementing this behavior in your own iOS applications becomes quite easy.

The view controller authorizes the image to rotate. If the user rotates the device, the active view controller gets asked if it's okay to change to the new orientation (which we'll do in this chapter). If the view controller responds in the affirmative, the application's window and views rotate, and the window and view resize to fit the new orientation.

On the iPhone and iPod touch, a view that starts in portrait mode exists taller than it is wide—you see the actual available space for any given device by referring to the Software Size column of Table 1-1 in Chapter 1. Note, however, that the vertical screen real estate available for your app decreases by 20 points vertically if your app is showing the status bar, which is the 20-point strip at the top of the screen (see Figure 5-1) that shows information like signal strength, time, and battery charge.

When the device rotates to landscape mode, the vertical and horizontal dimensions switch around, so, for example, an application running on an iPhone 6/6s would see a screen that's 375 points wide, 667 points high in portrait, but 667 points wide, 375 points high in landscape. Again though, on iPads the vertical space actually available to your app gets reduced by 20 points if you're showing the status bar, which most apps do. On iPhones, as of iOS 8, the status bar hides when in landscape orientation.

Points, Pixels, and the Retina Display

You might be wondering why we're talking about "points" instead of pixels. Earlier versions of this book did, in fact, refer to screen sizes in pixels rather than points. The reason for this change is Apple's introduction of the Retina display, which is Apple's marketing term for the high-resolution screen on all versions of the iPhone starting with iPhone 4 and later-generation iPod touches, as well as newer variants of the iPad. As you can see by looking back at Table 1-1 again, it doubles the hardware screen resolution for most models and almost triples it for the iPhone 6/6s Plus.

Fortunately, we don't need to do a thing in most situations to account for this. When we work with on-screen elements, we specify dimensions and distances in *points*, not in pixels. For older iPhones, and the iPad, iPad 2, and iPad Mini 1, points and pixels are equivalent—one point is one pixel. On more recent-model Apple devices, however, a point equates to a 4-pixel square (2 pixels wide × 2 pixels high) and the iPhone 5s screen (for example) still appears to be 320 points wide, even though it's actually 640 pixels across. On iPhone 6/6s Plus, the scaling factor is 3, so each point maps to a 9-pixel square. Think of it as a "virtual resolution," with iOS automatically mapping points to the physical pixels of your screen. We'll talk more about this in Chapter 16.

In typical applications, most of the work in actually moving the pixels around the screen is managed by iOS. Our app's main function in all this is making sure everything fits nicely and looks proper in the resized window.

Handling Rotation

To handle device rotation, we need to specify the correct **constraints** for all of the objects making up our interface. Constraints tell iOS how the controls should behave when their enclosing view is resized. How does that relate to device rotation? When the device rotates, the dimensions of the screen are (more or less) interchanged—so the area in which your views are laid out changes size.

The simplest way of using constraints is to configure them in Interface Builder (IB). Interface Builder lets you define constraints that describe how your GUI components will be repositioned and resized as their parent view changes or as other views move around. We did a little bit of this in Chapter 4 and we will delve further into the subject of constraints in this chapter. You can think of constraints as equations that make statements about view geometry and the iOS view system itself as a "solver" that will rearrange things as necessary to make those statements true. You can also add constraints in code, but we're not going to cover that in this book.

Constraints were added to iOS 6, but have been present on the Mac for a bit longer than that. On both iOS and macOS, constraints can be used in place of the old "springs and struts" system that was found in earlier releases. Constraints can do everything the old technology could do, and more.

Creating Our Orientations Project

We'll create a simple app to show you how to pick the orientations that you want your app to work with. Start a new Single View Application project in Xcode, and call it **Orientations**. Choose Universal from the Devices pop-up, and save it along with your other projects.

Before we lay out our GUI in the storyboard, we need to tell iOS that our view supports interface rotation. There are actually two ways of doing this. You can create an app-wide setting that will be the default for all view controllers and you can further tweak things for each individual view controller. We'll do both of these things, starting with the app-wide setting.

Supported Orientations at the App Level

First, we need to specify which orientations our application supports. When your new Xcode project window appeared, it should have opened to your project settings. If not, click the top line in the Project Navigator (the one named after your project), and then make sure you're on the General tab. Among the options available in the summary, you should see a section called Deployment Info, and within that, a section called Device Orientation (see Figure 5-2) with a list of check boxes.

Figure 5-2. *The General tab for our project shows, among other things, the supported device orientations*

This is how we identify which orientations our app supports. It doesn't necessarily mean that every view will use all of the selected orientations; but if we are going to support an orientation in any of the views, that orientation must be selected here. Notice that the Upside Down orientation is off by default. That's because Apple does not encourage the user to hold the phone upside down because if the phone rings while it is in that orientation, the user would have to twist it through a full half turn to answer it.

Open the Devices drop-down that's just above the check boxes (see Figure 5-3) and you'll see that you can actually configure separate sets of allowed orientations for the iPhone and the iPad. If you choose iPad, you'll see that all four check boxes are selected, because the iPad is meant to be used in any orientation.

Figure 5-3. *You can configure different orientations for iPhone and iPad*

■ **Note**   The four check boxes shown in Figures 5-2 and 5-3 are actually just a shortcut to adding and deleting entries in your application's Info.plist file. If you single-click Info.plist in the Project Navigator, you should see two entries called **Supported interface orientations** and **Supported interface orientations (iPad)**, with subentries for the orientations that are currently selected. Selecting and deselecting those check boxes in the project summary simply adds and removes items from these arrays. Using the check boxes is easier and less prone to error, so using the check boxes is definitely recommended. However, you should know what they do.

Again, we'll work with an iPhone 6s as our device. Now, select Main.storyboard. Find a label in the Object Library and drag it into your view, dropping it so that it's horizontally centered and somewhere near the top, as shown in Figure 5-4. Select the label's text and change it to **This way up**. Changing the text may shift the label's position, so drag it to make it horizontally centered again.

Figure 5-4. *Setting our Portrait orientation label*

We need to add Auto Layout constraints to pin the label in place before running the application, so Control-drag from the label upward until the background of the containing view turns blue, and then release the mouse. Hold down the Shift key and select Vertical Spacing to Top Layout Guide and Center Horizontally in Container in the pop-up, and then press Return. Now, press ⌘R to build and run this simple app on the iPhone simulator. When it comes up in the simulator, try rotating the device a few times by pressing ⌘-Left Arrow or ⌘-Right Arrow. You'll see that the entire view (including the label you added) rotates to every orientation except upside down, just as we configured it to do. Run it on the iPad simulator to confirm that it rotates to all four possible orientations.

We've identified the orientations our app will support, but that's not all we need to do. We can also specify a set of accepted orientations for each view controller, giving us more fine-grained control over which orientations will work in different parts of our apps.

Per-Controller Rotation Support

Let's configure our view controller to allow a different, smaller set of accepted orientations. The global configuration for the app specifies a sort of absolute upper limit for allowed orientations. If the global configuration doesn't include upside-down orientation, for example, there's no way that any individual view controller can force the system to rotate the display to upside down. All we can do in the view controller is place further limits on what is acceptable.

In the Project Navigator, single-click ViewController.swift. Here we'll implement a method defined in the UIViewController superclass that lets us specify which subset of the global set of orientations we'll accept *for this view controller*:

```
override func supportedInterfaceOrientations() -> UIInterfaceOrientationMask {
    return UIInterfaceOrientationMask(rawValue:
        (UIInterfaceOrientationMask.portrait.rawValue
            | UIInterfaceOrientationMask.landscapeLeft.rawValue))
}
```

This method lets us return a UIInterfaceOrientationMask that specifies the acceptable orientations. Calling this method is iOS's way of asking a view controller if it's allowed to rotate to a specific orientation. In this case, we're returning a value that indicates that we'll accept two orientations: the default portrait orientation and the orientation you get when you turn your phone 90° clockwise, so that the phone's left edge is at the top. We use the Boolean OR operator (the vertical bar symbol) to combine the raw values of these two orientation masks and use the result to create a new UIInterfaceOrientationMask that represents the combined value.

UIKit defines the following orientation masks, which you can combine in any way you like using the OR operator (shown in the preceding example):

- UIInterfaceOrientationMask.portrait.rawValue

- UIInterfaceOrientationMask.landscapeLeft.rawValue

- UIInterfaceOrientationMask.landscapeRight.rawValue

- UIInterfaceOrientationMask.portraitUpsideDown.rawValue

In addition, there are some predefined combinations of these for common use cases. These are functionally equivalent to OR-ing them together on your own, but can save you some typing and make your code more readable:

- UIInterfaceOrientationMask.landscape.rawValue

- UIInterfaceOrientationMask.all.rawValue

- UIInterfaceOrientationMask.allButUpsideDown.rawValue

When the iOS device changes to a new orientation, the supportedInterfaceOrientations() method is called on the active view controller. Depending on whether the returned value includes the new orientation, the application determines whether it should rotate the view. Because every view controller subclass can implement this differently, it is possible for one application to support rotation with some of its views but not with others, or for one view controller to support certain orientations under certain conditions. Run the example application again and verify that you can now only rotate the simulator to the two orientations that are returned by the supportedInterfaceOrientations() method. The .rawValue at the end of each orientation returns the integer value for the orientation to be used in comparison.

> ■ **Note** You can actually rotate the device, but the view itself does not rotate so the label is back to the top except for the two selected orientations.

CODE COMPLETION IN ACTION

Have you noticed that the defined system constants on the iPhone are always designed so that values that work together start with the same letters? One reason why `UIInterfaceOrientationMask.portrait`, `UIInterfaceOrientationMask.portraitUpsideDown`, `UIInterfaceOrientationMask.landscapeLeft`, and `UIInterfaceOrientationMask.landscapeRight` all begin with `UIInterfaceOrientationMask` is to let you take advantage of Xcode's **code completion** feature.

You've probably noticed that as you type, Xcode frequently tries to complete the word you are typing. That's code completion in action.

Developers cannot possibly remember all the various defined constants in the system, but you can remember the common beginning for the groups you use frequently. When you need to specify an orientation, simply type **UIInterfaceOrientationMask** (or even **UIInterf**). You'll see a list of all matches pop up. (In Xcode's preferences, you can configure the list to pop up only when you press the Esc key.) You can use the arrow keys to navigate the list that appears and make a selection by pressing the Tab or Return key. This is much faster than needing to look up the values in the documentation or header files.

Feel free to play around with this method by returning different orientation mask combinations. You can force the system to constrict your view's display to whichever orientations make sense for your app, but don't forget the global configuration we talked about earlier. Remember that if you haven't enabled upside down there (for example), none of your views will ever appear upside down, no matter what their view controller's `supportedInterfaceOrientations()` method declares.

> ■ **Note** iOS actually supports two different types of orientations. The one we're discussing here is the **interface orientation**. There's also a separate but related concept of **device orientation**. Device orientation specifies how the device is currently being held. Interface orientation is which way the views on the screen are rotated. If you turn a standard iPhone upside down, the device orientation will be upside down, but the interface orientation will almost always be one of the other three, since iPhone apps don't support portrait upside down by default.

Creating Our Layout Project

In Xcode, make another new project based on the Single View Application template and name it **Layout**. Select Main.storyboard to edit the storyboard in Interface Builder. A great thing about constraints is that they accomplish quite a lot using very little code. To see how this works, drag four labels from the library over to your view, and place them, as shown in Figure 5-5. Use the dashed blue guidelines to help you line up each one near its respective corner. In this example, we're going to use instances of the UILabel class to show how to use constraints to build your GUI layout, but the same rules apply to many GUI objects.

Figure 5-5. *Adding four labels to our Storyboard*

Double-click each label and assign a title to each one so that you can tell them apart later. We've used UL for the upper-left label, UR for the upper-right label, LL for the lower-left label, and LR for the lower-right label. After setting the text for each label, drag all of them into position so that they are lined up evenly with respect to the container view's corners.

Let's see what happens now, given that we haven't yet set any Auto Layout constraints. Build and run the app on the iPad Air simulator. Once the simulator starts up, you'll find that you can only see the labels on the left—the other two are off-screen to the right. Furthermore, the label at the bottom left is not where it should be—right in the bottom-left corner of the screen. Select Hardware ➤ Rotate Left, which will simulate turning the iPad to landscape mode. You'll find that you can now see the top-left and top-right labels, as shown in Figure 5-6.

Figure 5-6. *Changing orientation without adding any constraints*

As you can see, things aren't looking so good. The top-left label is in the right spot after rotating, but all of the others are in the wrong places and some of them aren't visible at all! What's happened is that every object has maintained its distance relative to the upper-left corner of the view in the storyboard. What we really want is to have each label sticking tightly to its nearest corner after rotating. The labels on the right should shift horizontally to match the view's new width, and the labels on the bottom should move vertically to match the new height. Fortunately, we can easily set up constraints in Interface Builder to make these changes happen for us.

As we've seen in earlier chapters, Interface Builder is smart enough to examine this set of objects and create a set of default constraints that will do exactly what we want. It uses some rules of thumb to figure out that if we have objects near edges, we probably want to keep them there. To make it apply these rules, first select all four labels. You can do this by clicking one label, and then holding down the Shift or⌘ key while clicking each of the other three. With all of them selected, choose Editor ➤ Resolve Auto Layout Issues ➤ Add Missing Constraints from the menu (you'll find there are two menu items with this name—in this case, because we have selected all of the labels, you can use either of them). Next, just press the Run button to launch the app in the simulator, and then verify that it works.

■ **Note**   Another way to easily select all the labels is to Shift-click the label names in the Document Outline, as shown in Figure 5-7.

Figure 5-7. *Using the Document Outline view (to the left of the Storyboard canvas) can sometimes make it easier to select and work with multiple UI objects*

Knowing that this works is one thing, but to use constraints like this most effectively, it's pretty important to understand how it works, too. So, let's dig into this a bit. Back in Xcode, click the upper-left label to select it. You'll notice that you can see some solid blue lines attached to the label. These blue lines are different from the dashed blue guidelines that you see when dragging objects around the screen, as shown in Figure 5-8.

Figure 5-8. *The solid blue lines show constraints that are configured for the chosen object*

Each of those solid blue lines represents a constraint. If you now press ⌥⌘**5** to open the Size Inspector, you'll see that it contains a list of constraints. Figure 5-9 shows the constraints that Xcode applied to the UL label in my storyboard, but the constraints that Xcode creates depends on exactly where you placed the labels, so you may see something different.

Figure 5-9. *Four constraints generated by Xcode to pin a label in its parent view*

In this case, two of the constraints deal with this label's position relative to its superview, the container view: it specifies the **leading space**, which generally means the space to the right, and the **top space** (i.e., the space above the label). These constraints cause the label to maintain the same distance to the top and right edges of its superview when the superview's size changes, as it does when the device is rotated. The other two constraints keep this label lined up with two of the other labels. Examine each of the other labels to see what constraints they have and make sure that you understand how those constraints work to keep the four labels in the corners of their superview.

You should know that in languages where text is written and read from right to left, "leading space" is on the right, so adding a trailing constraint will cause a GUI to be laid out in the opposite direction if the user has picked a language such as Arabic for their device. This is, in fact, what the user would expect. And it's automatic, so you don't need to do anything special to make it happen.

Overriding Default Constraints

Grab another label from the library and drag it over to the layout area. This time, instead of moving toward a corner, drag it toward the left edge of your view, lining up the label's left edge with the left edges of the other labels on the left side, and centering it vertically in the view. Dashed lines will appear to help you out. Figure 5-10 shows you what this looks like.

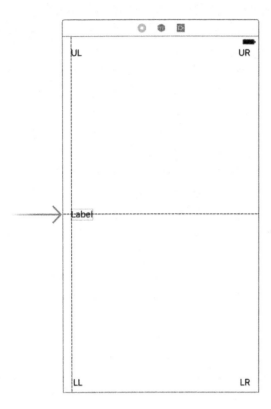

Figure 5-10. *Placing the Left label*

Let's add a new constraint to force this label to stay vertically centered. Select the label, click the Align icon below the storyboard, check Vertically in Container in the pop-up that appears, and then click Add 1 Constraint. Now make sure that the Size Inspector is on display (by pressing ⌥⌘5 if necessary). You'll see that this label now has a constraint aligning its center Y value to that of its superview. The label also needs a horizontal constraint. You can add this by making sure the label is selected, and then choosing Editor ➤ Resolve Auto Layout Issues ➤ Add Missing Constraints from the All Views section of the menu. Press ⌘R to run the app again. Do some rotating and you'll see that all the labels now move perfectly into their expected places for the various device types.

Now, let's complete our ring of labels by dragging out a new one to the right side of the view, lining up its right edge with the other labels on the right, and aligning it vertically with the Left label. Change this label's title to Right, and then drag it a bit to make sure that the right edge is vertically aligned with the right edges of the other two labels, using the dashed blue line as your guide. We want to use the automatic constraints that Xcode can provide us with, so select Editor ➤ Resolve Auto Layout Issues ➤ Add Missing Constraints to generate them.

Build and run again. Do some rotating again. You'll see that all the labels stay on the screen and are correctly positioned relative to each other (see Figure 5-11). If you rotate back, they should return to their original positions. This technique works great for many applications you're likely to encounter.

Figure 5-11. *The labels in their new positions after rotating*

Full-Width Labels

We're going to create some constraints that make sure that our labels stay the same width as each other, with tight spacing to keep them stretched across the top of the view even when the device rotates. Figure 5-12 should give you an idea of what we're trying to do.

Figure 5-12. *The top labels, spread across the entire width of the display, in both portrait and landscape orientations*

We need to be able to visually verify that we've got the result we want—namely, each label is precisely centered within its half of the screen. In order to make it easier to see whether we've got it right, let's temporarily set a background color for the labels. In the storyboard, select both the UL and UR labels, open the Attributes Inspector, and scroll down to the View section. Use the Background control to select a nice, bright color. You'll see that the (currently very small) frame of each label fills with the color you chose.

Drag the resizing control of the UL label from its right edge, pulling it almost to the horizontal midpoint of the view. You don't have to be exact here, for reasons that will become clear soon. After doing this, resize the UR label by dragging its left-edge resizing control to the left until you see the dashed blue guideline appear (if you don't see the guide disappear, just drag it reasonably close) which tells you that it's the recommended width from the label to its left. Now we'll add a constraint to make these labels retain their relative positions. Control-drag from the UL label until the mouse is over the UR label, and then release the mouse. In the pop-up, select Horizontal Spacing and press Return. That constraint tells the layout system to hold these labels beside one another with the same horizontal space they have right now. Build and run to see what happens. You should see something like Figure 5-13; the longer label may appear on the left or right depending upon your configuration.

143

Figure 5-13. *The labels are stretched across the display, but not evenly*

That's heading in the right direction but not yet what we had in mind. So what's missing? We've defined constraints that control each label's position relative to its superview and the allowed distance between the two labels, but we haven't said anything about the sizes of the labels. This leaves the layout system free to size them in whatever way it wants (which, as we've just seen, can be quite wrong). To remedy this, we need to add one more constraint.

Make sure the UL label is selected, and then hold down the Shift key (⇧) and click the UR label. With both labels selected, you can make a constraint that affects both of them. Click the Pin icon below the storyboard and check the Equal Widths check box in the pop-up that appears (which we saw in Chapter 3), and then click Add 1 Constraint. You'll now see a new constraint appear, as shown in Figure 5-14. You may notice two orange lines have appeared below the labels; this means that the current positions and sizes of the labels in the storyboard do not match what you will see at runtime. To fix this, select the View icon in the Document Outline, and then select Editor ➤ Resolve Auto Layout Issues ➤ Update Frames in Xcode's menu. The constraints should change to blue and the labels will resize themselves so that their widths are equal.

Figure 5-14. The top labels are now made equal in width by a constraint

If you run again at this point, you should see the labels spread across the entire screen, in both portrait and landscape orientations (see Figure 5-12).

In this project, all of our labels are visible and are correctly laid out in multiple orientations; however, there is a lot of unused space on the screen. Perhaps it would be better if we also set up the other two rows of labels to fill the width of the view or allowed the height of our labels to change so that there will be less empty space on the interface? Feel free to experiment with the constraints of these six labels and perhaps even add some others. Apart from what we've covered so far, you'll find more actions that create constraints in the pop-ups that appear when you click the Pin and Align icons below the storyboard. And if you end up making a constraint that doesn't do what you want, you can delete it by selecting it and pressing the Delete key, or try configuring it in the Attributes Inspector. Play around until you feel comfortable with the basics of how constraints work. We'll use constraints constantly throughout the book, but if you want the full details, just search for **Auto Layout** in the Xcode documentation window.

Creating Adaptive Layouts

The layout for the simple example that we just created works well in portrait and landscape orientations. It also works on both iPhone and iPad, despite their differing screen dimensions. As we already noted, handling device rotation and creating a user interface that works on devices with different screen sizes are really the same problem—after all, from the point of view of your application, when the device rotates, the screen effectively changes size. In the simplest cases, you handle them both at the same time by assigning Auto Layout constraints to make sure that all of your views are positioned and sized where you want them to be. However, that's not always possible. Some layouts work well when the device is in portrait mode, but not so well when it's rotated to landscape; and similarly, some designs suit the iPhone but not the iPad. When this happens, you really have no choice but to create separate designs for each case. Prior to iOS 8, this meant either implementing your whole layout in code, having multiple storyboards, or a combination of the two. Fortunately, Apple has made it possible to design **adaptive** applications that work in both orientations and on different devices while still using only a single storyboard. Let's take a look at how this works.

Creating the Restructure Application

To get started, we'll design a user interface that works well for an iPhone in portrait mode, but not so well when the phone is rotated or when the application runs on an iPad. Then we'll see how to use Interface Builder to adapt the design so that it works well everywhere.

Start by making a new Single View project like you've done before, naming this one **Restructure**. We're going to construct a GUI that consists of one large content area and a small set of buttons that perform various (fictional) actions. We'll place the buttons at the bottom of the screen and let the content area take up the rest of the space, as shown in Figure 5-15.

■ **Note**   You may have noticed that some of the various illustrations of Apple devices we use in this book have different configurations. While some, like Figure 5-15 have an appearance closer to a "real" device, others such as in Figure 5-11 appear more basic. The differences should not be a concern as you're likely to come across any of them in technical documentation, including that from Apple.

Figure 5-15. *The initial GUI of the Restructure app, in portrait orientation on the iPhone*

Select Main.storyboard to start editing the GUI. Since we don't really have an interesting content view we want to display, we'll just use a large colored rectangle. Drag a single UIView from the Object Library into your container view. While it's still selected, resize it so that it fills the top part of the available space, leaving a small margin above it and on both sides, as shown in Figure 5-15. Next, switch over to the Attributes Inspector and use the Background pop-up to pick some other background color. You can choose anything you like, as long as it's not white, so that the view stands out from the background. In the storyboard in the example source code archive, this view is green, so from now on we'll call it the green view.

Drag a button from the Object Library and place it in the lower left of the empty space below the green view. Double-click to select the text in its label, and change it to **Action One**. Now Option-drag three copies of this button and place them in two columns, like those in Figure 5-15. You don't have to line them up perfectly because we're going to use constraints to finalize their positions, but you should try to place the two button groups approximately equal distances from their respective sides of the containing view. Change their titles to **Action Two**, **Action Three**, and **Action Four**. Also, let's add a different background color to each button so they're easy to see; I've used red, blue, orange, and yellow in order, but you can choose any colors you prefer. If you use a dark background color like blue, you want to make the text lighter as well. Finally, drag the lower edge of the green view downward until it just touches the top row of buttons. Use the blue guidelines to line everything up, as shown in Figure 5-15.

Now let's set up the Auto Layout constraints. Start by selecting the green view. We're going to start by pinning this to the top and to the left and right sides of the main view. That's still not enough to fully constrain it because its height isn't specified yet; we're going to fix that by anchoring it to the top of the buttons, once we've fixed the buttons themselves. Click the Pin button at the bottom right of the storyboard editor. At the top of the pop-up, you'll see the now familiar group of four input fields surrounding a small square. Leave the Constrain to Margins check box checked. Click the red dashed lines above, to the left, and to the right of the small square to attach the view to the top, left, and right sides of its superview (see Figure 5-16). Click Add 3 Constraints.

Figure 5-16. *Adding constraints to fix the green view to the top, left, and right sides*

For now, we'll set a constant height for our buttons, starting with Action One, as shown in Figure 5-17. I've used the value of 43 points simply because that's where it was when I created the button. Anything around this number should be okay for what we're trying to do in this example, which is deal with different devices and orientations. Then repeat the operation for each of the other three buttons.

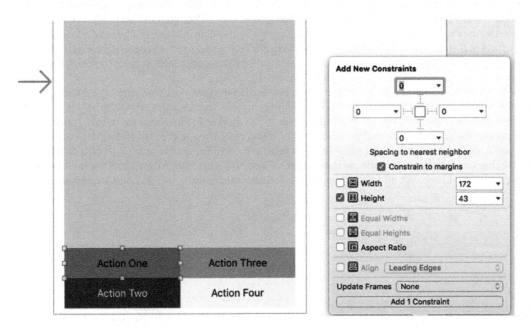

Figure 5-17. *Setting a height value for one of our buttons*

If you performed the operations correctly so far, you should be able to see the results of all of the constraints in the Document Outline, as shown in Figure 5-18, where we see each of our four button heights, as well as the three sides for the green view.

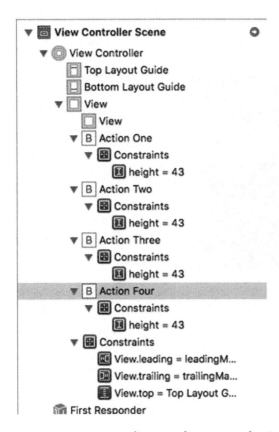

Figure 5-18. *You can always see the progress of setting your constraints in the Document Outline*

Next pin the bottom-left (Action Two) and bottom-right (Action Four) buttons to the lower corners by Control-dragging from each button to the lower left and lower right, respectively. For Action Two, Shift-select the two options, as shown in Figure 5-19.

Figure 5-19. *Control-drag down and to the left to pin the Action Two button to the lower left of the container view*

Perform the similar operation, Control-dragging out to the right and down to set the Leading and Vertical spacing for the Action Four button, as shown in Figure 5-20.

Figure 5-20. *Control-drag down and to the right to pin the Action Four button to the lower right of the container view*

Next, Shift-select all four buttons, click the Pin icon, and set all the widths to be equal (see Figure 5-21). Note that we haven't set a width yet, so they could vary from small to extremely wide; but in a moment, we'll take care of that through additional constraints.

Figure 5-21. *Set all the buttons to be equal widths, although we haven't yet set any value for width in our storyboard*

For the top row of buttons, Action One and Action Three, Control-drag to the left and right, respectively, to set the Leading Space to Container Margin and Trailing Space to Container Margin (see Figure 5-22). This ties the left edge of Action One and the right edge of Action Three to the edge of the view, setting one of our width anchor points.

Figure 5-22. *Setting the left edge of Action One and the right edge of Action Three to the edges of the containing view*

These final two constraints will be all we need to make sure that the buttons are half the width of the green view and match each other. Control-drag from Action One to Action Three and set Horizontal Spacing. Do the same thing between Action Two and Action Four, as shown in Figure 5-23. What we've done is to set the edge anchor to a fixed location, the left and right edges of the container in Figure 5-22. And, as we saw in Figure 5-21, we set the buttons to be equal width. By setting the horizontal spacing so that the buttons on the same row are up against each other, they work out to meet in the center of the view. And since the green view is also pinned to the left and right edges, the buttons meet in the middle of the green view as well.

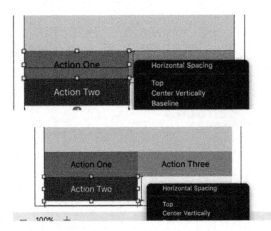

Figure 5-23. *Attach each row of buttons together at the center of the view; this, by default, sets the width of each button to be half the width of the view*

Just a couple more things and we'll be ready to test out our app in the various devices. Control-drag from Action Three to Action Four to set the Vertical Spacing, like we just did with the Horizontal Spacing of rows, as shown in Figure 5-24. Do the same between Action One and Action Two.

Figure 5-24. *Set the vertical spacing between buttons in the same column like we did with the button rows*

Finally, Control-drag between the green view and the Action One button to set the spacing so that the green view and the top row of buttons are adjacent, as shown in Figure 5-25.

Figure 5-25. *Setting the spacing between our green view and the top row of buttons*

Now you should be able to select any full screen iPhone or iPad in either portrait or landscape orientation and the buttons should maintain their position, as shown in Figure 5-26.

Figure 5-26. *Selecting different devices in portrait orientation; the layouts should maintain their positioning*

One other thing to note when looking at the Issue Navigator in Xcode is that there aren't any issues. By systematically setting just the constraints we needed, we were able to create a layout with minimal effort. However, don't expect it to be this easy all the time.

On last thing to do: Let's build and run our project in the simulator before moving forward just to make sure it works as we expect. Figure 5-27 shows the two iPhone 6s orientations, while Figure 5-28 shows the two orientations for a full screen iPad Air.

Figure 5-27. *Our two orientations for an iPhone 6s*

Figure 5-28. *Our two orientations for an iPad Air*

While these look as we would expect them to, they're not what we're after. For an iPhone in landscape, still a wC hC configuration, we want a single column of buttons pressed up against the right side. For an iPad, in any orientation, wR hR, we want a single row of buttons against the bottom of the view.

■ **Note** The notation w- h-, refers to the width and height of the configuration being considered. To simplify things, in Auto Layout this will be either C for compact or R for regular, so that you have the options: wC hC, wC hR, wR hC, and wR hR. By looking in the Device Configuration Bar you can see how these apply to actual Apple devices.

Setting the iPhone Landscape (wC hC) Configuration

We'll get to setting up our wC hC landscape configuration quickly, but first save your work and then close the Xcode project. You can just click the red ball at the upper left of the Xcode window to close this project. You don't have to exit Xcode completely.

Go to finder on your Mac to locate the Restructure folder and create a compressed version, as shown in Figure 5-29. This creates our "master" copy of the project that we can come back to at any time if, during the following changes, things get out of whack.

Figure 5-29. *Create a master copy of our project as it exists now*

And because we may want to do this again through the course of our following work, I renamed the .zip file to **RestructureBaseline**, as shown in Figure 5-30, so I know that this is the original project we made that works with all devices and orientations in the same manner.

Figure 5-30. *Saving our baseline project under a unique name*

First, let's create our iPhone landscape orientation. Select the iPhone 6s and the landscape orientation. To the right of the Device Configuration Bar, click the Vary for Traits and note that the bar turns blue, as shown in Figure 5-31. In the popup select both height and width. You should see, again in Figure 5-31, that now, only iPhone devices are shown and only in landscape orientation. In this variation of traits, we'll develop our UI just for this configuration.

Figure 5-31. *The starting point for creating the UI for our iPhone landscape configuration*

Next, and yes this will seem scary, click all five UI elements (our green view and the four buttons) and press Delete. Don't worry too much because you saved the project and created a compressed baseline version that we can always get back to later. If you didn't, it might be a good idea to do that now. When completed, your canvas will look, as you'd expect, like Figure 5-32. But, if you look at the Document Outline, you'll still see the elements and even the constraints. That's because they exist for the baseline configuration and we're creating a new configuration or a new trait collection for just our wC hC landscape.

Figure 5-32. *Starting over for just our iPhone landscape configuration. Note that we still have all the UI elements and constraints showing in our Document Outline but for our baseline configuration*

As we did for our baseline, drag out a UIView and four buttons setting them up with colors and titles as we did earlier. Place them in the approximate positions shown in Figure 5-33 but don't set any constraints just yet.

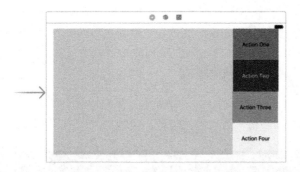

Figure 5-33. *Drag new UI elements onto the storyboard and position them approximately as shown*

In this section, let's make our measurements a little more accurate. Select the green view. Using the Size Inspector, set the dimensions to 500 × 340 points, as shown in Figure 5-34. The width (500pts) is arbitrary; the height is 340, which when divided by 4 comes out to 85, which is what we will set as the height of the buttons. Note that this is not necessarily a constraint, but rather, the appearance on the storyboard. In fact, we don't want any fixed size for the green view since it will vary depending on whether we go up in size to a Plus or down to a SE.

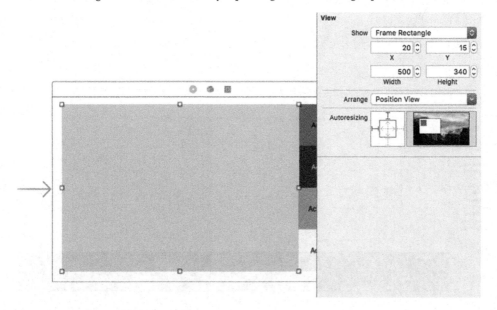

Figure 5-34. *Set the dimensions of the green view*

Select the green view and pin the top, left and right sides to the edge, as shown in Figure 5-35.

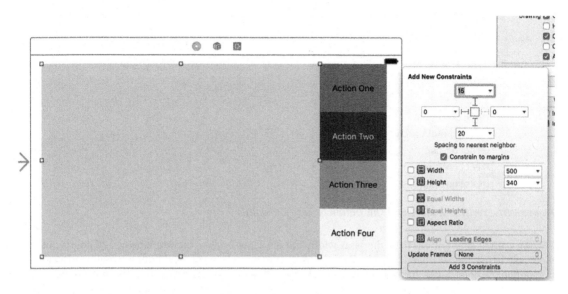

Figure 5-35. *Pin the green view to the top, left, and right for the landscape orientation*

Next, we're going to fix the width of the Action One button, but we're going to do it a little differently than previously. Inside the Action One button, Control-drag from one point to another both the starting and ending points within the red boundary and release. You're presented with a similar popover (see Figure 5-36), on which you select Width. The width of the Action One button should now be 120 points, as seen in Figure 5-37.

Figure 5-36. *Set the width of the Action One button*

Figure 5-37. *Verify that the Action One button is set to 120 points*

We want all four buttons to be the same width and the same height—the width being 120 points but the height being adjust dynamically based on the available vertical area of the iPhone when in landscape orientation. As before, we'll handle the equal height by setting the spacing between the buttons in the column. For now, Shift-click all four buttons to select them all, click the Pin icon, and set the Equal Widths and Equal Heights constraints, as shown in Figure 5-38.

Figure 5-38. *Set all four buttons to equal width and height*

Pin the Action One button to the top and right of its containing view (see Figure 5-39) and the Action Four button to the right and bottom (see Figure 5-40).

Figure 5-39. Pinning the Action One button to the top and right

Figure 5-40. *Pinning the Action Four button to the bottom and right*

For the Action Two button, Control-drag to the right and choose Trailing Space to Container Margin to pin it to the right side of the container, as shown in Figure 5-41. Repeat this operation with the Action Three button.

Figure 5-41. *Pin the middle buttons to the right side using the control-drag and set the Trailing Space to Container Margin pop-up, as shown here for Action Two. Do the same operation for the Action Three button*

Between the Action One and Action Two buttons, Control-drag to set the Vertical Spacing, as shown in Figure 5-42. Repeat for the spacing between Action Two and Action Three, and Action Three and Action Four.

Figure 5-42. *Set the Vertical Spacing between each of the pairs of buttons in the column. This forces the height of each button to be one-fourth of the height of the container*

Finally, set the Horizontal Spacing between the green view and the Action One button (you could use any of the four buttons), as shown in Figure 5-43.

Figure 5-43. *Set the Horizontal Spacing between the green view and the row of buttons*

Click the Done Varying button in the Device Configuration Bar to finish adding, placing and setting constraints for this iPhone landscape configuration, as shown in Figure 5-44.

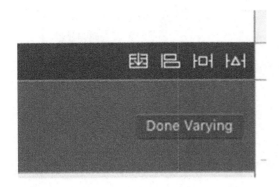

Figure 5-44. *Finish by clicking the Done Varying button in the Device Configuration Bar*

The buttons should now be properly placed for any of the three iPhone wC hC configurations, as shown in Figure 5-45. Note that if we were to select a 6/6s Plus, because that is a wR hC device, we would see the earlier baseline layout.

Figure 5-45. *Changing the device type in the Device Configuration Bar shows that we have correctly set up our constraints for the landscape orientation of wC hC iPhone devices*

Running the apps in the simulator should yield the results shown in Figure 5-46. Although we could have made the alignment a little tighter to the edges, which would be appropriate for a production app, in this example we wanted to stress the manipulations of UI elements for the various device and orientation configurations. As you become more and more familiar with Auto Layout, you'll naturally get much better with your designs.

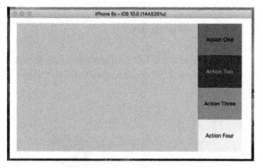

Figure 5-46. *If we've done everything correctly, we should see the proper layout for any iPhone (except 6/6s Plus) landscape configurations*

The last thing we want to do before moving on to iPad is to save this project version by compressing it for later and assigning a recognizable name. As shown in Figure 5-47, I used the name Restructure_wChC. zip for our file, which represents the compact width and height. Feel free to use any naming convention you like, as long as you're able to keep track of the various iterations.

Figure 5-47. *Save this version of the project in case we need to get back to this baseline*

Setting the iPad (iPhone Plus Landscape) (wR hR) Configurations

In the previous two sections I walked you through each step along the way to creating our layouts for the baseline and iPhone landscape configurations. You need to be able to quickly use Auto Layout when designing your UI so if you need any review, I might suggest running through the preceding sections another couple of times, trying it without looking at the text or figures.

For this configuration, to save space, I've shown the key steps in Table 5-1 along with pointing to the reference figures in case you might need a little help with understanding what the step is about. We'll work this way from now on, at least most of the time unless we need to address something new.

Follow the steps in Table 5-1 to set up the configuration for iPad all orientations and the iPhone 6/6s Plus in landscape orientation.

Table 5-1. *Setting up All Orientations on an iPad and the Landscape Orientation on iPhone 6/6s Plus*

STEP	Action	Figure
1	Click Vary For Traits and introduce variations based on width.	5-48
2	Delete the five UI elements in the Storyboard. Then add back five new elements from the object library as we did in the last section.	5-49
3	Select the green view we just added and in the Size Inspector, set the width to 728 and the height to 926. These are not constraints; they'll just help us with visually laying out the elements on the Storyboard. (Note: These values work for the iPhone 6s. If using a different device size, you will need to vary your height and width accordingly.)	5-50
4	Select the Action Four button and set its width to 182 using the Size Inspector…again, this is for the iPhone 6s device. This is only for visual placement and not a constraint.	5-51
5	Making sure we still have a blue Device Configuration Bar indicating that we're still in the Vary for Traits mode, align the UI elements as shown: the green view along the top and a single row of buttons along the bottom.	5-52
6	Similar to what we did before, pin the green view to the top, left and right sides of the containing view.	5-53
7	Pin the Action One button to the lower-left corner of the containing view.	5-54
8	Pin the Action Four button to the lower-right corner of the containing view.	5-55
9	Pin the Action Two button to the bottom edge of the containing view.	5-56
10	Pin the Action Three button to the bottom edge of the containing view.	5-57
11	Add a constraint to set the height of the Action One button to a fixed value. I used 63 points because it fit the layout on my Storyboard. There is no "right" answer; adjust it to your needs for your layout.	5-58
12	Shift-select all four action buttons along the bottom row and set to equal height and width.	5-59
13	Click-drag from the green view to the Action One button and set the Vertical Spacing. This forces the green view to sit against the row of buttons.	5-60
14	Click-drag from Action One to Action Two setting the Horizontal Spacing. Repeat for Action Two to Action Three and Action Three to Action Four. This causes the buttons to sit next to each other on the sides and to be one-quarter the width of the enclosing container.	5-61
15	Click the Done Varying button to end the modifications for this set of traits.	5-62

Figure 5-48. *Select an iPad, click Vary For Traits, and choose Width*

Figure 5-49. *Delete the five UI elements*

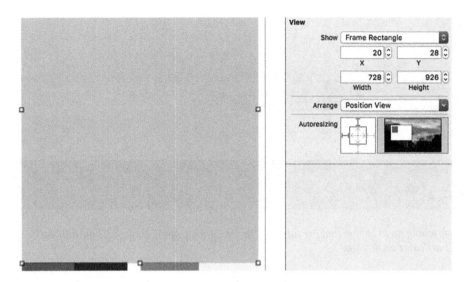

Figure 5-50. *Add in the five new UI elements from the UI object library and set the width and height of the green view using the Size Inspector. This does not set constraints, only the visual aspects so we can adjust our Storyboard*

Figure 5-51. *Similarly, set the width and height of the Action Four button so we have a visual reference with which to work and manipulate our Storyboard*

Figure 5-52. *Align everything up as shown making sure our Device Configuration Bar is still blue indicating we're working with a particular set of traits*

Figure 5-53. *Similar to what we did in the previous sections, pin the green view to the top, left and right sides of the containing view*

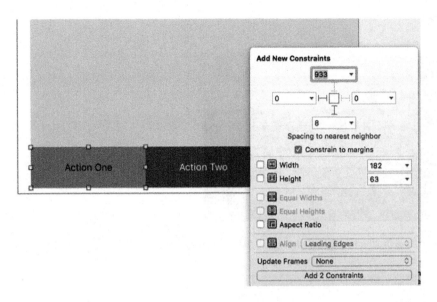

Figure 5-54. Pin the Action One button to the lower-left corner of the containing view

Figure 5-55. Pin the Action Four button to the lower right corner of the containing view

Figure 5-56. *Pin the Action Two button to the bottom edge of the containing view*

Figure 5-57. *Pin the Action Three button to the bottom edge of the containing view*

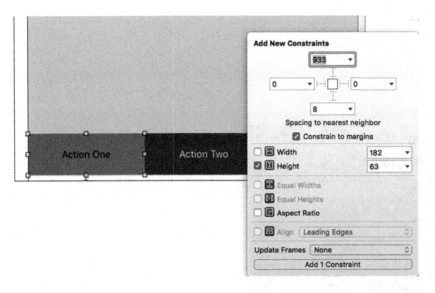

Figure 5-58. *Add a constraint to set the height of the Action One button to a fixed value. I used 63 points because it fit the layout on my Storyboard*

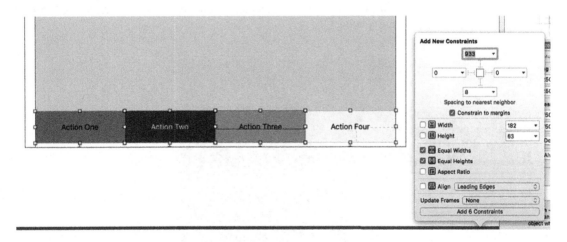

Figure 5-59. *Shift-select all four action buttons along the bottom row and set to equal height and width*

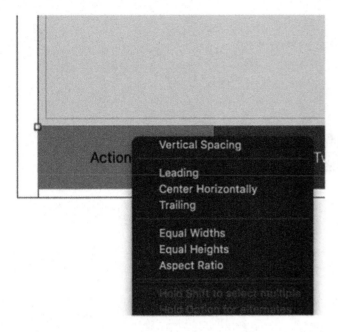

Figure 5-60. *Click-drag from the green view to the Action One button and set the Vertical Spacing. This forces the green view to sit against the row of buttons*

Figure 5-61. *Click-drag from Action One to Action Two setting the Horizontal Spacing. Repeat for Action Two to Action Three and Action Three to Action Four*

Figure 5-62. *Click the Done Varying button to end the modifications for this set of traits*

I hope you were able to follow this abbreviated form of using Auto Layout. If you found any issues, the best thing is to go back, delete your project, and start at the last baseline project. Until you work with Auto Layout for a dozen or so times, you'll most likely make several mistakes and get frustrated. You're not alone. When I'm away from Xcode and especially Auto Layout for a few weeks, I'm often walking away only to restart and re-layout things until I get it the way I need or want it to be.

Assuming you made it to this point successfully, click a few different iPad and orientation configurations to verify that things appear as we expect them, as shown in Figure 5-63.

Figure 5-63. *Check to make sure your orientations appear correctly in the Storyboard canvas*

Finally, run the simulator for various devices making sure things appear as they should. Figure 5-64 shows what things should look like for an iPad Air in portrait and landscape orientations.

Figure 5-64. *Verify things work as expected by running the simulator using various device types and checking orientations*

Summary

In this chapter we covered the basics of handling device rotations including getting heavily involved with using the new Xcode 8 Auto Layout and traits editor with the Device Configuration Bar. We started by talking the basics of rotations and what happens when you change orientation on an Apple device. Our first project, Orientations, showed the basics of working with simple device rotations and maintaining positioning of labels. In our second project, Layout, we refined our knowledge of label positioning by putting labels into all four corners, as well as the left and right edges to handle rotations.

Finally, in our Restructure project, we got very deep into understanding the use of Auto Layout for creating device and orientation specific layout configurations. As you will be using Auto Layout for the rest of this book, as well as your career, make sure that you're comfortable with its use before proceeding. While it can be very daunting at first, through practice, like anything else, it will become second nature—until Apple changes things next year.

CHAPTER 6

■ ■ ■

Creating a Multiview Application

Up until this point, we've written applications using a single view controller. While single view apps can often do what you need them to, the real power of the iOS platform emerges when you switch out views based on user input. Multiview applications come in several different flavors, but the underlying mechanism functions the same, regardless of how the app appears on the screen. In this chapter, we'll focus on the structure of multiview applications and the basics of swapping content views by building our own multiview app from scratch. Writing our own custom controller class that switches between two different content views, we'll establishing a strong foundation for taking advantage of the various multiview controllers provided by Apple.

First, let's look at some examples of our new area of exploration...multiviews.

Common Types of Multiview Apps

Strictly speaking, we have worked with multiple views in our previous applications, since buttons, labels, and other controls are all subclasses of UIView and they can all go into the view hierarchy. But when Apple uses the term **view** in documentation, they refer to a UIView or one of its subclasses having a corresponding view controller. These types of views are also sometimes referred to as **content views** because they are the primary container for the content of your application.

A utility app provides the simplest example of how a multiview application appears. It focuses primarily on a single view, but offers a second view typically used to configure the application or to provide more detail than the primary view. The Stocks application that ships with iPhone shows a good example of this (see Figure 6-1). Clicking button in the lower-right corner, the view transitions to a new view that lets you set the list of stocks tracked by the application.

© Molly Maskrey, Kim Topley, David Mark, Fredrik Olsson and Jeff Lamarche 2016
M. Maskrey et al., *Beginning iPhone Development with Swift 3*, DOI 10.1007/978-1-4842-2223-2_6

Figure 6-1. *The Stocks application that ships with iPhone provides two views: one to display the data and another to configure the stock list*

Several tab bar applications ship with the iPhone, including the Phone application (see Figure 6-2) and the Clock application. A tab bar application displays a row of buttons, called the **tab bar**, at the bottom of the screen. Tapping one of the buttons causes a new view controller to become active and a new view to be shown. In the Phone application, for example, tapping Contacts shows a different view than the one shown when you tap Keypad.

Figure 6-2. *The Phone application provides an example of a multiview application using a tab bar*

Another common type of multiview app uses a navigation-based mechanism featuring a navigation controller that uses a bar to control a hierarchical series of views, as seen in the Settings app (see Figure 6-3). In Settings, you first see a series of rows, each row corresponding to a cluster of settings or a specific app. Touching one of those rows takes you to a new view where you might customize one particular set of settings. Some views present a list that allows you to dive even deeper. The navigation controller keeps track of how deep you go and gives you a control to let you make your way back to the previous view.

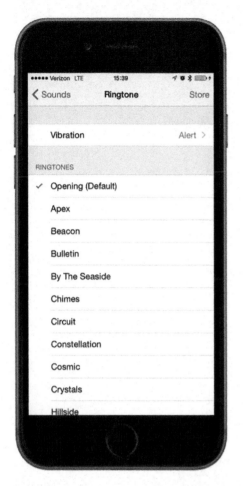

Figure 6-3. *The iPhone Settings application provides a great example of a multiview application using a navigation bar*

For example, selecting the Sounds preference takes you to a view with a list of sound-related options. The top of that view displays a navigation bar with a left arrow labeled Settings that takes you back to the previous view if you tap it. Within the sound options you'll see a row labeled Ringtone. Tap Ringtone. You're taken to a new view featuring a list of ringtones and a navigation bar that takes you back to the main Sounds preference view, as shown in Figure 6-4. A navigation-based application provides a useful mechanism when you want to present a hierarchy of views.

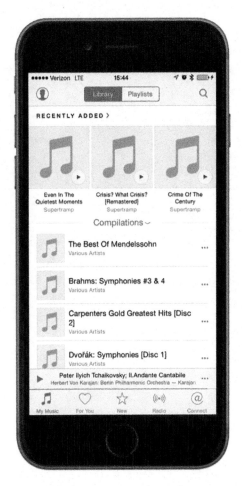

Figure 6-4. *The Music application uses both a navigation bar and a tab bar*

On the iPad, we implement most navigation-based applications, such as Mail, using a split view, where the navigation elements appear on the left side of the screen, and the item you select to view or edit appears on the right. We'll talk about split views in Chapter 11.

Because views are themselves hierarchical in nature, we might combine different mechanisms for swapping views within a single application. For example, the iPhone's Music application uses a tab bar to switch between different methods of organizing your music. It also uses a navigation controller and its associated navigation bar to allow you to browse your music based on that selection. In Figure 6-4, the tab bar is at the bottom of the screen and the navigation bar is at the top of the screen.

Some applications use a toolbar, which is often confused with a tab bar. A tab bar selects one and only one choice from among two or more options. A toolbar holds buttons and certain other controls, but those items are not mutually exclusive. A perfect example of a toolbar is at the bottom of the main Safari view, as shown in Figure 6-5. If you compare the toolbar at the bottom of the Safari view with the tab bar at the bottom of the Phone or Music application, you'll find the two pretty easy to tell apart. The tab bar has multiple segments, exactly one of which (the selected one) is highlighted with a tint color; but on a toolbar, normally every enabled button is highlighted.

Figure 6-5. *Mobile Safari features a toolbar at the bottom, acting like a free-form bar that allows you to include a variety of controls*

Each of these multiview application types uses a specific controller class from the UIKit. Tab bar interfaces are implemented using the UITabBarController class and navigation interfaces are implemented using UINavigationController. We'll describe their use in detail in the next few chapters.

The Architecture of a Multiview Application

The application we're going to build in this chapter, **View Switcher**, exhibits a fairly simple appearance; however, in terms of the code this is the most complex application we've yet tackled. View Switcher consists of three different controllers, a storyboard, and an application delegate.

When first launched, View Switcher appears, as shown in Figure 6-6, with a toolbar at the bottom containing a single button. The rest of the view displays a blue background and a button to be pressed.

Figure 6-6. *When you first launch the View Switcher application, you'll see a blue view with a button and a toolbar with its own button*

Pressing the Switch Views button causes the background to turn yellow and the button's title to change, as shown in Figure 6-7.

Figure 6-7. *Pressing the Switch Views button causes the blue view to flip, revealing the yellow view*

If either the Press Me or Press Me, Too button activates, an alert appears indicating which view's button was pressed, as shown in Figure 6-8.

Figure 6-8. *Pressing the Press Me or Press Me, Too button displays the alert*

Although we could achieve this same functionality writing a single-view application, I took this more complex approach to demonstrate the actual mechanics of a multiview application. Three view controllers interact in this simple application: one controlling the blue view, one, the yellow view, and a third special controller that swaps the other two in and out when the Switch Views button is pressed.

Before we start building our application, let's discuss how iOS multiview applications get put together. Most multiview applications use the same basic pattern.

The Root Controller

The storyboard acts as the key player here since it contains all the views and view controllers for our application. We'll create a storyboard with an instance of a controller class that is responsible for managing which other view currently appears to the user. We call this controller the **root controller** (as in "the root of the tree") because it is the first controller the user sees and the controller that is loaded when the application loads. This root controller often acts as an instance of UINavigationController or UITabBarController, although it can also be a custom subclass of UIViewController.

In a multiview application, the root controller takes two or more other views and presents them to the user as appropriate, based on the user's input. A tab bar controller, for example, swaps in different views and view controllers based on which tab bar item was last tapped. A navigation controller does the same thing when the user drills down and backs up through hierarchical data.

■ **Note**   The root controller provides the primary view controller for the application and, as such, specifies whether it is OK to automatically rotate to a new orientation. However, the root controller may pass responsibility for tasks like that to the currently active controller.

In multiview applications, the content view takes up most of the screen and each content view has its own view controller containing outlets and actions. In a tab bar application, for example, taps on the tab bar will go to the tab bar controller, but taps anywhere else on the screen get processed by the controller corresponding to the content view currently displayed.

Content View Anatomy

In a multiview application, each view controller (Swift code) manages a content view, and these content views are where the bulk of your application's user interface resides. Taken together, each of these pairings is called a **scene** within a storyboard. Each scene consists of a view controller and a content view, which may be an instance of UIView or one of its subclasses. Although you can create your interface in code rather than using Interface Builder, the power, flexibility, and stability of the tools preclude ever needing to do that.

In this project, we'll create a new controller class for each content view. Our root controller manages a content view consisting of a toolbar that occupies the bottom of the screen. The root controller then loads a blue view controller, placing the blue content view as a subview to the root controller view. When you press the root controller's Switch Views button (the button is in the toolbar), the root controller swaps out the blue view controller and swaps in a yellow view controller, instantiating that controller if it needs to do so. Let's build the project and see this all become much clearer.

Creating the View Switcher Application

To start our project, in Xcode: File ➤ New ➤ Project... or press ••N. When the template selection sheet opens, select Single View Application and then click Next. On the next page of the assistant, enter **View Switcher** as the Product Name, set the Language to Swift and the Devices pop-up button to **Universal**. When everything is set up correctly, click Next to continue. On the next screen, navigate to wherever you're saving your projects on disk and click the Create button to create a new project directory.

Renaming the View Controller

As you've already seen, the Single View Application template supplies an application delegate, a view controller, and a storyboard. The view controller class is called ViewController. In this application, we are going to be dealing with three view controllers, but most of the logic will be in the main view controller. Its task will be to switch the display so that the view from one of the other view controllers is showing at all times. To make the role of the main view controller clear, we'd like to give it a better name, such as SwitchingViewController. There are several places in the project where the view controller's class name is referenced. To change its name, we would need to update all of those places. Xcode has a nifty feature called **refactoring** that would do that for us, but, at the time of writing, refactoring is not supported for Swift projects in the Xcode beta I'm using. Instead, we're going to delete the controller that the template created for us and add a new one.

Start by selecting ViewController.swift in the Project Navigator. Right-click it and select Delete in the pop-up (see Figure 6-9). When prompted, choose to move the source file to the Trash.

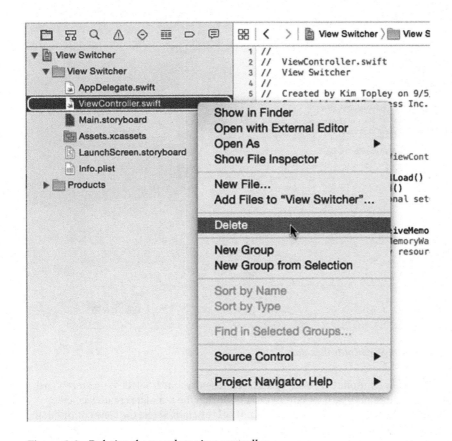

Figure 6-9. *Deleting the template view controller*

Now right-click the View Switcher group and select New File.... In the template chooser, select Cocoa Touch Class from the iOS Source section. Name the class `SwitchingViewController` and make it a subclass of `ViewController`. Make sure that **Also create XIB file** is not checked, since we are going to add this controller to the storyboard a little later and that Language is set to Swift, as shown in Figure 6-10, and then press Next followed by Create.

Choose options for your new file:

Class: SwitchingViewController

Subclass of: UIViewController

☐ Also create XIB file

Language: Swift

Cancel   Previous   Next

Figure 6-10. *Creating the SwitchingViewController class*

Now that we have our new view controller, we need to add it to the storyboard. Select Main.storyboard in the Document Outline to open the storyboard for editing. You'll see that the template created a view controller for us—we just need to link it to our SwitchingViewController class. Select the view controller in the Document Outline and open the Identity Inspector. In the Custom Class section, change the class from UIViewController to SwitchingViewController, as shown in Figure 6-11.

Figure 6-11. *Changing the view controller class in the storyboard*

Now if you check the Document Outline, you should see that the view controller's name has changed to Switching View Controller, as shown in Figure 6-12.

Figure 6-12. *The new view controller in the Document Outline*

Adding the Content View Controllers

We'll need two additional view controllers to display the content views. In the Project Navigator, right-click the View Switcher group and select New File.... In the template dialog, choose Cocoa Touch Class from the iOS Source section and press Next. Name the new class BlueViewController, make it a subclass of UIViewController, and make sure that the **Also create XIB file** check box is not checked. Press Next and then press Create to save the files for the new view controller. Repeat this process to create the second content view controller, giving it the name YellowViewController. To keep things organized you may want to move the files under the View Switcher folder in the Project Navigator, as shown in Figure 6-13.

Figure 6-13. *You may want to move the new swift files under the View Switcher folder in the Xcode Project Navigator*

Modifying SwitchingViewController.swift

The SwitchingViewController class will need an action method that will toggle between the blue and yellow views. We won't create any outlets, but we will need two properties—one for each of the view controllers that we'll be swapping in and out. These don't need to be outlets because we're going to create the view controllers in code rather than in the storyboard. Add the following property declarations to SwitchingViewController.swift:

```
private var blueViewController: BlueViewController!
private var yellowViewController: YellowViewController!
```

Add the following method at the bottom of the class:

```
@IBAction func switchViews(sender: UIBarButtonItem) {
}
```

Previously, we added action methods by Control-dragging from a view to the view controller's source code, but here you'll see that we can work the other way around just as well, since IB can see what outlets and actions are already defined in our source code. Now that we've declared the action we need, we can set up the minimal user interface for this controller in our storyboard.

Building a View with a Toolbar

We now need to set up the view for SwitchingViewController. As a reminder, this view controller will be our root view controller—the controller that is in play when our application is launched. SwitchingViewController's content view will consist of a toolbar that occupies the bottom of the screen and the view from either the yellow or blue view controller. Its job is to switch between the blue view and the yellow view, so it will need a way for the user to change the views. For that, we're going to use a toolbar with a button. Let's build the toolbar now.

In the Project Navigator, select Main.storyboard. In the IB editor view, you'll see our switching view controller. As you can see in Figure 6-14, it's currently empty and quite dull. This is where we'll start building our GUI.

Figure 6-14. *Our empty root view controller (Switching View Controller) Storyboard*

Grab a Toolbar from the library, drag it onto your view, and place it at the bottom so that it looks like Figure 6-15.

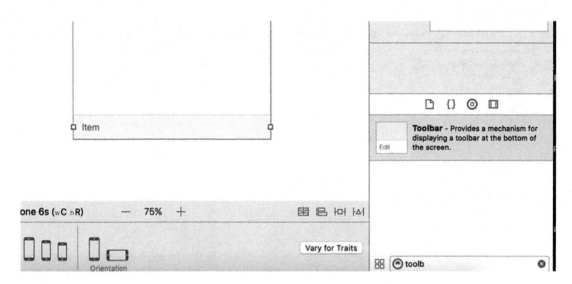

Figure 6-15. *Add a toolbar to the bottom of our root view controller*

We want to keep this toolbar stretched across the bottom of the content view no matter what size the view has. To do that, we need to add three layout constraints—one that pins the toolbar to the bottom of the view and another two that pin it to the view's left and right sides. To do this, select the toolbar in the Document Outline, click the Pin button on the toolbar beneath the storyboard, and change the values in the pop-up, as shown in Figure 6-16.

Figure 6-16. *Constrain the toolbar to the bottom, left, and right of its containing view*

Uncheck the Constrain to margins check box, because we want to position the toolbar relative to the edges of the content view, not the blue guidelines that appear near its edges. Next, set the distances to the nearest left, right, and bottom neighbors to zero (if you have correctly positioned the toolbar, they should already be zero). In this case, the nearest neighbor of the toolbar is the content view. You can see this by clicking the small arrow in one of the distance boxes. It opens a pop-up that shows the nearest neighbor and any other neighbors relative to which you could place the toolbar; in this case, there are no neighbors. To indicate that these distance constraints should be active, click the three dashed red lines that link the distance boxes to the small square in the center, so that they become solid lines. Finally, change Update Frames to Items of New Constraints (so that the toolbar's representation in the storyboard moves to its new constrained location) and click Add 3 Constraints.

Now, to make sure you're on the right track, click the Run button to make this app launch in the iOS simulator. You should see a plain white app start up, with a pale gray toolbar at the bottom containing a lone button. If not, go back and retrace your steps to see what you missed. Rotate the simulator. Verify that the toolbar stays fixed at the bottom of the view and stretched right across the screen. If this doesn't happen, you need to fix the constraints that you just applied to the toolbar.

Linking the Toolbar Button to the View Controller

You can see that the toolbar has a single button and we'll use that button to switch between the different content views. Double-click the button in the storyboard, as shown in Figure 6-17, and change its title to **Switch Views**. Press the Return key to commit your change. Now we can link the toolbar button to our action method in `SwitchingViewController`. Before doing that, though, you should be aware that toolbar buttons aren't like other iOS controls. They support only a single target action, and they trigger that action only at one well-defined moment—the equivalent of a touch up inside event on other iOS controls.

Figure 6-17. *Change the title of the button in the toolbar to Switch Views*

Selecting a toolbar button in Interface Builder can be tricky. The easiest way to do it is to expand the Switching View Controller icon in the Document Outline until you can see the button, which is now labeled Switch Views, and then click it. Once you have the Switch Views button selected, Control-drag from it over to the yellow Switching View Controller icon at the top of the scene, as shown in Figure 6-18. Release the mouse and select the `switchViewsWithSender:` action from the pop-up. If the `switchViewsWithSender:` action doesn't appear, and instead you see an outlet called **delegate**, you've most likely Control-dragged from the toolbar rather than the button. To fix it, just make sure you have the button rather than the toolbar selected, and then redo your Control-drag.

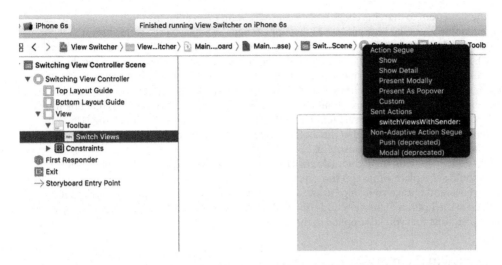

Figure 6-18. *Linking the toolbar button to the switchViewsWithSender: method in the view controller class*

■ **Note**   You may have noticed that when we entered the function manually earlier we called it `switchViews`, but because this is an Action, we get the sender parameter added for us whether or not we actually decide to use the parameter.

We have one more thing to point out in this scene, which is `SwitchingViewController`'s view outlet. This outlet is already connected to the view in the scene. The `view` outlet is inherited from the parent class, `UIViewController`, and gives the controller access to the view it controls. When we created the project, Xcode created both the controller and its view, and hooked them up for us. That's all we need to do here, so save your work. Next, let's get started writing our implementation code in the `SwitchingViewController`.

Writing the Root View Controller Implementation

In the Project Navigator, select SwitchingViewController.swift and modify the `viewDidLoad()` method to set some things up by adding the lines shown in Listing 6-1.

Listing 6-1. The Code for the viewDidLoad Method of Our Root View Controller

```
override func viewDidLoad() {
    super.viewDidLoad()

    // Do any additional setup after loading the view.
    blueViewController =
        storyboard?.instantiateViewController(withIdentifier: "Blue")
        as! BlueViewController
    blueViewController.view.frame = view.frame
    switchViewController(from: nil, to: blueViewController)  // helper method

}
```

▉ **Note** When you enter the code into the Swift file, as shown in Listing 6-1, you'll get an error on the line containing the call to switchViewController. This is because we have not written that helper method yet, which we'll do shortly.

Our implementation of viewDidLoad() overrides a UIViewController method that is called when the storyboard is loaded. How could we tell? Hold down the ⌥ key (the Option key) and single-click the method named viewDidLoad(). A documentation pop-up window will appear, as shown in Figure 6-19. Alternatively, you can select View ➤ Utilities ➤ Show Quick Help Inspector to view similar information in the Quick Help panel. viewDidLoad() is defined in our superclass, UIViewController, and is intended to be overridden by classes that need to be notified when the view has finished loading.

Figure 6-19. *This documentation window appears when you Option-click the viewDidLoad method name*

This version of viewDidLoad() creates an instance of BlueViewController. We use the instant iateViewController(withIdentifier:) method to load the BlueViewController instance from the same storyboard that contains our root view controller. To access a particular view controller from a storyboard, we use a string as an identifier—in this case "Blue" —which we'll set up when we configure our storyboard a little more. Once the BlueViewController is created, we assign this new instance to our blueViewController property:

```
blueViewController =
    storyboard?.instantiateViewController(withIdentifier: "Blue")
    as! BlueViewController
```

Next, we set the frame of the blue view controller's view to be the same as that of the switch view controller's content view, and switch to the blue view controller so that its view appears on the screen:

```
blueViewController.view.frame = view.frame
switchViewController(from: nil, to: blueViewController)
```

Since we need to perform a view controller switch in several places, the code to do this is in the helper method switchViewController(from:, to:) that we'll write shortly.

Now, why didn't we load the yellow view controller here also? We're going to need to load it at some point, so why not do it now? Good question. The answer is that the user may never tap the Switch Views button. The user might just use the view that's visible when the application launches, and then quit. In that case, why use resources to load the yellow view and its controller? Instead, we'll load the yellow view the first time we actually need it. This is called **lazy loading**, which is a standard way of keeping memory overhead down. The actual loading of the yellow view happens in the switchViews() method. Fill in the stub of this method that you created earlier by adding the code shown in Listing 6-2.

Listing 6-2. Our switchViews Implementation

```
@IBAction func switchViews(sender: UIBarButtonItem) {
    // Create the new view controller, if required
    if yellowViewController?.view.superview == nil {
        if yellowViewController == nil {
            yellowViewController =
                storyboard?.instantiateViewController(withIdentifier: "Yellow")
                as! YellowViewController
        }
    } else if blueViewController?.view.superview == nil {
        if blueViewController == nil {
            blueViewController =
                storyboard?.instantiateViewController(withIdentifier: "Blue")
                as! BlueViewController
        }
    }

    // Switch view controllers
    if blueViewController != nil
        && blueViewController!.view.superview != nil {
        yellowViewController.view.frame = view.frame
        switchViewController(from: blueViewController,
                            to: yellowViewController)
    } else {
        blueViewController.view.frame = view.frame
        switchViewController(from: yellowViewController,
                            to: blueViewController)
    }
}
```

switchViews() first checks which view is being swapped in by seeing whether yellowViewController's view's superview is nil. This will be true if one of two things is true:

- If yellowViewController exists, but its view is not being shown to the user, that view will not have a superview because it's not presently in the view hierarchy, and the expression will evaluate to true.

- If yellowViewController doesn't exist because it hasn't been created yet or was flushed from memory, it will also return true.

We then check to see whether yellowViewController exists:

```
if yellowViewController?.view.superview == nil {
```

If the result is nil, that means there is no instance of yellowViewController, so we need to create one. This could happen because it's the first time the button has been pressed or because the system ran low on memory and it was flushed. In this case, we need to create an instance of YellowViewController as we did for the BlueViewController in the viewDidLoad method:

```
if yellowViewController == nil {
    yellowViewController =
        storyboard?.instantiateViewController(withIdentifier: "Yellow")
        as! YellowViewController
}
```

If we're switching in the blue controller, we need to perform the same check to see whether it still exists (since it could have been flushed from memory) and create it if it does not. This is just the same code again, referencing the blue controller instead:

```
} else if blueViewController?.view.superview == nil {
    if blueViewController == nil {
        blueViewController =
            storyboard?.instantiateViewController(withIdentifier: "Blue")
            as! BlueViewController
    }
}
```

At this point, we know that we have a view controller instance because either we already had one or we just created it. We then set the view controller's frame to match that of the switch view controller's content view and then we use our switchViewController(from:, to:) method to actually perform the switch, as shown in Listing 6-3.

Listing 6-3. Switching View Controllers Depending On Which One We're Currently Presenting

```
// Switch view controllers
if blueViewController != nil
    && blueViewController!.view.superview != nil {
    yellowViewController.view.frame = view.frame
    switchViewController(from: blueViewController,
                           to: yellowViewController)
} else {
    blueViewController.view.frame = view.frame
    switchViewController(from: yellowViewController,
                           to: blueViewController)
}
}
```

The first branch of the if statement is taken if we are switching from the blue view controller to the yellow and vice versa for the else branch.

In addition to not using resources for the yellow view and controller if the Switch Views button is never tapped, lazy loading also gives us the ability to release whichever view is not being shown to free up its memory. iOS will call the UIViewController method didReceiveMemoryWarning(), which is inherited by every view controller, when memory drops below a system-determined level.

Since we know that either view will be reloaded the next time it is shown to the user, we can safely release either controller, provided it is not currently on display. We can do this by adding a few lines to the existing didReceiveMemoryWarning() method, as shown in Listing 6-4.

Listing 6-4. Safely Releasing Unneeded Controllers During Low Memory Conditions

```
override func didReceiveMemoryWarning() {
    super.didReceiveMemoryWarning()
    // Dispose of any resources that can be recreated.

    if blueViewController != nil
        && blueViewController!.view.superview == nil {
        blueViewController = nil
    }
    if yellowViewController != nil
        && yellowViewController!.view.superview == nil {
        yellowViewController = nil
    }
}
```

This newly added code checks to see which view is currently shown to the user, and then releases the controller for the other view by assigning `nil` to its property. This will cause the controller, along with the view it controls, to be deallocated, freeing up its memory.

■ **Tip** Lazy loading is a key component of resource management on iOS, which you should implement anywhere you can. In a complex, multiview application, being responsible and flushing unused objects from memory can be the difference between an application that works well and one that crashes periodically because it runs out of memory.

The final piece of the puzzle is the `switchViewController(from:, to:)` method, which is responsible for the view controller switch. Switching view controllers is a two-step process. First, we need to remove the view for the controller that's currently displayed, and then we need to add the view for the new view controller. But that's not quite all—we need to take care of some housekeeping as well. Add the implementation of this method, as shown in Listing 6-5.

Listing 6-5. The switchViewController Helper Method

```
private func switchViewController(from fromVC:UIViewController?,
                                    to toVC:UIViewController?) {
    if fromVC != nil {
        fromVC!.willMove(toParentViewController: nil)
        fromVC!.view.removeFromSuperview()
        fromVC!.removeFromParentViewController()
    }

    if toVC != nil {
        self.addChildViewController(toVC!)
        self.view.insertSubview(toVC!.view, at: 0)
        toVC!.didMove(toParentViewController: self)
    }
}
```

The first block of code removes the outgoing view controller; but let's look at the second block first, where we add the incoming view controller. Here's the first line of code in that block:

```
self.addChildViewController(toVC!)
```

This code makes the incoming view controller a child of the switching view controller. View controllers like SwitchingViewController that manage other view controllers are referred to as **container view controllers**. The standard classes UITabBarController and UINavigationController are both container view controllers and they have code that does something similar to what the switchViewController(from:, to:) method is doing. Making the new view controller a child of the SwitchingViewController ensures that certain events that are delivered to the root view controller are correctly passed to the child controller when required—for example, making sure that rotation is handled properly.

Next, the child view controller's view is added to that of the SwitchingViewController:

```
self.view.insertSubview(toVC!.view, atIndex: 0)
```

Note that the view is inserted in the subviews list of SwitchingViewController at index zero, which tells iOS to put this view *behind* everything else. Sending the view to the back ensures that the toolbar we created in Interface Builder a moment ago will always be visible on the screen, since we're inserting the content views behind it.

Finally, we notify the incoming view controller that it has been added as the child of another controller:

```
toVC!.didMoveToParentViewController(self)
```

This is necessary in case the child view controller overrides this method to take some action when it becomes the child of another controller.

Now that you've seen how a view controller is added, the code that removes a view controller from its parent is much easier to understand—all we do is reverse each of the steps that we performed when adding it:

```
if fromVC != nil {
    fromVC!.willMoveToParentViewController(nil)
    fromVC!.view.removeFromSuperview()
    fromVC!.removeFromParentViewController()
}
```

Implementing the Content Views

At this point, the code is complete, but we can't run the application yet because we don't have the blue and yellow content controllers in the storyboard. These two controllers are extremely simple. They each have one action method that is triggered by a button, and neither one needs any outlets. The two views are also nearly identical. In fact, they are so similar that they could have been represented by the same class. We chose to make them two separate classes because that's how most multiview applications are constructed.

The two action methods we're going to implement do nothing more than show an alert (as we did in Chapter 4's Control Fun application), so go ahead and add method in Listing 6-6 to BlueViewController.swift.

Listing 6-6. Pressing the Button on Our Blue Controller Presents an Alert

```
@IBAction func blueButtonPressed(sender: UIButton) {
    let alert = UIAlertController(title: "Blue View Button Pressed",
                                 message: "You pressed the button on the blue view",
```

```
                                  preferredStyle: .alert)
    let action = UIAlertAction(title: "Yes, I did", style: .default,
                               handler: nil)
    alert.addAction(action)
    present(alert, animated: true, completion: nil)
}
```

Save the file. Next, switch over to YellowViewController.swift and add this very similar method—shown in Listing 6-7—to that file, and save it as well.

Listing 6-7. Pressing the Button on Our Yellow Controller also Presents an Alert

```
@IBAction func yellowButtonPressed(sender: UIButton) {
    let alert = UIAlertController(title: "Yellow View Button Pressed",
                                  message: "You pressed the button on the yellow view",
                                  preferredStyle: .alert)
    let action = UIAlertAction(title: "Yes, I did", style: .default,
                               handler: nil)
    alert.addAction(action)
    present(alert, animated: true, completion: nil)
}
```

Next, select Main.storyboard to open it in Interface Builder so that we can make a few changes. First, we need to add a new scene for BlueViewController. Up until now, each storyboard we've dealt with contained just a single controller-view pairing, but the storyboard has more tricks up its sleeve, and holding multiple scenes is one of them. From the Object Library, drag out another View Controller and drop it in the editing area next to the existing one. Now your storyboard has two scenes, each of which can be loaded dynamically and independently while your application is running. In the row of icons at the top of the new scene, single-click the yellow View Controller icon and press ⌥⌘3 to bring up the Identity Inspector. In the Custom Class section, the Class menu defaults to UIViewController; change it to BlueViewController, as shown in Figure 6-20.

Figure 6-20. *Add our new view controller and associate it with the BlueViewController class file*

We also need to create an identifier for this new view controller so that our code can find it inside the storyboard. Just below the Custom Class section in the Identity Inspector, you'll see a Storyboard ID field. Click there and type **Blue** to match what we used in our code, as shown in Figure 6-21.

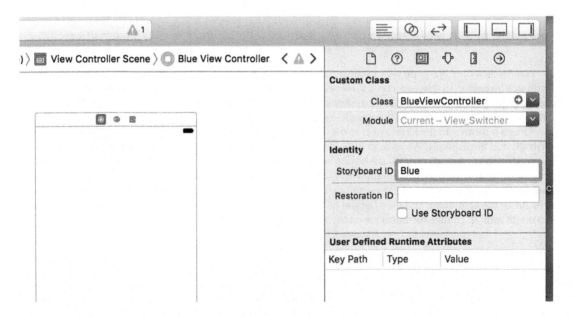

Figure 6-21. *Set the Storyboard ID of our Blue View Controller Storyboard to Blue*

So now you have two scenes. We showed you earlier how to configure your app to load this storyboard at launch time, but we didn't mention anything about scenes there. How will the app know which of these two views to show? The answer lies in the big arrow pointing at the first scene, as shown in Figure 6-22. That arrow points out the storyboard's default scene, which is what the app shows when it starts up. If you want to choose a different default scene, all you have to do is drag the arrow to point at the scene you want.

Figure 6-22. *We just added a second scene to our storyboard. The big arrow points at the default scene*

Single-click the big square view in the new scene you just added and then press ⌥⌘4 to bring up the Attributes Inspector. In the inspector's View section, click the color picker that's labeled Background, and use the pop-up color picker to change the background color of this view to a nice shade of blue. Once you are happy with your blue, close the color picker.

Drag a button from the library over to the view, using the guidelines to center it in the view, both vertically and horizontally. We want to make sure that the button stays centered no matter what, so make two constraints to that effect. With the button selected, click the Align icon below the storyboard. In the pop-up, check Horizontally in Container and Vertically in Container, change Update Frames to Items of New Constraints, and then click Add 2 Constraints (see Figure 6-23). It may help to change the background back to white for the alignment, and then back to blue once you're finished. Also, because of the blue background you might want to change the button text to white to be more visible.

Figure 6-23. *Aligning the button to the center of the view*

Double-click the button and change its title to **Press Me**. Next, with the button still selected, switch to the connections inspector (by pressing ⌥⌘6), drag from the Touch Up Inside event to the yellow View Controller icon at the top of the scene, and connect to the blueButtonPressedWithSender action method.

Now it's time to do pretty much the same set of things for YellowViewController. Grab yet another View Controller from the object library and drag it into the editor area. Don't worry if things are getting crowded; you can stack those scenes on top of each other if necessary. Click the View Controller icon for the new scene in the Document Outline and use the Identity Inspector to change its class to YellowViewController and its Storyboard ID to Yellow.

Next, select the YellowViewController's view and switch to the Attributes Inspector. There, click the Background color picker, select a yellow, and then close the picker.

Next, drag out a Button from the library and use the guidelines to center it in the view. Use the Align icon pop-up to create constraints aligning its horizontal and vertical center, just like for the last button. Now change its title to **Press Me, Too**. With the button still selected, use the Connections Inspector to drag from the Touch Up Inside event to the View Controller icon, and connect to the yellowButtonPressedWithSender action method.

When you're finished, save the storyboard and hit the Run button in Xcode to start the app presenting a full screen of blue. When you tap the Switch Views button, it will change to show the yellow view that we built. Tap it again and it goes back to the blue view. If you tap the button centered on the blue or yellow view, you'll get an alert view with a message indicating which button was pressed. This alert shows that the correct controller class is being called for the view that is being shown.

The transition between the two views is kind of abrupt, so we're going to animate the transition to give the user a better visual feedback of the change.

Animating the Transition

UIView has several class methods we can call to indicate that the transition between views should be animated, to indicate the type of transition that should be used, and to specify how long the transition should take.

Go back to SwitchingViewController.swift and enhance your switchViews() method by changing it, as shown in Listing 6-8.

Listing 6-8. Our Modified switchViews Method with Animation Added

```swift
@IBAction func switchViews(sender: UIBarButtonItem) {
    // Create the new view controller, if required
    if yellowViewController?.view.superview == nil {
        if yellowViewController == nil {
            yellowViewController =
                storyboard?.instantiateViewController(withIdentifier: "Yellow")
                as! YellowViewController
        }
    } else if blueViewController?.view.superview == nil {
        if blueViewController == nil {
            blueViewController =
                storyboard?.instantiateViewController(withIdentifier: "Blue")
                as! BlueViewController
        }
    }

    UIView.beginAnimations("View Flip", context: nil)
    UIView.setAnimationDuration(0.4)
    UIView.setAnimationCurve(.easeInOut)
    // Switch view controllers
    if blueViewController != nil
        && blueViewController!.view.superview != nil {
        UIView.setAnimationTransition(.flipFromRight,
                                    for: view, cache: true)
        yellowViewController.view.frame = view.frame
        switchViewController(from: blueViewController,
                            to: yellowViewController)
    } else {
        UIView.setAnimationTransition(.flipFromLeft,
                                    for: view, cache: true)
        blueViewController.view.frame = view.frame
        switchViewController(from: yellowViewController,
                            to: blueViewController)
    }
    UIView.commitAnimations()
}
```

Build and run this version. When you tap the Switch Views button, instead of the new view just snapping into place, the old view will flip over to reveal the new view.

To tell iOS that we want a change animated, we need to declare an **animation block** and specify how long the animation should take. Animation blocks are declared by using the UIView class method presentViewController(_:animated:completion:), like so:

```
UIView.beginAnimations("View Flip", context: nil)
UIView.setAnimationDuration(0.4)
```

presentViewController(_:animated:completion:) takes two parameters. The first is an animation block title. This title comes into play only if you take more direct advantage of Core Animation, the framework behind this animation. For our purposes, we could have used nil. The second parameter is a pointer that allows you to specify an object (or any other C data type) whose address you would like associated with this animation block. It is possible to add some code of our own that will be run during the transition, but we're not doing that here, so we set this parameter to nil. We also set the duration of the animation, which tells UIView how long (in seconds) the animation should last.

After that, we set the **animation curve**, which determines the timing of the animation. The default, which is a linear curve, causes the animation to happen at a constant speed. The option we set here, UIViewAnimationCurve.EaseInOut, specifies that the animation should start slow but speed up in the middle, and then slow down again at the end. This gives the animation a more natural, less mechanical appearance:

```
UIView.setAnimationCurve(.easeInOut)
```

Next, we need to specify the transition to use. At the time of this writing, five iOS view transitions are available:

- UIViewAnimationTransition.flipFromLeft

- UIViewAnimationTransition.flipFromRight

- UIViewAnimationTransition.curlUp

- UIViewAnimationTransition.curlDown

- UIViewAnimationTransition.none

We chose to use two different effects, depending on which view was being swapped in. Using a left flip for one transition and a right flip for the other makes the view seem to flip back and forth. The value UIViewAnimationTransition.none causes an abrupt transition from one view controller to another. Of course, if you wanted that effect, you wouldn't bother creating an animation block at all.

The cache option speeds up drawing by taking a snapshot of the view when the animation begins, and uses that image rather than redrawing the view at each step of the animation. You should always cache the animation unless the appearance of the view needs to change during the animation:

```
UIView.setAnimationTransition(.flipFromRight,
                        forView: view, cache: true)
```

When we're finished specifying the changes to be animated, we call commitAnimations() on UIView. Everything between the start of the animation block and the call to commitAnimations() animates together.

Thanks to Cocoa Touch's use of Core Animation under the hood, we're able to do fairly sophisticated animation with only a handful of code.

Summary

You should now have a very good grasp of how multiview applications are put together, now that you've built one from scratch. Although Xcode contains project templates for the most common types of multiview applications, we needed to understand the overall structure of these types of applications so we can build them ourselves from the ground up. The standard container controllers (`UITabBarController`, `UINavigationController`, and `UIPageViewController`) are incredible time-savers that you should use when you can, but at times, they simply won't meet your needs.

In the next few chapters, we're going to continue building multiview applications to reinforce the concepts from this chapter and to give you a feel for how more complex applications are put together. In Chapter 7, we'll construct a tab bar application.

CHAPTER 7

■ ■ ■

Using Tab Bars and Pickers

In the previous chapter, you built your first multiview application. In this chapter, we'll build another one—this time, creating a full tab bar application with five different tabs and five different content views. Building this application reinforces a lot of what we covered in Chapter 6. We'll use those five content views to demonstrate a type of iOS control not yet covered, a picker view, or just a picker. You may not be familiar with the name, but you've almost certainly used a picker if you own an iPhone or iPod touch for more than 10 minutes. Pickers contain controls with dials that spin. You use them to input dates in the Calendar application or to set a timer in the Clock application, as shown in Figure 7-1. It is not quite as common on an iPad, since the larger display lets you present other ways of choosing among multiple items, but even there, it's used by the Calendar application.

© Molly Maskrey, Kim Topley, David Mark, Fredrik Olsson and Jeff Lamarche 2016
M. Maskrey et al., *Beginning iPhone Development with Swift 3*, DOI 10.1007/978-1-4842-2223-2_7

Figure 7-1. *The Clock app uses a picker to set the time the alarm should go off*

Pickers provide a bit more complexity than the iOS controls we've seen so far; and as such, they deserve a little more attention. Pickers can be configured to display one dial or many. By default, pickers display lists of text, but they can also be made to display images.

The Pickers Application

This chapter's application, Pickers, features a tab bar and as you build Pickers, you'll change the default tab bar so that it has five tabs, add an icon to each of the tab bar items, and then create a series of content views and connect each view to a tab. The application's content views feature five different pickers:

- **Date picker:** The first content view we'll build uses a date picker, the easiest type of picker to implement (see Figure 7-2). The view also has a button that, when tapped, displays an alert showing the date that was picked.

Figure 7-2. *The first tab displays a date picker*

- **Single-component picker**: The second tab features a picker with a single list of values, as shown in Figure 7-3 and provides a little more work to implement than the date picker. You'll learn how to specify the values to be displayed in the picker by using a delegate and a data source.

Figure 7-3. *A picker displaying a single list of values*

- **Multicomponent picker**: In the third tab, we'll create a picker with two separate wheels. The technical term is **picker component**. Here, we create a picker with two components. You'll see how to use the data source and delegate by providing two independent lists of data to the picker (see Figure 7-4), each changeable without impacting the other one.

Figure 7-4. *A two-component picker, showing an alert that reflects our selection*

- **Picker with dependent components**: In the fourth content view, we'll build another picker with two components. But this time, the values displayed in the component on the right change based on the value selected in the component on the left. In our example, we're going to display a list of states in the left component and a list of that state's ZIP codes in the right component, as shown in Figure 7-5.

Figure 7-5. *In this picker, one component depends on the other. As you select a state in the left component, the right component changes to a list of ZIP codes in that state*

- **Custom picker with images**wwwww In the fifth content view, I'll demonstrate how to add image data to a picker, and we're going to do it by writing a little game that uses a picker with five components. Apple's documentation describes the picker's appearance as looking a bit like a slot machine. So, we'll be creating a slot machine, as shown in Figure 7-6. For this picker, the user won't be able to manually change the values of the components, but will be able to select the Spin button to make the five wheels rotate to a new, randomly selected value. If three copies of the same image appear in a row, the user wins.

Figure 7-6. *Our fifth component picker uses the picker like a slot machine*

Delegates and Data Sources

Before we start building the application, let's look at what makes pickers more complex than the other controls we've used so far. With the exception of the date picker, you can't use a picker by just grabbing one in the object library, dropping it on your content view, and configuring it. You also need to provide each picker with both a delegate and a data source.

We've already used application delegates and the basic idea works the same for pickers. The control itself defers several jobs to its delegate, the most important of these being the determination what to actually draw for each of the rows in each of its components. The picker asks the delegate for either a string or a view that will be drawn at a given spot on a given component. The picker gets its data from the delegate.

In addition to the delegate, pickers must have a data source. The data source tells the picker how many components it will be working with and how many rows make up each component. The data source works like the delegate in that its methods are called at certain, pre-specified times. Without a data source and a delegate, pickers cannot do their job; in fact, they won't even be drawn.

It's very common for the data source and the delegate to be the same object and exist in the same actual Swift file, typically the view controller for the picker's enclosing view. We use that approach in this application: the view controllers for each of our application's content panes will be the data source and the delegate for their picker.

■ **Note**   The question often arises as to whether the picker data source is part of the model, view, or controller portion of the application? A data source sounds like it must be part of the model, but it's actually part of the controller. The data source isn't usually an object designed to hold data. In simple applications, the data source might hold data, but its true job is to retrieve data from the model and pass it along to the picker.

Creating the Pickers Application

Although Xcode provides a template for tab bar applications, we're going to build ours from scratch. It's not much extra work and it will be good practice.

Create a new project, select the Single View Application template again, and choose Next to go to the next screen. In the Product Name field, type **Pickers**. Make sure the check box that says Use Core Data is unchecked, and set the Language to Swift and the Devices pop-up to Universal. Then choose Next again. Xcode will let you select the folder where you want to save your project.

We're going to walk you through the process of building the whole application; but at any step of the way, if you feel like challenging yourself by moving ahead, by all means do so. If you get stumped, you can always come back.

Creating the View Controllers

In the previous chapter, we created a root view controller ("root controller" for short) to manage the process of swapping our application's other views. We'll be doing that again this time, but we won't need to create our own root view controller class. Apple provides a very good class for managing tab bar views, so we're just going to use an instance of UITabBarController as our root controller. First, we need to create five new classes in Xcode: the five view controllers that the root controller will swap in and out. Expand the Pickers folder in the Project Navigator. There, you'll see the source code files that Xcode created to start off the project. Single-click the Pickers folder, and press ⌘N or select File ➤ New ➤ File....

Select iOS and then select Source in the left pane of the new file assistant. Then, select the Cocoa Touch Class icon and click Next to continue. The next screen lets you give your new class a name. Enter **DatePickerViewController** in the Class field. Ensure the Subclass of field contains UIViewController. Make sure that the **Also create XIB file** check box is unchecked, set the Language to Swift, and then click Next.

You'll be shown a folder selection window, which lets you choose where the class should be saved. Choose the Pickers directory, which already contains the AppDelegate class and a few other files. Make sure also that the Group pop-up has the Pickers folder selected and that the target check box for Pickers is checked. After you click the Create button, the file DatePickerViewcontroller.swift will appear in the Pickers folder.

Repeat those steps four more times, using the names SingleComponentPickerViewController, DoubleComponentPickerViewController, DependentComponentPickerViewController, and CustomPickerViewController. At the end of all this, the Pickers folder should contain all of the view controller class files, as shown in Figure 7-7.

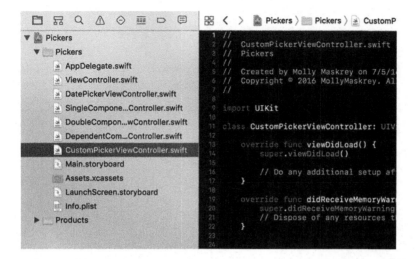

Figure 7-7. The Project Navigator should contain all these files after creating the five view controller classes

Creating the Tab Bar Controller

Now, let's create our tab bar controller. The project template already contains a view controller called
ViewController, which is a subclass of UIViewController. To convert it to a tab bar controller, all we need
to do is change its base class. Open ViewController.swift and make the following change shown in bold:

class ViewController: UITabBarController {

Next, to set the tab bar controller up in the storyboard, open Main.storyboard. The template added an
initial view controller, which we're going to replace, so select it in the Document Outline or the editor area,
and delete it by pressing the Delete key. In the Object Library, locate a Tab Bar Controller and drag it over to
the editing area (see Figure 7-8).

Figure 7-8. *Dragging a tab bar controller from the library onto the canvas*

While you're dragging, you'll see that, unlike the other controllers we've been asking you to drag out from the object library, this one actually pulls out three complete view-controller pairs at once, all of which are connected to each other with curved lines. This is actually more than just a tab bar controller; it's also two child controllers, already connected and ready to use.

Once you drop the tab bar controller onto the editing area, three new scenes are added to the storyboard. If you expand the document view on the left, you will see a nice overview of all the scenes contained in the storyboard (see Figure 7-8). You'll also see the curvy lines still in place connecting the tab bar controller with each of its children. Those lines will always adjust themselves to stay connected if you move the scenes around, which you are always free to do. The on-screen position of each scene within a storyboard has no impact on your app's appearance when it runs.

This tab bar controller will be our root controller. As a reminder, the root controller controls the very first view that the user will see when your program runs and it is responsible for switching the other views in and out. Since we'll connect each of our views to one of the tabs in the tab bar, the tab bar controller makes a logical choice as a root controller. We need to tell iOS that the tab bar controller is the one that it should load from Main.storyboard when the application starts. To do this, select the Tab Bar Controller icon in the Document Outline and open the Attributes Inspector; and then in the View Controller section, check the Is Initial View Controller check box. With the view controller still selected, switch to the Identity Inspector and change the class to ViewController.

Tab bars can use icons to represent each of the tabs, so we should also add the icons we're going to use before editing the storyboard. You can find some suitable icons in the 07 - ImageSets folder of the source code archive for this book. Each subfolder of 07 - ImageSets contains three images (one for devices with a standard display, two for Retina devices). In the Xcode Project Navigator, select Assets.xcassets and drag each subfolder from the 07 - ImageSets folder and drop it into the left column of the editing area, underneath AppIcon, to copy them all into the project (see Figure 7-9).

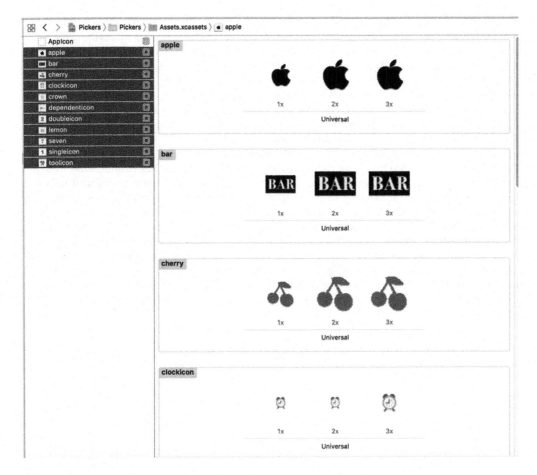

Figure 7-9. Drag the images below AppIcon within Assets.xcassets in Xcode

If you want to make your own icons instead, there are some guidelines for how they should be created. The icons you use should be 24 × 24 pixels and saved in .png format. The icon file should have a transparent background. Don't worry about trying to color the icons so that they match the appearance of the tab bar. Just as it does with the application icon, iOS will take your image and make it look just right.

▇ **Tip**   An image size of 24 × 24 pixels is actually for standard displays; for Retina displays on iPhone 4 and later and for the new iPads, you need a double-sized image, or it will appear pixelated. For the iPhone 6/6s Plus, you need to provide an image that's three times the size of the original. This is very easy: for any image foo.png, you should also provide an image named foo@2x.png that is doubled in size and another called foo@3x.png that is three times the size. Calling UIImage(named:"foo") will return the normal-sized image or the double-sized image automatically to best suit the device on which your app is currently executing.

Back in the storyboard, you can see that each of the child view controllers shows a name like "Item 1" at the top and has a single bar item at the bottom of its view, with a label matching what is present in the tab bar. We might as well set these two up so that they have the right names from the start, so select the Item 1

219

view controller, and then click the tab bar item labeled Item 1 in the Document Outline. Open the Attributes Inspector and you'll see a text field for setting the Title of the Bar Item, which currently contains the text Item 1. Replace the text with **Date** and press the Enter key. This immediately changes the text of the bar item at the bottom of this view controller, as well as the corresponding tab bar item in the tab bar controller. While you're still in the inspector, click the Image pop-up and select clockicon to set the icon, too. Now repeat the same steps for the second child view controller, but name this one **Single** and use the singleicon image for its bar item.

Our next step is to complete our tab bar controller so it reflects the five tabs shown in Figure 7-2. Each of those five tabs will contain one of our pickers. The way we're going to do this is by simply adding three more view controllers to the storyboard (in addition to the two that were added along with the tab bar controller), and then connecting each of them so that the tab bar controller can activate them. Get started by dragging out a normal View Controller from the Object Library and dropping on the storyboard. Next, Control-drag from the tab bar controller to your new view controller, release the mouse button, and select view controllers from the Relationship Segue section of the small pop-up window that appears. This tells the tab bar controller that it has a new child to maintain, so the tab bar immediately acquires a new item. Your new view controller gets a bar item in the bottom of its view and in the Document Outline, just like the others already had. Now do the same steps outlined previously to name this latest view controller's bar item **Double** with doubleicon as its image.

Drag out two more view controllers and connect each of them to the tab bar controller, as described previously. One at a time, select each of their bar items, naming one of them **Dependent** with dependenticon as its image, and name the other **Custom** with toolicon as its image. When finished, you should have one view controller with your tab bar at the bottom and five connected view controllers, as shown in Figure 7-10.

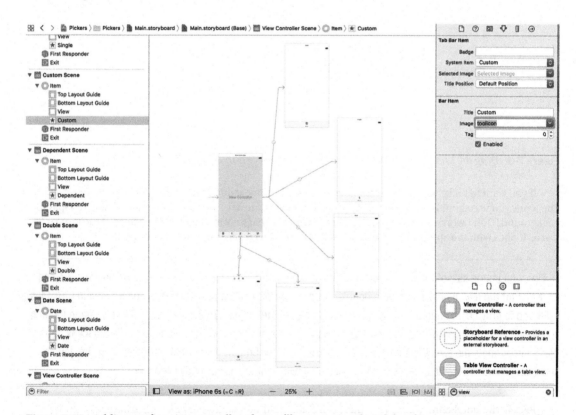

Figure 7-10. *Adding our five view controllers that we'll access using the tab bar from our root view controller*

Now that all our view controllers are in place, it's time to set up each of them with the correct controller class from the set that we created earlier. This will let us implement different functionality for each controller. In the Document Outline, select the view controller labeled Date and bring up the Identity Inspector. In the Custom Class section of the inspector, change the class to DatePickerViewController, and press Return or Tab to finish (see Figure 7-11).

Figure 7-11. *Connecting our Date view to its view controller*

Repeat this same process for the other four view controllers, in the order in which they appear at the bottom of the tab bar controller. You can select each view controller in turn by clicking on it in the storyboard, making sure to click in the bar at the top of the controller that contains the controller's name. In the Identity Inspector for each, use the class names SingleComponentPickerViewController, DoubleComponentPickerViewController, DependentComponentPickerViewController, and CustomPickerViewController, respectively. Before moving on to the next bit of GUI editing, save your storyboard file.

Initial Simulator Test

At this point, the tab bar and the content views should all be hooked up and working. Compile and run, and your application should launch with a tab bar that functions, as shown in Figure 7-12. Click each of the tabs in turn. Each tab should be selectable.

Figure 7-12. *The application with five empty but selectable tabs*

There's nothing in the content views now, so the changes won't be very dramatic. In fact, you won't see any difference at all, except for the highlighting tab bar items. But if everything went correctly, the basic framework for your multiview application is now set up and working. We can start designing the individual content views.

■ **Tip** If your simulator crashes when you click one of the tabs, most likely you've either missed a step or made a typo. Go back and make sure the connections are right and the class names are all set correctly.

If you want to make doubly sure everything is working, you can add a different label or some other object to each of the content views, and then relaunch the application. In that case, you should see the content of the different views change as you select different tabs.

Implementing the Date Picker

To implement the date picker, we'll need a single outlet and a single action. The outlet will be used to grab the value from the date picker. The action will be triggered by a button and will put up an alert to show the date value pulled from the picker. We'll add both of these from inside Interface Builder while editing the Main.storyboard file, so select it in the Project Navigator if it's not already front-and-center.

The first thing we need to do is find a Date Picker in the Object Library and drag it over to the Date Scene in the editing area. Click the Date icon in the Document Outline to bring the correct view controller to the front, and then drag the date picker from the Object Library and place it at the top of the view, right up against the top of the display. It's OK if it overlaps the status bar because this control has so much built-in vertical padding at the top that no one will notice.

Now we need to apply Auto Layout constraints so that the date picker is correctly sized and placed when the application runs on any kind of device. We want the picker to be horizontally centered and anchored to the top of the view. We also want it to be sized based on its content, so we need three constraints. With the date picker selected, first select Editor ➤ Size to Fit Content from the Xcode menu bar. If this option is not enabled, move the picker slightly and try again. Next, click the Align button below the storyboard, check the Horizontally in Container box, and then click Add 1 Constraint. Click the Pin button (which is next to the Align button). Using the four distance boxes at the top of the pop-up, set the distance between the picker and the top of edge of the view above it to zero by entering zero in the top box, and below it so that it becomes a solid line. At the bottom of the pop-up, set Update Frames to Items of New Constraints, and then click Add 1 Constraint. The date picker will resize and move to its correct position, as shown in Figure 7-13.

Figure 7-13. *The date picker, positioned at the top of its view controller's view*

Single-click the date picker, if it's not already selected, and go back to the Attributes Inspector. As you can see in Figure 7-14, a number of attributes can be configured for a date picker. We're going to leave most of the values at their defaults (but feel free to play with the options when we're finished, to see what they do). The one thing we will do is limit the range of the picker to reasonable dates. Look for the heading that says Constraints and check the box that reads Minimum Date. Leave the value at the default of 1/1/1970. Also check the box that reads Maximum Date and set that value to 12/31/2200.

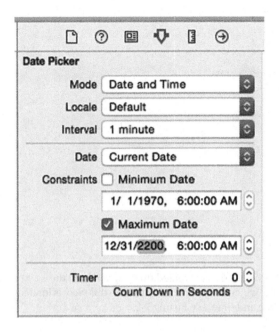

Figure 7-14. The Attributes Inspector for a date picker. Set the maximum date, but leave the rest of the settings at their default values

Now let's connect this picker to its controller. Press ⌥⌘Enter to open the Assistant Editor and make sure the jump bar at the top of the Assistant Editor is set to Automatic. That should make DatePickerViewController.swift show up there. Next, Control-drag from the picker to the blank line between the class declaration and the viewDidLoad() method, releasing the mouse button when the Insert Outlet, Action, or Outlet Collection tooltip appears. In the pop-up window that appears after you let go, make sure the Connection is set to Outlet, enter **datePicker** as the Name, and then press Enter to create the outlet and connect it to the picker.

Next, grab a Button from the library and place it a small distance below the date picker. Double-click the button and give it a title of Select. We want this button to be horizontally centered and to stay a fixed distance below the date picker. With the button selected, click the Align button at the bottom of the storyboard, check the Horizontally in Container box, and then click Add 1 Constraint. To fix the distance between them, Control-drag from the button to the date picker and release the mouse. In the pop-up that appears, select Vertical Spacing. Finally, click the Resolve Auto Layout Issues button at the bottom of the storyboard and then click Update Frames in the top section of the pop-up (if this item is not enabled, it means that the button is already in its correct location). The button should move to its correct location and there should no longer be any Auto Layout warnings.

Make sure that DatePickerViewController.swift is still visible in the Assistant Editor; if it's not, use the Manual selection in the jump bar to locate and open it. Now Control-drag from the button to the line above the closing brace at the end of the class in the assistant view, until you see the Insert Outlet, Action, or Outlet Collection tooltip appear. Change the Connection type to Action, name the new action onButtonPressed, and press Enter to connect it. Doing so creates an empty method called onButtonPressed(), which you should complete with the code in Listing 7-1.

Listing 7-1. Our Select Button Action Code

```
@IBAction func onButtonPressed(_ sender: UIButton) {
    let date = datePicker.date
    let message = "The date and time you selected is \(date)"
    let alert = UIAlertController(
        title: "Date and Time Selected",
        message: message,
        preferredStyle: .alert)
    let action = UIAlertAction(
        title: "That's so true!",
        style: .default,
        handler: nil)
    alert.addAction(action)
    present(alert, animated: true, completion: nil)

}
```

In viewDidLoad(), we create a new NSDate object. An NSDate object created this way will hold the current date and time. We then set datePicker to that date, which ensures that every time this view is loaded from the storyboard, the picker will reset to the current date and time, see Listing 7-2.

Listing 7-2. Setting Our Date in the viewDidLoad() Method

```
override func viewDidLoad() {
    super.viewDidLoad()

    // Do any additional setup after loading the view.
    let date = NSDate()
    datePicker.setDate(date as Date, animated: false)
}
```

And that is all there is. Go ahead and build and run to make sure your date picker checks out. If everything went OK, your application should look like Figure 7-2 when it executes. If you choose the Select button, an alert will pop up, telling you the date and time currently selected in the date picker.

■ **Note**   The date picker does not allow you to specify seconds or a time zone. The alert displays the time with seconds and in Greenwich Mean Time (GMT). We could have added some code to simplify the string displayed in the alert, but isn't this chapter long enough already? If you're interested in customizing the formatting of the date, take a look at the NSDateFormatter class.

Implementing the Single-Component Picker

Our next picker lets the user select from a list of values. In this example, we'll use an array to hold the values we want to display in the picker. Pickers don't hold any data themselves. Instead, they call methods on their data source and delegate to get the data they need to display. The picker doesn't really care where the underlying data lives. It asks for the data when it needs it, and the data source and delegate (which are often, in practice, the same object) work together to supply that data. As a result, the data could be coming from a static list, as we'll do in this section, or it could be loaded from a file or a URL, or even made up or calculated on the fly.

For the picker class to ask its controller for data, we must ensure that the controller implements the right methods. One part of doing that is declaring in the controller's class definition that it will implement a couple of protocols. In the Project Navigator, single-click SingleComponentPickerViewController.swift. This controller class will act as both the data source and the delegate for its picker, so we need to make sure it conforms to the protocols for those two roles. Add the following code:

```
class SingleComponentPickerViewController: UIViewController,
        UIPickerViewDelegate, UIPickerViewDataSource {
```

When you do this, you'll see an error appear in the editor. That's because we haven't yet implemented the required protocol methods. We'll do that soon, so just ignore the error for now.

Building the View

Select Main.storyboard again, since it's time to edit the content view for the second tab in our tab bar. In the Document Outline, click the Single icon to bring the view controller into the foreground in the editor area. Next, bring over a Picker View from the library (see Figure 7-15), and add it to your view, placing it snugly into the top of the view, as you did with the date picker view.

Figure 7-15. *Adding a picker view from the library to your second view*

Now we need to apply Auto Layout constraints so that the picker is correctly sized and placed when the application runs on any kind of device. We want the picker to be horizontally centered and anchored to the top of the view. We also want it to be sized based on its content, so we need three constraints. With the picker selected, first select Editor ➤ Size to Fit Content from the Xcode menu bar. If this option is not enabled, move the picker slightly and try again. Next, click the Align button below the storyboard, check the Horizontally in Container box, and then click Add 1 Constraint. Click the Pin button (which is next to the Align button). Using the four distance boxes at the top of the pop-up, set the distance between the picker and the top of edge of the view above it to zero by entering zero in the top box, and then click the dashed red line below it so that it becomes a solid line. At the bottom of the pop-up, set Update Frames to Items of New Constraints, and then click Add 1 Constraint. The picker will resize and move to its correct position, as shown in Figure 7-16.

Figure 7-16. The picker, positioned at the top of its view controller's view

Now let's connect this picker to its controller. The procedure here is just like for the previous picker view: open the Assistant Editor, set the jump bar to show the SingleComponentPickerViewController.swift file, Control-drag from the picker to the top of the `SingleComponentPickerViewController` class and create an outlet named `singlePicker`.

Next, with the picker selected, press ⌥⌘6 to bring up the Connections Inspector. If you look at the connections available for the picker view, you'll see that the first two items are `dataSource` and `delegate`. If you don't see those outlets, make sure you have the picker selected, rather than the `UIView`. Drag from the circle next to `dataSource` to the View Controller icon at the top of the scene in the storyboard or in the Document Outline (see Figure 7-17), and then drag from the circle next to `delegate` to the View Controller icon. Now this picker knows that the instance of the `SingleComponentPickerViewController` class in the storyboard is its data source and delegate, and the picker will ask it to supply the data to be displayed. In other words, when the picker needs information about the data it is going to display, it asks the `SingleComponentPickerViewController` instance that controls this view for that information.

Figure 7-17. *Connecting the dataSource to the View Controller*

Drag a button to the view, place it just below the picker. Double-click the button and name it **Select**. Press Return to commit the change. In the Connections Inspector, drag from the circle next to Touch Up Inside to code in the assistant view, releasing it just above the closing bracket at the end of the class definition to make a new action method. Name this action `onButtonPressed` and you'll see that Xcode fills in an empty method. You've just seen another way to add an action method to a view controller and link it to its source view. We want this button to be horizontally centered and to stay a fixed distance below the date picker. With the button selected, click the Align button at the bottom of the storyboard, check the Horizontally in Container box, and then click Add 1 Constraint (see Figure 7-18).

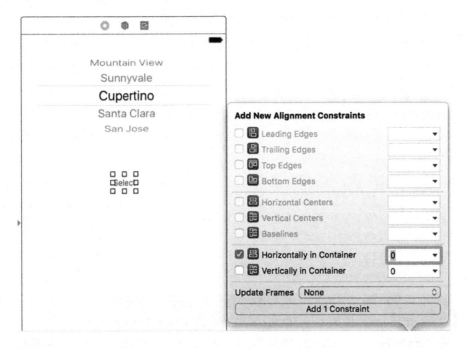

Figure 7-18. *Center the button horizontally in the view*

To fix the distance between them, Control-drag from the button to the picker and then release the mouse. In the pop-up that appears, select Vertical Spacing (see Figure 7-19). Finally, if you have any layout issues as shown by the Issue Inspector, click the Resolve Auto Layout Issues button at the bottom of the storyboard, and then click Update Frames in the top section of the pop-up (if this item is not enable, it means that the button is already in its correct location). The button should move to its correct location and there should no longer be any Auto Layout warnings.

Figure 7-19. *Set a consistent vertical spacing from the button to the picker*

Implementing the Data Source and Delegate

To make our controller work properly as the picker's data source and delegate, we'll start with some code you should feel comfortable with, and then add a few methods that you've never seen before.

Single-click SingleComponentPickerViewController.swift in the Project Navigator and add the following property at the top of the class definition. This gives us an array with the names of several well-known movie characters:

```
@IBOutlet weak var singlePicker: UIPickerView!
private let characterNames = [
        "Luke", "Leia", "Han", "Chewbacca", "Artoo",
        "Threepio", "Lando"]
```

And then change the onButtonPressed() method to what's shown in Listing 7-3.

Listing 7-3. The onButtonPressed Method for Our Single Picker View

```
@IBAction func onButtonPressed(_ sender: UIButton) {
    let row = singlePicker.selectedRow(inComponent: 0)
    let selected = characterNames[row]
    let title = "You selected \(selected)!"

    let alert = UIAlertController(
        title: title,
        message: "Thank you for choosing",
        preferredStyle: .alert)
    let action = UIAlertAction(
        title: "You're welcome",
        style: .default,
        handler: nil)
    alert.addAction(action)
    present(alert, animated: true, completion: nil)
}
```

As we saw earlier, a Date Picker contains the data we need to get to, but here, our regular picker hands off that job to the delegate and data source. The onButtonPressed() method needs to ask the picker which row is selected, and then grabs the corresponding data from your pickerData array. Here is how we ask it for the selected row:

```
let row = singlePicker.selectedRow(inComponent: 0)
```

Notice that we needed to specify which component we want to know about. We have only one component (i.e. one spinning wheel) in this picker, so we simply pass in 0, which is the index of the first (and only) component.

In the class declaration, we created an array of character names so that we have data to feed the picker. Usually, your data will come from other sources, like a property list or a web service query. By embedding an array of items in our code the way we've done here, we are making it much harder on ourselves if we need to update this list or if we want to have our application translated into other languages. But this approach is the quickest and easiest way to get data into an array for demonstration purposes. Even though you won't usually create your arrays like this, you will almost always configure some form of access to your application's model objects here in the viewDidLoad() method, so that you're not constantly going to disk or to the network every time the picker asks you for data.

> ■ **Tip** If you're not supposed to create arrays from lists of objects in your code, as we just did, how should you do it? Embed the lists in property list files and add those files to your project. Property list files can be changed without recompiling your source code, which means there is little risk of introducing new bugs when you do so. You can also provide different versions of the list for different languages, as you'll see in Chapter 22. I'll discuss property lists in more detail when we get to Chapter 13.

Finally, insert the code shown in Listing 7-4 at the bottom of the file.

Listing 7-4. Picker Data Source and Delegate Methods

```
// MARK:-
// MARK: Picker Data Source Methods

func numberOfComponents(in pickerView: UIPickerView) -> Int {
    return 1
}
func pickerView(_ pickerView: UIPickerView,
                numberOfRowsInComponent component: Int) -> Int {
    return characterNames.count
}

// MARK: Picker Delegate Methods
func pickerView(_ pickerView: UIPickerView, titleForRow row: Int, forComponent component:
Int) -> String? {
    return characterNames[row]
}
```

These three methods are required to implement the picker. The first two methods are from the UIPickerViewDataSource protocol, and they are both required for all pickers (except date pickers). Here's the first one:

```
func numberOfComponents(in pickerView: UIPickerView) -> Int {
    return 1
}
```

Pickers can have more than one spinning wheel, or component, and this is how the picker asks how many components it should display. We want to display only one list this time, so we return a value of 1. Notice that a UIPickerView is passed in as a parameter. This parameter points to the picker view that is asking us the question, which makes it possible to have multiple pickers being controlled by the same data source. In our case, we know that we have only one picker, so we can safely ignore this argument because we already know which picker is calling us.

The second data source method is used by the picker to ask how many rows of data there are for a given component:

```
func pickerView(_ pickerView: UIPickerView,
                numberOfRowsInComponent component: Int) -> Int {
    return characterNames.count
}
```

Once again, we are told which picker view is asking and which component that picker is asking about. Since we know that we have only one picker and one component, we don't bother with either of the arguments and simply return the count of objects from our sole data array.

// MARK: WHAT??

Did you notice the following lines of code from SingleComponentPickerViewController.swift?

```
// MARK:-
// MARK: Picker Data Source Methods
```

Any line of code that begins with // is a comment. Comments that start with // MARK: are treated specially by Xcode—they tell it to put an entry in the pop-up menu of methods and properties at the top of the editor pane. The first one (with the dash) puts a break in the menu. The second creates a text entry containing whatever the rest of the line holds, which you can use as a sort of descriptive header for groups of methods in your source code.

Some of your classes, especially some of your controller classes, are likely to get rather long, and the methods and functions pop-up menu makes navigating around your code much easier. Putting in // MARK: comments and logically organizing your code will make that pop-up more efficient to use.

After the two data source methods, we implement one delegate method. Unlike the data source methods, all of the delegate methods are optional. The term **optional** is a bit deceiving because you do need to implement at least one delegate method. You will usually implement the method that we are implementing here. However, if you want to display something other than text in the picker, you must implement a different method instead, as you'll see when we get to the custom picker later in this chapter:

```
func pickerView(_ pickerView: UIPickerView, titleForRow row: Int, forComponent component:
Int) -> String? {
    return characterNames[row]
}
```

In this method, the picker asks us to provide the data for a specific row in a specific component. We are provided with a pointer to the picker that is asking, along with the component and row that it is asking about. Since our view has one picker with one component, we simply ignore everything except the row argument and use that to return the appropriate item from our data array.

Build and run the application. When the simulator comes up, switch to the second tab—the one labeled Single—and check out your new custom picker, which should look like Figure 7-3.

In the next section we'll implement a picker with two components. If you feel up to a challenge , this next content view is actually a good one for you to attempt on your own. You've already seen all the methods you'll need for this picker, so go ahead if you'd like to give it a try. You might want to start with a good look at Figure 7-4, just to refresh your memory. When you're finished, read on, and you'll see how we tackled this problem.

Implementing a Multicomponent Picker

The next tab will have a picker with two components, or wheels, each independent of the other. The left wheel will have a list of sandwich fillings and the right wheel will have a selection of bread types. We'll write the same data source and delegate methods that we did for the single-component picker. We'll just need to write a little additional code in some of those methods to make sure we're returning the correct value and row count for each component. Start by single-clicking DoubleComponentPickerViewController.swift and adding the following code:

```
class DoubleComponentPickerViewController: UIViewController,
            UIPickerViewDelegate, UIPickerViewDataSource {
```

Here, we simply conform our controller class to both the delegate and data source. Save this and click Main.storyboard to work on the GUI.

Building the View

Select the Double Scene in the Document Outline and click the Double icon to bring its view controller to the front in the editor area. Now add a picker view and a button to the view, change the button label to Select, and then make the necessary connections. We're not going to walk you through it this time, but you can refer to the previous section if you need a step-by-step guide, since the two view controllers are identical in terms of connections in the storyboard. Here's a summary of what you need to do:

1. Create an outlet called doublePicker in the class extension of the DoubleComponentPickerViewController class to connect the view controller to the picker.

2. Connect the dataSource and delegate connections on the picker view to the view controller (use the Connections Inspector).

3. Connect the Touch Up Inside event of the button to a new action method called onButtonPressed on the view controller (use the Connections Inspector).

4. Add Auto Layout constraints to the picker and the button to pin them in place.

Make sure that you save your storyboard before you dive back into the code. You may want to bookmark this page because you may be referring to it in a bit.

Implementing the Controller

Select DoubleComponentPickerViewController.swift and add the code in Listing 7-5 at the top of the class definition, below our picker outlet.

Listing 7-5. Parameters Needed for Our Two-Component Picker

```
@IBOutlet weak var doublePicker: UIPickerView!
private let fillingComponent = 0
private let breadComponent = 1
private let fillingTypes = [
    "Ham", "Turkey", "Peanut Butter", "Tuna Salad",
    "Chicken Salad", "Roast Beef", "Vegemite"]
private let breadTypes = [
    "White", "Whole Wheat", "Rye", "Sourdough",
    "Seven Grain"]
```

As you can see, we start out by defining two constants that will represent the indices of the two components, which is just to make our code easier to read. Picker components are referred to by number, with the leftmost component being assigned zero and increasing by one each move to the right. Next, we declare two arrays that hold the data for our two picker components.

Now implement the onButtonPressed() method, as shown in Listing 7-6.

Listing 7-6. What to Do When the Select Button Is Pressed

```swift
@IBAction func onButtonPressed(_ sender: UIButton) {
    let fillingRow =
        doublePicker.selectedRow(inComponent: fillingComponent)
    let breadRow =
        doublePicker.selectedRow(inComponent: breadComponent)

    let filling = fillingTypes[fillingRow]
    let bread = breadTypes[breadRow]
    let message = "Your \(filling) on \(bread) bread will be right up."

    let alert = UIAlertController(
        title: "Thank you for your order",
        message: message,
        preferredStyle: .alert)
    let action = UIAlertAction(
        title: "Great",
        style: .default,
        handler: nil)
    alert.addAction(action)
    present(alert, animated: true, completion: nil)
}
```

Also, add the data source and delegate methods at the bottom of the class, as shown in Listing 7-7.

Listing 7-7. The dataSource and delegate Methods

```swift
// MARK:-
// MARK: Picker Data Source Methods
func numberOfComponents(in pickerView: UIPickerView) -> Int {
    return 2
}

func pickerView(_ pickerView: UIPickerView, numberOfRowsInComponent component: Int) ->
Int {
    if component == breadComponent {
        return breadTypes.count
    } else {
        return fillingTypes.count
    }
}

// MARK:-
// MARK: Picker Delegate Methods

func pickerView(_ pickerView: UIPickerView, titleForRow row: Int, forComponent component:
Int) -> String? {
    if component == breadComponent {
        return breadTypes[row]
```

```
    } else {
        return fillingTypes[row]
    }
}
```

The onButtonPressed() method is a bit more involved this time, but there's very little there that's new to you. We just need to specify which component we are talking about when we request the selected row using those constants we defined earlier—breadComponent and fillingComponent:

```
let fillingRow =doublePicker.selectedRow(inComponent: fillingComponent)
let breadRow = doublePicker.selectedRow(inComponent: breadComponent)
```

You can see here that using the two constants instead of 0 and 1 makes our code considerably more readable. From this point on, the onButtonPressed() method is fundamentally the same as the last one we wrote.

When we get down to the data source methods, that's where things start to change a bit. In the first method, we specify that our picker should have two components rather than just one:

```
func numberOfComponents(in pickerView: UIPickerView) -> Int {
    return 2
}
```

This time, when we are asked for the number of rows, we need to check which component the picker is asking about and return the correct row count for the corresponding array:

```
func pickerView(_ pickerView: UIPickerView, numberOfRowsInComponent component: Int) ->
Int {
    if component == breadComponent {
        return breadTypes.count
    } else {
        return fillingTypes.count
    }
}
```

Next, in our delegate method, we do the same thing. We check the component and use the correct array for the requested component to fetch and return the correct value:

```
func pickerView(_ pickerView: UIPickerView, titleForRow row: Int, forComponent component:
Int) -> String? {
    if component == breadComponent {
        return breadTypes[row]
    } else {
        return fillingTypes[row]
    }
}
```

That wasn't so hard, was it? Compile and run your application, and make sure the Double content pane looks like Figure 7-4.

Notice that the wheels are completely independent of each other. Turning one has no effect on the other. That's appropriate in this case, but there will be times when one component is dependent on another. A good example of this is in the date picker. When you change the month, the dial that shows the number of days in the month may need to change, because not all months have the same number of days. Implementing this isn't really hard once you know how, but it's not the easiest thing to figure out on your own, so let's do that next.

Implementing Dependent Components

As we're picking up momentum, I'm not going to hold your hand quite as much when it comes to material we've already covered. Instead, we'll focus on addressing new features. Our new picker will display a list of US states in the left component and a list of corresponding ZIP codes in the right component.

We'll need a separate list of ZIP code values for each item in the left-hand component. We'll declare two arrays, one for each component, as we did last time. We'll also need a **dictionary**. In the dictionary, we're going to store an **array** for each state (see Figure 7-20). Later, we'll implement a delegate method that will notify us when the picker's selection changes. If the value in the left picker wheel changes, we will grab the correct array out of the dictionary and assign it to the array being used for the right-hand picker wheel. Don't worry if you didn't catch all that; we'll talk about it more as we get into the code.

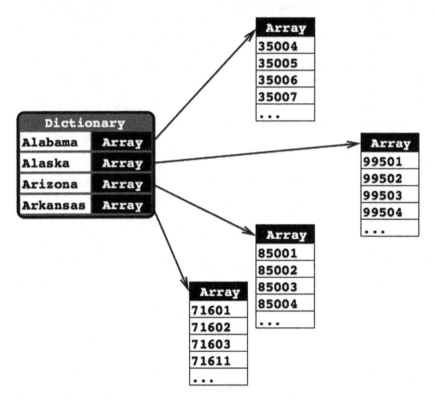

Figure 7-20. *Our application's data. For each state, there will be one entry in a dictionary with the name of the state as the key. Stored under that key will be an Array<String> instance containing all the ZIP codes from that state*

237

Add the following code to your DependentComponentPickerViewController.swift file:

```
class DependentComponentPickerViewController: UIViewController,
UIPickerViewDelegate, UIPickerViewDataSource {
private let stateComponent = 0
private let zipComponent = 1
private var stateZips:[String : [String]]!
private var states:[String]!
private var zips:[String]!
```

Now it's time to build the content view. That process is identical to the previous two component views we built. If you get lost, flip back to the Building the View section for the single-component picker and follow those step-by-step instructions. Here's a hint: start off by opening Main.storyboard, find the view controller for the DependentComponentPickerViewController class, and then repeat the same basic steps you've done for all the other content views in this chapter. You should end up with an outlet property called dependentPicker connected to a picker, an empty onButtonPressed: method connected to a button, and both the delegate and dataSource properties of the picker connected to the view controller. Don't forget to add the Auto Layout constraints to both views! When you're finished, save the storyboard.

Now we'll implement this controller class. This implementation may seem a little complicated at first. To make one component dependent on the other, we need to add a whole new level of complexity to our controller class. Although the picker displays only two lists at a time, our controller class must know about and manage 51 lists. The technique we're going to use here actually simplifies that process. The data source methods look almost identical to the one we implemented for the DoublePickerViewController. All of the additional complexity is handled elsewhere, between viewDidLoad and a new delegate method called picke rView(_:didSelectRow:inComponent:).

Before we write the code, we need some data to display. Up until now, we've created arrays in code by specifying a list of strings. Because we didn't want you to need to type in several thousand values, we're going to load the data from a property list. Both NSArray and NSDictionary objects can be created from property lists.

The data that we need is included in a property list called **statedictionary.plist** in the project archive, under the 07 – Picker Data folder. Drag that file into the Pickers folder in your Xcode project. If you single-click the .plist file in the Project Navigator, you can see and even edit the data that it contains (see Figure 7-21).

Key	Type	Value
▼ Root	Dictionary	(50 items)
▶ Alabama	Array	(657 items)
▶ Alaska	Array	(251 items)
▶ Arizona	Array	(376 items)
▶ Arkansas	Array	(618 items)
▶ California	Array	(1757 items)
▶ Colorado	Array	(501 items)
▶ Connecticut	Array	(276 items)
▶ Delaware	Array	(68 items)
▶ Florida	Array	(972 items)
▶ Georgia	Array	(736 items)
▶ Hawaii	Array	(92 items)
▶ Idaho	Array	(292 items)
▶ Illinois	Array	(1375 items)
▶ Indiana	Array	(780 items)
▶ Iowa	Array	(972 items)
▶ Kansas	Array	(721 items)
▶ Kentucky	Array	(799 items)
▶ Louisiana	Array	(542 items)
▶ Maine	Array	(415 items)
▶ Maryland	Array	(466 items)
▶ Massachusetts	Array	(519 items)
▶ Michigan	Array	(987 items)
▶ Minnesota	Array	(892 items)
▶ Mississippi	Array	(447 items)
▶ Missouri	Array	(1040 items)
▶ Montana	Array	(364 items)
▶ Nebraska	Array	(590 items)
▶ Nevada	Array	(158 items)
▶ New Hampshire	Array	(238 items)
▶ New Jersey	Array	(604 items)
▶ New Mexico	Array	(366 items)
▶ New York	Array	(1677 items)
▶ North Carolina	Array	(809 items)
▶ North Dakota	Array	(392 items)
▼ Ohio	Array	(1189 items)
Item 0	String	43001
Item 1	String	43002
Item 2	String	43003
Item 3	String	43004

The navigation bar above reads: Pickers ⟩ Pickers ⟩ statedictionary.plist ⟩ No Selection

Figure 7-21. *The statedictionary.plist file, showing our list of states. Within Ohio, you can see the start of a list of ZIP codes*

239

In DependentComponentPickerViewController.swift, we're going to first show you some whole methods to implement, and then we'll break it down into more digestible chunks. Start with the implementation of onButtonPressed(),as shown in Listing 7-8.

Listing 7-8. The onButtonPressed Method for Our ZIP Code View

```
@IBAction func onButtonPressed(_ sender: UIButton) {
    let stateRow =
        dependentPicker.selectedRow(inComponent: stateComponent)
    let zipRow =
        dependentPicker.selectedRow(inComponent: zipComponent)

    let state = states[stateRow]
    let zip = zips[zipRow]

    let title = "You selected zip code \(zip)"
    let message = "\(zip) is in \(state)"

    let alert = UIAlertController(
        title: title,
        message: message,
        preferredStyle: .alert)
    let action = UIAlertAction(
        title: "OK",
        style: .default,
        handler: nil)
    alert.addAction(action)
    present(alert, animated: true, completion: nil)
}
```

Next, add the following code to the existing viewDidLoad() method, as shown in Listing 7-9.

Listing 7-9. Add to the viewDidLoad() Method

```
override func viewDidLoad() {
    super.viewDidLoad()

    // Do any additional setup after loading the view.
    let bundle = Bundle.main
    let plistURL = bundle.urlForResource("statedictionary",
                                         withExtension: "plist")
    stateZips = NSDictionary.init(contentsOf: (plistURL)!) as! [String : [String]]
    let allStates = stateZips.keys
    states = allStates.sorted()
    let selectedState = states[0]
    zips = stateZips[selectedState]
}
```

And, finally, add the data source and delegate methods at the bottom of the file, as shown in Listing 7-10.

Listing 7-10. Our dataSource and delegate Methods for Displaying State ZIP Codes

```
// MARK:-
// MARK: Picker Data Source Methods
func numberOfComponents(in pickerView: UIPickerView) -> Int {
    return 2
}

func pickerView(_ pickerView: UIPickerView, numberOfRowsInComponent component: Int) -> Int {
    if component == stateComponent {
        return states.count
    } else {
        return zips.count
    }
}
// MARK:-
// MARK: Picker Delegate Methods
func pickerView(_ pickerView: UIPickerView, titleForRow row: Int, forComponent component:
Int) -> String? {
    if component == stateComponent {
        return states[row]
    } else {
        return zips[row]
    }
}

func pickerView(_ pickerView: UIPickerView, didSelectRow row: Int, inComponent component:
Int) {
    if component == stateComponent {
        let selectedState = states[row]
        zips = stateZips[selectedState]
        dependentPicker.reloadComponent(zipComponent)
        dependentPicker.selectRow(0, inComponent: zipComponent,
                                  animated: true)
    }
}
```

There's no need to talk about the onButtonPressed() method since it's fundamentally the same as the previous one. We should talk about the viewDidLoad() method, though. There's some stuff going on there that you need to understand, so pull up a chair and let's chat. The first thing we do in this new viewDidLoad() method is grab a reference to our application's main bundle:

```
let bundle = Bundle.main
```

A **bundle** is just a special type of folder, the contents of which follow a specific structure. Applications and frameworks are both bundles, and this call returns a bundle object that represents our application.

■ **Note**   In the latest revision of Xcode and the iOS libraries, Apple provided a more user friendly way of referring to elements such as NSBundle from Swift. Instead of something like "let bundle = NSBundle. mainBundle()", we use the much easier and more readable preceding versions.

One of the primary uses of a bundle (NSBundle) is to get to resources that you added to your project. Those files will be copied into your application's bundle when you build your application. If we want to get to those resources in our code, we usually need to use a bundle. We use the main bundle to retrieve the URL of the resource in which we're interested:

```
let plistURL = bundle.urlForResource("statedictionary",
                                 withExtension: "plist")
```

This will return a URL containing the location of the statedictionary.plist file. We can then use that URL to load our dictionary. Once we do that, the entire contents of that property list will be loaded into the newly created Dictionary object; that is, it is assigned to stateZips:

```
stateZips = NSDictionary.init(contentsOf: (plistURL)!) as! [String : [String]]
```

The Swift Dictionary type has no convenient way to load data from an external source, but the Foundation class NSDictionary does. This code takes advantage of that by loading the content of the statedictionary.plist file into an NSDictionary, which we then cast to the Swift type [String : [String]] that is, a dictionary in which each key is a string representing a state and the corresponding value is an array containing the ZIP codes for that state, as strings. This reflects the structure shown in Figure 7-18.

To populate the array for the left-hand component of the picker, which will display the states, we get the list of all keys from our dictionary and assign those to the states array. Before we assign it, though, we sort it alphabetically:

```
let allStates = stateZips.keys
states = allStates.sorted()
```

Unless we specifically set the selection to another value, pickers start with the first row (row 0) selected. To get the zips array that corresponds to the first row in the states array, we grab the object from the states array that's at index 0. That will return the name of the state that will be selected at launch time. We then use that state name to grab the array of ZIP codes for that state, which we assign to the zips array that will be used to feed data to the right-hand component:

```
let selectedState = states[0]
zips = stateZips[selectedState]
```

The two data source methods are practically identical to the previous version. We return the number of rows in the appropriate array. The same is true for the first delegate method we implemented. The second delegate method is the new one, which is where the magic happens:

```
func pickerView(_ pickerView: UIPickerView, didSelectRow row: Int, inComponent component:
Int) {
    if component == stateComponent {
        let selectedState = states[row]
        zips = stateZips[selectedState]
        dependentPicker.reloadComponent(zipComponent)
        dependentPicker.selectRow(0, inComponent: zipComponent,
                                 animated: true)
    }
}
```

In this method, which is called any time the picker's selection changes, we look at the component and see whether the left-hand component is the one that changed, which would mean that the user selected a new state. If it is, we grab the array that corresponds to the new selection and assign it to the zips array. Next, we set the right-hand component back to the first row and tell it to reload itself. By swapping the zips array whenever the state changes, the rest of the code remains pretty much the same as it was in the DoublePicker example.

We're not quite finished yet. Build and run the application, and then check out the Dependent tab, as shown in Figure 7-22. The two components are equal in size. Even though the ZIP code will never be more than five characters long, it has been given equal billing with the state. Since state names like Mississippi and Massachusetts won't fit in half of the picker on most iPhone screens, this seems less than ideal.

Figure 7-22. *Do we really want the two components to be of equal size? Notice the clipping of a long state name*

Fortunately, there's another delegate method we can implement to indicate how wide each component should be. Add the method in Listing 7-11 to the delegate section of DependentComponentPickerViewController.swift. You can see the difference in Figure 7-23.

Listing 7-11. Setting the Width of Our Picker's Components

```
func pickerView(_ pickerView: UIPickerView, widthForComponent component: Int) -> CGFloat
{
    let pickerWidth = pickerView.bounds.size.width
```

```
    if component == zipComponent {
        return pickerWidth/3
    } else {
        return 2 * pickerWidth/3
    }
}
```

Figure 7-23. *With the adjustment in width of our picker components, our UI has become more visually useful*

In this method, we return a number that represents how many pixels wide each component should be, and the picker will do its best to accommodate this. We've chosen to give the state component two-thirds of the available width and the rest goes to the ZIP component. Feel free to experiment with other values to see how the distribution of space between the components changes as you modify them. Save, build, and run; the picker on the Dependent tab will look more like the one shown in Figure 7-5.

By this point, you should be fairly comfortable with both pickers and tab bar applications. We have one more thing to do with pickers.

Creating a Simple Game with a Custom Picker

Next up, we're going to create a simulated slot machine. Take a look back at Figure 7-6 before proceeding, so you know what we're building.

Preparing the View Controller

Begin by adding the following code to CustomPickerViewController.swift:

```
class CustomPickerViewController: UIViewController,
    UIPickerViewDelegate, UIPickerViewDataSource {
private var images:[UIImage]!
```

At this point, all we've added to the class is a property for an array that will hold the images to use for the symbols on the spinners of the slot machine. The rest will come a little later.

Building the View

Even though the picker in Figure 7-6 looks quite a bit fancier than the other ones we've built, there's actually very little difference in the way we'll design our storyboard. All the extra work is done in the delegate methods of our controller.

Make sure that you've saved your new source code, and then select Main.storyboard in the Project Navigator and use the Document Outline to select the Custom icon in the Custom Scene to edit the GUI. Add a picker view, a label below that, and a button below that. Name the button **Spin**.

With the label selected, bring up the Attributes Inspector. Set the alignment to centered. Then click Text Color and set the color to something bright. Next, let's make the text a little bigger. Look for the Font setting in the inspector, and click the icon inside it (it looks like the letter T inside a little box) to pop up the font selector. This control lets you switch from the device's standard system font to another if you like, or simply change the size. For now, just change the size to 48 and delete the word Label, since we don't want any text displayed until the first time the user wins. With the label selected, click Editor ➤ Size to Fit Content to make sure the label is always large enough to display its content.

Now add Auto Layout constraints to center the picker, label, and button horizontally and to fix the vertical gaps between them and between the label and the picker, and the picker and the top of the view. You'll probably find it easiest to drag from the label in the Document Outline when adding its Auto Layout constraints, because the label on the storyboard is empty and difficult to find.

After that, make all the connections to outlets and actions. Create a new outlet called picker to connect the view controller to the picker view, another called winLabel to connect the view controller to the label. Again, you'll find it easiest to use the label in the Document Outline than the one on the storyboard. Next, connect the button's Touch Up Inside event to a new action method called spin(). After that, just make sure to connect the delegate and data source for the picker.

There's one additional thing that you need to do. Select the picker and bring up the Attributes Inspector. You need to uncheck the check box labeled User Interaction Enabled within the View settings, so that the user can't manually change the dial and cheat. Once you've done all that, save the changes you've made to the storyboard.

FONTS SUPPORTED BY IOS DEVICES

Be careful when using the fonts palette in Interface Builder for designing iOS interfaces. The Attribute Inspector's font selector will let you assign from a wide range of fonts, but not all iOS devices have the same set of fonts available. At the time of writing, for instance, there are several fonts that are available on the iPad, but not on the iPhone or iPod touch. You should limit your font selections to one of the font families found on the iOS device you are targeting. This post on Jeff LaMarche's excellent iOS blog shows you how to grab this list programmatically: http://iphonedevelopment.blogspot. com/2010/08/fonts-and-font-families.html.

In a nutshell, create a view-based application and add this code to the method application(_: didFinishLaunchingWithOptions:) in the application delegate:

```
for family in UIFont.familyNames() as [String] {
    println(family)
    for font in UIFont.fontNamesForFamilyName(family) {
        println("\t\(font)")
    }
}
```

Run the project in the appropriate simulator or device, and the available font families and fonts will be displayed in the project's console log.

Implementing the Controller

We have a bunch of new stuff to cover in the implementation of this controller. Select CustomPickerViewController.swift and get started by filling in the contents of the spin() method, as shown in Listing 7-12.

Listing 7-12. The spin() Method

```
@IBAction func spin(_ sender: UIButton) {
    var win = false
    var numInRow = -1
    var lastVal = -1

    for i in 0..<5 {
        let newValue = Int(arc4random_uniform(UInt32(images.count)))
        if newValue == lastVal {
// numInRow++   *** NOTE THAT increment/decrement operators are deprecated in Swift 3
            numInRow += 1
        } else {
            numInRow = 1
        }
        lastVal = newValue

        picker.selectRow(newValue, inComponent: i, animated: true)
```

```
        picker.reloadComponent(i)
        if numInRow >= 3 {
            win = true
        }
    }
    winLabel.text = win ? "WINNER!" : " "  // Note the space between the quotes
}
```

■ **Note**   The common use of unary increment (foo++) and decrement (foo--) has been deprecated in Swift 3 to the use of += and -=, respectively.

Change the `viewDidLoad()` method to what's shown in Listing 7-13.

Listing 7-13. The Modifications to viewDidLoad() to Set up the Images and Label

```
override func viewDidLoad() {
    super.viewDidLoad()

    // Do any additional setup after loading the view.
    images = [
        UIImage(named: "seven")!,
        UIImage(named: "bar")!,
        UIImage(named: "crown")!,
        UIImage(named: "cherry")!,
        UIImage(named: "lemon")!,
        UIImage(named: "apple")!
    ]
    winLabel.text = " " // Note the space between the quotes
    arc4random_stir()
}
```

Finally, add the dataSource and delegate code to the end of the class declaration, before the closing brace, as shown in Listing 7-14.

Listing 7-14. Our dataSource and delegate Methods

```
// MARK:-
// MARK: Picker Data Source Methods
func numberOfComponents(in pickerView: UIPickerView) -> Int {
    return 5
}
func pickerView(_ pickerView: UIPickerView, numberOfRowsInComponent component: Int) ->
Int {
    return images.count
}
// MARK:-
// MARK: Picker Delegate Methods
func pickerView(_ pickerView: UIPickerView, viewForRow row: Int, forComponent component:
Int, reusing view: UIView?) -> UIView {
```

```
        let image = images[row]
        let imageView = UIImageView(image: image)
        return imageView
}
func pickerView(_ pickerView: UIPickerView, rowHeightForComponent component: Int) ->
CGFloat {
        return 64
}
```

The spin Method

The spin() method executes when the user taps the Spin button. In it, we first declare a few variables that will help us keep track of whether the user has won. We'll use win to keep track of whether we've found three in a row by setting it to true if we have. We'll use numInRow to keep track of how many of the same value we have in a row so far. We will keep track of the previous component's value in lastVal, so that we have a way to compare the current value to the previous value. We initialize lastVal to -1 because we know that value won't match any of the real values:

```
var win = false
var numInRow = -1
var lastVal = -1
```

Next, we loop through all five components and set each one to a new, randomly generated row selection. We get the count from the images array to do that, which is a shortcut we can use because we know that all five columns use the same number of images:

```
for i in 0..<5 {
        let newValue = Int(arc4random_uniform(UInt32(images.count)))
```

We compare the new value to the previous value and increment numInRow if it matches. If the value didn't match, we reset numInRow back to 1. We then assign the new value to lastVal, so we'll have it to compare the next time through the loop:

```
if newValue == lastVal {
        numInRow += 1
} else {
        numInRow = 1
}
lastVal = newValue
```

After that, we set the corresponding component to the new value, telling it to animate the change; we tell the picker to reload that component:

```
picker.selectRow(newValue, inComponent: i, animated: true)
picker.reloadComponent(i)
```

The last thing we do each time through the loop is check whether we have three in a row, and then set win to true if we do:

```
if numInRow >= 3 {
        win = true
}
```

248

Once we're finished with the loop, we set the label to say whether the spin was a win:

```
winLabel.text = win ? "WINNER!" : " "
                    // Note the space between the quotes
```

The viewDidLoad() Method

The first thing was to load six different images, which we added to Images.xcassets right back at the beginning of the chapter. We did this using the imageNamed() convenience method of the UIImage class:

```
images = [
    UIImage(named: "seven")!,
    UIImage(named: "bar")!,
    UIImage(named: "crown")!,
    UIImage(named: "cherry")!,
    UIImage(named: "lemon")!,
    UIImage(named: "apple")!
]
```

The next thing we did in this method was to make sure the label contains exactly one space. We want the label to be empty, but if we really make it empty, it collapses to zero height. By including a space, we make sure the label is shown at its correct height:

```
winLabel.text = " " // Note the space between the quotes
```

Finally, we called the arc4random_stir() function to seed the random number generator so that we don't get the same sequence of random numbers every time we run the application.

So what do we do with those six images? If you scroll down through the code you just typed, you'll see that two data source methods look pretty much the same as before; however, if you look further into the delegate methods, you'll see that we're using completely different delegate code to provide data to the picker. The one that we've used up to now returned a string, but this one returns a UIView.

Using this method instead, we can supply the picker with anything that can be drawn into a UIView. Of course, there are limitations on what will work here and look good at the same time, given the small size of the picker. But this method gives us a lot more freedom in what we display, although it is a bit more work:

```
func pickerView(_ pickerView: UIPickerView, viewForRow row: Int, forComponent component:
Int, reusing view: UIView?) -> UIView {
    let image = images[row]
    let imageView = UIImageView(image: image)
    return imageView
}
```

This method returns one UIImageView object initialized with one of the images for the symbols. To do that, we first get the image for the symbol for the row. Next, create and return an image view with that symbol. For views more complex than a single image, it can be beneficial to create all needed views first (e.g., in viewDidLoad()), and then return these pre-created views to the picker view when requested. But for our simple case, creating the needed views dynamically works fine.

You got through all of it in one piece, and now you get to take it for a test. So, build and run the application and see how it works (see Figure 7-24).

Figure 7-24. *Not the prettiest slot machine app, but it gives you an idea of the versatility of working with pickers*

Additional Details for Our Game

Our game works okay, especially when you think about how little effort it took to build it. Now let's improve it with a couple more tweaks. There are two things about this game right now that we should address:

- It's so quiet. Real slot machines aren't quiet, so ours shouldn't be either.

- It tells us that we've won before the dials have finished spinning, which is a minor thing, but it does tend to eliminate the anticipation. To see this in action, run your application again. It is subtle, but the label really does appear before the wheels finish spinning.

The 07 - Picker Sounds folder in the project archive that accompanies the book contains two sound files: crunch.wav and win.wav. Drag both of these files to your project's Pickers folder. These are the sounds we'll play when the users tap the Spin button and when they win, respectively.

To work with sounds, we'll need access to the iOS Audio Toolbox classes. Insert the following AudioToolbox line, to a position after the existing import line at the top of CustomPickerViewController.swift:

```
import UIKit
import AudioToolbox
```

Next, we need to add an outlet that will point to the button. While the wheels are spinning, we're going to hide the button. We don't want users tapping the button again until the current spin is all done. Add the following bold line of code to CustomPickerViewController.swift:

```
class CustomPickerViewController: UIViewController,
            UIPickerViewDelegate, UIPickerViewDataSource {
    private var images:[UIImage]!
    @IBOutlet weak var picker: UIPickerView!
    @IBOutlet weak var winLabel: UILabel!
    @IBOutlet weak var button: UIButton!
```

After you type that and save the file, click Main.storyboard to edit the GUI. Open the Assistant Editor and make sure it shows the CustomPickerViewController.swift file. Click and drag from the little ball to the left of the Outlet we just added to the button on the Storyboard, as shown in Figure 7-25.

Figure 7-25. *Connecting the button outlet to the button on the Storyboard canvas*

Now, we need to do a few things in the implementation of our controller class. First, we need some instance variables to hold references to the loaded sounds. Open CustomPickerViewController.swift again and add the following new properties (shown in bold):

```
class CustomPickerViewController: UIViewController,
            UIPickerViewDelegate, UIPickerViewDataSource {
    private var images:[UIImage]!
    @IBOutlet weak var picker: UIPickerView!
    @IBOutlet weak var winLabel: UILabel!
    @IBOutlet weak var button: UIButton!
    private var winSoundID: SystemSoundID = 0
    private var crunchSoundID: SystemSoundID = 0
```

We also need a couple of methods added to our controller class. Add the two methods in Listing 7-12 to CustomPickerViewController.swift file.

Listing 7-12. Hiding the Spin Button And Playing Sounds in Our Slot Machine Game

```
func showButton() {
    button.isHidden = false
}

func playWinSound() {
    if winSoundID == 0 {
        let soundURL = Bundle.main.urlForResource(
            "win", withExtension: "wav")! as CFURL
        AudioServicesCreateSystemSoundID(soundURL, &winSoundID)
    }
    AudioServicesPlaySystemSound(winSoundID)
    winLabel.text = "WINNER!"
    DispatchQueue.main.after(when: .now() + 1.5) {
        self.showButton()
    }
}
```

We use the first method to show the button. As noted previously, we'll need to hide the button when the user taps it because, if the wheels are already spinning, there's no point in letting them spin again until they've stopped.

The second method will be called when the user wins. First, we check if we have already loaded the winning sound. The `winSoundID` and `crunchSoundID` properties are initialized as zero and valid identifiers for loaded sounds are not zero, so we can check whether a sound is loaded yet by comparing its identifier to zero. To load a sound, we first ask the main bundle for the path to the sound, in this case win.wav, just as we did when we loaded the property list for the Dependent picker view. Once we have the path to that resource, the next three lines of code load the sound file in and play it. Next, we set the label to **WINNER!** and call the `showButton()` method; however, we call the `showButton()` method in a special way using a function called `DispatchQueue(when: )`. This is a very handy function that lets you run code sometime in the future—in this case, one and a half seconds in the future, which will give the dials time to spin to their final locations before telling the user the result. This function is one of a group of useful functions collectively referred to as Grand Central Dispatch (or GCD for short), which I'll discuss in Chapter 15.

■ **Note** You may have noticed something a bit odd about the way we called the `AudioServicesCreateSystemSoundID()` function. That function takes a URL as its first parameter, but it doesn't want an instance of NSURL. Instead, it wants a CFURL (previously CFURLRef), which is a pointer to a structure that belongs to the C-language Core Foundation framework. NSURL is part of the Foundation framework, which is written in Objective-C. Fortunately, many of the C components in Core Foundation are "bridged" to their Objective-C counterparts in the Foundation framework, so that a CFURL is functionally equivalent to an NSURL pointer. That means that certain kinds of objects created in Swift or Objective-C can be used with C APIs simply by casting them to the corresponding C type using the **as** keyword.

We also need to make some changes to the `spin()` method. We will write code to play a sound and to call the `playWinSound` method if the player wins. Make the following changes to the `spin()` method, as shown in Listing 7-14.

Listing 7-14. Our Updated spin() Method to Add Sounds

```
@IBAction func spin(sender: AnyObject) {
    var win = false
    var numInRow = -1
    var lastVal = -1

    for i in 0..<5 {
        let newValue = Int(arc4random_uniform(UInt32(images.count)))
        if newValue == lastVal {
            numInRow += 1
        } else {
            numInRow = 1
        }
        lastVal = newValue

        picker.selectRow(newValue, inComponent: i, animated: true)
        picker.reloadComponent(i)
        if numInRow >= 3 {
            win = true
        }
    }

    if crunchSoundID == 0 {
        let soundURL = Bundle.main.urlForResource(
            "crunch", withExtension: "wav")! as CFURL
        AudioServicesCreateSystemSoundID(soundURL, &crunchSoundID)
    }
    AudioServicesPlaySystemSound(crunchSoundID)

    if win {
        DispatchQueue.main.after(when: .now() + 0.5) {
                    self.playWinSound()
        }
    } else {
        DispatchQueue.main.after(when: .now() + 0.5) {
            self.showButton()
        }
    }
    button.isHidden = true
    winLabel.text = " " // Note the space between the quotes
}
```

First, we load the crunch sound if needed, just as we did with the win sound before. Now play the crunch sound to let the player know the wheels have been spun. Next, instead of setting the label to **WINNER!** as soon as we know the user has won, we do something tricky. We call one of the two methods we just created, but we do it after a delay using DispatchQueue.main.after(when:). If the user won, we call our playWinSound() method half a second into the future, which will give time for the dials to spin into place; otherwise, we just wait a half a second and re-enable the Spin button. While waiting for the result, we hide the button and clear the label's text.

Now we're done so build and run the app, and then click the final tab to see and hear this slot machine in action. Tapping the Spin button should play a little cranking sound, and a win should produce a winning sound.

Summary

By now, you should be comfortable with tab bar applications and pickers. In this chapter, we built a full-fledged tab bar application containing five different content views from scratch. We practiced using pickers in a number of different configurations and creating pickers with multiple components. We even know how to make the values in one component dependent on the value selected in another component. We also saw how to make the picker display images rather than just text.

Along the way, we talked about picker delegates and data sources, and saw how to load images, play sounds, and create dictionaries from property lists. It was a long chapter, so congratulations on making it through. In the next chapter we'll start working with one of the most common elements for iPhone devices: table views.

CHAPTER 8

■ ■ ■

Introducing Table Views

Over the course of the next few chapters, we'll build some hierarchical navigation-based applications similar to the Mail application that ships on iOS devices. Applications of this type, usually called **master-detail applications**, allow the user to drill down into nested lists of data and edit that data. But before we can build these types of applications, we'll need to master the concept of table views.

Table views provide iOS devices the most common mechanism used to display lists of data to the user. They are highly configurable objects able to look practically any way you want them to. Mail uses table views to show lists of accounts, folders, and messages; however, table views are not limited to just the display of textual data. The Settings, Music, and Clock apps also use table views, even though those applications exhibit very different appearances, as shown in Figure 8-1.

Figure 8-1. *Though they all look different, the Settings, Music, and Clock applications use table views to display their data*

Table View Basics

Tables display lists of data, each item in a table's list known as a row. iOS allows tables to have an unlimited number of rows, constrained only by the amount of available memory, but only one column wide.

Table Views and Table View Cells

A table view object displays a table's data and functions as instance of the class UITableView; each visible row in a table being implemented by an instance of the class UITableViewCell, as shown in Figure 8-2.

Figure 8-2. *Each table view is an instance of UITableView, and each visible row is an instance of UITableViewCell*

Though not responsible for storing all of your table's data, table view contain only enough data to draw the rows currently visible. Somewhat like pickers, table views get their configuration data from an object that conforms to the UITableViewDelegate protocol, and their row data from an object that conforms to the UITableViewDataSource protocol. We'll see how all this works when developing our sample programs later in the chapter.

As mentioned, all tables contain just a single column. The Clock application, shown on the right side of Figure 8-1, gives the appearance of having two columns, but in reality, that's not the case—each row in the table is represented by a single UITableViewCell. By default, a UITableViewCell object can be configured with an image, some text, and an optional accessory icon, which is a small icon on the right side, which we'll cover in detail in chapter 9.

You increase the amount data in a cell by adding subviews to UITableViewCell by using one of two basic techniques: 1) adding subviews programmatically when creating the cell or, 2) loading them from a storyboard or nib file. You lay out the table view cell however appropriate including any subviews needed. This makes the single-column limitation far less limiting than it sounds at first. We'll explore how to use both of these techniques in this chapter.

Grouped and Plain Tables

Table views come in two basic styles:

- **Grouped**: A grouped table view contains one or more sections of rows. Within each section, all rows rest tightly together in a compact grouping; but between sections, clear visible gaps exist, as shown in the leftmost picture in Figure 8-3. Note that a grouped table can consist of a single group.

- **Plain**: A plain table view (see Figure 8-3, middle), the default style, sections are slightly closer together, and each section's header optionally styled in a custom manner. When an index is used, we refer to this style as **indexed** (see Figure 8-3, right).

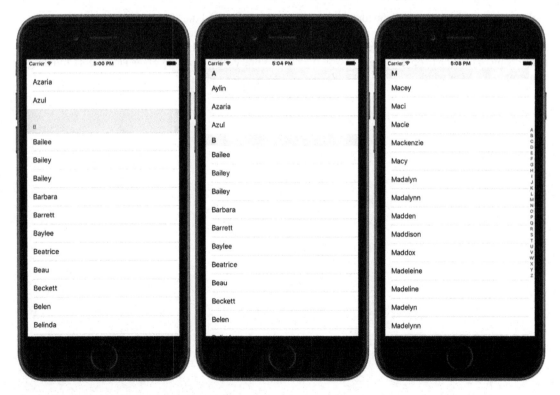

Figure 8-3. *One table view displayed as a grouped table (left); a plain table without an index (middle); and a plain table with an index, which is also called an indexed table (right)*

If your data source provides the necessary information, the table view allows the user to navigate your list by an index that is displayed along the right side.

iOS breaks up your table into divisions called sections. In a grouped table, each section presents itself visually as a group. In an indexed table, each indexed grouping of data Apple refers to as a section. For example, in the indexed table shown in Figure 8-3, all the names beginning with A would be one section, those beginning with B would be another, and so on.

■ **Caution**   Even though it is technically possible to create a grouped table with an index, you should not do so. The *iOS Human Interface Guidelines* specifically state that grouped tables should not provide indexes.

Implementing a Simple Table

Let's look at the simplest possible example of a table view to get a feel for how it works. In this first example, we'll only display a list of text values.

Create a new project in Xcode. For this chapter, we're going back to the Single View Application template, so select that one. Call your project **Simple Table**, set Swift as the Language, set the Devices field to Universal, and make sure that Use Core Data is unchecked.

Designing the View

In the Project Navigator, expand the top-level Simple Table project and the Simple Table folder. This is such a simple application that we're not going to need any outlets or actions. Go ahead and select Main. storyboard to edit the storyboard. If the View window isn't visible in the layout area, single-click its icon in the Document Outline to open it. Next, look in the object library for a Table View (see Figure 8-4) and drag that over to the View window.

Figure 8-4. *Dragging a table view from the library onto our main view*

Drop the table view onto the view controller and line it up to be more or less centered in its parent view. Now let's add Auto Layout constraints to make sure that the table view is positioned and sized correctly no matter what size the screen is. Select the table in the Document Outline, and then click the Pin icon at the bottom right of the storyboard editor (see Figure 8-5).

Figure 8-5. *Pinning the table view so that it fits the screen*

At the top of the pop-up, clear the Constrain to margins check box, click all four dashed lines, and set the distances in the four input fields to zero. This will have the effect of pinning all four edges of the table view to those of its parent view. To apply the constraints, change Update Frames to Items of New Constraints, and click the Add 4 Constraints button. The table should resize to fill the whole view.

Select the table view again in the Document Inspector and press ⌥⌘6 to bring up the Connections Inspector. You'll notice that the first two available connections for the table view are the same as the first two for the picker views that we used in the last chapter: dataSource and delegate. Drag from the circle next to each of those connections over to the View Controller icon in the Document Outline or above the view controller in the storyboard editor. This makes our controller class both the data source and delegate for this table, as shown in Figure 8-6.

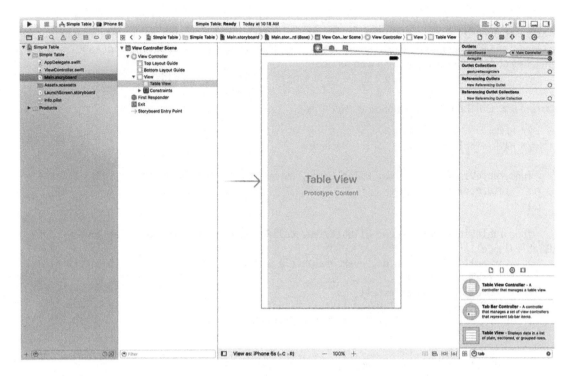

Figure 8-6. *Connecting our Table View's dataSource and delegate outlets*

Next, we'll start writing the Swift code for our Table View.

Implementing the Controller

If you've gone through the previous chapters, a lot of this will sound familiar and maybe a bit boring. However, because some readers skip ahead, I'm going to try and maintain a consistent approach at least for these early, more basic chapters. Single-click ViewController.swift and add the code in Listing 8-1 to the class declaration.

Listing 8-1. Add to the Top of the Class Declaration to Create Our Element Array

```
class ViewController: UIViewController,
            UITableViewDataSource, UITableViewDelegate {
    private let dwarves = [
            "Sleepy", "Sneezy", "Bashful", "Happy",
            "Doc", "Grumpy", "Dopey",
            "Thorin", "Dorin", "Nori", "Ori",
            "Balin", "Dwalin", "Fili", "Kili",
            "Oin", "Gloin", "Bifur", "Bofur",
            "Bombur"
    ]
    let simpleTableIdentifier = "SimpleTableIdentifier"
```

In Listing 8-1 we're conforming our class to the two protocols that are needed for it to act as the data source and delegate for the table view, declaring an array that holds the data that will be displayed in the table and an identifier that we'll use shortly. In a real application, the data would come from another source, such as a text file, a property list, or a web service.

Next, add the code in Listing 8-2 above the closing brace at the end of the file.

Listing 8-2. Our Table View's dataSource Methods

```
// MARK:-
// MARK: Table View Data Source Methods

func tableView(_ tableView: UITableView, numberOfRowsInSection section: Int) -> Int {
    return dwarves.count
}

func tableView(_ tableView: UITableView, cellForRowAt indexPath: IndexPath) ->
UITableViewCell {
    var cell = tableView.dequeueReusableCell(withIdentifier: simpleTableIdentifier)
    if (cell == nil) {
        cell = UITableViewCell(
            style: UITableViewCellStyle.default,
            reuseIdentifier: simpleTableIdentifier)
    }

    cell?.textLabel?.text = dwarves[indexPath.row]
    return cell!
}
```

These methods are part of the UITableViewDataSource protocol. The first one, tableView(_ tableView: UITableView, numberOfRowsInSection section: Int) -> Int is used by the table to ask how many rows are in a particular section. As you might expect, the default number of sections is one, and this method will be called to get the number of rows in the one section that makes up the list. We just return the number of items in our array.

The next method probably requires a little explanation, so let's look at it more closely:

```
func tableView(_ tableView: UITableView,
            cellForRowAt indexPath: IndexPath) -> UITableViewCell {
```

This method is called by the table view when it needs to draw one of its rows. Notice that the second argument to this method is an NSIndexPath instance. NSIndexPath is a structure that table views use to wrap the section and row indexes into a single object. To get the row index or the section index out of an NSIndexPath, you just access its row property or its section property, both of which return an integer value.

The first parameter, tableView, is a reference to the table that's being constructed. This allows us to create classes that act as a data source for multiple tables.

A table view displays only a few rows at a time, but the table itself can conceivably hold considerably more. Remember that each row in the table is represented by an instance of UITableViewCell, a subclass of UIView, which means each row can contain subviews. With a large table, this could represent a huge amount of overhead if the table were to try to keep one table view cell instance for every row in the table, regardless of whether that row was currently being displayed. Fortunately, tables don't work that way.

Instead, as table view cells scroll off the screen, they are placed into a queue of cells available to be reused. If the system runs low on memory, the table view will get rid of the cells in the queue. But as long as the system has some memory available for those cells, it will hold on to them in case you want to use them again.

Every time a table view cell rolls off the screen, there's a pretty good chance that another one just rolled onto the screen on the other side. If that new row can just reuse one of the cells that has already rolled off the screen, the system can avoid the overhead associated with constantly creating and releasing those views. To take advantage of this mechanism, we'll ask the table view to give us a previously used cell of the specified type using the identifier we declared earlier. In effect, we're asking for a reusable cell of type simpleTableIdentifier:

```
var cell = tableView.dequeueReusableCell(withIdentifier: simpleTableIdentifier)
```

In this example, the table uses only a single type of cell, but in a more complex table, you might need to format different types of cells according to their content or position, in which case you would use a separate table cell identifier for each distinct cell type.

Now, it's completely possible that the table view won't have any spare cells (e.g., when it's being initially populated), so we check the cell variable after the call to see whether it's nil. If it is, we manually create a new table view cell using the same identifier string. At some point, we'll inevitably reuse one of the cells we create here, so we need to make sure that we create it using simpleTableIdentifier:

```
if (cell == nil) {
    cell = UITableViewCell(
        style: UITableViewCellStyle.default,
        reuseIdentifier: simpleTableIdentifier)
}
```

Curious about UITableViewCellStyle.default? We'll get to it when we look at the table view cell styles shortly.

We now have a table view cell that we can return for the table view to use. So, all we need to do is place whatever information we want displayed in this cell. Displaying text in a row of a table is a very common task, so the table view cell provides a UILabel property called textLabel that we can set to display strings. That just requires getting the correct string from our dwarves array and using it to set the cell's textLabel.

To get the correct value, however, we need to know which row the table view is asking for. We get that information from the indexPath's row property. We use the row number of the table to get the corresponding string from the array, assign it to the cell's textLabel.text property, and then return the cell:

```
cell?.textLabel?.text = dwarves[indexPath.row]
return cell!
```

Compile and run your application, and you should see the array values displayed in a table view, as shown on the left of Figure 8-7.

Figure 8-7. The Simple Table application showing our dwarves array

You may be wondering why we need all the ? operators in this line of code:

```
cell?.textLabel?.text = dwarves[indexPath.row]
```

Each use of the ? operator is an example of Swift's **optional chaining**, which allows you to write compact code even if you have to invoke the methods or access the properties of an object reference that could be nil. The first ? operator is required because, as far as the compiler is concerned, cell could be nil. The reason for that is we obtained it by calling the dequeueReusableCellWithIdentifier() method, which returns a value of type UITableViewCell?. Of course, the compiler doesn't take into account the fact that we explicitly check for a nil return value and create a new UITableViewCell object if we find one, thus ensuring that cell will, in fact, never be nil when we reach this line of code. If you look at the documentation for the UITableViewCell class, you'll see that its textLabel property is of type UILabel?, so it could also be nil. Again, that won't actually be the case because we are using a default UITableViewCell instance, which always includes a label. Naturally, the compiler doesn't know that, so we use a ? operator when dereferencing it. This is something we'll see throughout our Swift experiences.

Adding an Image

It would be nice if we could add an image to each row. You might think that we would need to create a subclass of UITableViewCell or add subviews to do that. Actually, if you can live with the image being on the left side of each row, we're already set. The default table view cell can handle that situation just fine. Let's see how it works.

Drag the files star.png and star2.png from the 08 - Star Image folder in the example source code archive to your project's Assets.xcassets, as shown in Figure 8-8.

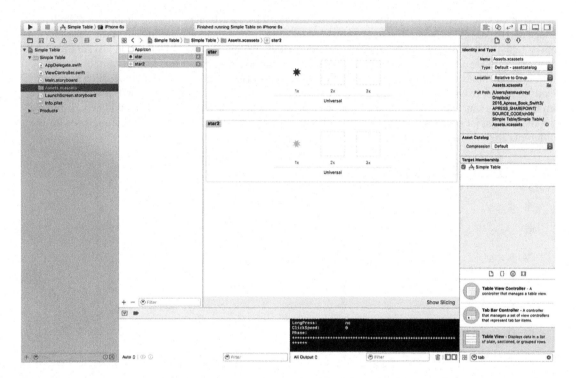

Figure 8-8. *Adding our images to the Assets.xcassets folder*

We're going to arrange for these icons to appear on every row of the table view. All we need to do is create a UIImage for each of them and assign it to the UITableViewCell when the table view asks its data source for the cell for each row. To do this, in the file ViewController.swift, modify the tableView(_:cellFor RowAtIndexPath:) method, as shown in Listing 8-3.

Listing 8-3. Our Modifications to Add the Image to Each Cell

```
func tableView(_ tableView: UITableView, cellForRowAt indexPath: IndexPath) ->
UITableViewCell {
    var cell = tableView.dequeueReusableCell(withIdentifier: simpleTableIdentifier)
    if (cell == nil) {
        cell = UITableViewCell(
            style: UITableViewCellStyle.default,
            reuseIdentifier: simpleTableIdentifier)
    }
```

```
        let image = UIImage(named: "star")
        cell?.imageView?.image = image
        let highlightedImage = UIImage(named: "star2")
        cell?.imageView?.highlightedImage = highlightedImage

        cell?.textLabel?.text = dwarves[indexPath.row]
        return cell!
    }
```

That's it. Each cell has an imageView property of type UIImage, which in turn has properties called image and highlightedImage. The image given by the image property appears to the left of the cell's text and is replaced by the highlightedImage, if one is provided, when the cell is selected. You just set the cell's imageView.image and imageView.highlightedImage properties to whatever images you want to display.

If you compile and run your application now, you should get a list with a bunch of nice little blue star icons to the left of each row, as shown in Figure 8-9. If you select any row, you'll see that its icon switches from blue to green, which is the color of the image in the star2.png file. Of course, we could have included a different image for each row in the table, or, with very little effort, we could have used different icons for the different categories of dwarves.

Figure 8-9. *We used the cell's imageView property to add an image to each of the table view's cells*

> **■ Note** UIImage uses a caching mechanism based on the file name, so it won't load a new `image` property each time `UIImage(named:)` is called. Instead, it will use the already cached version.

Using Table View Cell Styles

The work you've done with the table view so far has used the default cell style shown in Figure 8-9, represented by the constant `UITableViewCellStyle.default`. But the `UITableViewCell` class includes several other predefined cell styles that let you easily add a bit more variety to your table views. These cell styles all use three different cell elements:

- **Image**: If an image is part of the specified style, the image is displayed to the left of the cell's text.

- **Text label**: This is the cell's primary text. In the case of the `UITableViewCellStyle.Default` style that we have been using so far, the text label is the only text shown in the cell.

- **Detail text label**: This is the cell's secondary text, usually used as an explanatory note or label.

To see what these new style additions look like, add the following code to `tableView(_:cellForRowAtIndexPath:)` in ViewController.swift:

```
if indexPath.row < 7 {
    cell?.detailTextLabel?.text = "Mr Disney"
} else {
    cell?.detailTextLabel?.text = "Mr Tolkien"
}
```

Place it just before the `cell?.textLabel?.text = dwarves[indexPath.row]` line in the method.

All we've done here is set the cell's detail text. We use the string "Mr. Disney" for the first seven rows and the string "Mr. Tolkien" for the rest. When you run this code, each cell will look just as it did before (see Figure 8-10). That's because we are using the style `UITableViewCellStyle.default`, which does not use the detail text.

Figure 8-10. *The default cell style shows the image and text label in a straight line*

Now change `UITableViewCellStyle.default` to `UITableViewCellStyle.subtitle` like this:

```
if (cell == nil) {
    cell = UITableViewCell(
        style: UITableViewCellStyle.subtitle,
        reuseIdentifier: simpleTableIdentifier)
}
```

Now run the app again. With the subtitle style, both text elements are shown, one below the other, as shown in Figure 8-11.

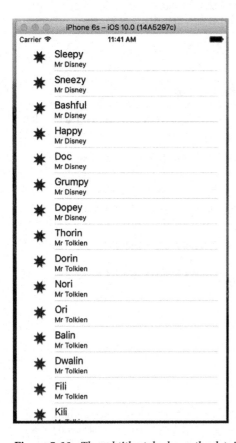

Figure 8-11. *The subtitle style shows the detail text in smaller letters below the text label*

Next, change `UITableViewCellStyle.subtitle` to `UITableViewCellStyle.value1`, and then build and run again. This style places the text label and detail text label on the same line, but on opposite sides of the cell, as shown in Figure 8-12.

Figure 8-12. *The style value1 places the text label on the left side in black letters and the detail text right-justified on the right side*

Finally, change `UITableViewCellStyle.value1` to `UITableViewCellStyle.value2`. This format is often used to display information along with a descriptive label. It doesn't show the cell's icon, but places the detail text label to the left of the text label, as shown in Figure 8-13. In this layout, the detail text label acts as a label describing the type of data held in the text label.

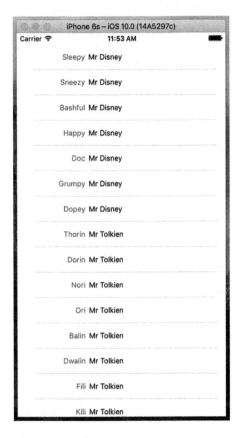

Figure 8-13. The style value 2 does not display the image and places the detail text label in blue letters to the left of the text label

Now that you've seen the cell styles that are available, go ahead and change back to the UITableViewCellStyle.default style before continuing. Later in this chapter, you'll see how to create custom table view cells. But before you do that, make sure you consider the available cell styles to see whether one of them will suit your needs.

You may have noticed that we made our controller both the data source and delegate for this table view; but up until now, we haven't actually implemented any of the methods from the UITableViewDelegate protocol. Unlike picker views, simpler table views don't require the use of a delegate to do their thing. The data source provides all the data needed to draw the table. The purpose of the delegate is to configure the appearance of the table view and to handle certain user interactions. Let's take a look at a few of the configuration options now. We'll discuss a few more in the next chapter.

Setting the Indent Level

The delegate can be used to specify that some rows should be indented. In the file ViewController.swift, add the following method to your code:

```
// MARK:-
// MARK: Table View delegate Methods
```

```
func tableView(_ tableView: UITableView, indentationLevelForRowAt indexPath: IndexPath) ->
Int {
    return indexPath.row % 4
}
```

This method sets the **indent level** for each row based on its row number; so row 0 will have an indent level of 0, row 1 will have an indent level of 1, and so on. Because of the % operator, row 4 will revert back to an indent level of 0 and the cycle begins again. An indent level is simply an integer that tells the table view to move that row a little to the right. The higher the number, the further to the right the row will be indented. You might use this technique, for example, to indicate that one row is subordinate to another row, as Mail does when representing subfolders.

When you run the application again, you'll see that the rows indent in blocks of four, as shown in Figure 8-14.

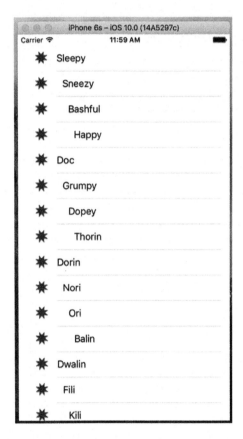

Figure 8-14. *Indented table rows*

Handling Row Selection

The table's delegate has two methods that allow you to handle row selection. One method is called before the row is selected, which can be used to prevent the row from being selected or even to change which row gets selected. Let's implement that method and specify that the first row is not selectable. Add the following method to the end of ViewController.swift:

```swift
func tableView(_ tableView: UITableView, willSelectRowAt indexPath: IndexPath) ->
IndexPath? {
    return indexPath.row == 0 ? nil : indexPath
}
```

This method is passed an `indexPath` that represents the item that's about to be selected. Our code looks at which row is about to be selected. If it's the first row, which is always index zero, then it returns `nil` to indicate that no row should actually be selected. Otherwise, it returns the unmodified `indexPath`, which is how we indicate that it's OK for the selection to proceed.

Before you compile and run, let's also implement the delegate method that is called after a row has been selected, which is typically where you'll actually handle the selection. In the next chapter, we'll use this method to handle drill-downs in a master-detail application, but in this chapter, we'll just put up an alert to show that the row was selected. Add the method in Listing 8-4 at the end of ViewController.swift.

Listing 8-4. Pop up an Alert When the User Taps a Row

```swift
func tableView(_ tableView: UITableView, didSelectRowAt indexPath: IndexPath) {
    let rowValue = dwarves[indexPath.row]
    let message = "You selected \(rowValue)"

    let controller = UIAlertController(title: "Row Selected",
                                        message: message, preferredStyle: .alert)
    let action = UIAlertAction(title: "Yes I Did",
                                style: .default, handler: nil)
    controller.addAction(action)
    present(controller, animated: true, completion: nil)
}
```

Once you've added this method, compile and run the app, and then take it for a spin. For example, see whether you can select the first row (you shouldn't be able to), and then select one of the other rows. The selected row should be highlighted. Also, your alert should pop up, telling you which row you selected while the selected row fades in the background, as shown in Figure 8-15.

Figure 8-15. *In this example, the first row is not selectable, and an alert is displayed when any other row is selected*

Note that you can also modify the index path before you pass it back, which would cause a different row and/or section to be selected. You won't do that very often, as you should have a very good reason for changing the user's selection. In the vast majority of cases where you use the `tableView(_:willSelectRowAtIndexPath:)` method, you will either return `indexPath` unmodified to allow the selection or return `nil` to disallow it. If you really want to change the selected row and/or section, use the `NSIndexPath(forRow:, inSection:)` initializer to create a new `NSIndexPath` object and return it. For example, the code in Listing 8-5 would ensure that if you tried to select an even-numbered row, you would actually select the row that follows it.

Listing 8-5. Returning the Following Row

```
func tableView(tableView: UITableView,
               willSelectRowAtIndexPath indexPath: NSIndexPath)
    -> NSIndexPath? {
        if indexPath.row == 0 {
            return nil
        } else if (indexPath.row % 2 == 0){
            return NSIndexPath(row: indexPath.row + 1,
                               section: indexPath.section)
        } else {
            return indexPath
        }
}
```

Changing the Font Size and Row Height

Let's say that we want to change the size of the font being used in the table view. In most situations, you shouldn't override the default font; it's what users expect to see. But sometimes there are valid reasons to change the font. Change the code for your tableView(_:cellForRowAtIndexPath:) method:

```
func tableView(_ tableView: UITableView, cellForRowAt indexPath: IndexPath) ->
UITableViewCell {
    var cell = tableView.dequeueReusableCell(withIdentifier: simpleTableIdentifier)
    if (cell == nil) {
        cell = UITableViewCell(
            style: UITableViewCellStyle.default,
            reuseIdentifier: simpleTableIdentifier)
    }

    let image = UIImage(named: "star")
    cell?.imageView?.image = image
    let highlightedImage = UIImage(named: "star2")
    cell?.imageView?.highlightedImage = highlightedImage

    if indexPath.row < 7 {
        cell?.detailTextLabel?.text = "Mr Disney"
    } else {
        cell?.detailTextLabel?.text = "Mr Tolkien"
    }

    cell?.textLabel?.text = dwarves[indexPath.row]
    cell?.textLabel?.font = UIFont.boldSystemFont(ofSize: 50) // <- add this line
    return cell!
}
```

When you run the application now, the values in your list are drawn in a really large font size, but they don't exactly fit in the row, as shown in Figure 8-16.

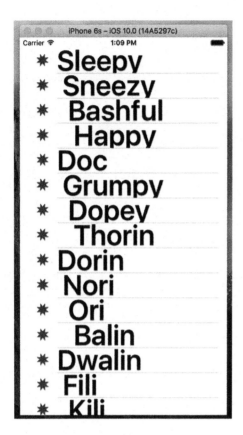

Figure 8-16. *Changing the font used to draw table view cells*

There are a couple of ways to fix this. First, we can tell the table that all of its rows should have a given, fixed height. To do that, we set its rowHeight property, like this:

```
tableView.rowHeight = 70
```

If you need different rows to have different heights, you can implement the UITableViewDelegate's tab leView(_:heightForRowAtIndexPath:) method. Go ahead and add this method to your controller class:

```
func tableView(_ tableView: UITableView, heightForRowAt indexPath: IndexPath) -> CGFloat
{
    return indexPath.row == 0 ? 120 : 70
}
```

We've just told the table view to set the row height for all rows to 70 points, except for the first row, which will be a little larger. Compile and run, and your table's rows should be a better fit for their content now, as shown in Figure 8-17.

Figure 8-17. *Changing the row size using the delegate. Notice that the first row is much taller than the rest*

There are more tasks that the delegate handles, but most of the remaining ones come into play when you start working with hierarchical data, which we'll do in the next chapter. To learn more, use the documentation browser to explore the UITableViewDelegate protocol and see what other methods are available.

Customizing Table View Cells

You can do a lot with table views right out of the box; but often, you will want to format the data for each row in ways that simply aren't supported by UITableViewCell directly. In those cases, there are three basic approaches: one that involves adding subviews to UITableViewCell programmatically when creating the cell, a second that involves loading a cell from a nib file, and a third that is similar, but loads the cell from a storyboard. We'll take a look at the first two techniques in this chapter and you'll see an example that creates a cell from a storyboard in Chapter 9.

Adding Subviews to the Table View Cell

To show how to use custom cells, we're going to create a new application with another table view. In each row, we'll display two lines of information along with two labels, as shown in Figure 8-18. Our application displays the name and color of a series of potentially familiar computer models. We'll show both of those pieces of information in the same row by adding subviews to its table view cell.

Figure 8-18. *Adding subviews to the table view cell can give you multiline rows*

Implementing a Custom Table Views Application

Create a new Xcode project using the Single View Application template. Name the project **Table Cells** and use the same settings as your last project. Click Main.storyboard to edit the GUI in Interface Builder.

Add a Table View to the main view and use the Connections Inspector to set its data source to the view controller, as we did for the Simple Table application. Then, use the Pin button at the bottom of the window to create constraints between the table view's edges and those of its parent view and the status bar. You can actually use the same settings as in Figure 8-5, since the values that you specify in the input boxes at the top of the pop-up are, by default, the distances between the table view and its nearest neighbor in all four directions. Finally, save the storyboard.

Creating a UITableViewCell Subclass

Until this point, the standard table view cells we've been using have taken care of all the details of cell layout for us. Our controller code has been kept clear of the messy details about where to place labels and images; we just pass off the display values to the cell. This keeps presentation logic out of the controller, and that's a really good design to stick to. For this project, we're going to make a new cell UITableViewCell subclass of our own that takes care of the details of the new layout, which will keep our controller as simple as possible.

277

Adding New Cells

Select the Table Cells folder in the Project Navigator, and press ⌘N to create a new file. In the assistant that pops up, select Cocoa Touch Class from the iOS Source section and press Next. On the following screen, enter **NameAndColorCell** as the name of the new class, select UITableViewCell in the Subclass of pop-up list, leave **Also create XIB file** unchecked, click Next again, and on the next screen, click Create.

Now select NameAndColorCell.swift in the Project Navigator and add the following code:

```swift
class NameAndColorCell: UITableViewCell {
    var name: String = ""
    var color: String = ""
    var nameLabel: UILabel!
    var colorLabel: UILabel!
```

Here, we've added two properties (name and color) to our cell's interface that our controller will use to pass values to each cell. We also added a couple of properties that we'll use to access some of the subviews we'll be adding to our cell. Our cell will contain four subviews, two of which are labels that have fixed content and another two for which the content will be changed for every row.

Those are all the properties we need to add, so let's move on to the code. We're going to override the table view cell's init(style:reuseIdentifier:) initializer to add some code to create the views that we'll need to display, as shown in Listing 8-6.

Listing 8-6. Our Table View Cell's init() Method

```swift
override init(style: UITableViewCellStyle, reuseIdentifier: String?) {
    super.init(style: style, reuseIdentifier: reuseIdentifier)

    let nameLabelRect = CGRect(x: 0, y: 5, width: 70, height: 15)
    let nameMarker = UILabel(frame: nameLabelRect)
    nameMarker.textAlignment = NSTextAlignment.right
    nameMarker.text = "Name:"
    nameMarker.font = UIFont.boldSystemFont(ofSize: 12)
    contentView.addSubview(nameMarker)

    let colorLabelRect = CGRect(x: 0, y: 26, width: 70, height: 15)
    let colorMarker = UILabel(frame: colorLabelRect)
    colorMarker.textAlignment = NSTextAlignment.right
    colorMarker.text = "Color:"
    colorMarker.font = UIFont.boldSystemFont(ofSize: 12)
    contentView.addSubview(colorMarker)

    let nameValueRect = CGRect(x: 80, y: 5, width: 200, height: 15)
    nameLabel = UILabel(frame: nameValueRect)
    contentView.addSubview(nameLabel)

    let colorValueRect = CGRect(x: 80, y: 25, width: 200, height: 15)
    colorLabel = UILabel(frame: colorValueRect)
    contentView.addSubview(colorLabel)
}
```

That should be pretty straightforward. We create four UILabels and add them to the table view cell. The table view cell already has a UIView subview called contentView, which it uses to group all of its subviews. As a result, we don't add the labels as subviews directly to the table view cell, but rather to its contentView.

Two of these labels contain static text. The label `nameMarker` contains the text Name:, and the label `colorMarker` contains the text Color:. Those are just labels that we won't change. Both of these labels have right-aligned text using `NSTextAlignment.right`.

We'll use the other two labels to display our row-specific data. Remember that we need some way of retrieving these fields later, so we keep references to both of them in the properties that we declared earlier.

Since we've overridden a designated initializer of the table view cell class, Swift requires us to also provide an implementation of the `init(coder:)` initializer. This initializer will never be called in our example application, so just add these three lines of code:

```
required init?(coder aDecoder: NSCoder) {
    fatalError("init(coder:) has not been implemented")
}
```

In Chapter 13, we'll discuss this initializer and why it's sometimes needed.

Now let's put the finishing touches on the `NameAndColorCell` class by adding some setter logic to the name and color properties. Change the declarations of these properties as follows:

```
var name: String = "" {
    didSet {
        if (name != oldValue) {
            nameLabel.text = name
        }
    }
}
var color: String = "" {
    didSet {
        if (color != oldValue) {
            colorLabel.text = color
        }
    }
}
```

All we're doing here is adding code to ensure that when the `name` or `color` property's value is changed, the text property of the corresponding label in the same custom table view cell is set to the same value.

Implementing the Controller's Code

Now, let's set up the simple controller to display values in our nice new cells. Start off by selecting ViewController.swift and add the code in Listing 8-7.

Listing 8-7. Displaying Values in Our Custom Cell

```
class ViewController: UIViewController, UITableViewDataSource {

    let cellTableIdentifier = "CellTableIdentifier"
    @IBOutlet var tableView:UITableView!
    let computers = [
        ["Name" : "MacBook Air", "Color" : "Silver"],
        ["Name" : "MacBook Pro", "Color" : "Silver"],
        ["Name" : "iMac", "Color" : "Silver"],
        ["Name" : "Mac Mini", "Color" : "Silver"],
```

```
        ["Name" : "Mac Pro", "Color" : "Black"]
    ]

    override func viewDidLoad() {
        super.viewDidLoad()
        // Do any additional setup after loading the view, typically from a nib.
        tableView.register(NameAndColorCell.self,
                                forCellReuseIdentifier: cellTableIdentifier)
    }
```

We conformed the view controller to the UITableViewDataSource protocol, and added a cell identifier name and an array of dictionaries. Each dictionary contains the name and color information for one row in the table. The name for that row is held in the dictionary under the key Name, and the color is held under the key Color. We also added an outlet for the table view, so we need to connect it in the storyboard. Select the Main.storyboard file. In the Document Outline, Control-drag from the View Controller icon to the Table View icon. Release the mouse and select tableView in the pop-up to link the table view to the outlet.

Now add the code in Listing 8-8 to the end of the ViewController.swift file.

Listing 8-8. Our Table View's Data Source Methods

```
// MARK: -
// MARK: Table View Data Source Methods

func tableView(_ tableView: UITableView, numberOfRowsInSection section: Int) -> Int {
    return computers.count
}

func tableView(_ tableView: UITableView, cellForRowAt indexPath: IndexPath) ->
UITableViewCell {
    let cell = tableView.dequeueReusableCell(
        withIdentifier: cellTableIdentifier, for: indexPath)
        as! NameAndColorCell

    let rowData = computers[indexPath.row]
    cell.name = rowData["Name"]!
    cell.color = rowData["Color"]!

    return cell
}
```

You have already seen these methods in our previous example—they belong to the UITableViewDataSource protocol. Let's focus on **tableView(_ tableView: UITableView, cellForRowAt indexPath: IndexPath)** since that's where we're really getting into some new stuff. Here we're using an interesting feature: a table view can use a sort of registry to create a new cell when needed. That means that as long as we've registered all the reuse identifiers that we're going to use for a table view, we can always get access to an available cell. In our previous example, the dequeue method we implemented also used the registry, but it returned nil if the identifier that we give it isn't registered. The nil return value is used as a signal that we need to create and populate a new UITableViewCell object. The following method that we're using never returns nil:

```
dequeueReusableCell(
            withIdentifier: cellTableIdentifier, for: indexPath)
```

So how does it get a table cell object? It uses the identifier that we pass to it as the key to its registry. We added an entry to the registry that's mapped to our table cell identifier in the viewDidLoad method:

```
tableView.register(NameAndColorCell.self,
                      forCellReuseIdentifier: cellTableIdentifier)
```

What happens if we pass an identifier that's not registered? In that case, the dequeueReusableCell method crashes. Crashing sounds bad, but in this case, it would be the result of a bug that you would discover right away during development. Therefore, we don't need to include code that checks for a nil return value since that will never happen.

Once we've got our new cell, we use the indexPath argument that was passed in to determine which row the table is requesting a cell for, and then use that row value to grab the correct dictionary for the requested row. Remember that the dictionary has two key/value pairs: one with name and another with color:

```
let rowData = computers[indexPath.row]
```

Now, all that's left to do is populate the cell with data from the chosen row, using the properties we defined in our subclass:

```
cell.name = rowData["Name"]!
cell.color = rowData["Color"]!
```

As you saw earlier, setting these properties causes the value to be copied to the name and color labels in the table view cell.

Build and run your application. You should see a table of rows, each with two lines of data, as shown in Figure 8-19.

Figure 8-19. *Our Table View of custom cells created in code*

Being able to add views to a table view cell provides a lot more flexibility than using the standard table view cell alone, but it can get a little tedious creating, positioning, and adding all the subviews programmatically. Gosh, it sure would be nice if we could design the table view cell graphically by using Xcode's GUI editing tools. Well, we're in luck. As mentioned earlier, you can use Interface Builder to design your table view cells, and then simply load the views from a storyboard or a XIB file when you create a new cell.

Loading a UITableViewCell from a XIB File

We're going to re-create that same two-line interface we just built in code using the visual layout capabilities that Xcode provides in Interface Builder. To do this, we'll create a new XIB file that will contain the table view cell, and lay out its views using Interface Builder. Then, when we need a table view cell to represent a row, instead of creating a standard table view cell, we'll just load the XIB file and use the properties we already defined in our cell class to set the name and color. In addition to using Interface Builder's visual layout, we'll also simplify our code in a few other places. Before proceeding, you might want to make a copy of the Table Cells project in which you can make the changes that follow. As we did previously, exit Xcode, and just compress the project file giving it a suitable name for reference. I called mine Table Cells Orig.zip as a reference to it being our original Table Cells project (see Figure 8-20).

Figure 8-20. *You can compress a project folder to create a version baseline in case you decide to go back to it later*

First, we'll make a few changes to the NameAndColorCell class, in NameAndColorCell.swift. The first step is to mark up the nameLabel and colorLabel properties as outlets, so we can use them in Interface Builder:

```
@IBOutlet var nameLabel: UILabel!
@IBOutlet var colorLabel: UILabel!
```

Now, remember that setup we did in init(style: UITableViewCellStyle, reuseIdentifier: String?), where we created our labels? All that can go. In fact, you should just delete the entire method since all that setup will now be done in Interface Builder. And since we are no longer overriding any of the base class initializers, you can delete the init(coder:) method too.

After all that, you're left with a cell class that's even smaller and cleaner than before. Its only real function now is to shuffle data to the labels. Now we need to re-create the cell and its labels in Interface Builder.

Designing the Table View Cell in Interface Builder

Right-click the Table Cells folder in Xcode and select New File… from the contextual menu. In the left pane of the new file assistant, click User Interface (making sure to pick it in the iOS section, rather than the watchOS, tvOS, or macOS section). From the upper pane, select User Interface and Empty, and then click Next (see Figure 8-21). On the following screen, use the file name NameAndColorCell.xib. Make sure that the main project directory is selected in the file browser and that the Table Cells group is selected in the Group pop-up. Press Create to create a new XIB file.

Figure 8-21. *Create an empty UI file that will become our custom cell XIB*

Next, select NameAndColorCell.xib in the Project Navigator to open the file for editing. Until now, we've been doing all of our GUI editing inside of storyboards, but now we're using a nib file instead. Most things are similar and will look very familiar to you, but there are a few differences. One of the main differences is that, while a storyboard file is centered around scenes that pair up a view controller and a view, inside a nib file there's no such forced pairing. In fact, a nib file often doesn't contain a real controller object at all, just a proxy that is called **File's Owner**. If you open the Document Outline, you'll see it there, right above First Responder.

Look in the library for a Table View Cell and drag one over to the GUI layout area, as shown in Figure 8-22.

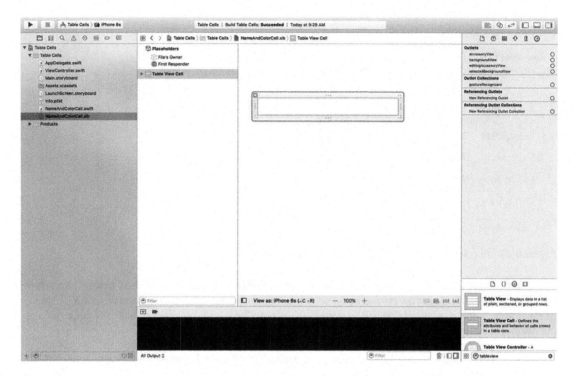

Figure 8-22. *Drag a table view cell from the library onto the canvas*

Next, press ⌥⌘4 to go to the Attributes Inspector (see Figure 8-23). One of the first fields you'll see there is Identifier. That's the reuse identifier that we've been using in our code. If this does not ring a bell, scan back through the chapter and look for CellTableIdentifier. Set the Identifier value to CellTableIdentifier.

Figure 8-23. *The Attributes Inspector for our table view cell*

The idea here is that, when we retrieve a cell for reuse, perhaps because of scrolling a new cell into view, we want to make sure we get the correct cell type. When this particular cell is instantiated from the XIB file, its reuse identifier instance variable will be prepopulated with the name you entered in the Identifier field of the Attributes Inspector—CellTableIdentifier, in this case.

Imagine a scenario where you created a table with a header and then a series of "middle" cells. If you scroll a middle cell into view, it's important that you retrieve a middle cell to reuse and not a header cell. The Identifier field lets you tag the cells appropriately.

Our next step is to edit our table cell's content view. First, select the table cell in the editing area and drag down its lower edge to make the cell a little taller. Keep dragging until the height is 65. Go to the library, drag out four Label controls, and place them in the content view, using Figure 8-24 as a guide. The labels will be too close to the top and bottom for those guidelines to be of much help, but the left guideline and the alignment guidelines should serve their purpose. Note that you can drag out one label, and then Option-drag to create copies, if that approach makes things easier for you.

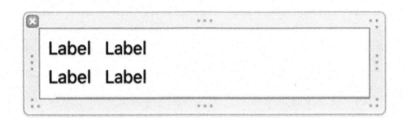

Figure 8-24. *The table view cell's content view, with four labels dragged in*

Next, double-click the upper-left label and change its title to **Name:**, and then change the lower-left label to **Color:**.

Now, select both the Name: and Color: labels and press the small T button in the Attribute Inspector's Font field. This will open a small panel containing a Font pop-up button. Click that and choose Headline as the typeface. If needed, select the two unchanged label fields on the right and drag them a little more to the right to give the design a bit of breathing room, and then resize the other two labels so that you can see the text that you just set. Next, resize the two right-side labels so that they stretch all the way to the right guideline. Figure 8-25 should give you a sense of our final cell content view.

Figure 8-25. *The table view cell's content view with the left label names changed and set to Headline style, which is bold, and with the right labels slightly moved and resized*

As always when we create a new layout, we need to add Auto Layout constraints. The general idea is to pin the left side labels to the left side of the cell and the right side labels to its right. We'll also make sure that the vertical separation between the labels and the top and bottom of the cell and between the labels is preserved. We'll link each left side label to the one on its right. Here are the steps:

1. Click the Name: label, hold down Shift, and then click the Color: label. Click the Pin icon below the nib editor, check the Equal Widths check box, and click Add 1 Constraint. You'll see some Auto Layout warnings appear when you do this—don't worry about them, because we'll fix them as we add more constraints.

2. With the two labels still selected, open the Size Inspector and find the section headed Content Hugging Priority. If you don't see it, try deselecting and reselecting both labels. The values in these fields determine how resistant the labels are to expanding into extra space. We don't want these labels to expand at all in the horizontal, so change the value in the Horizontal field from 251 to 500. Any value greater than 251 will do—we just need it to be greater than the Content Hugging Priority of the two labels on the right, so that any extra horizontal space is allocated to them.

3. Control-drag from the Color: label up to the Name: label, select Vertical Spacing from the pop-up, and press Return.

4. Control-drag diagonally up and left from the Name: label toward the top-left corner of the cell until the cell's background turns completely blue. In the pop-up, hold down Shift and select Leading Space to Container Margin and Top Space to Container Margin, and then press Return.

5. Control-drag diagonally down and left from the Color: label toward the bottom-left corner of the cell until its background is blue. In the pop-up, hold down Shift, select Leading Space to Container Margin and Bottom Space to Container Margin, and then press Return.

6. Control-drag from the Name: label to the label to its right. In the pop-up, hold down Shift, select Horizontal Spacing and Baseline, and then press Return. Control-drag from the top label on the right toward the right edge of the cell until the cell's background turns blue. In the pop-up, select Trailing Space to Container Margin.

7.   Similarly, Control-drag from the Color: label to the label to its right. In the pop-up, hold down Shift, select Horizontal Spacing and Baseline, and then press Return. Control-drag from the bottom label on the right toward the right edge of the cell until the cell's background turns blue. In the pop-up, select Trailing Space to Container Margin and press Return.

8.   Finally, select the Content View icon in the Document Outline and then choose Editor ➤ Resolve Auto Layout Issues ➤ Update Frames from the menu, if it's enabled. The four labels should move to their final locations, as shown in Figure 8-26. If you see something different, delete all of the constraints in the Document Outline and try again.

Figure 8-26. *Final label positioning within our custom cell*

Now, we need to let Interface Builder know that this table view cell isn't just a normal cell, but an instance of our special subclass. Otherwise, we wouldn't be able to connect our outlets to the relevant labels. Select the table view cell by clicking `CellTableIdentifier` in the Document Outline, bring up the Identity Inspector by pressing ⌥⌘**3**, and choose `NameAndColorCell` from the Class control (see Figure 8-27).

Figure 8-27. *Set to our custom class*

Next, switch to the Connections Inspector (⌥⌘**6**), where you'll see the `colorLabel` and `nameLabel` outlets (see Figure 8-28).

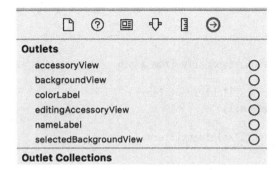

Figure 8-28. Our colorLabel and nameLabel outlets

Drag from the `nameLabel` outlet to the top label on the right in the table cell and from the `colorLabel` outlet to the bottom label on the right, as shown in Figure 8-29.

Figure 8-29. Connecting our name and color label outlets

Using the New Table View Cell

To use the cell we designed, we just need to make a few pretty simple changes to the `viewDidLoad()` method in ViewController.swift, as shown in Listing 8-9.

Listing 8-9. Modifying viewDidLoad() to Use Our New Cell

```
override func viewDidLoad() {
    super.viewDidLoad()
    // Do any additional setup after loading the view, typically from a nib.
    tableView.register(NameAndColorCell.self,
                             forCellReuseIdentifier: cellTableIdentifier)
let xib = UINib(nibName: "NameAndColorCell", bundle: nil)
    tableView.register(xib,
                             forCellReuseIdentifier: cellTableIdentifier)
    tableView.rowHeight = 65
}
```

Just as it can associate a class with a reuse identifier (as you saw in the previous example), a table view can keep track of which nib files are meant to be associated with particular reuse identifiers. This allows you to register cells for each row type you have using classes or nib files once, and dequeueReusableCell (_:forIndexPath:) will always provide a cell ready for use.

That's it. Build and run. Now your two-line table cells are based on your Interface Builder design skills, as shown in Figure 8-30.

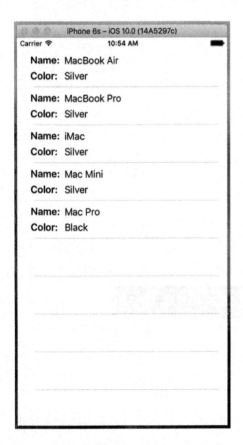

Figure 8-30. *The results of using our custom cell*

Grouped and Indexed Sections

Our next project will explore another fundamental aspect of tables. We're still going to use a single table view—no hierarchies yet—but we'll divide data into sections. Create a new Xcode project using the Single View Application template again, this time calling it **Sections**. As usual, set the Language to Swift and the Devices to Universal.

Building the View

Open the Sections folder and click Main.storyboard to edit the file. Drop a table view onto the View window, as we did before and add the same Auto Layout constraints that we used in the Table Cell example. Then press ⌥⌘6 and connect the dataSource connection to the View Controller icon.

Next, make sure the table view is selected and press ⌥⌘4 to bring up the Attributes Inspector. Change the table view's Style from Plain to Grouped, as shown in Figure 8-31. Save the storyboard.

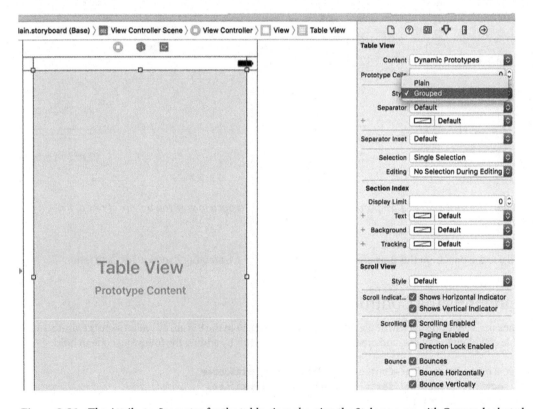

Figure 8-31. *The Attributes Inspector for the table view, showing the Style pop-up with Grouped selected*

Importing the Data

This project needs a fair amount of data. To save you a few hours of typing, we've provided another property list for your tabling pleasure. Grab the file named sortednames.plist from the 08 - Sections Data subfolder in this book's example source code archive and drag it into your project's Sections folder in Xcode.

Once sortednames.plist is added to your project, single-click it just to get a sense of what it looks like, as shown in Figure 8-32. It's a property list that contains a dictionary, with one entry for each letter of the alphabet. Underneath each letter is a list of names that start with that letter.

Figure 8-32. *The sortednames.plist property list file. The letter J is open to give you a sense of one of the dictionaries*

We'll use the data from this property list to feed the table view, creating a section for each letter.

Implementing the Controller

Single-click the ViewController.swift file. Make the class conform to the UITableViewDataSource protocol, add a table cell identifier name, and create a couple of properties by adding the following code in bold:

```
class ViewController: UIViewController, UITableViewDataSource {
    let sectionsTableIdentifier = "SectionsTableIndentifier"
    var names: [String: [String]]!
    var keys: [String]!
```

Select the Main.storyboard file again and then bring up the Assistant Editor. If not shown, use the jump bar to select ViewController.swift file. Control-drag from the table view to the Assistant Editor to create an outlet for the table just below the definition of the keys property:

```
@IBOutlet weak var tableView: UITableView!
```

Now modify the viewDidLoad() method, as shown in Listing 8-10.

Listing 8-10. Our New viewDidLoad Method

```
override func viewDidLoad() {
    super.viewDidLoad()
    // Do any additional setup after loading the view, typically from a nib.
    tableView.register(UITableViewCell.self,
                        forCellReuseIdentifier: sectionsTableIdentifier)

    let path = Bundle.main.path(forResource:
        "sortednames", ofType: "plist")
    let namesDict = NSDictionary(contentsOfFile: path!)
    names = namesDict as! [String: [String]]
    keys = (namesDict!.allKeys as! [String]).sorted()
}
```

Most of this isn't too different from what you've seen before. Earlier, we added property declarations for both a dictionary and an array. The dictionary will hold all of our data, while the array will hold the sections sorted in alphabetical order. In the viewDidLoad() method, we first registered the default table view cell class that should be displayed for each row, using our declared identifier. After that, we created an NSDictionary instance from the property list we added to our project and assigned it to the names property, casting it to the appropriate Swift dictionary type as we do so. Next, we grabbed all the keys from the dictionary and sorted them to give us an ordered array with all the key values in the dictionary in alphabetical order. Remember that our data uses the letters of the alphabet as its keys, so this array will have 26 letters sorted from A to Z. We'll use the array to help us keep track of the sections.

Next, add the code in Listing 8-11 to the end of the ViewController.swift file.

Listing 8-11. Our Table View's Data Source Methods

```
// MARK: Table View Data Source Methods
func numberOfSections(in tableView: UITableView) -> Int {
    return keys.count
}

func tableView(_ tableView: UITableView, numberOfRowsInSection section: Int) -> Int {
    let key = keys[section]
    let nameSection = names[key]!
    return nameSection.count
}

func tableView(_ tableView: UITableView, titleForHeaderInSection section: Int) -> String? {
    return keys[section]
}

func tableView(_ tableView: UITableView, cellForRowAt indexPath: IndexPath) ->
UITableViewCell {
    let cell = tableView.dequeueReusableCell(withIdentifier: sectionsTableIdentifier, for:
    indexPath)
        as UITableViewCell
```

```
    let key = keys[indexPath.section]
    let nameSection = names[key]!
    cell.textLabel?.text = nameSection[indexPath.row]

    return cell
}
```

These are all table data source methods. The first one we added to our class specifies the number of sections. We didn't implement this method in the earlier examples because we were happy with the default setting of 1. This time, we're telling the table view that we have one section for each key in our dictionary:

```
func numberOfSectionsInTableView(tableView: UITableView) -> Int {
    return keys.count
}
```

The next method calculates the number of rows in a specific section. In the previous example, we had only one section, so we just returned the number of rows in our array. This time, we need to break it down by section. We can do this by retrieving the array that corresponds to the section in question and returning the count from that array:

```
func tableView(_ tableView: UITableView, numberOfRowsInSection section: Int) -> Int {
    let key = keys[section]
    let nameSection = names[key]!
    return nameSection.count
}
```

The method tableView(_:titleForHeaderInSection:) allows you to specify an optional header value for each section. We simply return the letter for this group, which is the group's key:

```
func tableView(_ tableView: UITableView, titleForHeaderInSection section: Int) -> String? {
    return keys[section]
}
```

In our tableView(_:cellForRowAtIndexPath:) method, we need to extract both the section key and the names array using the section and row properties from the index path, and then use those to determine which value to use. The section number will tell us which array to pull out of the names dictionary, and then we can use the row to figure out which value from that array to use. Everything else in that method is basically the same as the version in the Table Cells application we built earlier in the chapter.

Build and run the project remembering that we changed the table's Style to Grouped, so we ended up with a grouped table with 26 sections, which should look like Figure 8-33.

Figure 8-33. *A grouped table with multiple sections*

As a contrast, let's change our table view back to the plain style and see what a plain table view with multiple sections looks like. Select Main.storyboard to edit the file in Interface Builder again. Select the table view and use the Attributes Inspector to switch the view to Plain. Save the project, and then build and run it—same data, but a different look, as shown in Figure 8-34.

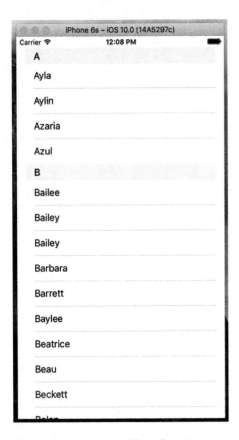

Figure 8-34. *A plain table with sections*

Adding an Index

One problem with our current table is the sheer number of rows. There are 2,000 names in this list. Your finger will get awfully tired looking for Zachariah or Zayne, not to mention Zoie.

One solution to this problem is to add an index down the right side of the table view. Now that we've set our table view style back to Plain, that's relatively easy to do, as shown in Figure 8-35. Add the following method to the bottom of ViewController.swift, and then build and run the app.

```
func sectionIndexTitles(for tableView: UITableView) -> [String]? {
    return keys
}
```

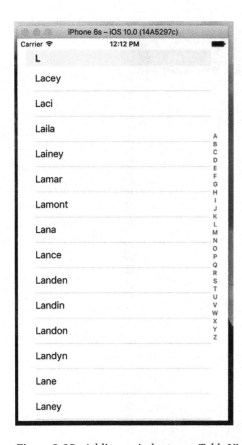

Figure 8-35. *Adding an index to our Table View*

Adding a Search Bar

The index is helpful, but even so, we still have a whole lot of names here. If we want to see whether the name Arabella is in the list, for example, we'll need to scroll for a while even after using the index. It would be nice if we could let the user pare down the list by specifying a search term, making it more user friendly. Well, it's a bit of extra work, but it's not that much. We're going to implement a standard iOS search bar using a search controller, like the one shown on the left in Figure 8-36.

Figure 8-36. *The application with a search bar added to the table*

As the user types into the search bar, the list of names reduces to only those that contain the entered text as a substring. As a bonus, the search bar also allows you to define scope buttons that you can use to qualify the search in some way. We'll add three scope buttons to our search bar—the Short button will limit the search to names that are less than six characters long, the Long button will consider only those names that have at least six characters, and the All button includes all names in the search. The scope buttons appear only when the user is typing into the search bar; you can see them in action on the right of Figure 8-36.

Adding search functionality is quite easy. You need only three things:

- Some data to be searched. In our case, that's the list of names.

- A view controller to display the search results. This view controller temporarily replaces the one that's providing the data. It can choose to display the results in any way, but usually the source data is presented in a table and the results view controller will use another table that looks very similar to it, thus creating the impression that the search is simply filtering the original table. As you'll see, though, that's not actually what's happening.

- A `UISearchController` that provides the search bar and manages the display of the search results in the results view controller.

Let's start by creating the skeleton of the results view controller. We are going to display our search results in a table, so our results view controller needs to contain a table. We could drag a view controller onto the storyboard and add a table view to it as we have done in the earlier examples in the chapter, but let's do something different this time. We're going to use a `UITableViewController`, which is a view controller with an embedded `UITableView` that is preconfigured as both the data source and the delegate for its table view. In the Project Navigator, right-click the Sections group and select New File... from the pop-up menu. In the file template chooser, select Cocoa Touch Class from the iOS Source group and press Next. Name your new class `SearchResultsController` and make it a subclass of `UITableViewController`. Press Next, choose the location for the new file, and let Xcode create it.

Select SearchResultsController.swift in the Project Navigator and make the following change to it:

```
class SearchResultsController: UITableViewController,
        UISearchResultsUpdating {
```

We're going to implement the search logic in this view controller, so we conformed it to the `UISearchResultsUpdating` protocol, which allows us to assign it as a delegate of the `UISearchController` class. As you'll see later, the single method defined by this protocol is called to update the search results as the user types into the search bar.

Since it's going to implement the search operation for us, `SearchResultsController` needs access to the list of names that the main view controller is displaying, so we'll need to give it properties that we can use to pass to it the names dictionary and the list of keys that we're using for display in the main view controller. Let's add these properties to SearchResultsController.swift now. You've probably noticed that this file already contains some incomplete code that provides a partial implementation of the `UITableViewDataSource` protocol and some commented-out code blocks for other methods that `UITableViewController` subclasses frequently need to implement. We're not going to use these in this example, so delete all of the commented-out code and the two `UITableViewDataSource` methods, and then add the following code at the top of the file:

```
class SearchResultsController: UITableViewController, UISearchResultsUpdating {
    let sectionsTableIdentifier = "SectionsTableIdentifier"
    var names:[String: [String]] = [String: [String]]()
    var keys: [String] = []
    var filteredNames: [String] = []
```

We added the `sectionsTableIdentifier` variable to hold the identifier for the table cells in this view controller. We're using the same identifier as we did in the main view controller, although we could have used any name at all. We also added the two properties that will hold the names dictionary and the list of keys that we'll use when searching, and another that will keep a reference to an array that will hold the search results.

Next, add a line of code to the viewDidLoad() method to register our table cell identifier with the results controller's embedded table view:

```
override func viewDidLoad() {
    super.viewDidLoad()
    tableView.register(UITableViewCell.self,
                          forCellReuseIdentifier: sectionsTableIdentifier)
}
```

That's all we need to do in the results view controller for now, so let's switch back to our main view controller for a while and add the search bar to it. Select ViewController.swift in the Project Navigator and add a property to hold a reference to the UISearchController instance that will do most of the hard work for us in this example at the top of the file:

```
class ViewController: UIViewController, UITableViewDataSource {
    let sectionsTableIdentifier = "SectionsTableIndentifier"
    var names: [String: [String]]!
    var keys: [String]!
    @IBOutlet weak var tableView: UITableView!
    var searchController: UISearchController!   // ← add this line
```

Next, modify the viewDidLoad() method to add the search controller, as shown in Listing 8-12.

Listing 8-12. Adding the Search Controller to Our Main viewDidLoad method in ViewController.swift

```
override func viewDidLoad() {
    super.viewDidLoad()
    // Do any additional setup after loading the view, typically from a nib.
    tableView.register(UITableViewCell.self,
                          forCellReuseIdentifier: sectionsTableIdentifier)

    let path = Bundle.main.pathForResource(
        "sortednames", ofType: "plist")
    let namesDict = NSDictionary(contentsOfFile: path!)
    names = namesDict as! [String: [String]]
    keys = (namesDict!.allKeys as! [String]).sorted()

    let resultsController = SearchResultsController()
    resultsController.names = names
    resultsController.keys = keys
    searchController =
        UISearchController(searchResultsController: resultsController)

    let searchBar = searchController.searchBar
    searchBar.scopeButtonTitles = ["All", "Short", "Long"]
    searchBar.placeholder = "Enter a search term"
    searchBar.sizeToFit()
    tableView.tableHeaderView = searchBar
    searchController.searchResultsUpdater = resultsController
}
```

We start by creating the results controller and set its names and keys properties. Then, we create the UISearchController, passing it a reference to our results controller—UISearchController presents this view controller when it has search results to display:

```
let resultsController = SearchResultsController()
resultsController.names = names
resultsController.keys = keys
searchController =
  UISearchController(searchResultsController: resultsController)
```

The next three lines of code get and configure the UISearchBar, which is created by the UISearchController and which we can get from its searchBar property:

```
let searchBar = searchController.searchBar
searchBar.scopeButtonTitles = ["All", "Short", "Long"]
searchBar.placeholder = "Enter a search term"
```

The search bar's scopeButtonTitles property contains the names to be assigned to its scope buttons. By default, there are no scope buttons, but here we install the names of the three buttons discussed earlier in this section. We also set some placeholder text to let the user know what the search bar is for. You can see the placeholder text on the left in Figure 8-36.

So far, we have created the UISearchController but we haven't connected it to our user interface. To do that, we get the search bar and install it as the header view of the table in our main view controller:

```
searchBar.sizeToFit()
tableView.tableHeaderView = searchBar
```

The table's header view is managed automatically by the table view. It always appears before the first row of the first table section. Notice that we use the sizeToFit() method to give the search bar the size that's appropriate for its content. We do this so that it is given the correct height—the width that's set by this method is not important, because the table view will make sure that it stretches the whole width of the table and will resize it automatically if the table changes size (typically because the device has been rotated.)

The final change to viewDidLoad assigns a value to the UISearchController's searchResultsUpdater property, which is of type UISearchResultsUpdating:

```
searchController.searchResultsUpdater = resultsController
```

Each time the user types something into the search bar, UISearchController uses the object stored in its searchResultsUpdater property to update the search results. As mentioned, we are going to handle the search in the SearchResultsController class, which is why we needed to make it conform to the UISearchResultsUpdating protocol.

That's all we need to do to in our main view controller to add the search bar and have the search results displayed. Next, we need to return to SearchResultsController.swift, where we have two tasks to complete—add the code that implements the search and the UITableDataSource methods for the embedded table view.

Let's start with the code for the search. As the user types into the search bar, the UISearchController calls the updateSearchResultsForSearchController() method of its search results updater, which is our SearchResultsController. In this method, we need to get the search text from the search bar and use it to construct a filtered list of names in the filteredNames array. We'll also use the scope buttons to limit the names that we include in the search. Add the following constant definitions at the top of SearchResultsController.swift:

```
class SearchResultsController: UITableViewController, UISearchResultsUpdating {
    private static let longNameSize = 6
    private static let shortNamesButtonIndex = 1
    private static let longNamesButtonIndex = 2
```

Now add code in Listing 8-13 to the end of the file.

Listing 8-13. Our Search Results Code

```
// MARK: UISearchResultsUpdating Conformance
func updateSearchResults(for searchController: UISearchController) {
        if let searchString = searchController.searchBar.text {
            let buttonIndex = searchController.searchBar.selectedScopeButtonIndex
            filteredNames.removeAll(keepingCapacity: true)

            if !searchString.isEmpty {
                let filter: (String) -> Bool = { name in
                    // Filter out long or short names depending on which
                    // scope button is selected.
                    let nameLength = name.characters.count
                    if (buttonIndex == SearchResultsController.shortNamesButtonIndex
                        && nameLength >= SearchResultsController.longNameSize)
                        || (buttonIndex == SearchResultsController.longNamesButtonIndex
                            && nameLength < SearchResultsController.longNameSize) {
                        return false
                    }

                    let range = name.range(of: searchString, options: NSString.
                    CompareOptions.caseInsensitive, range: nil, locale: nil)
                    //                      let range = name.rangeOfString(searchString,
                    //                                              options: NSString.
                    CompareOptions.CaseInsensitiveSearch)
                    return range != nil
                }

                for key in keys {
                    let namesForKey = names[key]!
                    let matches = namesForKey.filter(filter)
                    filteredNames += matches
                }
            }
        }
        tableView.reloadData()
}
```

Let's walk through this code to see what it's doing. First, we get the search string from the search bar and the index of the scope button that's selected, and then we clear the list of filtered names. We only search if the text control returns a string; theoretically, it is possible for the text to be nil, so we bracket the rest of the code in an `if let` construction:

```
if let searchString = searchController.searchBar.text {
    let buttonIndex = searchController.searchBar.selectedScopeButtonIndex
    filteredNames.removeAll(keepingCapacity: true)
```

Next, we check that the search string is not empty—we do not display any matching results for an empty search string:

```
if !searchString.isEmpty {
```

Now we define a closure for matching names against the search string. The closure will be called for each name in the names directory, and will be given a name (as a string) and return true if the value matches and false if there's no match. We first check that the length of the name is consistent with the selected scope button and return false if it isn't:

```
let filter: (String) -> Bool = { name in
    // Filter out long or short names depending on which
    // scope button is selected.
    let nameLength = name.characters.count
    if (buttonIndex == SearchResultsController.shortNamesButtonIndex
        && nameLength >= SearchResultsController.longNameSize)
       || (buttonIndex == SearchResultsController.longNamesButtonIndex
           && nameLength < SearchResultsController.longNameSize) {
        return false
    }
```

If the name passes this test, we look for the search string as a substring of the name. If we find it, then we have a match:

```
let range = name.range(of: searchString, options:
NSString.CompareOptions.caseInsensitive,
        range: nil, locale: nil)
        return range != nil
}
```

That's all the code that we need in the closure to handle the name search. Next, we iterate over all the keys in the names dictionary, each of which corresponds to an array of names (key A maps to the names that start with the letter A, and so on). For each key, we get its array of names and filter it using our closure. This gets us a (possibly empty) filtered array of the names that match, which we add to the filteredNames array:

```
for key in keys {
    let namesForKey = names[key]!
    let matches = namesForKey.filter(filter)
    filteredNames += matches
}
```

In this code, namesForKey is of type [String] and contains the names that correspond to whichever key value we are processing. We use the filter() method of Array to apply our closure to each of the elements in namesToKey. The result is another array containing only the elements that match the filter—that is, only the names should match the search text and the selected scope button, which we then add to filteredNames.

Once all the name arrays have been processed, we have the complete set of matching names in the filteredNames array. Now all we need to do is arrange for them to be displayed in the table in our SearchResultsController. We start by telling the table that it needs to redisplay its content:

```
    }
    tableView.reloadData()
}
```

We need the table view to display one name from the `filteredNames` array in each row. To do that, we implement the methods of the `UITableViewDataSource` protocol in our `SearchResultsController` class. Recall that `SearchResultsController` is a subclass of `UITableViewController`, so it automatically acts as its table's data source. Add the code in Listing 8-14 to SearchResultsController.swift, above the updateSearchResults method.

Listing 8-14. Our Table View Data Source Methods

```
// MARK: Table View Data Source Methods
override func tableView(_ tableView: UITableView, numberOfRowsInSection section: Int) -> Int {
    return filteredNames.count
}

override func tableView(_ tableView: UITableView, cellForRowAt indexPath: IndexPath) ->
UITableViewCell {
    let cell = tableView.dequeueReusableCell(withIdentifier: sectionsTableIdentifier)
    cell!.textLabel?.text = filteredNames[indexPath.row]
    return cell!

}
```

You can now run the app and try filtering the list of names, as shown in Figure 8-37.

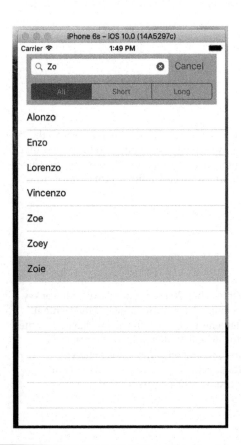

Figure 8-37. *The application with a search bar added to the table*

View Debugging

The UISearchController class does a good job of switching between the two tables in our last example—so good that you might find it hard to believe that there is a switch going on at all. Apart from the fact that you've seen all the code, there are also a couple of visual clues—the search table is a plain table, so you don't see the names grouped like they are in the main table. It also has no section index. If you want even more proof, you can get it by using a neat feature of Xcode called View Debugging, which lets you take snapshots of the view hierarchy of a running application and examine them in the Xcode editor area. This feature works on both the simulator and real devices. You'll probably find it invaluable at some point or another when you're trying to find out why one of your views appears to be missing or is not where you expect it to be.

Let's start by looking at what View Debugging makes of our application when it's showing the full name list. Run the application again and in the Xcode menu bar, select Debug ➤ View Debugging ➤ Capture View Hierarchy. Xcode grabs the view hierarchy from the simulator or device, and displays it, as shown in Figure 8-38.

Figure 8-38. *The view hierarchy of the Sections application*

That probably doesn't look very useful—we can't really see anything more than we could in the simulator. To reveal the view hierarchy, you need to rotate the image of the application so that you can look at it "from the side." To do so, click the mouse in the editor area, somewhere just to the left of the captured image, and drag it to the right. As you do so, the layering of views in the application will reveal itself. If you rotate through about 45 degrees, you'll see something like Figure 8-39.

Figure 8-39. *Examining the application's view hierarchy*

If you click the various views in the stack, you'll see that the jump bar at the top changes to show you the class name of the view that you've clicked and those of all of its ancestor views. Click each of the views from the back to the front to get familiar with how the table is constructed. You should be able to find the view controller's main view, the table view itself, some table view cells, the search bar, the search bar index, and various other views that are part of the table's implementation.

Now let's see what the view hierarchy looks like while we are searching. Xcode pauses your application to let you examine the view snapshot, so first resume execution by clicking Debug ➤ Continue. Now start typing into the application's search bar and capture the view hierarchy again using Debug ➤ View Debugging ➤ Capture View Hierarchy. When the view hierarchy appears, rotate it a little and you'll see something like what's shown in Figure 8-40.

Figure 8-40. *Our View Hierarchy when searching for "Zoe"*

Now it's pretty clear that there are indeed two tables in use. You can see the original table near the bottom of the view stack and above (i.e., to the right of) it, you can see the table view that belongs to the search results view controller. Just behind that, there's a translucent gray view that covers the original table— that's the view that dims the original table when you first start typing in the search bar.

Experiment a little with the buttons at the bottom of the editor area—you can use them to turn on and off the display of Auto Layout constraints, reset the view to the top-down view shown earlier, and zoom in and zoom out. You can also use the slider on the left to change the spacing between views, and use the one on the right to remove layers at the top or bottom of the hierarchy so that you can see what's behind them. View Debugging is a very powerful tool.

Summary

This was a pretty hefty chapter and you've learned a great deal. You should have a very solid understanding of the way that flat tables work. You should know how to customize tables and table view cells, as well as how to configure table views. You also saw how to implement a search bar, which is a vital tool in any iOS application that presents large volumes of data. Finally, you met View Debugging, an extremely useful feature of Xcode. Make sure you understand everything we did in this chapter because we're going to build on it.

We're going to continue working with table views in the next chapter. For example, you'll learn how to use them to present hierarchical data. And you'll see how to create content views that allow the user to edit data selected in a table view, as well as how to present checklists in tables, embed controls in table rows, and delete rows.

CHAPTER 9

■ ■ ■

Adding Navigation Controllers to Table Views

In the previous chapter, we worked through the basics of using table views. In this chapter, we'll go further by adding **navigation controllers**.

Table views and navigation controllers work together, but strictly speaking, a navigation controller doesn't need a table view to function. As a practical matter, however, when using a navigation controller, you normally include at least one or more tables because the strength of the navigation controller lies in the ease with which it handles complex hierarchical data. On the iPhone's small screen, hierarchical data is best presented using a succession of table views.

In this chapter, we'll build an application step by step, just as we did with the Pickers application back in Chapter 7. When we have the basic navigation controller and the root view controller working, we'll start adding more controllers and layers to the hierarchy. Each view controller we create reinforces some aspect of table use or configuration:

- How to drill down from table views into child table views

- How to drill down from table views into content views, where detailed data can be viewed and even edited

- How to use multiple sections within a table view

- How to use edit mode to allow rows to be deleted from a table view

- How to use edit mode to let the user reorder rows within a table view

Navigation Controller Basics

The main tool you'll use to build hierarchical applications, the `UINavigationController`, functions similarly to the `UITabBarController` in that it manages, and swaps in and out, multiple content views. The main difference between the two being the child view controllers of a `UINavigationController` are organized in a stack, which makes it well suited to working with hierarchies.

If you're a previous software developer and understand stacks, you may want to skip over the next section or just scan it. But if you're new to stacks, continue reading. Fortunately, stacks are a pretty easy concept to grasp.

© Molly Maskrey, Kim Topley, David Mark, Fredrik Olsson and Jeff Lamarche 2016
M. Maskrey et al., *Beginning iPhone Development with Swift 3*, DOI 10.1007/978-1-4842-2223-2_9

Stacks

The stack, a commonly used data structure, functions using the principle of "last in, first out." A common Pez dispenser (see Figure 9-1) provides a great example of a stack. Ever try to load one? According to the little instruction sheet that comes with each and every Pez dispenser, there are a few easy steps. First, unwrap the pack of Pez candy. Second, open the dispenser by tipping its head straight back. Third, grab the stack of candy, holding it firmly between your pointer finger and thumb, and insert the column into the open dispenser.

Figure 9-1. *A Pez dispenser represents a simple implementation of a stack*

Remember that we said a stack was last in, first out? That also means first in, last out. The first piece of candy you push into the dispenser will be the last piece that pops out. The last piece of candy you push in becomes be the first piece you pop out. A computer stack follows the same rules:

- When you add an object to a stack, it's called a **push**. You push an object onto the stack.

- The first object you push onto the stack is called the **base** of the stack.

- The object you most recently pushed onto the stack is called the top of the stack (at least until it is replaced by the next object you push onto the stack).

- When you remove an object from the stack, it's called a **pop**. When you pop an object off the stack, it's always the last one you pushed onto the stack. Conversely, the first object you push onto the stack will always be the last one you pop off the stack.

A Stack of Controllers

Navigation controllers maintain a stack of view controllers and when you design your controller, you must specify the very first view the user sees. As discussed previously, we call that view's controller the **root view controller**, or just **root controller**, which becomes the base of the navigation controller's stack. As the user selects a new view to display, another controller gets pushed onto the stack, and its view appears. We refer to these new view controllers as **subcontrollers.** In this chapter's application, Fonts, we include a navigation controller and several subcontrollers.

In Figure 9-2, notice the title centered in the navigation bar and the back button on the left side of the navigation bar. The title of the navigation bar gets populated with the title property of the top view controller in the navigation controller's stack, and the title of the back button displays the name of the previous view controller. The back button acts similar to a web browser's back button. When the user taps that button, the current view controller gets popped off the stack, and the previous view becomes the current view.

Back Button Title

Figure 9-2. The Settings application uses a navigation controller. The back button at the upper left pops the current view controller off the stack, returning you to the previous level of the hierarchy. The title of the current content view controller is also displayed

This design pattern allows us to build complex hierarchical applications iteratively so we don't need to know the entire structure to get everything up and running. Each controller only needs to know about its child controllers, so it can push the appropriate new controller object onto the stack when the user makes a selection. We can build up a large application from many small pieces this way, which we'll be doing in this chapter.

The navigation controller provides the core to many iPhone apps; however, when it comes to iPad apps, the navigation controller plays a more marginal role. The Mail app depicts a typical example featuring a hierarchical navigation controller to let users navigate among all their mail servers, folders, and messages. In the iPad version of Mail, the navigation controller never fills the screen, but appears either as a sidebar or a temporary view covering part of the main view. We'll work with that in Chapter 11.

Fonts: A Simple Font Browser

The application we're about to build shows how to do most of the common tasks associated with displaying a hierarchy of data. When the application launches, we're presented with a list of all the font families that are included with iOS, as shown in Figure 9-3. A font family groups closely related fonts, or fonts that are stylistic variations of one another such as Helvetica, Helvetica-Bold, Helvetic-Oblique, and other variations all included in the Helvetica font family.

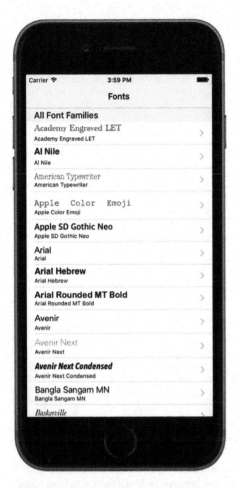

Figure 9-3. *In our project, the root view controller displays accessory icons on the right side of each row in the view. This particular type of accessory icon is called a disclosure indicator, letting us know that touching that row drills down to another view of some kind*

Selecting any row in this top-level view will push a new view controller onto the navigation controller's stack. The small images on the far right of each row are called **accessory icons**. This particular accessory icon (the gray arrow) displays a disclosure indicator letting the user know that touching that row drills down to another view.

Subcontrollers of Our Fonts App

Before we actually start working on this chapter's project, let's examine each of the subcontrollers that we'll be using.

The Font List Controller

Touching any row of the table shown in Figure 9-3 will bring up the child view shown in Figure 9-4.

Figure 9-4. *The first of the Fonts application's subcontrollers implements a table in which each row contains a detail disclosure button*

The accessory icon to the right of each row in Figure 9-4, called a **detail disclosure**, functions differently than the arrow we saw previously. Unlike the **disclosure indicator**, the detail disclosure button provides not just an icon but acts as a control that the user can tap independently. This means that you can have two different options available for a given row: one action triggered when the user selects the row, and another that is triggered when the user taps the icon. Tapping the small info button within this accessory should allow the user to view, and perhaps edit, more detailed information about the current row. Meanwhile, the presence of the right-pointing arrow should indicate to the user that there is some deeper navigation to be found by tapping elsewhere in the row.

The Font Sizes View Controller

Touching any row of the table shown in Figure 9-4 brings up the child view shown in Figure 9-5.

Figure 9-5. *Located one layer deeper than the Font List View Controller, the Font Sizes View Controller shows multiple sizes of the chosen font, one per row*

Using Disclosure Indicators and Detail Disclosure

Some guidelines for when to use each of these buttons:

- To offer a single choice for a row tap, don't use an accessory icon if a row tap will only lead to a more detailed view of that row.

- Mark the row with a disclosure indicator (right-pointing arrow) if a row tap leads to a new view listing more items (not a detail view).

- To offer two choices for a row, mark the row with either a detail disclosure indicator or a detail button. This allows the user to tap the row for a new view or the disclosure button for more details.

The Font Info View Controller

Our final application subcontroller—the only one not a table view—appears(see Figure 9-6) when you tap on the info icon for any row in the Font List View Controller shown in Figure 9-2.

Figure 9-6. *The final view controller in the Fonts application allows you to view the chosen font at any size you want*

This view lets the user drag a slider to adjust the size of the displayed font. It also includes a switch that allows the user to specify whether this font should be listed among the user's favorites. If any fonts are set as favorites, they appear within a separate group in the root view controller.

The Fonts Application's Skeleton

Xcode offers a perfectly good template for creating navigation-based applications, and you will likely use it much of the time when you need to create hierarchical applications. However, we're not going to use that template today. Instead, we'll construct our navigation-based application from the ground up, so we get a feel for how everything fits together. We'll also walk through it one piece at a time, so it should be easy to keep up.

In Xcode, press ⌘⇧N to create a new project. Select Single View Application from the iOS template list, and then click Next to continue. Set Fonts as the Product Name, Swift as the Language, and select Universal for Devices. Make sure that Use Core Data is not checked, click Next, and choose the location to save your project.

Setting Up the Navigation Controller

We'll now create the basic navigation structure for our application. At the core of this will be a UINavigationController, managing the stack of view controllers that a user can navigate between, and a UITableViewController displaying the top-level list of rows we're going to show. As it turns out, Interface Builder makes this easy to create.

Select Main.storyboard. The template has created a basic view controller for us, but we need to use a UINavigationController instead, so select the view controller in either the editor area or the Document Outline, and delete it to leave the storyboard empty. Now use the Object Library to search for UINavigationController and drag an instance into the editing area. You'll see that you actually get two scenes instead of one, similar to what you saw when creating a tab view controller in Chapter 7. On the left is the UINavigationController itself. Select this controller, open the Attributes Inspector, and check Is Initial View Controller in the View Controller section to make this the controller that appears when the application is launched.

The UINavigationController has a connection wired to the second scene, which contains a UITableViewController. You'll see that the table has the title Root View Controller. Click the Root View Controller icon in the Document Outline (the one below the Table View, not the one above it), open the Attributes Inspector, and then set the title to Fonts. If you don't see the title change in the storyboard, you chose the wrong Root View Controller icon.

By setting it up this way, we get the view created by the navigation controller, a composite view that contains a combination of two things: the navigation bar at the top of the screen (which usually contains some sort of title and often a back button of some kind on the left) and the content of whatever the navigation controller's current view controller wants to display. In our case, the lower part of the display will be filled with the table view that was created alongside the navigation controller.

We'll see more about how to control what the navigation controller shows in the navigation bar as we go forward. You'll also gain an understanding of how the navigation controller shifts focus from one subordinate view controller to another. For now, we've laid enough groundwork so that we can start defining what our custom view controllers are going to do.

At this point, the application skeleton is essentially complete. You'll see a warning about setting a reuse identifier for a prototype table cell, but we can ignore that for now. Save all your files, and then build and run the app. If all is well, the application should launch, and a navigation bar with the title Fonts should appear. You haven't given the table view any information about what to show yet, so no rows will display at this point, as shown in Figure 9-7.

Figure 9-7. *Our application skeleton without any data*

Keeping Track of Favorite Fonts

At several points in this application, we're going to let the user maintain a list of favorite fonts by letting them add chosen fonts, view a whole list of already-chosen favorites, and remove fonts from the list. In order to manage this list in a consistent way, we're going to make a new class that will hang onto an array of favorites and store them in the user's preference for this application. You'll learn a lot more about user preferences in Chapter 12, but here we'll just touch on some basics.

Start by creating a new class. Select the Fonts folder in the Project Navigator and press ⌘N to bring up the new file assistant. Select Swift File from the iOS Source section and then click Next. On the following screen, name the new file FavoritesList.swift and press Create. Select the new file in the Project Navigator and make the additions shown in Listing 9-1.

Listing 9-1. Our FavoritesList Class File

```
import Foundation
import UIKit

class FavoritesList {
    static let sharedFavoritesList = FavoritesList()
    private(set) var favorites:[String]

    init() {
        let defaults = UserDefaults.standard
        let storedFavorites = defaults.object(forKey: "favorites") as? [String]
        favorites = storedFavorites != nil ? storedFavorites! : []
    }

    func addFavorite(fontName: String) {
        if !favorites.contains(fontName) {
            favorites.append(fontName)
            saveFavorites()
        }
    }

    func removeFavorite(fontName: String) {
        if let index = favorites.index(of: fontName) {
            favorites.remove(at: index)
            saveFavorites()
        }
    }

    private func saveFavorites() {
        let defaults = UserDefaults.standard
        defaults.set(favorites, forKey: "favorites")
        defaults.synchronize()
    }
}
```

In the preceding snippet, we declared the API for our new class. For starters, we declared a class property called sharedFavoritesList that returns an instance of this class. No matter how many times this method is called, the same instance will always be returned. The idea is that FavoritesList should work as a singleton—instead of using multiple instances, we'll just use one instance throughout the application.

Next, we declared a property to hold the names of our favorite fonts. Pay close attention to the definition of this array:

```
private(set) var favorites:[String]
```

The private(set) qualifier means that the array can be read by code outside the class, but only code in the class implementation can modify it. That's exactly what we want, because we need users of our class to be able to read the favorites list:

```
let favorites = FavoritesList.sharedFavoritesList.favorites  // Read-access is OK
```

But we don't want either of these to be allowed:

```
FavoritesList.sharedFavoritesList.favorites = []     // Not allowed
FavoritesList.sharedFavoritesList.favorites.append("Comic Sans MS")    // Not allowed
```

The class initializer is responsible for setting the initial content of the `favorites` array:

```
init() {
    let defaults = UserDefaults.standard
    let storedFavorites = defaults.object(forKey: "favorites") as? [String]
    favorites = storedFavorites != nil ? storedFavorites! : []
}
```

As you'll see shortly, any time we add something to or remove something from this array, we save its contents to the application's user defaults (which is discussed in detail in Chapter 12) so that the content of the list is preserved over application restarts. In the initializer, we check whether we have a stored favorites list, and if so, we use it to initialize the `favorites` property. If not, we simply make it empty.

The remaining three methods deal with adding to and removing from the `favorites` array. The implementations should be self-explanatory. Note that the first two methods both call `saveFavorites()`, which saves the updated value to the user defaults under the same key (favorites) as the initializer uses to read it. You'll learn more about how this works in Chapter 12; but for now, it's enough to know that the `UserDefaults` (`NSUserDefaults`) object that we use here acts like a sort of persistent dictionary, and anything that we put in there will be available the next time we ask for it, even if the application has been stopped and restarted.

■ **Note**   In Xcode 8 Apple made many of the former NS- objects more user-friendly for use in Swift; for example `NSUserDefaults` is now `UserDefaults`.

Creating the Root View Controller

Let's get started developing our first view controller. In the previous chapter, we used simple arrays of strings to populate our table rows. We're going to do something similar here, but this time we'll use the `UIFont` class to get a list of font families, and then use the names of those font families to populate each row. We'll also use the fonts themselves to display the font names, so that each row will contain a small preview of what the font family contains.

It's time to create the first controller class for this application. The template created a view controller for us, but its name—ViewController—isn't very useful, because there are going to be several view controllers in this application. So first select ViewController.swift in the Project Navigator and press Delete to delete it and move it to the trash. Next, select the Fonts folder in the Project Navigator and press ⌘N to bring up the new file assistant. Select Cocoa Touch Class from the iOS Source section and then click Next. On the following screen, name the new class RootViewController and enter **UITableViewController** for Subclass of. Click Next and then click Create to create the new class. In the Project Navigator, select RootViewController. swift and add the **bold** lines in the snippet that follows to add a few properties:

```
class RootViewController: UITableViewController {
    private var familyNames: [String]!
    private var cellPointSize: CGFloat!
    private var favoritesList: FavoritesList!
    private static let familyCell = "FamilyName"
    private static let favoritesCell = "Favorites"
```

We'll assign values to the first three of those properties from the onset, and then use them at various times while this class is in use. The `familyNames` array will contain a list of all the font families we're going to display; the `cellPointSize` property will contain the font size that we want to use in all of our table view cells; and `favoritesList` will contain a pointer to the `FavoritesList` singleton. The last two are constants that represent the cell identifiers that we will use for the table view cells in this controller.

Set up all of this class's properties by adding the bold code shown here to the `viewDidLoad()`, as shown in Listing 9-2.

Listing 9-2. The viewDidLoad Method for the RootViewController.swift File

```
override func viewDidLoad() {
    super.viewDidLoad()

    familyNames = (UIFont.familyNames() as [String]).sorted()
    let preferredTableViewFont =
        UIFont.preferredFont(forTextStyle: UIFontTextStyleHeadline)
    cellPointSize = preferredTableViewFont.pointSize
    favoritesList = FavoritesList.sharedFavoritesList
    tableView.estimatedRowHeight = cellPointSize
}
```

In Listing 9-2, we populated `familyNames` by asking the `UIFont` class for all known family names, and then sorting the resulting array. We then used `UIFont` once again to ask for the preferred font for use in a headline. We did this using a piece of functionality added in iOS 7, which uses a font size setting that can be configured by the user in the Settings app. This dynamic font sizing lets the user set an overall font scaling for system-wide use. Here, we used that font's `pointSize` property to establish a baseline font size that we'll use elsewhere in this view controller. Finally, we grabbed the singleton favorites list object and we set the `estimatedRowHeight` property of the table view to indicate roughly how tall our table's rows will be. As it turns out, the table will calculate the correct size for each cell based on the cell's content, provided that we set this property, leave the table view's `rowHeight` property set to its default value of `UITableViewAutomaticDimension,` and use default table view cells (or use auto layout to construct custom table view cells).

Before we go on, let's delete the `didReceiveMemoryWarning()` method, as well as all of the table view delegate or data source methods that the template gave us—we're not going to use any of them in this class.

The idea behind this view controller is to show two sections. The first section is a list of all available font families, each of which leads to a list of all the fonts in the family. The second section is for favorites, and contains just a single entry that will lead the user to a list of their favorite fonts. However, if the user has no favorites (for example, when the app is launched for the first time), we'd rather not show that second section at all, since it would just lead the user to an empty list. So, we'll have to do a few things throughout the rest of this class to compensate for this eventuality. The first of these is to implement this method, which is called just before the root view controller's view appears on the screen:

```
override func viewWillAppear(_ animated: Bool) {
    super.viewWillAppear(animated)
    tableView.reloadData()
}
```

The reason for this is that there may be times when the set of things we're going to display might change from one viewing to the next. For example, the user may start with no favorites, but then drill down, view a font, set it as a favorite, and then come back out to the root view. At that time, we need to reload the table view, so that the second section will appear.

Next, we're going to implement a sort of utility method for use within this class. At a couple of points, while configuring the table view via its data source methods, we'll need to be able to figure out which font we want to display in a cell. We put that functionality into a method of its own, as shown in Listing 9-3.

Listing 9-3. Figuring out Which Font We Want to Display

```
func fontForDisplay(atIndexPath indexPath: NSIndexPath) -> UIFont? {
    if indexPath.section == 0 {
        let familyName = familyNames[indexPath.row]
        let fontName = UIFont.fontNames(forFamilyName: familyName).first
        return fontName != nil ?
            UIFont(name: fontName!, size: cellPointSize) : nil
    } else {
        return nil
    }
}
```

This method uses the `UIFont` class to find all the font names for the given family name, and then grab the first font name within that family. We don't necessarily know that the first named font in a family is the best one to represent the whole family, but it's as good a guess as any. If the family has no font names, we return `nil`.

Now, let's move on to the primary code in this view controller: the table view data source methods. First up, let's look at the number of sections:

```
override func numberOfSections(in tableView: UITableView) -> Int {
    return favoritesList.favorites.isEmpty ? 1 : 2
}
```

We use the favorites list to determine whether we want to show the second section. Next, we tackle the number of rows in each section:

```
override func tableView(_ tableView: UITableView, numberOfRowsInSection section: Int) -> Int {
    // Return the number of rows in the section.
    return section == 0 ? familyNames.count : 1
}
```

That one's also pretty simple. We just use the section number to determine whether the section is showing all family names, or a single cell linking to the list of favorites. Now let's define one other method, an optional method in the `UITableViewDataSource` protocol that lets us specify the title for each of our sections:

```
override func tableView(_ tableView: UITableView, titleForHeaderInSection section: Int) ->
String? {
    return section == 0 ? "All Font Families" : "My Favorite Fonts"
}
```

This is another straightforward method. It uses the section number to determine which header title to use. The final core method that every table view data source must implement is the one for configuring each cell, and ours looks like Listing 9-4.

Listing 9-4. Our cellForRow (atIndexPath:) Function

```
override func tableView(_ tableView: UITableView, cellForRowAt indexPath: IndexPath) ->
UITableViewCell {
    if indexPath.section == 0 {
        // The font names list
```

```
        let cell = tableView.dequeueReusableCell(withIdentifier: RootViewController.
        familyCell, for: indexPath)
        cell.textLabel?.font = fontForDisplay(atIndexPath: indexPath)
        cell.textLabel?.text = familyNames[indexPath.row]
        cell.detailTextLabel?.text = familyNames[indexPath.row]
        return cell
    } else {
        // The favorites list
        return tableView.dequeueReusableCell(withIdentifier: RootViewController.
        favoritesCell, for: indexPath)
    }
}
```

When we created this class, we defined two different cell identifiers that we use to load two different cell prototypes from the storyboard (much like we loaded a table cell from a nib file in Chapter 8). We haven't configured those cell prototypes yet, but we will soon. Next, we use the section number to determine which of those cells we want to show for the current indexPath. If the cell is meant to contain a font family name, then we put the family name into both its textLabel and its detailTextLabel. We also use a font from the family (the one we get from the fontForDisplay(atIndexPath:) method that we added earlier) within the text label, so that we'll see the font family name shown in the font itself, as well as a smaller version in the standard system font.

Initial Storyboard Setup

Now that we have a view controller that we think should show something, let's configure the storyboard to make things happen. Select Main.storyboard in the Project Navigator. You'll see the navigation controller and the table view controller that we added earlier. The first thing we need to configure is the table view controller. By default, the controller's class is set to UITableViewController. We need to change that to our root view controller class. In the Fonts Scene in the Document Outline, select the yellow icon labeled Fonts, and then use the Identity Inspector to change the view controller's Class to RootViewController.

The other configuration we'll need to do right now is to set up a pair of prototype cells to match the cell identifiers we used in our code. From the start, the table view has a single prototype cell. Select it and press ⌘D to duplicate it, and you'll see that you now have two cells. Select the first one, and then use the Attributes Inspector to set its Style to Subtitle, its Identifier to FamilyName, and its Accessory to Disclosure Indicator. Next, select the second prototype cell, and then set its Style to Basic, its Identifier to Favorites, and its Accessory to Disclosure Indicator. Also, double-click the title shown in the cell itself and change the text from Title to Favorites.

■ **Tip** The prototype cells that we are using in this example both have standard table view cell styles. If you set the Style to Custom, you can design the layout of the cell right in the cell prototype, just like you did when you created a cell in a nib file in Chapter 8.

Now build and run this app, and you should see a nice list of fonts. Scroll around a bit and you'll see that not all of the fonts produce text of the same height, as shown in Figure 9-8. All of the cells are tall enough to contain their content. If you've forgotten why this works, refer back to the discussion of the code we added to the viewDidLoad() method earlier in this section.

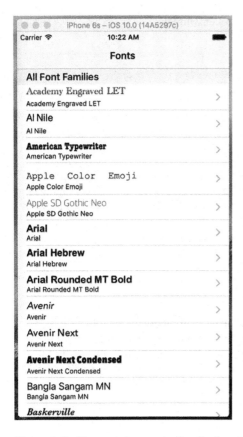

Figure 9-8. *The root view controller displays the installed font families*

First Subcontroller: The Font List View

Our app currently just shows a list of font families, and nothing more. We want to add the ability for a user to touch a font family and see all the fonts it contains, so let's make a new view controller that can manage a list of fonts. Create a new Cocoa Touch class called FontListViewController as a subclass of UITableViewController. In the Project Navigator, select FontListViewController.swift, and add the following properties:

```
class FontListViewController: UITableViewController {
    var fontNames: [String] = []
    var showsFavorites:Bool = false
    private var cellPointSize: CGFloat!
    private static let cellIdentifier = "FontName"
```

The fontNames property is what we'll use to tell this view controller what to display. We also created a showsFavorites property that we'll use to let this view controller know if it's showing the list of favorites instead of just a list of fonts in a family, since this will be useful later on. We'll use the cellPointSize property to hold the preferred display size for displaying each font, once again using UIFont to find the preferred size. Finally, cellIdentifier is the identifier used for the table view cells in this controller.

To initialize the cellPointSize property and set the table view's estimated row height, add the code in Listing 9-5 to the viewDidLoad() method.

Listing 9-5. Our viewDidLoad Method for the FontListViewController.swift File

```
override func viewDidLoad() {
    super.viewDidLoad()

    let preferredTableViewFont =
        UIFont.preferredFont(forTextStyle: UIFontTextStyleHeadline)
    cellPointSize = preferredTableViewFont.pointSize
    tableView.estimatedRowHeight = cellPointSize
}
```

The next thing we want to do is create a little utility method for choosing the font to be shown in each row, similar to what we have in RootViewController. Here it's a bit different, though. Instead of holding onto a list of font families in this view controller we're holding onto a list of font names in the fontNames property. We'll use the UIFont class to get each named font, like this:

```
func fontForDisplay(atIndexPath indexPath: NSIndexPath) -> UIFont {
    let fontName = fontNames[indexPath.row]
    return UIFont(name: fontName, size: cellPointSize)!
}
```

Now it's time for a small addition in the form of a viewWillAppear() implementation. In RootViewController, we implemented this method in case the list of favorites might change, requiring a refresh. The same applies here. This view controller might be showing the list of favorites, and the user might switch to another view controller, change a favorite (we'll get there later), and then come back here. We need to reload the table view then, and this method takes care of that, as shown in Listing 9-6.

Listing 9-6. Refreshing the View in Case Something Changes

```
override func viewWillAppear(_ animated: Bool) {
    super.viewWillAppear(animated)
    if showsFavorites {
        fontNames = FavoritesList.sharedFavoritesList.favorites
        tableView.reloadData()
    }
}
```

The basic idea is that this view controller, in normal operation, is passed a list of font names before it displays, and that the list stays the same the whole time this view controller is around. In one particular case (which we'll see later), this view controller needs to reload its font list.

Moving on, we can delete the numberOfSectionsInTableView() method entirely. We'll only have one section here, and just skipping that method is the equivalent of implementing it and returning 1. Next, we implement the two other main data source methods, like Listing 9-7.

Listing 9-7. Our dataSource Methods

```
override func tableView(_ tableView: UITableView, numberOfRowsInSection section: Int) -> Int {
    // Return the number of rows in the section.
    return fontNames.count
}
```

```
override func tableView(_ tableView: UITableView, cellForRowAt indexPath: IndexPath) ->
UITableViewCell {

    let cell = tableView.dequeueReusableCell(
        withIdentifier: FontListViewController.cellIdentifier,
        for: indexPath)

  cell.textLabel?.font = fontForDisplay(atIndexPath: indexPath)
  cell.textLabel?.text = fontNames[indexPath.row]
  cell.detailTextLabel?.text = fontNames[indexPath.row]

  return cell
}
```

Neither of these methods really needs any explanation, because they are similar to what we used in RootViewController, but even simpler.

We'll add some more to this class later, but first we want to see it in action. To make this happen, we'll need to configure the storyboard some more, and then make some modifications to RootViewController. Switch over to Main.storyboard to get started.

Creating the Font List Storyboard

The storyboard currently contains a table view controller that displays the list of font families, embedded inside a navigation controller. We need to add one new layer of depth to incorporate the view controller that will display the fonts for a given family. Find a Table View Controller in the Object Library and drag one out into the editing area, to the right of the existing table view controller. Select the new table view controller and use the Identity Inspector to set its class to FontListViewController. Select the prototype cell in the table view and open the Attributes Inspector to make some adjustments. Change its Style to Subtitle, its Identifier to FontName, and its Accessory to Detail Disclosure. Using the detail disclosure accessory will let rows of this type respond to two kinds of taps so that users can trigger two different actions, depending on whether they tap the accessory or any other part of the row.

One way to make a user action in one view controller cause the instantiation and display of another view controller is to create a **segue** connecting the two of them. This is probably an unfamiliar word for many people, so let's get this out of the way: segue essentially means "transition." It is sometimes used by writers and filmmakers to describe making a smooth movement from one paragraph or scene to the next. Apple could have been a little straightforward and just called it a transition; but since that word appears elsewhere in the UIKit APIs, maybe Apple decided to use a distinct term to avoid confusion. I should also mention here that the word "segue" is pronounced exactly the same as the name of the Segway personal transportation product (and now you know why the Segway is called what it is).

Often, segues are created entirely within Interface Builder. The idea is that an action in one scene can trigger a segue to load and display another scene. If you're using a navigation controller, the segue can push the next controller onto the navigation stack automatically. We'll be using this functionality in our app, starting right now.

In order for the cells in the root view controller to make the Font List View Controller appear, you need to create a couple of segues connecting the two scenes. This is done simply by Control-dragging from the first of the two prototype cells in the Fonts scene over to the new scene; you'll see the entire scene highlight when you drag over it, indicating it's ready to connect, as shown in Figure 9-9.

Figure 9-9. *Creating a show segue from the font list controller to the font names controller*

Release the mouse button and select Show from the Selection Segue section of the pop-up menu that appears. Now do the same for the other prototype cell. Creating these segues means that as soon as the user taps any of these cells, the view controller at the other end of the connection will be allocated and made ready.

Making the Root View Controller Prepare for Segues

Save your changes and switch back to RootViewController.swift. Note that we're not talking about our latest class, FontListViewController, but instead its "parent" controller. This is the place where you'll need to respond to the user's touches in the root table view by preparing the new FontListViewController (specified by one of the segues you just created) for display and by passing it the values it needs to display.

The actual preparation of the new view controller is done using the prepareForSegue(_:sender:) method. Add an implementation of this method, as shown in Listing 9-8.

Listing 9-8. Preparing the New View Controller for Display

```swift
// MARK: - Navigation

override func prepare(for segue: UIStoryboardSegue, sender: AnyObject?) {
    // Get the new view controller using [segue destinationViewController].
    // Pass the selected object to the new view controller.
    let indexPath = tableView.indexPath(for: sender as! UITableViewCell)!
    let listVC = segue.destinationViewController as! FontListViewController

    if indexPath.section == 0 {
        // Font names list
        let familyName = familyNames[indexPath.row]
```

```
        listVC.fontNames = (UIFont.fontNames(forFamilyName: familyName) as [String]).
        sorted()
        listVC.navigationItem.title = familyName
        listVC.showsFavorites = false
    } else {
        // Favorites list
        listVC.fontNames = favoritesList.favorites
        listVC.navigationItem.title = "Favorites"
        listVC.showsFavorites = true
    }
}
```

This method uses the sender (the UITableViewCell that was tapped) to determine which row was tapped and asks the segue for its destinationViewController, which is the FontListViewController instance that is about to be displayed. We then pass some values along to the new view controller, depending on whether the user tapped a font family (section 0) or the favorites cell (section 1). As well as setting the custom properties for the target view controller, we also access the controller's navigationItem property in order to set its title. The navigationItem property is an instance of UINavigationItem, which is a UIKit class that contains information about what should be displayed in the navigation bar for any given view controller.

Now run the app. You'll see that touching the name of any font family shows you a list of all the individual fonts it contains (see Figure 9-10). Furthermore, you can tap the Fonts label in the header of the fonts list navigation controller to go back to its parent controller to select another font.

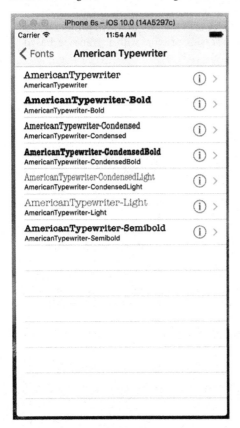

Figure 9-10. *Showing the individual fonts contained in a font family*

Creating the Font Sizes View Controller

What you'll notice, however, is that the app currently doesn't let you go any further. Figures 9-4 and 9-5 show additional screens that let you view a chosen font in various ways; we're not there yet. But soon, we will be! Let's create the view shown in Figure 9-4, which shows multiple font sizes at once. Using the same steps as you used to create FontListViewController, add a new view controller that subclasses UITableViewController, and name it FontSizesViewController. The only parameter this class will need from its parent controller is a font. We'll also need a couple of private properties.

For starters, switch over to FontSizesViewController.swift and go ahead and delete the didReceiveMemoryWarning and numberOfSectionsInTableView: methods, along with all of the commented-out methods at the bottom. Again, you're not going to need any of those. Now add the following properties at the top of the class definition:

```
import UIKit

class FontSizesViewController: UITableViewController {
    var font: UIFont!
    private static let pointSizes: [CGFloat] = [
            9, 10, 11, 12, 13, 14, 18, 24, 36, 48, 64, 72, 96, 144
    ]
    private static let cellIdentifier = "FontNameAndSize"
```

The font property will be set by FontListViewController before it pushes this view controller onto the navigation controller's stack. The pointSizes property is an array of point sizes in which the font will be displayed. We also need the following utility method, which gets a version of a font with a given size, based on a table row index:

```
func fontForDisplay(atIndexPath indexPath: NSIndexPath) -> UIFont {
    let pointSize = FontSizesViewController.pointSizes[indexPath.row]
    return font.withSize(pointSize)
}
```

We also need to set the table view's estimatedRowHeight property so that the table will automatically calculate the correct row heights for each row based on what it contains. To do that, add the following line to the viewDidLoad() method:

tableView.estimatedRowHeight = FontSizesViewController.pointSizes[0]

It doesn't actually matter what value we assign to this property, so we arbitrarily choose to use the smallest font point size that the table will need to display.

For this view controller, we're going to skip the method that lets us specify the number of sections to display, since we're going to just use the default number (1). However, we must implement the methods for specifying the number of rows and the content of each cell. Those two methods are shown in Listing 9-9.

Listing 9-9. The dataSource Methods for the FontSizeViewController Table View

```
// MARK: - Table view data source

override func tableView(_ tableView: UITableView, numberOfRowsInSection section: Int) -> Int {
    return FontSizesViewController.pointSizes.count
}
```

```
override func tableView(_ tableView: UITableView, cellForRowAt indexPath: IndexPath) ->
UITableViewCell {
    let cell = tableView.dequeueReusableCell(
        withIdentifier: FontSizesViewController.cellIdentifier,
        for: indexPath)

    cell.textLabel?.font = fontForDisplay(atIndexPath: indexPath)
    cell.textLabel?.text = font.fontName
    cell.detailTextLabel?.text =
        "\(FontSizesViewController.pointSizes[indexPath.row]) point"

    return cell
}
```

There's really nothing in any of these methods we haven't seen before, so let's move on to setting up the Storyboard for our user interface.

Creating the Font Sizes View Controller Storyboard

Go back to Main.storyboard and drag another Table View Controller into the editing area. Use the Identity Inspector to set its class to FontSizesViewController. You'll need to make a segue connection from its parent, the FontListViewController. So find that controller and Control-drag from its prototype cell to the newest view controller, and then select Show from the Selection Segue section of the pop-up menu that appears. Next, select the prototype cell in the new scene you just added, and then use the Attributes Inspector to set its Style to Subtitle and its Identifier to FontNameAndSize.

Implementing the Font Sizes View Controller Prepare for Segue

Now, just like the last time we extended our storyboard's navigation hierarchy, we need to jump up to the parent controller so that it can configure its child. That means we need to go to FontListViewController.swift and implement the prepareForSegue(_:sender:) method, as shown in Listing 9-10.

Listing 9-10. The FontListViewsController's preparedForSeque Method

```
// MARK: - Navigation

override func prepare(for segue: UIStoryboardSegue, sender: AnyObject?) {
    // Get the new view controller using [segue destinationViewController].
    // Pass the selected object to the new view controller.
    let tableViewCell = sender as! UITableViewCell
    let indexPath = tableView.indexPath(for: tableViewCell)!
    let font = fontForDisplay(atIndexPath: indexPath)

    let sizesVC = segue.destinationViewController as! FontSizesViewController
    sizesVC.title = font.fontName
    sizesVC.font = font
}
```

That probably all looks pretty familiar by now, so we won't dwell on it further.

Run the app, select a font family, select a font (by tapping a row anywhere except the accessory on the right), and you'll now see the multisize listing shown in Figure 9-11.

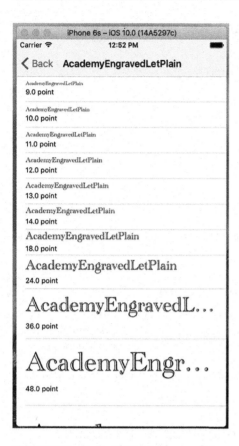

Figure 9-11. *Our multisize table view list*

Creating the Font Info View Controller

The final view controller we're going to create is the one shown in Figure 9-5. This one isn't based on a table view. Instead, it features a large text label, a slider for setting text size, and a switch for toggling whether the font that it uses should be included in the list of favorites. Create a new Cocoa Touch class in your project using UIViewController as the superclass, and then name it FontInfoViewController. Like most of the other controllers in this app, this one needs to have a couple of parameters passed in by its parent controller. Enable this by defining these properties and four outlets that we'll use when we construct the user interface in FontInfoViewController.swift:

```
class FontInfoViewController: UIViewController {
    var font: UIFont!
    var favorite: Bool = false
    @IBOutlet weak var fontSampleLabel: UILabel!
    @IBOutlet weak var fontSizeSlider: UISlider!
    @IBOutlet weak var fontSizeLabel: UILabel!
    @IBOutlet weak var favoriteSwitch: UISwitch!
```

Next, implement viewDidLoad() and a pair of action methods that will be triggered by the slider and switch, respectively, as shown in Listing 9-10.

Listing 9-10. Our viewDidLoad(), slider, and switch Methods

```
override func viewDidLoad() {
    super.viewDidLoad()

    // Do any additional setup after loading the view.
    fontSampleLabel.font = font
    fontSampleLabel.text =
        "AaBbCcDdEeFfGgHhIiJjKkLlMmNnOoPpQqRrSsTtUuVv"
        + "WwXxYyZz 0123456789"
    fontSizeSlider.value = Float(font.pointSize)
    fontSizeLabel.text = "\(Int(font.pointSize))"
    favoriteSwitch.isOn = favorite
}
@IBAction func slideFontSize(slider: UISlider) {
    let newSize = roundf(slider.value)
    fontSampleLabel.font = font.withSize(CGFloat(newSize))
    fontSizeLabel.text = "\(Int(newSize))"
}

    @IBAction func toggleFavorite(sender: UISwitch) {
        let favoritesList = FavoritesList.sharedFavoritesList
        if sender.isOn {
            favoritesList.addFavorite(fontName: font.fontName)
        } else {
            favoritesList.removeFavorite(fontName: font.fontName)
        }
    }
}
```

These methods are all pretty straightforward. The viewDidLoad() method sets up the display based on the chosen font; slideFontSize() changes the size of the font in the fontSampleLabel label based on the value of the slider; and toggleFavorite() either adds the current font to the favorites list or removes it from the favorites list, depending on the value of the switch.

Creating the Font Info View Controller Storyboard

Now head back over to Main.storyboard to build the GUI for this app's final view controller. Use the Object Library to find a plain View Controller. Drag it into the editing area and use the Identity Inspector to set its class to FontInfoViewController. Next, use the Object Library to find some more objects and drag them into your new scene. You need three labels, a switch, and a slider. Lay them out roughly, as shown in Figure 9-12. Don't worry about adding auto layout constraints yet—we'll do that later.

Figure 9-12. *Label, switch, and slider layout*

Notice that we left some space above the upper label, since we're going to end up having a navigation bar up there. Also, we want the upper label to be able to display long pieces of text across multiple lines, but by default the label is set to show only one line. To change that, select the label, open the Attributes Inspector, and set the number in the Lines field to 0.

Figure 9-12 also shows changed text in the lower two labels. Go ahead and make the same changes yourself. What you can't see here is that the Attributes Inspector was used to right-align the text in both of them. You should do the same, since they will both have layout constraints that essentially tie them to their right edges. Also, select the slider at the bottom, and then use the Attributes Inspector to set its Minimum to 1 and its Maximum to 200.

Now it's time to wire up all the connections for this GUI. Start by selecting the view controller and opening the Connections Inspector. When we have so many connections to make, the overview shown by that inspector is pretty nice. Make connections for each of the outlets by dragging from the small circles next to favoriteSwitch, fontSampleLabel, fontSizeLabel, and fontSizeSlider to the appropriate objects in the scene. In case it's not obvious, fontSampleLabel should be connected to the label at the top, fontSizeLabel to the label at the bottom right, and the favoriteSwitch and fontSizeSlider outlets to the only places they can go. To connect the actions to the controls, you can continue to use the Connections Inspector. In the Received Actions section of the Connections Inspector for the view controller, drag from the little circle next to slideFontSize: over to the slider, release the mouse button, and select Value Changed from the context menu that appears. Next, drag from the little circle next to toggleFavorite: over to the switch and again select Value Changed. The connections should look as shown in Figure 9-13.

Figure 9-13. *The completed connections for our Font Info View Controller Storyboard*

One more thing we need to do here is create a segue so that this view can be shown. Remember that this view is going to be displayed whenever a user taps the detail accessory (the little blue "i" in a circle) when the Font List View Controller is displayed. So, find that controller, Control-drag from its prototype cell to the new font info view controller you've been working on, and select Show from the Accessory Action section of the context menu that appears. Note that we just said Accessory Action, not Selection Segue (see Figure 9-14). The accessory action is the segue that is triggered when the user taps the detail accessory, whereas the selection segue is the segue that is triggered by a tap anywhere else in the row. We already set this cell's selection segue to open a FontSizesViewController.

Figure 9-14. *Setting the Accessory Action Show Segue*

Now we have two different segues that can be triggered by touches in different parts of a row. Since these will present different view controllers, with different properties, we need to have a way to differentiate them. Fortunately, the `UIStoryboardSegue` class, which represents a segue, has a way to accomplish this: we can use an identifier, just as we do with table view cells.

All you have to do is select a segue in the editing area and use the Attributes Inspector to set its Identifier. You may need to shift your scenes around a bit, so that you can see both of the segues that are snaking their way out of the right-hand side of the Font List View Controller. Select the one that's pointing at the Font Sizes View Controller and set its Identifier to ShowFontSizes. Next, select the one that's pointing at the Font Info View Controller and set its Identifier to ShowFontInfo, as shown in Figure 9-15.

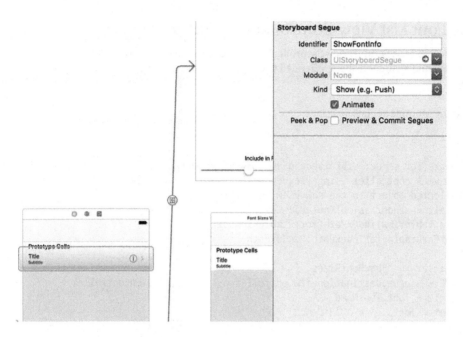

Figure 9-15. *Identifying the segues*

Setting Up Constraints

Setting up that segue lets Interface Builder know that our new scene will be used within the context of the navigation controller like everything else, so it automatically receives a blank navigation bar at the top. Now that the real confines of our view are in place, it's a good time to set up the constraints. This is a fairly complex view with several subviews, especially near the bottom, so we can't quite rely on the system's automatic constraints to do the right thing for us. We'll use the Pin button at the bottom of the editing area and the pop-up window it triggers to build most of the constraints we'll need.

Start with the uppermost label. If you placed it too close to the top, first drag it down until it's a comfortable distance below the navigation bar. Click Pin, and then, in the pop-up window, select the little red bars above, to the left, and to the right of the little square—but not the one below it. Now click the Add 3 Constraints button at the bottom.

Next, select the slider at the bottom and click the Pin button. This time, select the red bars below, to the left, and to the right of the little square—but not the one above it. Again, click Add 3 Constraints to put them in place.

For each of the two remaining labels and for the switch, follow this procedure: select the object, click Pin, select the red bars below and to the right of the little square, turn on the check boxes for Width and Height, and finally, click Add 4 Constraints. Setting those constraints for all three of those objects will bind them to the lower-right corner.

There's just one more constraint to make. We want the top label to grow to contain its text, but to never grow so large that it overlaps the views at the bottom. We can accomplish this with a single constraint. Control-drag from the upper label to the Include in favorites label, release the mouse button, and select Vertical Spacing from the context menu that appears. Next, click the new constraint to select it (it's a blue vertical bar connecting the two labels) and open the Attributes Inspector, where you'll see some configurable attributes for the constraint. Change the Relation pop-up to Greater Than or Equal, and then set the Constant value to 10. That ensures that the expanding upper label won't push past the other views at the bottom.

Adapting the Font List View Controller for Multiple Segues

Now head back over to good old FontListViewController.swift. Since this class will now be able to trigger segues to two different child view controllers, you need to adapt the prepareForSegue(_:sender:) method, as shown in Listing 9-11.

Listing 9-11. Handling Multiple Segues

```
// MARK: - Navigation

override func prepare(for segue: UIStoryboardSegue, sender: AnyObject?) {
    // Get the new view controller using [segue destinationViewController].
    // Pass the selected object to the new view controller.
    let tableViewCell = sender as! UITableViewCell
    let indexPath = tableView.indexPath(for: tableViewCell)!
    let font = fontForDisplay(atIndexPath: indexPath)

    if segue.identifier == "ShowFontSizes" {
        let sizesVC =  segue.destinationViewController as! FontSizesViewController
        sizesVC.title = font.fontName
        sizesVC.font = font
    } else {
        let infoVC = segue.destinationViewController as! FontInfoViewController
        infoVC.title = font.fontName
        infoVC.font = font
        infoVC.favorite =
            FavoritesList.sharedFavoritesList.favorites.contains(font.fontName)
    }
}
```

Build and run the app to see how things worked out. Select a font family that contains many fonts (for example, Gill Sans), and then tap the middle of the row for any font. You'll be taken to the same list you saw earlier, which shows the font in multiple sizes. Press the navigation button at the upper left (it's labeled Gill Sans) to go back, and then tap another row; however, this time tap on the right-hand side where the detail accessory is shown. This should bring up the final view controller, which shows a sample of the font with a slider at the bottom that lets you pick whatever size you want.

Also, you can now use the Include in favorites switch to mark this font as a favorite. Do that, and then hit the navigation button at the top-left corner a couple of times to get back to the root controller view.

My Favorite Fonts

Scroll down to the bottom of the root view controller and you'll see something new: the My Favorite Fonts section is now there. Selecting it shows you a list of all the favorite fonts that have been selected so far, as shown in Figure 9-16.

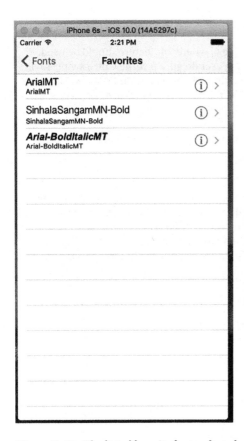

Figure 9-16. *The list of favorite fonts selected so far*

Adding Features

Now the basic functionality of our app is complete. But before we can really call it a day, there are a couple more features we should implement. If you've been using iOS for a while, you're probably aware that you can often delete a row from a table view by swiping from right to left. For example, in Mail you can use this technique to delete a message in a list of messages. Performing this gesture brings up a small GUI, right inside the table view row. This GUI asks you to confirm the deletion, and then the row disappears and the remaining rows slide up to fill the gap. That whole interaction—including handling the swipe, showing the confirmation GUI, and animating any affected rows—is taken care of by the table view itself. All you need to do is implement two methods in your controller to make it happen.

Also, the table view provides easy-to-use functionality that lets the user reorder rows within a table view by dragging them up and down. As with swipe-to-delete, the table view takes care of the entire user interaction for us. All we have to do is one line of setup (to create a button that activates the reordering GUI), and then implement a single method that is called when the user has finished dragging.

Implementing Swipe-to-Delete

In this app, the `FontListViewController` class is a typical example of where this feature should be used. Whenever the app is showing the list of favorites, we should let the user delete a favorite with a swipe, saving them the step of tapping the detail accessory and then turning off the switch. Select FontListViewController. swift in Xcode to get started. Start by adding an implementation of the `tableView(_:canEditRowAt: indexPath:)` method:

```
override func tableView(_ tableView: UITableView, canEditRowAt indexPath: IndexPath) -> Bool {
    return showsFavorites
}
```

That method will return `true` if it's showing the list of favorites, and `false` otherwise. This means that the editing functionality that lets you delete rows is only enabled while displaying favorites. If you were to try to run the app and delete rows with just this change, you wouldn't see any difference. The table view won't bother to deal with the swipe gesture because it sees that we haven't implemented the other method that is required to complete a deletion. So, let's put that in place, too. Add an implementation for the `tableView(_: commitEditingStyle:forRowAtIndexPath:)` method as in Listing 9-12.

Listing 9-12. Allowing the deletion of rows from our favorites list

```
override func tableView(_ tableView: UITableView, commit editingStyle:
UITableViewCellEditingStyle, forRowAt indexPath: IndexPath) {
if !showsFavorites {
    return
}

if editingStyle == UITableViewCellEditingStyle.delete {
    // Delete the row from the data source
    let favorite = fontNames[indexPath.row]
    FavoritesList.sharedFavoritesList.removeFavorite(fontName: favorite)
    fontNames = FavoritesList.sharedFavoritesList.favorites

    tableView.deleteRows(at: [indexPath],
                    with: UITableViewRowAnimation.fade)
}

}
```

This method is called when an editing action in the table is being completed. It's pretty straightforward, but there are some subtle things going on. The first thing we do is check to make sure we're showing the favorites list and if not, we just bail. Normally, this should never happen, since we specified with the previous method that only the favorites list should be editable. Nevertheless, we're doing a bit of defensive programming here. After that, we check the editing style to make sure that the particular edit operation we're going to conclude really was a deletion. It's possible to do insertion edits in a table view, but not without additional setup that we're not doing here, so we don't need to worry about that case. Next, we determine which font should be deleted, remove it from our `FavoritesList` singleton, and update our local copy of the favorites list.

Finally, we tell the table view to delete the row and make it disappear with a visual fade animation. It's important to understand what happens when you tell the table view to delete a row. Intuitively, you might think that calling that method would delete some data, but that's not what happens. In fact, we've already deleted the data! This final method call is really our way of telling the table view, "Hey, I've made a change, and I want you to animate away this row. Ask me if you need anything more." When that happens, the table view will start animating any rows that are below the deleted row by moving them up, which means that it's possible that one or more rows that were previously off-screen will now come on-screen, at which time it will indeed ask the controller for cell data via the usual methods. For that reason, it's important that our implementation of the ta bleView(_:commitEditingStyle:forRowAtIndexPath:) method makes necessary changes to the data model (in this case, the FavoritesList singleton) *before* telling the table view to delete a row.

Build and run the app again, make sure you have some favorite fonts set up, and then go into the Favorites list and delete a row by swiping from right to left. The row slides partly off-screen, and a Delete button appears on the right (see Figure 9-17). Tap the Delete button so that the row disappears.

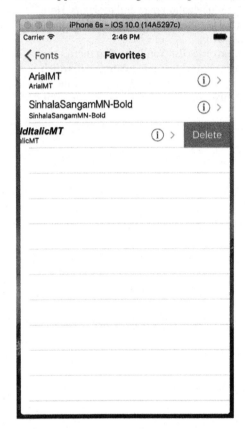

Figure 9-17. *A favorite font row with the Delete button showing*

Implementing Drag-to-Reorder

The final feature we're going to add to the font list will let users rearrange their favorites just by dragging them up and down. In order to accomplish this, we're going to add one method to the FavoritesList class, which will let us reorder its items however we want. Open FavoritesList.swift and add the following method:

```
func moveItem(fromIndex from: Int, toIndex to: Int) {
    let item = favorites[from]
    favorites.remove(at: from)
    favorites.insert(item, at: to)
    saveFavorites()
}
```

This new method provides the underpinnings for what we're going to do. Now select FontListViewController.swift and add the following lines at the end of the viewDidLoad method:

```
if showsFavorites {
    navigationItem.rightBarButtonItem = editButtonItem()
}
```

I've mentioned the navigation item. It's an object that holds the information about what should appear in the navigation bar for a view controller. It has a property called rightBarButtonItem that can hold an instance of UIBarButtonItem, a special sort of button meant only for navigation bars and tool bars. Here, we're pointing that at editButtonItem, a property of UIViewController that gives us a special button item that's preconfigured to activate the table view's editing/reordering GUI:.

With that in place, try running the app again and go into the Favorites list. You'll see that there's now an Edit button in the upper-right corner. Pressing that button toggles the table view's editing GUI, which right now means that each row acquires a delete button on the left, while its content slides a bit to the right to make room (see Figure 9-18). This enables yet another way that users can delete rows, using the same methods we already implemented.

Figure 9-18. *We've added the Edit feature in our favorites table*

But our main interest here is in adding reordering functionality. For that, all we need to do is add the following method in FontListViewController.swift:

```
override func tableView(_ tableView: UITableView, moveRowAt sourceIndexPath: IndexPath, to
destinationIndexPath: IndexPath) {
    FavoritesList.sharedFavoritesList.moveItem(fromIndex: sourceIndexPath.row,
                                   toIndex: destinationIndexPath.row)
    fontNames = FavoritesList.sharedFavoritesList.favorites:

}
```

This method is called as soon as the user finishes dragging a row. The arguments tell us which row was moved and where it ended up. All we do here is tell the FavoritesList singleton to do the same reordering of its content, and then refresh our list of font names, just as we did after deleting an item. To see this in action, run the app, go into the Favorites list, and tap the Edit button. You'll see that the edit mode now includes little "dragger" icons on the right side of each row, which you can use to rearrange items.

Summary

Although we worked a lot with table views in this chapter, our focus has really been on the use of navigation controllers and how we drill down into hierarchical content in a limited width space as we might have on most iPhone devices, especially in portrait orientation.

We created a font list view application that showed us not only how to drill down into more detailed views, but how to handle multiple segues from a single table view cell as we did with looking at either font sizes or font information.

Finally, we looked at tweaking our table views a bit to include the capabilities of deleting and moving rows within the view.

CHAPTER 10

■ ■ ■

Collection Views

For years, iOS developers used the UITableView component to create a huge variety of interfaces. With its ability to let you define multiple cell types, create them on the fly as needed, and handily scroll them vertically, UITableView became a key component of thousands of apps. While Apple has increased the capability of table views with every major new iOS release, it's still not the ultimate solution for all large sets of data. If you want to present data in multiple columns, for example, you need to combine all the columns for each row of data into a single cell. There's also no way to make a UITableView scroll its content horizontally. In general, much of the power of UITableView came with a particular trade-off: developers have no control of the overall layout of a table view. You define the look of each individual cell, but the cells are just going to be stacked on top of each other in one big scrolling list.

In iOS 6, Apple introduced a new class called UICollectionView addressing these shortcomings. Similar to a table view, UICollectionView allows you to display a bunch of "cells" of data and handles functionality such as queuing up unused cells to use later. But unlike a table view, UICollectionView doesn't lay these cells out in a vertical stack for you. In fact, UICollectionView doesn't lay them out at all. Instead, UICollectionView uses a helper class to do layout.

Creating the DialogViewer Project

Let's start by talking about UICollectionView. To show some of its capabilities, we're going to use it to lay out some paragraphs of text. Each word will be placed in a cell of its own, and all the cells for each paragraph will be clustered together in a section. Each section will also have its own header. This may not seem too exciting, considering that UIKit already contains other perfectly good ways of laying out text. However, this process will be instructive anyway, since you'll get a feel for just how flexible this thing is. You certainly wouldn't get very far doing something like Figure 10-1 with a table view.

© Molly Maskrey, Kim Topley, David Mark, Fredrik Olsson and Jeff Lamarche 2016
M. Maskrey et al., *Beginning iPhone Development with Swift 3*, DOI 10.1007/978-1-4842-2223-2_10

Figure 10-1. *Each word is a separate cell, with the exception of the headers, which are, well, headers. All of this is laid out using a single UICollectionView, and no explicit geometry calculations of our own*

In order to make this work, we'll define a couple of custom cell classes, we'll use UICollectionViewFlowLayout (the one and only layout helper class included in UIKit at this time), and, as usual, we'll use our view controller class to make it all come together.

Use Xcode to create a new Single View Application, as you've done many times by now. Name your project DialogViewer and use the standard settings we've used throughout the book (set Language to Swift and choose Universal for Devices.). Open ViewController.swift and change its super class to UICollectionView:

```
class ViewController: UICollectionViewController {
```

Open Main.storyboard. We need to set up the view controller to match what we just specified in ViewController.swift. Select the one and only View Controller in the Document Outline and delete it, leaving an empty storyboard. Now use the Object Library to locate a Collection View Controller and drag it into the editing area. If you examine the Document Outline, you'll see that the collection view controller comes with a nested collection view. Its relation to the collection view is very much like the relationship between

UITableViewController and its nested UITableView. Select the icon for the collection view controller and use the Identity Inspector to change its class to ViewController, which we just made into a subclass of UICollectionViewController. In the Attributes Inspector, ensure that the Is Initial View Controller check box is checked. Next, select the collection view in the Document Outline and use the Attributes Inspector to change its background color to white. Finally, you'll see that the collection view has a child called Collection View Cell. This is a prototype cell that you can use to design the layout for your actual cells in Interface Builder, just like we have been doing with table view cells. We're not going to do that in this chapter, so select that cell and delete it.

Defining Custom Cells

Now let's define some cell classes. As you saw in Figure 10-1, we're displaying two basic kinds of cells: a "normal" one containing a word and another that is used as a sort of header. Any cell you're going to create for use in a UICollectionView needs to be a subclass of the system-supplied UICollectionViewCell class, which provides basic functionality similar to UITableViewCell. This functionality includes a backgroundView, a contentView, and so on. Because our two types of cell will have some shared functionality, we'll actually make one a subclass of the other and use the subclass to override some of the functionality of the base class.

Start by creating a new Cocoa Touch class in Xcode. Name the new class ContentCell and make it a subclass of UICollectionViewCell. Select the new class's source file and add declarations for three properties and a stub for a class method, as shown in Listing 10-1.

Listing 10-1. Our ContentCell Class Definition

```
class ContentCell: UICollectionViewCell {
    var label: UILabel!
    var text: String!
    var maxWidth: CGFloat!

    class func sizeForContentString(s: String,
                    forMaxWidth maxWidth: CGFloat) -> CGSize {
        return CGSize.zero
    }
}
```

The label property will point at a UILabel. We'll use the text property to tell the cell what to display, the maxWidth property to control the cell's maximum width. We'll use the sizeForContentString(_:forMaxWidth:) method—which we'll implement shortly—to ask how big the cell needs to be to display a given string. This will come in handy when creating and configuring instances of our cell classes.

Now add overrides of the UIView init(frame:) and init(coder:) methods, as shown in Listing 10-2.

Listing 10-2. Init Override Routines for Our Cell ContentCell Class

```
override init(frame: CGRect) {
    super.init(frame: frame)
    label = UILabel(frame: self.contentView.bounds)
    label.isOpaque = false
    label.backgroundColor =
        UIColor(red: 0.8, green: 0.9, blue: 1.0, alpha: 1.0)
    label.textColor = UIColor.black()
```

```
        label.textAlignment = .center
        label.font = self.dynamicType.defaultFont()
        contentView.addSubview(label)
}

required init?(coder aDecoder: NSCoder) {
    super.init(coder: aDecoder)
}
```

The code in Listing 10-2 is pretty simple. It creates a label, sets its display properties, and adds the label to the cell's contentView. The only mysterious thing here is that it uses the defaultFont() method to get a font, which is used to set the label's font. The idea is that this class should define which font will be used for displaying content, while also allowing any subclasses to declare their own display font by overriding the defaultFont() method. We haven't created the defaultFont() method yet, so let's do so:

```
class func defaultFont() -> UIFont {
    return UIFont.preferredFontForTextStyle(UIFontTextStyleBody)
}
```

Pretty straightforward. This uses the preferredFontForTextStyle() method of the UIFont class to get the user's preferred font for body text. The user can use the Settings app to change the size of this font. By using this method instead of hard-coding a font size, we make our apps a bit more user-friendly. Notice how this method is called:

```
label.font = self.dynamicType.defaultFont()
```

The defaultFont() method is a type method of the ContentCell class. To call it, you would normally use the name of the class, like this:

```
ContentCell.defaultFont()
```

In this case, that won't work—if this call is made from a subclass of ContentCell (such as the HeaderCell class that we will create shortly), we want to actually call the subclass' override of defaultFont(). To do that, we need a reference to the subclass's type object. That's what the expression self.dynamicType gives us. If this expression is executed from an instance of the ContentCell class, it resolves to the type object of ContentCell and we'll call the defaultFont() method of that class; but in the HeaderCell subclass, it resolves to the type object for HeaderCell and we'll call HeaderCell's defaultFont() method instead, which is exactly what we want. To finish off this class, let's implement the method that we added a stub for earlier, the one that computes an appropriate size for the cell, as shown in Listing 10-3.

Listing 10-3. Compute an Approximate Cell Size

```
class func sizeForContentString(s: String,
                                forMaxWidth maxWidth: CGFloat) -> CGSize {
    let maxSize = CGSize(width: maxWidth, height: 1000.0)
    let opts = NSStringDrawingOptions.usesLineFragmentOrigin

    let style = NSMutableParagraphStyle()
    style.lineBreakMode = NSLineBreakMode.byCharWrapping
    let attributes = [ NSFontAttributeName: defaultFont(),
                NSParagraphStyleAttributeName: style]
```

```
let string = s as NSString
let rect = string.boundingRect(with: maxSize, options: opts,
                                    attributes: attributes, context: nil)


return rect.size
}
```

The method in Listing 10-3 does a lot of things, so it's worth walking through it. First, we declare a maximum size so that no word will be allowed to be wider than the value of the maxWidth argument, which will be set from the width of the UICollectionView. We also create a paragraph style that allows for character wrapping, so in case our string is too big to fit in our given maximum width, it will wrap around to a subsequent line. We also create an attributes dictionary that contains the default font we defined for this class and the paragraph style we just created. Finally, we use some NSString functionality provided in UIKit that lets us calculate sizes for a string. We pass in an absolute maximum size and the other options and attributes that we set up, and we get back a size.

All that's left for this class is some special handling of the text property. Instead of letting this use an implicit instance variable as we normally do, we're going to define methods that get and set the value based on the UILabel we created earlier, basically using the UILabel as storage for the displayed value. By doing so, we can also use the setter to recalculate the cell's geometry when the text changes. Replace the definition of the text property in ContentCell.swift with the code in Listing 10-4.

Listing 10-4. The Text Property Definition in the ContentCell.swift File

```
var label: UILabel!
var text: String! {
    get {
        return label.text
    }
    set(newText) {
        label.text = newText
        var newLabelFrame = label.frame
        var newContentFrame = contentView.frame
        let textSize = self.dynamicType.sizeForContentString(s: newText,
                                                forMaxWidth: maxWidth)
        newLabelFrame.size = textSize
        newContentFrame.size = textSize
        label.frame = newLabelFrame
        contentView.frame = newContentFrame
    }
}
```

The getter is nothing special; but the setter is doing some extra work. Basically, it's modifying the frame for both the label and the content view, based on the size needed for displaying the current string.

That's all we need for our base cell class. Now let's make a cell class to use for a header. Use Xcode to make another new Cocoa Touch class, naming this one HeaderCell and making it a subclass of ContentCell. Let's open HeaderCell.swift and make some changes. All we're going to do in this class is override some methods from the ContentCell class to change the cell's appearance, making it look different from the normal content cell, as shown in Listing 10-5.

347

Listing 10-5. The HeaderCell Class

```
class HeaderCell: ContentCell {

    override init(frame: CGRect) {
        super.init(frame: frame)
        label.backgroundColor = UIColor(red: 0.9, green: 0.9,
                                        blue: 0.8, alpha: 1.0)
        label.textColor = UIColor.black()
    }

    required init?(coder aDecoder: NSCoder) {
        super.init(coder: aDecoder)
    }

    override class func defaultFont() -> UIFont {
        return UIFont.preferredFont(forTextStyle: UIFontTextStyleHeadline)
    }

}
```

That's all we should have to do to give the header cell a distinct look, with its own colors and font.

Configuring the View Controller

Select ViewController.swift and start by declaring an array to contain the content we want to display, as shown in Listing 10-6.

Listing 10-6. Our Content to Be Displayed— Place This in the ViewController.swift File

```
private var sections = [
    ["header": "First Witch",
     "content" : "Hey, when will the three of us meet up later?"],
    ["header" : "Second Witch",
     "content" : "When everything's straightened out."],
    ["header" : "Third Witch",
     "content" : "That'll be just before sunset."],
    ["header" : "First Witch",
     "content" : "Where?"],
    ["header" : "Second Witch",
     "content" : "The dirt patch."],
    ["header" : "Third Witch",
     "content" : "I guess we'll see Mac there."]
]
```

The sections array contains a list of dictionaries, each of which has two keys: header and content. We'll use the values associated with those keys to define our display content.

Much like UITableView, UICollectionView lets us register the class of a reusable cell based on an identifier. Doing this lets us call a dequeuing method later on, when we're going to provide a cell. If no cell is available, the collection view will create one for us—just like UITableView. Add this line to the end of the viewDidLoad() method to make this happen:

```
self.collectionView?.register(ContentCell.self, forCellWithReuseIdentifier: "CONTENT")
```

Since this application has no navigation bar, the content of the main view will be visible beneath the status bar. To prevent that, add the following lines to the end of `viewDidLoad()`:

```
var contentInset = collectionView!.contentInset
contentInset.top = 20
collectionView!.contentInset = contentInset
```

That's enough configuration in `viewDidLoad()` for now. Before we get to the code that populates the collection view, we need to write one little helper method. All of our content is contained in lengthy strings, but we're going to need to deal with them one word at a time to be able to put each word into a cell. So let's create an internal method of our own to split those strings apart. This method takes a section number, pulls the relevant content string from our section data, and splits it into words:

```
func wordsInSection(section: Int) -> [String] {
    let content = sections[section]["content"]
    let spaces = NSCharacterSet.whitespacesAndNewlines
    let words = content?.components(separatedBy: spaces)
    return words!
}
```

Providing Content Cells

Now it's time to create the group of methods that will actually populate the collection view. These next three methods are all defined by the `UICollectionViewDataSource` protocol, which is adopted by the `UICollectionViewController` class. The `UICollectionViewController` assigns itself as the data source of its nested `UICollectionView`, so these methods will be called automatically by the `UICollectionView` when it needs to know about its content.

First, we need a method to let the collection view know how many sections to display:

```
override func numberOfSections(in collectionView: UICollectionView) -> Int {
    return sections.count
}
```

Next, we have a method to tell the collection how many items each section should contain. This uses the `wordsInSection()` method we defined earlier:

```
override func collectionView(_ collectionView: UICollectionView, numberOfItemsInSection
section: Int) -> Int {
    let words = wordsInSection(section: section)
    return words.count
}
```

Listing 10-7 shows the method that actually returns a single cell, configured to contain a single word. This method also uses our `wordsInSection()` method. As you can see, it uses a dequeuing method on `UICollectionView`, similar to the one in `UITableView`. Since we've registered a cell class for the identifier we're using here, we know that the dequeuing method always returns an instance:

Listing 10-7. Setting up the Collection View Cell

```
override func collectionView(_ collectionView: UICollectionView, cellForItemAt indexPath:
IndexPath) -> UICollectionViewCell {
    let words = wordsInSection(section: indexPath.section)

    let cell = collectionView.dequeueReusableCell(
        withReuseIdentifier: "CONTENT", for: indexPath) as! ContentCell
    cell.maxWidth = collectionView.bounds.size.width
    cell.text = words[indexPath.row]
    return cell
}
```

Judging by the way that UITableView works, you might think that at this point we'd have something that works, in at least a minimal way. Build and run the app. You'll see that we're not really at a useful point yet, as shown in Figure 10-2.

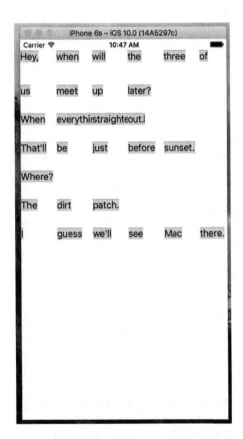

Figure 10-2. *Not quite what we're looking for...yet*

We can see some of the words, but there's no "low" going on here. Each cell is the same size, and everything is all jammed together. The reason for this is that we have some collection view delegate responsibilities we have to take care of to make things work.

Creating the Layout Flow

Until now, we've been dealing with the UICollectionView, but this class has a sidekick that takes care of the actual layout. UICollectionViewFlowLayout, which is the default layout helper for UICollectionView, includes delegate methods of its own that it will use to try to pull out more information from us. We're going to implement one of these right now. The layout object calls this method for each cell to find out how large it should be. Here we're once again using our wordsInSection() method to get access to the word in question, and then using a method we defined in the ContentCell class to see how large it needs to be.

When the UICollectionViewController is initialized, it makes itself the delegate of its UICollectionView. The collection view's UICollectionViewFlowLayout will treat the view controller as its own delegate if it declares that it conforms to the UICollectionViewDelegateFlowLayout protocol. The first thing we need to do is change the declaration of our view controller in ViewController.swift so that it declares conformance to that protocol:

```
class ViewController: UICollectionViewController,
          UICollectionViewDelegateFlowLayout {
```

All of the methods of the UICollectionViewDelegateFlowLayout protocol are optional and we only need to implement one of them. Add the method in Listing 10-8 to ViewController.swift.

Listing 10-8. Resizing the Cells Using the UICollectionViewDelegateFlowLayout Protocol

```
func collectionView(collectionView: UICollectionView,
        layout collectionViewLayout: UICollectionViewLayout,
        sizeForItemAtIndexPath indexPath: NSIndexPath) -> CGSize {
    let words = wordsInSection(indexPath.section)
    let size = ContentCell.sizeForContentString(words[indexPath.row],
                  forMaxWidth: collectionView.bounds.size.width)
    return size
}
```

Now build and run the app again. You'll see that we've taken a step forward, as shown in Figure 10-3.

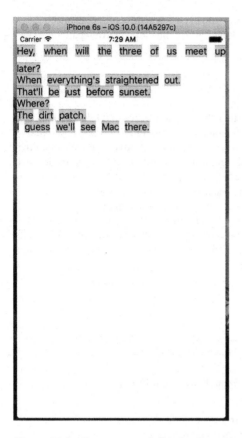

Figure 10-3. *Our paragraph flow begins taking shape*

You can see that the cells are now flowing and wrapping around so that the text is readable, and that the beginning of each section drops down a bit. But each section is jammed really tightly against the ones before and after it. They're also pressing all the way out to the sides, which doesn't look too nice. Let's fix that by adding a bit more configuration. Add these lines to the end of the viewDidLoad() method:

```
let layout = collectionView!.collectionViewLayout
let flow = layout as! UICollectionViewFlowLayout
flow.sectionInset = UIEdgeInsetsMake(10, 20, 30, 20)
```

Here we're grabbing the layout object from our collection view. We assign this first to a temporary variable, which will be inferred to be of type UICollectionViewLayout. We do this primarily to highlight a point: UICollectionView only knows about this generic layout class, but it's really using an instance of UICollectionFlowLayout, which is a subclass of UICollectionViewLayout. Knowing the true type of the layout object, we can use a typecast to assign it to another variable of the correct type, enabling us to access properties that only that subclass has. In this case, we use the sectionInset property to tell the UICollectionViewLayout to leave some empty space around each item in the collection view. In our case, that means that there will now be a little space around every word, as you'll see if you run the example again (see Figure 10-4).

Figure 10-4. *Things are much less cramped*

Implementing the Header Views

The only thing missing now is the display of our header objects, so it's time to fix that. You will recall that UITableView has a system of header and footer views, and it asks for those specifically for each section. UICollectionView has made this concept a bit more generic, allowing for more flexibility in the layout. The way this works is that, along with the system of accessing normal cells from the delegate, there is a parallel system for accessing additional views that can be used as headers, footers, or anything else. Add this bit of code to the end of viewDidLoad() to let the collection view know about our header cell class:

```
self.collectionView?.register(HeaderCell.self,
                forSupplementaryViewOfKind: UICollectionElementKindSectionHeader,
                withReuseIdentifier: "HEADER")
```

As you can see, in this case we're not only specifying a cell class and an identifier, but we're also specifying a "kind." The idea is that different layouts may define different kinds of supplementary views and may ask the delegate to supply views for them. UICollectionFlowLayout is going to ask for one section header for each section in the collection view, which we'll supply, as shown in Listing 10-9.

353

Listing 10-9. Getting Our Header Cell View

```
override func collectionView(_ collectionView: UICollectionView,
viewForSupplementaryElementOfKind kind: String, at indexPath: IndexPath) ->
UICollectionReusableView {
    if (kind == UICollectionElementKindSectionHeader) {
        let cell =
            collectionView.dequeueReusableSupplementaryView(
                ofKind: kind, withReuseIdentifier: "HEADER",
                for: indexPath) as! HeaderCell
        cell.maxWidth = collectionView.bounds.size.width
        cell.text = sections[indexPath.section]["header"]
        return cell
    }
    abort()
}
```

Note the abort() call at the end of this method. This function causes the application to terminate immediately. It's not the sort of thing you should use frequently in production code. Here, we only expect to be called to create header cells and there is nothing we can do if we are asked to create a different kind of cell—we can't even return nil, because the method's return type does not permit it. If we are called to create a different kind of header, it's a programming error on our part or a bug in UIKit.

Build and run. You'll see... wait! Where are those headers? As it turns out, UICollectionFlowLayout won't give the headers any space in the layout unless we tell it exactly how large they should be. So go back to viewDidLoad() and add the following line at the end:

flow.headerReferenceSize = CGSize(width: 100, height: 25)

Build and run once more. You'll see the headers in place, as Figure 10-1 showed earlier and Figure 10-5 shows again.

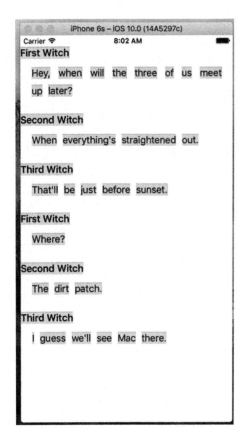

Figure 10-5. *The completed DialogViewer app*

Summary

In this chapter, we've really just touched on `UICollectionView` and what can be accomplished with the default `UICollectionFlowLayout` class. You can get even fancier with it by defining your own layout classes, but that is a topic for another book.

Stack Views are something else you should look into when considering applications using Collection Views. They may offer an alternative approach that could save you time. As this book is tending to get larger and larger with the new Swift, Xcode and iOS features, I'm leaving Stack Views as an exercise for the reader.

CHAPTER 11

■ ■ ■

Split Views and Popovers for iPad Apps

In Chapter 9, we spent a lot of time dealing with app navigation based on selections in table views, where each selection causes the top-level view, which filled the entire screen, to slide left and bring in the next view in the hierarchy. Many iPhone and iPod touch apps work this way such as Mail, which lets you drill down through mail accounts and folders until you make your way to the message. Although, this approach works on the iPad, it leads to a user interaction problem.

On a screen the size of the iPhone or iPod touch, having a screen-sized view slide away to reveal another screen-sized view works well. But with an iPad, that same interaction can seem less smooth, perhaps a little exaggerated, and even a little overwhelming. Consuming such a large display with a single table view wastes space. As a result, you'll see that the built-in iPad apps don't behave this way. Instead, any drill-down navigation functionality, like that used in Mail, becomes relegated to a narrow column whose contents slide left or right as the user drills down into or backs out of the hierarchy. With the iPad in landscape mode, the navigation column stays at a fixed position on the left, with the content of the selected item displayed on the right in what's known as a **split-view** (see Figure 11-1), and applications built this way are called **master-detail** applications.

© Molly Maskrey, Kim Topley, David Mark, Fredrik Olsson and Jeff Lamarche 2016
M. Maskrey et al., *Beginning iPhone Development with Swift 3*, DOI 10.1007/978-1-4842-2223-2_11

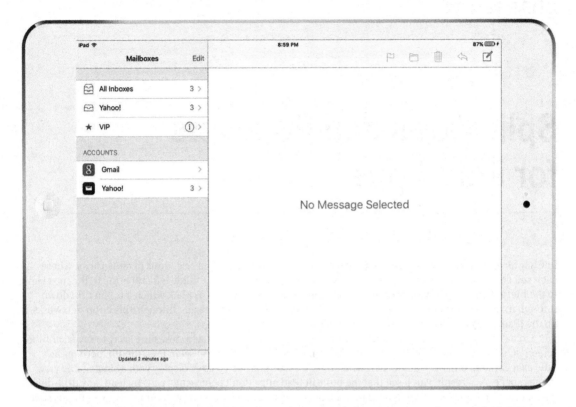

Figure 11-1. *This iPad, in landscape mode, shows a split view with the navigation column on the left. Tap an item in the navigation column and that item's content displays in the area on the right*

Split view provides a perfect visual for developing master-detail applications like Mail. Prior to iOS 8, the split view class, `UISplitViewController`, was only available on the iPad, meaning that if you wanted to build a universal master-detail application, you had to do it one way on the iPad and another way on the iPhone. Now, with `UISplitViewController` available everywhere, you no longer need to write special code to handle the iPhone.

When used on the iPad, the left side of the split view provides a width of 320 points by default. The split view itself, with navigation and content side by side, typically appears only in landscape mode. If you turn the device to portrait orientation, the split view still functions, but it's no longer visible in the same way. The navigation view loses its permanent location. It can be activated only by swiping in from the left side of the view or by pressing a toolbar button, causing it to slide in from the left in a view that floats in front of everything else on the screen, as shown in Figure 11-2.

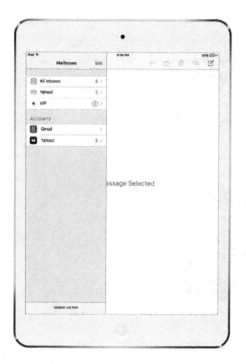

Figure 11-2. *Split view on an iPad in portrait mode appears differently from landscape mode, in that the information from the left side of the split view in landscape mode appears only when the user swipes in from the left or taps a toolbar button*

Some applications don't strictly follow this rule such as the iPad Settings app which uses a split view visible all the time. The left side neither disappears nor covers the content view on the right. But for this chapter's project we'll stick to the standard usage pattern.

We'll create a master-detail application using a split view controller, and then we'll test the application on the iPad simulator. But when it's finished, we'll see that the same code also works on the iPhone, although it doesn't quite look the same. You'll learn how to customize the split view's appearance and behavior, and create and display a popover that's like the one that we saw in Chapter 4 when we discussed alert views and action sheets. Unlike the popover in Figure 4-29, which wrapped an action sheet, this one will contain content that is specific to the example application—specifically, a list of presidents, as shown in Figure 11-3.

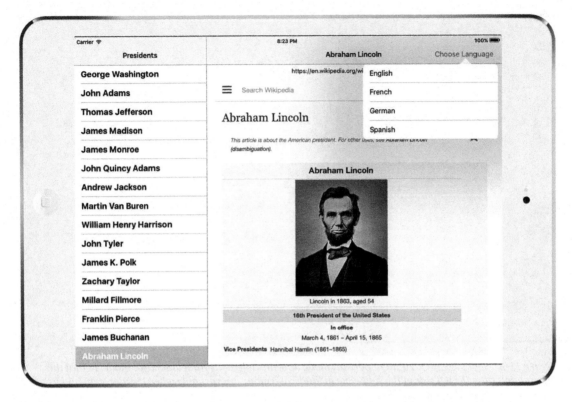

Figure 11-3. *A popover visually appears to sprout from the button that triggered it*

Building Master-Detail Applications with UISplitViewController

We're going to start off with an easy task: taking advantage of one of Xcode's predefined templates to create a split view project. We'll build an app that lists all the US presidents and shows the Wikipedia entry for whichever one you select.

Open Xcode and select File ➤ New ➤ Project.... From the iOS Application section, select Master-Detail Application and click Next. On the next screen, name the new project **Presidents**, set the Language to Swift and Devices to Universal. Make sure that all of the check boxes are unchecked. Click Next, choose the location for your project, and then click Create. Xcode will do its usual thing, creating a handful of classes and a storyboard file for you, and then showing the project. If it's not already open, expand the Presidents folder and take a look at what it contains.

From the start, the project contains an app delegate (as usual), a class called MasterViewController, and a class called DetailViewController. Those two view controllers represent, respectively, the views that will appear on the left and right sides of the split view in landscape orientation. MasterViewController defines the top level of a navigation structure and DetailViewController defines what's displayed in the larger area when a navigation element is selected. When the app launches, both of these are contained inside a split view, which, as you may recall, does a bit of shape-shifting as the device is rotated.

To see what this particular application template gives you in terms of functionality, build the app and run it in the iPad simulator. If the application launches into portrait mode, you'll see just the detail view controller, as shown on the left in Figure 11-4. Tap the Master button on the toolbar or swipe from the left edge of the view to the right to slide in the master view controller over the top of the detail view, as shown on the right in Figure 11-4.

Figure 11-4. *The default master-detail application in portrait mode. The layout on the right is similar to Figure 11-2*

Rotate the simulator left or right, into landscape orientation. In this mode, the split view works by showing the navigation view on the left and the detail view on the right, as shown in Figure 11-5.

Figure 11-5. *The default master-detail application in landscape mode. Note the similar layouts shown in this figure and Figure 11-1*

The Storyboard Defines the Structure

From the onset, you have a pretty complex set of view controllers in play:

- A split view controller that contains all the elements

- A navigation controller to handle what's happening on the left side of the split

- A master view controller (displaying a master list of items) inside the navigation controller

- A detail view controller on the right

- Another navigation controller as a container for the detail view controller on the right

In the default master-detail application template that we used, these view controllers are set up and interconnected in the main storyboard file, rather than in code. Apart from doing GUI layout, Interface Builder functions as a way of letting you connect different components without writing a bunch of code establishing relationships. Let's look at the project's storyboard to see how things are set up.

Select Main.storyboard to open it in Interface Builder. This storyboard really has a lot of stuff going on. You'll definitely want to open the Document Outline for the best results, as shown in Figure 11-6. Zooming out can also help you see the big picture.

Figure 11-6. *Main.storyboard open in Interface Builder. This complex object hierarchy can be best viewed using the Document Outline on the left*

To get a better sense of how these controllers relate to one another, open the Connections Inspector, and then spend some time clicking each of the view controllers in turn. Here's a quick summary of what you'll find:

- The UISplitViewController has relationship segues called **master view controller** and **detail view controller** to two UINavigationControllers. These are used to tell the UISplitViewController what it should use for the narrow strip it displays on the left (the master view controller) and for the larger display area (the detail view controller).

- The UINavigationController linked via the **master view controller** segue has a **root view controller relationship** to its own root view controller, which is the MasterViewController class generated by the template. The master view controller is a subclass of UITableViewController, which you should be familiar with from Chapter 9.

- Similarly, the other UINavigationController has a **root view controller relationship** to the detail view controller, which is the template's DetailVIewController class. The detail view controller generated by the template is a plain UIViewController subclass, but you are at liberty to use any view controller that meets your application's requirements.

- There is a storyboard segue from the cells in the master view controller to the detail view controller, of type **showDetail**. This segue causes the item in the clicked cell to be shown in the detail view. More about this later when we take a more detailed look at the master view controller.

At this point, the content of Main.storyboard provides a definition of how the app's various controllers are interconnected. As in most cases where you're using storyboards, this eliminates a lot of code, which is usually a good thing.

The Code Defines the Functionality

One of the main reasons for keeping the view controller interconnections in a storyboard is that they don't clutter up your source code with configuration information that doesn't need to be there. What's left is just the code that defines the actual functionality. Let's look at what we have as a starting point. Xcode defined several classes for us when the project was created. We're going to peek into each of them before we start making any changes.

The App Delegate

First up is AppDelegate.swift, the application delegate. Its source file starts something like Listing 11-1.

Listing 11-1. AppDelegate.swift

```
import UIKit

@UIApplicationMain
class AppDelegate: UIResponder, UIApplicationDelegate, UISplitViewControllerDelegate {

    var window: UIWindow?

    func application(_ application: UIApplication, didFinishLaunchingWithOptions
    launchOptions: [NSObject: AnyObject]?) -> Bool {
        // Override point for customization after application launch.
        let splitViewController = self.window!.rootViewController as! UISplitViewController
        let navigationController = splitViewController.viewControllers[splitViewController.
        viewControllers.count-1] as! UINavigationController
        navigationController.topViewController!.navigationItem.leftBarButtonItem =
        splitViewController.displayModeButtonItem()
        splitViewController.delegate = self
        return true
    }
}
```

Let's look at the last part of this code first:

```
splitViewController.delegate = self;
```

This line sets the UISplitViewController's delegate property, pointing it at the application delegate itself. But why make this connection here in code, instead of having it hooked up directly in the storyboard? After all, just a few paragraphs ago, you were told that elimination of boring code—"connect this thing to that thing"—is one of the main benefits of both XIBs and storyboards. And we've hooked up delegates in Interface Builder plenty of times, so why can't we do that here?

To understand why using a storyboard to make the connections can't really work here, you need to consider how a storyboard differs from a XIB file. A XIB file is really a frozen object graph. When you load a XIB into a running application, the objects it contains all "thaw out" and spring into existence, including all the interconnections specified in the file. The system creates a fresh instance of every single object in the file, one after another, and connects all the outlets and connections between objects. A storyboard, however, is something more than that. You could say that each scene in a storyboard corresponds roughly to a XIB file. When you add in the metadata describing how the scenes are connected via segues, you end up with a storyboard. However, unlike a single XIB, a complex storyboard is not normally loaded all at once. Instead, any activity that causes a new scene to be activated will end up loading that particular scene's frozen object graph from the storyboard. This means that the objects you see when looking at a storyboard won't necessarily all exist at the same time.

Since Interface Builder has no way of knowing which scenes will coexist, it actually forbids you from making any outlet or target/action connections from an object in one scene to an object in another scene. In fact, segues are the only connection that it allows you to make from one scene to another.

You can try this for yourself. First, select the Split View Controller in the storyboard (you'll find it within the dock in the Split View Controller Scene). Now bring up the Connections Inspector and try to drag a connection from the delegate outlet to another view controller or object. You can drag all over the layout view and the list view, and you won't find any spot that highlights (which would indicate it was ready to accept a drag). The only way to make this connection is in code. All in all, this extra bit of code is a small price to pay, considering how much other code is eliminated by our use of storyboards.

Now let's rewind and look at what happens at the start of the `application(_:didFinishLaunchingWith Options:)` method:

```
let splitViewController = self.window!.rootViewController as! UISplitViewController
```

This grabs the window's `rootViewController`, which is the one indicated in the storyboard by the free-floating arrow. If you look back at Figure 11-6, you'll see that the arrow points at our `UISplitViewController` instance. This code comes next:

```
let navigationController = splitViewController.viewControllers[splitViewController.
viewControllers.count-1] as! UINavigationController
```

On this line, we dig into the `UISplitViewController`'s `viewControllers` array. When the split view is loaded from the storyboard, this array has references to the navigation controllers, wrapping the master and detail view controllers. We grab the last item in this array, which points to the `UINavigationController` for our detail view. Finally, we see this:

```
navigationController.topViewController!.navigationItem.leftBarButtonItem =
    splitViewController.displayModeButtonItem()
```

This assigns the `displayModeButtonItem` of the split view controller to the navigation bar of the detail view controller. The `displayModeButtonItem` is a bar button item that is created and managed by the split view itself. This code is actually adding the Master button that you can see on the navigation bar on the left in Figure 11-4. On the iPad, the split view shows this button when the device is in portrait mode and the master view controller is not visible. When the device rotates to landscape orientation or the user presses the button to make the master view controller visible, the button is hidden.

The Master View Controller

Now, let's take a look at `MasterViewController`, which controls the setup of the table view containing the app's navigation. Listing 11-2 shows the code from the top of the file MasterViewController.swift.

Listing 11-2. MasterViewController.swift

```
import UIKit

class MasterViewController: UITableViewController {

    var detailViewController: DetailViewController? = nil
    var objects = [AnyObject]()

    override func viewDidLoad() {
        super.viewDidLoad()
        // Do any additional setup after loading the view, typically from a nib.
        self.navigationItem.leftBarButtonItem = self.editButtonItem()

        let addButton = UIBarButtonItem(barButtonSystemItem: .add, target: self, action:
                        #selector(insertNewObject(_:)))
        self.navigationItem.rightBarButtonItem = addButton
        if let split = self.splitViewController {
            let controllers = split.viewControllers
            self.detailViewController = (controllers[controllers.count-1] as!
            UINavigationController).topViewController as? DetailViewController
        }
    }
}
```

The main point of interest here is the viewDidLoad() method. In previous chapters, when you implemented a table view controller that responded to a user row selection, you typically created a new view controller and pushed it onto the navigation controller's stack. In this app, however, the view controller we want to show is already in place and it will be reused each time the user makes a selection on the left. It's the instance of DetailViewController contained in the storyboard file. Here, we're grabbing that DetailViewController instance and saving it in a property, anticipating that we'll want to use it later, although, this property is not used in the rest of the template code.

The viewDidLoad() method also adds a button to the toolbar. This is the + button that you can see on the right of master view controller's navigation bar in Figure 11-4 and Figure 11-5. The template application uses this button to create and add a new entry to the master view controller's table view. Since we don't need this button in our Presidents application, we'll be removing this code shortly.

There are several more methods included in the template for this class, but don't worry about those right now. We're going to delete some of those and rewrite the others, but only after taking a look at the detail view controller.

The Detail View Controller

The final class created for us by Xcode is DetailViewController, which takes care of the actual display of the item the user chooses from the table in the master view controller. Here's what you'll find in DetailViewController.swift, as shown in Listing 11-3.

Listing 11-3. DetailViewController.swift

```
import UIKit

class DetailViewController: UIViewController {

    @IBOutlet weak var detailDescriptionLabel: UILabel!
```

```
func configureView() {
    // Update the user interface for the detail item.
    if let detail = self.detailItem {
        if let label = self.detailDescriptionLabel {
            label.text = detail.description
        }
    }
}

override func viewDidLoad() {
    super.viewDidLoad()
    // Do any additional setup after loading the view, typically from a nib.
    self.configureView()
}

override func didReceiveMemoryWarning() {
    super.didReceiveMemoryWarning()
    // Dispose of any resources that can be recreated.
}

var detailItem: NSDate? {
    didSet {
        // Update the view.
        self.configureView()
    }
}

}
```

The detailDescriptionLabel property is an outlet that connects to a label in the storyboard. In the template application, the label simply displays a description of the object in the detailItem property. The detailItem property itself is where the view controller stores its reference to the object that the user selected in the master view controller. Its property observer (the code in the didSet block), which is called after its value has been changed, calls configureView(), another method that's generated for us. All it does is call the description method of the detail object and then uses the result to set the text property of the label in the storyboard:

```
func configureView() {
    // Update the user interface for the detail item.
    if let detail = self.detailItem {
        if let label = self.detailDescriptionLabel {
            label.text = detail.description
        }
    }
}
```

The description method is implemented by every subclass of NSObject. If your class doesn't override it, it returns a default value that's probably not very useful. However, in the template code, the detail objects are all instances of the NSDate, class and NSDate's implementation of the description method returns the date and time, formatted in a generic way.

How the Master-Detail Template Application Works

Now you've seen all of the pieces of the template application, but you're probably still not very clear on how it works, so let's run it and take a look at what it actually does. Run the application on an iPad simulator and rotate the device to landscape mode so that the master view controller appears. You can see that the label in the detail view controller currently has the default text that's assigned to it in the storyboard. What we're going to see in this section is how the act of selecting an item in the master view controller causes that text to change. There currently aren't any items in the master view controller. To fix that, press the + button at the top right of its navigation bar a few times. Every time you do that, a new item is added to the controller's table view, as shown in Figure 11-7.

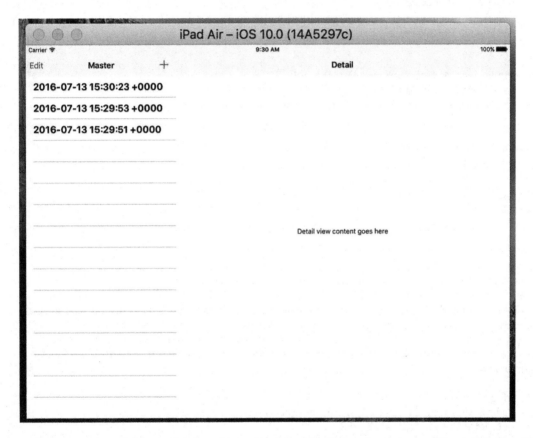

Figure 11-7. *The template application with an item selected in the master view controller and displayed in the detail view controller*

All of the items in the master view controller table are dates. Select one of them, and the label in the detail view updates to show the same date. You've already seen the code that does this—it's the configureView method in DetailViewController.swift, which is called when a new value is stored in the detail view controller's detailItem property. What is it that causes a new value of the detailItem property to be set? Take a look back at the storyboard in Figure 11-6. There's a segue that links the prototype table cell in the master view controller's table cell to the detail view controller. If you click this segue and open the Attributes Inspector, you'll see that this is a Show Detail segue with the identifier showDetail, as shown in Figure 11-8.

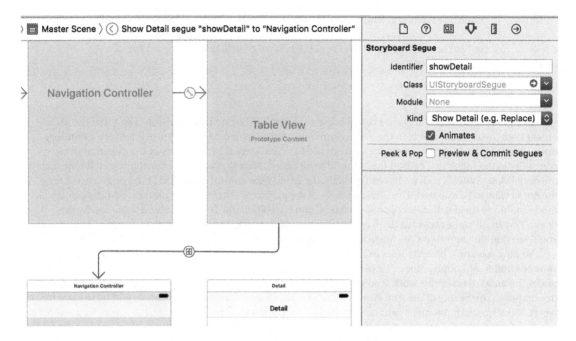

Figure 11-8. *The Show Detail segue linking the master and detail view controllers*

As you saw in Chapter 9, a segue that's linked to a table view cell is triggered when that cell is selected, so when you select a row in the master view controller's table view, iOS performs the Show Detail segue, with the navigation controller wrapping the detail view controller as the segue destination. This causes two things to happen:

- A new instance of the detail view controller is created and its view is added to the view hierarchy.

- The prepareForSegue(_:sender:) method in the master view controller is called.

The first step takes care of making sure the detail view controller is visible. In the second step, your master view controller needs to display the object selected in the master view controller in some way. Here's how the template code in MasterViewController.swift handles this, as shown in Listing 11-4.

Listing 11-4. The MasterViewcontroller.swift File's prepare(forSegue:)

```
// MARK: - Segues

override func prepare(for segue: UIStoryboardSegue, sender: AnyObject?) {
    if segue.identifier == "showDetail" {
        if let indexPath = self.tableView.indexPathForSelectedRow {
            let object = objects[indexPath.row] as! NSDate
            let controller = (segue.destinationViewController as! UINavigationController).
                        topViewController as! DetailViewController
            controller.detailItem = object
```

```
            controller.navigationItem.leftBarButtonItem = self.splitViewController?.
                                                displayModeButtonItem()
            controller.navigationItem.leftItemsSupplementBackButton = true
            }
        }
    }
```

First, the segue identifier is checked to make sure that it's the one that is expected and that the NSDate object from the selected object in the view controller's table is obtained. Next, the master view controller finds the DetailViewController instance from the topViewController property of the destination view controller in the segue that caused this method to be called. Now that we have both the selected object and the detail view controller, all we have to do is set the detail view controller's detailItem property to cause the detail view to be updated. The final two lines of the prepare(forSegue:) method add the display mode button to the detail view controller's navigation bar. When the device is in landscape mode, this doesn't do anything because the display mode button isn't visible, but if you rotate to portrait orientation, you'll see that the button (it's the Master button) appears.

So now you know how the selected item in the master view controller gets displayed in the detail view controller. Although it doesn't look like much is going on here, in fact there is a great deal happening under the hood to make this work correctly on both the iPad and the iPhone, in portrait and landscape orientations. The beauty of the split view controller is that it takes care of all the details and leaves you free to worry about how to implement your custom master and detail view controllers.

That concludes the overview of what the Xcode Master-Detail Application template provides. It might be a lot to understand at first, but, ideally, presenting it one piece at a time has helped you understand how all the pieces fit together.

Adding the President Data

Now that you've seen the basic layout of our project, it's time to fill in the blanks and turn the template app into something all your own. Start by looking in the book's source code archive, where the folder 11 – Presidents Data contains a file called PresidentList.plist. Drag that file into your project's Presidents folder in Xcode to add it to the project, making sure that the check box telling Xcode to copy the file itself is checked. This file contains information about all the US presidents so far, consisting of just the name and the Wikipedia entry URL for each of them.

Now, let's look at the master view controller and see how we need to modify it to handle the presidential data properly. It's going to be a simple matter of loading the list of presidents, presenting them in the table view, and passing a URL to the detail view for display. In MasterViewController.swift, start off by adding the bold line shown here at the top of the class and removing the crossed-out line:

```
class MasterViewController: UITableViewController {
    var detailViewController: DetailViewController? = nil
    var objects = [AnyObject]()
    var presidents: [[String: String]]!
```

Now look at the viewDidLoad() method, where the changes are a little more involved (but still not too bad). You're going to add a few lines to load the list of presidents, and then remove a few other lines that set up edit and insertion buttons in the toolbar, as shown in Listing 11-5.

Listing 11-5. The MasterViewController.swift viewDidLoad Method

```
override func viewDidLoad() {
    super.viewDidLoad()
    // Do any additional setup after loading the view, typically from a nib.
    let path = Bundle.main.path(forResource: "PresidentList", ofType: "plist")
    let presidentInfo = NSDictionary(contentsOfFile: path)!
    presidents = presidentInfo["presidents"]! as! [[String: String]]

    if let split = self.splitViewController {
        let controllers = split.viewControllers
        self.detailViewController = (controllers[controllers.count-1] as!
                                UINavigationController).topViewController as?
                                DetailViewController
    }
}
```

This code may be a little confusing at first:

```
let path = Bundle.main.path(forResource:"PresidentList", ofType: "plist")!
let presidentInfo = NSDictionary(contentsOfFile: path)!
presidents = presidentInfo["presidents"]! as! [[String: String]]
```

The `Bundle.main pathForResource(_:ofType:)` method gets the path to the PresidentList.plist file, the content of which is then loaded into an `NSDictionary`. This dictionary has one entry, with key "presidents". The value of that entry is an array, which has one `NSDictionary` for each president; that dictionary contains key-value pairs, where both the key and value are strings. We cast the array to the correct Swift type, `[[String: String]]`, and assign it to the `presidents` variable.

This template-generated class also includes a method called `insertNewObject()` for adding items to the `objects` array. We don't even have that array anymore, so delete the entire method.

Also, we have a couple of data source methods that deal with letting users edit rows in the table view. We're not going to allow any editing of rows in this app, so let's just remove the `canEditRowAt` and `commit editingStyle:` methods.

Now it's time to get to the main table view data source methods, adapting them for our purposes. Let's start by editing the method that tells the table view how many rows to display:

```
override func tableView(_ tableView: UITableView, numberOfRowsInSection section: Int) -> Int {
    return presidents.count
}
```

After that, edit the `tableView(_:cellForRowAtIndexPath:)` method to make each cell display a president's name:

```
override func tableView(_ tableView: UITableView, cellForRowAt indexPath: IndexPath) ->
UITableViewCell {
    let cell = tableView.dequeueReusableCell(withIdentifier: "Cell", for: indexPath)

    let president = presidents[indexPath.row]
    cell.textLabel!.text = president["name"]
    return cell
}
```

Finally, edit the prepareForSegue(_:sender:)method to pass the data for the selected president (which, as described earlier, is a dictionary of type [String: String]) to the detail view controller, as in Listing 11-6.

Listing 11-6. The prepare (forSegue:) Method

```
// MARK: - Segues


override func prepare(for segue: UIStoryboardSegue, sender: AnyObject?) {
    if segue.identifier == "showDetail" {
        if let indexPath = self.tableView.indexPathForSelectedRow {
            let object = presidents[indexPath.row]
            let controller = (segue.destinationViewController
                as! UINavigationController).topViewController as! DetailViewController
            controller.detailItem = object
            controller.navigationItem.leftBarButtonItem =
                self.splitViewController?.displayModeButtonItem()
            controller.navigationItem.leftItemsSupplementBackButton = true
        }
    }
}
```

■ **Note**   If your template for the DetailViewController.swift file's detailItem method had the value NSDate or similar, you should change it to 'AnyObject?' to remove potential errors.

That's all we need to do in the master view controller.

Next, select Main.storyboard and click the Master icon in the Master Scene in the Document Outline to select the master view controller (it's the one on the right of the top row of the storyboard), and then double-click its title bar and replace Master with Presidents, and save the storyboard.

At this point, you can build and run the app. Switch to landscape mode to bring up the master view controller, showing a list of presidents, as in Figure 11-9. Tap a president's name to display a not-very-useful string in the detail view.

Figure 11-9. *Our first run of the app, showing a list of presidents in the master view controller, but nothing in the detail view*

Let's finish this example by making the detail view do something a little more useful with the data that it's given. Add the following line shown in bold to DetailViewContoller.swift to create an outlet for a web view to display the Wikipedia page for the selected president:

```
class DetailViewController: UIViewController {
    @IBOutlet weak var detailDescriptionLabel: UILabel!
    @IBOutlet weak var webView: UIWebView!
```

Next, scroll down to the configureView() method and replace it with the code in Listing 11-7.

Listing 11-7. The configureView Method

```
func configureView() {
    // Update the user interface for the detail item.
    if let detail = self.detailItem {
if let label = self.detailDescriptionLabel {
            let dict = detail as! [String: String]
            let urlString = dict["url"]!
            label.text = urlString

            let url = NSURL(string: urlString)!
            let request = URLRequest(url: url as URL)
            webView.loadRequest(request)
```

```
            let name = dict["name"]!
            title = name
        }
    }
}
```

The detailItem that was set by the master view controller is a dictionary containing two key-value pairs: one with a key name that stores the president's name and another with a key url that gives the URL of the president's Wikipedia page. We use the URL to set the text of the detail description label and to construct an URLRequest that the UIWebView will use to load the page. We use the name to set the detail view controller's title. When a view controller is a container in a UINavigationController, the value in its title property is displayed in the navigation controller's navigation bar. That's all we need to get our web view to load the requested page.

The final changes we need to make are in Main.storyboard. Open it for editing and find the detail view at the lower right. Let's first take care of the label in the GUI (the text of which reads, "Detail view content goes here"). Start by selecting the label. You might find it easiest to select the label in the Document Outline, in the section labeled Detail Scene. Once the label is selected, drag it to the top of the window. The label should run from the left-to-right blue guideline and fit snugly under the navigation bar (resize it to make sure that is the case). This label is being repurposed to show the current URL. But when the application launches, before the user has chosen a president, we want this field to give the user a hint about what to do.

Double-click the label and change its text to Select a President. You should also use the Size Inspector to make sure that the label's position is constrained to both the left and right sides of its superview, as well as the top edge, as shown in Figure 11-10. If you need to adjust these constraints, use the methods described earlier to set them up. You can probably get almost exactly what you want by selecting the label and then choosing Editor ➤ Resolve Auto Layout Issues ➤ Reset to Suggested Constraints from the menu.

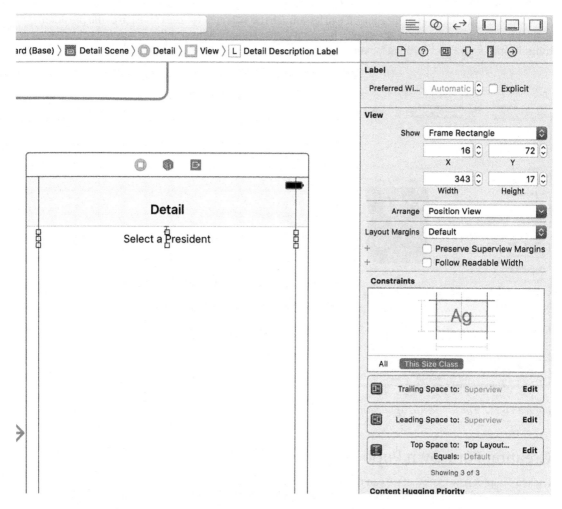

Figure 11-10. *The Size Inspector, showing the constraints settings for the "Select a President" label*

Next, find a `UIWebView` in the Object Library and drag it into the space below the label you just moved. After dropping the web view there, use the resize handles to make it fill the rest of the view below the label. Make it go from the left edge to the right edge, and from the blue guideline just below the bottom of the label all the way to the very bottom of the window. Now use the Size Inspector to constrain the web view to the left, bottom, and right edges of the superview, as well as to the label for the top edge. Once again, you can probably get exactly what you need by selecting Editor ➤ Resolve Auto Layout Issues ➤ Reset to Suggested Constraints from the menu.

Now select the Master view controller in the Document Outline and open the Attributes Inspector. In the View Controller section, change the Title from Master to Presidents. This changes the title of the navigation button at the top of the detail view controller to something more useful.

We have one last step to complete. To hook up the outlet for the web view that you created, Control-drag from the Detail icon (the one immediately below the Detail Scene icon in the Document Outline) to our new Web View (same section, just below the label in the Document Outline, or in the storyboard), and connect the `webView` outlet. Save your changes.

Now you can build and run the app. It will let you see the Wikipedia entries for each of the presidents, as shown in Figure 11-11. Rotate the display between the two orientations. You'll see how the split view controller takes care of everything for you, with a little help from the detail view controller.

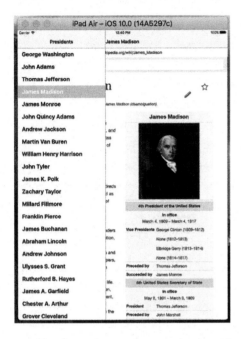

Figure 11-11. *The Presidents application, showing the Wikipedia page for James Madison*

Creating Your Own Popover

Back in Chapter 4, we saw that we can display an action sheet in what looks like a cartoon speech bubble (see Figure 4-29). That speech bubble is the visual representation of a **popover controller**, or **popover** for short. The popover that you get with an action sheet is created for you when the action sheet is presented by a `UIPopoverPresentationController`. It turns out that you can use the same controller to create popovers of your own.

To see how this works, we're going to add a popover that will be activated by a permanent toolbar item (unlike the one in the `UISplitView`, which is meant to come and go). This popover will display a table view containing a list of languages. If the user picks a language from the list, the web view will load whatever Wikipedia entry that was already showing, in the new language. This is simple enough to do, since switching from one language to another in Wikipedia is just a matter of changing a small piece of the URL that contains an embedded country code. Figure 11-3 shows what we are aiming for.

■ **Note**   In this example, we're using a `UIPopoverPresentationController` to display a table view controller, but don't let that mislead you—it can be used to handle the display of any view controller content you like. We're sticking with table views for this example because it's a common use case, it's easy to show in a relatively small amount of code, and it's something with which you should already be quite familiar.

Start by right-clicking the Presidents folder in Xcode and selecting New File... from the pop-up menu. When the assistant appears, select Cocoa Touch Class from the iOS Source section, and then click Next. On the next screen, name the new class `LanguageListController` and select `UITableViewController` from the Subclass of field. Click Next, double-check the location where you're saving the file, and click Create.

The `LanguageListController` will be a pretty standard table view controller class. It will display a list of items and let the detail view controller know when a choice is made, by using a pointer back to the detail view controller. Edit LanguageListController.swift, adding the three lines shown below the class name:

```
class LanguageListController: UITableViewController {
    weak var detailViewController: DetailViewController? = nil
    private let languageNames: [String] = ["English", "French", "German", "Spanish"]
    private let languageCodes: [String] = ["en", "fr", "de", "es"]
```

These additions define a pointer back to the detail view controller (which we'll set from code in the detail view controller itself when we're about to display the language list), as well as a pair of arrays containing the values that will be displayed (English, French, etc.) and the underlying values that will be used to build an URL from the chosen language (`en`, `fr`, and so on).

If you copied and pasted this code from the book's source archive (or e-book) into your own project or typed it yourself a little sloppily, you may not have noticed an important difference in how the `detailViewController` property was declared earlier. Unlike most properties that reference an object pointer, we declared this one using `weak` instead of `strong`. This is something that we must do to avoid a **retain** cycle.

What's a retain cycle? It's a situation where a set of two or more objects have references to each other, in a circular fashion. Each object is keeping the memory of the other object from being freed. Most potential retain cycles can be avoided by carefully considering the creation of your objects, often by trying to figure out which object "owns" which. In this sense, an instance of `DetailViewController` owns an instance of `LanguageListController` because it's the `DetailViewController` that actually creates the `LanguageListController` to get a piece of work done. Whenever you have a pair of objects that need to refer to one another, you'll usually want the owner object to retain the other object, while the other object should specifically not retain its owner. Since we're using the ARC feature that Apple introduced way back in Xcode 4.2, the compiler does most of the work for us. Instead of paying attention to the details about releasing and retaining objects, all we need to do is declare a property that refers to an object that we do not own with the `weak` keyword instead of `strong`. ARC does the rest.

Next, scroll down a bit to the `viewDidLoad()` method and add this setup code:

```
override func viewDidLoad() {
    super.viewDidLoad()

    clearsSelectionOnViewWillAppear = false
    preferredContentSize = CGSize(width: 320, height: (languageCodes.count * 44))
    tableView.register(UITableViewCell.self, forCellReuseIdentifier: "Cell")
}
```

Here, we define the size that the view controller's view will use if shown in a popover (which, as we know, it will be). Without defining the size, we would end up with a popover stretching vertically to fill nearly the whole screen, even if it can be displayed in full with a much smaller view. And finally, we register a default table view cell class to use, as explained in Chapter 8.

Further down, we have a few methods generated by Xcode's template that don't contain particularly useful code—just a warning and some placeholder text. Let's replace those with something real:

```
override func numberOfSections(in tableView: UITableView) -> Int {
    return 1
}
override func tableView(_ tableView: UITableView, numberOfRowsInSection section: Int) -> Int {
    return languageCodes.count
}
```

Now implement the `tableView(_:cellForRow atIndexPath:)` method to get a cell object and put a language name into a cell, as shown in Listing 11-8.

Listing 11-8. Getting Our Cell for the Table View

```
override func tableView(_ tableView: UITableView, cellForRowAt indexPath: IndexPath) ->
UITableViewCell {
    let cell = tableView.dequeueReusableCell(withIdentifier: "Cell", for: indexPath)
    // Configure the cell...
    cell.textLabel!.text = languageNames[indexPath.row]

    return cell
}
```

Next, implement `tableView(_:didSelectRowAtIndexPath:)` so that you can respond to a user's touch by passing the language selection back to the detail view controller and dismissing the presented `LanguageListController` by calling its `dismissViewControllerAnimated(_:completion:)` method:

```
override func tableView(_ tableView: UITableView, didSelectRowAt indexPath: IndexPath) {
    detailViewController?.languageString = languageCodes[indexPath.row]
    dismiss(animated: true, completion: nil)
}
```

■ **Note**   `DetailViewController` doesn't actually have a `languageString` property yet, so you will see a compiler error. We'll take care of that in just a bit.

Now it's time to make the changes required for `DetailViewController` to display the popover, as well as to generate the correct URL whenever the user either changes the display language or picks a different president. Start by adding the following three lines of code in DetailViewController.swift below the `UIWebView` declaration.

```
private var languageListController: LanguageListController?
private var languageButton: UIBarButtonItem?
var languageString = ""
```

We added some properties to keep track of the GUI components required for the popover and the user's selected language. All that we need to do now is fix DetailViewController.swift so that it can handle the language popover and the URL construction.

Start by adding a function that takes as arguments a URL pointing to a Wikipedia page and a two-letter language code, and then returns a URL that combines the two. We'll use this at appropriate spots in our controller code later, as shown in Listing 11-9.

Listing 11-9. Function to Get Our Language-Specific URL

```
private func modifyUrlForLanguage(url: String, language lang: String?) -> String {
    var newUrl = url

    // We're relying on a particular Wikipedia URL format here. This
    // is a bit fragile!
    if let langStr = lang {
        // URL is like https://en.wikipedia...
        let range = NSMakeRange(8, 2)
        if !langStr.isEmpty && (url as NSString).substring(with: range) != langStr {
            newUrl = (url as NSString).replacingCharacters(in: range,
                                                           with: langStr)
        }
    }

    return newUrl
}
```

Our next move is to update the `configureView()` method. This method will use the function we just defined to combine the URL that's passed in with the chosen `languageString` to generate the correct URL, as shown in Listing 11-10.

Listing 11-10. Update configureView Method for the Language-Specific URL

```
    func configureView() {
        // Update the user interface for the detail item.
        if let detail = self.detailItem {
            if let label = self.detailDescriptionLabel {
                let dict = detail as! [String: String]
//              let urlString = dict["url"]!
                let urlString = modifyUrlForLanguage(url: dict["url"]!, language: languageString)
                label.text = urlString

                let url = URL(string: urlString)!
                let request = URLRequest(url: url )
                webView.loadRequest(request)
                let name = dict["name"]!
                title = name
            }
        }
    }
```

Now let's update the `viewDidLoad()` method. Here, we're going to create a `UIBarButtonItem` and put it into the `UINavigationItem` at the top of the screen. The button will call the controller's `showLanguagePopover()` method, which we'll implement shortly, when it is clicked, as shown in Listing 11-11.

Listing 11-11. The Modified viewDidLoad Method

```
override func viewDidLoad() {
    super.viewDidLoad()
    // Do any additional setup after loading the view, typically from a nib.
    self.configureView()
    languageButton = UIBarButtonItem(title: "Choose Language", style: .plain,
                                        target: self, action:
            #selector(DetailViewController.showLanguagePopover))
    navigationItem.rightBarButtonItem = languageButton

}
```

Next, we implement a property observer for the languageString property, which is called when the value of the property is changed. The property observer calls configureView() so that the URL is regenerated to include the selected language and the new page loaded:

```
var languageString = "" {
    didSet {
        if languageString != oldValue {
            configureView()
        }
    }
}
```

Now, let's implement the method that's called when the user taps the Choose Language button. Simply put, we display the LanguageListController, creating it the first time we do so. Then, we get its popover presentation controller and set the properties that control where the popover will appear. Place this method after the viewDidLoad() method, as shown in Listing 11-12.

Listing 11-12. The showLanguagePopover Method

```
func showLanguagePopover() {
    if languageListController == nil {
        // Lazy creation when used for the first time
        languageListController = LanguageListController()
        languageListController!.detailViewController = self
        languageListController!.modalPresentationStyle = .popover
    }
    present(languageListController!, animated: true, completion: nil)
    if let ppc = languageListController?.popoverPresentationController {
        ppc.barButtonItem = languageButton
    }
}
```

In the first part of this method, we check whether we have already created the LanguageListController. If we haven't, we create an instance and then set its detailViewController property to point to ourselves. We also set its modalPresentationStyle property to .popover. This property determines how the controller is displayed when it is modally presented. There are several possible values, which you can read about on the documentation page for the UIViewController class. Not surprisingly, the value .popover is the one you need to use if you want the controller to be presented in a popover.

Next, we use the `presentViewController(_:animated:completion:)` method to make the `LanguageListController` visible, just as we did when displaying an alert back in Chapter 4. Calling this method does not make the controller visible immediately—UIKit does that when it's finished processing the button click event—but it does create the `UIPopoverPresentationController` that will manage the controller's popover. Before the popover appears, we need to tell UIKit where it should appear. In Chapter 4, we used this technique to place a popover near a specific view by setting its `UIPopoverPresentationController`'s `sourceRect` and `sourceView` properties. In this example, we want the popover to appear near the language button and we can do that by assigning a reference to that button to the controller's `barButtonItem` property.

Now run the example on the iPad simulator and press the Choose Language button. You'll find that the language list controller is displayed in a popover, as shown in Figure 11-12. You should be able to use the language pop-up to select any of the four available languages and watch the web view update to show the version of the President's page for that language.

Figure 11-12. *Choosing to load a page in a different language*

Switching from one language to another should always leave the chosen president intact. Likewise, switching from one president to another should leave the language intact—but actually, it doesn't. Try this: choose a president, change the language to (say) Spanish, and then choose another president. Unfortunately, the language is no longer Spanish.

Why did this happen? The Show Detail segue creates a new instance of the detail view controller every time it's called. That means that the language setting, which is stored as a property of the detail view controller, is going to be lost each time a new president is selected. To fix it, we need to add a few lines of code in the master view controller. Open MasterViewController.swift and make the changes in Listing 11-13 to the `prepareForSegue` method.

Listing 11-13. Updated prepareForSegue Method

```
override func prepare(for segue: UIStoryboardSegue, sender: AnyObject?) {
    if segue.identifier == "showDetail" {
        if let indexPath = self.tableView.indexPathForSelectedRow {
            let object = presidents[indexPath.row]
            let controller = (segue.destinationViewController as!
                UINavigationController).topViewController as! DetailViewController
            if let oldController = detailViewController {
                controller.languageString = oldController.languageString
            }
            controller.detailItem = object
            controller.navigationItem.leftBarButtonItem =
                self.splitViewController?.displayModeButtonItem()
            controller.navigationItem.leftItemsSupplementBackButton = true
            detailViewController = controller
        }
    }
}
```

Summary

In this chapter, you learned about the split view controller and its role in the creation of Master-Detail applications. You also saw that a complex application with several interconnected view controllers can be configured entirely within Interface Builder. Although split views are now available on all devices, they are probably still most useful in the larger screen space of the iPhone 6/6s Plus and the iPad.

■ ■ ■

CHAPTER 12

App Customization with Settings and Defaults

All but the simplest apps you're likely to use typically include a preferences window where the user sets application-specific options. On macOS, you'll usually find a **Preferences...** menu item in the application's menu. Selecting it brings up a window where the user enters and changes various options. The iPhone and iPad include a dedicated application called Settings that you've likely used before. In this chapter, we'll show you how to add settings for your iOS application to the Settings app and how to access those settings from within your application.

The Settings Bundle

The Settings application lets the user enter and change preferences for any application that includes a settings bundle. The settings bundle contains a group of files built in to an application that tells the Settings application which preferences the application wishes to collect from the user, as shown in Figure 12-1. The Settings application acts as a common user interface for the iOS User Defaults mechanism. User Defaults stores and retrieves preferences for the application.

© Molly Maskrey, Kim Topley, David Mark, Fredrik Olsson and Jeff Lamarche 2016
M. Maskrey et al., *Beginning iPhone Development with Swift 3*, DOI 10.1007/978-1-4842-2223-2_12

Figure 12-1. *The Settings app on a typical iPhone display*

In an iOS application, the NSUserDefaults class provides the user defaults service. If you've programmed in Cocoa on macOS, you're probably already familiar with NSUserDefaults because it's the same class used to store and read preferences on macOS. Your applications use NSUserDefaults to read and store preference data using pairs of keys and values, just as you would access keyed data from a dictionary, the difference being NSUserDefaults data persists to the file system rather than stored in an object instance in memory. In this chapter, we'll create an application, add and configure a settings bundle, and then access and edit those preferences from the Settings application, and from within our own application.

Because the Settings app provides a standard interface, you don't need to design your own UI for your app's preferences. You create a property list describing your application's available settings, and the Settings app creates the interface for you. Immersive applications, such as games, generally should provide their own preferences view so that the user doesn't need to quit to make a change. Even utility and productivity applications might, at times, have preferences that a user should be able to change without leaving the application. We'll also show you to how to collect preferences from the user directly in your application and store those in iOS's User Defaults.

iOS allows the user to switch from one application to the Settings app, change a preference, and then switch back to your still-running application. We'll see how to do this at the end of the chapter.

The Bridge Control Application

In this chapter, we're going to build a simple application that keeps track of some aspects of managing the bridge of a simulated starship. First, we'll create a settings bundle so that, when the user launches the Settings application, there will be an entry for our app, Bridge Control, as shown in Figure 12-2.

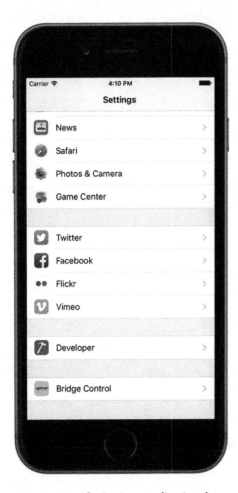

Figure 12-2. *The Settings application shows an entry for our Bridge Control application in the simulator*

If the user selects our application from the display in Figure 12-2, Settings drills down into a view showing the preferences relevant to our application. The Settings application uses text fields, secure text fields, switches, and sliders to update values, as shown in Figure 12-3.

Figure 12-3. Our application's primary settings view

Notice that two items in the view contain disclosure indicators. The first one, Rank, takes the user to another table view that displays the options available for that item. From that table view, the user selects a single value, as shown in Figure 12-4.

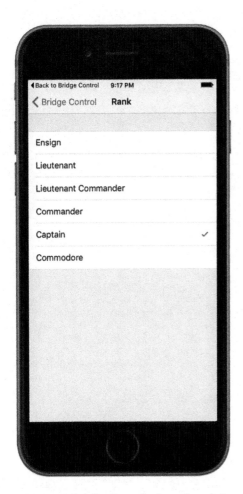

Figure 12-4. *Selecting a single preference item from a list*

The More Settings disclosure indicator allows the user to drill down to another set of preferences, as shown in Figure 12-5. This child view can have the same kinds of controls as the main settings view or even its own child views. The Settings application uses a navigation controller, which it needs because it supports the construction of hierarchical preference views.

Figure 12-5. *The child settings view for our Bridge Control application*

When users launch Bridge Control, it presents a list of the preferences gathered in the Settings application, as shown in Figure 12-6.

Figure 12-6. *The app's main view presents the list of preferences to the user*

To show how to update preferences from within our application, Bridge Control provides a second view where the user can change additional preferences directly in the application, as shown in Figure 12-7

Figure 12-7. *Bridge Control allows setting some preferences from within the app itself*

Creating the Bridge Control Project

In Xcode, press ⇧⌘N or select File ➤ New ➤ Project.... When the new project assistant comes up, select Application from under the iOS heading in the left pane, click the Tabbed Application icon, and then click Next. On the next screen, name your project **Bridge Control**. Set Devices to Universal, and then click the Next button. Finally, choose a location for your project and click Create.

The Bridge Control application is based on the UITabBarController class that we used in Chapter 7. The template creates two tabs, which is all we'll need. Each tab requires an icon. You'll find these in the 12 - Images folder in the example source code archive. In Xcode, select Assets.xcassets, and then delete the first and second images that were added by the Xcode template. Now add the replacement images by dragging the singleicon.imageset and doubleicon.imageset folders from 12 - Images into the editing area.

Next, we'll assign the icons to their tab bar items. Select Main.storyboard. You'll see the tab bar controller and the two child controllers for its tabs: one labeled First View and the other Second View. Select the first child controller, and then click its tab bar item, which currently shows a square and the title First. In the Bar Item section of the Attributes Inspector, change the Title to Main and the Image to singleicon, as shown in Figure 12-8. Now select the tab bar item for the second child controller and change the title from Second to Settings and the image from second to doubleicon. That's enough work on the application itself for now—before doing anything more, let's create its settings bundle.

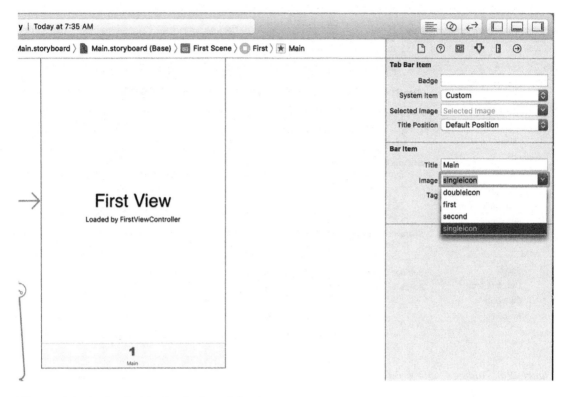

Figure 12-8. *Setting the icon for the first tab bar item*

Working with the Settings Bundle

The Settings application uses the contents of each application's settings bundle to construct a settings view for that application. If an application has no settings bundle, then the Settings app doesn't show anything for it. Each settings bundle must contain a property list called Root.plist that defines the root-level preferences view. This property list must follow a very precise format, which we'll talk about when we set up the property list for our app's settings bundle.

When the Settings application starts up, it checks each application for a settings bundle and adds a settings group for each application that includes a settings bundle. If we want our preferences to include any subviews, we need to add property lists to the bundle and add an entry to Root.plist for each child view. You'll see exactly how to do that in this chapter.

Adding a Settings Bundle to Our Project

In the Project Navigator, click the Bridge Control folder, and then select File ➤ New ➤ File… or press ⌘N. In the left pane, select Resource under the iOS heading, and then select the Settings Bundle icon (see Figure 12-9). Click the Next button, leave the default name of Settings.bundle, and click Create.

Figure 12-9. *Adding a Settings Bundle to our project*

You should now see a new item in the project window called Settings.bundle. Expand the Settings. bundle item. You should see two subitems: a folder named en.lproj, containing a file named Root.strings, and another named Root.plist. We'll discuss en.lproj later when we talk about localizing an application into other languages. Here, we'll concentrate on Root.plist.

Select Root.plist and take a look at the editor pane. You're looking at the Xcode property list editor, as shown in Figure 12-10.

Key		Type	Value
▼ iPhone Settings Schema		Dictionary	(2 items)
Strings Filename	⬍ ⊕ ⊖	String	Root
▶ Preference Items	⬍	Array	(4 items)

⊞ ⟨ ⟩ 📄 Bridge Control ⟩ 📁 Bridge Control ⟩ ◯ Settings.bundle ⟩ 📄 Root.plist ⟩ No Selection

Figure 12-10. *Root.plist in the property list editor pane. If your editing pane looks slightly different, don't panic. Simply Control-click in the editing pane and select Show Raw Keys/Values from the contextual menu that appears*

Notice the organization of the items in the property list. Property lists are essentially dictionaries, storing item types and values and using a key to retrieve them, just as a `Dictionary` does. Several different types of nodes can be put into a property list. The Boolean, Data, Date, Number, and String node types are meant to hold individual pieces of data, but you also have a couple of ways to deal with whole collections of nodes, as well. In addition to `Dictionary` node types, which allow you to store other dictionaries, there are `Array` nodes, which store an ordered list of other nodes similar to an array. The `Dictionary` and `Array` types are the only property list node types that can contain other nodes.

■ **Note**   Although you can use most kinds of objects as keys in a `Dictionary` node type, keys in property list dictionary nodes must be strings. However, you are free to use any node type for the values.

When creating a settings property list, you need to follow a very specific format. Fortunately, Root. plist, the property list that came with the settings bundle you just added to your project, follows this format exactly. Let's take a look.

In the Root.plist editor pane, names of keys can either be displayed in their true, "raw" form or in a slightly more human-readable form. We're big fans of seeing things as they truly are whenever possible, so right-click anywhere in the editor and make sure that the Show Raw Keys/Values option in the contextual menu is checked, as shown in Figure 12-11. The rest of our discussion here uses the real names for all the keys we're going to talk about, so this step is important.

Figure 12-11. *Right-click or Control-click anywhere in the property list editing pane and make sure the Show Raw Keys/Values item is checked. This will ensure that real names are used in the property list editor, which makes your editing experience more precise*

■ **Caution**   Leaving the property list, either by editing a different file or by quitting Xcode, may reset the Show Raw Keys/Values item to be unchecked. If your text suddenly looks a little different, take another look at that menu item and make sure it is checked.

One of the items in the dictionary is StringsTable. A strings table is used in translating your application into another language. We'll discuss the translation of strings in Chapter 22 when we get into localization. We won't be using it in this chapter, but feel free to leave it in your project since it won't do any harm. In addition to StringsTable, the property list contains a node named PreferenceSpecifiers, which is an array. This array node is designed to hold a set of dictionary nodes, where each node represents either a single preference item that the user can modify or a single child view that the user can drill down into.

Click the disclosure triangle to the left of PreferenceSpecifiers to expand that node. You'll notice that Xcode's template kindly gave us four child nodes, as shown in Figure 12-12. Those nodes don't reflect the preferences that we need in this example, so delete Item 1, Item 2, and Item 3 (select each one and press the Delete key, one after another), leaving just Item 0 in place.

Key	Type	Value
▼ iPhone Settings Schema	Dictionary	(2 items)
StringsTable ⬍	String	**Root**
▼ PreferenceSpecifiers ⬍	Array	(4 items)
▶ Item 0 (Group - Group)	Dictionary	(2 items)
▶ Item 1 (Text Field - Name)	Dictionary	(8 items)
▶ Item 2 (Toggle Switch - Enabled)	Dictionary	(4 items)
▶ Item 3 (Slider)	Dictionary	(7 items)

Figure 12-12. *Root.plist in the editor pane, this time with PreferenceSpecifiers expanded*

■ **Note**　To select an item in the property list, it is best to click one side or the other of the Key column to avoid bringing up the Key column's drop-down menu.

Single-click Item 0 but don't expand it. The Xcode property list editor lets you add rows simply by pressing the Return key. The current selection state—including which row is selected and whether it's expanded—determines where the new row will be inserted. When an unexpanded array or dictionary is selected, pressing Return adds a sibling node after the selected row. In other words, it will add another node at the same level as the current selection. If you were to press Return (but don't do that now), you would get a new row called Item 1 immediately after Item 0. Figure 12-13 shows an example of hitting Return to create a new row. Notice the drop-down menu that allows you to specify the kind of preference specifier this item represents—more on this in a bit.

Key		Type		Value
▼ iPhone Settings Schema		Dictionary		(2 items)
StringsTable	↕	String		**Root**
▼ PreferenceSpecifiers	↕	Array		(2 items)
▶ Item 0 (Group - Group)		Dictionary		(2 items)
▶ Item 1 (Text Field -)	⌄	Dictionary	↕	(3 items)

> Group
> Multi Value
> Slider
> ✓ Text Field
> Title
> Toggle Switch

Figure 12-13. *We selected Item 0 and hit Return to create a new sibling row. Note the drop-down menu that appears, allowing us to specify the kind of preference specifier this item represents*

Now expand Item 0 and see what it contains, as shown in Figure 12-14. The editor is now ready to add child nodes to the selected item. If you were to press Return at this point (again, don't actually press it now), you would get a new first child row inside Item 0.

Key		Type		Value
▼ iPhone Settings Schema		Dictionary		(2 items)
StringsTable	↕ ⊕ ⊖	String		**Root**
▼ PreferenceSpecifiers	↕	Array		(1 item)
▼ Item 0 (Group - Group)	⌄	Dictionary	↕	(2 items)
Type	↕	String		**PSGroupSpecifier**
Title	↕	String		**Group**

Figure 12-14. *When you expand Item 0, you'll find a row with a key of Type and a second row with a key of Title. This represents a group with a title of Group*

One of the items inside Item 0 has a key of Type. Every property list node in the PreferenceSpecifiers array must have an entry with this key. The Type key tells the Settings application what type of data is associated with this item. In Item 0, the Type item has a value of PSGroupSpecifier. This indicates that the item represents the start of a new group. Each item that follows will be part of this group—until the next item with a Type of PSGroupSpecifier. If you look back at Figure 12-3, you'll see that the Settings application presents the application settings in a grouped table. Item 0 in the PreferenceSpecifiers array in a settings bundle property list should always be a PSGroupSpecifier, so that the settings start in a new group. This is important because you need at least one group in every Settings table.

The only other entry in Item 0 has a key of Title, and this is used to set an optional header just above the group that is being started. Now take a closer look at the Item 0 row itself and you'll see that it's actually shown as Item 0 (Group – Group). The values in parentheses represent the value of the Type item (the first Group) and the Title item (the second Group). This is a nice shortcut that Xcode gives you so that you can visually scan the contents of a settings bundle.

As shown back in Figure 12-3, we called our first group General Info. Double-click the value next to Title, and change it from Group to General Info (see Figure 12-15). When you enter the new title, you may notice a slight change to Item 0. It's now shown as Item 0 (Group – General Info) to reflect the new title. In the Settings application, the title is shown in uppercase, so the user will actually see GENERAL INFO instead. You can see this in Figure 12-3.

Key		Type	Value
▼ iPhone Settings Schema		Dictionary	(2 items)
StringsTable	⬍	String	Root
▼ PreferenceSpecifiers	⬍	Array	(1 item)
▼ Item 0 (Group - General Info)		Dictionary	(2 items)
Type	⬍	String	PSGroupSpecifier
Title	⬍ ⊕ ⊖	String	◇ General Info

Figure 12-15. *We changed the title of the Item 0 group from Group to General Info*

Adding a Text Field Setting

We now need to add a second item in this array, which will represent the first actual preference field. We're going to start with a simple text field. If you were to single-click the PreferenceSpecifiers row in the editor pane (don't do this, just keep reading) and press Return to add a child, the new row would be inserted at the beginning of the list, which is not what we want. We want to add a row at the end of the array.

To add the row, click the disclosure triangle to the left of Item 0 to close it, and then select Item 0 and press Return. This gives you a new sibling row after the current row, as shown in Figure 12-16. As usual, when the item is added, a drop-down menu appears, showing the default value of Text Field.

Figure 12-16. *Adding a new sibling row to Item 0*

Click somewhere outside the drop-down menu to make it go away, and then click the disclosure triangle next to Item 1 to expand it. You'll see that it contains a Type row set to PSTextFieldSpecifier. This is the Type value used to tell the Settings application that we want the user to edit this setting in a text field. It also contains two empty rows for Title and Key, as shown in Figure 12-17.

Figure 12-17. *Our text field item, expanded to show the type, title, and key*

Select the Title row, and then double-click in the whitespace of the Value column. Type in Commanding Officer to set the Title value. This is the text that will appear in the Settings app.

Now do the same for the Key row (no, that's not a misprint, you're really looking at a key called **Key**). In the value field, type **officer** (note the lowercase first letter). which key to use when it stores the value entered in this text field.

Recall what we said about NSUserDefaults? It lets you store values using a key, similar to a Dictionary. Well, the Settings application does the same thing for each of the preferences it saves on your behalf. If you give it a key value of foo, then later in your application, you can request the value for foo, and it will give you the value the user entered for that preference. We will use key value officer later to retrieve this setting from the user defaults in our application.

■ **Note** Our Title has a value of Commanding Officer and our Key has a value of officer. This uppercase/lowercase difference will happen frequently, and here we're even compounding the difference by using two words for the displayed title, and a single word for the key. The Title is what appears on the screen; so the capital C and O, and putting a space between the words, all makes sense. The Key is a text string we'll use to retrieve preferences from the user defaults, so all lowercase makes sense there. Could we use all lowercase for Title? You bet. And we could use all capitals for Key. As long as you capitalize it the same way when you save and when you retrieve, it doesn't matter which convention you use for your preference keys.

Now select the last of the three Item 1 rows (the one with a key of Key) and press Return to add another entry to the Item 1 dictionary, giving this one a key of AutocapitalizationType. Note that, as soon as you start typing **AutocapitalizationType**, Xcode presents you with a list of matching choices, so you can simply pick one from the list instead of typing the whole name. After you've entered AutocapitalizationType, press the Tab key or click the small up/down arrow icon on the right of the Value column to open a list where you can select from the available options. Choose Words. This specifies that the text field should automatically capitalize each word that the user types in this field.

Create one last new row and give it a key of AutocorrectionType and a value of No. This will tell the Settings application not to autocorrect values entered into this text field. In any situation where you do want the text field to use autocorrection, you would set the value in this row to Yes. Again, Xcode presents you with a list of matching choices as you begin entering **AutocorrectionType**. It shows you a list of valid options in a pop-up.

When you're finished, your property list should look like the one shown in Figure 12-18.

Key		Type	Value
▼ iPhone Settings Schema		Dictionary	(2 items)
StringsTable	↕	String	Root
▼ PreferenceSpecifiers	↕	Array	(9 items)
▶ Item 0 (Group - General Info)		Dictionary	(2 items)
▼ Item 1 (Text Field - Commanding		Dictionary	(5 items)
Type	↕	String	PSTextFieldSpecifier
Title	↕	String	Commanding Officer
Key	↕	String	officer
AutocapitalizationType	↕ ⊕ ⊖	String	↕ Words
AutocorrectionType	↕	String	No

Figure 12-18. *The finished text field specified in Root.plist*

Adding an Application Icon

Before we try our new setting, let's add an application icon to the project. You've done this before, so the steps should be familiar. First, save Root.plist, the property file you just edited. Next, use the Project Navigator to select the Assets.xcassets item, and then select the AppIcon item it contains. There, you'll find a set of drop targets where icons can be placed.

In the Finder, navigate first to the source code archive, and then into the 12 - Images folder. Working from top to bottom of the slots in the editor view Assets.xcassets in Xcode, drag and drop the files from 12 - Images as follows:

- Drag Settings-iPhone@2x.png and Settings-iPhone@3x.png respectively onto the 2x and 3x slots in the top left group.

- Drag Spotlight-iPhone@2x.png and Spotlight-iPhone@3x.png respectively onto the 2x and 3x slots in the top-right group.

- Drag AppIcon-iPhone@2x.png and AppIcon-iPhone@3x.png onto the 2x and 3x slots in the group on the second row.

- Drag Settings-iPad.png and Settings-iPad@2x.png onto the 1x and 2x slots in the left group on the third row.

- Drag Spotlight-iPad.png and Spotlight-iPad@2x.png onto the 1x and 2x slots in the right group on the third row.

- Drag AppIcon-iPad.png and AppIcon-iPad@2x.png onto the 1x and 2x slots in the group on the bottom row.

- Drag AppIcon-iPadPro.png onto the iPad Pro slot on the bottom right.

While you're doing this, keep an eye on the Xcode Activity View: if you drop an image on the wrong slot, you'll see a warning triangle appear. If this happens, fix the problem before continuing. When you're done, the editor should look like Figure 12-19.

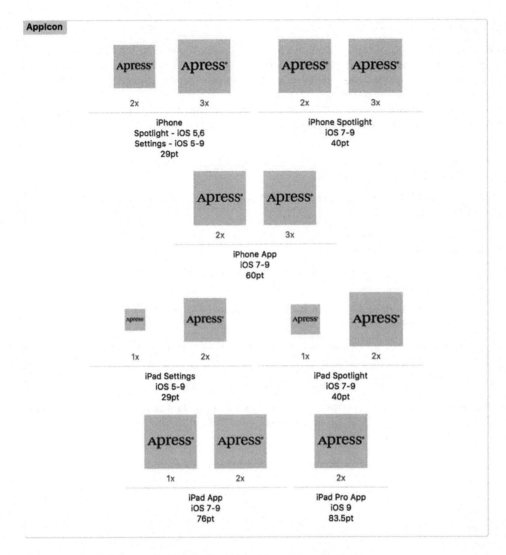

Figure 12-19. *Adding the settings and app icons for our application*

That's it. Build and run the application by selecting Product ➤ Run. You haven't built any sort of GUI for the app yet, so you'll just see the first tab of the tab bar controller. Press the Home button (or press ⌘ ⇧ H on the simulator), and then tap the icon for the Settings application. Scroll down and you will find an entry for our application, which uses the icon added earlier (see Figure 12-2). Click the Bridge Control row. You will be presented with a simple settings view with a single text field, as shown in Figure 12-20.

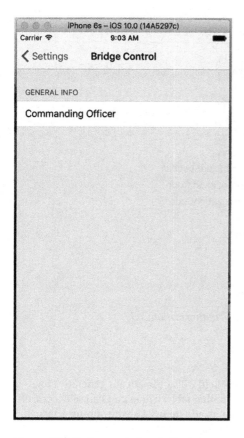

Figure 12-20. *Our root view in the Settings application after adding a group and a text field*

We're not finished yet, but you should now have a sense of how easy it is to add preferences to your application. Let's add the rest of the fields for our root settings view. The first one we'll add is a secure text field for the user's authorization code.

Adding a Secure Text Field Setting

Go back to Xcode and click Root.plist to return to your setting specifiers (don't forget to turn on Show Raw Keys/Values, assuming Xcode's editing area has reset this). Collapse Item 0 and Item 1, and then select Item 1. Press ⌘C to copy it to the clipboard, and then press ⌘V to paste it back. This will create a new Item 2 that is identical to Item 1. Expand the new item and change the Title to Authorization Code and the Key to authorizationCode. Remember that the Title is what's shown in an on-screen label, and the Key is what's used for saving the value.

Next, add one more child to the new item. Remember that the order of items does not matter, so feel free to place it directly below the Key item you just edited. To do this, select the Key/authorizationCode row, and then hit Return.

Give the new item a Key of IsSecure (note the leading uppercase I) and press Tab. You'll see that Xcode automatically changes the Type to Boolean. Now change its Value from NO to YES, which tells the Settings application that this field needs to hide the user's input like a password field, rather than behaving like an ordinary text field. Finally, change AutocapitalizationType to None. Our finished Item 2 is shown in Figure 12-21.

Key		Type	Value
▼ iPhone Settings Schema		Dictionary	(2 items)
StringsTable	⬍	String	Root
▼ PreferenceSpecifiers	⬍	Array	(3 items)
▶ Item 0 (Group - General Info)		Dictionary	(2 items)
▶ Item 1 (Text Field - Commanding		Dictionary	(5 items)
▼ Item 2 (Text Field - Authorization		Dictionary	(6 items)
Type	⬍	String	PSTextFieldSpecifier
Title	⬍	String	Authorization Code
Key	⬍	String	authorizationCode
IsSecure	⬍	Boolean	YES
AutocapitalizationType	⬍	String	None
AutocorrectionType	⬍	String	No

Figure 12-21. *Our finished Item 2, a text field designed to accept an authorizationCode*

Adding a Multivalue Field

The next item we're going to add is a **multivalue field**. This type of field will automatically generate a row with a disclosure indicator. Clicking it will let users drill down to another table, where they can select one of several rows. Collapse Item 2, select the row, and then press Return to add Item 3. Use the pop-up attached to the Key field to select Multi Value, and then expand Item 3 by clicking the disclosure triangle.

The expanded Item 3 already contains a few rows. One of them, the Type row, is set to PSMultiValueSpecifier. Look for the Title row and set its value to Rank. Then find the Key row and give it a value of rank. The next part is a little tricky, so let's talk about it before we do it.

We're going to add two more children to Item 3, but they will be Array type nodes, not String type nodes, as follows:

- One array, called **Titles**, will hold a list of the values from which the user can select.

- The other array, called **Values**, will hold a corresponding list of the values that are stored in the user defaults.

So, if the user selects the first item in the list, which corresponds to the first item in the Titles array, the Settings application will actually store the first value from the Values array. This pairing of Titles and Values lets you present user-friendly text to the user, but actually stores something else, like a number, date, or different string. Both of these arrays are required. If you want them to be the same, you can create one array, copy it, paste it back in, and then change the key so that you have two arrays with the same content, but stored under different keys. We'll actually do just that.

Select Item 3 (leave it open) and press Return to add a new child. You'll see that, once again, Xcode is aware of the type of file we're editing and even seems to anticipate what we want to do: the new child row already has Key set to Titles and is configured to be an Array, which is just what we wanted! Press Return to stop editing the Key field, and then expand the Titles row and hit Return to add a child node. Repeat this five more times, so you have a total of six child nodes. All six nodes should be String type and should be given the following values: Ensign, Lieutenant, Lieutenant Commander, Commander, Captain, and Commodore.

Once you've created all six nodes and entered their values, collapse Titles and select it. Next, press ⌘C to copy it and press ⌘V to paste it back. This will create a new item with a key of Titles - 2. Double-click the key Titles - 2 and change it to Values.

We're almost finished with our multivalue field. There's just one more required value in the dictionary, which is the default value. Multivalue fields must have one—and only one—row selected. So, we need to specify the default value to be used if none has yet been selected; it needs to correspond to one of the items in the Values array (not the Titles array, if they are different). Xcode already added a DefaultValue row when we created this item, so all we need to do now is give it a value of Ensign. Go ahead and do that now. Figure 12-22 shows our finalized version of Item 3.

Key		Type	Value
▼ iPhone Settings Schema		Dictionary	(2 items)
Strings Filename	↕	String	**Root**
▼ Preference Items	↕	Array	(4 items)
▶ Item 0 (Group - General Info)		Dictionary	(2 items)
▶ Item 1 (Text Field - Commanding		Dictionary	(5 items)
▶ Item 2 (Text Field - Authorization		Dictionary	(6 items)
▼ Item 3 (Multi Value - Rank)		Dictionary	(6 items)
▼ Titles	↕	Array	(6 items)
Item 0		String	Ensign
Item 1		String	Lieutenant
Item 2		String	Lieutenant Commander
Item 3		String	Commander
Item 4	⊕ ⊖	String	↕ Captain
Item 5		String	Commodore
▼ Values	↕	Array	(6 items)
Item 0		String	Ensign
Item 1		String	Lieutenant
Item 2		String	Lieutenant Commander
Item 3		String	Commander
Item 4		String	Captain
Item 5		String	Commodore
Type	↕	String	Multi Value
Title	↕	String	Rank
Identifier	↕	String	rank
Default Value	↕	String	Ensign

Figure 12-22. *Our finished Item 3, a multivalue field designed to let the user select from one of six possible values*

Let's check our work. Save the property list, and build and run the application again. When your application starts, press the Home button and launch the Settings application. When you select Bridge Control, you should see three fields on your root-level view, as shown in Figure 12-23. Go ahead and play with it a bit, and then let's move on.

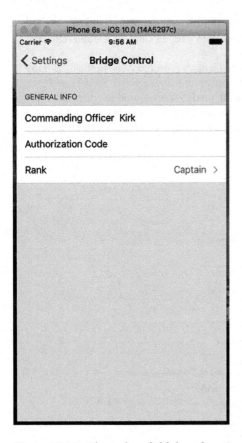

Figure 12-23. *Three of our fields have been implemented*

Adding a Toggle Switch Setting

The next item we need to get from the user is a Boolean value that indicates whether our warp engines should be turned on. To capture a Boolean value in our preferences, we are going to tell the Settings application to use a UISwitch by adding another item to our PreferenceSpecifiers array with a type of PSToggleSwitchSpecifier.

Collapse Item 3 if it's currently expanded, and then single-click it to select it. Press Return to create Item 4. Use the drop-down menu to select Toggle Switch, and then click the disclosure triangle to expand Item 4. You'll see there's already a child row with a Key of Type and a Value of PSToggleSwitchSpecifier. Give the empty Title row a value of Warp Drive and set the value of the Key row to warp.

We have one more required item in this dictionary, which is the default value. Just as with the Multi Value setup, here Xcode has already created a DefaultValue row for us. Let's turn on our warp engines by default by giving the DefaultValue row a value of YES. Figure 12-24 shows our completed Item 4.

Key		Type	Value
▼ iPhone Settings Schema		Dictionary	(2 items)
Strings Filename	↕	String	**Root**
▼ Preference Items	↕	Array	(5 items)
▶ Item 0 (Group - General Info)		Dictionary	(2 items)
▶ Item 1 (Text Field - Commanding		Dictionary	(5 items)
▶ Item 2 (Text Field - Authorization		Dictionary	(6 items)
▶ Item 3 (Multi Value - Rank)		Dictionary	(6 items)
▼ Item 4 (Toggle Switch - Warp	⌄	Dictionary ⌄	(4 items)
Type	↕	String	**Toggle Switch**
Title	↕	String	**Warp Drive**
Identifier	↕	String	**warp**
Default Value	↕	Boolean	**YES**

Figure 12-24. *Our finished Item 4, a toggle switch to turn the warp engines on and off*

Adding the Slider Setting

The next item we need to implement is a slider. In the Settings application, a slider can have a small image at each end, but it can't have a label. Let's put the slider in its own group with a header, so that the user will know what the slider does. Start by collapsing Item 4. Now single-click Item 4 and press Return to create a new row. Use the pop-up to turn the new item into a Group, and then click the item's disclosure triangle to expand it. You'll see that Type is already set to PSGroupSpecifier. This will tell the Settings application to start a new group at this location. Double-click the value in the row labeled Title and change the value to Warp Factor.

Collapse Item 5 and select it, and then press Return to add a new sibling row. Use the pop-up to change the new item into a Slider, which indicates to the Settings application that it should use a UISlider to get this information from the user. Expand Item 6 and set the value of the Key row to warpFactor, so that the Settings application knows which key to use when storing this value.

We're going to allow the user to enter a value from 1 to 10. We'll set the default to warp 5. Sliders need to have a minimum value, a maximum value, and a starting (or default) value; and all of these need to be stored as numbers, not strings, in your property list. Fortunately, Xcode has already created rows for all these values. Give the DefaultValue row a value of 5, the MinimumValue row a value of 1, and the MaximumValue row a value of 10.

If you want to test the slider, go ahead. We're going to do just a bit more customization. As noted, you can place an image at each end of the slider. Let's provide little icons to indicate that moving the slider to the left slows us down and moving it to the right speeds us up.

Adding Icons to the Settings Bundle

In the 12 - Images folder in the project archive that accompanies this book, you'll find two icons called rabbit.png and turtle.png. We need to add both of these to our settings bundle. Because these images need to be used by the Settings application, we can't just put them in our Bridge Control folder; we need to put them in the settings bundle, so the Settings application can access them. To do that, we'll need to open the settings bundle in the Finder. Control-click the Settings.bundle icon in the Project Navigator and when the contextual menu appears, select Show in Finder (see Figure 12-25), to show the bundle in the Finder.

Figure 12-25. *The Settings.bundle contextual menu*

Remember that bundles look like files in the Finder, but they are really folders. When the Finder window opens to show the Settings.bundle file, Control-click the file and select Show Package Contents from the contextual menu that appears. This will open the settings bundle in a new Finder window. You should see the same two items that you see in Settings.bundle in Xcode. Copy the two icon files, rabbit.png and turtle. png, from the 12 - Images folder into the Settings.bundle package contents in the Finder window, next to en.proj and Root.plist. You can leave this window open in the Finder, as we'll need to copy another file here soon. Now we'll return to Xcode and tell the slider to use these two images.

Back in Xcode, return to Root.plist and add two more child rows under Item 6. Give one a key of MinimumValueImage and a value of turtle. Give the other a key of MaximumValueImage and a value of rabbit. Figure 12-26 shows our finished Item 6.

Key		Type	Value
▼ iPhone Settings Schema		Dictionary	(2 items)
StringsTable	⬍	String	Root
▼ PreferenceSpecifiers	⬍	Array	(7 items)
▶ Item 0 (Group - General Info)		Dictionary	(2 items)
▶ Item 1 (Text Field - Commanding		Dictionary	(5 items)
▶ Item 2 (Text Field - Authorization		Dictionary	(6 items)
▶ Item 3 (Multi Value - Rank)		Dictionary	(6 items)
▶ Item 4 (Toggle Switch - Warp		Dictionary	(4 items)
▶ Item 5 (Group - Warp Factor)		Dictionary	(2 items)
▼ Item 6 (Slider)		Dictionary	(7 items)
Type	⬍	String	PSSliderSpecifier
Key	⬍	String	warpFactor
DefaultValue	⬍	Number	5
MinimumValue	⬍	Number	1
MaximumValue	⬍	Number	10
MinimumValueImage	⬍	String	turtle
MaximumValueImage	⬍	String	rabbit

Figure 12-26. *Our finished Item 6: a slider with turtle and rabbit icons to represent slow and fast*

Save your property list, and then build and run the app to make sure everything functions as expected. You should be able to navigate to the Settings application and find the slider waiting for you, with the sleepy turtle and the happy rabbit at their respective ends, as shown in Figure 12-27.

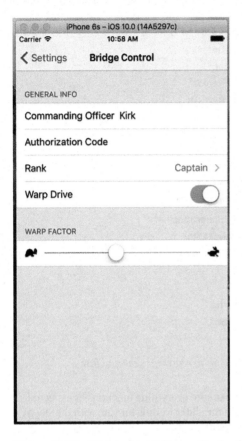

Figure 12-27. *We have text fields, multivalue fields, a toggle switch, and a slider*

Adding a Child Settings View

We're going to add another preference specifier to tell the Settings application that we want it to display a child settings view. This specifier will present a row with a disclosure indicator that, when tapped, will take the user down to a whole new view full of preferences.

Since we don't want this new preference to be grouped with the slider, first we'll copy the group specifier in Item 0 and paste it at the end of the PreferenceSpecifiers array to create a new group for our child settings view. In Root.plist, collapse all open items, and then single-click Item 0 to select it, and press ⌘C to copy it to the clipboard. Next, select Item 6, and then press ⌘V to paste in a new Item 7. Expand Item 7 and double-click the Value column next to the key Title, changing it from General Info to Additional Info.

Now collapse Item 7 again. Select it and press Return to add Item 8, which will be our actual child view. Expand it by clicking the disclosure triangle. Find the Type row, give it a value of PSChildPaneSpecifier, and then set the value of the Title row to More Settings. We need to add one final row to Item 8, which will tell the Settings application which property list to load for the More Settings view. Add another child row, and give it a key of File (you can do this by changing the key of the last row in the group from Key to File) and a value of More (see Figure 12-28). The file extension .plist is assumed and must not be included (if it is, the Settings application won't find the .plist file).

Key		Type	Value
▼ iPhone Settings Schema		Dictionary	(2 items)
StringsTable	◆	String	Root
▼ PreferenceSpecifiers	◆	Array	(9 items)
▶ Item 0 (Group - General Info)		Dictionary	(2 items)
▶ Item 1 (Text Field - Commanding		Dictionary	(5 items)
▶ Item 2 (Text Field - Authorization		Dictionary	(6 items)
▶ Item 3 (Multi Value - Rank)		Dictionary	(6 items)
▶ Item 4 (Toggle Switch - Warp		Dictionary	(4 items)
▶ Item 5 (Group - Warp Factor)		Dictionary	(2 items)
▶ Item 6 (Slider)		Dictionary	(7 items)
▶ Item 7 (Group - Additional Info)		Dictionary	(2 items)
▼ Item 8 (Child Pane - More		Dictionary	(4 items)
Type	◆	String	PSChildPaneSpecifier
Title	◆	String	More Settings
Key	◆	String	
File	◆	String	More

Figure 12-28. Our finished Items 7 and 8, setting up the new Additional Info settings group and providing the child pane link to the file, More.plist

We are adding a child view to our main preference view. We've configured the settings bundle to indicate that the settings in that child view are specified in the More.plist file so we need to add a file called More.plist into the settings bundle. We can't add new files to the bundle in Xcode, and the Property List Editor's Save dialog will not let us save into a bundle, so we need to create a new property list, save it somewhere else, and then drag it into the Settings.bundle window using the Finder. When you create your own child settings views, the easiest approach is to make a copy of Root.plist and give it a new name then delete all of the existing preference specifiers except the first one and add whatever preference specifiers you need for that new file. To save yourself the trouble of doing all this, you can grab the More.plist file in the 12 - Images folder in the project archive that accompanies this book, and then drag it into that Settings. bundle window we left open earlier, alongside Root.plist.

We're now finished with our settings bundle. Feel free to build, run, and test the Settings application. You should be able to reach the child view and set values for all the other fields. Go ahead and play with it, and make changes to the property list if you want.

■ **Tip** We've covered almost every configuration option available (at least at the time of this writing). You can find the full documentation of the settings property list format in the document called *Settings Application Schema Reference* in the iOS Dev Center. You can get that document, along with a ton of other useful reference documents, from this page: `http://developer.apple.com/library/ios/navigation/`.

Before continuing, select the Assets.xcassets item in Xcode's Project Navigator, and then copy the rabbit. png and turtle.png icons from the 12 - Images folder in the project archive into the left side of the editor area. This will add these icons to the project as new images resources, ready for use. We'll be using them in our application to show the value of the current settings.

You might have noticed that the two icons you just added are exactly the same ones you added to your settings bundle earlier. You might be wondering why we've added them to our Xcode project twice. Remember that iOS applications can't read files out of other applications' sandboxes. The settings bundle doesn't become part of our application's sandbox—it becomes part of the Settings application's sandbox. Since we also want to use those icons in our application, we need to add them separately to Assets.xcassets, so they are copied into our application's sandbox too.

Reading Settings in Our Application

We've now solved half of our problem. The user can use the Setting app to declare their preferences, but how do we get to them from within our application? As it turns out, that's the easy part. Before we write the code to retrieve our settings, open the Settings application, locate our application's settings and set a value for every setting so that the application has something to display in the user interface that we're about to create.

Retrieving User Settings

We'll use a class called UserDefaults (NSUserDefaults) to access the user's settings. UserDefaults is implemented as a singleton, which means there is only one instance of UserDefaults that holds the settings for our application. To get access to that one instance, we call the class method standard, like so:

```
let defaults = UserDefaults.standard
```

Once we have a pointer to the standard user defaults, we use it much like a Dictionary. To get a value from it, we can call object(forKey:), which will return an object, a String or a Foundation object such as Date (NSDate), or NSNumber. If we want to retrieve the value as a scalar—like an int, float, or Boolean—we can use another method, such as int(forKey:), float(forKey:), or bool(forKey:).

While you were creating the property list for this application, you were actually creating an array of PreferenceSpecifiers inside a .plist file. Within the Settings application, some of those specifiers were used to create groups, while others were used to create interface objects for user interaction. Those are the specifiers we are really interested in because they hold the keys for the real settings data. Every specifier that was tied to a user setting has a Key named Key. Take a minute to go back and check. For example, the Key for our slider has a value of warpFactor and the Key for our Authorization Code field is authorizationCode. We'll use those keys to retrieve the user settings.

Instead of using strings for each key directly in our methods, we'll define some constants for those values. That way we can use these constants in our code instead of inline strings, where we would run the risk of mistyping something. We'll set these up in a separate Swift file, since we're going to use some of them in more than one class later on. So, in Xcode, press ⌘N and, from the iOS section of the file creation window, choose Source and then Swift File. Press Next, call the file Constants.swift and press Create. Open the newly created file and add code in Listing 12-1.

Listing 12-1. Our Constants

```
let officerKey = "officer"
let authorizationCodeKey = "authorizationCode"
let rankKey = "rank"
let warpDriveKey = "warp"
let warpFactorKey = "warpFactor"
let favoriteTeaKey = "favoriteTea"
let favoriteCaptainKey = "favoriteCaptain"
let favoriteGadgetKey = "favoriteGadget"
let favoriteAlienKey = "favoriteAlien"
```

These constants are the keys that we used in our .plist file for the different preference fields. Now that we have a place to display the settings, let's quickly set up our main view with a bunch of labels. Before going over to Interface Builder, let's create outlets for all the labels we'll need. Single-click FirstViewController. swift, and make the changes in Listing 12-2.

Listing 12-2. Adding Outlets to the FirstViewController.swift File

```
class FirstViewController: UIViewController {
    @IBOutlet var officerLabel:UILabel!
    @IBOutlet var authorizationCodeLabel:UILabel!
    @IBOutlet var rankLabel:UILabel!
    @IBOutlet var warpDriveLabel:UILabel!
    @IBOutlet var warpFactorLabel:UILabel!
    @IBOutlet var favoriteTeaLabel:UILabel!
    @IBOutlet var favoriteCaptainLabel:UILabel!
    @IBOutlet var favoriteGadgetLabel:UILabel!
    @IBOutlet var favoriteAlienLabel:UILabel!
```

There's nothing new here—we declared nine properties, all of them labels with the @IBOutlet keyword to make them connectable in Interface Builder. Save your changes. Now that we have our outlets declared, let's head over to the storyboard file to create the user interface.

Creating the Main View

Select Main.storyboard to edit it in Interface Builder. When it comes up, you'll see the tab bar view controller on the left and the view controllers for the two tabs on the right, one above the other. The upper one is for the first tab, corresponding to the FirstViewController class, and the lower one is for the second tab, which will be implemented in the SecondViewController class.

We're going to start by adding a bunch of labels to the View of FirstViewController, so it looks like the one shown in Figure 12-29. We'll need a grand total of 18 labels. Half of them, on the left side of the screen, will be right-aligned and bold; the other half, on the right side of the screen, will be used to display the actual values retrieved from the user defaults and will have outlets pointing to them. All of the changes that we make here will be to the view controller for the first tab, which is the upper one on the right of the storyboard.

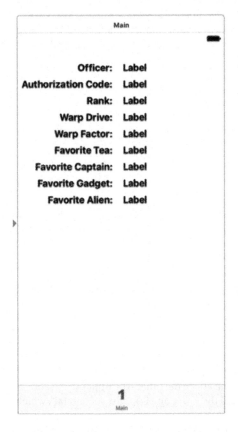

Figure 12-29. *The view controller for the first tab in Interface Builder, showing the 18 labels we added*

Start by expanding the node for Main Scene in the Document Outline, and then expand the View item. You'll find two child views already in place—delete them both. Now drag a Label from the Object Library and drop it near the top left of the view in the storyboard. Drag it all the way to the left of the window (or at least to the left blue guideline), and then widen it by dragging its right edge toward the center of the view, like the Officer label in Figure 12-29. In the Attributes Inspector, make the text right aligned and change the font to System Bold 17. Now Option-drag the label downward to create eight more copies, lining them up neatly to form the left column. Change the label texts so that they match the ones in Figure 12-29.

Building the right-hand column is slightly easier. Drag another label onto the View and place it to the right of the Officer label, leaving a small gap between them. In the Attributes Inspector, set the font to System 17. Option-drag this label downward to create eight more copies, each of them lined up with the corresponding label in the left column.

Now we need to set the auto layout constraints. Let's start by linking the top two labels together. Control-drag from the Officer label to the label to its right. Release the mouse and hold down the Shift key. In the pop-up menu, select Horizontal Spacing and Baseline, and then click outside the pop-up. Do the same for the other eight rows, to link each pair of labels together.

Next, we'll fix the positions of the labels in the left column relative to the left and top of the view. In the Document Outline, Control-drag from the Officer label to its parent View. Release the mouse, hold down the Shift key and select Leading Space to Container Margin and Vertical Spacing to Top Layout Guide, and then press Return to apply the constraints. Do the same with the other eight labels in the left column.

Finally, we need to fix the widths of the labels in the left column. Select the Officer label and click the Pin button below the storyboard editor. In the pop-up, check the Width check box followed by Add 1 Constraint. Repeat this process for all of the labels in the left column.

All of the labels should now be properly constrained, so select the view controller Main in the Document Outline, and then click Editor ➤ Resolve Auto Layout Issues ➤ Update Frames in the Xcode menu. (If this option is not enabled, all of the labels are already in their correct positions in the storyboard). If all is well, the labels will move to their final positions.

The next thing we need to do is link the labels in the right column to their outlets. Open FirstViewController.swift in the Assistant Editor and Control-drag from the top label in the right column to the officerLabel outlet to connect them. Control-drag from the second label in the right column to authorizationLabel, and repeat until all nine labels in the right column are connected to their outlets. Save the Main.storyboard file.

Updating the First View Controller

In Xcode, select FirstViewController.swift and add the code in Listing 12-3 at the bottom of the class.

Listing 12-3. Displaying Data in Our Label Fields

```
func refreshFields() {
    let defaults = UserDefaults.standard
    officerLabel.text = defaults.string(forKey: officerKey)
    authorizationCodeLabel.text = defaults.string(forKey: authorizationCodeKey)
    rankLabel.text = defaults.string(forKey: rankKey)
    warpDriveLabel.text = defaults.bool(forKey: warpDriveKey)
        ? "Engaged" : "Disabled"
    warpFactorLabel.text = defaults.object(forKey: warpFactorKey)?.stringValue
    favoriteTeaLabel.text = defaults.string(forKey: favoriteTeaKey)
    favoriteCaptainLabel.text = defaults.string(forKey: favoriteCaptainKey)
    favoriteGadgetLabel.text = defaults.string(forKey: favoriteGadgetKey)
    favoriteAlienLabel.text = defaults.string(forKey: favoriteAlienKey)
}

override func viewWillAppear(_ animated: Bool) {
    super.viewWillAppear(animated)
    refreshFields()
}
```

There's not really much here that should throw you. The refreshFields() method does two things. First, it grabs the standard user defaults. Second, it sets the text properties of all the labels to the appropriate object from the user defaults using the same key values that we put in our .plist file. Notice that for warpFactorLabel, we're calling string on the object returned. Most of our other preferences are strings, which come back from the user defaults as String objects. The preference stored by the slider, however, comes back as an NSNumber, but we need a string for display purposes, so we call string on it to get a string representation of the value it holds.

After that, we overrode our superclass's viewWillAppear() method, and there we called our refreshFields() method. This causes the displayed values to be updated whenever the view appears—which includes when the application starts and when the user switches from the second tab to the first tab.

Now run the application. You should see the user interface that you built for the first tab, with most of the fields filled with the values that you entered into the Settings application earlier. However, some of the fields will be empty. Don't worry, this is not a bug. It is correct behavior, believe it or not. You'll see why, and how to fix it, in the upcoming "Registering Default Values" section.

Changing Defaults from Our Application

Now that we have the main view up and running, let's build the second tab. As you can see in Figure 12-30, the second tab features our warp drive switch, as well as the warp factor slider. We'll use the same controls that the Settings application uses for these two items: a switch and a slider. In addition to declaring our outlets, we'll also declare a method called refreshFields(), just as we did in FirstViewController, and two action methods that will be triggered by the user touching the controls.

Figure 12-30. *Designing the second view controller in Interface Builder*

Select SecondViewController.swift and make the following changes:

```
class SecondViewController: UIViewController {
    @IBOutlet var engineSwitch:UISwitch!
    @IBOutlet var warpFactorSlider:UISlider!
```

Now, save your changes and select Main.storyboard to edit the GUI in Interface Builder, this time focusing on the Settings Scene in the Document Outline. Hold down the Option key and click the disclosure triangle to expand Settings Scene and everything below it. Locate the View node and delete both of its child nodes. Next, select the View node, and then bring up the Attributes Inspector. Change the background color by using the Background pop-up to select Light Gray Color.

Next, drag two labels from the library and place them on the view in the storyboard. Make sure you drag them onto the Settings Scene controller, which is the one at the bottom right of the storyboard. Double-click one of them, and change it to read Warp Engines:. Double-click the other, and call it Warp Factor:. Place both labels against the left guideline, one above the other. You can use Figure 12-30 as a placement guide.

Next, drag over a Switch from the library and place it against the right side of the view, across from the label that reads Warp Engines. Control-drag from the View Controller icon (it's the yellow one) at the top of the Settings Scene to the new switch and connect it to the engineSwitch outlet. Next, open SecondViewController in the Assistant Editor and Control-drag from the switch to a point just above the closing brace at the bottom of the file. Release the mouse and create an action called onEngineSwitchTapped, leaving all the other selections in the pop-up at their default values.

Drag over a slider from the library and place it below the label that reads Warp Factor:. Resize the slider so that it stretches from the blue guideline on the left margin to the one on the right. Now Control-drag from the View Controller icon at the top of the Settings Scene to the slider, and then connect it to the warpFactorSlider outlet. Next, Control-drag from the slider to the end of the SecondViewController class and create an action called onWarpSliderDragged, leaving all the other selections in the pop-up at their default values.

Single-click the slider, if it's not still selected, and then bring up the Attributes Inspector. Set Minimum to 1.00, Maximum to 10.00, and Current to 5.00. Next, select **turtle** for Min Image and **rabbit** for Max Image. If those don't show up in the pop-up buttons, make sure you dragged the images into the Assets.xcassets assets catalog.

To complete the user interface, drag a button from the Object Library, drop it at the bottom of the view, and change its name to Open Settings Application. Control-drag from the button to just below the onWarpSliderDragged method in SecondViewController and create an action called onSettingsButtonTapped. We'll use this button at the end of the chapter.

It's time to add the auto layout constraints. Start by selecting Main.storyboard. In the Document Outline, Control-drag from the Warp Engines label to its parent view and release the mouse. Hold down the Shift key and select Leading Space to Container Margin and Vertical Spacing to Top Layout Guide, and then press the return key to apply the constraints. Repeat this for the Warp Factor label.

Next, Control-drag from the switch to Main View and release the mouse. Hold down the Shift key and select Trailing Space to Container Margin and Vertical Spacing to Top Layout Guide, and then press Return. Control-drag from the slider to Main View and release the mouse. Hold down the Shift key and this time select Leading Space to Container Margin, Trailing Space to Container Margin and Vertical Spacing to Top Layout Guide, and press Return.

Finally, we need to fix the position of the button at the bottom of the view. Control-drag from the button to Main View, release the mouse, and select Vertical Spacing to Bottom Layout Guide and Center Horizontally in Container while holding down the Shift key, and then press Return. That completes the auto layout constraints, so go ahead and select the view controller Main in the Document Outline, and then click Editor ➤ Resolve Auto Layout Issues ➤ Update Frames in the Xcode menu. Make sure that everything is where it should be in the view.

Now, let's finish the settings view controller. Select SecondViewController.swift and add the code in Listing 12-4 at the bottom of the class.

Listing 12-4. Our refreshFields and viewWillAppear Methods for the SecondViewController

```swift
override func viewWillAppear(_ animated: Bool) {
    super.viewWillAppear(animated)
    refreshFields()
}

func refreshFields() {
    let defaults = UserDefaults.standard
    engineSwitch.isOn = defaults.bool(forKey: warpDriveKey)
    warpFactorSlider.value = defaults.float(forKey: warpFactorKey)
}
```

Next, add the following code in the onEngineSwitchTapped() and onWarpSliderDragged() methods:

```
@IBAction func onEngineSwitchTapped(_ sender: AnyObject) {
    let defaults = UserDefaults.standard
    defaults.set(engineSwitch.isOn, forKey: warpDriveKey)
}
@IBAction func onWarpSliderDragged(_ sender: AnyObject) {
    let defaults = UserDefaults.standard
    defaults.set(warpFactorSlider.value, forKey: warpFactorKey)
}
```

When the view controller's view appears (e.g., when the tab is selected), we call our refreshFields() method. This method's three lines of code get a reference to the standard user defaults, and then use the outlets for the switch and slider to make them display the values stored in the user defaults. We also implemented the onEngineSwitchTapped() and onWarpSliderDragged() action methods, so that we could stuff the values from our controls back into the user defaults when the user changes them.

Now you should be able to run the app, switch to the second tab, edit the values presented there, and see them reflected in the first tab when you switch back.

Registering Default Values

We've created a settings bundle, including some default settings for a few values, to give the Settings app access to our app's preferences. We've also set up our own app to access the same information, with a GUI to let the user see and edit it. However, one piece is missing: our app is completely unaware of the default values that we specified in the settings bundle. You can see this for yourself by deleting the Bridge Control app from the iOS simulator or the device you're running on (thereby deleting the preferences stored for the app), and then running it from Xcode again. At the start of a fresh launch, the app will show you blank values for most of the settings. Even the default values for the warp drive settings, which we defined in the settings bundle, are nowhere to be seen. If you then switch over to the Settings app, you'll see the default values; however, unless you actually change the values there, you'll never see them back in the Bridge Control app.

The reason our default settings disappeared is that our app knows nothing about the settings bundle it contains. So, when it tries to read the value from UserDefaults for warpFactor and finds nothing saved under that key, it has nothing to show us. Fortunately, UserDefaults includes a method called register() that lets us specify the default values that we should find if we try to look up a key/value that hasn't been set. To make this work throughout the app, it's best if this is called early during app start-up. Select AppDelegate. swift and modify the application(_:didFinishLaunchingWithOptions:) method:

```
func application(application: UIApplication,
            didFinishLaunchingWithOptions launchOptions: [NSObject: AnyObject]?) -> Bool {
    // Override point for customization after application launch.

    let defaults = [warpDriveKey: true, warpFactorKey: 5, favoriteAlienKey: "Vulcan"]
    UserDefaults.standard.register(defaults)
    return true
}
```

The first thing we do here is create a dictionary that contains three key/value pairs, one for each of the keys available in Settings that requires a default value. We're using the same key names we defined earlier to reduce the risk of mistyping a key name. We pass the entire dictionary to the standard NSUserDefaults instance's registerDefaults() method. From that point on, NSUserDefaults will give us the values we specify here, as long as we haven't set different values either in our app or in the Settings app.

This class is complete. Delete the Bridge Control application and run it again. It will look something like Figure 12-6, except yours will be showing whatever values you entered in your Settings application, of course.

■ **Note** To remove an app, click an app icon from the main device screen and hold until the icons start wiggling. Then, release the mouse and click the X on the app that you wish to delete.

Keeping It Real

Now you should be able to run your app, view the settings, and then press the Home button and open the Settings app to tweak some values. Hit the Home button again to launch your app again from the Home screen. You may be in for a surprise. When you go back to your app, you won't see the settings change. They'll remain as they are, showing the old values.

In iOS, hitting the Home button while an app is running doesn't actually quit the app. Instead, the operating system suspends the app in the background, leaving it ready to be quickly fired up again. This is great for switching back and forth between applications, since the amount of time it takes to reawaken a suspended app is much shorter than what it takes to launch it from scratch. However, in our case, we need to do a little more work, so that when our app wakes up, it effectively gets a slap in the face, reloads the user preferences, and redisplays the values they contain.

You'll learn more about background applications in Chapter 15, but we'll give you a sneak peek at the basics of how to make your app notice that it has been brought back to life. To do this, we're going to sign up each of our controller classes to receive a notification that is sent by the application when it wakes up from its state of suspended execution.

A **notification** is a lightweight mechanism that objects can use to communicate with each other. Any object can define one or more notifications that it will publish to the application's **notification center**, which is a singleton object that exists only to pass these notifications between objects. Notifications are usually indications that some event occurred, and objects that publish notifications include a list of notifications in their documentation. The UIApplication class publishes a number of notifications (you can find them in the Xcode documentation viewer, toward the bottom of the UIApplication page). The purpose of most notifications is usually pretty obvious from their names, but the documentation contains further information if you're unclear about a given notification's purpose.

Our application needs to refresh its display when the application is about to come to the foreground, so we are interested in the notification called UIApplicationWillEnterForeground. We'll modify the viewWillAppear() method of our view controllers to subscribe to that notification and tell the notification center to call another method when that notification happens. Add the following code to both FirstViewController.swift and SecondViewController.swift:

```
func applicationWillEnterForeground(notification:NSNotification) {
    let defaults = UserDefaults.standard
    defaults.synchronize()
    refreshFields()
}
```

The method itself is quite simple. First, it gets a reference to the standard user defaults object and calls its synchronize() method, which forces the User Defaults system to save any unsaved changes and also reload any unmodified preferences from storage. In effect, we're forcing it to reread the stored preferences so that we can pick up the changes that were made in the Settings app. Next, the applicationWillEnterForeground() method calls the refreshFields() method, which each class uses to update its display.

Now we need to make each of our controllers subscribe to the notification. Add the following two lines of code to the viewWillAppear: method in both FirstViewController.swift and SecondViewController.swift:

```
let app = UIApplication.shared()
NotificationCenter.default.addObserver(self, selector: #selector(self.applicationWillEn
terForeground(notification:)), name: Notification.Name.UIApplicationWillEnterForeground,
object: app)
```

We start by getting a reference to our application instance, and then use that to subscribe to the applicationWillEnterForeground notification, using the default NotificationCenter instance and a method called addObserver(_:selector:name:object:). We then pass the following to this method:

- For the observer, we pass self, which means that our controller class (each of them individually, since this code is going into both of them) is the object that needs to be notified.

- For selector, we pass a selector to the applicationWillEnterForeground() method we just wrote, telling the notification center to call that method when the notification is posted.

- The third parameter, applicationWillEnterForeground, is the name of the notification that we're interested in receiving.

- The final parameter, app, is the object from which we're interested in getting the notification. We use a reference to our own application for this. If we passed nil for the final parameter instead, we would get notified any time any application posted the UIApplicationWillEnterForeground.

That takes care of updating the display, but we also need to consider what happens to the values that are put into the user defaults when the user manipulates the controls in our app. We need to make sure that they are saved to storage before control passes to another app. The easiest way to do that is to call synchronize as soon as the settings are changed, by adding one line to the first two of our action methods in SecondViewController.swift:

```
@IBAction func onEngineSwitchTapped(_ sender: AnyObject) {
    let defaults = UserDefaults.standard
    defaults.set(engineSwitch.isOn, forKey: warpDriveKey)
    defaults.synchronize()
}
@IBAction func onWarpSliderDragged(_ sender: AnyObject) {
    let defaults = UserDefaults.standard
    defaults.set(warpFactorSlider.value, forKey: warpFactorKey)
    defaults.synchronize()
}
```

■ **Note** Calling the synchronize() method is a potentially expensive operation because the entire contents of the user defaults in memory must be compared with what's in storage. When you're dealing with a whole lot of user defaults at once and want to make sure everything is in sync, it's best to try to minimize calls to synchronize(), so that this whole comparison isn't performed over and over again. However, calling it once in response to each user action, as we're doing here, won't cause any noticeable performance problems.

There's one more thing to take care of to make this work as cleanly as possible. You already know that you must clean up your memory by setting properties to `nil` when they're no longer in use, as well as performing other clean-up tasks. The notification system is another place where you need to clean up after yourself by telling the default `NotificationCenter` that you don't want to listen to any more notifications. In our case, where we've registered each view controller to observe this notification in its `viewWillAppear()` method, we should unregister in the matching `viewDidDisappear()` method. So, in both FirstViewController.swift and SecondViewController.swift, add the following method:

```swift
override func viewDidDisappear(_ animated: Bool) {
    super.viewDidDisappear(animated)
    NotificationCenter.default.removeObserver(self)
}
```

Note that it's possible to unregister for specific notifications using the `removeObserver(_:name:obje ct:)` method by passing in the same values that were used to register your observer in the first place. In any case, the preceding line is a handy way to make sure that the notification center forgets about our observer completely, no matter how many notifications it was registered for.

With that in place, it's time to build and run the app and see what happens when you switch between your app and the Settings app. Changes you make in the Settings app should now be immediately reflected in your app when you switch back to it.

Switching to the Settings Application

To switch from the Bridge Control application to its settings, you need to go to the Home screen, launch the Settings application, find the Bridge Control entry, and select it. That's a lot of steps. It's so tiresome that many applications have opted to include their own settings screen rather than make the user go through all of that. Wouldn't it be much nicer if you could just take the user directly to screen for your settings in the Settings application? Well, it turns out that you can do just that. Remember the Open Settings Application button we added to `SecondViewController` in Figure 12-30? We wired it up to the `onSettingsButtonTapped()` method in the view controller, but we didn't put any code in that method. Let's fix that now. Add the following code shown to the `onSettingsButtonTapped()` method:

```swift
@IBAction func onSettingsButtonTapped(_ sender: AnyObject) {
    let application = UIApplication.shared()
    let url = URL(string: UIApplicationOpenSettingsURLString)! as URL
    if application.canOpenURL(url) {
        application.open(url, options:["":""] , completionHandler: nil)
    }
}
```

This code uses a system-defined URL stored in the external constant `UIApplicationOpenSettingsURLString` (the value is actually `app-settings:`) to launch the Settings application right from our view controller. Run the application, switch to the second tab, and click the Open Settings Application button—you'll be taken directly to our settings screen, the one shown in Figure 12-3. That's a great improvement. Even better, as of iOS 9, at the top of the Settings screen, you'll see a small button that lets you return directly to our application (see Figure 12-31). Now you can easily navigate back and forth between the Bridge Control and Settings applications, changing values and seeing the effect on our application's user interface.

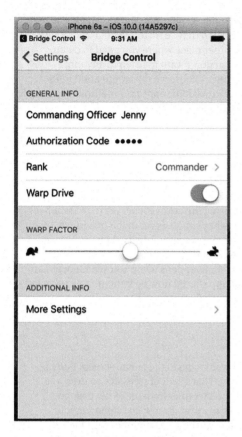

Figure 12-31. *When the Settings application is opened from Bridge Control, there's a button in the status bar that lets us go right back to our application*

Summary

At this point, you should have a very solid grasp on both the Settings application and the User Defaults mechanism. You know how to add a settings bundle to your application and how to build a hierarchy of views for your application's preferences. You also learned how to read and write preferences using UserDefaults, as well as how to let the user change preferences from within your application. You even got a chance to use a new project template in Xcode. There really shouldn't be much in the way of application preferences that you are not equipped to handle now.

CHAPTER 13

■ ■ ■

Persistence: Saving Data Between App Launches

So far, we've focused on the controller and view aspects of the MVC paradigm. Although several of our applications read data from their own application bundle, only the Bridge Control example in Chapter 12 places any data in persistent storage. When any of our other apps launched, they appeared with exactly the same data they had when first launched. That approach worked up to this point, but in the real world, your apps need to persist data. When users make changes, they want to see those changes when they launch the program again.

A number of different mechanisms exist for persisting data on an iOS device. If you've programmed in Cocoa for macOS, you've likely used some or all of these techniques. In this chapter, we'll look at four different mechanisms for persisting data to the iOS file system:

- Property lists

- Object archives (or archiving)

- SQLite3 (iOS's embedded relational database)

- Core Data (Apple's provided persistence tool)

■ **Note** Property lists, object archives, SQLite3, and Core Data are not the only ways you can persist data on iOS; they are just the most common and easiest. You always have the option of using traditional C I/O calls like `fopen()` to read and write data. You can also use Cocoa's low-level file-management tools. In almost every case, doing so will result in a lot more coding effort and is rarely necessary, but those tools are there if you want them.

Your Application's Sandbox

All four of this chapter's data-persistence mechanisms share an important common element: your application's Documents folder. Every application gets its own Documents folder, and applications are allowed to read and write from their own Documents directory.

© Molly Maskrey, Kim Topley, David Mark, Fredrik Olsson and Jeff Lamarche 2016
M. Maskrey et al., *Beginning iPhone Development with Swift 3*, DOI 10.1007/978-1-4842-2223-2_13

First, let's look at how applications are organized in iOS by examining the folder layout used by the iPhone simulator. To see this, you'll need to look inside the Library directory contained in your home directory. On OS X 10.6 and earlier, this was no problem; however, starting with OS X 10.7, Apple decided to make the Library folder hidden by default, so there's a small extra hoop to jump through. Open a Finder window and navigate to your home directory. If you can see your Library folder, that's great. If not, hold down the Option key (⌥) and select Go ➤ Library. The Library option is hidden unless you hold down the Option key.

Within the Library folder, drill down into Developer/CoreSimulator/Devices/. Within that directory, you'll see one subdirectory for each simulator in your current Xcode installation. The subdirectory names are globally unique identifiers (GUIDs) that are generated automatically by Xcode, so it's impossible to know just by looking at them which directory corresponds to which simulator. To find out, look for a file called device.plist in any of the simulator directories and open it. You'll find a key that maps to the simulated device's name. Figure 13-1 shows the device.plist file for the iPad Pro simulator.

Figure 13-1. *Using the device.plist file to map a directory to a simulator*

Choose a device and drill down into its data directory until you reach the subdirectory data/Containers/Data/Application. Here again you'll see subdirectories with names that are GUIDs. In this case, each one of them represents either a preinstalled application or an application that you have run on that simulator. Select one of the directories and open it. You'll see something like Figure 13-2.

Figure 13-2. *The sandbox for an application on the simulator*

> ■ **Note** It may take a little searching when starting from the Devices in Figure 13-1 to find a Containers subdirectory. If you don't see it at first, keep going down the list of device GUIDs and you should eventually find your way to the Containers subdirectory.

Although the previous listing represents the simulator, the file structure functions similarly to what's on an actual device. To see the sandbox for an application on a device, plug it onto your Mac and open the Xcode Devices window (Window ➤ Devices). You should see your device in the window sidebar. Select it and then choose an application from the Installed Apps table. Near the bottom of the window on the right-hand side, you'll see a section called Installed Apps (you may have to click a down arrow near the bottom of the window to see this section) that contains a table with a row for each of the apps you have installed from Xcode. Below the table, there's an icon that looks like a gear. Click it and select Show Container from the pop-up to see the contents of the sandbox for whichever application you select in the table (see Figure 13-3). You can also download everything in the sandbox to your Mac. Figure 13-4 shows the application sandbox for an application called townslot2 from my book *App Development Recipes for iOS and watchOS* (Apress, 2016).

Figure 13-3. *Configuration and contents of an actual device showing the townslot2 app*

423

townslot2 1 container:

Name	Kind
📁 Documents	Folder
▼ 📁 Library	Folder
📁 Caches	Folder
▼ 📁 Preferences	Folder
📄 com.globalteklabs.townslot2.plist	File
📁 tmp	Folder

[Done]

Figure 13-4. *The sandbox for the townslot2 application on an iPhone 6s*

Every application sandbox contains these three directories:

- Documents: Your application stores data in the Documents directory. If you enable iTunes file sharing for your application, the user can see the contents of this directory (and any subdirectories that your application creates) in iTunes and may upload files to it.

■ **Tip** To enable file sharing for your application, open its Info.plist file and add the key Application supports iTunes file sharing with the value YES.

- Library: This provides another place that your application stores data. Use it for files that you do not want to share with the user. You can create your own subdirectories if required. As you can see in Figure 13-4, the system creates subdirectories called Cache and Preferences which contains the .plist file storing the application's preferences, and sets using the UserDefaults class, which we discussed in Chapter 12.

- tmp: The tmp directory offers a place where your application can store temporary files. Files written into tmp will not be backed up by iTunes when your iOS device syncs; but to avoid filling up the file system, your application does need to take responsibility for deleting the files in tmp once they are no longer needed.

Getting the Documents and Library Directories

Although our application exists in a folder with a seemingly random name, it's quite easy to retrieve the full path to the Documents directory so that we can read and write our files using this method urls(for:in:) of the FileManager class locates the various directories for you. FileManager is a Foundation class, so it is shared with Cocoa for OS X. Many of its available options are designed for macOS and some of the return values on iOS that aren't very useful, because your application doesn't have rights to access the directory due to iOS's sandboxing mechanism. Listing 13-1 shows an example code snippet in Swift 3 to access the iOS Documents directory.

Listing 13-1. Code to Get an NSURL that Points to the Documents Directory

```
let urls = FileManager.default.urls(for:
    .documentDirectory, ins: .userDomainMask)
if let documentUrl = urls.first {
    print(documentUrl)
```

The first argument to the urlsForDirectory(_:in:) method specifies which directory we are looking for. The searchPathDirectory enumeration defines the possible values; here, we use the value SearchPathDirectory.documentDirectory (shortened to .documentDirectory) indicating that we are looking for the Documents directory. The second argument gives the domain or domains (called the domainMask in the Apple documentation) to be used for the search. The possible domains are all values of the SearchPathDomainMask enumeration and here we specify .userDomainMask. On iOS, this domain maps to the running application's sandbox. The urls(for: in:) method returns an array containing one or more URLs that map to the requested directory in the specified domain. On iOS, there is always only one Documents directory for each application, so we can safely assume that exactly one NSURL object will be returned, but just be on the safe side, we use an if let construction to safely access the first element of the NSURL array, just in case it happens to be empty. On a real iOS device, the URL for the Documents directory would be something like file:///var/mobile/Containers/Data/Application/69BFDDB0-E4A8-4359-8382-F6DDDF031481/Documents/.

We can create a URL for a file in the Documents directory by appending another component onto the end of the URL we just retrieved. We'll use an NSURL method called appendingPathComponent(), which was designed for just that purpose:

```
let fileUrl = try documentUrl.appendingPathComponent("theFile.txt")
```

■ **Note**   Error handling in Swift 3 operates similar to other languages that use the try, catch, and throw keywords.

After this call, fileUrl should contain the full URL (see Listing 13-2) for a file called theFile.txt in our application's Documents directory, and we can use this URL to create, read, and write from that file. It's important to note that the file doesn't need to exist for you to be able to get an NSURL object for it.

Listing 13-2. You can use the same method with first argument .libraryDirectory to locate the application's Library directory.

```
let urls = FileManager.default.urls(for:
    .libraryDirectory, in: .userDomainMask)
if let libraryUrl = urls.first {
    print(libraryUrl)
}
```

This code would return a URL like this:

```
file:///var/mobile/Containers/Data/Application/69BFDDB0-E4A8-4359-8382-F6DDDF031481/Library/.
```

It's possible to specify more than one search domain. When you do so, FileManager looks for the directory in all of the domains and may return more than one NSURL. For reasons already explained, this is not really very useful on iOS but for the sake of completeness, consider the example in Listing 13-3.

Listing 13-3. Getting Multiple URLs

```
let urls = FileManager.default.urls(for:
    .libraryDirectory,in: [.userDomainMask, .systemDomainMask])
print(urls)
```

Here, we ask FileManager to look for the Library directory in both the user and system domains and the result is that we get back an array containing two NSURLs:

- file:///var/mobile/Containers/Data/Application/69BFDDB0-E4A8-4359-8382-F6DDDF031481/Library/

- file:///System/Library/

The second URL refers to the system's Library directory, which, of course, we can't access. When more than one URL is returned, the order in which they appear in the returned array is undefined.

Notice how we wrote the value of the inDomains argument in Listing 13-3:

```
[.userDomainMask, .systemDomainMask]
```

This might look like an initializer for an array but it's actually creating a set—the syntax for initializing an array and a set in Swift are the same.

Getting the tmp Directory

Getting a reference to your application's temporary directory is even easier than getting a reference to the Documents directory. The Foundation function called NSTemporaryDirectory() returns a string containing the full path to your application's temporary directory. To create an NSURL for a file that will be stored in the temporary directory, first find the temporary directory:

```
let tempDirPath = NSTemporaryDirectory()
```

Next, convert the path to a URL and create a path to a file in the temporary directory by appending a path component to it as we did before, as shown in Listing 13-4.

Listing 13-4. Appending a Path Component to a URL

```
let tempDirUrl = NSURL(fileURLWithPath: tempDirPath)
let tempFileUrl = tempDirUrl.appendingPathComponent("tempFile.txt")
```

The resulting URL will be something like this:

```
file:///private/var/mobile/Containers/Data/Application/29233884-23EB-4267-8CC9-86DCD507D84C/
tmp/tempFile.txt
```

File-Saving Strategies

All four persistence approaches we're going to look at in this chapter use the iOS file system. In the case of SQLite3, we'll create a single SQLite3 database file and let SQLite3 worry about storing and retrieving your data. In its simplest form, Core Data takes care of all the file system management for you. With the other two persistence mechanisms—property lists and archiving—you need to put some thought into whether you are going to store your data in a single file or in multiple files.

Single-File Persistence

Using a single file for data storage provides the easiest approach and with many applications, a perfectly acceptable one. You start by creating a root object, usually an `Array` or `Dictionary` (your root object can also be based on a custom class when using archiving). Next, you populate your root object with all the program data that needs to be persisted. Whenever you need to save, your code rewrites the entire contents of that root object to a single file. When your application launches, it reads the entire contents of that file into memory. When it quits, it writes out the entire contents. This is the approach we'll use.

The downside of using a single file is that you need to load all of your application's data into memory and that you must write all of it to the file system for even the smallest changes. But if your application isn't likely to manage more than a few megabytes of data, this approach works fine and its simplicity certainly makes things easier.

Multiple-File Persistence

Using multiple files for persistence provides another approach. For example, an e-mail application might store each e-mail message in its own file.

There are obvious advantages to this method. It allows the application to load only data that the user has requested (another form of lazy loading); and when the user makes a change, only the files that changed need to be saved. This method also gives you the opportunity to free up memory when you receive a low-memory notification. Any memory that is being used to store data that the user is not currently viewing can be flushed and then simply reloaded from the file system the next time it's needed. The downside of multiple-file persistence is that it adds a fair amount of complexity to your application. For now, we'll work with single-file persistence.

Next, we'll get into the specifics of each of our persistence methods: property lists, object archives, SQLite3, and Core Data. We'll explore each of these in turn and build an application that uses each mechanism to save some data to the device's file system. We'll start with property lists.

Using Property Lists

Several of our sample applications have used property lists, most recently when we created a property list to specify our application settings and preferences in Chapter 12. Property lists provide convenience in that they can be edited manually using Xcode or the Property List Editor application. Also, both `Dictionary` and `Array` instances can be written to and created from property lists, as long as they contain only specific serializable objects.

Property List Serialization

A **serialized object** is one that has been converted into a stream of bytes so that it can be stored in a file or transferred over a network. Although any object can be made serializable, only certain objects can be placed into a collection class, such as an NSDictionary or NSArray, and then stored to a property list using the collection class's writeToURL(_:atomically:) or writeToFile(_:atomically:) methods. The following classes can be serialized this way:

- Array or NSArray
- NSMutableArray
- Dictionary or NSDictionary
- NSMutableDictionary
- NSData
- NSMutableData
- String or NSString
- NSMutableString
- NSNumber
- Date or NSDate

If you can build your data model from just these objects, you can use property lists to save and load your data.

■ **Note** The writeToURL(_:atomically:) and writeToFile(_:atomically:) methods do the same thing, but the first requires you to give the file location as an NSURL, the second as a String. Previously, file locations were always given as string paths, but more recently Apple started preferring to use NSURLs instead, so the examples in this book do the same, except where there is only an API that requires a path. You can easily get the path for a file-based NSURL from its path property, as you'll see in the first example in this chapter.

If you're going to use property lists for persisting application data, use either an Array or a Dictionary to hold the data that needs to be persisted. Assuming that all the objects that you put into the Array or Dictionary are serializable objects from the preceding list, you can write out a property list by calling the write(to url: URL, atomically: Bool) -> Bool method on the dictionary or array instance, as shown in Listing 13-5.

Listing 13-5. Writing to a Property List

```
let array: NSArray = [1,2,3]
let tempDirPath = NSTemporaryDirectory()
let tempDirUrl = NSURL(fileURLWithPath: tempDirPath)
let tempFileUrl = tempDirUrl.appendingPathComponent("tempFile.txt")
array.write(to: tempFileUrl!, atomically:true)
```

■ **Note** The atomically parameter causes the method to first write the data to an auxiliary file, not to the specified location and after successfully being written to that file, gets a copy to the location specified by the first parameter. This provides a safer way to write a file, because if the application crashes during the save, the existing file (if there was one) will not be corrupted. It adds a bit of overhead; but in most situations, it's worth the cost.

One problem with the property list approach is that custom objects cannot be serialized into property lists. You also can't use other classes from Cocoa Touch, which means that classes like NSURL, UIImage, and UIColor cannot be used directly.

Apart from the serialization issue, keeping all your model data in the form of property lists means you can't easily create derived or calculated properties (such as a property that is the sum of two other properties), and some of your code that really should be contained in model classes must be moved to your controller classes. Again, these restrictions work for simple data models and apps. But most of the time your app will be much easier to maintain by creating dedicated model classes.

Simple property lists still provide usefulness in complex applications as they are a great way to include static data in your application. For example, when your application includes a picker, often the best way to include the list of items for it is to create a .plist file placing that file into your project's Resources folder causing it to be compiled into your application.

We'll now build a simple application that uses property lists to store its data.

Creating the First Version of a Persistence Application

We're going to build a program that lets you enter data into four text fields, saves those fields to a .plist file when the application quits, and then reloads the data back from that .plist file the next time the application launches (see Figure 13-5).

Figure 13-5. *Our Persistence application*

■ **Note** In this chapter's applications, we won't be taking the time to set up all the user interface niceties that we have added in previous examples. Tapping the Return key, for example, will neither dismiss the keyboard nor take you to the next field. If you want to add such polish to the application, doing so would be good practice, so we encourage you to do that on your own.

In Xcode, create a new project using the Single View Application template and name it Persistence. Before we build the view with the four text fields, let's create the single outlet we need. In the Project Navigator, single-click the ViewController.swift file and add the following outlet:

```
class ViewController: UIViewController {
    @IBOutlet var lineFields:[UITextField]!
```

Designing the Persistence Application View

Now select Main.storyboard to edit the GUI. Once Xcode switches over to Interface Builder mode, you'll see the View Controller scene in the editing pane. Drag a Text Field from the library and place it against the top and right blue guidelines. Bring up the Attributes Inspector. Make sure the box labeled Clear When Editing Begins is unchecked.

Now drag a Label to the window and place it to the left of the text field using the left blue guideline, and then use the horizontal blue guideline to line up the label's vertical center with that of the text field. Double-click the label and change it to say Line 1:. Finally, resize the text field using the left resize handle to bring it close to the label. Use Figure 13-6 as a guide. Next, select the label and text field, hold down the Option key, and drag down to make a copy below the first set. Use the blue guidelines to guide your placement. Now select both labels and both text fields, hold down the Option key, and drag down again. You should now have four labels next to four text fields. Double-click each of the remaining labels and change their names to Line 2:, Line 3:, and Line 4:. Again, compare your results with Figure 13-6.

Figure 13-6. *Designing the Persistence application's view*

Once you have all four text fields and labels placed, Control-drag from the View Controller icon in the Document Outline to each of the four text fields. Connect them all to the lineFields outlet collection, making sure to connect them in order from top to bottom. Save the changes you made to Main.storyboard.

Now let's add the Auto Layout constraints to make sure that the design works the same way on all devices. Starting by Control-dragging from the Line 1 label to the text field to its right, and then release the mouse. Hold down the Shift key and select Horizontal Spacing and Baseline, and then click the Return key. Do the same for the other three labels and text fields.

Next, we'll fix the positions of the text fields. In the Document Outline, Control-drag from the top text field to its parent View icon, release the mouse, hold down the Shift key, and select Trailing Space to Container Margin and Vertical Spacing to Top Layout Guide. Do the same for the other three text fields.

We need to fix the widths of the labels so that they don't resize if the user types more text than will fit in any of the text fields. Select the top label and click the Pin button below the storyboard editor. In the pop-up, select the Width check box and press Add 1 Constraint. Do the same for all of the labels.

Finally, back in the Document Outline, Control-drag from the Line 1 label to the View icon, release the mouse, and select Leading Space to Container Margin. Do the same for all of the labels and that's it—all the required Auto Layout constraints have been set. Select the view controller icon in the Document Outline followed by Editor ➤ Resolve Auto Layout Issues ➤ Update Frames in the menu to remove the warnings in the Xcode Activity View. Now build and run the application and compare the result with Figure 13-6.

Editing the Persistence Classes

In the Project Navigator, select ViewController.swift and add the code in Listing 13-6.

Listing 13-6. Getting the URL for Our data.plist File

```
func dataFileURL() -> NSURL {
    let urls = FileManager.default.urls(for:
        .documentDirectory, in: .userDomainMask)
    var url:NSURL?
    url = URL(fileURLWithPath: "")        // create a blank path
    do {
        try url = urls.first!.appendingPathComponent("data.plist")
    } catch  {
        print("Error is \(error)")
    }
    return url!
}
```

The dataFileURL() method returns the URL of the data file that we'll be creating in this example by finding the Documents directory and appending the file name to it. This method will be called from any code that needs to load or save data. We are playing it a little loose here with the url. Note that we've encapsulated the appendingPathComponent method within a Swift do-catch block. We have to do this because the append method throws an error that needs to be caught. But since we know that our app bundle must have a document directory and we're creating the data.plist file ourselves, we're not going to see this error as long as we write the code correctly. Normally, we want to handle things a little more securely so our customers don't see crashes, but for the sake of brevity we're not going to deal with that here since it's not the subject of our discussion.

■ **Note**   In Swift we use a do-catch block (which can be found in the Xcode code snippet library) to try a method call that throws an exception (an error) and then "catch" that exception and handle it in some way that prevents the app from crashing.

Find the viewDidLoad() method and add the following code to it, as well as a new method for receiving notifications named applicationWillResignActive() just below it, as shown in Listing 13-7.

Listing 13-7. The viewDidLoad method in the ViewController.swift file and the applicationWillResignActive method.

```
override func viewDidLoad() {
    super.viewDidLoad()
    // Do any additional setup after loading the view, typically from a nib.
    let fileURL = self.dataFileURL()
    if (FileManager.default.fileExists(atPath: fileURL.path!)) {
        if let array = NSArray(contentsOf: fileURL as URL) as? [String] {
            for i in 0..<array.count {
                lineFields[i].text = array[i]
            }
        }
    }
}
```

```
let app = UIApplication.shared()
    NotificationCenter.default.addObserver(self, selector: #selector(self.applicationWill
    ResignActive(notification:)), name: Notification.Name.UIApplicationWillResignActive,
    object: app)
}

func applicationWillResignActive(notification:NSNotification) {
    let fileURL = self.dataFileURL()
    let array = (self.lineFields as NSArray).value(forKey: "text") as! NSArray
    array.write(to: fileURL as URL, atomically: true)
}
```

In the viewDidLoad() method, we do a few more things. First, we use the fileExists(atPath:) method of the FileManager class to check whether our data file already exists, which would be the case if we have already run the application at least once. This method requires the file's path name, which we get from the path property of its URL (unfortunately, there isn't a variant of this method that accepts a URL argument). If there isn't one, we don't want to bother trying to load it. If the file does exist, we instantiate an array with the contents of that file, and then copy the objects from that array to our four text fields. Because arrays are ordered lists, we copy them in the same order as we saved them

To read the file, we use an Array initializer that creates an NSArray object from the contents of a file at a given URL. The Array initializer expects the file content to be in property list format, which is fine because that's the form in which it is saved, in the code we'll write shortly.

Our application needs to save its data before it is terminated or sent to the background, so we are interested in the notification called applicationWillResignActive. This notification is posted whenever an app is no longer the one with which the user is interacting. This happens when the user taps the Home button, as well as when the application is pushed to the background by some other event, such as an incoming phone call. We can find out that this has happened by registering for a notification from iOS's notification center. The notification center delivers a notification by calling a method that you register with it, passing an argument of type Notification that includes the details of the event that's being notified. To register for this notification, we get a reference to our application instance and use that to subscribe to UIApplicationWillResignActive, using the default NotificationCenter instance and a method called addObserver(_:selector:name:object:). We pass self as the first parameter, specifying that our ViewController instance is the observer that should be notified. For the second parameter, we pass a selector to the applicationWillResignActive() method, telling the notification center to call that method when the notification is posted. The third parameter, UIApplicationWillResignActive, is the name of the notification that we're interested in receiving. This is a string constant defined by the UIApplication class.

Finally, we added the implementation of the applicationWillResignActive() method, which the notification center will call:

```
func applicationWillResignActive(notification:NSNotification) {
    let fileURL = self.dataFileURL()
    let array = (self.lineFields as NSArray).value(forKey: "text") as! NSArray
    array.write(to: fileURL as URL, atomically: true)
}
```

This method is pretty short, but really does a lot with just a few method calls. We construct an array of strings by calling the text method on each of the text fields in our lineFields array. To accomplish this, we use a clever shortcut: instead of explicitly iterating through our array of text fields, asking each for its text value, and adding that value to a new array, we cast the Swift lineFields array (of UITextFields) to an NSArray and call value(forKey:) on it, passing "text" as a parameter. The NSArray implementation of valueForKey() does the iteration for us, asks each UITextField instance it contains for its text value, and returns a new NSArray containing all the values. After that, we write the contents of that array out to our .plist file in property list format, using the write(_ to:atomically:) method. That's all there is to saving our data using property lists.

Let's summarize how this works. When our main view is finished loading, we look for a .plist file. If it exists, we copy data from it into our text fields. Next, we register to be notified when the application becomes inactive (either by being quit or pushed to the background). When that happens, we gather the values from our four text fields, stick them in a mutable array, and write that mutable array to a property list.

Build and run the application. It should build and then launch in the simulator. Once it comes up, you should be able to type into any of the four text fields. When you've typed something in them, press ⌘⇧H (Command-Shift-H) to return to the home screen. It's very important that you do this. If you just exit the simulator, that's the equivalent of forcibly quitting your application. In that case, the view controller will never receive the notification that the application is going inactive, and your data will not be saved. After returning to the home screen, you may then quit the simulator, or stop the app from Xcode and run it again. Your text will be restored and will appear in the text fields the next time the app starts.

■ **Note** It's important to understand that returning to the home screen doesn't typically quit the app—at least not at first. The app is put into a background state, ready to be instantly reactivated in case the user switches back to it. We'll dig into the details of these states and their implications for running and quitting apps in Chapter 15.

Property list serialization is pretty cool and easy to use. However, it's a little limiting, since only a small selection of objects can be stored in property lists. Let's look at a somewhat more robust approach.

Archiving Model Objects

In the Cocoa world, the term **archiving** refers to another form of serialization, but it's a more generic type that any object can implement. Any model object specifically written to hold data should support archiving. The technique of archiving model objects lets you easily write complex objects to a file and then read them back in. As long as every property you implement in your class is either a scalar (e.g., Int or Float) or an instance of a class that conforms to the NSCoding protocol, you can archive your objects completely. Since most Foundation and Cocoa Touch classes capable of storing data do conform to NSCoding (though there are a few noteworthy exceptions, such as UIImage), archiving is relatively easy to implement for most classes.

Although not strictly required to make archiving work, another protocol should be implemented along with NSCoding: the NSCopying protocol, which allows your object to be copied. Being able to copy an object gives you a lot more flexibility when using data model objects.

Conforming to NSCoding

The NSCoding protocol declares two methods, which are both required. One encodes your object into an archive; the other one creates a new object by decoding an archive. Both methods are passed an instance of NSCoder, which you work with in very much the same way as NSUserDefaults, introduced in the previous chapter. You can encode and decode both objects and native data types like Int and Float values using **key-value coding**.

To support archiving in an object, we need to make it a subclass of NSObject (or any other class that is derived from NSObject) and we need to encode each of our instance variables into encoder using the appropriate encoding method. Let's see how this works. Suppose we create a simple container class, like this:

```
class MyObject : NSObject, NSCoding, NSCopying {
    var number = 0;
    var string = ""
    var child: MyObject?

    override init() {
    }
}
```

This class contains an integer property, a string property, and a reference to another instance of the same class. It is derived from NSObject and conforms to the NSCoding and NSCopying protocols. The NSCoding protocol method to encode an object of type MyObject might look like this:

```
func encode(with aCoder: NSCoder) {
    aCoder.encode(string, forKey: "stringKey")
    aCoder.encode(32, forKey: "intKey")
    if let myChild = child {
        aCoder.encode(myChild, forKey: "childKey")
    }
}
```

If MyObject were a subclass of a class that also conforms to NSCoding, we would need to make sure that also we called encodeWithCoder() on its superclass to ensure that the superclass encodes its data. In that case, this method would look like this instead:

```
func encode(with aCoder: NSCoder) {
    super.encode(with aCoder: NSCoder)
    aCoder.encode(string, forKey: "stringKey")
    aCoder.encode(32, forKey: "intKey")
    if let myChild = child {
        aCoder.encode(myChild, forKey: "childKey")
    }
}
```

The NSCoding protocol also requires us to implement an initializer that initializes an object from an NSCoder, allowing us to restore an object that was previously archived. Implementing this method is very similar to implementing encodeWithCoder(). If your object has no base class or you are subclassing some other class that doesn't conform to NSCoding, your initializer would look something like the following:

```
required init?(coder aDecoder: NSCoder) {
        string = aDecoder.decodeObject(forKey: "stringKey") as! String
        number = aDecoder.decodeInteger(forKey: "intKey")
        child = aDecoder.decodeObject(forKey: "childKey") as? MyObject
}
```

The initializer sets the properties of the object being initialized by decoding values from the passed-in instance of NSCoder. Since we are allowing the child property of the original object to be nil, we need to use conditional casting when assigning to the decoded object's child property because the archived object may not have a stored child object.

435

When implementing NSCoding for a class with a superclass that also conforms to NSCoding, you need to add an extra line to allow the superclass to initialize its own state:

```
required init?(coder aDecoder: NSCoder) {
    string = aDecoder.decodeObject(forKey: "stringKey") as! String
    number = aDecoder.decodeInteger(forKey: "intKey")
    child = aDecoder.decodeObject(forKey: "childKey") as? MyObject
    super.init(code: aDecoder)
}
```

And that's basically it. As long as you implement these two methods to encode and decode all your object's properties, your object is archivable and can be written to and read from archives.

Implementing NSCopying

As mentioned earlier, conforming to NSCopying is a very good idea for any data model objects. NSCopying has one method, called copyWithZone(), which allows objects to be copied. Implementing NSCopying is similar to implementing init(coder:). You just need to create a new instance of the same class, and then set all of that new instance's properties to the same values as this object's properties. Even though you implement the copy(with zone:) method, the application code actually calls a method called copy(), which forwards the operation to copy(with zone:):

```
let anObject = MyObject()
let objectCopy = anObject.copy() as! MyObject
```

Here's what the copy(withZone:) method for the MyObject class would look like:

```
func copy(with zone: NSZone? = nil) -> AnyObject {
    let copy = MyObject()
    copy.number = number
    copy.string = string
    copy.child = child?.copy() as? MyObject
    return copy
}
```

Notice that with this implementation, if there is a property that references a child object (such as the child property in this example), the new object will have a copy of that child, not the original one. If the child object is of a type that is immutable, or if you only need to provide a shallow copy of the object, then you would simply assign the original child object reference to the new object.

■ **Note** Don't worry too much about the NSZone parameter. This pointer is to a struct that is used by the system to manage memory. Only in rare circumstances did developers ever need to worry about zones or create their own, and nowadays, it's almost unheard of to have multiple zones. Calling copy on an object is the same as calling copy(with zone:)using the default zone, which is always what you want. In fact, on the modern iOS, zones are completely ignored. The fact that NSCopying uses zones at all is a historical oddity for the sake of backward compatibility.

Archiving and Unarchiving Data Objects

Creating an archive from an object (or objects) that conforms to NSCoding is relatively easy. First, we create an instance of the Foundation class NSMutableData to hold the encoded data, and then we create an NSKeyedArchiver instance to archive objects into that NSMutableData instance:

```
let data = NSMutableData()
let archiver = NSKeyedArchiver(forWritingWith: data)
```

After creating both of those, we then use key-value coding to archive any objects we wish to include in the archive, like this:

```
archiver.encode(anObject, forKey: "keyValueString")
```

Once we've encoded all the objects we want to include, we just tell the archiver we're finished, and then we write the NSMutableData instance to the file system:

```
archiver.finishEncoding()
let success = data.write(to: archiveUrl as URL, atomically: true)
```

If you're feeling a little overwhelmed by archiving, don't worry. It's actually fairly straightforward. We're going to retrofit our Persistence application to use archiving, so you'll get to see it in action. Once you've done it a few times, archiving will become second nature, as all you're really doing is storing and retrieving your object's properties using key-value coding.

The Archiving Application

Let's redo the Persistence application, so that it uses archiving instead of property lists. We're going to be making some fairly significant changes to the Persistence source code, so you should make a copy of your entire project folder before continuing. I've compressed it before making any changes—using the property list technique—to PersistencePL.zip.

Implementing the FourLines Class

Once you're ready to proceed and have a copy of your Persistence project open in Xcode, press ⌘N or select File ➤ New ➤ File.... When the new file assistant comes up, from the iOS section, select Swift File and click Next. On the next screen, name the file FourLines.swift, choose the Persistence folder to save it, and then click Create. This class is going to be our data model. It will hold the data that we're currently storing in a dictionary in the property list application.

Single-click FourLines.swift and add the code in Listing 13-8.

Listing 13-8. Our FourLines Class

```
class FourLines : NSObject, NSCoding, NSCopying {
    private static let linesKey = "linesKey"
    var lines:[String]?

    override init() {
    }
```

```swift
    required init?(coder aDecoder: NSCoder) {
        lines = aDecoder.decodeObject(forKey: FourLines.linesKey) as? [String]
    }
    func encode(with aCoder: NSCoder) {
        if let saveLines = lines {
            aCoder.encode(saveLines, forKey: FourLines.linesKey)
        }
    }
    func copy(with zone: NSZone? = nil) -> AnyObject {
        let copy = FourLines()
        if let linesToCopy = lines {
            var newLines = Array<String>()
            for line in linesToCopy {
                newLines.append(line)
            }
            copy.lines = newLines
        }
        return copy
    }
}
```

We just implemented all the methods necessary to conform to the NSCoding and NSCopying protocols. We encoded the lines property in encode(with aCoder:) and decoded it using the same key value in init(with aCoder:). In copy(with zone:), we created a new FourLines object and copied the string array to it, carefully making a deep copy so that changes to the original will not affect the new object. See? It's not hard at all; just make sure you did not forget to change anything if you did a lot of copying and pasting.

Implementing the ViewController Class

Now that we have an archivable data object, let's use it to persist our application data. Select ViewController. swift and make the changes in Listing 13-9.

Listing 13-9. Our Save and Retrieve Code for Archiving Object in ViewController.swift

```swift
override func viewDidLoad() {
    super.viewDidLoad()
    // Do any additional setup after loading the view, typically from a nib.
    let fileURL = self.dataFileURL()
    if (FileManager.default.fileExists(atPath: fileURL.path!)) {
        if let array = NSArray(contentsOf: fileURL as URL) as? [String] {
            for i in 0..<array.count {
                lineFields[i].text = array[i]
            }
        }
        let data = NSMutableData(contentsOf: fileURL as URL)
        let unarchiver = NSKeyedUnarchiver(forReadingWith: data as! Data)
        let fourLines = unarchiver.decodeObject(forKey: ViewController.rootKey) as!
                        FourLines
        unarchiver.finishDecoding()
```

```
        if let newLines = fourLines.lines {
            for i in 0..<newLines.count {
                lineFields[i].text = newLines[i]
            }
        }
    }
    let app = UIApplication.shared()
    NotificationCenter.default.addObserver(self, selector: #selector(self.applicationWill
    ResignActive(notification:)), name: Notification.Name.UIApplicationWillResignActive,
    object: app)
}

func applicationWillResignActive(notification:NSNotification) {
    let fileURL = self.dataFileURL()
    let fourLines = FourLines()
    let array = (self.lineFields as NSArray).value(forKey: "text")
        as! [String]
    fourLines.lines = array

    let data = NSMutableData()
    let archiver = NSKeyedArchiver(forWritingWith: data)
    archiver.encode(fourLines, forKey: ViewController.rootKey)
    archiver.finishEncoding()
    data.write(to: fileURL as URL, atomically: true)
}

func dataFileURL() -> NSURL {
    let urls = FileManager.default.urls(for:
        .documentDirectory, in: .userDomainMask)
    var url:NSURL?
    url = URL(fileURLWithPath: "")       // create a blank path
    do {
        try url = urls.first!.appendingPathComponent("data.archive")
    } catch  {
        print("Error is \(error)")
    }
    return url!
}
```

Save your changes, then build and run this version of the app. Not very much has changed, really. We started off by specifying a new file name in the dataFileURL() method, so that our program doesn't try to load the old property list as an archive. We also defined a new constant that will be the key value we use to encode and decode our object. Next, we redefined the loading and saving by using FourLines to hold the data and using its NSCoding methods to do the actual loading and saving. The GUI is identical to the previous version.

This new version takes several more lines of code to implement than property list serialization, so you might be wondering if there really is an advantage to using archiving over just serializing property lists. For this application, the answer is simple: no, there really isn't any advantage. But imagine we had an array of archivable objects, such as the FourLines class that we just built, we could archive the entire array by archiving the array instance itself. Collection classes like Array, when archived, archive all of the objects they contain. As long as every object you put into an array or dictionary conforms to NSCoding, you can archive the array or dictionary and restore it so that all the objects that were in it when you archived it will be in the restored array or dictionary. The same is not true of property link persistence, which only works for a small set of Foundation object types—you cannot use it to persist custom classes without writing additional code to convert instances of those classes to and from a `Dictionary`, with one key for each object property.

In other words, the `NSCoding` approach scales beautifully (in terms of code size, at least). No matter how many objects you add, the work to write those objects to disk (assuming you're using single-file persistence) is exactly the same. With property lists, the amount of work increases with every object you add.

Using iOS's Embedded SQLite3

The third persistence option we're going to discuss is using iOS's embedded SQL database, called SQLite3. SQLite3 is very efficient at storing and retrieving large amounts of data. It's also capable of doing complex aggregations on your data, with much faster results than you would get doing the same thing using objects. Consider a couple scenarios. What if you need to calculate the sum of a particular field across all the objects in your application? Or, what if you need the sum from just the objects that meet certain criteria? SQLite3 allows you to get this information without loading every object into memory. Getting aggregations from SQLite3 is several orders of magnitude faster than loading all the objects into memory and summing their values. Being a full-fledged embedded database, SQLite3 contains tools to make it even faster by, for example, creating table indexes that can speed up your queries.

SQLite3 uses the Structured Query Language (SQL), the standard language used to interact with relational databases. Whole books have been written on the syntax of SQL (hundreds of them, in fact), as well as on SQLite itself. So if you don't already know SQL and you want to use SQLite3 in your application, you have a little work ahead of you. I'll show you how to set up and interact with the SQLite database from your iOS applications. I'll also show you some of the basics of the syntax in this chapter. But to really make the most of SQLite3, you'll need to do some additional research and exploration. A couple of good starting points are "An Introduction to the SQLite3 C/C++ Interface" (`www.sqlite.org/cintro.html`) and "SQL As Understood by SQLite" (`www.sqlite.org/lang.html`).

Relational databases (including SQLite3) and object-oriented programming languages use fundamentally different approaches to storing and organizing data. The approaches are different enough that numerous techniques and many libraries and tools for converting between the two have been developed. These different techniques are collectively called **object-relational mapping** (ORM). There are currently several ORM tools available for Cocoa Touch. In fact, we'll look at one ORM solution provided by Apple, called Core Data, later in the chapter.

But before we do that, we're going to focus on the SQLite3 basics, including setting it up, creating a table to hold your data, and using the database in an application. Obviously, in the real world, an application as simple as the one we're working on wouldn't warrant the investment in SQLite3. But this application's simplicity is exactly what makes it a good learning example.

Creating or Opening the Database

Before you can use SQLite3, you must open the database. The function that's used to do that, `sqlite3_open()`, will open an existing database; or, if none exists at the specified location, the function will create a new one. Here's what the code to open a database might look like:

```
var database:OpaquePointer? = nil
let result = sqlite3_open("/path/to/database/file", &database)
```

If result is equal to the constant SQLITE_OK, then the database was successfully opened. Notice the type of the database variable. In the SQLite3 API, this variable is a C language structure of type sqlite3. When this C API is imported into Swift, this variable is mapped to UnsafeMutablePointer<COpaquePointer>, which is how Swift expresses the C pointer type void *. This means that we have to treat it as an opaque pointer. That's OK, because we won't need to access the internals of this structure from our Swift code—we just need to pass the pointer to other SQLite3 functions, like sqlite3_close().

```
sqlite3_close(database)
```

Databases store all their data in tables. You can create a new table by crafting an SQL CREATE statement and passing it in to an open database using the function sqlite3_exec, like so:

```
let createSQL = "CREATE TABLE IF NOT EXISTS PEOPLE" +
                "(ID INTEGER PRIMARY KEY AUTOINCREMENT, FIELD_DATA TEXT)"
var errMsg:UnsafeMutablePointer<Int8> = nil
result = sqlite3_exec(database, createSQL, nil, nil, &errMsg)
```

The function sqlite3_exec is used to run any command against SQLite3 that doesn't return data, including updates, inserts, and deletes. Retrieving data from the database is a little more involved. You first need to prepare the statement by feeding it your SQL SELECT command:

```
let createSQL = "SELECT ID, FIELD_DATA FROM FIELDS ORDER BY ROW"
var statement: OpaquePointer? = nil
result = sqlite3_prepare_v2(database, createSQL, -1, &statement, nil)
```

If result equals SQLITE_OK, your statement was successfully prepared, and you can start stepping through the result set. This code shows another instance where we have to treat an SQLite3 structure as an opaque pointer—in the SQLite3 API, the statement variable would be of type sqlite3_stmt.

Here is an example of stepping through a result set and retrieving an Int and a String from the database:

```
while sqlite3_step(statement) == SQLITE_ROW {
    let row = Int(sqlite3_column_int(statement, 0))
    let rowData = sqlite3_column_text(statement, 1)
    let fieldValue = String.init(cString: UnsafePointer<CChar>(rowData!))
    lineFields[row].text = fieldValue!
}
sqlite3_finalize(statement)
```

Once again, we have to take care to bridge between the requirements of a C language API and what Swift supports. In this case, the sqlite3_column_text() function returns a value of type const unsigned char *, which Swift translates to UnsafePointer<UInt8>. We need to create a String from the returned character data and we can do this by using the method String.init(cString:) (UnsafePointer<CChar>). We have an UnsafePointer<UInt8> instead of an UnsafePointer<CChar>, but fortunately there is an initializer that lets us create the latter from the former. Once we've got the String, we assign it to the UITextField's text property.

Using Bind Variables

Although it's possible to construct SQL strings to insert values, it is common practice to use something called **bind variables** for this purpose. Handling strings correctly—making sure they don't have invalid characters and that quotes are inserted properly—can be quite a chore. With bind variables, those issues are taken care of for us.

To insert a value using a bind variable, you create your SQL statement as normal, but put a question mark (?) into the SQL string. Each question mark represents one variable that must be bound before the statement can be executed. Next, you prepare the SQL statement, bind a value to each of the variables, and execute the command.

Here's an example that prepares an SQL statement with two bind variables, binds an Int to the first variable and a string to the second variable, and then executes and finalizes the statement:

```
var statement:OpaquePointer? = nil
let sql = "INSERT INTO FOO VALUES (?, ?);"
if sqlite3_prepare_v2(database, sql, -1, &statement, nil)
        == SQLITE_OK {
    sqlite3_bind_int(statement, 1, 235)
    sqlite3_bind_text(statement, 2, "Bar", -1, nil)
}
if sqlite3_step(statement) != SQLITE_DONE {
    print("This should be real error checking!")
}
sqlite3_finalize(statement);
```

There are multiple bind statements available, depending on the data type that you wish to use. Most bind functions take only three parameters:

- The first parameter to any bind function, regardless of the data type, is a pointer to the sqlite3_stmt used previously in the sqlite3_prepare_v2() call.

- The second parameter is the index of the variable to which you're binding. This is a one-indexed value, meaning that the first question mark in the SQL statement has index 1, and each one after it is one higher than the one to its left.

- The third parameter is always the value that should be substituted for the question mark.

A few bind functions, such as those for binding text and binary data, have two additional parameters:

- The first additional parameter is the length of the data being passed in the third parameter. In the case of C strings, you can pass -1 instead of the string's length, and the function will use the entire string. In all other cases, you need to tell it the length of the data being passed in.

  The final parameter is an optional function callback in case you need to do any memory cleanup after the statement is executed. Typically, such a function would be used to free memory allocated using malloc().

The syntax that follows the bind statements may seem a little odd since we're doing an insert. When using bind variables, the same syntax is used for both queries and updates. If the SQL string had an SQL query, rather than an update, we would need to call sqlite3_step() multiple times until it returned SQLITE_DONE. Since this is an update, we call it only once.

Creating the SQLite3 Application

In Xcode, create a new project using the Single View Application template and name it SQLite Persistence. This project will start off identical to the previous project, so begin by opening the ViewController.swift file, and add an outlet:

```
class ViewController: UIViewController {
    @IBOutlet var lineFields:[UITextField]!
```

Next, select Main.storyboard. Design the view and connect the outlet collection by following the instructions in the "Designing the Persistence Application View" section earlier in this chapter. Once your design is complete, save the storyboard file.

We've covered the basics, so let's see how this would work in practice. We're going to modify our Persistence application again, this time storing its data using SQLite3. We'll use a single table and store the field values in four different rows of that table. We'll also give each row a row number that corresponds to its field. For example, the value from the first line will get stored in the table with a row number of 0, the next line will be row number 1, and so on. Let's get started.

Linking to the SQLite3 Library

SQLite 3 is accessed through a procedural API that provides interfaces to a number of C function calls. To use this API, we'll need to link our application to a dynamic library called libsqlite3.dylib. Select the SQLite Persistence item at the very top of the Project Navigator list (leftmost pane), and then select SQLite Persistence from the TARGETS section in the main area (see Figure 13-7, middle pane). (Be careful that you have selected SQLite Persistence from the TARGETS section, not from the PROJECT section.)

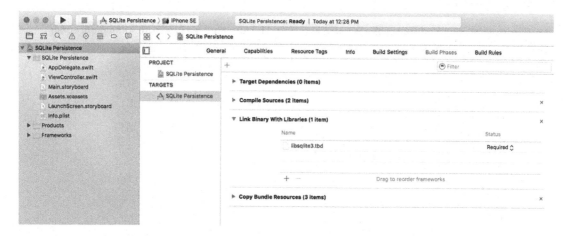

Figure 13-7. *Selecting the SQLite Persistence project in the Project Navigator; selecting the SQLite Persistence target; and finally, selecting the Build Phases tab*

With the SQLite Persistence target selected, click the Build Phases tab in the rightmost pane. You'll see a list of items, initially all collapsed, which represent the various steps Xcode goes through to build the application. Expand the item labeled Link Binary With Libraries. This section contains the libraries and frameworks that Xcode links with your application. By default, it's empty because the compiler automatically links with any iOS frameworks that your application uses, but the compiler doesn't know anything about the SQLite3 library, so we need to add it here.

Click the + button at the bottom of the linked frameworks list, and you'll be presented with a sheet that lists all available frameworks and libraries. Find libsqlite3.tbd in the list (or use the handy search field) and click the Add button. Note that there may be several other entries in that directory that start with libsqlite3. Be sure you select libsqlite3.tbd. It is an alias that always points to the latest version of the SQLite3 library.

Modifying the Persistence View Controller

Next, we need to import the header files for SQLite3 into the view controller so that the compiler can see the function and other definitions that make up the API. There is no way to directly import the header file into Swift code, because the SQLite3 library is not packaged as a framework. The easiest way to deal with this is to add a **bridging header** to the project. Once you have a bridging header, you can add other header files to it, and those header files will be read by the Swift compiler. There are a couple of ways to add a bridging file. We'll use the simpler of the two, which is to temporarily add an Objective-C class to the project. Let's do that now.

Press ⌘N or select File ➤ New ➤ File…. In the iOS Source section of the dialog, choose Cocoa Touch Class and press Next. Name the class Temporary, make it a subclass of NSObject, change the language to Objective-C, and press Next. In the next screen, press the Create button. When you do this, Xcode will pop up a window asking whether you want to create a bridging header. Click Create Bridging Header. Now, in the Project Navigator, you'll see the files for the new class (Temporary.m and Temporary.h) and the bridging header, which is called SQLite Persistence-Bridging-Header.h. Delete the Temporary.m and Temporary.h files—you don't need them anymore. Select the bridging header to open it in the editor, and then add the following line to it:

```
#import <sqlite3.h>
```

Now that the compiler can see the SQLite3 library and header files, we can write some more code. Select ViewController.swift and make the changes shown in Listing 13-10.

Listing 13-10. Using SQLite3 to Save and Retrieve Our Information

```
override func viewDidLoad() {
    super.viewDidLoad()
    // Do any additional setup after loading the view, typically from a nib.
    var database:OpaquePointer? = nil
    var result = sqlite3_open(dataFilePath(), &database)
    if result != SQLITE_OK {
        sqlite3_close(database)
        print("Failed to open database")
        return
    }
    let createSQL = "CREATE TABLE IF NOT EXISTS FIELDS " +
                        "(ROW INTEGER PRIMARY KEY, FIELD_DATA TEXT);"
    var errMsg:UnsafeMutablePointer<Int8>? = nil
    result = sqlite3_exec(database, createSQL, nil, nil, &errMsg)
    if (result != SQLITE_OK) {
        sqlite3_close(database)
        print("Failed to create table")
        return
    }

    let query = "SELECT ROW, FIELD_DATA FROM FIELDS ORDER BY ROW"
    var statement:OpaquePointer? = nil
    if sqlite3_prepare_v2(database, query, -1, &statement, nil) == SQLITE_OK {
        while sqlite3_step(statement) == SQLITE_ROW {
            let row = Int(sqlite3_column_int(statement, 0))
            let rowData = sqlite3_column_text(statement, 1)
            let fieldValue = String.init(cString: UnsafePointer<CChar>(rowData!))
            lineFields[row].text = fieldValue
```

```swift
        }
        sqlite3_finalize(statement)
    }
    sqlite3_close(database)

    let app = UIApplication.shared()
    NotificationCenter.default.addObserver(self, selector: #selector(self.applicationWill
    ResignActive(notification:)), name: Notification.Name.UIApplicationWillResignActive,
    object: app)

}

func dataFilePath() -> String {
    let urls = FileManager.default.urls(for:
        .documentDirectory, in: .userDomainMask)
    var url:String?
    url = ""       // create a blank path
    do {
        try url = urls.first?.appendingPathComponent("data.plist").path!
    } catch  {
        print("Error is \(error)")
    }
    return url!
}

func applicationWillResignActive(notification:NSNotification) {
    var database:OpaquePointer? = nil
    let result = sqlite3_open(dataFilePath(), &database)
    if result != SQLITE_OK {
        sqlite3_close(database)
        print("Failed to open database")
        return
    }
    for i in 0..<lineFields.count  {
        let field = lineFields[i]
        let update = "INSERT OR REPLACE INTO FIELDS (ROW, FIELD_DATA) " +
        "VALUES (?, ?);"
        var statement:OpaquePointer? = nil
        if sqlite3_prepare_v2(database, update, -1, &statement, nil) == SQLITE_OK {
            let text = field.text
            sqlite3_bind_int(statement, 1, Int32(i))
            sqlite3_bind_text(statement, 2, text!, -1, nil)
        }
        if sqlite3_step(statement) != SQLITE_DONE {
            print("Error updating table")
            sqlite3_close(database)
            return
        }
        sqlite3_finalize(statement)
    }
    sqlite3_close(database)
}
```

The first piece of new code is in the viewDidLoad() method. We begin by getting the path to the database file using the dataFilePath() method that we added. This is just like the dataFileURL() method that we added to our earlier examples, except that it returns the file's path not its URL. That's because the SQLite3 APIs that work with files require paths, not URLs. Next, we use the path to open the database, creating it if it does not exist. If we hit a problem with opening the database, we close it, print an error message, and return:

```
var database:OpaquePointer? = nil
var result = sqlite3_open(dataFilePath(), &database)
if result != SQLITE_OK {
    sqlite3_close(database)
    print("Failed to open database")
    return
}
```

Next, we need to make sure that we have a table to hold our data. We use an SQL CREATE TABLE statement to do that. By specifying IF NOT EXISTS, we prevent the database from overwriting existing data—if there is already a table with the same name, this command quietly completes without doing anything. That means it's safe to use it every time our application launches without explicitly checking to see if a table exists:

```
let createSQL = "CREATE TABLE IF NOT EXISTS FIELDS " +
                    "(ROW INTEGER PRIMARY KEY, FIELD_DATA TEXT);"
var errMsg:UnsafeMutablePointer<Int8>? = nil
result = sqlite3_exec(database, createSQL, nil, nil, &errMsg)
if (result != SQLITE_OK) {
    sqlite3_close(database)
    print("Failed to create table")
    return
}
```

Each row in the database table contains an integer and a string. The integer is the number of the row in the GUI from which the data was obtained (starting from zero), and the string is the content of the text field on that row. Finally, we need to load our data. We do this using an SQL SELECT statement. In this simple example, we create an SQL SELECT statement that requests all the rows from the database and then we ask SQLite3 to prepare our SELECT. We also tell SQLite3 to order the rows by the row number, so that we always get them back in the same order. Absent this, SQLite3 will return the rows in the order in which they are stored internally.

```
let query = "SELECT ROW, FIELD_DATA FROM FIELDS ORDER BY ROW"
var statement:OpaquePointer? = nil
if sqlite3_prepare_v2(database, query, -1, &statement, nil) == SQLITE_OK {
```

Next, we use the sqlite3_step() function to execute the SELECT statement and step through each of the returned rows:

```
while sqlite3_step(statement) == SQLITE_ROW {
```

Now we grab the row number, store it in an int, and then grab the field data as a C string, which we then convert to a Swift String, as described earlier in the chapter:

```
let row = Int(sqlite3_column_int(statement, 0))
let rowData = sqlite3_column_text(statement, 1)
let fieldValue = String.init(cString: UnsafePointer<CChar>(rowData!))
```

Next, we set the appropriate field with the value retrieved from the database:

```
lineFields[row].text = fieldValue
```

Finally, we close the database connection, and we're finished:

```
    }
    sqlite3_finalize(statement)
}
sqlite3_close(database)
```

Note that we close the database connection as soon as we're finished creating the table and loading any data it contains, rather than keeping it open the entire time the application is running. It's the simplest way of managing the connection; and in this little app, we can just open the connection those few times we need it. In a more database-intensive app, you might want to keep the connection open all the time.

The other changes we made are in the applicationWillResignActive() method, where we need to save our application data.

The applicationWillResignActive() method starts by once again opening the database. To save the data, we loop through all four fields and issue a separate command to update each row of the database:

```
for i in 0..<lineFields.count  {
    let field = lineFields[i]
```

We craft an INSERT OR REPLACE SQL statement with two bind variables. The first represents the row that's being stored; the second is for the actual string value to be stored. By using INSERT OR REPLACE instead of the more standard INSERT, we don't need to worry about whether a row already exists:

```
let update = "INSERT OR REPLACE INTO FIELDS (ROW, FIELD_DATA) " +
             "VALUES (?, ?);"
```

Next, we declare a pointer to a statement, prepare our statement with the bind variables, and bind values to both of the bind variables:

```
var statement:OpaquePointer? = nil
if sqlite3_prepare_v2(database, update, -1, &statement, nil) == SQLITE_OK {
    let text = field.text
    sqlite3_bind_int(statement, 1, Int32(i))
    sqlite3_bind_text(statement, 2, text!, -1, nil)
}
```

Now we call sqlite3_step to execute the update, check to make sure it worked, and finalize the statement, ending the loop:

```
if sqlite3_step(statement) != SQLITE_DONE {
    print("Error updating table")
    sqlite3_close(database)
    return
}
sqlite3_finalize(statement)
```

Notice that we simply print an error message here if anything goes wrong. In a real application, if an error condition is one that a user might reasonably experience, you should use some other form of error reporting, such as popping up an alert box.

```
sqlite3_close(database)
```

■ **Note**   There is one condition that could cause an error to occur in the preceding SQLite code that is not a programmer error. If the device's storage is completely full—to the extent that SQLite can't save its changes to the database—then an error will occur here, as well. However, this condition is fairly rare and will probably result in deeper problems for the user, outside the scope of our app's data. Our app probably wouldn't even launch successfully if the system were in that state. So we're going to just sidestep the issue entirely.

Build and run the app. Enter some data and then press the iPhone simulator's Home button. Quit the simulator (to force the app to actually quit), and then relaunch the SQLite Persistence application. That data should be right where you left it. As far as the user is concerned, there's absolutely no difference between the various versions of this application; however, each version uses a different persistence mechanism.

Using Core Data

The final technique demonstrated in this chapter shows how to implement persistence using Apple's Core Data framework. Core Data is a robust, full-featured persistence tool. Here, I will show you how to use Core Data to re-create the same persistence you've seen in our Persistence application so far.

■ **Note**   For more comprehensive coverage of Core Data, check out *Pro iOS Persistence: Using Core Data* by Michael Privet and Robert Warner (Apress, 2014).

In Xcode, create a new project. Select the Single View Application template from the iOS section and click Next. Name the product **Core Data Persistence**, make sure that Swift is selected as the language and choose Universal in the Devices control but don't click the Next button just yet. If you look just below the Devices control, you'll see a check box labeled Use Core Data. There's a certain amount of complexity involved in adding Core Data to an existing project, so Apple has kindly provided an application project template to do much of the work for you. Check the Use Core Data check box (see Figure 13-8), and then click the Next button. When prompted, choose a directory to store your project and then click Create.

Choose options for your new project:

Product Name:	Core Data Persistence
Team:	Molly Maskrey
Organization Name:	MollyMaskrey
Organization Identifier:	com.mollymaskrey
Bundle Identifier:	com.mollymaskrey.Core-Data-Persistence
Language:	Swift
Devices:	Universal

☑ Use Core Data
☐ Include Unit Tests
☐ Include UI Tests

Cancel   Previous   Next

Figure 13-8. *Select Single View Application and the option to use Core Data for persistence*

Before we move on to our code, let's take a look at the project window, which contains some new items. Expand the Core Data Persistence folder if it's closed (see Figure 13-9).

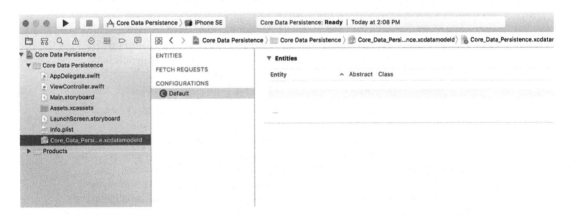

Figure 13-9. *Our project template with the files needed for Core Data. The Core Data model is selected, and the data model editor is shown in the editing pane*

Entities and Managed Objects

Most of what you see in the Project Navigator should be familiar: the application delegate, the view controller, two storyboards and the assets catalog. In addition, you'll find a file called Core_Data_Persistence.xcdatamodeld, which contains our data model. Within Xcode, Core Data lets us design our data models visually, without writing code, and stores that data model in the .xcdatamodeld file.

Single-click the .xcdatamodeld file now, and you will be presented with the **data model editor** (see the right side of Figure 13-9). The data model editor gives you two distinct views into your data model, depending on the setting of the Editor Style control in the lower-right corner of the project window. In Table mode, the mode shown in Figure 13-9, the elements that make up your data model will be shown in a series of editable tables. In Graph mode, you'll see a graphical depiction of the same elements. At the moment, both views reflect the same empty data model.

Before Core Data, the traditional way to create data models was to create subclasses of NSObject and conform them to NSCoding and NSCopying so that they could be archived, as we did earlier in this chapter. Core Data uses a fundamentally different approach. Instead of classes, you begin by creating **entities** here in the data model editor and then, in your code, you create **managed objects** from those entities.

■ **Note** The terms **entity** and **managed object** can be a little confusing, since both refer to data model objects. Entity refers to the description of an object. Managed object refers to actual concrete instances of that entity created at runtime. So, in the data model editor, you create entities; but in your code, you create and retrieve managed objects. The distinction between entities and managed objects is similar to the distinction between a class and instances of that class.

An entity is made up of properties. There are three types of properties:

- **Attributes**: An attribute serves the same function in a Core Data entity as a property does in a Swift class. They both hold the data.

- **Relationships**: As the name implies, a relationship defines the relationship between entities. For example, to create a Person entity, you might start by defining a few attributes such as hairColor, eyeColor, height, and weight. You might also define address attributes, such as state and zipCode, or you might embed them in a separate HomeAddress entity. Using the latter approach, you would then create a relationship between a Person and a HomeAddress. Relationships can be **to-one** and **to-many**. The relationship from Person to HomeAddress is probably to-one, since most people have only a single home address. The relationship from HomeAddress to Person might be to-many, since there may be more than one Person living at that HomeAddress.

- **Fetched properties**: A fetched property is an alternative to a relationship. Fetched properties allow you to create a query that is evaluated at fetch time to see which objects belong to the relationship. To extend our earlier example, a Person object could have a fetched property called Neighbors that finds all HomeAddress objects in the data store that have the same ZIP code as the Person's own HomeAddress. Due to the nature of how fetched properties are constructed and used, they are always one-way relationships. Fetched properties are also the only kind of relationship that lets you traverse multiple data stores.

Typically, attributes, relationships, and fetched properties are defined using Xcode's data model editor. In our Core Data Persistence application, we'll build a simple entity, so you can get a sense of how this all works together.

Key-Value Coding

In your code, instead of using accessors and mutators, you will use key-value coding to set properties or retrieve their existing values. Key-value coding may sound intimidating, but you've already used it quite a bit in this book. Every time we used Dictionary, for example, we were using a form of key-value coding because every object in a dictionary is stored under a unique key value. The key-value coding used by Core Data is a bit more complex than that used by `Dictionary`, but the basic concept is the same. When working with a managed object, the key you will use to set or retrieve a property's value is the name of the attribute you wish to set. So, here's how to retrieve the value stored in the attribute called name from a managed object:

```
let name = myManagedObject.valueForKey("name")
```

Similarly, to set a new value for a managed object's property, do this:

```
myManagedObject.setValue("Gregor Overlander", forKey:"name")
```

Putting It All in Context

So where do these managed objects live? They live in something called a **persistent store**, also referred to as a **backing store**. Persistent stores can take several different forms. By default, a Core Data application implements a backing store as an SQLite database stored in the application's Documents directory. Even though your data is stored via SQLite, classes in the Core Data framework do all the work associated with loading and saving your data. If you use Core Data, you don't need to write any SQL statements like the ones you saw in the SQLite Persistence application. You just work with objects, and Core Data figures out what it needs to do behind the scenes.

SQLite isn't the only option Core Data has for storage. Backing stores can also be implemented as binary flat files or even stored in an XML format. Another option is to create an in-memory store, which you might use if you're writing a caching mechanism; however, it doesn't save data beyond the end of the current session. In almost all situations, you should just leave it as the default and use SQLite as your persistent store.

Although most applications will have only one persistent store, it is possible to have multiple persistent stores within the same application. If you're curious about how the backing store is created and configured, take a look at the file AppDelegate.swift in your Xcode project. The Xcode project template we chose provided us with all the code needed to set up a single persistent store for our application.

Other than creating it, you generally won't work with your persistent store directly. Rather, you will use something called a **managed object context**, often referred to as just a **context**. The context manages access to the persistent store and maintains information about which properties have changed since the last time an object was saved. The context also registers all changes with the **undo manager**, which means that you always have the ability to undo a single change or roll back all the way to the last time data was saved.

■ **Note**   You can have multiple contexts pointing to the same persistent store, though most iOS applications will use only one.

Many Core Data method calls require an `NSManagedObjectContext` as a parameter or must be executed against a context. With the exception of more complicated, multithreaded iOS applications, you can just use the `managedObjectContext` property provided by your application delegate, which is a default context that is created for you automatically, also courtesy of the Xcode project template.

You may notice that in addition to a managed object context and a persistent store coordinator, the provided application delegate also contains an instance of `NSManagedObjectModel`. This class is responsible for loading and representing, at runtime, the data model you will create using the data model editor in Xcode. You generally won't need to interact directly with this class. It's used behind the scenes by the other Core Data classes, so they can identify which entities and properties you've defined in your data model. As long as you create your data model using the provided file, there's no need to worry about this class at all.

Creating New Managed Objects

Creating a new instance of a managed object is pretty easy, though not quite as straightforward as creating a normal object instance. Instead, you use the insertNewObject(forEntityName: into:) factory method in a class called NSEntityDescription. NSEntityDescription's job is to keep track of all the entities defined in the app's data model and to let you create instances of those entities. This method creates and returns an instance representing a single entity in memory. It returns either an instance of NSManagedObject that is set up with the correct properties for that particular entity; or, if you've configured your entity to be implemented with a specific subclass of NSManagedObject, an instance of that class. Remember that entities are like classes. An entity is a description of an object and defines which properties a particular entity has.

To create a new object, do this:

```
let thing = NSEntityDescription.insertNewObject (forEntityName: "Thing",
                                  into:managedObjectContext)
```

The method is called insertNewObject(forEntityName: into:) because, in addition to creating the object, it inserts the newly created object into the context and then returns that object. After this call, the object exists in the context, but is not yet part of the persistent store. The object will be added to the persistent store the next time the managed object context's save() method is called.

Retrieving Managed Objects

To retrieve managed objects from the persistent store, you'll use a **fetch request**, which is Core Data's way of handling a predefined query. For example, you might say, "Give me every Person whose eyeColor is blue." To create a fetch request, you provide it with an NSEntityDescription that specifies the entity of the object or objects you wish to retrieve. Here is an example that creates a fetch request:

```
let context = appDelegate.managedObjectContext
let request: NSFetchRequest<NSFetchRequestResult> = NSFetchRequest(entityName:"Thing")
```

You **execute** the fetch request using an instance method on NSManagedObjectContext:

```
do {
    let objects = try context.fetch(request)
    // No error - use "objects"
} catch {
    // Error - the "error" variable contains an NSError object
  print(error)
}
```

fetch() will load the specified objects from the persistent store and return them in an optional array. If an error is encountered, fetch() throws an NSError object that describes the specific problem. You need to either catch this error and handle it if at all possible, or let it propagate to the caller of the function that contains this code. Here, we just write the error to the console. If you are not familiar with Swift's error handling mechanisms, refer to the section "Error Handling" in the Appendix. If no error occurs, you will get a valid array, though it may not have any objects in it since it is possible that none meets the specified criteria. From this point on, any changes you make to the managed objects returned in that array will be tracked by the managed object context you executed the request against, and saved when you send that context a save: message.

The Core Data Application

Before getting into the code, we'll create our data model.

Designing the Data Model

Select Core_Data_Persistence.xcdatamodel to open Xcode's data model editor. The data model editing pane shows all the entities, fetch requests, and configurations that are contained within your data model.

■ **Note** The Core Data concept of **configurations** lets you define one or more named subsets of the entities contained in your data model, which can be useful in certain situations. For example, if you want to create a suite of apps that shares the same data model, but some apps shouldn't have access to everything (perhaps there's one app for normal users and another for administrators), this approach lets you do that. You can also use multiple configurations within a single app as it switches between different modes of operation. In this book, we're not going to deal with configurations at all; but since the list of configurations (including the single default configuration that contains everything in your model) is right there, staring you in the face beneath the entities and fetch requests, we thought it was worth a mention here.

As shown in Figure 13-9, those lists are empty now because we haven't created anything yet. Remedy that by clicking the plus icon labeled Add Entity in the lower-left corner of the editor pane. This will create a brand-new entity with the name Entity, as shown in Figure 13-10.

Figure 13-10. *The data model editor, showing our newly added entity*

As you build your data model, you'll probably find yourself switching between Table view and Graph view using the Editor Style control at the bottom right of the editing area. Switch to Graph view now. Graph view presents a little box representing our entity, which itself contains sections for showing the entity's attributes and relationships, also currently empty (see Figure 13-11). Graph view is really useful if your model contains multiple entities, because it shows a graphic representation of all the relationships between your entities.

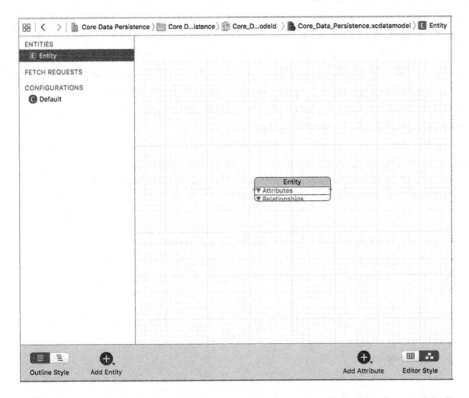

Figure 13-11. *Using the control in the lower-right corner, we switched the data model editor into Graph mode. Note that Graph mode shows the same entities as Table mode, just in a graphic form. This is useful if you have multiple entities with relationships between them*

■ **Note**   If you prefer working graphically, you can actually build your entire model in Graph view. We're going to stick with Table view in this chapter because it's easier to explain. When you're creating your own data models, feel free to work in Graph view if that approach suits you better.

Whether you're using Table view or Graph view for designing your data model, you'll almost always want to bring up the Core Data data model inspector. This inspector lets you view and edit relevant details for whatever item is selected in the data model editor—whether it's an entity, attribute, relationship, or anything else. You can browse an existing model without the data model inspector; but to really work on a model, you'll invariably need to use this inspector, much as you frequently use the Attributes Inspector when editing nib files.

Press ⌥⌘3 to open the data model inspector. At the moment, the inspector shows information about the entity we just added. The single entity in our model contains the data from one line on the GUI, so we'll call it Line. Change the Name field from Entity to Line, as shown in Figure 13-12.

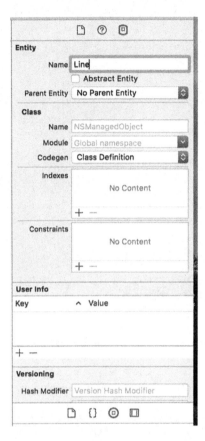

Figure 13-12. Using the data model inspector to change our entity's name to Line

If you're currently in Graph view, use the Editor Style control to switch back to Table view. Table view shows more details for each piece of the entity we're working on, so it's usually more useful than Graph view when creating a new entity. In Table view, most of the data model editor is taken up by the table showing the entity's attributes, relationships, and fetched properties. This is where we'll set up our entity.

Notice that at the lower right of the editing area, next to the Editor Style control, there's an icon containing a plus sign, labeled Add Attribute. If you select your entity and then hold down the mouse button over this control, a pop-up menu will appear, allowing you to add an attribute, relationship, or fetched property to your entity (see Figure 13-13). Alternatively, if you just want to add an attribute, you can simply click the plus icon.

Figure 13-13. *With an entity selected, press and hold the right plus-sign icon to add an attribute, relationship, or fetched property to your entity*

Go ahead and use this technique to add an attribute to your Line entity. A new attribute, creatively named attribute, is added to the Attributes section of the table and selected. In the table, you'll see that not only is the row selected, but the attribute's name is selected as well. This means that immediately after clicking the plus sign, you can start typing the name of the new attribute without further clicking. Change the new attribute's name from attribute to lineNumber, and click the pop-up next to the name to change its Type from Undefined to Integer 16. Doing so turns this attribute into one that will hold an integer value. We will be using this attribute to identify which of the managed object's four fields holds data. Since we have only four options, we selected the smallest integer type available.

Now direct your attention to the data model inspector, which is in the pane to the right of the editor area. Here, additional details can be configured. The inspector should be showing properties for the attribute you just added. If it's still showing details of the Line entity, click the attribute row in the editor to select it and the inspector should switch its focus to the attribute. The check box below the Name field on the right, Optional, is selected by default. Click it to deselect it. We don't want this attribute to be optional—a line that doesn't correspond to a label on our interface is useless.

Selecting the Transient check box creates a transient attribute. This attribute is used to specify a value that is held by managed objects while the app is running, but is never saved to the data store. We do want the line number saved to the data store, so leave the Transient check box unchecked. Selecting the Indexed check box will cause an index in the underlying SQL database to be created on the column that holds this attribute's data. Leave the Indexed check box unchecked. The amount of data is small and we won't provide the user with a search capability; therefore, there's no need for an index.

Beneath that are more settings that allow us to do some simple data validation by specifying minimum and maximum values for the integer, a default value, and more. We won't be using any of these settings in this example.

Now make sure the Line entity is selected and click the Add Attribute control to add a second attribute. Change the name of your new attribute to lineText and change its Type to String. This attribute will hold the actual data from the text field. Leave the Optional check box checked for this one; it is altogether possible that the user won't enter a value for a given field.

■ **Note**   When you change the Type to String, you'll notice that the inspector shows a slightly different set of options for setting a default value or limiting the length of the string. Although we won't be using any of those options for this application, it's nice to know they're there.

Our data model is complete. That's all there is to it. Core Data lets you point and click your way to an application data model. Let's finish building the application so you can see how to use our data model from our code.

Modifying the AppDelegate.swift File

Locate the following line in the AppDelegate.swift file:

```
// MARK: - Core Data stack
```

Below this line you should see two sections of code. The first creates an NSPersistentContainer, a new feature that essentially provides a wrapper around a lot of the Core Data structure. We won't be using that in this example so delete that section of code.

■ **Note**   The new container feature is a good thing that will eventually make life easier as you develop Core Data applications, however, at the time of writing, I found it to not be consistently stable and as such will follow the methods of creating our project as was done in the previous version of this book. The approach we'll be using works just fine.

Also delete the template saveContext method and replace it with that shown in Listing 13-11. This is where all our "stuff" gets saved. We'll call it from our View Controller when we are ready to resign active status of our app.

Listing 13-11.   Our saveContext Method in the AppDelegate.swift File

```swift
func saveContext () {
    if managedObjectContext.hasChanges {
        do {
            try managedObjectContext.save()
        } catch {
            // Replace this implementation with code to handle the error appropriately.
            // abort() causes the application to generate a crash log and terminate. You
            should not use this function in a shipping application, although it may be
            useful during development.
```

```
            let nserror = error as NSError
            NSLog("Unresolved error \(nserror), \(nserror.userInfo)")
            abort()
        }
    }
}
```

Next, add the following methods in Listing 13-12 to the AppDelegate.swift file below the following line:

```
// MARK: - Core Data stack
```

Listing 13-12. Our Core Data Stack

```
// MARK: - Core Data stack

lazy var applicationDocumentsDirectory: URL = {
    // The directory the application uses to store the Core Data store file. This code uses
    a directory in the application's documents Application Support directory.
    let urls = FileManager.default.urls(for: .documentDirectory, in: .userDomainMask)
    return urls[urls.count-1]
}()

lazy var managedObjectModel: NSManagedObjectModel = {
    // The managed object model for the application. This property is not optional. It is a
    fatal error for the application not to be able to find and load its model.
    let modelURL = Bundle.main.url(forResource: "Core_Data_Persistence", withExtension: "momd")!
    return NSManagedObjectModel(contentsOf: modelURL)!
}()

lazy var persistentStoreCoordinator: NSPersistentStoreCoordinator = {
    // The persistent store coordinator for the application. This implementation creates and
    returns a coordinator, having added the store for the application to it. This property
    is optional since there are legitimate error conditions that could cause the creation of
    the store to fail.
    // Create the coordinator and store
    let coordinator = NSPersistentStoreCoordinator(managedObjectModel: self.
    managedObjectModel)
    let url = try! self.applicationDocumentsDirectory.appendingPathComponent("SingleViewCore
    Data.sqlite")
    var failureReason = "There was an error creating or loading the application's saved data."
    do {
        try coordinator.addPersistentStore(ofType: NSSQLiteStoreType, configurationName:
        nil, at: url, options: nil)
    } catch {
        // Report any error we got.
        var dict = [String: AnyObject]()
        dict[NSLocalizedDescriptionKey] = "Failed to initialize the application's saved data"
        dict[NSLocalizedFailureReasonErrorKey] = failureReason
```

```
        dict[NSUnderlyingErrorKey] = error as NSError
        let wrappedError = NSError(domain: "YOUR_ERROR_DOMAIN", code: 9999, userInfo: dict)
        // Replace this with code to handle the error appropriately.
        // abort() causes the application to generate a crash log and terminate. You should
        not use this function in a shipping application, although it may be useful during
        development.
        NSLog("Unresolved error \(wrappedError), \(wrappedError.userInfo)")
        abort()
    }

    return coordinator
}()

lazy var managedObjectContext: NSManagedObjectContext = {
    // Returns the managed object context for the application (which is already bound
    to the persistent store coordinator for the application.) This property is optional
    since there are legitimate error conditions that could cause the creation of the
    context to fail.
    let coordinator = self.persistentStoreCoordinator
    var managedObjectContext = NSManagedObjectContext(concurrencyType:
    .mainQueueConcurrencyType)
    managedObjectContext.persistentStoreCoordinator = coordinator
    return managedObjectContext
}()
```

■ **Note** In previous versions of Xcode, the Single View template generated much of this code. Whether a change or a bug, we found that most of this was not generated for a Single View in the beta release of Xcode. However, if you were to select Master-Detail to create a project, you will find that much more of this is provided by Xcode.

The following line defines the path to the Core Data store file:

```
lazy var applicationDocumentsDirectory: URL = {
```

This variable represents our managed object model:

```
lazy var managedObjectModel: NSManagedObjectModel = {
    // The managed object model for the application.
    // This property is not optional. It is a fatal error for
    //the application not to be able to find and load its model.
    let modelURL = Bundle.main.url(forResource: "Core_Data_Persistence", withExtension: "momd")!
    return NSManagedObjectModel(contentsOf: modelURL)!
}()
```

Similarly, the following section of code provides the reference to our persistent store coordinator:

```
lazy var persistentStoreCoordinator: NSPersistentStoreCoordinator = {
    // The persistent store coordinator for the application. This implementation creates
    and returns a coordinator, having added the store for the application to it. This
    property is optional since there are legitimate error conditions that could cause
    the creation of the store to fail.
    // Create the coordinator and store
    let coordinator = NSPersistentStoreCoordinator(managedObjectModel: self.managedObjectModel)
    let url = try! self.applicationDocumentsDirectory.appendingPathComponent("SingleVie
wCoreData.sqlite")
    var failureReason = "There was an error creating or loading the application's saved data."
    do {
        try coordinator.addPersistentStore(ofType: NSSQLiteStoreType, configurationName:
        nil, at: url, options: nil)
    } catch {
        // Report any error we got.
        var dict = [String: AnyObject]()
        dict[NSLocalizedDescriptionKey] = "Failed to initialize the application's saved data"
        dict[NSLocalizedFailureReasonErrorKey] = failureReason

        dict[NSUnderlyingErrorKey] = error as NSError
        let wrappedError = NSError(domain: "YOUR_ERROR_DOMAIN", code: 9999, userInfo: dict)
        // Replace this with code to handle the error appropriately.
        // abort() causes the application to generate a crash log and terminate. You
        should not use this function in a shipping application, although it may be
        useful during development.
        NSLog("Unresolved error \(wrappedError), \(wrappedError.userInfo)")
        abort()
    }

    return coordinator
}()
```

Finally, the last remaining piece is our managed object context shown here:

```
lazy var managedObjectContext: NSManagedObjectContext = {
    // Returns the managed object context for the application (which is already bound
    to the persistent store coordinator for the application.) This property is optional
    since there are legitimate error conditions that could cause the creation of the
    context to fail.
    let coordinator = self.persistentStoreCoordinator
    var managedObjectContext = NSManagedObjectContext(concurrencyType: .mainQueueConcurrencyType)
    managedObjectContext.persistentStoreCoordinator = coordinator
    return managedObjectContext
}()
```

That's really all we need for our application delegate. We create the various bits and pieces needed so the rest of our app can have access to the Core Data capabilities.

Creating the Persistence View

Select ViewController.swift and make the following change shown in bold:

```
class ViewController: UIViewController {
    @IBOutlet var lineFields:[UITextField]!
```

Save this file. Next, select Main.storyboard to edit the GUI in Interface Builder. Design the view and connect the outlet collection by following the instructions in the "Designing the Persistence Application View" section earlier in this chapter. You might also find it useful to refer back to Figure 13-6. Once your design is complete, save the storyboard file.

Now go back to ViewController.swift, and make the changes in Listing 13-13.

Listing 13-13. Modifying Our ViewController.swift file to Use Core Data

```
import UIKit
import CoreData

class ViewController: UIViewController {
    private static let lineEntityName = "Line"
    private static let lineNumberKey = "lineNumber"
    private static let lineTextKey = "lineText"
    @IBOutlet var lineFields:[UITextField]!

    override func viewDidLoad() {
        super.viewDidLoad()
        // Do any additional setup after loading the view, typically from a nib.

        let appDelegate =
                    UIApplication.shared().delegate as! AppDelegate
        let context = appDelegate.managedObjectContext
        let request: NSFetchRequest<NSFetchRequestResult> = NSFetchRequest(entityName:
        ViewController.lineEntityName)

        do {
            let objects = try context.fetch(request)
            for object in objects {
                let lineNum: Int = object.value(forKey: ViewController.lineNumberKey)! as! Int
                let lineText = object.value(forKey: ViewController.lineTextKey) as? String ?? ""
                let textField = lineFields[lineNum]
                textField.text = lineText
            }

            let app = UIApplication.shared()
            NotificationCenter.default.addObserver(self,
                        selector: #selector(UIApplicationDelegate.
                        applicationWillResignActive(_:)),
                        name: NSNotification.Name.UIApplicationWillResignActive,
                        object: app)
```

```
    } catch {
        // Error thrown from executeFetchRequest()
        print("There was an error in executeFetchRequest(): \(error)")
    }
}


func applicationWillResignActive(_ notification:Notification) {
    let appDelegate =
        UIApplication.shared().delegate as! AppDelegate
    let context = appDelegate.managedObjectContext
    for i in 0 ..< lineFields.count {
        let textField = lineFields[i]

        let request: NSFetchRequest<NSFetchRequestResult> = NSFetchRequest(entityName:
        ViewController.lineEntityName)
        let pred = Predicate(format: "%K = %d", ViewController.lineNumberKey, i)
        request.predicate = pred

        do {
            let objects = try context.fetch(request)
            var theLine:NSManagedObject! = objects.first as? NSManagedObject
            if theLine == nil {
                // No existing data for this row - insert a new managed object for it
                theLine =
                    NSEntityDescription.insertNewObject(
                            forEntityName: ViewController.lineEntityName,
                            into: context)
                            as NSManagedObject
            }

            theLine.setValue(i, forKey: ViewController.lineNumberKey)
            theLine.setValue(textField.text, forKey: ViewController.lineTextKey)
        } catch {
            print("There was an error in executeFetchRequest(): \(error)")
        }
    }
    appDelegate.saveContext()
}
}
```

So that we can use Core Data, we imported the Core Data framework. Next, we modified the viewDidLoad()
method, which needs to check whether there is any existing data in the persistent store. If there is, it
should load the data and populate the text fields with it. The first thing we do in that method is get a
reference to our application delegate, which we then use to get the managed object context (of type
NSManagedObjectContext) that was created for us:

```
    let appDelegate =
                UIApplication.shared().delegate as! AppDelegate
    let context = appDelegate.managedObjectContext
```

The next order of business is to create a fetch request and pass it the entity name, so it knows which type of objects to retrieve:

```
let request: NSFetchRequest<NSFetchRequestResult> =
NSFetchRequest(entityName: ViewController.lineEntityName)
```

Since we want to retrieve all Line objects in the persistent store, we do not create a predicate. By executing a request without a predicate, we're telling the context to give us every Line object in the store. Having created the fetch request, we use the fetch() method of the managed object context to execute it. Since fetch() can throw an error, we place the call and the code that uses its results in a do-catch block, so that we can log the error, if there is one:

```
do {
    let objects = try context.fetch(request)
```

Next, we loop through the array of retrieved managed objects, pull the lineNum and lineText values from each managed object, and use that information to update one of the text fields on our user interface:

```
for object in objects {
    let lineNum: Int = object.value(forKey: ViewController.lineNumberKey)! as! Int
    let lineText = object.value(forKey: ViewController.lineTextKey) as? String ?? ""
    let textField = lineFields[lineNum]
    textField.text = lineText
}
```

Of course, the first time we execute this code, we won't have saved anything in the data store, so the objects list will be empty.

Next, just as with all the other applications in this chapter, we register to be notified when the application is about to move out of the active state (either by being shuffled to the background or exited completely), so we can save any changes the user has made to the data:

```
let app = UIApplication.shared()
NotificationCenter.default.addObserver(self,
        selector: #selector(UIApplicationDelegate.applicationWillResignActive(_:)),
        name: NSNotification.Name.UIApplicationWillResignActive,
        object: app)
```

Finally, the catch clause prints any error that is thrown from the fetch() method:

```
} catch {
    // Error thrown from executeFetchRequest()
    print("There was an error in executeFetchRequest(): \(error)")
}
```

Now let's look at applicationWillResignActive(). We start out the same way as the previous method: by getting a reference to the application delegate and using that to get a pointer to our application's default managed object context:

```
let appDelegate =
    UIApplication.shared().delegate as! AppDelegate
let context = appDelegate.managedObjectContext
```

After that, we go into a loop that executes once for each text field, and then get a reference to the correct field:

```
for i in 0 ..< lineFields.count {
    let textField = lineFields[i]
```

Next, we create our fetch request for our Line entry. We need to find out if there's already a managed object in the persistent store that corresponds to this field, so we create a predicate that identifies the correct object for the field by using the index of the text field as the record key:

```
let request: NSFetchRequest<NSFetchRequestResult> =
let pred = Predicate(format: "%K = %d", ViewController.lineNumberKey, i)
request.predicate = pred
```

Now we execute the fetch request against the context. As before, we wrap this code in a do-catch block so that we can report any error that is reported by Core Data:

```
do {
    let objects = try context.fetch(request)
```

After that, we declare a variable called theLine of type NSManagedObject that will reference the managed object for this row's data. We may not have previously stored any data for this row, so at this point, we don't know whether we're going to get a managed object for it from the persistent store. For that reason, theLine needs to be declared as optional. But for convenience, we'll make it force unwrapped, since we're going to use the insertNewObject (forEntityName: inManagedObjectContext:) method to create a new managed object for this row in the persistent store if we didn't get one. We'll use that managed object to initialize theLine in that case:

```
var theLine:NSManagedObject! = objects.first as? NSManagedObject
if theLine == nil {
    // No existing data for this row - insert a new managed object for it
    theLine =
        NSEntityDescription.insertNewObject(
                forEntityName: ViewController.lineEntityName,
                into: context)
            as NSManagedObject
```

Next, we use key-value coding to set the line number and text for this managed object. We log any error that was caught in the catch clause:

```
theLine.setValue(i, forKey: ViewController.lineNumberKey)
theLine.setValue(textField.text, forKey: ViewController.lineTextKey)
```

Finally, once we're finished looping, we tell the context to save its changes:

```
appDelegate.saveContext()
```

That's it. Build and run the app to make sure it works. The Core Data version of your application should behave exactly the same as the previous versions.

Summary

You should now have a solid handle on four different ways of preserving your application data between sessions—five ways if you include the user defaults that you learned how to use in the previous chapter. We built an application that persisted data using property lists and modified the application to save its data using object archives. We then made a change and used the iOS's built-in SQLite3 mechanism to save the application data. Finally, we rebuilt the same application using Core Data. These mechanisms are the basic building blocks for saving and loading data in almost all iOS applications.

CHAPTER 14

■ ■ ■

Documents and iCloud

Apple's iCloud service introduced with iOS 5 (see Figure 14-1) provides cloud storage for iOS devices, as well as for computers running macOS. Most iOS users probably encounter the iCloud device backup option immediately when setting up a new device or upgrading an old device to a more recent version of iOS, quickly discovering the advantages of automatic backup that doesn't require the use of a computer.

Figure 14-1. *First introduced with iOS 5, Apple's iCloud provides easy to use server storage for iOS and macOS applications*

Computerless backup provides a great feature, but it only scratches the surface of what iCloud does. More importantly, iCloud provides app developers with a mechanism for transparently saving data to Apple's cloud servers with little effort. You configure your apps to save information to iCloud and have that data automatically transfer to any other devices registered to the same iCloud user. Users may create a document on their iPad and later view the same document on their iPhone or Mac without any intervening steps—the document just appears.

© Molly Maskrey, Kim Topley, David Mark, Fredrik Olsson and Jeff Lamarche 2016
M. Maskrey et al., *Beginning iPhone Development with Swift 3*, DOI 10.1007/978-1-4842-2223-2_14

A system process takes care of making sure the user has a valid iCloud login and manages the file transfers, so you don't need to worry about networks or authentication. Apart from a small amount of app configuration, just a few small changes to your methods for saving files and locating available files gets you into the iCloud space.

The UIDocument class provides a component of the iCloud filing system. UIDocument takes a portion of the work out of creating a document-based app by handling some of the common aspects of reading and writing files. That way, you spend more of your time focusing on the unique features of your app, instead of building the same plumbing for every app you create.

Whether you're using iCloud or not, UIDocument provides some powerful tools for managing document files in iOS. To demonstrate these features, the first portion of this chapter is dedicated to creating TinyPix, a simple document-based app that saves files to local storage. This is an approach that can work well for all kinds of iOS-based apps, and recently Apple has enabled testing iCloud syncing from within Simulator before executing on physical devices.

This chapter shows you how to iCloud-enable the TinyPix app.

Managing Document Storage with UIDocument

Any piece of software letting you deal with multiple collections of data, saving each collection to a separate file, could be considered a document-based application. Often, there's a one-to-one correspondence between an on-screen window and the document it contains; however, sometimes (e.g., Xcode) a single window can display multiple documents that are all related in some way.

On iOS devices, apps usually don't make use of multiple windows, but plenty of apps can still benefit from a document-based approach. Thanks to the UIDocument class, which takes care of the most common aspects of document file storage, you won't need to deal with files directly (just URLs), and all the necessary reading and writing happens on a background thread, so your app can remain responsive even during file access. UIDocument automatically saves edited documents periodically and whenever the app is suspended (such as when the device is shut down, the Home button is pressed, and so on), so there's no need for any sort of save button. All of this helps make applications behave the way users expect their iOS apps to behave.

Creating the TinyPix Application

We're going to build an app called TinyPix that lets you edit simple 8 × 8 images, in 1-bit color, as shown in Figure 14-2. For the user's convenience, each picture is blown up to the full screen size for editing. We'll be using UIDocument to represent the data for each image.

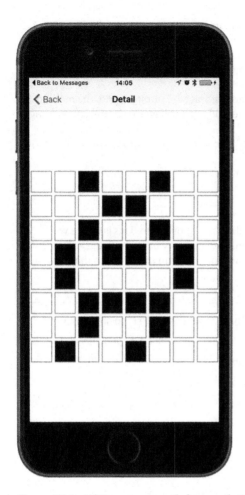

Figure 14-2. *Editing an extremely low-resolution icon in TinyPix*

Start off by creating a new project in Xcode. From the iOS Application section, select the Master-Detail Application template and click Next. Name this new app **TinyPix** and set the Devices pop-up to Universal. Make sure the Use Core Data check box is unchecked. Now click Next again and choose the location to save your project.

In Xcode's Project Navigator, you'll see that your project contains files for AppDelegate, MasterViewController, and DetailViewController, as well as the Main.storyboard file. We'll make changes to all of these files and we will create a few new classes along the way.

Creating TinyPixDocument

The first new class we're going to create is the document class that will contain the data for each TinyPix image that's loaded from file storage. Select the TinyPix folder in Xcode and press ⌘N to create a new file. From the iOS Source section, select Cocoa Touch Class and click Next. Enter **TinyPixDocument** in the Class field, enter **UIDocument** in the **Subclass of** field, and click Next. Finally, click Create to create the file.

Let's think about the public API of this class before we get into its implementation details. This class is going to represent an 8 × 8 grid of pixels, where each pixel consists of a single on or off value. So, we'll give it a method that takes a pair of row and column indexes and returns a Bool value. We'll also provide a method to set a specific state at a specified row and column and, as a convenience, another method that simply toggles the state at a particular place.

Switch over to TinyPixDocument.swift, where we'll implement storage for our 8 × 8 grid, the methods that we need for our public API, and the required UIDocument methods that will enable loading and saving our documents.

Let's start by defining the storage for our 8 × 8 bitmap data. We'll hold this data in an array of UInt8. Add the following property to the TinyPixDocument class:

```
class TinyPixDocument: UIDocument {
    private var bitmap: [UInt8]
```

The UIDocument class has a designated initializer that all subclasses should use. This is where we'll create our initial bitmap. In true bitmap style, we're going to minimize memory usage by using a single byte to contain each row. Each bit in the byte represents the on/off value of a column index within that row. In total, our document contains just 8 bytes.

■ **Note** This section contains a small number of bitwise operations, as well as some C pointer and array manipulation. This is all pretty mundane for C developers; but if you don't have much C experience, it may seem puzzling or even impenetrable. In that case, feel free to simply copy and use the code provided (it works just fine). If you really want to understand what's going on, you may want to dig deeper into C itself.

Add this initializer to our document's implementation:

```
override init(fileURL: URL) {
    bitmap = [0x01, 0x02, 0x04, 0x08, 0x10, 0x20, 0x40, 0x80]
    super.init(fileURL: fileURL as URL)
}
```

This starts off the bitmap with a simple diagonal pattern stretching from one corner to another. Now, it's time to implement the methods that make up the public API. Let's first create a method that reads the state of a single bit from the bitmap. Add the method in Listing 14-1.

Listing 14-1. Read the State of a Single Bit

```
func stateAt(row: Int, column: Int) -> Bool {
    let rowByte = bitmap[row]
    let result = UInt8(1 << column) & rowByte
    return result != 0
}
```

This code simply grabs the relevant byte from our array of bytes, and then does a bit shift and an AND operation to determine whether the specified bit was set, returning true or false accordingly. Next comes the inverse: a method that sets the value specified at a given row and column. Here, we once again grab the byte for the specified row and do a bit shift. But this time, instead of using the shifted bit to examine the contents of the row, we use it to either set or unset a bit in the row. Add the method in Listing 14-2 to the end of the class definition.

Listing 14-2. Set or Unset a Bit in the Row

```
func setState(state: Bool, atRow row: Int, column: Int) {
    var rowByte = bitmap[row]
    if state {
        rowByte |= UInt8(1 << column)
    } else {
        rowByte &= ~UInt8(1 << column)
    }
    bitmap[row] = rowByte
}
```

Now, let's add a convenience method that lets outside code simply toggle a single cell:

```
func toggleStateAt(row: Int, column: Int) {
    let state = stateAt(row: row, column: column)
    setState(state: !state, atRow: row, column: column)
}
```

Our document class requires two final pieces before it fits into the puzzle of a document-based app: methods for reading and writing. As mentioned earlier, you don't need to deal with files directly. You don't even need to worry about the URL that was passed into the init(fileURL:) initializer earlier. All that you need to do is implement one method that transforms the document's internal data structure (in our case, this is the bitmap byte array) into an NSData object, ready for saving, and another that takes a freshly loaded NSData object and pulls the object's data structure out of it. Add the two methods in Listing 14-3 to implement the required UIDocument contract.

Listing 14-3. Conversion to and from NSData Objects

```
override func contents(forType typeName: String) throws -> AnyObject {
    print("Saving document to URL \(fileURL)")
    let bitmapData = NSData(bytes: bitmap, length: bitmap.count)
    return bitmapData
}

override func load(fromContents contents: AnyObject, ofType typeName: String?) throws {
    print("Loading document from URL \(fileURL)")
    if let bitmapData = contents as? NSData {
        bitmapData.getBytes(UnsafeMutablePointer<UInt8>(bitmap), length: bitmap.count)
    }
}
```

The first of these methods, contents(forType: typeName:), is called whenever our document is about to be saved to storage. It simply returns a copy of our bitmap wrapped in an NSData object, which the system will take care of storing later. The second method, load(fromContents contents:), is called whenever the system has just loaded data from storage and wants to provide this data to an instance of our document class. Here, we just grab a copy of the bytes from the NSData object that has been passed in. We've included some logging statements in both methods, just so you can see what's happening in the Xcode log later on.

Each of these methods allows you to do some things that we're ignoring in this app. They both provide a typeName parameter, which you could use to distinguish between different types of data storage that your document can load from or save to. They also both declare that they can throw an error in the event that something goes wrong. In our case, however, what we're doing is so simple that there are no error conditions for which we need to check.

That's all to do for our document class. Sticking to MVC principles, our document sits squarely in the model camp (of MVC), knowing nothing about how it's displayed. And thanks to the UIDocument superclass, the document is even shielded from most of the details about how it's stored.

Code Master

Now that we have our document class ready to go, it's time to address the first view that a user sees when running our app: the list of existing TinyPix documents, which is taken care of by the MasterViewController class. We need to let this class know how to grab the list of available documents, let the user choose an existing document for viewing or editing, and create and name a new document. When a document is created or chosen, it's then passed along to the detail controller for display.

Start by selecting MasterViewController.swift. This file, generated as part of the Master–Detail application template, contains starter code for displaying an array of items. We're not going to use any of that, but instead do these things all on our own. Therefore, delete everything in the file apart from the import of the UIKit framework and the class declaration. When you're done, you should have a clean slate that looks like this:

```
import UIKit

class MasterViewController: UITableViewController {

}
```

We'll also include a segmented control in our GUI, which will allow the user to choose a tint color that will be used as a highlight color for portions of the TinyPix GUI. Although this is not a particularly useful feature in and of itself, it will help demonstrate the iCloud mechanism, as the highlight color setting makes its way from the device on which you set it to another of your connected devices running the same app. The first version of the app will use the color as a local setting on each device. Later in the chapter, we'll add the code to make the color setting propagate through iCloud to the user's other devices.

To implement the color selection control, we'll add an outlet and an action to our code as well. We'll also add properties for holding onto a list of document file names and a pointer to the document the user has chosen. Make these changes to MasterViewController.swift:

```
class MasterViewController: UITableViewController {
    @IBOutlet var colorControl: UISegmentedControl!
    private var documentFileURLs: [URL] = []
    private var chosenDocument: TinyPixDocument?
```

Before we implement the table view methods and other standard methods that we need to deal with, we'll write a couple of private utility methods. The first of these takes a file name, combines it with the URL of the app's Documents directory, and returns a URL pointing to that specific file. As you saw in Chapter 13, the Documents directory is a special location that iOS sets aside, one for each app installed on an iOS device. You can use it to store documents created by your app, and rest assured that those documents will be automatically included whenever users back up their iOS device, whether it's to iTunes or iCloud.

Add this method to MasterViewController.swift:

```
private func urlForFileName(fileName: String) -> URL {
    let urls = FileManager.default.urls (for:
        .documentDirectory, inDomains: .userDomainMask)
    var url: URL = URL(fileURLWithPath: "")      // create a blank path
    do {
```

```
        try url = urls.first!.appendingPathComponent(fileName)
    } catch  {
        print("Error is \(error)")
    }
    return url
}
```

The second private method is a bit longer. It also uses the Documents directory, this time to search for files representing existing documents. The method takes the files it finds and sorts them by creation date, so that the user will see the list of documents sorted "blog-style" with the newest items first. The document file URLs are stashed away in the documentFileURLs property, and then the table view (which we haven't yet dealt with) is reloaded. Add the code in Listing 14-4 to the class definition:

Listing 14-4. Reload Files Method

```
private func reloadFiles() {
    let fm = FileManager.default
    let documentsURL = fm.urls(for:
        .documentDirectory, inDomains: .userDomainMask).first!

    do {
        let fileURLs = try fm.contentsOfDirectory(at: documentsURL,
                                                  includingPropertiesForKeys: nil,
                                                  options: [])
        let sortedFileURLs = fileURLs.sorted(isOrderedBefore: { (file1URL, file2URL) -> Bool in
            let attr1 = try! fm.attributesOfItem(atPath: file1URL.path!)
            let attr2 = try! fm.attributesOfItem(atPath: file2URL.path!)
            let file1Date = attr1[FileAttributeKey.creationDate] as! NSDate
            let file2Date = attr2[FileAttributeKey.creationDate] as! NSDate
            let result = file1Date.compare(file2Date as Date)
            return result == ComparisonResult.orderedAscending

        })

        documentFileURLs = sortedFileURLs
        tableView.reloadData()

    } catch {
        print("Error listing files in directory \(documentsURL.path!): \(error)")
    }
}
```

Now, let's add the table view data source methods. These should be pretty familiar to you by now. Add the methods shown in Listing 14-5 to the MasterViewController.swift file.

Listing 14-5. Table View Data Source Methods

```
override func numberOfSections(in tableView: UITableView) -> Int {
    return 1
}
```

```
override func tableView(_ tableView: UITableView, numberOfRowsInSection section: Int) -> Int {
    return documentFileURLs.count
}

override func tableView(_ tableView: UITableView, cellForRowAt indexPath: IndexPath) ->
UITableViewCell {
    let cell = tableView.dequeueReusableCell(withIdentifier: "FileCell")!
    let fileURL = documentFileURLs[indexPath.row]
    do {
        try cell.textLabel!.text = fileURL.deletingPathExtension().lastPathComponent
    } catch {
        print("Error is \(error)")
    }
    return cell
}
```

These methods are based on the contents of the array stored in the documentFileURLs property that we created in the reloadFiles() method. This array contains one NSURL for each file in the Documents directory, sorted by creation time, with the oldest file first. The call to the tableView(_:cellForForAtIndex Path:) method to get a UITableViewCell instance relies on the existence of a cell attached to the table view with "FileCell" set as its identifier, so we must be sure to set that up in the storyboard a little later.

If not for the fact that we haven't touched our storyboard yet, the code we have now would almost be something we could run and see in action; however, with no preexisting TinyPix documents, we would have nothing to display in our table view. And so far, we don't have any way to create new documents, either. Also, we have not yet dealt with the color-selection control we're going to add. So, let's do a bit more work before we try to run our app.

The user's choice of highlight color will be used to immediately set a tint color for the segmented control. The UIView class has a tintColor property. When it's set for any view, the value applies to that view and will propagate down to all of its subviews. When we set the segmented control's tint color, we'll also store it in NSUserDefaults for later retrieval. Add these two methods to the end of the class definition:

```
@IBAction func chooseColor(sender: UISegmentedControl) {
    let selectedColorIndex = sender.selectedSegmentIndex
    setTintColorForIndex(colorIndex: selectedColorIndex)

    let prefs = UserDefaults.standard
    prefs.set(selectedColorIndex, forKey: "selectedColorIndex")
    prefs.synchronize()
}

private func setTintColorForIndex(colorIndex: Int) {
    colorControl.tintColor = TinyPixUtils.getTintColorForIndex(index: colorIndex)
}
```

The first method triggers when the user changes the selection in the segmented control. It saves the selected index in the user defaults and passes it to the second method, which converts the index to a color and applies it to the segmented control as its tint color, thus making the control take on the color that the user chose. We'll need to use the code that does the conversion from index to color in the detail view controller as well, so it's implemented in a separate class. To create that class, press ⌘N to open the new file dialog. From the iOS Source section, select Swift File and click Next. Enter **TinyPixUtils.swift** as the file name and click Create to create the file.

Now switch over to TinyPixUtils.swift to implement the method that we need:

```
import UIKit

class TinyPixUtils {
    class func getTintColorForIndex(index: Int) -> UIColor {
        let color: UIColor
        switch index {
        case 0:
            color = UIColor .red

        case 1:
            color = UIColor(red: 0, green: 0.6, blue: 0, alpha: 1)

        case 2:
            color = UIColor.blue

        default:
            color = UIColor.red
        }
        return color
    }
}
```

We realize that we haven't yet set anything up in the storyboard. First, we have some more work to do in MasterViewController.swift. Let's start with the viewDidLoad method. After calling the superclass's implementation, we'll need to add a button to the right side of the navigation bar. The user will press this button to create a new TinyPix document. We'll also load the saved tint color from the user defaults and use it to set the tint color of the segmented control. We finish by calling the reloadFiles() method that we implemented earlier to get a list of TinyPix documents that the user has already created. Add this code to implement viewDidLoad():

Listing 14-6. Our MasterViewController.swift File's viewDidLoad Method

```
override func viewDidLoad() {
    super.viewDidLoad()

    let addButton = UIBarButtonItem(
        barButtonSystemItem: UIBarButtonSystemItem.add,
        target: self, action: #selector(MasterViewController.insertNewObject))
    navigationItem.rightBarButtonItem = addButton

    let prefs = UserDefaults.standard
    let selectedColorIndex = prefs.integer(forKey: "selectedColorIndex")
    setTintColorForIndex(colorIndex: selectedColorIndex)
    colorControl.selectedSegmentIndex = selectedColorIndex

    reloadFiles()
}
```

As you'll see when you run the app for the first time, the segmented control's tint color starts out being red. That's because there's nothing stored in the user defaults yet, so the integerForKey() method returns 0, which the setTintColorForIndex() method interprets as red.

You may have noticed that, when we created the UIBarButtonItem, we told it to call the insertNewObject() method when it's pressed. We haven't written that method yet, so let's do so now. Add this method definition:

```
func insertNewObject() {
    let alert = UIAlertController(title: "Choose File Name",
                                message: "Enter a name for your new TinyPix document",
                                preferredStyle: .alert)
    alert.addTextField(configurationHandler: nil)

    let cancelAction = UIAlertAction(title: "Cancel", style: .cancel, handler: nil)
    let createAction = UIAlertAction(title: "Create", style: .default) { action in
        let textField = alert.textFields![0] as UITextField
        self.createFileNamed(textField.text!)
    };

    alert.addAction(cancelAction)
    alert.addAction(createAction)

    present(alert, animated: true, completion: nil)
}
```

This method uses the UIAlertController class to display an alert that includes a text-input field, a Create button, and a Cancel button. If the Create button is pressed, the responsibility of creating a new item instead falls to the method that the button's handler block calls when it's finished, which we'll also add now. Add this method:

```
private func createFileNamed(fileName: String) {
    let trimmedFileName = fileName.trimmingCharacters(in: NSCharacterSet.whitespaces)
    if !trimmedFileName.isEmpty {
        let targetName = trimmedFileName + ".tinypix"
        let saveUrl = urlForFileName(fileName: targetName)
        chosenDocument = TinyPixDocument(fileURL: saveUrl)
        chosenDocument?.save(to: saveUrl,
                        for: UIDocumentSaveOperation.forCreating,
                            completionHandler: { success in
                                if success {
                                    print("Save OK")
                                    self.reloadFiles()
                                    self.performSegue(withIdentifier: "masterToDetail",
                                    sender: self)
                                } else {
                                    print("Failed to save!")
                                }
        })
    }
}
```

This method starts out simply enough. It strips leading and trailing whitespace characters from the name that it's passed. If the result is not empty, it then creates a file name based on the user's entry, a URL based on that file name (using the `urlForFilename()` method we wrote earlier), and a new `TinyPixDocument` instance using that URL.

What comes next is a little more subtle. It's important to understand here that just creating a new document with a given URL doesn't create the file. In fact, at the time that `init(fileURL:)` is called, the document doesn't yet know if the given URL refers to an existing file or to a new file that needs to be created. We need to tell it what to do. In this case, we tell it to save a new file at the given URL with this code:

```
chosenDocument?.save(to: saveUrl,
            for: UIDocumentSaveOperation.forCreating,
            completionHandler: { success in
.
.
.
    })
```

Of interest is the purpose and usage of the closure that is passed in as the last argument. The method we're calling, `save(to: saveUrl  )` doesn't have a return value to tell us how it all worked out. In fact, the method returns immediately after it's called, long before the file is actually saved. Instead, it starts the file-saving work and later, when it's done, calls the closure that we gave it, using the `success` parameter to let us know whether it succeeded. To make it all work as smoothly as possible, the file-saving work is actually performed on a background thread. The closure we pass in, however, is executed on the thread that called `save(to: saveUrl  )` in the first place. In this particular case, that means that the block is executed on the main thread, so we can safely use any facilities that require the main thread, such as UIKit. With that in mind, take a look again at what happens inside that block:

```
if success {
    print("Save OK")
    self.reloadFiles()
    self.performSegue(withIdentifier: "masterToDetail", sender: self)
} else {
    print("Failed to save!")
}
```

This is the content of the block we passed in to the file-saving method, and it's called later, after the file operation is completed. We check to see if it succeeded; if so, we do an immediate file reload, and then initiate a segue to another view controller. This is an aspect of segues that we didn't cover in Chapter 9, but it's pretty straightforward. The idea is that a segue in a storyboard file can have an identifier, just like a table view cell, and you can use that identifier to trigger a segue programmatically. In this case, we'll just need to remember to configure that segue in the storyboard when we get to it. But before we do that, let's add the last method this class needs, to take care of that segue. Add this method to MasterViewController.swift, as shown in Listing 14-7.

Listing 14-7. Our prepareForSeque Method in the MasterViewController.swift File

```
override func prepare(for segue: UIStoryboardSegue, sender: AnyObject?) {
    let destination =
        segue.destinationViewController as! UINavigationController
    let detailVC =
        destination.topViewController as! DetailViewController
```

```
    if sender === self {
        // if sender === self, a new document has just been created,
        // and chosenDocument is already set.
        detailVC.detailItem = chosenDocument
    } else {
        // Find the chosen document from the tableview
        if let indexPath = tableView.indexPathForSelectedRow {
            let docURL = documentFileURLs[(indexPath as NSIndexPath).row]
            chosenDocument = TinyPixDocument(fileURL: docURL)
            chosenDocument?.open() { success in
                if success {
                    print("Load OK")
                    detailVC.detailItem = self.chosenDocument
                } else {
                    print("Failed to load!")
                }
            }
        }
    }
}
```

This method, has two clear paths of execution that are determined by the condition at the top. Remember from our discussion of storyboards in Chapter 9 that this method is called on a view controller whenever a segue is about to be performed from that view controller. The `sender` parameter refers to the object that initiated the segue and we use that to figure out just what to do here. If the segue is initiated by the programmatic method call we performed in the alert view delegate method, then `sender` will be equal to `self`, because that's the value of the `sender` argument in the `performSegue(withIdentifier:)` call in the `createFileNamed()` method. In that case, we know that the `chosenDocument` property is already set, and we simply pass its value to the destination view controller.

Otherwise, we know we're responding to the user touching a row in the table view, and that's where things get a little more complicated. That's the time to create a new instance of our document class, and try to open the file that the user selected. You'll see that the method we call to open the file, `open()`, works similarly to the save method we used earlier. We pass it a closure that it will save for later execution. Just as with the file-saving method, the loading occurs in the background, and this closure will be executed on the main thread when it's complete. At that point, if the loading succeeded, we pass the document along to the detail view controller.

Note that both of these methods use the key-value coding technique that we've used a few times before, letting us set the `detailItem` property of the segue's destination controller, even though we don't include its header. This will work out just fine for us, since `DetailViewController`—the detail view controller class created as part of the Xcode project—happens to include a property called `detailItem` right out of the box, but we may need to convert that from `NSDate` to `AnyObject?` as in:

```
var detailItem: AnyObject? {
```

With the amount of code we now have in place, we'll now set up the storyboard so that we can run our app and make something happen. Save your code and continue.

Setting Up the Storyboard

Select Main.storyboard in the Xcode Project Navigator and take a look at what's already there. You'll find scenes for a split view controller, two navigation controllers, the master view controller, and the detail view controller (see Figure 14-3). All of our work will be with the master and detail view controllers.

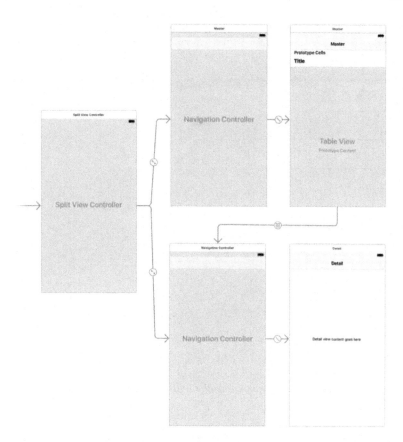

Figure 14-3. *The TinyPix storyboard, showing split view controller, navigation controllers, master view controller, and detail view controller*

Let's start by dealing with the master view controller scene, the one on the top right in Figure 14-3. This is where the table view showing the list of all our TinyPix documents is configured. By default, this scene's table view is configured to use dynamic cells instead of static cells. We want our table view to get its contents from the data source methods we implemented, so this default setting is just what we want. We do need to configure the cell prototype though, so select it, and open the Attributes Inspector. Change the cell's Identifier from Cell to FileCell. This will let the data source code we wrote earlier access the table view cell.

We also need to create the segue that we're triggering in our code. Do this by Control-dragging from the master view controller's icon (a yellow circle at the top of its scene or the Master icon under Master Scene in the Document Outline) over to the Navigation Controller for the detail view (the controller at the bottom left in Figure 14-3, which you can also find in the Document Outline by expanding the Navigation Controller Scene), and then selecting Show Detail from the storyboard segues menu.

You'll now see two segues that seem to connect the two scenes. By selecting each of them, you can tell where they're coming from. Selecting one segue highlights the whole master scene; selecting the second one highlights just the table view cell. Select the segue that highlights the whole scene (i.e., the segue that you just created), and use the Attributes Inspector to set its Identifier, which is currently empty, to masterToDetail.

The final touch needed for the master view controller scene is to let the user pick which color will be used to represent an "on" point in the detail view. Instead of implementing some kind of comprehensive color picker, we're just going to add a segmented control that will let the user pick from a set of predefined colors.

Find a Segmented Control in the object library, drag it out, and place it in the navigation bar at the top of the master view (see Figure 14-4).

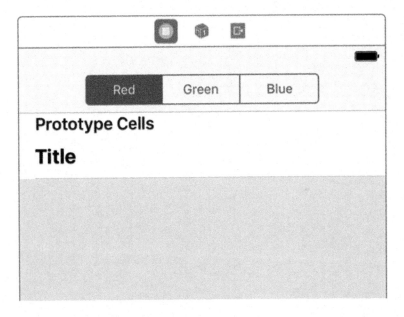

Figure 14-4. *The TinyPix storyboard, showing the master view controller with a segmented control on the controller's navigation bar*

Make sure the segmented control is selected and then open the Attributes Inspector. In the Segmented Control section at the top of the inspector, use the stepper control to change the number of Segments from 2 to 3. Next, double-click the title of each segment in turn, changing them to Red, Green, and Blue, respectively. After setting those titles, click one of the resizing handles for the segmented control and make it wide enough so that all three titles are comfortably visible.

Next, Control-drag from the segmented control to the icon representing the master controller (the yellow circle labeled Master above the controller in the storyboard, or the Document Outline icon labeled Master under Master Scene) and select the chooseColor() method. Then Control-drag from the master controller back to the segmented control, and select the colorControl outlet. We've now connected the segmented control to its outlet in the master controller, and to the action method that will be called when a segment is selected.

We've finally reached a point where we can build and run the app. You'll see it start up and display an empty table view with a segmented control at the top and a plus (+) button in the upper-right corner, as shown in Figure 14-5.

Figure 14-5. *The TinyPix app when it first appears. Click the plus icon to add a new document. You'll be prompted to name your new TinyPix document. At the moment, all the detail view does is display the document name in a label*

Tap the Back button to return to the master list, where you'll see the item you added. Go ahead and create one or two more items to see that they're correctly added to the list. Finally, head back to Xcode because we've got more to do.

Creating the TinyPix View

Our next order of business is the creation of a view class to display our grid and let the user edit it. Select the TinyPix folder in the Project Navigator, and press ⌘N to create a new file. In the iOS Source section, select Cocoa Touch Class and click Next. Name the new class TinyPixView and choose UIView in the **Subclass of** pop-up. Click Next, verify that the save location is OK, and then click Create.

■ **Note** The implementation of our view class includes some drawing and touch handling that hasn't been covered yet. Rather than bog down this chapter with too many details about these topics, I'm just going to quickly show you the code. I'll cover the details of drawing with Core Graphics in Chapter 16. I'll talk about how to respond to touches and drags in Chapter 18.

Select TinyPixView.swift and add the following structure definition at the top of the file, before the class definition:

```
struct GridIndex {
    var row: Int
    var column: Int
}
```

We'll use this structure whenever we need to refer to a (row, column) pair in the grid. Now add the following property definitions, which we'll make use of shortly, to the class:

```
var document: TinyPixDocument!
var lastSize: CGSize = CGSize.zero
var gridRect: CGRect!
var blockSize: CGSize!
var gap: CGFloat = 0
var selectedBlockIndex: GridIndex = GridIndex(row: NSNotFound, column: NSNotFound)
```

A UIView subclass is usually initialized by calling its init(frame:) method, which is its default initializer. However, since this class is going to be loaded from a storyboard, it will instead be initialized using its init(coder:) method. We'll implement both of these initializers, making them both call a third method that initializes our properties. Add the code in Listing 14-8 to TinyPixView.swift.

Listing 14-8. Initializers for TinyPixView.swift

```
override init(frame: CGRect) {
    super.init(frame: frame)
    commonInit()
}

required init?(coder aDecoder: NSCoder) {
    super.init(coder: aDecoder)
    commonInit()
}

private func commonInit() {
    calculateGridForSize(bounds.size)
}
```

The calculateGridForSize() method figures out how large the cells in the color grid should be, based on the size of TinyPixView. Calculating the grid size allows us to use the same application with screens of different sizes and also handles the case where the size of the view changes when the device is rotated. Add the implementation of the calculateGridForSize() method to TinyPixView.swift:

```
private func calculateGridForSize(_ size: CGSize) {
    let space = min(size.width, size.height)
    gap = space/57
    let cellSide = gap * 6
    blockSize = CGSize(width: cellSide, height: cellSide)
    gridRect = CGRect(x: (size.width - space)/2, y: (size.height - space)/2,
                      width: space, height: space)
}
```

The idea behind this method is to make the grid fill either the full width or the full height of the view, whichever is the smaller, and to center it along the longer axis. To do that, we calculate the size of each cell, plus the gaps between the cells, by dividing the smaller dimension of the view by 57. Why 57? Well, we want to have space for eight cells and we want each cell to be six times the size of the intercell gap. Given that we need gaps between each pair of cells, plus a gap at the start and end of each row or column, that effectively means we need space for $(6 \times 8) + 9 = 57$ gaps. Once we have the gap size, we get the size of each cell (by multiplying by 6). We use that information to set the value of the blockSize property, which represents the size of each cell, and the gridRect property, which corresponds to the region within the view in which the grid cells will actually be drawn.

Now let's take a look at the drawing routines. We override the standard UIView drawRect() method, use that to simply walk through all the blocks in our grid, and then call another method that will draw each cell block. Add the following bold code and don't forget to remove the comment marks around the drawRect() method:

```swift
override func draw(_ rect: CGRect) {
    if document != nil {
        let size = bounds.size
        if !size.equalTo(lastSize) {
            lastSize = size
            calculateGridForSize(size)
        }

        for row in 0 ..< 8 {
            for column in 0 ..< 8 {
                drawBlockAt(row: row, column: column)
            }
        }
    }
}
```

Before we draw the cells, we compare the current size of the view to the value in the lastSize property and, if it's different, we call calculateGridForSize(). This will happen when the view is first drawn and any time it changes size, which will most likely be when the device is rotated.

Now add the code that draws the block for each cell in the grid:

```swift
private func drawBlockAt(row: Int, column: Int) {
    let startX = gridRect.origin.x + gap
            + (blockSize.width + gap) * (7 - CGFloat(column)) + 1
    let startY = gridRect.origin.y + gap
            + (blockSize.height + gap) * CGFloat(row) + 1

    let blockFrame = CGRect(x: startX, y: startY,
                        width: blockSize.width, height: blockSize.height)
    let color = document.stateAt(row: row, column: column)
                    ? UIColor.black() : UIColor.white()

    color.setFill()
    tintColor.setStroke()
    let path = UIBezierPath(rect:blockFrame)
    path.fill()
    path.stroke()
}
```

This code uses the grid origin and the cell size and gap values set by the `calculateGridForSize()` method to figure out where each cell should be, and then draws it using the current tint color for the outline and either black or white for the interior fill, depending on whether the cell should be filled or not. We'll discuss the drawing methods in Chapter 16.

Finally, we add a set of methods that respond to touch events by the user. Both `touchesBegan(_:withEvent:)` and `touchesMoved(_:withEvent:)` are standard methods that every `UIView` subclass can implement to capture touch events that happen within the view's frame. We'll discuss these methods in detail in Chapter 19. Our implementation uses two other methods that we're adding here to calculate a grid location based on a touch location and to toggle a specific value in the document. Again, these methods use the values set by the `calculateGridForSize()` method to decide whether a touch falls within a grid cell or not. Add these four methods at the bottom of the file, just above the closing brace, as shown in Listing 14-9.

Listing 14-9. Our Touch Events Methods to Add to TinyPixView.swift

```
private func touchedGridIndexFromTouches(_ touches: Set<UITouch>) -> GridIndex {
    var result = GridIndex(row: -1, column: -1)
    let touch = touches.first!
    var location = touch.location(in: self)
    if gridRect.contains(location) {
        location.x -= gridRect.origin.x
        location.y -= gridRect.origin.y
        result.column = Int(8 - (location.x * 8.0 / gridRect.size.width))
        result.row = Int(location.y * 8.0 / gridRect.size.height)
    }
    return result
}

private func toggleSelectedBlock() {
    if selectedBlockIndex.row != -1
            && selectedBlockIndex.column != -1 {
        document.toggleStateAt(row: selectedBlockIndex.row,
                column: selectedBlockIndex.column)
        document.undoManager?.prepare(withInvocationTarget: document)
                .toggleStateAt(row: selectedBlockIndex.row,
                             column: selectedBlockIndex.column)
        setNeedsDisplay()
    }
}

override func touchesBegan(_ touches: Set<UITouch>, with event: UIEvent?) {
    selectedBlockIndex = touchedGridIndexFromTouches(touches)
    toggleSelectedBlock()
}

override func touchesMoved(_ touches: Set<UITouch>, with event: UIEvent?) {
    let touched = touchedGridIndexFromTouches(touches)
    if touched.row != selectedBlockIndex.row
            && touched.column != selectedBlockIndex.column {
        selectedBlockIndex = touched
        toggleSelectedBlock()
    }
}
```

Sharp-eyed readers may have noticed that the toggleSelectedBlock ()method does something a bit special. After calling the document's toggleStateAt(row:column:)method to change the value of a particular grid point, it does something more. Let's take another look:

```
private func toggleSelectedBlock() {
    if selectedBlockIndex.row != -1
            && selectedBlockIndex.column != -1 {
        document.toggleStateAt(row: selectedBlockIndex.row,
                column: selectedBlockIndex.column)
        document.undoManager?.prepare(withInvocationTarget: document)
                .toggleStateAt(row: selectedBlockIndex.row,
                                column: selectedBlockIndex.column)
        setNeedsDisplay()
    }
}
```

The call to document.undoManager returns an instance of NSUndoManager. We haven't dealt with this directly anywhere else in this book, but NSUndoManager is the structural underpinning for the undo/redo functionality in both iOS and macOS. The idea is that anytime the user performs an action in the GUI, you use NSUndoManager to leave a sort of breadcrumb by "recording" a method call that will undo what the user just did. NSUndoManager will store that method call on a special undo stack, which can be used to backtrack through a document's state whenever the user activates the system's undo functionality.

The way it works is that the prepare(withInvocationTarget:) method returns a proxy object to which you can send any message, and the message will be packed up with the target and pushed onto the undo stack. So, while it may look like you're calling toggleStateAt(row:column:) twice in a row, the second time it's not being called but instead is just being queued up for later potential use.

So, why are we doing this? We haven't been giving any thought to undo/redo issues up to this point, so why now? The reason is that registering an undoable action with the document's NSUndoManager marks the document as "dirty" and ensures that it will be saved automatically at some point in the next few seconds. The fact that the user's actions are also undoable is just icing on the cake, at least in this application, because we're not going to add any controls to the user interface to allow the user to make use of it. However, in an app with a more complex document structure, allowing document-wide undo support can be hugely beneficial.

Save your changes. Now that our view class is ready, we'll go back to the storyboard to configure the detail view.

Storyboard Detail View

Select Main.storyboard, find the detail scene (it's the one at the bottom left), and take a look at what's there right now. All the GUI contains is a label ("Detail view content goes here"), which is the one that contained the document's description when you ran the app earlier. That label isn't particularly useful, so select it in the storyboard or in the Document Outline and press the Delete key to remove it. Next, use the object library to find a UIView and drag it into the detail view. Position and size it so that it fills the entire area below the title bar, as shown in Figure 14-6.

Figure 14-6. *Replaced the label in the detail view with another view, centered in its containing view. After dropping it, resize it to fill the entire area below the title bar*

Switch over to the Identity Inspector, so we can change this UIView instance into an instance of our custom class. In the Custom Class section at the top of the inspector, select the Class pop-up list, and choose TinyPixView. Now open the Attributes Inspector and change the Mode setting to Redraw. This causes TinyPixView to redraw itself when its size changes. This is necessary because the position of the grid inside the view depends on the size of the view itself, which changes when the device is rotated. At this point, the view hierarchy for the Detail Scene should look like Figure 14-7.

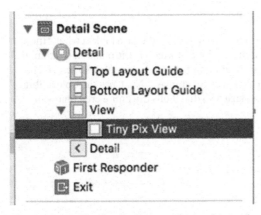

Figure 14-7. *The detail view scene's view hierarchy*

Before we go on, we need to adjust the auto layout constraints for the new view. We want it to fill the available area in the detail view. So, in the Document Outline, Control-drag from TinyPixView to its parent view and release the mouse. Hold down the Shift key and in the pop-up, select Leading Space to Container Margin, Trailing Space to Container Margin, Vertical Spacing to Top Layout Guide, and Vertical Spacing to Bottom Layout Guide, and then click return to apply the constraints.

Now we need to wire up the custom view to our detail view controller. We haven't prepared an outlet for our custom view yet, but that's OK since the Xcode drag-to-code feature will do that for us. Activate the Assistant Editor. A text editor should slide into place alongside the GUI editor, displaying the contents of DetailViewController.swift. If it's showing you anything else, use the jump bar at the top of the text editor to make DetailViewController.swift come into view. To make the connection, Control-drag from the TinyPixView icon in the Document Outline to the code, releasing the drag below the existing IBOutlet at the top of the file. In the pop-up window that appears, make sure that Connection is set to Outlet, name the new outlet pixView, and click the Connect button. While we're here, delete the detailDescriptionLabel outlet, since we're not going to be using it.

You should see that making that connection has added this line to DetailViewController.swift:

```
@IBOutlet weak var pixView: TinyPixView!
```

Now let's modify the configureView() method. This isn't a standard UIViewController method. It's just a private method that the project template included in this class as a convenient spot to put code that needs to update the detail view after anything changes. Since we're not using the description label, we delete the code that refers to it. Next, we add a bit of code to pass the chosen document along to our custom view and tell it to redraw itself by calling setNeedsDisplay():

```
func configureView() {
    // Update the user interface for the detail item.
    if detailItem != nil && isViewLoaded() {
        pixView.document = detailItem! as! TinyPixDocument
        pixView.setNeedsDisplay()
    }
}
```

Notice the call to isViewLoaded() before updating the document in the TinyPixView object. This is needed because it's possible for configureView() to be called before the detail view controller has loaded its view. In that case, the pixView property will still be nil and the app will crash if we try to use it. We can safely defer updating the document in this case, because configureView() will be called again from viewDidLoad when the view is actually loaded.

Next, we need to arrange for the tint color selected in the segmented control to be applied to the TinyPixView. We need to do this both when the view is first loaded and whenever the tint color is changed. We know that we can get the initial tint color from the user defaults, because we saved the index of the color that the user selected there in the action method that's connected to the segmented control, so let's add a method that gets the value, converts it to a UIColor and applies it to the TinyPixView. Add this method somewhere in the body of the class:

```
private func updateTintColor() {
    let prefs = UserDefaults.standard
    let selectedColorIndex = prefs.integer(forKey: "selectedColorIndex")
    let tintColor = TinyPixUtils.getTintColorForIndex(selectedColorIndex)
    pixView.tintColor = tintColor
    pixView.setNeedsDisplay()
}
```

We need to call this method to set the initial tint color when the view is first loaded. We also need to call it when the tint changes. How will we know that's happened—the segmented control is owned by the master view controller, so we don't have any connection to it? It turns out that we don't need one: we can tell that the tint color has changed because the new value gets stored in the user defaults and you can find out that something in the user defaults has changed by registering an observer for the NSUserDefaultsDidChangeNotification notification with the default notification center. Add the following code to the bottom of the viewDidLoad method:

```
updateTintColor()
NotificationCenter.default.addObserver(self,
        selector: #selector(DetailViewController.onSettingsChanged(_:)),
        name: UserDefaults.didChangeNotification , object: nil)
```

Now, when anything in the user defaults changes, the onSettingsChanged() method is called. When this happens, we need to set the new tint color, in case it's changed. Add the implementation of this method to the class:

```
func onSettingsChanged(notification: NSNotification) {
    updateTintColor()
}
```

Having added a notification observer, we have to remove it before the class is deallocated. We can do this by implementing the class deinitializer:

```
deinit {
    NotificationCenter.default.removeObserver(self,
                name: UserDefaults.didChangeNotification, object: nil)
}
```

We're nearly finished with this class, but we need to make one more change. Remember when I mentioned the autosaving that takes place when a document is notified that some editing has occurred, triggered by registering an undoable action? The save normally happens within about 10 seconds after the edit occurs. Like the other saving and loading procedures described earlier in this chapter, it happens in a background thread, so that normally the user won't even notice. However, that works only as long as the document is still around.

With our current set up, there's a risk that when the user hits the Back button to go back to the master list, the document instance will be deallocated without any save operation occurring, and the user's latest changes will be lost. To make sure this doesn't happen, we need to add some code to the viewWillDisappear() method to close the document as soon as the user navigates away from the detail view. Closing a document causes it to be automatically saved, and again, the saving occurs on a background thread. In this particular case, we don't need to do anything when the save is done, so we pass in nil instead of a block:

```
override func viewWillDisappear(_ animated: Bool) {
    super.viewWillDisappear(animated)
    if let doc = detailItem as? UIDocument {
        doc.close(completionHandler: nil)
    }
}
```

And with that, this version of our first truly document-based app is ready to try out. Build and run the app. You can create new documents, edit them, flip back to the list, and then select another document (or the same document), and it all just works. Experiment with changing the tint color and verify that it is properly saved and restored when you stop and restart the app. If you open the Xcode console while doing this, you'll see some output each time a document is loaded or saved. Using the autosaving system, you don't have direct control over just when saves occur (except for when closing a document), but it can be interesting to watch the logs just to get a feel for when they happen.

Adding iCloud Support

You now have a fully working document-based app, but we're not going to stop here. Modifying TinyPix to work with iCloud is pretty straightforward. Considering all that's happening behind the scenes, this requires a surprisingly small number of changes. We'll need to make some revisions to the method that loads the list of available files and the method that specifies the URL for loading a new file, but that's about it.

Apart from the code changes, we will also need to deal with some additional administrative details. Apple allows an app to save to iCloud only if it contains an embedded provisioning profile that is configured to allow iCloud usage. This means that to add the iCloud support to our app, you must have a paid iOS developer membership and have installed your developer certificate. It also works only with actual devices, not the simulator, so you'll need to have at least one iOS device registered with iCloud to run the new iCloud-backed TinyPix. With two devices, you'll have even more fun, as you can see how changes made on one device propagate to the other. Start by using the Finder to make a copy of the TinyPix project so that we can make these changes without disturbing our working application. Open the copy of the project that you just made in Xcode and we'll get started enabling it for iCloud.

Creating a Provisioning Profile

First, you need to create an iCloud-enabled provisioning profile for TinyPix. This used to require a lot of convoluted steps on Apple's developer web site, but nowadays Xcode makes it easy. In the Project Navigator, select the TinyPix item at the top, and then click the Capabilities tab in the editing area. You should see something like what's shown in Figure 14-8.

Figure 14-8. *The Xcode presentation of easily configurable app technologies and services*

If you are not using a paid developer account, you'll see a smaller list of capabilities that doesn't include iCloud. If that's the case, sign up for a developer account at Apple's web site and try again. If your developer account does not have the same name as the free account you have been using to run applications on your devices so far, you'll need to add it in Xcode. To do that, click Xcode ➤ Preferences… in the menu bar to open the Preferences dialog, and then select the Accounts tab, which should look something like Figure 14-9.

Figure 14-9. *The Accounts tab shows your available developer accounts*

Click the + icon at bottom left and select Add Apple ID… from the pop-up that appears. Then, enter the name and password for your paid developer account, which will be added to the list of available accounts in the Accounts tab. Now close the Preferences dialog and select the General tab in the Xcode editor. In the Identity section, you'll see a Team selector, as shown in Figure 14-10.

▼ **Identity**

Display Name	TinyPix
Bundle Identifier	com.mollymaskrey.TinyPix
Version	1.0
Build	1

▼ **Signing**

☑ Automatically manage signing
Xcode will create and update
profiles, app IDs, and certificates.

Team   Molly Maskrey

Provisioning Profile   Xcode Managed Profile ⓘ

Signing Certificate   iPhone Developer: Molly Maskrey (5...

Figure 14-10. *Using the Team selector to enable your paid developer account in the Xcode project*

Select your paid developer account and switch back to the Capabilities tab. If everything worked, you should now see the full list of capabilities shown in Figure 14-8.

The capabilities shown in Figure 14-7 can be configured directly in Xcode, all without needing to go to a web site, create and download provisioning profiles, and so on. Before you can do this, you need to give your app a unique App ID. To change the App ID to co.myCo, for example, you would set the Bundle Identifier, as shown in Figure 14-11.

☐	General	Capabilities	Resource Tags	Info	Build Settings	Build Phases
PROJECT	▼ **Identity**					
📄 TinyPix						
TARGETS		Bundle Identifier	co.myCo.TinyPix			
🅰 TinyPix		Version	1.0			
		Build	1			

Figure 14-11. *Changing the application's bundle ID*

Of course, you should use a value that's unique to you rather than co.myCo. Now switch back to the Capabilities tab. For TinyPix, we want to enable iCloud, the first capability listed, so click the disclosure triangle next to the cloud icon. Here you'll see some information about what this capability is for. Click the switch at the right to turn it on. Xcode will then communicate with Apple's servers to configure the provisioning profile for this app. If the bundle ID that you selected earlier is already in use, you'll see a red icon and an error message at the bottom of the iCloud section. Switch back to the General tab, select a different bundle ID and try again. Next, click to turn on the Key-value storage and iCloud Documents check boxes, as shown in Figure 14-12.

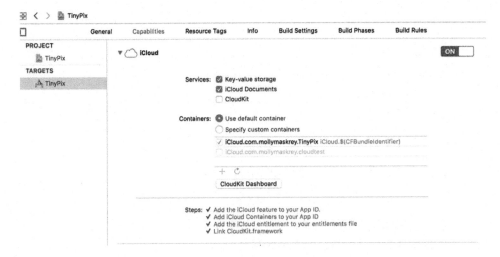

Figure 14-12. *The app is now configured to use iCloud*

Our app now has the necessary permissions to access iCloud from your code. The rest is a simple matter of programming.

How to Query

Select MasterViewController.swift so that we can start making changes for iCloud. The biggest change is going to be the way we look for available documents. In the first version of TinyPix, we used `FileManager` to see what's available on the local file system. This time, we're going to do things a little differently. Here, we will fire up a special sort of query to look for documents.

Start by adding a property to the class that will hold a pointer to an ongoing query:

```
@IBOutlet var colorControl: UISegmentedControl!
private var documentFileURLs: [URL] = []
private var chosenDocument: TinyPixDocument?
private var query: NSMetadataQuery!
```

Now, let's look at the new file-listing method. Remove the entire `reloadFiles()` method and replace it with Listing 14-10.

Listing 14-10. The iCloud reloadFiles Method

```
private func reloadFiles() {
    let fileManager = FileManager.default

    // Passing nil is OK here, matches the first entitlement
    let cloudURL = fileManager.urlForUbiquityContainerIdentifier(nil)
    print("Got cloudURL \(cloudURL)")
    if (cloudURL != nil) {
        query = NSMetadataQuery()
        query.predicate = Predicate(format: "%K like '*.tinypix'",
                                    NSMetadataItemFSNameKey)
```

```
    query.searchScopes = [NSMetadataQueryUbiquitousDocumentsScope]

    NotificationCenter.default.addObserver(self,
            selector: #selector(MasterViewController.updateUbiquitousDocuments(_:)),
            name: NSNotification.Name.NSMetadataQueryDidFinishGathering,
            object: nil)
    NotificationCenter.default.addObserver(self,
            selector: #selector(MasterViewController.updateUbiquitousDocuments(_:)),
            name: NSNotification.Name.NSMetadataQueryDidUpdate,
            object: nil)

    query.start()
  }
}
```

There are some new things here that are definitely worth mentioning. The first is seen in this line:

```
let cloudURL = fileManager.urlForUbiquityContainerIdentifier(nil)
```

Ubiquity? What are we talking about here? When it comes to iCloud, a lot of Apple's terminology for identifying resources in iCloud storage includes words like "ubiquity" and "ubiquitous" to indicate that something is omnipresent—accessible from any device using the same iCloud login credentials.

In this case, we're asking the file manager to give us a base URL that will let us access the iCloud directory associated with a particular container identifier. A container identifier is normally a string containing your company's unique bundle seed ID and the application identifier. The container identifier is used to pick one of the iCloud entitlements contained within your app. Passing nil here is a shortcut that just means "give me the first one in the list." Since our app contains only one checked item in that list (which you can see listed under "Containers" at the bottom of Figure 14-12), that shortcut suits our needs perfectly.

After that, we create and configure an instance of NSMetadataQuery:

```
query = NSMetadataQuery()
query.predicate = Predicate(format: "%K like '*.tinypix'",
                            NSMetadataItemFSNameKey)
query.searchScopes = [NSMetadataQueryUbiquitousDocumentsScope]
```

The NSMetaDataQuery class was originally written for use with the Spotlight search facility on OS X (macOS), but it's now doing extra duty as a way to let iOS apps search iCloud directories. We give the query a predicate, which limits its search results to include only those with the correct sort of file name. And we give it a search scope that limits it to look just within the Documents folder in the app's iCloud storage. Next, we set up some notifications to let us know when the query is complete and then we initiate the query:

```
NotificationCenter.default.addObserver(self,
        selector: #selector(MasterViewController.updateUbiquitousDocuments(_:)),
        name: NSNotification.Name.NSMetadataQueryDidFinishGathering,
        object: nil)
NotificationCenter.default.addObserver(self,
        selector: #selector(MasterViewController.updateUbiquitousDocuments(_:)),
        name: NSNotification.Name.NSMetadataQueryDidUpdate,
        object: nil)

query.start()
```

Now we need to implement the method that those notifications call when the query is done. Add this method just below the `reloadFiles()` method, as shown in Listing 14-11.

Listing 14-11. Update Method for When the Notifications Occur

```
func updateUbiquitousDocuments(_ notification: Notification) {
    documentFileURLs = []

    print("updateUbiquitousDocuments, results = \(query.results)")
    let results = query.results.sorted() { obj1, obj2 in
        let item1 = obj1 as! NSMetadataItem
        let item2 = obj2 as! NSMetadataItem
        let item1Date =
            item1.value(forAttribute: NSMetadataItemFSCreationDateKey) as! Date
        let item2Date =
            item2.value(forAttribute: NSMetadataItemFSCreationDateKey) as! Date
        let result = item1Date.compare(item2Date)
        return result == ComparisonResult.orderedAscending
    }
    for item in results as! [NSMetadataItem] {
        let url = item.value(forAttribute: NSMetadataItemURLKey) as! URL
        documentFileURLs.append(url)
    }
    tableView.reloadData()
}
```

The query's results contain a list of `NSMetadataItem` objects, from which we can get items like file URLs and creation dates. We use this to sort the items by date, and then grab all the URLs and save them in the existing `documentFileURLs` property for later use.

Save Location

The next change is to the `urlForFilename:` method, which once again is completely different. Here, we're using a ubiquitous URL to create a full path URL for a given file name. We insert `"Documents"` in the generated path as well, to make sure we're using the app's Documents directory in iCloud. Delete the old method and replace it with this new one:

```
private func urlForFileName(_ fileName: String) -> URL {
    // Be sure to insert "Documents" into the path
    let fm = FileManager.default
    let baseURL = fm.urlForUbiquityContainerIdentifier(nil)
    let pathURL = try! baseURL?.appendingPathComponent("Documents")
    let destinationURL = try! pathURL?.appendingPathComponent(fileName)
    return destinationURL!
}
```

Now, build and run your app on an actual iOS device (not the simulator). If you've run the previous version of the app on that device, you'll find that any TinyPix masterpieces you created earlier are now nowhere to be seen. This new version ignores the local Documents directory for the app and relies completely on iCloud. However, you should be able to create new documents and find that they stick around after quitting and restarting the app. Moreover, you can even delete the TinyPix app from your device entirely, run it again from Xcode, and find that all your iCloud-saved documents are available at once. If you have an additional iOS device configured with the same iCloud user, use Xcode to run the app on that device—and you'll see all the same documents appear there, as well! It's pretty sweet. You can also find these documents in the iCloud section of your iOS device's Settings app (look under Storage ➤ Manage Storage ➤ TinyPix), as well as the iCloud section of your Mac's System Preferences app if you're running OS X 10.8 or later.

Storing Preferences on iCloud

We can use iCloud to add one more piece of functionality with just a bit of effort. iOS's iCloud support includes a class called NSUbiquitousKeyValueStore, which works a lot like UserDefaults; however, its keys and values are stored in the cloud. This is great for application preferences, login tokens, and anything else that doesn't belong in a document, but could be useful when shared among all of a user's devices.

In TinyPix, we'll use this feature to store the user's preferred highlight color. That way, instead of needing to be configured on each device, the user sets the color once, and it shows up everywhere. Here's the plan of action:

- Whenever the user changes the tint color, we'll save the new value in NSUserDefaults. We'll also save it in the NSUbiquitousKeyValueStore, the iCloud version of user defaults, which will make it available to instances of the application on other devices.

- We'll register to be notified of changes in the NSUbiquitousKeyValueStore. When we're notified of a change, we'll get the new tint color value. At this point, we need to update the segmented control and the tint color used by the master view controller and the drawing color in the detail view controller. Rather than do this directly, we'll just save the new tint color in UserDefaults. Changing UserDefaults causes a notification to be generated. The detail view controller is already observing this notification, so it will update itself automatically. We're going to make some small changes to the master view controller so that it does the same thing.

It's important to be aware that updates to NSUbiquitousKeyValueStore do not propagate immediately to other devices and, in fact, if a device is not connected to iCloud for any reason, it won't see the update until it next connects. So don't expect changes to be seen immediately.

Let's start by registering to receive change notifications from the iCloud key-value store. Open AppDelegate.swift and add the following code to the application(application:, didFinishLaunchingWithOptions:) method, as shown in Listing 14-12.

Listing 14-12. Our Update application(_ application:, didFinishLaunchingWithOptions:) Method

```
func application(_ application: UIApplication, didFinishLaunchingWithOptions
launchOptions: [NSObject: AnyObject]?) -> Bool {
    // Override point for customization after application launch.
    let splitViewController = self.window!.rootViewController as! UISplitViewController
    let navigationController = splitViewController.viewControllers[splitViewController.
                          viewControllers.count-1] as! UINavigationController
    navigationController.topViewController!.navigationItem.leftBarButtonItem =
    splitViewController.displayModeButtonItem()
    splitViewController.delegate = self

    // Register for notification of iCloud key-value changes
    NotificationCenter.default.addObserver(self,
        selector: #selector(AppDelegate.iCloudKeysChanged(_:)),
        name: NSUbiquitousKeyValueStore.didChangeExternallyNotification,
        object: nil)
```

```
    // Start iCloud key-value updates
    NSUbiquitousKeyValueStore.default().synchronize()
    updateUserDefaultsFromICloud()

    return true
}
```

The first new line of code arranges for the application delegate's iCloudKeysChanged() method to be called when an NSUbiquitousKeyValueStoreDidChangeExternallyNotification occurs—that is, when iCloud notifies a change in any of the application's key/value pairs. The synchronize method causes local changes to the NSUbiquitousKeyValueStore to be written to iCloud in the background and notification of remote updates to start. The updateUserDefaultsFromICloud() method, which you'll see shortly, gets the current state of the selected tint color from the iCloud key-value store, if it's set, and stores it in the local user defaults, so that it will be used immediately.

Next, add the implementation of the iCloudKeysChanged() and updateUserDefaultsFromCloud() methods, as shown in Listing 14-13.

Listing 14-13. Updates from iCloud

```
func iCloudKeysChanged(_ notification: Notification) {
    updateUserDefaultsFromICloud()
}

private func updateUserDefaultsFromICloud() {
    let values = NSUbiquitousKeyValueStore.default().dictionaryRepresentation
    if values["selectedColorIndex"] != nil {
        let selectedColorIndex =
            Int(NSUbiquitousKeyValueStore.default().longLong(
                    forKey: "selectedColorIndex"))
        let prefs = UserDefaults.standard
        prefs.set(selectedColorIndex, forKey: "selectedColorIndex")
        prefs.synchronize()
    }
}
```

When a notification occurs, we use the longLongForKey() method to get the new selected tint color index from the key store. The API is very similar to that of UserDefaults, but there is no method to store an integer value, so we treat the tint color index as a long long instead. Once we have the value, we simply copy it to the UserDefaults and synchronize the change, so that a notification is generated. We already know that the detail view controller will update itself when it receives this notification. Next, we need to change the master view controller so that it does the same. Back in MasterViewController.swift, start by registering the controller to be notified of UserDefaults changes in its viewDidLoad() method:

```
reloadFiles()

NotificationCenter.default.addObserver(self,
    selector: #selector(MasterViewController.onSettingsChanged(_:)),
    name: UserDefaults.didChangeNotification ,
    object: nil)
```

Next, add the onSettingsChanged: method:

```
func onSettingsChanged(_ notification: Notification) {
    let prefs = UserDefaults.standard
    let selectedColorIndex = prefs.integer(forKey: "selectedColorIndex")
    setTintColorForIndex(selectedColorIndex)
    colorControl.selectedSegmentIndex = selectedColorIndex
}
```

This method updates the tint color of the segmented control using the same method that's called when the user taps one of its segments, but it gets the color index from UserDefaults instead of from the control.

Finally, when the user changes the tint color, we need to save the new index in the iCloud key-value store. Make the following changes to the chooseColor() method to take care of this:

```
@IBAction func chooseColor(_ sender: UISegmentedControl) {
    let selectedColorIndex = sender.selectedSegmentIndex
    setTintColorForIndex(selectedColorIndex)

    let prefs = UserDefaults.standard
    prefs.set(selectedColorIndex, forKey: "selectedColorIndex")
    prefs.synchronize()

    NSUbiquitousKeyValueStore.default()
            .set(Int64(selectedColorIndex),
            forKey: "selectedColorIndex")
    NSUbiquitousKeyValueStore.default().synchronize()
}
```

That's it. You can now run the app on multiple devices configured for the same iCloud user, and will see that setting the color on one device results in the new color appearing on the other device soon afterward.

Summary

We now have the basics of an iCloud-enabled, document-based application up and running, but there are a few more issues that you may want to consider. We're not going to cover these topics in this book; but if you're serious about making a great iCloud-based app, you'll want to think about these areas:

- Documents stored in iCloud are prone to conflicts. What happens if you edit the same TinyPix file on several devices at once? Fortunately, Apple has already thought of this and provides some ways to deal with these conflicts in your app. It's up to you to decide whether you want to ignore conflicts, try to fix them automatically, or ask the user to help sort out the problem. For full details, search for a document titled "Resolving Document Version Conflicts" in the Xcode documentation viewer.

- Apple recommends that you design your application to work in a completely offline mode in case the user isn't using iCloud for some reason. It also recommends that you provide a way for a user to move files between iCloud storage and local storage. Sadly, Apple doesn't provide or suggest any standard GUI for helping a user manage this, and current apps that provide this functionality, such as Apple's iWork apps, don't seem to handle it in a particularly user-friendly way. See Apple's "Managing the Life Cycle of a Document" in the Xcode documentation for more on this.

- Apple supports using iCloud for Core Data storage and even provides a class called UIManagedDocument that you can subclass if you want to make that work. See the UIManagedDocument class reference for more information. This architecture is a lot more complex and problematic than normal iCloud document storage. Apple has taken steps to improve things in recent versions of iOS, but it's still not perfectly smooth, so look before you leap.

CHAPTER 15

Multithreaded Programming Using Grand Central Dispatch

While the idea of programming multithreaded functions in any environment may seem daunting at first (see Figure 15-1), Apple came up with a new approach that makes multithreaded programming much easier. **Grand Central Dispatch** comprises language features, runtime libraries, and system enhancements that provide systemic, comprehensive improvements to the support for concurrent code execution on multicore hardware in iOS and macOS.

Figure 15-1. *Programming multithreaded applications can seem to be a disheartening experience*

© Molly Maskrey, Kim Topley, David Mark, Fredrik Olsson and Jeff Lamarche 2016
M. Maskrey et al., *Beginning iPhone Development with Swift 3*, DOI 10.1007/978-1-4842-2223-2_15

A big challenge facing developers today is writing software able to perform complex actions in response to user input while remaining responsive, so that the user isn't constantly kept waiting while the processor does some behind-the-scenes task. That challenge has been with us all along; and in spite of the advances in computing technology that bring us faster CPUs, the problem persists. Look at the nearest computer screen; chances are that the last time you sat down to work at your computer, at some point, your work flow was interrupted by a spinning mouse cursor of some kind or another.

One of the reasons this has become so problematic is the way software is typically written: as a sequence of events to be performed sequentially. Such software can scale up as CPU speeds increase, but only to a certain point. As soon as the program gets stuck waiting for an external resource, such as a file or a network connection, the entire sequence of events is effectively paused. All modern operating systems now allow the use of multiple threads of execution within a program, so that even if a single thread is stuck waiting for a specific event, the other threads can keep going. Even so, many developers see multithreaded programming as a mystery and shy away from it.

■ **Note**   A thread is a sequence of instructions managed independently by the operating system.

Apple provides Grand Central Dispatch (GCD) giving the developer an entirely new API for splitting up the work the application needs to do into smaller chunks that can be spread across multiple threads and, with the right hardware, multiple CPUs.

We access this API using Swift closures, providing a convenient way to structure interactions between different objects while keeping related code closer together in our methods.

Creating the SlowWorker Application

As a platform for demonstrating how GCD works, we'll create the SlowWorker application that consists of a simple interface driven by a single button and a text view. Click the button, and a synchronous task is immediately started, locking up the app for about ten seconds. Once the task completes, some text appears in the text view, as shown in Figure 15-2.

Figure 15-2. *The SlowWorker application hides its interface behind a single button. Click the button, and the interface hangs for about ten seconds while the application does its work*

Start by using the Single View Application template to make a new application in Xcode, as you've done many times before. Name this one SlowWorker, set Devices to Universal, click Next to save your project, and so on. Next, make the changes to ViewController.swift, as shown in Listing 15-1.

Listing 15-1. Add These Methods to the ViewController.swift File

```
@IBOutlet var startButton: UIButton!
@IBOutlet var resultsTextView: UITextView!

func fetchSomethingFromServer() -> String {
    Thread.sleep(forTimeInterval: 1)
    return "Hi there"
}
```

```
func processData(_ data: String) -> String {
    Thread.sleep(forTimeInterval: 2)
    return data.uppercased()
}

func calculateFirstResult(_ data: String) -> String {
    Thread.sleep(forTimeInterval: 3)
    return "Number of chars: \(data.characters.count)"
}

func calculateSecondResult(_ data: String) -> String {
    Thread.sleep(forTimeInterval: 4)
    return data.replacingOccurrences(of: "E", with: "e")
}

@IBAction func doWork(_ sender: AnyObject) {
        let startTime = NSDate()
        self.resultsTextView.text = ""
        let fetchedData = self.fetchSomethingFromServer()
        let processedData = self.processData(fetchedData)
        let firstResult = self.calculateFirstResult(processedData)
        let secondResult = self.calculateSecondResult(processedData)
        let resultsSummary =
            "First: [\(firstResult)]\nSecond: [\(secondResult)]"
        self.resultsTextView.text = resultsSummary
        let endTime = NSDate()
        print("Completed in \(endTime.timeIntervalSince(startTime as Date)) seconds")
}
```

As you can see, the work of this class (such as it is) is split up into a number of small pieces. This code simulates some slow activities, and none of those methods really do anything time-consuming at all. To make things interesting, each method contains a call to the sleep(forTimeInterval:) class method in Thread, which simply makes the program (specifically, the thread from which the method is called) effectively pause and do nothing at all for the given number of seconds. The doWork() method also contains code at the beginning and end to calculate the amount of time it took for all the work to be done.

Now open Main.storyboard and drag a Button and a Text View into the empty View window. Position the controls as shown in Figure 15-3. You'll see some default text. Clear the text in the Text View and change the button's title to Start Working. To set the auto layout constraints, start by selecting the Start Working button, and then click the Align button at the bottom right of the editor area. In the pop-up, check Horizontally in Container and Click Add 1 Constraint. Next, Control-drag from the button to the top of the View window, release the mouse and select Vertical Spacing to Top Layout Guide. To complete the constraints for this button, Control-drag from the button down to the text view, release the mouse, and select Vertical Spacing. To fix the position and size of the text view, expand the View Controller Scene in the Document Outline and Control-drag from the text view in the storyboard to the View icon in the Document Outline. Release the mouse and, when the pop-up appears, hold down the Shift key and select Leading Space to Container Margin, Trailing Space to Container Margin, and Vertical Spacing to Bottom Layout Guide, and then click return to apply the constraints. That completes the auto layout constraints for this application.

Figure 15-3. *The SlowWorker interface consists of a button and a text view*

Control-drag from View Controller icon in the Document Outline to connect the view controller's two outlets (i.e., the startButton and resultsTextView instance variables) to the button and the text view.

Next, Control-drag from the button to the View Controller, release the mouse and select the doWork() method in the pop-up so that it's called when the button is pressed. Finally, select the text view, use the Attributes Inspector to uncheck the Editable check box (it's in the upper-right corner), and delete the default text from the text view.

Save your work, and then select Run. Your app should start up, and pressing the button will make it work for about ten seconds (the sum of all those sleep amounts) before showing you the results. During your wait, you'll see that the Start Working button fades visibly, never turning back to its normal color until the "work" is done. Also, until the work is complete, the application's view is unresponsive. Tapping anywhere on the screen or rotating the device has no effect. In fact, the only way you can interact with your application during this time is by tapping the home button to switch away from it. This is exactly the state of affairs we want to avoid.

Threading Basics

Before we start implementing solutions, let's go over some concurrency basics. This is far from a complete description of threading in iOS or threading in general. I just want to explain enough for you to understand what we're doing in this chapter. Most modern operating systems (including, of course, iOS) support the notion of threads of execution. Each process can contain multiple threads, which all run concurrently. If there's just one processor core, the operating system will switch between all executing threads, much like it switches between all executing processes. If more than one core is available, the threads will be distributed among them, just as processes are.

All threads in a process share the same executable program code and the same global data. Each thread can also have some data that is exclusive to the thread. Threads can make use of a special structure called a **mutex** (short for **mutual exclusion**) or a lock, which can ensure that a particular chunk of code can't be run by multiple threads at once. This is useful for ensuring correct outcomes when multiple threads access the same data simultaneously, by locking out other threads when one thread is updating a value (in what's called a **critical section** of your code).

A common concern when dealing with threads is the idea of code being **thread-safe**. Some software libraries are written with thread concurrency in mind and have all their critical sections properly protected with mutexes. Some code libraries aren't thread-safe. For example, in Cocoa Touch, the Foundation framework is generally considered to be thread-safe. However, the UIKit framework (containing the classes specific to building GUI applications, such as UIApplication, UIView and all its subclasses, and so on) is, for the most part, not thread-safe. (Some UIKit functionality such as drawing is considered thread-safe however.) This means that in a running an iOS application, all method calls that deal with any UIKit objects should be executed from within the same thread, which is commonly known as the **main thread**. If you access UIKit objects from another thread, all bets are off. You are likely to encounter seemingly inexplicable bugs (or, even worse, you won't experience any problems, but some of your users will be affected by them after you ship your app).

■ **Tip**   A lot has been written about thread safety. It's well worth your time to dig in and try to digest as much of it as you can. One great place to start is Apple's own documentation. Take a few minutes and read through this page (it will definitely help):

https://developer.apple.com/library/ios/documentation/Cocoa/Conceptual/Multithreading/
ThreadSafetySummary/ThreadSafetySummary.html

Units of Work

The problem with the threading model described earlier is that, for the average programmer, writing error-free, multithreaded code is nearly impossible. This is not meant as a critique of our industry or of the average programmer's abilities; it's simply an observation. The complex interactions you must account for in your code when synchronizing data and actions across multiple threads are really just too much for most people to tackle. Imagine that 5% of all people have the capacity to write software at all. Only a small fraction of those 5% are really up to the task of writing heavy-duty multithreaded applications. Even people who have done it successfully will often advise others to not follow their example.

Fortunately, there are alternatives. It is possible to implement some concurrency without too much low-level detailed work. Just as we have the ability to display data on the screen without directly poking bits into video RAM and to read data from disk without interfacing directly with disk controllers, we can also leverage software abstractions that let us run our code on multiple threads without requiring us to do much directly with the threads.

The solutions Apple encourages us to use center around the idea of splitting up long-running tasks into units of work and putting those units into queues for execution. The system manages the queues for us, executing units of work on multiple threads. We don't need to start or manage the background threads directly, and we are freed from much of the bookkeeping that's usually involved in implementing multithreaded applications; the system takes care of that for us.

GCD: Low-Level Queuing

This idea of putting units of work into queues that can be executed in the background, with the system managing the threads for you, provides power and greatly simplifies many development situations where concurrency is needed. GCD made its debut on OS X (now macOS) several years ago, providing the infrastructure to do just that. A couple of years later, this technology came to the iOS platform as well. GCD puts some great concepts—units of work, painless background processing, and automatic thread management—into a C interface that can be used not only with Objective-C, but also with C, C++, and, of course, Swift. To top things off, Apple has made its implementation of GCD open source, so it can be ported to other Unix-like operating systems, as well.

One of the key concepts of GCD is the **queue**. The system provides a number of predefined queues, including a queue that's guaranteed to always do its work on the main thread. It's perfect for the non-thread-safe UIKit. You can also create your own queues—as many as you like. GCD queues are strictly first-in, first-out (FIFO). Units of work added to a GCD queue will always be started in the order they were placed in the queue. That said, they may not always finish in the same order, since a GCD queue will automatically distribute its work among multiple threads, if possible.

GCD accesses a pool of threads that are reused throughout the lifetime of the application. It tries to maintain a number of threads appropriate for the machine's architecture. It automatically takes advantage of a more powerful machine by utilizing more processor cores when it has work to do. Until a few years ago, iOS devices were all single-core, so this wasn't much of an issue. But now that all iOS devices released in the past few years feature multicore processors, GCD has become truly useful.

GCD uses closures to encapsulate the code to be added to a queue. Closures are first-class language citizens in Swift—you can assign a closure to a variable, pass one to a method, or return one as the result of a method call. Closures are the equivalent of Objective-C's blocks and similar features, sometimes referred to using the term **lambdas**, in other programming languages, such as Python. Much like a method or function, a closure can take one or more parameters and specify a return value, although closures used with GCD can neither accept arguments nor return a value. To declare a closure variable, you simply assign to it some code wrapped in curly braces, optionally with arguments:

```
// Declare a closure variable "loggerClosure" with no parameters
// and no return value.
let loggerClosure = {
    print("I'm just glad they didn't call it a lambda")
}
```

You can execute the closure in the same way as you call a function:

```
// Execute the closure, producing some output in the console.
loggerClosure()
```

Improving SlowWorker

To see how to use closures with GCD, let's revisit SlowWorker's doWork() method. It currently looks like this:

```
@IBAction func doWork(_ sender: AnyObject) {
        let startTime = NSDate()
        self.resultsTextView.text = ""
        let fetchedData = self.fetchSomethingFromServer()
        let processedData = self.processData(fetchedData)
        let firstResult = self.calculateFirstResult(processedData)
```

```
    let secondResult = self.calculateSecondResult(processedData)
    let resultsSummary =
        "First: [\(firstResult)]\nSecond: [\(secondResult)]"
    self.resultsTextView.text = resultsSummary
    let endTime = NSDate()
    print("Completed in \(endTime.timeIntervalSince(startTime as Date)) seconds")
}
```

We can make this method run entirely in the background by wrapping all the code in a closure and passing it to a GCD function called DispatchQueue. This function takes two parameters: a GCD queue and the closure to assign to the queue. Make the changes in Listing 15-2 to your copy of doWork().

Listing 15-2. Modifications to the doWork Method to Use GCD

```
@IBAction func doWork(sender: AnyObject) {
    let startTime = NSDate()
    resultsTextView.text = ""
    let queue = DispatchQueue.global(qos: .default)
    queue.async {
        let fetchedData = self.fetchSomethingFromServer()
        let processedData = self.processData(fetchedData)
        let firstResult = self.calculateFirstResult(processedData)
        let secondResult = self.calculateSecondResult(processedData)
        let resultsSummary =
            "First: [\(firstResult)]\nSecond: [\(secondResult)]"
        self.resultsTextView.text = resultsSummary
        let endTime = NSDate()
        print("Completed in \(endTime.timeIntervalSince(startTime as Date)) seconds")
    }
}
```

The first changed line grabs a preexisting global queue that's always available, using the DispatchQueue.global() function. That function takes one arguments letting you specify a priority. If you specify a different priority in the argument you will actually get a different global queue, which the system will prioritize differently. For now, we'll stick with the default global queue.

The queue is then passed to the queue.async() function, along with the closure. GCD takes the closure and puts it on the queue, from where it will be scheduled to run on a background thread and executed one step at a time, just as when it was running in the main thread.

Note that we defined a variable called startTime just before the closure is created, and then use its value at the end of the closure. Intuitively, this doesn't seem to make sense because, by the time the closure is executed, the doWork() method has returned, so the NSDate instance that the startTime variable is pointing to should already be released! This is a crucial point to understand about closures: if a closure accesses any variables from "the outside" during its execution, then some special setup happens when the closure is created, allowing it to continue to access to them. All of this is done automatically by the Swift compiler and runtime—you don't need to do anything special to make it happen.

Don't Forget That Main Thread

Getting back to the project at hand, there's one problem here: UIKit thread-safety. Remember that messaging any GUI object from a background thread, including our resultsTextView, is a no-no. In fact, if you run the example now, you'll see an exception appear in the Xcode console after about ten seconds, when the closure tries to update the text view. Fortunately, GCD provides a way to deal with this, too. Inside the closure, we can call another dispatching function, passing work back to the main thread. Make one additional change to your version of doWork(), as shown in Listing 15-3.

Listing 15-3. The modified doWork Method

```
@IBAction func doWork(sender: AnyObject) {
    let startTime = NSDate()
    resultsTextView.text = ""
    let queue = DispatchQueue.global(attributes: DispatchQueue.GlobalAttributes.qosDefault)
    queue.async {
        let fetchedData = self.fetchSomethingFromServer()
        let processedData = self.processData(fetchedData)
        let firstResult = self.calculateFirstResult(processedData)
        let secondResult = self.calculateSecondResult(processedData)
        let resultsSummary =
            "First: [\(firstResult)]\nSecond: [\(secondResult)]"
        DispatchQueue.main.async {
            self.resultsTextView.text = resultsSummary
        }
        let endTime = NSDate()
        print("Completed in \(endTime.timeIntervalSince(startTime as Date)) seconds")

    }
}
```

Giving Some Feedback

If you build and run your app at this point, you'll see that it now seems to work a bit more smoothly, at least in some sense. The button no longer gets stuck in a highlighted position after you touch it, which perhaps leads you to tap again, and again, and so on. If you look in the Xcode console log, you'll see the result of each of those taps, but only the results of the last tap will be shown in the text view. What we really want to do is enhance the GUI so that, after the user presses the button, the display is immediately updated in a way that indicates that an action is underway. We also want the button to be disabled while the work is in progress so that the user can't keep clicking it to spawn more and more work into background threads. We'll do this by adding a UIActivityIndicatorView to our display. This class provides the sort of spinner seen in many applications and web sites. Start by adding an outlet for it at the top of ViewController.swift:

@IBOutlet var spinner : UIActivityIndicatorView!

Next, open Main.Storyboard, locate an Activity Indicator View in the library, and drag it into our view, next to the button. You'll need to add layout constraints to fix the activity indicator's position relative to the button. One way to do this is to Control-drag from the button to the activity indicator and select Horizontal Spacing from the pop-up menu to fix the horizontal separation between them, and then Control-drag again and select Center Vertically to make sure that their centers remain vertically aligned.

With the activity indicator spinner selected, use the Attributes Inspector to check the Hides When Stopped check box so that our spinner will appear only when we tell it to start spinning (no one wants an unspinning spinner in their GUI). Next, Control-drag from the View Controller icon to the spinner and connect the spinner outlet. Save your changes.

Now open ViewController.swift. Here, we'll first work on the doWork() method a bit, adding a few lines to manage the appearance of the button and the spinner when the user taps the button and when the work is done. We'll first set the button's enabled property to false, which prevents it from registering any taps and also shows that the button is disabled by making its text gray and somewhat transparent. Next, we get the spinner moving by calling its **startAnimating**() method. At the end of the closure, we re-enable the button and stop the spinner, which causes it to disappear again, as shown in Listing 15-4.

Listing 15-4. Adding the Spinner Functions to our doWork Method

```
@IBAction func doWork(sender: AnyObject) {
    let startTime = NSDate()
    resultsTextView.text = ""
    startButton.isEnabled = false
    spinner.startAnimating()
    let queue = DispatchQueue.global(qos: .default)
    queue.async {
        let fetchedData = self.fetchSomethingFromServer()
        let processedData = self.processData(fetchedData)
        let firstResult = self.calculateFirstResult(processedData)
        let secondResult = self.calculateSecondResult(processedData)
        let resultsSummary =
            "First: [\(firstResult)]\nSecond: [\(secondResult)]"
        DispatchQueue.main.async {
            self.resultsTextView.text = resultsSummary
            self.startButton.isEnabled = true
            self.spinner.stopAnimating()
        }
        let endTime = NSDate()
        print("Completed in \(endTime.timeIntervalSince(startTime as Date)) seconds")

    }
}
```

Build and run the app, and press the button. Even though the work being done takes a few seconds, the user isn't just left hanging. The button is disabled and looks the part as well. Also, the animated spinner lets the user know that the app hasn't actually hung up and can be expected to return to normal at some point.

Concurrent Closures

The sharp-eyed among you will notice that, after going through these motions, we still haven't really changed the basic sequential layout of our algorithm (if you can even call this simple list of steps an algorithm). All that we're doing is moving a chunk of this method to a background thread and then finishing up in the main thread. The Xcode console output proves it: this work takes ten seconds to run, just as it did at the outset. The issue is that the calculateFirstResult() and calculateSecondResult() methods don't depend on each and therefore don't need to be called in sequence. Doing them concurrently gives us a substantial speedup.

Fortunately, GCD has a way to accomplish this by using what's called a **dispatch group**. All closures that are dispatched asynchronously within the context of a group, via the dispatch_group_async() function, are set loose to execute as fast as they can, including being distributed to multiple threads for concurrent execution, if possible. We can also use dispatch_group_notify() to specify an additional closure that will be executed when all the closures in the group have been run to completion.

Make these final changes to the doWork method, as shown in Listing 15-5.

Listing 15-5. The Final Version of Our doWork Method

```
@IBAction func doWork(_ sender: AnyObject) {
    let startTime = Date()
    self.resultsTextView.text = ""
    startButton.isEnabled = false
    spinner.startAnimating()
    let queue = DispatchQueue.global(qos: .default)
    queue.async {
        let fetchedData = self.fetchSomethingFromServer()
        let processedData = self.processData(fetchedData)
        var firstResult: String!
        var secondResult: String!
        let group = DispatchGroup()

        queue.async(group: group) {
            firstResult = self.calculateFirstResult(processedData)
        }
        queue.async(group: group) {
            secondResult = self.calculateSecondResult(processedData)
        }

        group.notify(queue: queue) {
            let resultsSummary = "First: [\(firstResult!)]\nSecond: [\(secondResult!)]"
            DispatchQueue.main.async {
                self.resultsTextView.text = resultsSummary
                self.startButton.isEnabled = true
                self.spinner.stopAnimating()
            }
            let endTime = Date()
            print("Completed in \(endTime.timeIntervalSince(startTime)) seconds")
        }
    }
}
```

One complication here is that each of the calculate methods returns a value that we want to grab, so we need to make sure that the variables firstResult and secondResult can be assigned from the closures. To do this, we declare them using var instead of let. However, Swift requires a variable that's referenced from a closure to be initialized, so the following declarations don't work:

```
var firstResult: String
var secondResult: String
```

You can, of course, work around this problem by initializing both variables with an arbitrary value, but it's easier to make them implicitly unwrapped optionals by adding ! to the declaration:

```
var firstResult: String!
var secondResult: String!
```

Now, Swift doesn't require an initialization, but we need to be sure that both variables will have a value when they are eventually read. In this case, we can be sure of that, because the variables are read in the completion closure for the async group, by which time they are certain to have been assigned a value. With this in place, build and run the app again. You'll see that your efforts have paid off. What was once a ten-second operation now takes just seven seconds, thanks to the fact that we're running both of the calculations simultaneously.

Obviously, our contrived example gets the maximum effect because these two "calculations" don't actually do anything but cause the thread they're running on to sleep. In a real application, the speedup would depend on what sort of work is being done and what resources are available. The performance of CPU-intensive calculations is helped by this technique only if multiple CPU cores are available. It will get better almost for free as more cores are added to future iOS devices. Other uses, such as fetching data from multiple network connections at once, would see a speed increase even with just one CPU.

As you can see, GCD is not a panacea. Using GCD won't automatically speed up every application. But by carefully applying these techniques at those points in your app where speed is essential, or where you find that your application feels like it's lagging in its responses to the user, you can easily provide a better user experience, even in situations where you can't improve the real performance.

Background Processing

Another important technology for handling concurrency is background processing. This allows your apps to run in the background—in some circumstances, even after the user has pressed the home button.

This functionality should not be confused with the true multitasking that modern desktop operating systems now feature, where all the programs you launch remain resident in the system RAM until you explicitly quit them (or until the operating system needs to free up some space and starts swapping them to disk). iOS devices still have too little RAM to be able to pull that off very well. Instead, this background processing is meant to allow applications that require specific kinds of system functionality to continue to run in a constrained manner when they are in the background. For instance, if you have an app that plays an audio stream from an Internet radio station, iOS will let that app continue to run, even if the user switches to another app. Beyond that, it will even provide standard pause and volume controls in the iOS control center (the translucent control panel that appears when you swipe up from the bottom of the screen) while your app is playing audio.

Assume you're creating an app that does one of the following things: plays audio even when the user is running another app, requests continuous location updates, responds to a special type of push request telling it to load new data from a server, or implements Voice over IP (VoIP) to let users send and receive phone calls on the Internet. In each of these cases, you can declare this situation in your app's Info.plist file, and the system will treat your app in a special way. This usage, while interesting, is probably not something that most readers of this book will be tackling right away, so we're not going to delve into it here.

Besides running apps in the background, iOS also includes the ability to put an app into a suspended state after the user presses the home button. This state of suspended execution is conceptually similar to putting your Mac into sleep mode. The entire working memory of the application is held in RAM; it just isn't executed while suspended. As a result, switching back to such an application is lightning-fast. This isn't limited to special applications. In fact, it is the default behavior of any app you build with Xcode (though this can be disabled by another setting in the Info.plist file). To see this in action, open your device's Mail application and drill down into a message. Next, press the home button, open the Notes application, and select a note. Now double-tap the home button and switch back to Mail. You'll see that there's no perceptible lag; it just slides into place as if it had been running all along.

For most applications, this sort of automatic suspension and resumption is all you're likely to need. However, in some situations, your app may need to know when it's about to be suspended and when it has just been awakened. The system provides ways of notifying an app about changes to its execution state via the UIApplication class, which has a number of delegate methods and notifications for just this purpose. I'll show you how to use them later in this chapter.

When your application is about to be suspended, one thing it can do, regardless of whether it's one of the special backgroundable application types, is request a bit of additional time to run in the background. The idea is to make sure your app has enough time to close any open files, network resources, and so on. We'll see an example of this shortly.

Application Life Cycle

Before we get into the specifics of how to deal with changes to your app's execution state, let's talk a bit about the various states in its life cycle:

- **Not Running**: This is the state that all apps are in on a freshly rebooted device. An application that has been launched at any point after the device is turned on will return to this state only under specific conditions:

  - If its Info.plist includes the UIApplicationExitsOnSuspend key (with its value set to YES)

  - If it was previously Suspended and the system needs to clear out some memory

  - If it crashes while running

- **Active**: This is the normal running state of an application when it's displayed on the screen. It can receive user input and update the display.

- **Background**: In this state, an app is given some time to execute some code, but it can't directly access the screen or get any user input. All apps enter this state briefly when the user presses the home button; most of them quickly move on to the Suspended state. Apps that want to do any sort of background processing stay in this state until they're made Active again.

- **Suspended**: A Suspended app is frozen. This is what happens to normal apps after their brief stint in the Background state. All the memory the app was using while it was active is held just as it was. If the user brings the app back to the Active state, it will pick up right where it left off. On the other hand, if the system needs more memory for whichever app is currently Active, any Suspended apps may be terminated (and placed back into the Not Running state) and their memory freed for other use.

- **Inactive**: An app enters the Inactive state only as a temporary rest stop between two other states. The only way an app can stay Inactive for any length of time is if the user is dealing with a system prompt (such as those shown for an incoming call or SMS message) or if the user has locked the screen. This state is basically a sort of limbo.

State-Change Notifications

To manage changes between these states, UIApplication defines a number of methods that its delegate can implement. In addition to the delegate methods, UIApplication also defines a matching set of notification names (see Table 15-1). This allows other objects besides the app delegate to register for notifications when the application's state changes.

Table 15-1. *Delegate Methods for Tracking Your Application's Execution State and Their Corresponding Notification Names*

Delegate Method	Notification Name
`application(_:didFinishLaunchingWithOptions:)`	`UIApplicationDidFinishLaunching`
`applicationWillResignActive()`	`UIApplicationWillResignActive`
`applicationDidBecomeActive()`	`UIApplicationDidBecomeActive`
`applicationDidEnterBackground()`	`UIApplicationDidEnterBackground`
`applicationWillEnterForeground()`	`UIApplicationWillEnterForeground`
`applicationWillTerminate()`	`UIApplicationWillTerminate`

Note that each of these methods is directly related to one of the running states: Active, Inactive, and Background. Each delegate method is called (and each notification posted) in only one of those states. The most important state transitions are between Active and other states. Some transitions, like from Background to Suspended, occur without any notice whatsoever. Let's go through these methods and discuss how they're meant to be used.

The first of these, `application(_:didFinishLaunchingWithOptions:)`, we've already seen many times in this book. It's the primary way of doing application-level coding directly after the app has launched. There is a similar method called `application(_:willFinishLaunchingWithOptions:)` that's called first and which is intended for applications that use the view controller-based state save and restore feature (which is beyond the scope of this book). That method is not listed here because it's not associated with a state change.

The next two methods, `applicationWillResignActive()` and `applicationDidBecomeActive()`, are both used in a number of circumstances. If the user presses the home button, `applicationWillResignActive()` gets called. If the user later brings the app back to the foreground, `applicationDidBecomeActive()` is called. The same sequence of events occurs if the user receives a phone call. `applicationDidBecomeActive()` is also called when the application launches for the first time. In general, this pair of methods brackets the movement of an application from the Active state to the Inactive state. They are good places to enable and disable any animations, in-app audio, or other items that deal with the app's presentation to the user. Because of the multiple situations where `applicationDidBecomeActive()` is used, you may want to put some of your app initialization code there instead of in `application(_:didFinishLaunchingWithOptions:)`. Note that you should not assume in `applicationWillResignActive()` that the application is about to be sent to the background; it may just be a temporary change that ends up with a move back to the Active state.

After those methods we see `applicationDidEnterBackground()` and `applicationWillEnterForeground()`, which have a slightly different usage area: dealing with an app that is definitely being sent to the background. `applicationDidEnterBackground()` is where your app should free all resources that can be re-created later, save all user data, close network connections, and so forth. This is also the spot where you can request more time to run in the background if you need it, as we'll see shortly. If you spend too much time doing things in `applicationDidEnterBackground()`—more than about five seconds—the system will decide that your app is misbehaving and terminate it. You should implement `applicationWillEnterForeground()` to re-create whatever was torn down in `applicationDidEnterBackground()`, such as reloading user data, reestablishing network connections, and so on. Note that when `applicationDidEnterBackground()` is called, you can safely assume that `applicationWillResignActive()` has also been recently called. Likewise, when `applicationWillEnterForeground()` gets called, you can assume that `applicationDidBecomeActive()` will soon be called, as well.

Finally, `applicationWillTerminate()`, which you'll probably rarely use, if ever, is called only if your application is already in the background and the system decides to skip suspension for some reason and simply terminate the app.

Now that you have a basic theoretical understanding of the states an application transitions between, let's put this knowledge to the test with a simple app that does nothing more than write a message to Xcode's console log each time one of these methods is called. We'll then manipulate the running app in a variety of ways, just as a user might, and see which transitions occur. To get the most out of this example, you'll need an iOS device. If you don't have one, you can use the simulator and skip over the parts that require a device.

Creating State Lab

In Xcode, create a new project based on the Single View Application template and name it State Lab. Initially at least, this app won't display anything but the default white screen it's born with. Later, we'll make it do something more interesting, but for now, all the output it's going to generate will end up in the Xcode console. The AppDelegate.swift file already contains all the methods we're interested in. We just need to add some logging, as shown in bold. Note that we've also removed the comments from these methods, as shown in Listing 15-6, just for the sake of brevity.

Listing 15-6. The AppDelegate.swift Logging Methods

```
func application(_ application: UIApplication,
                 didFinishLaunchingWithOptions launchOptions: [NSObject: AnyObject]?) -> Bool {
    print(#function)
    return true
}

func applicationWillResignActive(_ application: UIApplication) {
    print(#function)
}

func applicationDidEnterBackground(_ application: UIApplication) {
    print(#function)
}

func applicationWillEnterForeground(_ application: UIApplication) {
    print(#function)
}

func applicationDidBecomeActive(_ application: UIApplication) {
    print(#function)
}

func applicationWillTerminate(_ application: UIApplication) {
    print(#function)
}
```

You may be wondering about the value that's being passed to the `print()` function in each of these methods: the literal expression `#function` evaluates to the name of the method in which it appears. Here, we are using it to get the current method name without needing to retype it or copy and paste it into each of the lifecycle methods.

Exploring Execution States

Now build and run the app and take a look at the console (View ➤ Debug Area ➤ Activate Console), where you should see something like this:

```
application(_:didFinishLaunchingWithOptions:)
applicationDidBecomeActive
```

among a number of other messages. You can use the search field below the console output to filter what you observe.

Here, you can see that the application has successfully launched and been moved into the Active state. Now press the home button (if you're using the simulator, you'll have to do this by selecting Hardware ➤ Home from the simulator's menu or ⇧⌘H on the keyboard). You should see the following in the console:

```
applicationWillResignActive
applicationDidEnterBackground
```

These two lines show the app actually transitioning between two states: it first becomes Inactive, and then goes to Background. What you can't see here is that the app also switches to a third state: Suspended. Remember that you do not get any notification that this has happened; it's completely outside your control. Note that the app is still live in some sense, and Xcode is still connected to it, even though it's not actually getting any CPU time. Verify this by tapping the app's icon to relaunch it, which should produce this output:

```
applicationWillEnterForeground
applicationDidBecomeActive
```

There you are, back in business. The app was previously Suspended, is woken up to Inactive, and then ends up Active again. So, what happens when the app is really terminated? Tap the home button again and you'll see this:

```
applicationWillResignActive
applicationDidEnterBackground
```

Now double-tap the home button (or on the simulator, press ⇧⌘HH—you need to press the H key twice). The sideways-scrolling screen of apps should appear. Press and swipe upward on the State Lab screenshot until it flies offscreen, killing the application. You should see something like:

```
2016-07-21 10:15:40.201746 temp[2825:864732] [Common] <FBSUIApplicationWorkspaceClient
[0x6080000f8700]>: Received exit event
applicationDidEnterBackground
applicationWillTerminate
```

■ **Tip** Do not rely on the `applicationWillTerminate()` method being called to save the state of your application—do this in `applicationDidEnterBackground()` instead.

There's one more interesting interaction to examine here. It's what happens when the system shows an alert dialog, temporarily taking over the input stream from the app and putting it into an Inactive state. This state can be readily triggered only when running on a real device instead of the simulator, using the built-in Messages app. Messages, like many other apps, can receive messages from the outside and display them in several ways.

To see how these are set up, run the Settings app on your device, choose Notifications from the list, and then select the Messages app from the list of apps. The hot "new" way to show messages, which debuted way back in iOS 5, is called **Banners**. This works by showing a small banner overlaid at the top of the screen, which doesn't need to interrupt whatever app is currently running. What we want to show is the bad old Alerts method, which makes a modal panel appear in front of the current app, requiring a user action. Under the heading ALERT STYLE WHEN UNLOCKED, select Alerts so that the Messages app turns back into the kind of pushy jerk that users of iOS 4 and earlier always had to deal with.

Now back to your computer. In Xcode, use the pop-up at the upper left to switch from the simulator to your device, and then hit the Run button to build and run the app on your device. Now all you need to do is send a message to your device from the outside. If your device is an iPhone, you can send it an SMS message from another phone. If it's an iPod touch or an iPad, you're limited to Apple's own iMessage communication, which works on all iOS devices, as well as OS X in the Messages app. Figure out what works for your setup, and send your device a message via SMS or iMessage. When your device displays the system alert showing the incoming message, this will appear in the Xcode console:

```
applicationWillResignActive
```

Note that our app didn't get sent to the background. It's in the Inactive state and can still be seen behind the system alert. If this app were a game or had any video, audio, or animations running, this is where we would probably want to pause them.

Press the Close button on the alert, and you'll get this:

```
applicationDidBecomeActive
```

Now let's see what happens if you decide to reply to the message instead. Send another message to your device, generating this:

```
applicationWillResignActive
```

This time, hit Reply, which switches you over to the Messages app. You should see the following flurry of activity:

```
applicationDidBecomeActive
applicationWillResignActive
applicationDidEnterBackground
```

Our app quickly becomes Active, becomes Inactive again, and finally goes to Background (and then, silently, Suspended).

Using Execution State Changes

So, what should we make of all this? Based on what was just demonstrated, it seems like there's a clear strategy to follow when dealing with these state changes:

Active ➤ Inactive

Use applicationWillResignActive()/UIApplicationWillResignActive notification to "pause" your app's display. If your app is a game, you probably already have the ability to pause the gameplay in some way. For other kinds of apps, make sure no time-critical demands for user input are in the works because your app won't be getting any user input for a while.

Inactive ➤ Background

Use `applicationDidEnterBackground()`/`UIApplicationDidEnterBackground` notification to release any resources that don't need to be kept around when the app is backgrounded (such as cached images or other easily reloadable data) or that might not survive backgrounding anyway (such as active network connections). Getting rid of excess memory usage here will make your app's eventual Suspended snapshot smaller, thereby decreasing the risk that your app will be purged from RAM entirely. You should also use this opportunity to save any application data that will help your users pick up where they left off the next time your app is relaunched. If your app comes back to the Active state, normally this won't matter; however, in case it's purged and must be relaunched, your users will appreciate starting off in the same place.

Background ➤ Inactive

Use `applicationWillEnterForeground()`/`UIApplicationWillEnterForeground` notification to undo anything you did when switching from Inactive to Background. For example, here you can reestablish persistent network connections.

Inactive ➤ Active

Use `applicationDidBecomeActive()`/`UIApplicationDidBecomeActive` notification to undo anything you did when switching from Active to Inactive. Note that, if your app is a game, this probably does not mean dropping out of pause straight to the game; you should let your users do that on their own. Also keep in mind that this method and notification are used when an app is freshly launched, so anything you do here must work in that context, as well.

There is one special consideration for the Inactive ➤ Background transition. Not only does it have the longest description in the previous list, but it's also probably the most code- and time-intensive transition in applications because of the amount of bookkeeping you may want your app to do. When this transition is underway, the system won't give you the benefit of an unlimited amount of time to save your changes here. It gives you a few seconds. If your app takes longer than that to return from the delegate method (and handle any notifications you've registered for), then your app will be summarily purged from memory and pushed into the Not Running state. If this seems unfair, don't worry because there is a reprieve available. While handling that delegate method or notification, you can ask the system to perform some additional work for you in a background queue, which buys you some extra time.

Handling the Inactive State

The simplest state change your app is likely to encounter is from Active to Inactive, and then back to Active. You may recall that this is what happens if your iPhone receives an SMS message while your app is running and displays it for the user. In this section, we're going to make State Lab do something visually interesting so that you can see what happens if you ignore that state change. Next, I'll show you how to fix it.

We'll also add a `UILabel` to our display and make it move using Core Animation, which is a really nice way of animating objects in iOS.

Start by adding a `UILabel` in ViewController.swift:

```
class ViewController: UIViewController {
    private var label:UILabel!
```

Now let's set up the label when the view loads. Modify the `viewDidLoad()` method as shown in Listing 15-7.

Listing 15-7. Our Modified viewDidLoad Method

```
override func viewDidLoad() {
    super.viewDidLoad()
    // Do any additional setup after loading the view, typically from a nib.
    let bounds = view.bounds

    let labelFrame = CGRect(origin: CGPoint(x: bounds.origin.x, y: bounds.midY - 50) ,
                   size: CGSize(width:  bounds.size.width, height: 100))
    label = UILabel(frame: labelFrame)
    label.font = UIFont(name: "Helvetica", size:70)
    label.text = "Bazinga!"
    label.textAlignment = NSTextAlignment.center
    label.backgroundColor = UIColor.clear()
    view.addSubview(label)
}
```

This vertically centers the label in its parent view and makes it stretch across the full width of its parent. Next, let's set up some animation. We'll define two methods: one to rotate the label to an upside-down position:

```
func rotateLabelDown() {
    UIView.animate(withDuration: 0.5, animations: {
            self.label.transform = CGAffineTransform(rotationAngle: CGFloat(M_PI))
        },
        completion: {(Bool) -> Void in
            self.rotateLabelUp()
        }
    )
}
```

This one rotates it back to normal:

```
func rotateLabelUp() {
    UIView.animate(withDuration: 0.5, animations: {
            self.label.transform = CGAffineTransform(rotationAngle: 0)
        },
        completion: {(Bool) -> Void in
                self.rotateLabelDown()
        }
    )
}
```

This deserves a bit of explanation. UIView defines a class method called animate(withDuration: completion:), which sets up an animation. Attributes that can be animated, which we set within the animations closure, don't have an immediate effect on the receiver. Instead, Core Animation will smoothly transition that attribute from its current value to the new value we specify. This is what's called an **implicit animation**, which is one of the main features of Core Animation. The completion closure lets us specify what will happen after the animation is complete. Note carefully the syntax of this closure:

```
completion: {(Bool) -> Void in
    if self.animate {
        self.rotateLabelDown()
    }
}
```

The code in bold is the signature of the closure—it says that the closure is called with a single Boolean argument and returns nothing. The argument has a value of `true` if the animation completed normally, `false` if it was cancelled. In this example, we don't make any use of this argument.

So, each of these methods sets the label's `transform` property to a particular rotation angle, specified in radians, and uses the completion closure to call the other method, so the text will continue to animate back and forth forever.

Finally, we need to set up a way to kick-start the animation. For now, we'll do this by adding this line at the end of `viewDidLoad()`:

```
rotateLabelDown();
```

Build and run the app. You should see the Bazinga! label rotate back and forth, as shown in Figure 15-4.

Figure 15-4. *The State Lab application rotating the label*

To test the Active ➤ Inactive transition, you really need to once again run this on an actual iPhone and send an SMS message to it from elsewhere. Build and run the app on an iPhone, and see that the animation is running along. Now send an SMS message to the device. When the system alert comes up to show the message, you'll see that the animation keeps on running. That may be slightly comical, but it's probably irritating for a user. We will use application state transition notifications to stop our animation when this occurs.

Our controller class will need to have some internal state to keep track of whether it should be animating at any given time. For this purpose, let's add a property to the ViewController class:

```
class ViewController: UIViewController {
    private var label:UILabel!
    private var animate = false
```

As you've seen, changes in the application state are notified to the application delegate, but since our class isn't the application delegate, we can't just implement the delegate methods and expect them to work. Instead, we sign up to receive notifications from the application when its execution state changes. Do this by adding the following code to the end of the viewDidLoad method in ViewController.swift:

```
    let center = NotificationCenter.default
    center.addObserver(self, selector: #selector(ViewController.applicationWillResignActive),
            name: Notification.Name.UIApplicationWillResignActive, object: nil)
      center.addObserver(self, selector: #selector(ViewController.applicationDidBecomeActive),
            name: NSNotification.Name.UIApplicationDidBecomeActive, object: nil)
```

This sets up the notifications so that each will call a method in our class at the appropriate time. Add the following methods to the ViewController class:

```
func applicationWillResignActive() {
    print("VC: \(#function)")
    animate = false
}

func applicationDidBecomeActive() {
    print("VC: \(#function)")
    animate = true
    rotateLabelDown()
}
```

These methods include the same method logging as before, just so you can see where the methods occur in the Xcode console. We added the preface "VC: " to distinguish this call from the similar calls in the delegate (VC is for view controller). The first of these methods just turns off the animate flag. The second turns the flag back on, and then actually starts up the animations again. For that first method to have any effect, we need to add some code to check the animate flag and keep on animating only if it's enabled:

```
func rotateLabelUp() {
    UIView.animate(withDuration: 0.5, animations: {
            self.label.transform = CGAffineTransform(rotationAngle: 0)
        },
        completion: {(Bool) -> Void in
            if self.animate {
                self.rotateLabelDown()
            }
```

```
        }
    )
}
```

We added this to the completion block of `rotateLabelUp()`, (and only there) so that our animation will stop only when the text is right-side up. Finally, since we are now starting the animation when the application becomes active, and this happens right after it is launched, we no longer need the call `rotateLabelDown()` in `viewDidLoad()`, so delete it:

```
override func viewDidLoad() {

    rotateLabelDown();
    let center = NSNotificationCenter.default
```

Now build and run the app again, and you should see that it's animating as before. Once again, send an SMS message to your iPhone. This time, when the system alert appears, you'll see that the animation in the background stops as soon as the text is right-side up. Tap the Close button, and the animation starts back up.

Now you've seen what to do for the simple case of switching from Active to Inactive and back. The bigger task, and perhaps the more important one, is dealing with a switch to the background and then back to foreground.

Handling the Background State

As mentioned earlier, switching to the Background state is pretty important to ensure the best possible user experience. This is the spot where you'll want to discard any resources that can easily be reacquired (or will be lost anyway when your app goes silent) and save information about your app's current state, all without occupying the main thread for more than five seconds.

To demonstrate some of these behaviors, we're going to extend State Lab in a few ways. First, we're going to add an image to the display so that I can later show you how to get rid of the in-memory image. Then I'm going to show you how to save some information about the app's state, so we can easily restore it later. Finally, I'll show you how to make sure these activities aren't taking up too much main thread time by putting all this work into a background queue.

Removing Resources When Entering the Background

Start by adding smiley.png from the 15 - Image folder in the book's source archive to your project's State Lab folder. Be sure to enable the check box that tells Xcode to copy the file to your project directory. Don't add it to the Assets.xcassets asset catalog because that would provide automatic caching, which would interfere with the specific resource management we're going to implement.

Now let's add properties for both the image and an image view to ViewController.swift:

```
class ViewController: UIViewController {
    private var label:UILabel!
    private var smiley:UIImage!
    private var smileyView:UIImageView!
    private var animate = false
```

Next, set up the image view and put it on the screen by modifying the `viewDidLoad()` method, as shown in Listing 15-7.

Listing 15-7. Modified viewDidLoad Methods

```
override func viewDidLoad() {
    super.viewDidLoad()
    // Do any additional setup after loading the view, typically from a nib.

    let bounds = view.bounds
    let labelFrame = CGRect(origin: CGPoint(x: bounds.origin.x, y: bounds.midY - 50) ,
                    size: CGSize(width:  bounds.size.width, height: 100))
    label = UILabel(frame:labelFrame)
    label.font = UIFont(name:"Helvetica", size:70)
    label.text = "Bazinga!"
    label.textAlignment = NSTextAlignment.center
    label.backgroundColor = UIColor.clear()

    // smiley.png is 84 x 84
    let smileyFrame = CGRect(x: bounds.midX - 42,
        y: bounds.midY/2 - 42, width: 84, height: 84)

    smileyView = UIImageView(frame:smileyFrame)
    smileyView.contentMode = UIViewContentMode.center
    let smileyPath =
        Bundle.main.pathForResource("smiley", ofType: "png")!
    smiley = UIImage(contentsOfFile: smileyPath)
    smileyView.image = smiley
    view.addSubview(smileyView)

    view.addSubview(label)

    let center = NotificationCenter.default
    center.addObserver(self, selector: #selector(ViewController.applicationWillResignActive),
            name: NSNotification.Name.UIApplicationWillResignActive, object: nil)
    center.addObserver(self, selector: #selector(ViewController.applicationDidBecomeActive),
            name: NSNotification.Name.UIApplicationDidBecomeActive, object: nil)
}
```

Build and run the app. You'll see the incredibly happy-looking smiley face toward the top of your screen, as shown in Figure 15-5.

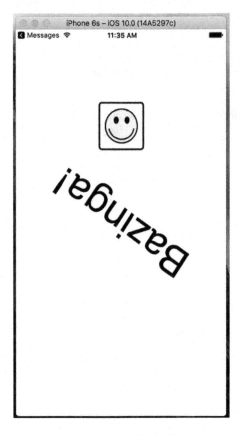

Figure 15-5. The State Lab application rotating the label with the addition of a smiley icon

Next, press the home button to switch your app to the background, and then tap its icon to launch it again. You'll see that when the app resumes, the label starts rotating again, as expected. All seems well, but in fact, we're not yet optimizing system resources as well as we could. Remember that the fewer resources we use while our app is suspended, the lower the risk that iOS will terminate our app entirely. By clearing any easily re-created resources from memory when we can, we increase the chance that our app will stick around and therefore relaunch super-quickly.

Let's see what we can do about that smiley face. We would really like to free up that image when going to the Background state and re-create it when coming back from the Background state. To do that, we'll need to add two more notification registrations inside viewDidLoad():

```
center.addObserver(self, selector: #selector(ViewController.applicationDidEnterBackground),
            name: NSNotification.Name.UIApplicationDidEnterBackground, object: nil)
center.addObserver(self, selector: #selector(ViewController.applicationWillEnterForeground),
            name: NSNotification.Name.UIApplicationWillEnterForeground, object: nil)
```

And we want to implement the two new methods:

```
func applicationDidEnterBackground() {
    print("VC: \(#function)")
    self.smiley = nil;
    self.smileyView.image = nil;
}
func applicationWillEnterForeground() {
    print("VC: \(__FUNCTION__)")
    let smileyPath =
        Bundle.main.path(forResource:"smiley", ofType:"png")!
    smiley = UIImage(contentsOfFile: smileyPath)
    smileyView.image = smiley
}
```

Build and run the app, and repeat the same steps of backgrounding your app and switching back to it. You should see that, from the user's standpoint, the behavior appears to be about the same. If you want to verify for yourself that this is really happening, comment out the contents of the applicationWillEnterForeground() method, and then build and run the app again. You'll see that the image really does disappear.

Saving State When Entering the Background

Now that you've seen an example of how to free up some resources when entering the Background state, it's time to think about saving state. Remember that the idea is to save information relevant to what the user is doing, so that if your application is later dumped from memory, users can still pick up right where they left off the next time they return.

The kind of state we're talking about here is really application-specific, not view-specific. Do not confuse this with saving and restoring the locations of views or which screen of your application the user was looking at when it was last active—for that, iOS provides the state saving and restoration mechanism, which you can read about in the *iOS App Programming Guide* on Apple's web site (https://developer.apple.com/library/ios/documentation/iPhone/Conceptual/iPhoneOSProgrammingGuide/StrategiesforImplementingYourApp/StrategiesforImplementingYourApp.html). Here, we're thinking about things like user preferences in applications for which you do not want to implement a separate settings bundle. Using the same UserDefaults API that we introduced you to in Chapter 12, you can quickly and easily save preferences from within the application and read them back later. Of course, if your application is not visually complex or you don't want to use the state saving and restoration mechanism, you can save information that will allow you to restore its visual state in the user preferences, too.

The State Lab example is too simple to have real user preferences, so let's take a shortcut and add some application-specific state to its one and only view controller. Add a property called index in ViewController. swift, along with a segmented control:

```
class ViewController: UIViewController {
    private var label:UILabel!
    private var smiley:UIImage!
    private var smileyView:UIImageView!
    private var segmentedControl:UISegmentedControl!
    private var index = 0
    private var animate = false
```

We're going to allow the user to set the value of this property using a segmented control and we're going to save it in the user defaults. We're then going to terminate and relaunch the application, to demonstrate that we can recover the value of the property.

Next, move to the middle of the viewDidLoad() method, where you'll create the segmented control, and add it to the view:

```
smileyView.image = smiley
segmentedControl =
    UISegmentedControl(items: ["One","Two", "Three", "Four"])
segmentedControl.frame = CGRect(x: bounds.origin.x + 20, y: 50,
    width: bounds.size.width - 40, height: 30)
segmentedControl.addTarget(self, action: #selector(ViewController.selectionChanged(_:)),
    for: UIControlEvents.valueChanged)

view.addSubview(segmentedControl)
view.addSubview(smileyView)
```

We also used the addTarget(_:action:forControlEvents) method to connect the segmented control to the selectionChanged() method, which we need to have called when the selected segment changes. Add the implementation of this method anywhere in the implementation of the ViewController class:

```
func selectionChanged(_ sender:UISegmentedControl) {
        index = segmentedControl.selectedSegmentIndex;
}
```

Now whenever the user changes the selected segment, the value of the index property will be updated.

Build and run the app. You should see the segmented control and be able to click its segments to select them one at a time. As you do so, the value of the index property will change, although you can't actually see this happening. Background your app again by clicking the home button, bring up the task manager (by double-clicking the home button) and kill your app, and then relaunch it. When the application restarts, the index property will have a value of zero again and there will be no selected segment. That's what we need to fix next.

Saving the value of the index property is simple enough; we just need one line of code to the end of the applicationDidEnterBackground() method in ViewController.swift:

```
func applicationDidEnterBackground() {
    print("VC: \(#function)")
    self.smiley = nil;
    self.smileyView.image = nil;
    UserDefaults.standard.set(self.index,
        forKey:"index")
}
```

But where should we restore the property value and use it to configure the segmented control? The inverse of this method, applicationWillEnterForeground(), isn't what we want. When that method is called, the app has already been running, and the setting is still intact. Instead, we need to access this when things are being set up after a new launch, which brings us back to the viewDidLoad() method. Add the bold lines shown here to that method:

```
view.addSubview(label)

index = UserDefaults.standard.integer(forKey: "index")
segmentedControl.selectedSegmentIndex = index;
```

When the application is being launched for the first time, there will not be a value saved in the user defaults. In this case, the `integerForKey()` method returns the value zero, which happens to be the correct initial value for the `index` property. If you wanted to use a different initial value, you could do so by registering it as the default value for the `index` key, as described in "Registering Default Values" in Chapter 12.

Now build and run the app. You'll notice a difference immediately—the first segment in the segmented control is preselected, because its selected segment index was set in the `viewDidLoad()` method. Now touch a segment, and then do the full background-kill-restart dance. There it is—the index value has been restored and, as a result, the correct segment in the segmented control is now selected.

Obviously, what we've shown here is pretty minimal, but the concept can be extended to all kinds of application states. It's up to you to decide how far you want to take it in order to maintain the illusion for the users that your app was always there, just waiting for them to come back.

Requesting More Backgrounding Time

Earlier, I mentioned the possibility of your app being dumped from memory if moving to the Background state takes too much time. For example, your app may be in the middle of doing a file transfer that it would really be a shame not to finish; however, trying to hijack the `applicationDidEnterBackground()` method to make it complete the work there, before the application is really backgrounded, isn't really an option. Instead, you should use `applicationDidEnterBackground()`as a point for telling the system that you have some extra work you would like to do, and then start up a block to actually do it. Assuming that the system has enough available RAM to keep your app in memory while the user does something else, the system will oblige you and keep your app running for a while.

Let's demonstrate this, not with an actual file transfer, but with a simple sleep call. Once again, we'll be using our new acquaintances GCD to make the contents of our `applicationDidEnterBackground()` method run in a separate queue.

In ViewController.swift, modify the `applicationDidEnterBackground()` method as shown in Listing 15-8.

Listing 15-8. The Updated applicationDidEnterBackground Method

```
func applicationDidEnterBackground() {
    print("VC: \(#function)")
    UserDefaults.standard.set(self.index,
        forKey:"index")

    let app = UIApplication.shared()
    var taskId = UIBackgroundTaskInvalid
    let id = app.beginBackgroundTask() {
        print("Background task ran out of time and was terminated.")
        app.endBackgroundTask(taskId)
    }
    taskId = id

    if taskId == UIBackgroundTaskInvalid {
        print("Failed to start background task!")
        return
    }

    DispatchQueue.global(qos: .default).async {
            print("Starting background task with " +
                "\(app.backgroundTimeRemaining) seconds remaining")
```

```
            self.smiley = nil;
            self.smileyView.image = nil;

            // simulate a lengthy (25 seconds) procedure
            Thread.sleep(forTimeInterval: 25)

            print("Finishing background task with " +
                    "\(app.backgroundTimeRemaining) seconds remaining")
            app.endBackgroundTask(taskId)
        });
    }
```

Let's look through this code piece by piece. First, we grab the shared UIApplication instance, since we'll be using it several times in this method. And then comes this:

```
    var taskId = UIBackgroundTaskInvalid
    let id = app.beginBackgroundTask() {
        print("Background task ran out of time and was terminated.")
        app.endBackgroundTask(taskId)
    }
    taskId = id
```

With the call to app.beginBackgroundTask(), we're basically telling the system that we need more time to accomplish something, and we promise to let it know when we're finished. The closure we give as a parameter may be called if the system decides that we've been going way too long anyway and decides to stop our background task. The call to app.beginBackgroundTask() returns an identifier that we save in the local variable taskId (if it better suits your class design, you could also store this value in a property of the view controller class).

Note that the closure ends with a call to endBackgroundTask(), passing along taskId. That tells the system that we're finished with the work for which we previously requested extra time. It's important to balance each call to app.beginBackgroundTask() with a matching call to endBackgroundTask() so that the system knows when we've completed the work.

■ **Note**   Depending on your computing background, the use of the word **task** here may evoke associations with what we usually call a **process**, consisting of a running program that may contain multiple threads, and so on. In this case, try to put that out of your mind. The use of task in this context really just means "something that needs to get done." Any task you create here is running within your still-executing app.

Next, we do this:

```
    if taskId == UIBackgroundTaskInvalid {
        print("Failed to start background task!")
        return
    }
```

If our earlier call to app.beginBackgroundTask() returned the special value UIBackgroundTaskInvalid, which means the system is refusing to grant us any additional time. In that case, you could try to do the quickest part of whatever needs doing anyway and hope that it completes quickly enough that your app won't be terminated before it's finished. This was more likely to be an issue when running on older devices, such as the iPhone 3G, that didn't support multitasking. In this example, however, we're just letting it slide. Next comes the interesting part where the work itself is actually done:

```
DispatchQueue.global(qos: .default).async {
        print("Starting background task with " +
               "\(app.backgroundTimeRemaining) seconds remaining")

        self.smiley = nil;
        self.smileyView.image = nil;

        // simulate a lengthy (25 seconds) procedure
        Thread.sleep(forTimeInterval: 25)

        print("Finishing background task with " +
               "\(app.backgroundTimeRemaining) seconds remaining")
        app.endBackgroundTask(taskId)
    });
```

All this does is take the same work our method was doing in the first place and place it in a background queue. Notice, though, that the code that uses UserDefaults to save state has not been moved into this closure. That's because it's important to save that state whether or not iOS grants the application additional time to run when it moves into the background. At the end of the closure, we call endBackgroundTask() to let the system know that we're finished.

With that in place, build and run the app, and then background your app by pressing the home button. Watch the Xcode console and after 25 seconds, you will see the final log in your output. A complete run of the app up to this point should give you console output along these lines:

```
application(_:didFinishLaunchingWithOptions:)
applicationDidBecomeActive
VC: applicationDidBecomeActive()
applicationWillResignActive
VC: applicationWillResignActive()
applicationDidEnterBackground
VC: applicationDidEnterBackground()
Starting background task with 179.808078499991 seconds remaining
Finishing background task with 154.796897583336 seconds remaining
```

As you can see, the system is much more generous with time when doing things in the background than it is in the main thread of your app—in this example, it should give you a couple minutes to complete whatever you need to get done in the background. Following this procedure can really help you out if you have any ongoing tasks to deal with.

Note that we used only a single background task, but in practice, you can use as many as you need. For example, if you have multiple network transfers happening at Background time and you need to complete them, you can create a background task for each and allow them to continue running in a background queue. So, you can easily allow multiple operations to run in parallel during the available time.

Summary

This has been a pretty intense chapter, with a lot of new concepts thrown your way. You've discovered a new conceptual paradigm for dealing with concurrency without worrying about threads. Techniques for making sure your apps play nicely in the multitasking world of iOS were also demonstrated. Now that we've gotten some of this heavy stuff out of the way, let's move on to the next chapter, which focuses on drawing.

CHAPTER 16

■ ■ ■

Graphics and Drawing

We've constructed all our application UIs so far using views and controls that are part of the UIKit framework. We can do a lot with UIKit, and a great many applications are constructed using only its predefined objects. Some visual elements (see Figure 16-1), however, can't be fully realized without going beyond what the UIKit stock components offer.

Figure 16-1. *Graphics-intense apps can require more drawing control than UIKit offers*

For example, sometimes an application needs to be able to do custom drawing. iOS includes the Core Graphics framework, allowing us to perform a wide array of drawing tasks. In this chapter, we'll explore a small part of this powerful graphics environment. We'll also build sample applications demonstrating key features of Core Graphics and explain the main concepts.

© Molly Maskrey, Kim Topley, David Mark, Fredrik Olsson and Jeff Lamarche 2016
M. Maskrey et al., *Beginning iPhone Development with Swift 3*, DOI 10.1007/978-1-4842-2223-2_16

Quartz 2D

Core Graphics includes a main set of APIs called Quartz 2D, which is a collection of functions, data types, and objects designed to let you draw directly into a view or an image in memory. Quartz 2D provides the view or image that is being drawn into as a virtual canvas. It follows what's called a **painter's model**, which means that the drawing commands are applied in much the same way that paint is applied to a canvas.

If a painter paints an entire canvas red, and then paints the bottom half of the canvas blue, the canvas will be half red and half either blue, if the blue paint is opaque, or purple if the blue paint is semitransparent. Quartz 2D's virtual canvas works the same way. If you paint the whole view red, and then paint the bottom half of the view blue, you'll have a view that's half red and half either blue or purple, depending on whether the second drawing action was fully opaque or partially transparent. Each drawing action gets applied to the canvas on top of any previous drawing actions.

Quartz 2D provides a variety of line, shape, and image drawing functions. Though easy to use, Quartz 2D is limited to two-dimensional drawing. We'll start with the basics of how Quartz 2D works, and then build a simple drawing application using it.

The Quartz 2D Approach to Drawing

When using Quartz 2D (Quartz for short), we'll usually add the Swift graphics code to the view doing the drawing. For example, we might create a subclass of UIView and add Quartz function calls to that class's **draw(_ rect:)** method. The **draw(_ rect:)** method is part of the UIView class definition and it is called every time a view needs to redraw itself. If you insert your Quartz code in **draw(_ rect:)** that code will be called, and then the view redraws itself.

Quartz 2D's Graphics Contexts

In Quartz, as in the rest of Core Graphics, drawing happens in a **graphics context**, usually referred to simply as a **context**. Every view includes an associated context. You retrieve the current context, use that context to make various Quartz drawing calls, and let the context handle rendering the drawing onto the view. You can think of this context as a sort of canvas. The system provides you with a default context where the contents will appear on the screen. However, it's also possible to create a context of your own for doing drawing that you don't want to appear immediately, but to save for later or use for something else. We'll focus on using the default context, which we get from within **draw(_ rect:)** by writing let context = UIGraphicsGetCurrentContext().

The graphics context is of type CGContext. This is the Swift mapping for the C-language pointer type CGContextRef, the native Core Graphics representation of a context. The actual inferred type of the context variable in the preceding code is CGContext!. It's optional because C-language calls can theoretically return NULL (although UIGraphicsGetCurrentContext() doesn't, provided you only use it where there is guaranteed to be a current context), and it's unwrapped so that you don't have to unwrap every reference to the context.

■ **Note** Core Graphics is a C-language API. All the functions with names starting with CG that you see in this chapter are C functions, not Swift functions.

Once you've got a graphics context, you can draw into it by passing the context to a variety of Core Graphics drawing functions. For example, the sequence in Listing 16-1 creates a path describing a simple line, and then draws that path.

Listing 16-1. Drawing into a Graphics Context

```
context?.setLineWidth(4.0)
context?.setStrokeColor(UIColor.red.cgColor)
context?.moveTo(x: 10.0, y: 10.0)
context?.addLineTo(x: 20.0, y: 20.0)
context?.strokePath()
```

The first call specifies that any subsequent drawing commands that create the current path should be performed with a brush that is 4 points wide. Think of this as selecting the size of the brush you're about to paint with. Until you call this function again with a different number, all lines will have a width of 4 points when drawn in this context. You then specify that the stroke color should be red. In Core Graphics, two colors are associated with drawing actions:

- The **stroke color** is used in drawing lines and for the outline of shapes.

- The **fill color** is used to fill in shapes.

A context has a sort of invisible pen associated with it that does the line drawing. As drawing commands are executed, the movements of this pen form a path. When you call .moveTo(x: , y:), you lift the virtual pen and move to the location you specify, without actually drawing anything. Whatever operation comes next; it will do its work relative to the point to which you last moved the pen. In the earlier example, for instance, we first moved the pen to (10, 10). The next function call added a line from the current pen location (10, 10) to the specified location (20, 20), which became the new pen location.

When you draw in Core Graphics, you're not drawing anything you can actually see—at least not immediately. You're creating a path, which can be a shape, a line, or some other object; however, it contains no color or other features to make it visible. It's like writing in invisible ink. Until you do something to make it visible, your path can't be seen. So, the next step is to call the .strokePath() function, which tells Quartz to draw the path you've constructed. This function will use the line width and the stroke color we set earlier to actually color (or "paint") the path and make it visible.

The Coordinate System

In Listing 16-1, we passed a pair of floating-point numbers as parameters to context!.moveTo(x:, y:) and context!.addLineTo(x:, y:). These numbers represent positions in the Core Graphics coordinate system. Locations in this coordinate system are denoted by their x and y coordinates, which we usually represent as (x, y). The upper-left corner of the context is (0, 0). As you move down, the y increases. As you move to the right, the x increases. What this code did was draw a diagonal line from (10, 10) to (20, 20), which would look like the one shown in Figure 16-2.

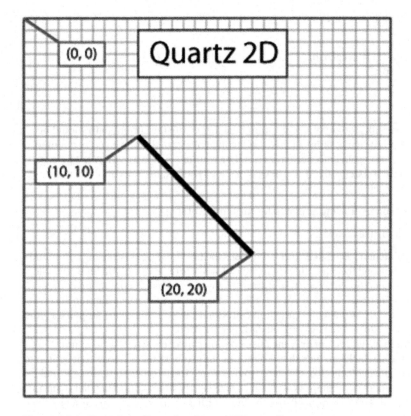

Figure 16-2. *Drawing a line using Quartz 2D's coordinate system*

The Quartz coordinate system can be a little confusing on iOS because its vertical component is flipped from what many graphics libraries use and from the traditional Cartesian coordinate system. In other systems such as OpenGL or the macOS version of Quartz, (0, 0) is in the lower-left corner; and as the y coordinate increases, you move toward the top of the context or view, as shown in Figure 16-3.

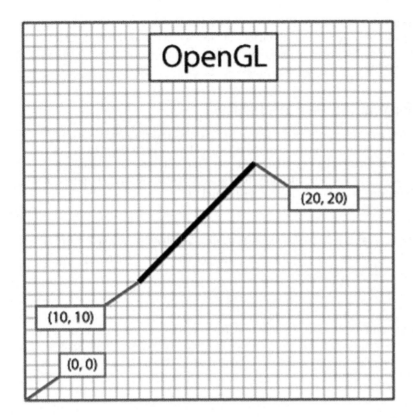

Figure 16-3. *In many graphics libraries, including OpenGL, drawing from (10, 10) to (20, 20) would produce a line that looks like this instead of the line in Figure 16-2*

To specify a point in the coordinate system, some Quartz functions require two floating-point numbers as parameters. Other Quartz functions ask for the point to be embedded in a CGPoint, a struct that holds two floating-point values: x and y. To describe the size of a view or other object, Quartz uses CGSize, a struct that also holds two floating-point values: width and height. Quartz also declares a data type called CGRect, which is used to define a rectangle in the coordinate system. A CGRect contains two elements: a CGPoint called origin, with x and y values that identify the top left of the rectangle; and a CGSize called size, which identifies the width and height of the rectangle, as shown in Listing 16-2.

Listing 16-2. Creating a Rectangle

```
var startingPoint = CGPoint(x: 1.0, y: 1.0)
var sizeOfrect = CGSize(width: 10.0, height: 10.0)
var rectangle = CGRect(origin: startingPoint, size: sizeOfrect)
```

Specifying Colors

An important part of drawing is color, so understanding the way colors work on iOS is critical. UIKit provides a class that represents a color: UIColor. You can't use a UIColor object directly in Core Graphic calls. However, UIColor is just a wrapper around a Core Graphics structure called cgColor (which is what the Core Graphic functions require). You can retrieve a cgColor reference from a UIColor instance by using its cgColor property, as we showed earlier, context!.setStrokeColor(UIColor.red.cgColor).

533

We got a reference to a predefined UIColor instance using a type method called red, and then retrieved its cgColor property and passed that into the function. If you look at the documentation for the UIColor class, you'll see that there are several convenience methods like redColor() that you can use to get UIColor objects for some commonly used colors.

A Bit of Color Theory for Your iOS Device's Display

In modern computer graphics, any color displayed on the screen has its data stored in some way based on something called a color model. A **color model** (sometimes called a **color space**) is simply a way of representing real-world color as digital values that a computer can use. One common way to represent colors is to use four components: red, green, blue, and alpha. In Quartz, each of these values is represented as CGFloat. These values should always contain a value between 0.0 and 1.0.

■ **Caution**   On 32-bit systems, CGFloat is a 32-bit floating-point number and therefore maps directly to the Swift Float type. However, on 64-bit systems, it is a 64-bit value, corresponding to the Swift Double type. Be careful when manipulating CGFloat values in Swift code.

The red, green, and blue components are fairly easy to understand, as they represent the **additive primary colors**, or the **RGB color model**, as shown in Figure 16-4. If you add together the light of these three colors in equal proportions, the result appears to the eye as either white or a shade of gray, depending on the intensity of the light mixed. Combining the three additive primaries in different proportions gives you a range of different colors, referred to as a **gamut**.

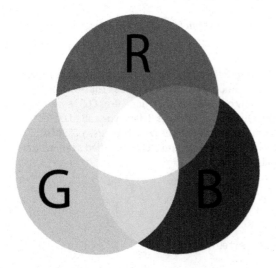

Figure 16-4. *A simple representation of the additive primary colors that make up the RGB color model*

You've probably learned that the primary colors are red, yellow, and blue, which are known as the **historical subtractive primaries**, or the **RYB color model**, and have little application in modern color theory and are almost never used in computer graphics. The color gamut of the RYB color model is much more limited than the RGB color model, and it also doesn't lend itself easily to mathematical definition. For our purposes, the primary colors are red, green, and blue, not red, yellow, and blue.

In addition to red, green, and blue, Quartz uses another color component, called **alpha**, which represents how transparent a color is. When drawing one color on top of another color, alpha is used to determine the final color that is drawn. With an alpha of 1.0, the drawn color is 100% opaque and obscures any colors beneath it. With any value less than 1.0, the colors below will show through and mix with the color above. If the alpha is 0.0, then this color will be completely invisible and whatever is behind it will show through completely. When an alpha component is used, the color model is sometimes referred to as the **RGBA color model**, although technically speaking, the alpha isn't really part of the color; it just defines how the color will interact with other colors when it is drawn.

Other Color Models

Although the RGB model is the most commonly used in computer graphics, it is not the only color model. Several others are in use, including the following:

- Hue, saturation, value (HSV)

- Hue, saturation, lightness (HSL)

- Cyan, magenta, yellow, black (CMYK), which is used in four-color offset printing

- Grayscale

There are also different versions of some of these models, including several variants of the RGB color space. Fortunately, for most operations, we don't need to worry about the color model that is being used. We can just call `cgColor` on our `UIColor` objects, and in most cases, Core Graphics will handle any necessary conversions.

Drawing Images in Context

Quartz allows you to draw images directly into a context. This is another example of a UIKit class (`UIImage`) that you can use as an alternative to working with a Core Graphics data structure (`cgImage`). The `UIImage` class contains methods to draw its image into the current context. You'll need to identify where the image should appear in the context using either of the following techniques:

- By specifying a `CGPoint` to identify the image's upper-left corner

- By specifying a `CGRect` to frame the image, resized to fit the frame if necessary

You can draw a `UIImage` into the current context as shown in Listing 16-3.

Listing 16-3. Draw a UIImage into the Current Context

```
var image:UIImage  = UIImage() // assuming this exists and points at a UIImage instance
let drawPoint = CGPoint(x: 100.0, y: 100.0)
image.draw(at: drawPoint)
```

Drawing Shapes: Polygons, Lines, and Curves

Quartz provides a number of functions to make it easier to create complex shapes. To draw a rectangle or a polygon, you don't need to calculate angles, draw lines, or do any math at all. You can just call a Quartz function to do the work for you. For example, to draw an ellipse, you define the rectangle into which the ellipse needs to fit and let Core Graphics do the work, as shown in Listing 16-4.

Listing 16-4. Drawing a Rectangle in the Current Context

```
let startingPoint = CGPoint(x: 1.0, y: 1.0)
let sizeOfrect = CGSize(width: 10.0, height: 10.0)
let theRect = CGRect(origin: startingPoint, size:sizeOfrect)
context!.addEllipse(inRect: theRect)
context!.addRect(theRect)
```

You use similar methods for rectangles. Quartz also provides methods that let you create more complex shapes, such as arcs and Bezier paths.

■ **Note** We won't be working with complex shapes in this chapter's examples. To learn more about arcs and Bezier paths in Quartz, check out the *Quartz 2D Programming Guide* in the iOS Dev Center at `http://developer.apple.com/documentation/GraphicsImaging/Conceptual/drawingwithquartz2d/` or in Xcode's online documentation.

Quartz 2D Tool Sampler: Patterns, Gradients, and Dash Patterns

Quartz offers quite an impressive array of tools. For example, Quartz supports filling polygons not only with solid colors, but also with gradients. And in addition to drawing solid lines, it can also use an assortment of dash patterns. Take a look at the screenshots in Figure 16-5, which are from Apple's QuartzDemo sample code, to see a sampling of what Quartz can do for you.

Figure 16-5. *Some examples of what Quartz 2D can do from the QuartzDemo sample project provided by Apple*

Now that you have a basic understanding of how Quartz works and what it is capable of doing, let's try it out.

The QuartzFun Application

For our next application we'll build a simple drawing program (see Figure 16-6) using Quartz to give you a feel for how the concepts we've been describing fit together.

Figure 16-6. *The QuartzFun application in action*

Creating the QuartzFun Application

In Xcode, create a new project using the Single View Application template and call it **QuartzFun**. The template has already provided us with an application delegate and a view controller. We're going to be executing our custom drawing in a custom view, so we need to also create a subclass of UIView where we'll do the drawing by overriding the **draw(_ rect:)** method. With the QuartzFun folder selected (the folder that currently contains the app delegate and view controller files), press ⌘N to bring up the new file assistant, and then select Cocoa Touch Class from the iOS Source section. Name the new class QuartzFunView and make it a subclass of UIView.

We're going to add a couple of enumerations—one for the types of shapes that can be drawn and another for the available colors. Also, since one of the color selections is Random, we'll also need a method that returns a random color each time it's called. Let's start by creating that method and the two enumerations.

Creating a Random Color

We could define a global function that returns a random color, but it's better to add this function as an extension to the UIColor class. Open the QuartzFunView.swift file and add the following code near the top:

```
// Random color extension of UIColor
extension UIColor {
    class func randomColor() -> UIColor {
        let red = CGFloat(Double(arc4random_uniform(255))/255)
        let green = CGFloat(Double(arc4random_uniform(255))/255)
        let blue = CGFloat(Double(arc4random_uniform(255))/255)
        return UIColor(red: red, green: green, blue: blue, alpha:1.0)
    }
}
```

This code is fairly straightforward. For each color component, we use the arc4random_uniform() function to generate a random floating-point number in the range 0 to 255. Each component of the color needs to be between 0.0 and 1.0, so we simply divide the result by 255. Why 255? Quartz 2D on iOS supports 256 different intensities for each of the color components, so using the number 255 ensures that we have a chance to randomly select any one of them. Finally, we use those three random components to create a new color. We set the alpha value to 1.0 so that all generated colors will be opaque.

Defining Shape and Color Enumerations

The possible shapes and drawing colors are represented by enumerations. Add the following definitions to the QuartzFunView.swift file:

```
enum Shape : Int {
    case line = 0, rect, ellipse, image
}

// The color tab indices
enum DrawingColor : Int {
    case red = 0, blue, yellow, green, random
}
```

Both enumerations are derived from UInt because, as you'll see later, we will need to use the raw enumeration values to map between a shape or a color and the selected segment of a segmented control.

Implementing the QuartzFunView Skeleton

Since we're going to do our drawing in a subclass of UIView, let's set up that class with everything it needs, except for the actual code to do the drawing, which we'll add later. Start out by adding the following six properties to the QuartzFunView class:

```
    // Application-settable properties
    var shape = Shape.line
    var currentColor = UIColor.red
    var useRandomColor = false
```

```
// Internal properties
private let image = UIImage(named:"iphone")
private var firstTouchLocation = CGPoint.zero
private var lastTouchLocation = CGPoint.zero
```

The shape property keeps track of the shape the user wants to draw, the currentColor property is the user's selected drawing color, and the useRandomColor property will be true if the user chooses to draw with a random color. These properties are all meant to be used outside the class (in fact, they will be used by the view controller).

The next three properties are required only by the class implementation and are therefore marked as private. The first two properties will track the user's finger as it drags across the screen. We'll store the location where the user first touches the screen in firstTouchLocation. We'll store the location of the user's finger while dragging and when the drag ends in lastTouchLocation. Our drawing code will use these two variables to determine where to draw the requested shape. The image property holds the image to be drawn on the screen when the user selects the rightmost toolbar item on the bottom toolbar, as shown in Figure 16-7.

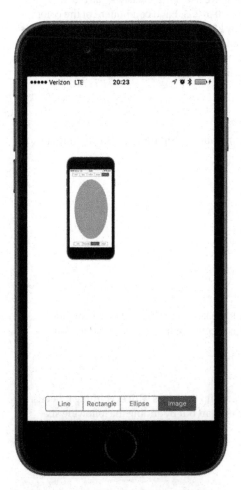

Figure 16-7. *Using QuartzFun to draw a UIImage*

Now on to the implementation itself. Let's first add a few methods to respond to the user's touches. After the property declarations, insert the three methods in Listing 16-5.

Listing 16-5. The Touch Methods for the QuartFunView.swift File

```
override func touchesBegan(_ touches: Set<UITouch>, with event: UIEvent?) {
if let touch = touches.first {
    if useRandomColor {
        currentColor = UIColor.randomColor()
    }
    firstTouchLocation = touch.location(in: self)
    lastTouchLocation = firstTouchLocation
    setNeedsDisplay()
}
}

override func touchesMoved(_ touches: Set<UITouch>, with event: UIEvent?) {
if let touch = touches.first {
    lastTouchLocation = touch.location(in: self)
    setNeedsDisplay()
}
}

override func touchesEnded(_ touches: Set<UITouch>, with event: UIEvent?) {
if let touch = touches.first {
    lastTouchLocation = touch.location(in: self)
    setNeedsDisplay()
}
}
```

These three methods are inherited from UIView, which in turn inherits them from its parent, UIResponder. They can be overridden to find out where the user is touching the screen. They work as follows:

- touchesBegan(_:withEvent:) is called when the user's finger first touches the screen. In that method, we change the color if the user has selected a random color using the new randomColor method we added to UIColor earlier. After that, we store the current location so that we know where the user first touched the screen, and we indicate that our view needs to be redrawn by calling setNeedsDisplay() on self.

- touchesMoved(_:withEvent:) is continuously called while the user is dragging a finger on the screen. All we do here is store the new location in lastTouchLocation and indicate that the screen needs to be redrawn.

- touchesEnded(_:withEvent:) is called when the user lifts the finger off the screen. Just as in the touchesMoved(_:withEvent:) method, all we do is store the final location in the lastTouchLocation variable and indicate that the view needs to be redrawn.

Don't worry if you don't fully understand the rest of the code here. We'll get into the details of working with touches and the specifics of the touchesBegan(_:withEvent:), touchesMoved(_:withEvent:), and touchesEnded(_:withEvent:) methods in Chapter 18.

We'll come back to this class once we have our application skeleton up and running. That **draw(_ rect:)** method, which is currently commented out, is where we will do this application's real work, and we haven't written that yet. Let's finish setting up the application before we add our drawing code.

Creating and Connecting Outlets and Actions

Before we can start drawing, we need to add the segmented controls to our GUI, and then hook up the actions and outlets. Single-click Main.storyboard to set these things up. The first order of business is to change the class of the view. In the document outline, expand the items for the scene and for the view controller it contains, and then single-click the View item. Press ⇧⌘3 to bring up the identity inspector and change the class from UIView to QuartzFunView.

Now use the object library to find a segmented control and drag it to the top of the view, just below the status bar. Place it somewhere near the center. You don't need to be too accurate with this because we'll shortly add a layout constraint that will center it.

With the segmented control selected, bring up the Attributes Inspector and change the number of segments from 2 to 5. Double-click each segment in turn, changing its label to (from left to right) Red, Blue, Yellow, Green, and Random, in that order. Now let's apply layout constraints. In the Document Outline, Control-drag from the segmented control item to the Quartz Fun View item, release the mouse, hold down the Shift key, and select Vertical Spacing to Top Layout Guide and Center Horizontally in Container then press Return. In the Document Outline, select the View Controller icon, and then back in the storyboard editor, click the Resolve Auto Layout Issues button (the one to the right of the Pin button) and select Update Frames. If this option is not enabled, make sure you have the View Controller selected in the Document Outline. The segmented control should now be properly sized and positioned, as shown in Figure 16-8.

Figure 16-8. *Our correctly labelled and positioned color segment control*

Bring up the assistant editor, if it's not already open, and select ViewController.swift from the jump bar. Now Control-drag from the segmented control in the Document Outline to the ViewController.swift file on the right to the line below the class declaration and release the mouse to create a new outlet. Name the new outlet colorControl, and leave all the other options at their default values. Your class should now look like this:

```
class ViewController: UIViewController {
    @IBOutlet weak var colorControl: UISegmentedControl!
```

Next, let's add an action. Open ViewController.swift in the assistant editor, select Main.storyboard again, and Control-drag from the segmented control over to the bottom of the class definition in the view controller file, directly above the closing brace. In the pop-up, change the connection type to Action and the name to changeColor. The pop-up should default to using the Value Changed event, which is what we want. You should also set the type to UISegmentedControl.

Now let's add a second segmented control. This one will be used to choose the shape to be drawn. Drag a segmented control from the library and drop it near the bottom of the view. Select the segmented control in the Document Outline, bring up the Attributes Inspector, and change the number of segments from 2 to 4. Now double-click each segment and change the titles of the four segments to Line, Rectangle, Ellipse, and Image, in that order. Now we need to add layout constraints to fix the size and position of the control, just like we did with the color selection control. Here's the sequence of steps that you need:

1. In the Document Outline, Control-drag from the new segmented control item to the Quartz Fun View item and release the mouse. Hold down the Shift key and select Vertical Spacing to Bottom Layout Guide and Center Horizontally in Container, and then press Return.

2. In the Document Outline, select the View Controller icon, and then back in the editor, click the Resolve Auto Layout Issues button and select Update Frames.

Once you've done that, open ViewController.swift in the assistant editor again, and then Control-drag from the new segmented control over to the bottom of ViewController.swift to create another action. Change the connection type to Action, name the action **changeShape**, change the type to UISegmentedControl, and click Connect. The storyboard should now look like Figure 16-9. Our next task is to implement the action methods.

Figure 16-9. *Our storyboard with both segmented controls in place*

Implementing the Action Methods

Save the storyboard and feel free to close the assistant editor. Now select ViewController.swift, look for the
stub implementation of changeColor() that Xcode created for you and add the code in Listing 16-6.

Listing 16-6. The changeColor Method Goes in the ViewController.swift File

```
@IBAction func changeColor(_ sender: UISegmentedControl) {
    let drawingColorSelection =
            DrawingColor(rawValue: UInt(sender.selectedSegmentIndex))
    if let drawingColor = drawingColorSelection {
        let funView = view as! QuartzFunView
        switch drawingColor {
        case .red:
            funView.currentColor = UIColor.red
            funView.useRandomColor = false
```

```
        case .blue:
            funView.currentColor = UIColor.blue
            funView.useRandomColor = false

        case .yellow:
            funView.currentColor = UIColor.yellow
            funView.useRandomColor = false

        case .green:
            funView.currentColor = UIColor.green
            funView.useRandomColor = false

        case .random:
            funView.useRandomColor = true
        }
    }
}
```

This is pretty straightforward. We simply look at which segment was selected and create a new color based on that selection to serve as our current drawing color. To map from the segmented control's selected index to the enumeration value for the corresponding color, we use the enumeration's constructor that takes a raw value:

```
        let drawingColorSelection =
            DrawingColor(rawValue: UInt(sender.selectedSegmentIndex))
```

After that, we set the currentColor property so that our class knows which color to use when drawing, unless random color has been selected. In that case, we set the useRandomColor property to true and a new color will be chosen each time the user starts a new drawing action (you'll find in this code in the touchesBegan(_:withEvent:) method, which we added a few pages ago). Since all the drawing code will be in the view itself, we don't need to do anything else in this method.

Next, look for the existing implementation of changeShape() and add the following code to it:

```
@IBAction func changeShape(_ sender: UISegmentedControl) {
    let shapeSelection = Shape(rawValue: UInt(sender.selectedSegmentIndex))
    if let shape = shapeSelection {
        let funView = view as! QuartzFunView
        funView.shape = shape
        colorControl.isHidden = shape == Shape.image
    }
}
```

In this method, all we do is set the shape type based on the selected segment of the control. The four elements of the Shape enumeration correspond to the four toolbar segments at the bottom of the application view. We set the shape to be the same as the currently selected segment, and we also hide or show the color selection control based on whether the Image segment was selected.

Make sure that everything is in order by compiling and running your app. You won't be able to draw shapes on the screen yet, but the segmented controls should work; and when you tap the Image segment in the bottom control, the color controls should disappear.

Now that we have everything working, let's do some drawing.

Adding Quartz 2D Drawing Code

We're ready to add the code that does the drawing. We'll draw a line, some shapes, and an image. We're going to work incrementally, adding a small amount of code, and then run the app to see what that code does.

Drawing the Line

Let's do the simplest drawing option first: drawing a single line. Select QuartzFunView.swift and replace the commented-out **draw(_ rect: CGRect)** method with the one shown in Listing 16-7.

Listing 16-7. The draw(rect:) Method

```
override func draw(_ rect: CGRect) {
    let context = UIGraphicsGetCurrentContext()
    context!.setLineWidth(2.0)
    context!.setStrokeColor(currentColor.cgColor)

    switch shape {
    case .line:
        context?.moveTo(x: firstTouchLocation.x,
                              y: firstTouchLocation.y)
        context?.addLineTo(x: lastTouchLocation.x,
                              y: lastTouchLocation.y)

        context?.strokePath()

    case .rect:
        break

    case .ellipse:
        break

    case .image:
        break
    }
}
```

We start things off by retrieving a reference to the current context, which will let us draw onto our QuartzFunView:

```
let context = UIGraphicsGetCurrentContext()
```

Next, we set the line width to 2.0, which means that any line that we stroke will be 2 points wide:

```
context!.setLineWidth(2.0)
```

After that, we set the color for stroking lines. Since UIColor has a CGColor property, which is what this function needs, we use that property of our currentColor property to pass the correct color on to this function.

```
context!.setStrokeColor(currentColor.cgColor)
```

We use a switch to jump to the appropriate code for each shape type. As mentioned earlier, we'll start off with the code to handle drawing a line, get that working, and then we'll add code for each shape in turn as we make our way through this example:

```
switch shape {
case .line:
```

To draw a line, we tell the graphics context to create a path starting at the first place the user touched. Remember that we stored that value in the touchesBegan(_:withEvent:) method, so it will always reflect the starting point of the most recent touch or drag:

```
context?.moveTo(x: firstTouchLocation.x,
                y: firstTouchLocation.y)
```

Next, we draw a line from that spot to the last spot the user touched. If the user's finger is still in contact with the screen, lastTouchLocation contains the finger's current location. If the user is no longer touching the screen, lastTouchLocation contains the location of the user's finger when it was lifted off the screen:

```
context?.addLineTo(x: lastTouchLocation.x,
                   y: lastTouchLocation.y)
```

This function doesn't actually draw the line—it just adds it to the context's current path. To make the line appear on the screen, we need to stroke the path. This function will stroke the line we just drew, using the color and width we set earlier:

```
context?.strokePath()
```

And that's it for now. At this point, you should be able to compile and run the app once more. The Rectangle, Ellipse, and Shape options won't work, but you should be able to draw lines just fine using any of the color choices (see Figure 16-10).

Figure 16-10. *The line-drawing part of our application is now complete. Here, we are drawing using a random color*

Drawing the Rectangle and Ellipse

Let's write the code to draw the rectangle and the ellipse at the same time, since Quartz implements both of these objects in basically the same way. Change the existing **draw(_ rect:**) method as shown in Listing 16-8.

Listing 16-8. Changes to the draw(_ rect:) to Handle the Rectangle and Ellipse

```
override func draw(_ rect: CGRect) {
    let context = UIGraphicsGetCurrentContext()
    context?.setLineWidth(2.0)
    context?.setStrokeColor(currentColor.cgColor)
    context?.setFillColor(currentColor.cgColor)
    let currentRect = CGRect(x: firstTouchLocation.x,
                            y: firstTouchLocation.y,
                        width: lastTouchLocation.x - firstTouchLocation.x,
                        height: lastTouchLocation.y - firstTouchLocation.y)
```

```
        switch shape {
        case .line:
            context?.moveTo(x: firstTouchLocation.x,
                                  y: firstTouchLocation.y)
            context?.addLineTo(x: lastTouchLocation.x,
                                  y: lastTouchLocation.y)
            context?.strokePath()

        case .rect:
            context?.addRect(currentRect)
            context?.drawPath(using: .fillStroke)

        case .ellipse:
            context?.addEllipse(inRect: currentRect)
            context?.drawPath(using: .fillStroke)

        case .image:
            break
        }
    }
```

Because we want to paint both the outline of the ellipse and the rectangle, and to fill their interiors, we add a call to set the fill color using currentColor:

```
context?.setFillColor(currentColor.cgColor)
```

Next, we declare a CGRect variable. We do this here because both the rectangle and ellipse are drawn based on a rectangle. We'll use currentRect to hold the rectangle described by the user's drag. Remember that a CGRect has two members: size and origin. A function called CGRect(x: y: width: height:) lets us create a CGRect by specifying the values needed to make our rectangle. The code to create the rectangle is pretty straightforward. We use the point stored in firstTouchLocation to create the origin. Next, we figure out the size by getting the difference between the two x values and the two y values. Note that, depending on the direction of the drag, one or both size values may end up with negative numbers, but that's OK. A CGRect with a negative size will simply be rendered in the opposite direction of its origin point (to the left for a negative width; upward for a negative height):

```
let currentRect = CGRect(x: firstTouchLocation.x,
        y: firstTouchLocation.y,
        width: lastTouchLocation.x - firstTouchLocation.x,
        height: lastTouchLocation.y - firstTouchLocation.y)
```

Once we have this rectangle defined, drawing either a rectangle or an ellipse is as easy as calling two functions: one to draw the rectangle or ellipse in the CGRect we defined, and the other to stroke and fill it:

```
    case .rect:
        context?.addRect(currentRect)
        context?.drawPath(using: .fillStroke)

    case .ellipse:
        context?.addEllipse(inRect: currentRect)
        context?.drawPath(using: .fillStroke)
```

Build and run your application. Try out the Rectangle and Ellipse tools to see how you like them. Don't forget to change colors, including using a random color.

549

Drawing the Image

For our last trick, let's draw an image. The 16 - Image folder contains three images named iphone.png, iphone@2x.png and iphone@3x.png that you can add to your project's asset catalog. Select Assets.xcassets in the Project Navigator to open it in the editor, and then select all three images in the Finder and drag them onto the editor area to create a new image group called iphone in the asset catalog. Now modify the draw(_ rect:) method, as shown in Listing 16-9.

Listing 16-9. Our Modified draw(_ rect:) Method to Handle Images

```
override func draw(_ rect: CGRect) {
    let context = UIGraphicsGetCurrentContext()
    context?.setLineWidth(2.0)
    context?.setStrokeColor(currentColor.cgColor)
    context?.setFillColor(currentColor.cgColor)
    let currentRect = CGRect(x: firstTouchLocation.x,
                             y: firstTouchLocation.y,
                             width: lastTouchLocation.x - firstTouchLocation.x,
                             height: lastTouchLocation.y - firstTouchLocation.y)

    switch shape {
    case .line:
        context?.moveTo(x: firstTouchLocation.x,
                        y: firstTouchLocation.y)
        context?.addLineTo(x: lastTouchLocation.x,
                           y: lastTouchLocation.y)
        context?.strokePath()

    case .rect:
        context?.addRect(currentRect)
        context?.drawPath(using: .fillStroke)

    case .ellipse:
        context?.addEllipse(inRect: currentRect)
        context?.drawPath(using: .fillStroke)

    case .image:
        let horizontalOffset = image!.size.width / 2
        let verticalOffset = image!.size.height / 2
        let drawPoint =
            CGPoint(x: lastTouchLocation.x - horizontalOffset,
                    y: lastTouchLocation.y - verticalOffset)
        image!.draw(at: drawPoint)
    }
}
```

First, we calculate the center of the image, since we want the image drawn centered on the point where the user last touched. Without this adjustment, the image would be drawn with the upper-left corner at the user's finger, also a valid option. We then make a new CGPoint by subtracting these offsets from the x and y values in lastTouchLocation:

```
let horizontalOffset = image!.size.width / 2
let verticalOffset = image!.size.height / 2
let drawPoint =
    CGPoint(x: lastTouchLocation.x - horizontalOffset,
            y: lastTouchLocation.y - verticalOffset)
```

Now we tell the image to draw itself. This line of code does that:

```
image!.draw(at: drawPoint)
```

Build and run the application, select Image from the segmented control, and check that you can place an image on the drawing canvas. For a little extra fun, move your finger around the screen and observe that the image follows it.

Optimizing the QuartzFun Application

Our application does what we want, but we should consider a bit of optimization. In our little application, you won't notice a slowdown; however, in a more complex application that is running on a slower processor, you might see some lag. The problem occurs in QuartzFunView.swift, in the methods touchesMoved(_:withEvent:) and touchesEnded(_:withEvent:). Both methods include this line of code:

```
setNeedsDisplay()
```

Obviously, this is how we tell our view that something has changed and that it needs to redraw itself. This code works, but it causes the entire view to be erased and redrawn, even if only a tiny bit has changed. We do want to erase the screen when we get ready to drag out a new shape, but we don't want to clear the screen several times a second as we drag out our shape.

Rather than forcing the entire view to be redrawn many times during our drag, we can use the setNeedsDisplayInRect() method instead. setNeedsDisplayInRect() is a UIView method that marks just one rectangular portion of a view's region as needing redisplay. By using this method, we can be more efficient by marking only the part of the view that is affected by the current drawing operation as needing to be redrawn.

We need to redraw not just the rectangle between firstTouchLocation and lastTouchLocation, but any part of the screen encompassed by the current drag. If the user touched the screen and then scribbled all over, but we redrew only the section between firstTouchLocation and lastTouchLocation, then we would leave a lot of stuff drawn on the screen by the previous redraw that we don't want to remain.

The solution is to keep track of the entire area that has been affected by a particular drag in a CGRect instance variable. In touchesBegan(_:withEvent:), we would reset that instance variable to just the point where the user touched. Then, in touchesMoved(_:withEvent:) and touchesEnded(_:withEvent:), we would use a Core Graphics function to get the union of the current rectangle and the stored rectangle, and store the resulting rectangle. We would then use it to specify which part of the view needs to be redrawn. This approach gives us a running total of the area impacted by the current drag.

At the moment, we calculate the current rectangle in the draw(_ rect:) method for use in drawing the ellipse and rectangle shapes. We'll move that calculation into a new method, so that it can be used in all three places without repeating code. Let's try it.

Add a new property called redrawRect to the QuartzFunView class:

```
// Internal properties
private let image = UIImage(named:"iphone")
private var firstTouchLocation = CGPoint.zero
private var lastTouchLocation = CGPoint.zero
private var redrawRect = CGRect.zero
```

We will use this property to keep track of the area that needs to be redrawn. We also need to move the calculation of the current redraw rectangle to a separate method, which you should add at the end of the QuartzFunView class:

```
func currentRect() -> CGRect {
    return CGRect(x: firstTouchLocation.x,
        y: firstTouchLocation.y,
        width: lastTouchLocation.x - firstTouchLocation.x,
        height: lastTouchLocation.y - firstTouchLocation.y)
}
```

Now, in the draw(_ rect:) method, change all references to currentRect to currentRect(), so that the code uses that new method we just created. Next, delete the lines of code where we calculated currentRect, as shown in Listing 16-10.

Listing 16-10. Our Final Modifications to draw(_ rect:)

```
override func draw(_ rect: CGRect) {
    let context = UIGraphicsGetCurrentContext()
    context?.setLineWidth(2.0)
    context?.setStrokeColor(currentColor.cgColor)
    context?.setFillColor(currentColor.cgColor)

    switch shape {
    case .line:
        context?.moveTo(x: firstTouchLocation.x,
                        y: firstTouchLocation.y)
        context?.addLineTo(x: lastTouchLocation.x,
                           y: lastTouchLocation.y)
        context?.strokePath()

    case .rect:
        context?.addRect(currentRect())
        context?.drawPath(using: .fillStroke)

    case .ellipse:
        context?.addEllipse(inRect: currentRect())
        context?.drawPath(using: .fillStroke)

    case .image:
        let horizontalOffset = image!.size.width / 2
        let verticalOffset = image!.size.height / 2
```

```
        let drawPoint =
            CGPoint(x: lastTouchLocation.x - horizontalOffset,
                    y: lastTouchLocation.y - verticalOffset)
        image!.draw(at: drawPoint)
    }
}
```

We also need to make some changes to touchesBegan(_:withEvent:), touchesEnded(_:withEvent:)
and touchesMoved(_:withEvent:). We will recalculate the space impacted by the current operation
and use that to indicate that only a portion of our view needs to be redrawn. Replace the existing
touchesEnded(_:withEvent:) and touchesMoved(_:withEvent:) methods with the new versions shown in
Listing 16-11.

Listing 16-11. The Updated Touches Routines

```
override func touchesBegan(_ touches: Set<UITouch>, with event: UIEvent?) {
    if let touch = touches.first {
        if useRandomColor {
            currentColor = UIColor.randomColor()
        }
        firstTouchLocation = touch.location(in: self)
        lastTouchLocation = firstTouchLocation
        redrawRect = CGRect.zero
        setNeedsDisplay()
    }
}

override func touchesMoved(_ touches: Set<UITouch>, with event: UIEvent?) {
    if let touch = touches.first {
        lastTouchLocation = touch.location(in: self)

        if shape == .image {
            let horizontalOffset = image!.size.width / 2
            let verticalOffset = image!.size.height / 2
            redrawRect = redrawRect.union(CGRect(x: lastTouchLocation.x - horizontalOffset,
                    y: lastTouchLocation.y - verticalOffset,
                    width: image!.size.width, height: image!.size.height))
        } else {
            redrawRect = redrawRect.union(currentRect())
        }
        setNeedsDisplay(redrawRect)
    }
}

override func touchesEnded(_ touches: Set<UITouch>, with event: UIEvent?) {
    if let touch = touches.first {
        lastTouchLocation = touch.location(in: self)

        if shape == .image {
            let horizontalOffset = image!.size.width / 2
            let verticalOffset = image!.size.height / 2
```

553

```
            redrawRect = redrawRect.union(CGRect(x: lastTouchLocation.x - horizontalOffset,
                            y: lastTouchLocation.y - verticalOffset,
                            width: image!.size.width, height: image!.size.height))
        } else {
            redrawRect = redrawRect.union(currentRect())
        }
        setNeedsDisplay(redrawRect)
    }
}
```

Build and run the application again to see the final result. You probably won't see any difference, but with only a few additional lines of code, we reduced the amount of work necessary to redraw our view by getting rid of the need to erase and redraw any portion of the view that hasn't been affected by the current drag. Being kind to your iOS device's precious processor cycles like this can make a big difference in the performance of your applications, especially as they get more complex.

■ **Note**   If you're interested in a more in-depth exploration of Quartz 2D topics, you might want to take a look at *Beginning iPad Development for iPhone Developers: Mastering the iPad SDK* by Jack Nutting, Dave Wooldridge, and David Mark (Apress, 2010). This book covers a lot of Quartz 2D drawing. All the drawing code and explanations in that book apply to the iPhone as well as the iPad.

Summary

In this chapter, we've really just scratched the surface of the drawing capabilities built into iOS. You should feel pretty comfortable with Quartz 2D now, and with some occasional references to Apple's documentation, you can probably handle most any drawing requirement that comes your way.

Now it's time to level up your graphics skills even further as Chapter 17 will introduce you to the Sprite Kit framework, introduced in iOS 7, which lets you do blazingly fast bitmap rendering for creating games or other fast-moving interactive content.

■ ■ ■

Simple Games Using SpriteKit

In iOS 7, Apple introduced SpriteKit, a framework for the high-performance rendering of 2D graphics. Unlike Core Graphics (which is focused on drawing graphics using a painter's model) or Core Animation (which is focused on animating attributes of GUI elements), SpriteKit focuses on a different area entirely—video games—and it is Apple's first foray into the graphical side of game programming in the iOS era. It was released for iOS 7 and OS X 10.9 (Mavericks) at the same time, providing the same API on both platforms, so that apps written for one can be easily ported to the other. Although Apple has never before supplied a framework quite like SpriteKit, it has clear similarities to various open source libraries such as Cocos2D. If you've used Cocos2D or something similar in the past, you'll feel right at home.

SpriteKit does not implement a flexible, general-purpose drawing system like Core Graphics—there are no methods for drawing paths, gradients, or filling spaces with color. Instead, what you get is a **scene graph** (analogous to UIKit's view hierarchy); the ability to transform each graph node's position, scale, and rotation; and the ability for each node to draw itself. Most drawing occurs in an instance of the SKSprite class (or one of its subclasses), which represents a single graphical image ready for putting on the screen.

In this chapter, we're going to use SpriteKit to build a simple shooting game called **TextShooter**. Instead of using premade graphics, we're going to build our game objects with pieces of text, using a subclass of SKSprite that is specialized for just this purpose. Using this approach, you won't need to pull graphics out of a project library or anything like that. The app we'll make will be simple in appearance, but easy to modify and use.

Creating the TextShooter App

In Xcode, press ⌘N or select File ➤ New ➤ Project... and choose the Game template from the iOS section. Press Next, name your project **TextShooter**, set Devices to Universal, set Game Technology to SpriteKit, and create the project. While you're here, it's worth looking briefly at the other available technology choices. OpenGL ES and Metal (the latter of which is new in iOS 8) are low-level graphics APIs that give you almost total control over the graphics hardware, but are much more difficult to use than SpriteKit. Also, don't select Integrate GamePlayKit, because we won't be working with that feature here. Whereas SpriteKit is a 2D API, SceneKit (which was also introduced in iOS 8) is a toolkit that you can use to build 3D graphics applications. After you've read this chapter, it's worth checking out the SceneKit documentation at https://developer. apple.com/library/prerelease/ios/documentation/SceneKit/Reference/SceneKit_Framework/index. html if you have any interest in 3D game programming.

If you run the TextShooter project now, you'll see the default SpriteKit application, which is shown in Figure 17-1. Initially, you'll just see the "Hello, World" text. If you click or tap on any portion of the screen, you'll see the text fade and a rotating shape appear for a few seconds. Over the course of this chapter, we'll replace everything in this template and progressively build up a simple application of our own.

© Molly Maskrey, Kim Topley, David Mark, Fredrik Olsson and Jeff Lamarche 2016
M. Maskrey et al., *Beginning iPhone Development with Swift 3*, DOI 10.1007/978-1-4842-2223-2_17

Figure 17-1. *The default SpriteKit app in action showing some text displayed in the center of the screen*

Now let's take a look at the project that Xcode created. You'll see it has a standard AppDelegate class and a small view controller class called GameViewController that does some initial configuration of an SKView object. This object, which is loaded from the application's storyboard, is the view that will display all our SpriteKit content. Here's the code from the GameViewController viewDidLoad() method that initializes the SKView:

```
override func viewDidLoad() {
    super.viewDidLoad()

    if let view = self.view as! SKView? {
        // Load the SKScene from 'GameScene.sks'
        if let scene = SKScene(fileNamed: "GameScene") {
            // Set the scale mode to scale to fit the window
            scene.scaleMode = .aspectFill
```

```
        // Present the scene
        view.presentScene(scene)
    }

    view.ignoresSiblingOrder = true

    view.showsFPS = true
    view.showsNodeCount = true
    }
}
```

This code gets the SKView instance from the storyboard and configures it to show some performance-related values while the game is running. SpriteKit applications are constructed as a set of **scenes**, represented by the SKScene class. When developing with SpriteKit, you'll probably make a new SKScene subclass for each visually distinct portion of your app. A scene can represent a fast-paced game display with dozens of objects animating around the screen, or something as simple as a start menu. We'll see multiple uses of SKScene in this chapter. The template generates an initially empty scene in the shape of a class called GameScene.

The relationship between SKView and SKScene has some parallels to the UIViewController classes we've been using throughout this book. The SKView class acts a bit like UINavigationController, in the sense that it is sort of a blank slate that simply manages access to the display for other controllers. At this point, things start to diverge, however. Unlike UINavigationController, the top-level objects managed by SKView aren't UIViewController subclasses. Instead, they're subclasses of SKScene, which knows how to manage a graph of objects that can be displayed, acted upon by the physics engine, and so on.

This method creates the initial scene:

```
        if let scene = SKScene(fileNamed: "GameScene") {
```

There are two ways to create a scene—you can allocate and initialize an instance programmatically, or you can load one from a SpriteKit scene file. The Xcode template takes the latter approach—it generates a SpriteKit scene file called **GameScene.sks** containing an archived copy of an SKScene object. SKScene, like most of the other SpriteKit classes, conforms to the NSCoder protocol, which we discussed in Chapter 13. The GameScene.sks file is just a standard archive, which you can read and write using the NSKeyedUnarchiver and NSKeyedArchiver classes. Usually, though, you'll use the SKScene(fileNamed:) initializer, which loads the SKScene from the archive for you and initializes it as an instance of the concrete subclass on which it is invoked—in this case, the archived SKScene data is used to initialize the GameScene object.

You may be wondering why the template code goes to the trouble of loading an empty scene object from the scene file when it could have just created one. The reason is the Xcode **SpriteKit Level Designer**, which lets you design a scene much like you construct a user interface in Interface Builder. Having designed your scene, you save it to the scene file and run your application again. This time, of course, the scene is not empty and you should see the design that you created in the Level Designer. Having loaded the initial scene, you are at liberty to programmatically add additional elements to it. We'll be doing a lot of that in this chapter. Alternatively, if you don't find the Level Designer useful, you can build all your scenes completely in code.

If you select the GameScene.sks file in the Project Navigator, Xcode opens it in the Level Designer, as shown in Figure 17-2.

Figure 17-2. *The Xcode SpriteKit Level Designer showing the initial GameScene with the label*

The scene is displayed in the editor area. To the right of it is the **SKNode Inspector**, which you can use to set properties of the node that's selected in the editor. SpriteKit scene elements are all nodes—instances of the SKNode class. SKScene itself is a subclass of SKNode. Here, the SKScene node is selected, so the SKNode Inspector is displaying its properties. Below the inspector, in the bottom right, is the usual Xcode Object Library, which is automatically filtered to show only the types of objects you can add to a SpriteKit scene. You design your scene by dragging objects from here and dropping them onto the editor.

Now let's go back and finish discussing the viewDidLoad method.

```
// Set the scale mode to scale to fit the window
scene.scaleMode = .aspectFill
```

This is the scene's scaleMode property, which we've set to .aspectFill, scaling each dimension so that the larger of the two (width, height) is chosen. We can also select .fill, .aspectFit, and .resizeFill. These have the following characteristics:

- SKSceneScaleMode.aspectFill resizes the scene so that it fills the screen while preserving its aspect (width-to-height ratio). This mode ensures that every pixel of the SKView is covered, but loses part of the scene—in this case, the scene has been cropped on the left and right. The content of the scene is also scaled, so the text is smaller than in the original scene, but its position relative to the scene is preserved.

- SKSceneScaleMode.aspectFit also preserves the scene's aspect ratio, but ensures that the whole scene is visible. The result is a letter-box view, with parts of the SKView visible above and below the scene content.

- SKSceneScaleMode.fill scales the scene along both axes so that it exactly fits the view. This ensures that everything in the scene is visible, but since the aspect ratio of the original scene is not preserved, there may be unacceptable distortion of the content. Here, you can see that the text has been horizontally compressed.

- Finally, SKSceneScaleMode.resizeFill places the bottom-left corner of the scene in the bottom-left corner of the view and leaves it at its original size.

This tells our rendering that we don't really care about parent-child scene relationships when the scenes are displayed:

```
view.ignoresSiblingOrder = true
```

Depending on how your game works, you may want to set this so the appropriate stacking order of elements is followed. This line animates the scene change:

```
view.presentScene(scene)
```

Calling this method when there's already a presented scene causes the new scene to immediately replace the old one. You'll see examples of this later in the chapter. In this case, since we are making the initial scene visible, there is nothing to transition from, so it's acceptable to use the presentScene() method.

```
view.showsFPS = true
view.showsNodeCount = true
```

These last two lines just display some information about the animation shown on the bottom of the display, as shown in Figure 17-3.

Figure 17-3. Additional information about the animation shown in the view

Initial Scene Customization

Select the GameScene class. We don't need most of the code that the Xcode template generated for us, so let's remove it. First, delete the entire didMoveToView() method. This method is called whenever the scene is presented in an SKView and it is typically used to make last-minute changes to the scene before it becomes visible. Next, change the touchesBegan(_:withEvent:) method, leaving just the for loop and the first line of code.

```
override func touchesBegan(_ touches: Set<UITouch>, with event: UIEvent?) {
    /* Called when a touch begins */
```

```
        for touch in touches {
            let location = touch.location(in: self)
        }
    }
}
```

Since we're not going to load our scene from GameScene.sks, we need a method that will create a scene for us, with some initial content. We'll also need to add properties for the current game-level number, the number of lives the player has, and a flag to let us know whether the level is finished. Modify the GameScene. swift file, as shown in Listing 17-1.

Listing 17-1. Our First Modifications to GameScene.swift

```
class GameScene: SKScene {

    private var levelNumber: Int
    private var playerLives: Int
    private var finished = false

    class func scene(size:CGSize, levelNumber:Int) -> GameScene {
        return GameScene(size: size, levelNumber: levelNumber)
    }

    override convenience init(size:CGSize) {
        self.init(size: size, levelNumber: 1)
    }

    init(size:CGSize, levelNumber:Int) {
        self.levelNumber = levelNumber
        self.playerLives = 5
        super.init(size: size)

        backgroundColor = SKColor.lightGray()

        let lives = SKLabelNode(fontNamed: "Courier")
        lives.fontSize = 16
        lives.fontColor = SKColor.black()
        lives.name = "LivesLabel"
        lives.text = "Lives: \(playerLives)"
        lives.verticalAlignmentMode = .top
        lives.horizontalAlignmentMode = .right
        lives.position = CGPoint(x: frame.size.width,
                                 y: frame.size.height)
        addChild(lives)

        let level = SKLabelNode(fontNamed: "Courier")
        level.fontSize = 16
        level.fontColor = SKColor.black()
        level.name = "LevelLabel"
        level.text = "Level \(levelNumber)"
        level.verticalAlignmentMode = .top
        level.horizontalAlignmentMode = .left
        level.position = CGPoint(x: 0, y: frame.height)
```

```
        addChild(level)
    }

    required init?(coder aDecoder: NSCoder) {
        levelNumber = aDecoder.decodeInteger(forKey: "level")
        playerLives = aDecoder.decodeInteger(forKey: "playerLives")
        super.init(coder: aDecoder)
    }

    override func encode(with aCoder: NSCoder) {
        aCoder.encode(Int(levelNumber), forKey: "level")
        aCoder.encode(playerLives, forKey: "playerLives")
    }
}
```

The first method, scene(size:levelNumber:), gives us a factory method that will work as a shorthand for creating a level and setting its level number at once. In the second method, init(), we override the class's default initializer, passing control to the third method (and passing along a default value for the level number). That third method in turn calls the designated initializer from its superclass's implementation, after setting the initial values of levelNumber and playerLives properties. This may seem like a roundabout way of doing things, but it's a common pattern when you want to add new initializers to a class while still using the class's designated initializer. After calling the superclass initializer, we set the scene's background color. Note that we're using a class called SKColor instead of UIColor here. In fact, SKColor isn't really a class at all; it's a type alias that is mapped to UIColor for an iOS app and NSColor for an OS X app. This allows us to port games between iOS and OS X a little more easily.

After that, we create two instances of a class called SKLabelNode. This is a handy class that works somewhat like a UILabel, allowing us to add some text to the scene and letting us choose a font, set a text value, and specify some alignments. We create one label for displaying the number of lives at the upper right of the screen and another that will show the level number at the upper left of the screen. Look closely at the code that we use to position these labels. Here is the code that sets the position of the lives label:

```
        lives.position = CGPoint(x: frame.size.width,
                                 y: frame.size.height)
```

If you think about the points we're passing in as the position for this label, you may be surprised to see that we're passing in the scene's height. In UIKit, positioning anything at the height of a UIView would put it at the bottom of that view; but in Scene Kit, the y axis is flipped—the coordinate origin is at the bottom left of the scene and the y axis points upward. As a result, the maximum value of the scene's height is a position at the top of the screen instead. What about the label's x coordinate? We're setting that to be the width of the view. If you did that with a UIView, the view would be positioned just off the right side of the screen. That doesn't happen here, because we also did this:

```
        lives.horizontalAlignmentMode = .right
```

Setting the horizontalAlignmentMode property of the SKLabelNode to SKLabelHorizontalAlignmentMode.right moves the point of the label node that's used to position it (it's actually a property called position) to the right of the text. Since we want the text to be right justified on the screen, we therefore need to set the x coordinate of the position property to be the width of the scene. By contrast, the text in the level label is left-aligned and we position it at the left edge of the scene by setting its x coordinate to zero:

```
        level.horizontalAlignmentMode = .left
        level.position = CGPoint(x: 0, y: frame.height)
```

You'll also see that we gave each label a name. This works similarly to a tag or identifier in other parts of UIKit, and it will let us retrieve those labels later by asking for them by name.

We added the init(coder:) and encode(with aCoder:) methods because all SpriteKit nodes, including SKScene, conform to the NSCoding protocol. This requires us to override init(coder:), so we also implement encode(with aCoder:) for the sake of consistency, even though we won't be archiving the scene object in this application. You'll see the same pattern in all of the SKNode subclasses that we create, although we won't implement the encode(with aCoder:) method when the subclass has no additional state of its own, since the base class version does everything that we need in that case.

Now select GameViewController.swift and make the following changes to the viewDidLoad method:

```swift
override func viewDidLoad() {
    super.viewDidLoad()

    let scene = GameScene(size: view.frame.size, levelNumber: 1)

    // Configure the view.
    let skView = self.view as! SKView
    skView.showsFPS = true
    skView.showsNodeCount = true

    /* Sprite Kit applies additional optimizations to improve rendering performance */
    skView.ignoresSiblingOrder = true

    /* Set the scale mode to scale to fit the window */
    scene.scaleMode = .aspectFill

    skView.presentScene(scene)
}
```

Instead of loading the scene from the scene file, we're using the scene(size:levelNumber:) method that we just added to GameScene to create and initialize the scene and make it the same size as the SKView. Since the view and scene are the same size, there is no longer any need to set the scene's scaleMode property, so you can go ahead and remove the line of code that does that. Near the end of GameViewController.swift, you'll find the following method:

```swift
override func prefersStatusBarHidden() -> Bool {
    return true
}
```

This code makes the iOS status bar disappear while our game is running. The Xcode template includes this method because hiding the status bar is usually what you want for action games like this. Now run the game. You'll see that we have a very basic structure in place, as shown in Figure 17-4.

Figure 17-4. *Our game doesn't have much fun factor right now, but at least it has a high frame rate*

■ **Tip** The node count and frame rate at the bottom right of the scene are useful for debugging, but you don't want them to be there when you release your game. You can switch them off by setting the `showsFPS` and `showsNodeCount` properties of the `SKView` to `false` in the `viewDidLoad` method of `GameViewController`. There are some other `SKView` properties that let you get more debugging information—refer to the API documentation for the details.

Player Movement

Now it's time to add a little interactivity. We're going to make a new class that represents a player. It will know how to draw itself as well as how to move to a new location in a nicely animated way. Next, we'll insert an instance of the new class into the scene and write some code to let the player move the object around by touching the screen. Every object that's going to be part of our scene must be a subclass of `SKNode`, so use Xcode's File menu to create a new Cocoa Touch class named `PlayerNode` that's a subclass of `SKNode`. In the nearly empty PlayerNode.swift file that's created, import the SpriteKit framework and add the following code:

```
import SpriteKit

class PlayerNode: SKNode {
    override init() {
        super.init()
        name = "Player \(self)"
        initNodeGraph()
    }

    required init?(coder aDecoder: NSCoder) {
        super.init(coder: aDecoder)
    }

    private func initNodeGraph() {
        let label = SKLabelNode(fontNamed: "Courier")
        label.fontColor = SKColor.darkGray()
        label.fontSize = 40
        label.text = "v"
        label.zRotation = CGFloat(M_PI)
        label.name = "label"
        self.addChild(label)
    }
}
```

Our PlayerNode doesn't display anything itself, because a plain SKNode has no way to do any drawing of its own. Instead, the init() method sets up a subnode that will do the actual drawing. This subnode is another instance of SKLabelNode, just like the one we created for displaying the level number and the number of lives remaining. SKLabelNode is a subclass of SKNode that *does* know how to draw itself. Another such subclass is SKSpriteNode. We're not setting a position for the label, which means that its position is coordinate (0, 0). Just like views, each SKNode lives in a coordinate system that is inherited from its parent object. Giving this node a zero position means that it will appear on-screen at the PlayerNode instance's position. A non-zero value would effectively be an offset from that point.

We also set a rotation value for the label, so that the lowercase letter "v" that it contains will be shown upside-down. The name of the rotation property, zRotation, may seem a bit surprising; however, it simply refers to the z axis of the coordinate space in use with SpriteKit. You only see the x and y axes on screen, but the z axis is useful for ordering items for display purposes, as well as for rotating things around. The values assigned to zRotation need to be in radians instead of degrees, so we assign the value M_PI, which is a constant that is approximately equal to π. Since π radians are equal to 180°, this is just what we want.

Adding the Player to the Scene

Now switch back to GameScene.swift. Here, we're going to add an instance of PlayerNode to the scene. Start off by adding a property to represent the player node:

```
private let playerNode: PlayerNode = PlayerNode()
```

Continue by adding the following bold code at the end of the init(size:levelNumber:) method:

```
level.position = CGPoint(x: 0, y: frame.height)
addChild(level)
```

```
playerNode.position = CGPoint(x: frame.midX,
                                y: frame.height * 0.1)
addChild(playerNode)
```

If you build and run the app now, you should see that the player appears near the lower middle of the screen, as shown in Figure 17-5.

Figure 17-5. *Added an upside-down V as our player*

Handling Touches: Player Movement

Next, we're going to put some logic back into the touchesBegan(_:withEvent:) method, which we earlier left nearly empty. Insert the bold lines shown here in GameScene.swift (you'll get a compiler error when you add this code—we'll fix it shortly):

```
override func touchesBegan(_ touches: Set<UITouch>, with event: UIEvent?) {
    /* Called when a touch begins */

    for touch in touches {
        let location = touch.location(in: self)
        if location.y < frame.height * 0.2 {
            let target = CGPoint(x: location.x, y: playerNode.position.y)
```

```
                playerNode.moveToward(target)
            }
        }
    }
```

The preceding code segment uses any touch location in the lower fifth of the screen as the basis of a new location toward which you want the player node to move. It also tells the player node to move toward it. The compiler complains because we haven't defined the player node's moveToward() method yet. So switch over to PlayerNode.swift and add the implementation of that method:

```
func moveToward(_ location: CGPoint) {
    removeAction(forKey: "movement")

    let distance = pointDistance(position, location)
    let screenWidth = UIScreen.main.bounds.size.width
    let duration = TimeInterval(2 * distance/screenWidth)

    run(SKAction.move(to: location, duration: duration),
        withKey:"movement")

}
```

We'll skip the first line for now, returning to it shortly. This method compares the new location to the current position and figures out the distance and the number of pixels to move. Next, it figures out how much time the movement should take, using a numeric constant to set the speed of the overall movement. Finally, it creates an SKAction to make the move happen. SKAction is a part of SpriteKit that knows how to make changes to nodes over time, letting you easily animate a node's position, size, rotation, transparency, and more. In this case, we are creating an action that animates a simple movement action over a particular duration, and then assigning that action to the player node, using the key "movement". As you see, this key is the same as the key used in the first line of this method to remove an action. We started off this method by removing any existing action with the same key, so that the user can tap several locations in quick succession without spawning a lot of competing actions trying to move in different ways.

Geometry Calculations

Now you'll notice that we've introduced another problem, because Xcode can't find any function called pointDistance(). This is one of several simple geometric functions that our app will use to perform calculations using points, vectors, and floats. Let's put this in place now. Use Xcode to create a new Swift file called **Geometry.swift** and give it the following content:

```
import UIKit

// Takes a CGVector and a CGFLoat.
// Returns a new CGFloat where each component of v has been multiplied by m.

func vectorMultiply(_ v: CGVector, _ m: CGFloat) -> CGVector {
    return CGVector(dx: v.dx * m, dy: v.dy * m)
}

// Takes two CGPoints.
// Returns a CGVector representing a direction from p1 to p2.
```

```
func vectorBetweenPoints(_ p1: CGPoint, _ p2: CGPoint) -> CGVector {
    return CGVector(dx: p2.x - p1.x, dy: p2.y - p1.y)
}

// Takes a CGVector.
// Returns a CGFloat containing the length of the vector, calculated using
// Pythagoras' theorem.
func vectorLength(_ v: CGVector) -> CGFloat {
    return CGFloat(sqrtf(powf(Float(v.dx), 2) + powf(Float(v.dy), 2)))
}

// Takes two CGPoints. Returns a CGFloat containing the distance between them,
// calculated with Pythagoras' theorem.
func pointDistance(_ p1: CGPoint, _ p2: CGPoint) -> CGFloat {
    return CGFloat(
    sqrtf(powf(Float(p2.x - p1.x), 2) + powf(Float(p2.y - p1.y), 2)))
}
```

These are simple implementations of some common operations that are useful in many games: multiplying vectors, creating vectors pointing from one point to another, and calculating distances. Now build and run the app. After the player's "ship" appears, tap anywhere in the bottom portion of the screen to see that the ship slides left or right to reach the point you tapped. You can tap again before the ship reaches its destination, and it will immediately begin a new animation to move toward the new spot. That's fine, but wouldn't it be nice if the player's ship were a bit livelier in its motion?

Making It Wobble

Let's give the ship a bit of a wobble as it moves by adding another animation. Add the bold lines to PlayerNode's moveToward: method.

```
func moveToward(_ location: CGPoint) {
    removeAction(forKey: "movement")
    removeAction(forKey: "wobbling")

    let distance = pointDistance(position, location)
    let screenWidth = UIScreen.main.bounds.size.width
    let duration = TimeInterval(2 * distance/screenWidth)

    run(SKAction.move(to: location, duration: duration),
                      withKey:"movement")

    let wobbleTime = 0.3
    let halfWobbleTime = wobbleTime/2
    let wobbling = SKAction.sequence([
            SKAction.scaleX(to: 0.2, duration: halfWobbleTime),
            SKAction.scaleX(to: 1.0, duration: halfWobbleTime)
    ])
    let wobbleCount = Int(duration/wobbleTime)
    run(SKAction.repeat(wobbling, count: wobbleCount),
                        withKey:"wobbling")
}
```

What we just did is similar to the movement action we created earlier, but it differs in some important ways. For the basic movement, we simply calculated the movement duration, and then created and ran a movement action in a single step. This time, it's a little more complicated. First, we define the time for a single "wobble" (the ship may wobble multiple times while moving, but will wobble at a consistent rate throughout). The wobble itself consists of first scaling the ship along the x axis (i.e., its width) to 2/10ths of its normal size, and then scaling it back to its full size. Each of these is a single action that is packed together into another kind of action called a **sequence**, which performs all the actions it contains one after another. Next, we figure out how many times this wobble can happen during the duration of the ship's travel and wrap the wobbling sequence inside a repeat action, telling it how many complete wobble cycles it should execute. And, as before, we start the method by canceling any previous wobbling action, since we wouldn't want competing wobblers.

Now run the app. You'll see that the ship wobbles pleasantly when moving back and forth. It kind of looks like it's walking.

Creating Your Enemies

So far so good, but this game is going to need some enemies for our players to shoot at. Use Xcode to make a new Cocoa Touch class called EnemyNode, using SKNode as the parent class. We're not going to give the enemy class any real behavior just yet, but we will give it an appearance. We'll use the same technique that we used for the player, using text to build the enemy's body. Surely, there's no text character more intimidating than the letter X, so our enemy will be a letter X... made of lowercase Xs. Add this code to EnemyNode.swift:

```swift
import SpriteKit

class EnemyNode: SKNode {
    override init() {
        super.init()
        name = "Enemy \(self)"
        initNodeGraph()
    }

    required init?(coder aDecoder: NSCoder) {
        super.init(coder: aDecoder)
    }
    private func initNodeGraph() {
        let topRow = SKLabelNode(fontNamed: "Courier-Bold")
        topRow.fontColor = SKColor.brown()
        topRow.fontSize = 20
        topRow.text = "x x"
        topRow.position = CGPoint(x: 0, y: 15)
        addChild(topRow)

        let middleRow = SKLabelNode(fontNamed: "Courier-Bold")
        middleRow.fontColor = SKColor.brown()
        middleRow.fontSize = 20
        middleRow.text = "x"
        addChild(middleRow)

        let bottomRow = SKLabelNode(fontNamed: "Courier-Bold")
        bottomRow.fontColor = SKColor.brown()
        bottomRow.fontSize = 20
```

```
        bottomRow.text = "x x"
        bottomRow.position = CGPoint(x: 0, y: -15)
        addChild(bottomRow)
    }
}
```

There's nothing much new there; we're just adding multiple "rows" of text by shifting the y value for each of their positions.

Putting Enemies in the Scene

Now let's make some enemies appear in the scene by making some changes to GameScene.swift. First, add a new property to hold the enemies that will be added to this level:

private let enemies = SKNode()

You might think that we'd use an Array<SKNode> for this, but it turns out that using a plain SKNode is perfect for the job. SKNode can hold any number of child nodes. And since we need to add all the enemies to the scene anyway, we may as well hold them all in an SKNode for easy access. The next step is to add the spawnEnemies() method, as shown here:

```
private func spawnEnemies() {
    let count = Int(log(Float(levelNumber))) + levelNumber
    for _ in 0..<count {
        let enemy = EnemyNode()
        let size = frame.size;
        let x = arc4random_uniform(UInt32(size.width * 0.8))
                                + UInt32(size.width * 0.1)
        let y = arc4random_uniform(UInt32(size.height * 0.5))
                                + UInt32(size.height * 0.5)
        enemy.position = CGPoint(x: CGFloat(x), y: CGFloat(y))
        enemies.addChild(enemy)
    }
}
```

Add these lines near the end of the init(size:levelNumber:) method to add the enemies node to the scene, and then call the spawnEnemies method:

```
addChild(playerNode)
```

addChild(enemies)
spawnEnemies()

Since we added the enemies node to the scene, any child enemy nodes we add to the enemies node will also appear in the scene. Notice that we're using the arc4random_uniform() function to get random values for the x and y coordinates of our enemy nodes. We'll get random numbers that are less predictable if we "stir" the random number generator before using it. To do that, open AppDelegate.swift and add the following line in bold to the application(_:didFinishLaunchingWithOptions:) method:

```
func application(application: UIApplication,
    didFinishLaunchingWithOptions launchOptions: [NSObject: AnyObject]?) -> Bool {
    // Override point for customization after application launch.
    arc4random_stir()
    return true
}
```

Now build and run the app. You'll see a dreadful enemy placed randomly in the upper portion of the screen, as shown in Figure 17-6. Don't you wish you could shoot it?

Figure 17-6. *I'm sure you'll agree that the X made of Xs just needs to be shot*

Start Shooting

It's time to implement the next logical step in the development of this game: letting the player attack the enemies. We want the player to be able to tap anywhere in the upper 80% of the screen to shoot a bullet at the enemies. We're going to use the **physics engine** included in SpriteKit both to move our player's bullets and to let us know when a bullet collides with an enemy.

But first, what is this thing we call a physics engine? Basically, a physics engine is a software component that keeps track of multiple physical objects (commonly referred to as **physics bodies**) in a world, along with the forces that are acting upon them. It also makes sure that everything moves in a realistic way. It can take into account the force of gravity, handle collisions between objects (so that objects don't occupy the same space simultaneously), and even simulate physical characteristics like friction and bounciness. It's important to understand that a physics engine is usually separate from a graphics engine. Apple provides convenient APIs to let us work with both, but they are essentially separate. It's common to have objects in your display, such as our labels that show the current level number and remaining lives, which are completely separate from the physics engine. And it's possible to create objects that have a physics body, but don't actually display anything at all.

Defining Your Physics Categories

One of the things that the SpriteKit physics engine lets us do is to assign objects to several distinct **physics categories**. A physics category is a way to group related objects so that the physics engine can handle collisions between them in different ways. In this game, for example, we'll create three categories: one for enemies, one for the player, and one for player missiles. We definitely want the physics engine to concern itself with collisions between enemies and player missiles, but we probably want it to ignore collisions between player missiles and the player itself. This is easy to set up using physics categories. So, let's create the categories we're going to need. Press ⌘N to bring up the new file assistant, choose Swift File from the iOS Source section, and press Next. Give the new file the name PhysicsCategories.swift and save it, and then add the following code to it:

```
import Foundation

let PlayerCategory: UInt32 = 1 << 1
let EnemyCategory: UInt32 = 1 << 2
let PlayerMissileCategory: UInt32 = 1 << 3
```

Here we declared three category constants. Note that the categories work as a bitmask, so each of them must be a power of two. We can easily do this by bit-shifting. These are set up as a bitmask in order to simplify the physics engine's API a little bit. With bitmasks, we can logically OR several values together. This enables us to use a single API call to tell the physics engine how to deal with collisions between many different pairs of nodes. We'll see this in action soon.

Creating the BulletNode Class

Now that we've laid some groundwork, let's create some bullets so we can start shooting. Create a new Cocoa Touch class called BulletNode, once again using SKNode as its superclass. Start by importing the SpriteKit framework and adding a property to hold this bullet's thrust vector:

```
import SpriteKit

class BulletNode: SKNode {
    var thrust: CGVector = CGVector(dx: 0, dy: 0)

}
```

Next, we implement the init() method. Like the other init() methods in this application, this is where we create the object graph for our bullet. This will consist of a single dot. While we're at it, let's also configure physics for this class by creating and configuring an SKPhysicsBody instance and attaching it to self. In the process, we tell the new body what category it belongs to and which categories should be checked for collisions with this object:

```
override init() {
    super.init()

    let dot = SKLabelNode(fontNamed: "Courier")
    dot.fontColor = SKColor.black()
    dot.fontSize = 40
    dot.text = "."
    addChild(dot)

    let body = SKPhysicsBody(circleOfRadius: 1)
    body.isDynamic = true
    body.categoryBitMask = PlayerMissileCategory
    body.contactTestBitMask = EnemyCategory
    body.collisionBitMask = EnemyCategory
    body.fieldBitMask = GravityFieldCategory
    body.mass = 0.01

    physicsBody = body
    name = "Bullet \(self)"
}
```

We'll also add the init(coder aDecoder:) and encode(with aCoder:) methods:

```
required init?(coder aDecoder: NSCoder) {
    super.init(coder: aDecoder)
    let dx = aDecoder.decodeFloat(forKey: "thrustX")
    let dy = aDecoder.decodeFloat(forKey: "thrustY")
    thrust = CGVector(dx: CGFloat(dx), dy: CGFloat(dy))
}

override func encode(with aCoder: NSCoder) {
    super.encode(with: aCoder)
    aCoder.encode(Float(thrust.dx), forKey: "thrustX")
    aCoder.encode(Float(thrust.dy), forKey: "thrustY")
}
```

Applying Physics

Next, we'll add the factory method that creates a new bullet and gives it a thrust vector that the physics engine will use to propel the bullet toward its target:

```
class func bullet(from start: CGPoint, toward destination: CGPoint) -> BulletNode {
    let bullet = BulletNode()
    bullet.position = start
    let movement = vectorBetweenPoints(start, destination)
    let magnitude = vectorLength(movement)
    let scaledMovement = vectorMultiply(movement, 1/magnitude)
```

```
    let thrustMagnitude = CGFloat(100.0)
    bullet.thrust = vectorMultiply(scaledMovement, thrustMagnitude)
    bullet.run(SKAction.playSoundFileNamed("shoot.wav",
                                    waitForCompletion: false))
    return bullet
}
```

The basic calculations are pretty simple. We first determine a movement vector that points from the start location to the destination, and then we determine its magnitude (length). Dividing the movement vector by its magnitude produces a normalized **unit vector**, a vector that points in the same direction as the original but is exactly one unit long (a unit, in this case, is the same as a "point" on the screen—for example, two pixels on a Retina device, one pixel on older devices). Creating a unit vector is very useful because we can multiply that by a fixed magnitude (in this case, 100) to determine a uniformly powerful thrust vector, no matter how far away the user tapped the screen. The final piece of code we need to add to this class is this method, which applies thrust to the physics body. We'll call this once per frame, from inside the scene:

```
func applyRecurringForce() {
    physicsBody!.applyForce(thrust)
}
```

Adding Bullets to the Scene

Now switch over to GameScene.swift to add bullets to the scene itself. For starters, add another property to contain all bullets in a single SKNode, just as you did earlier for enemies:

private let playerBullets = SKNode()

Find the section of the init(size:levelNumber:) method where you previously added the enemies. That's the place to set up the playerBullets node, too.

```
addChild(enemies)
spawnEnemies()
```

addChild(playerBullets)
}

Now we're ready to code the actual missile launches. Add this else clause to the touchesBegan(_:withEvent:) method, so that all taps in the upper part of the screen shoot a bullet instead of moving the ship:

```
        } else {
            let bullet = BulletNode.bullet(from: playerNode.position, toward: location)
            playerBullets.addChild(bullet)
        }
```

That adds the bullet, but none of the bullets we add will actually move unless we tell them to by applying thrust every frame. Our scene already contains an empty method called update() that was added as part of the project template. If the update() method is not present, add it as shown in the following. SpriteKit calls this method every frame and it's the perfect place to do any game logic that needs to occur in each frame. Rather than updating all our bullets right in that method, however, we put that code in a separate method that we call from the update() method:

```
override func update(_ currentTime: TimeInterval) {
    /* Called before each frame is rendered */
    updateBullets()
}
private func updateBullets() {
    var bulletsToRemove:[BulletNode] = []
    for bullet in playerBullets.children as! [BulletNode] {
        // Remove any bullets that have moved off-screen
        if !frame.contains(bullet.position) {
            // Mark bullet for removal
            bulletsToRemove.append(bullet)
            continue
        }

        // Apply thrust to remaining bullets
        bullet.applyRecurringForce()
    }

    playerBullets.removeChildren(in: bulletsToRemove)
}
```

Before telling each bullet to apply its recurring force, we also check whether it is still on-screen. Any bullet that's gone off-screen is put into a temporary array; and then, at the end, those are swept out of the playerBullets node. Note that this two-stage process is necessary because the for loop at work in this method is iterating over all children in the playerBullets node. Making changes to a collection while you're iterating over it is never a good idea, and it can easily lead to a crash. Now build and run the app. You'll see that, in addition to moving the player's ship, you can make it shoot missiles upward by tapping on the screen (see Figure 17-7).

Figure 17-7. *Firing bullets*

Attacking Enemies with Physics

A couple of important gameplay elements are still missing from our game. The enemies never attack us, and we can't yet get rid of the enemies by shooting them. Let's take care of the latter right now. We're going to set things up so that shooting an enemy has the effect of dislodging it from the spot where it's currently fixed on the screen. This feature will use the physics engine for most of the work, and involves making changes to PlayerNode, EnemyNode, and GameScene.

For starters, let's add physics bodies to our nodes that don't already have them. Start with EnemyNode. swift. Add the following line to the init() method:

initPhysicsBody()

Now add the code to really set up the physics body. This is pretty similar to what you did earlier for the PlayerBullet class:

```
private func initPhysicsBody() {
    let body = SKPhysicsBody(rectangleOf: CGSize(width: 40, height: 40))
    body.affectedByGravity = false
    body.categoryBitMask = EnemyCategory
    body.contactTestBitMask = PlayerCategory | EnemyCategory
    body.mass = 0.2
    body.angularDamping = 0
    body.linearDamping = 0
    body.fieldBitMask = 0
    physicsBody = body
}
```

Then select PlayerNode.swift, where you're going to do a pretty similar set of things. First, add the line shown here to the init() method:

initPhysicsBody()

Finally, add the new initPhysicsBody() method:

```
private func initPhysicsBody() {
    let body = SKPhysicsBody(rectangleOf: CGSize(width: 20, height: 20))
    body.affectedByGravity = false
    body.categoryBitMask = PlayerCategory
    body.contactTestBitMask = EnemyCategory
    body.collisionBitMask = 0
    body.fieldBitMask = 0
    physicsBody = body
}
```

At this point, you can run the app and see that your bullets now have the ability to knock enemies into space. However, you'll also see there's a problem here. When you start the game and then send the lone enemy hurtling into space, you're stuck so it's probably a good time to add level management to the game.

Finishing Levels

Begin by adding this updateEnemies() method to GameScene.swift. It works a lot like the updateBullets() method added earlier:

```
private func updateEnemies() {
    var enemiesToRemove:[EnemyNode] = []
    for node in enemies.children as! [EnemyNode] {
        if !frame.contains(node.position) {
            // Mark enemy for removal
```

```
            enemiesToRemove.append(node)
        }
    }
    enemies.removeChildren(in: enemiesToRemove)
}
```

That takes care of removing each enemy from the level's enemies array each time one goes off-screen. Now let's modify the update() method, telling it to call updateEnemies(), as well as a new method we haven't yet implemented:

```
override func update(currentTime: CFTimeInterval) {
    if finished {
        return
    }
    updateBullets()
    updateEnemies()
    checkForNextLevel()
}
```

We started out that method by checking the finished property. Since we're about to add code that can officially end a level, we want to be sure that we don't keep doing additional processing after the level is complete. Then, just as we're checking each frame to see if any bullets or enemies have gone off-screen, we're going to call checkForNextLevel each frame to see if the current level is complete. Let's add this method:

```
    private func checkForNextLevel() {
        if enemies.children.isEmpty {
            goToNextLevel()
        }
    }
```

Transitioning to the Next Level

The checkForNextLevel() method in turn calls another method we haven't yet implemented. The goToNextLevel() method marks this level as finished, displays some text on the screen to let the player know, and then starts the next level:

```
    private func goToNextLevel() {
        finished = true

        let label = SKLabelNode(fontNamed: "Courier")
        label.text = "Level Complete!"
        label.fontColor = SKColor.blue()
        label.fontSize = 32
        label.position = CGPoint(x: frame.size.width * 0.5,
                                 y: frame.size.height * 0.5)
        addChild(label)

        let nextLevel = GameScene(size: frame.size, levelNumber: levelNumber + 1)
        nextLevel.playerLives = playerLives
        view!.presentScene(nextLevel, transition:
            SKTransition.flipHorizontal(withDuration: 1.0))
    }
```

The second half of the goToNextLevel() method creates a new instance of GameScene and gives it all the start values it needs. It then tells the view to present the new scene, using a transition to smooth things over. The SKTransition class lets us pick from a variety of transition styles. Run the app and complete a level to see what this one looks like, as shown in Figure 17-8.

Figure 17-8. *The end-of-level screen-flipping transition*

The transition in use here makes it looks like we're flipping a card over its horizontal axis, but there are plenty more to choose from. See the documentation for SKTransition to view more possibilities.

Customizing Collisions

Now we've got a game that you can really play. You can clear level after level by knocking enemies upward off the screen. That's OK, but there's really not much challenge. I mentioned earlier that having enemies attack the player is one piece of missing gameplay, and now it's time to make that happen. We're going to make things a little harder by making the enemies fall down when they're bumped, either from being hit by a bullet or from being touched by another enemy. We also want to make it so that being hit by a falling enemy takes a life away from the player. You also may have noticed that after a bullet hits an enemy, the bullet squiggles its way around the enemy and continues on its upward trajectory, which is pretty weird. We're going to tackle all these things by implementing a collision-handling method in GameScene.swift.

The method for handling detected collisions is a delegate method for the SKPhysicsWorld class. Our scene has a physics world by default, but we need to set it up a little bit before it will tell us anything. For starters, it's good to let the compiler know that we're going to implement a delegate protocol, so let's add this declaration to the GameScene class:

```
class GameScene: SKScene, SKPhysicsContactDelegate {
```

We still need to configure the world a bit (giving it a slightly less cruel amount of gravity) and tell it who its delegate is. To do so, we add these bold lines near the end of the init(size:levelNumber:) method:

```
physicsWorld.gravity = CGVector(dx: 0, dy: -1)
physicsWorld.contactDelegate = self
```

Now that we've set the physics world's contactDelegate to be the GameScene, we can implement the relevant delegate method. The core of the method looks like this:

```
func didBegin(_ contact: SKPhysicsContact) {
    if contact.bodyA.categoryBitMask == contact.bodyB.categoryBitMask {
        // Both bodies are in the same category
        let nodeA = contact.bodyA.node!
        let nodeB = contact.bodyB.node!

        // What do we do with these nodes?
    } else {
        var attacker: SKNode
        var attackee: SKNode

        if contact.bodyA.categoryBitMask
                > contact.bodyB.categoryBitMask {
            // Body A is attacking Body B
            attacker = contact.bodyA.node!
            attackee = contact.bodyB.node!
        } else {
            // Body B is attacking Body A
            attacker = contact.bodyB.node!
            attackee = contact.bodyA.node!
        }

        if attackee is PlayerNode {
            playerLives -= 1
        }

        // What do we do with the attacker and the attackee?
    }
}
```

Go ahead and add that method, but if you look at it right now, you'll see that it doesn't really do much yet. In fact, the only concrete result of that method would be to reduce the number of player lives each time a falling enemy hits the player's ship. But the enemies aren't falling yet.

The idea behind this implementation is to look at the two colliding objects and to figure out whether they are of the same category (in which case, they are "friends" to one another) or if they are of different categories. If they are of different categories, we have to determine who is attacking whom. If you look at the order of the categories declared in PhysicsCategories.swift, you'll see that they are specified in order of increased "attackyness": Player nodes can be attacked by Enemy nodes, which in turn can be attacked by nodes that have the PlayerMissile category (i.e., BulletNodes). That means that we can use a simple greater-than comparison to figure out who is the "attacker" in this scenario.

For the sake of simplicity and modularity, we don't really want the scene to decide how each object should react to being attacked by an enemy or bumped by another object. It's much better to build those details into the affected node classes themselves. But, as you see in the method we've got, the only thing we're sure of is that each side has an SKNode instance. Rather than coding up a big chain of if-else statements to ask each node which SKNode subclass it belongs to, we can use regular polymorphism to let each of our node classes handle things in its own way. In order for that to work, we have to add methods to SKNode, with default implementations that do nothing, and let our subclasses override them where appropriate. This calls for a class extension.

Adding a Class Extension to SKNode

To add an extension to SKNode, right-click the TextShooter folder in the Xcode Project Navigator and choose New File... from the pop-up menu. From the assistant's iOS Source section, choose Swift File, and then click Next. Name the file SKNode+Extra.swift, and press Create. Open the file in the editor and add the code shown here:

```
import SpriteKit

extension SKNode {
    func receiveAttacker(_ attacker: SKNode, contact: SKPhysicsContact) {
        // Default implementation does nothing
    }

    func friendlyBumpFrom(_ node: SKNode) {
        // Default implementation does nothing
    }
}
```

Now head back over to GameScene.swift to finish up its part of the collision handling. Go back to the didBegin(_ contact:) method, where you'll add the bits that actually do some work:

```
func didBegin(_ contact: SKPhysicsContact) {
    if contact.bodyA.categoryBitMask == contact.bodyB.categoryBitMask {
        // Both bodies are in the same category
        let nodeA = contact.bodyA.node!
        let nodeB = contact.bodyB.node!

        // What do we do with these nodes?
        nodeA.friendlyBumpFrom(nodeB)
        nodeB.friendlyBumpFrom(nodeA)
    } else {
```

```swift
        var attacker: SKNode
        var attackee: SKNode

        if contact.bodyA.categoryBitMask
                > contact.bodyB.categoryBitMask {
            // Body A is attacking Body B
            attacker = contact.bodyA.node!
            attackee = contact.bodyB.node!
        } else {
            // Body B is attacking Body A
            attacker = contact.bodyB.node!
            attackee = contact.bodyA.node!
        }

        if attackee is PlayerNode {
            playerLives -= 1
        }

        // What do we do with the attacker and the attackee?
        attackee.receiveAttacker(attacker, contact: contact)
        playerBullets.removeChildren(in: [attacker])
        enemies.removeChildren(in: [attacker])
    }
}
```

All we added here were a few calls to our new methods. If the collision is "friendly fire," such as two enemies bumping into each other, we'll tell each of them that it received a friendly bump from the other. Otherwise, after figuring out who attacked whom, we tell the attackee that it's come under attack from another object. Finally, we remove the attacker from both the playerBullets node and the enemies node. We tell each of those nodes to remove the attacker, even though it can only be in one of them, but that's OK. Telling a node to remove a child it doesn't have isn't an error—it just has no effect.

Adding Custom Collision Behavior to Enemies

Now that all that's in place, we can implement some specific behaviors for our nodes by overriding the extension methods we added to SKNode. Select EnemyNode.swift and add the following two overrides:

```swift
override func friendlyBumpFrom(_ node: SKNode) {
    physicsBody!.affectedByGravity = true
}
override func receiveAttacker(_ attacker: SKNode, contact: SKPhysicsContact) {
    physicsBody!.affectedByGravity = true
    let force = vectorMultiply(attacker.physicsBody!.velocity,
                                    contact.collisionImpulse)
    let myContact =
        scene!.convert(contact.contactPoint, to: self)
    physicsBody!.applyForce(force, at: myContact)
}
```

The first of those methods, friendlyBumpFrom(), simply turns on gravity for the affected enemy. So, if one enemy is in motion and bumps into another, the second enemy will suddenly notice gravity and start falling downward.

The receiveAttacker(_:contact:) method, which is called if the enemy is hit by a bullet, first turns on gravity for the enemy. However, it also uses the contact data that was passed in to figure out just where the contact occurred and applies a force to that point, giving it an extra push in the direction that the bullet was fired.

Showing Accurate Player Lives

Run the game again. You'll see that you can shoot at enemies to knock them down. You'll also see that any other enemies bumped into by a falling enemy will fall, as well.

■ **Note** At the start of each level, the game world performs one step of its physics simulation to make sure that there aren't physics bodies overlapping each other. This will produce an interesting side effect at higher levels, since there will be an increasing chance that multiple randomly placed enemies will occupy overlapping spaces. Whenever that happens, the enemies will be immediately shifted so they no longer overlap, and our collision-handling code will be triggered, which subsequently turns on gravity and lets them fall! This behavior wasn't anything we planned on when we started building this game, but it turns out to be a happy accident that makes higher levels progressively more difficult, so we're letting physics run its course.

If you let enemies hit you as they fall, the number of player lives decreases, but... hey wait, it just shows 5 all the time! The Lives display is set up when the level is created, but it's never updated after that. Fortunately, this is easily fixed by adding a property observer to the playerLives property in GameScene. swift, like this:

```
private var playerLives: Int {
    didSet {
        let lives = childNode(withName: "LivesLabel") as! SKLabelNode
        lives.text = "Lives: \(playerLives)"
    }
}
```

The preceding snippet uses the name we previously associated with the label (in the init(size:levelNumber:) method) to find the label again and set a new text value. Play the game again, and you'll see that, as you let enemies rain down on your player, the number of lives will decrease to zero. And then the game doesn't end. After several hits, you end up with negative number of lives, as you can see in Figure 17-9.

Figure 17-9. *Since we don't have a way to end the game, we can end up with a negative number of lives*

The reason this problem appears is because we haven't written any code to detect the end of the game; that is, the point in time when the number of player lives hits zero. We'll do that soon, but first let's make our on-screen collisions a bit more stimulating.

Spicing Things Up with Particles

One of the nice features of SpriteKit is the inclusion of a particle system. Particle systems are used in games to create visual effects simulating smoke, fire, explosions, and more. Right now, whenever our bullets hit an enemy or an enemy hits the player, the attacking object simply blinks out of existence. Let's make a couple of particle systems to improve this situation.

Start out by pressing ⌘N to bring up the new file assistant. Select the iOS Resource section on the left, and then choose SpriteKit Particle File on the right. Click Next, and on the following screen choose the SparkKit particle file. Click Next again and name this file MissileExplosion.sks.

Your First Particle

You'll see that Xcode creates the particle file and also adds a new resource called **spark.png** to the project. At the same time, the entire Xcode editing area switches over to the new particle file, showing you a huge, animated exploding thing. We don't want something quite this extravagant and enormous when our bullets hit enemies, so let's reconfigure this thing. All the properties that define this particle's animation are available in the SKNode Inspector, which you can bring up by pressing Opt-Cmd-7. Figure 17-10 shows both the massive explosion and the inspector.

Figure 17-10. *The parameters shown on the right define how the default particle looks*

Now, for our bullet hit, let's make it a much smaller explosion. It will have a whole different set of parameters, all of which you configure right in the inspector. First, fix the colors to match what our game looks like by clicking the small color well in the Color Ramp at the bottom and setting it to black. Next, change the Background color to white and change the Blend Mode to Alpha. Now you'll see that the flaming fountain has turned all inky. The rest of the parameters are all numeric. Change them one at a time, setting them all, as shown in Figure 17-11. At each step of the way, you'll see the particle effect change until it eventually reaches its target appearance.

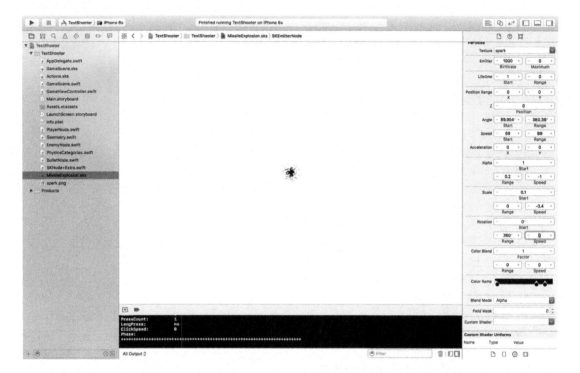

Figure 17-11. *This is the final missile explosion particle effect we want*

Now make another particle system, once again using the Spark template. Name this one EnemyExplosion.sks and set its parameters, as shown in Figure 17-12.

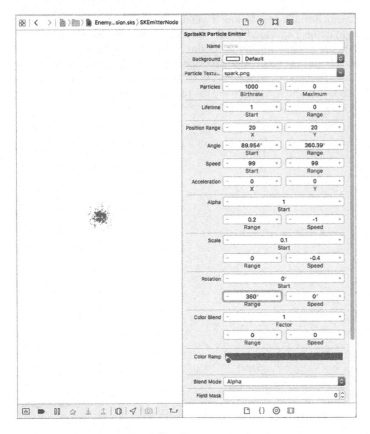

Figure 17-12. *Here's the enemy explosion we want to create. In case you're seeing this book in black and white, the color we've chosen in the Color Ramp at the bottom is deep red*

Putting Particles into the Scene

Now let's start putting these particles to use. Switch over to EnemyNode.swift and add the bold code shown here to the bottom of the receiveAttacker(_:contact:) method:

```
override func receiveAttacker(_ attacker: SKNode, contact: SKPhysicsContact) {
    physicsBody!.affectedByGravity = true
    let force = vectorMultiply(attacker.physicsBody!.velocity,
                              contact.collisionImpulse)
    let myContact =
        scene!.convert(contact.contactPoint, to: self)
    physicsBody!.applyForce(force, at: myContact)
    let path = Bundle.main.path(forResource: "MissileExplosion",
                                        ofType: "sks")
    let explosion = NSKeyedUnarchiver.unarchiveObject(withFile: path!)
        as! SKEmitterNode
    explosion.numParticlesToEmit = 20
    explosion.position = contact.contactPoint
    scene!.addChild(explosion)
}
```

Run the game and shoot some enemies. You'll see a nice little explosion where each bullet hits an enemy, as shown in Figure 17-13.

Figure 17-13. *Bullet explosions after impact*

Now let's do something similar for those times an enemy smashes into a player's ship. Select PlayerNode.swift and add this method:

```
override func receiveAttacker(_ attacker: SKNode, contact: SKPhysicsContact) {
    let path = Bundle.main.path (forResource: "EnemyExplosion",
                                        ofType: "sks")
    let explosion = NSKeyedUnarchiver.unarchiveObject(withFile: path!)
        as! SKEmitterNode
    explosion.numParticlesToEmit = 50
    explosion.position = contact.contactPoint
    scene!.addChild(explosion)
}
```

Play it again. You'll see a nice red splat every time an enemy hits the player, as shown in Figure 17-14.

Figure 17-14. *The explosion when an enemy ship hits the player*

These changes are pretty simple, but they improve the feel of the game substantially. Now when things collide, you have visual consequences and can see that something happened.

Ending the Game

As mentioned before, we currently have a small problem in the game. When the number of lives hits zero, we need to end the game. What we'll do is create a new scene class to transition to when the game is over. You've seen us do a scene transition before, when moving from one level to the next. This will be similar, but with a new class. So, create a new iOS/Cocoa Touch class. Use SKScene as the parent class and name the new class GameOverScene. We'll start with a very simple implementation that just displays "Game Over" text and does nothing more. We'll accomplish this by adding this code to GameOverScene.swift:

```
import SpriteKit

class GameOverScene: SKScene {

    override init(size: CGSize) {
        super.init(size: size)
        backgroundColor = SKColor.purple
        let text = SKLabelNode(fontNamed: "Courier")
        text.text = "Game Over"
        text.fontColor = SKColor.white
        text.fontSize = 50
        text.position = CGPoint(x: frame.size.width/2, y: frame.size.height/2)
        addChild(text)
    }

    required init?(coder aDecoder: NSCoder) {
        super.init(coder: aDecoder)
    }
}
```

Now let's switch back to GameScene.swift. The basic action of what to do when the game ends is defined by a new method called triggerGameOver(). Here, we show both an extra explosion and kick off a transition to the new scene we just created:

```
private func triggerGameOver() {
    finished = true

    let path = Bundle.main.path(forResource:"EnemyExplosion",
                                    ofType: "sks")
    let explosion = NSKeyedUnarchiver.unarchiveObject(withFile: path!)
        as! SKEmitterNode
    explosion.numParticlesToEmit = 200
    explosion.position = playerNode.position
    scene!.addChild(explosion)
    playerNode.removeFromParent()

    let transition = SKTransition.doorsOpenVertical(withDuration: 1)
    let gameOver = GameOverScene(size: frame.size)
    view!.presentScene(gameOver, transition: transition)
}
```

Next, create this new method that will check for the end of the game, call triggerGameOver() if it's time, and return either true to indicate the game ended or false to indicate that it's still on:

```
private func checkForGameOver() -> Bool {
    if playerLives == 0 {
        triggerGameOver()
        return true
    }
    return false
}
```

Finally, make the following change shown in bold to the existing update() method. It checks for the game-over state and only looks for a potential next-level transition if the game is still going. Otherwise, there's a risk that the final enemy on a level could take the player's final life and trigger two scene transitions at once.

```
override func update(_ currentTime: TimeInterval) {
    /* Called before each frame is rendered */
    if finished {
        return
    }
    updateBullets()

    updateEnemies()
    if (!checkForGameOver()) {
        checkForNextLevel()
    }
}
```

Now run the game again, let falling enemies damage your ship five times. You'll see the Game Over screen, as shown in Figure 17-15.

Figure 17-15. *The Game Over screen*

Create a StartScene

This leads us to another problem: What do we do after the game is over? We could allow the player to tap to restart the game; but while thinking of that, a thought crossed my mind. Shouldn't this game have some sort of start screen, so the player isn't immediately thrust into a game at launch time? And shouldn't the game-over screen lead you back there? Of course, the answer to both questions is yes. Go ahead and create another new iOS/Cocoa Touch class, once again using SKScene as the superclass, and this time naming it StartScene. We're going to make a super-simple start scene here. All it will do is display some text and start the game when the user taps anywhere. Add all the code shown here to StartScene.swift to complete this class:

```swift
import SpriteKit

class StartScene: SKScene {

    override init(size: CGSize) {
        super.init(size: size)
        backgroundColor = SKColor.green()

        let topLabel = SKLabelNode(fontNamed: "Courier")
        topLabel.text = "TextShooter"
        topLabel.fontColor = SKColor.black()
        topLabel.fontSize = 48
        topLabel.position = CGPoint(x: frame.size.width/2,
                                    y: frame.size.height * 0.7)
        addChild(topLabel)

        let bottomLabel = SKLabelNode(fontNamed: "Courier")
        bottomLabel.text = "Touch anywhere to start"
        bottomLabel.fontColor = SKColor.black()
        bottomLabel.fontSize = 20
        bottomLabel.position = CGPoint(x: frame.size.width/2,
                                       y: frame.size.height * 0.3)
        addChild(bottomLabel)
    }

    required init?(coder aDecoder: NSCoder) {
        super.init(coder: aDecoder)
    }

    override func touchesBegan(_ touches: Set<UITouch>, with event: UIEvent?) {
        let transition = SKTransition.doorway(withDuration: 1.0)
        let game = GameScene(size:frame.size)
        view!.presentScene(game, transition: transition)
    }
}
```

Now go back to GameOverScene.swift, so we can make the game-over scene perform a transition to the start scene. Add the following code:

```swift
override func didMove(to view: SKView) {
    DispatchQueue.main.after(
        when: DispatchTime.now() + Double(3 * Int64(NSEC_PER_SEC)) / Double(NSEC_PER_SEC)) {
```

591

```
            let transition = SKTransition.flipVertical(withDuration: 1)
            let start = StartScene(size: self.frame.size)
            view.presentScene(start, transition: transition)
        }
    }
```

As you saw earlier, the didMoveToView() method is called on any scene after it's been put in place in a view. Here, we simply trigger a three-second pause, followed by a transition back to the start scene. There's just one more piece of the puzzle to make all our scenes transition to each other as they should. We need to change the app startup procedure so that, instead of jumping right into the game, it shows us the start screen instead. This takes us back to GameViewController.swift. In the viewDidLoad() method, we just replace the code to create one scene class with another:

```
/* Pick a size for the scene */
let scene = GameScene(size: view.frame.size, levelNumber: 1)
let scene = StartScene(size: view.frame.size)
```

Now give it a try. Launch the app and you'll be greeted by the start scene. Touch the screen, play the game, die a lot, and you'll eventually get to the game-over scene. Wait a few seconds and you're back to the start screen, as shown in Figure 17-16.

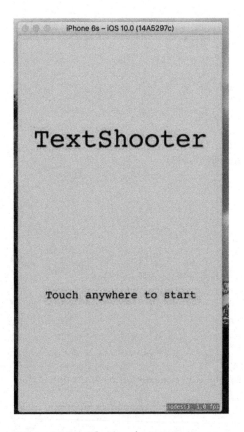

Figure 17-16. *The game's start screen*

Adding Sound Effects

We've been working on a video game, and video games are known for being noisy, but ours is completely silent. Fortunately, SpriteKit contains audio playback code that's extremely easy to use. In the 17 – Sound Effects folder in the source code for this chapter, you'll find the prepared audio files: enemyHit.wav, gameOver.wav, gameStart.wav, playerHit.wav, and shoot.wav. Drag all of them into the Xcode Project Navigator.

Now we'll bake in easy playback for each of these sound effects. Starting with BulletNode.swift, add the bold code to the end of the bullet(from:toward:) method, just before the return line:

```
bullet.run(SKAction.playSoundFileNamed("shoot.wav",
                        waitForCompletion: false))
```

Next, switch over to EnemyNode.swift, adding these lines to the end of the receiveAttacker(_:contact:) method:

```
run(SKAction.playSoundFileNamed("enemyHit.wav",
                        waitForCompletion: false))
```

Now do something extremely similar in PlayerNode.swift, adding these lines to the end of the receiveAttacker(_:contact:) method:

```
run(SKAction.playSoundFileNamed("playerHit.wav",
                        waitForCompletion: false))
```

Those are enough in-game sounds to satisfy for the moment. Go ahead and run the game at this point to try them out. We think you'll agree that the simple addition of particles and sounds gives the game a much better feel.

Now let's just add some effects for starting the game and ending the game. In StartScene.swift, add these lines at the end of the touchesBegan(_:withEvent:) method:

```
run(SKAction.playSoundFileNamed("gameStart.wav",
                        waitForCompletion: false))
```

And finally, add these lines to the end of the triggerGameOver() method in GameScene.swift:

```
run(SKAction.playSoundFileNamed("gameOver.wav",
                        waitForCompletion: false))
```

Making the Game a Little Harder: Force Fields

One of the most interesting features of SpriteKit is the ability to place force fields in a scene. A force field has a type, a location, a region in which it takes effect, and several other properties that specify how it behaves. The idea is that the field perturbs the motion of objects as they move through its sphere of influence, which is defined by its region property. There are various standard force fields that you can use, just by creating and configuring an instance and adding it to a scene. If you are feeling ambitious, you can even create custom force fields. For a list of the standard force fields and their behaviors, which include gravity fields, electric and magnetic fields, and turbulence, look at the API documentation for the SKFieldNode class.

To make our game a little more challenging, we're going to add some **radial gravity fields** to the scene. Radial gravity fields act like a large mass concentrated at a point. As an object moves through the region of a radial gravity field, it will be deflected toward it (or away from it, if you want to configure it that way), much like a meteor passing close enough to the Earth would be as it flies past. We're going to arrange for our gravity fields to act on missiles, so that you won't always be able to directly aim at an enemy and be sure of hitting it. Let's get started.

First, we need to add a new category to PhysicsCategories.swift. Make the following change in that file:

let GravityFieldCategory: UInt32 = 1 << 4

A field acts on a node if the fieldBitMask in the node's physics body has any category in common with the field's categoryBitMask. By default, a physics body's fieldBitMask has all categories set, which means it will be affected by any field that it comes within range of. We don't want the player or enemies to be affected by the gravity field, so we need to clear their fieldBitMask by adding the following code in EnemyNode.swift:

```
private func initPhysicsBody() {
    let body = SKPhysicsBody(rectangleOf: CGSize(width: 40, height: 40))
    body.affectedByGravity = false
    body.categoryBitMask = EnemyCategory
    body.contactTestBitMask = PlayerCategory | EnemyCategory
    body.mass = 0.2
    body.angularDamping = 0
    body.linearDamping = 0
    body.fieldBitMask = 0
    physicsBody = body
}
```

Make a similar change in PlayerNode.swift:

```
private func initPhysicsBody() {
    let body = SKPhysicsBody(rectangleOf: CGSize(width: 20, height: 20))
    body.affectedByGravity = false
    body.categoryBitMask = PlayerCategory
    body.contactTestBitMask = EnemyCategory
    body.collisionBitMask = 0
    body.fieldBitMask = 0
    physicsBody = body
}
```

The missile nodes will respond to the gravity field even if we don't do anything, since their physics nodes have all field categories set by default, but it's cleaner if we make this explicit, so make the following change in BulletNode.swift:

```
override init() {
    super.init()

    let dot = SKLabelNode(fontNamed: "Courier")
    dot.fontColor = SKColor.black()
    dot.fontSize = 40
    dot.text = "."
    addChild(dot)

    let body = SKPhysicsBody(circleOfRadius: 1)
    body.isDynamic = true
    body.categoryBitMask = PlayerMissileCategory
```

```
        body.contactTestBitMask = EnemyCategory
        body.collisionBitMask = EnemyCategory
        body.fieldBitMask = GravityFieldCategory
        body.mass = 0.01

        physicsBody = body
        name = "Bullet \(self)"
    }
```

The rest of the changes are going to be in the file GameScene.swift. We're going to add three gravity fields centered at random points just below the center of the scene. As we did with the missiles and enemies, we'll add the force field nodes to a parent node that we'll then add to the scene. Add the definition of the parent node as a new property:

```
class GameScene: SKScene, SKPhysicsContactDelegate  {
    private var levelNumber: Int
    private var playerLives: Int {
        didSet {
            let lives = childNode(withName: "LivesLabel") as! SKLabelNode
            lives.text = "Lives: \(playerLives)"
        }
    }
    private var finished = false
    private let playerNode: PlayerNode = PlayerNode()
    private let enemies = SKNode()
    private let playerBullets = SKNode()
    private let forceFields = SKNode()
```

At the end of the init(size:levelNumber:) method, add code to add the forceFields node to the scene and create the actual force field nodes:

```
        addChild(forceFields)
        createForceFields()

        physicsWorld.gravity = CGVector(dx: 0, dy: -1)
        physicsWorld.contactDelegate = self
    }
```

Finally, add the implementation of the createForceFields() method:

```
private func createForceFields() {
    let fieldCount = 3
    let size = frame.size
    let sectionWidth = Int(size.width)/fieldCount
    for i in 0..<fieldCount {
        let x = CGFloat(UInt32(i * sectionWidth) +
                        arc4random_uniform(UInt32(sectionWidth)))
        let y = CGFloat(arc4random_uniform(UInt32(size.height * 0.25))
                        + UInt32(size.height * 0.25))

        let gravityField = SKFieldNode.radialGravityField()
```

```
        gravityField.position = CGPoint(x: x, y: y)
        gravityField.categoryBitMask = GravityFieldCategory
        gravityField.strength = 4
        gravityField.falloff = 2
        gravityField.region = SKRegion(size: CGSize(width: size.width * 0.3,
        height: size.height * 0.1))
        forceFields.addChild(gravityField)

        let fieldLocationNode = SKLabelNode(fontNamed: "Courier")
        fieldLocationNode.fontSize = 16
        fieldLocationNode.fontColor = SKColor.red()
        fieldLocationNode.name = "GravityField"
        fieldLocationNode.text = "*"
        fieldLocationNode.position = CGPoint(x: x, y: y)
        forceFields.addChild(fieldLocationNode)
    }
}
```

All force fields are represented by instances of the SKFieldNode class. For each type of field, the SKFieldNode class has a factory method that lets you create a node of that field's type. Here, we use the radialGravityField() method to create three instances of a radial gravity field. We place them in a band just below the center of the scene. The strength and falloff properties control how strong the gravity field is and how rapidly it diminishes with the distance from the field node. A falloff value of 2 makes the force proportional to the inverse square of the distance between the field node and the affected object, just like in the real world. A positive force makes the field node attract the other object. Experiment with different strength values, including negative ones, to see how the effect varies. We also create three SKLabelNodes at the same positions as the gravity force fields, so that the player can see where they are. That's all we need to do. Build and run the app and watch what happens when your bullets fly close to one of the red asterisks in the scene.

Summary

Although TextShooter may be simple in appearance, the techniques we've covered in this chapter form the basis for all sorts of game development using SpriteKit. You've learned how to organize your code across multiple node classes, group objects together using the node graph, and more. You've also been given a taste of what it's like to build this sort of game one feature at a time, discovering each step along the way. Of course, we're not showing you all of our own missteps made along the way—this book is already over 800 pages long without that—but even counting those, this app really was built from scratch, in roughly the order shown in this chapter, in just a few short hours.

Once you get going, SpriteKit allows you to build up a lot of structure in a short amount of time. As you've seen, you can use text-based sprites if you don't have images handy. And if you want to swap them out for real graphics later, it's no problem. One early reader even pointed out a middle path: "Instead of plain old ASCII text in the strings in your source code, you can insert emoji characters by using Apple's Character Viewer input source." Accomplishing this is left as an exercise to the reader.

CHAPTER 18

■ ■ ■

Taps, Touches, and Gestures

The screens of the iPhone, iPod touch, and iPad—with their crisp, bright, touch-sensitive display—represent masterpieces of engineering. The multitouch screen common to all iOS devices provides one of the key factors in the platform's tremendous usability. Because the screen can detect multiple touches at the same time and track them independently, applications are able to detect a wide range of gestures, giving the user power that goes beyond the interface.

Suppose you are in the Mail application staring at a long list of junk e-mail that you want to delete. You can tap each one individually to read it, tap the trash icon to delete it, and then wait for the next message to download, deleting each one in turn. This method is best if you want to read each message before you delete it. If you have an iPhone 6s or iPhone 6s Plus, you can even take advantage of its 3D Touch feature to preview an e-mail without actually opening it. Alternatively, from the list of messages, you can tap the Edit button in the upper-right corner, tap each e-mail row to mark it, and then hit the Trash button to delete all marked messages. This method is best if you don't need to read each message before deleting it. Another alternative is to swipe across a message in the list from right to left. That gesture produces a More button and a Trash button for that message. Tap the Trash button, and the message is deleted.

This example is just one of the many gestures that are made possible by the multitouch display. You can pinch your fingers together to zoom out while viewing a picture or reverse-pinch to zoom in. On the home screen, you can long-press an icon to turn on "jiggly mode," allowing you to delete applications from your iOS device; on the iPhone 6s and iPhone 6s, you can summon a list of shortcuts for an application that supports 3D Touch. In this chapter, we're going to look at the underlying architecture that lets you detect gestures. You'll learn how to detect the most common gestures, as well as how to create and detect a completely new gesture.

Multitouch Terminology

Before we dive into the architecture, let's cover some basic vocabulary. First, a **gesture** is any sequence of events that happens from the time you touch the screen with one or more fingers until you lift your fingers off the screen. No matter how long it takes, as long as one or more fingers remain against the screen, you are still within a gesture (unless a system event, such as an incoming phone call, interrupts it). In some sense, a gesture is a verb, and a running app can watch the user input stream to see if one is happening. A gesture is passed through the system inside a series of events. Events are generated when you interact with the device's multitouch screen. They contain information about the touch or touches that occurred.

The term **touch** refers to a finger being placed on the screen, dragging across the screen, or being lifted from the screen. The number of touches involved in a gesture is equal to the number of fingers on the screen at the same time. You can actually put all five fingers on the screen, and as long as they aren't too close to each other, iOS recognizes and tracks them all. Experimentation has shown that the iPad can handle up to 11 simultaneous touches! This may seem excessive, but could be useful if you're working on a multiplayer game, in which several players are interacting with the screen at the same time. The newest iOS devices can report how hard the user is pressing on the screen, making it possible for you to implement gestures that depend on that information.

A **tap** happens when you touch the screen with a finger and then immediately lift your finger off the screen without moving it around. The iOS device keeps track of the number of taps and can tell you if the user double-tapped, triple-tapped, or even 20-tapped. It handles all the timing and other work necessary to differentiate between two single-taps and a double-tap, for example.

A **gesture recognizer** object knows how to watch the stream of events generated by a user and recognize when the user is touching and dragging in a way that matches a predefined gesture. The UIGestureRecognizer class and its various subclasses can help take a lot of work off your hands when you want to watch for common gestures. This class encapsulates the work of looking for a gesture and can be easily applied to any view in your application.

In the first part of this chapter, we'll see the events that are reported when the user touches the screen with one or more fingers, and how to track the movement of fingers on the screen. We can use these events to handle gestures in a custom view or in our application delegate. Next, we'll look at some of the gesture recognizers that come with the iOS SDK, and finally, you'll see how to build your own gesture recognizer.

The Responder Chain

Since gestures are passed through the system inside events, and events are passed through the **responder chain**, you need to have an understanding of how the responder chain works in order to handle gestures properly. If you've worked with Cocoa for macOS (or previously OS X), you're probably familiar with the concept of a responder chain, as the same basic mechanism is used in both Cocoa and Cocoa Touch. If this is new material, don't worry; we'll explain how it works.

Responding to Events

Several times in this book, we've mentioned the first responder, which is usually the object with which the user is currently interacting. The first responder is the start of the responder chain, but it's not alone. There are always other responders in the chain as well. In a running application, the responder chain is a changing set of objects that are able to respond to user events. Any class that has UIResponder as one of its superclasses is a **responder**. UIView is a subclass of UIResponder, and UIControl is a subclass of UIView, so all views and all controls are responders. UIViewController is also a subclass of UIResponder, meaning that it is a responder, as are all of its subclasses, such as UINavigationController and UITabBarController. Responders, then, are so named because they respond to system-generated events, such as screen touches.

If a responder doesn't handle a particular event, such as a gesture, it usually passes that event up the responder chain. If the next object in the chain responds to that particular event, it will usually consume the event, which stops the event's progression through the responder chain. In some cases, if a responder only partially handles an event, that responder will take an action and forward the event to the next responder in the chain. That's not usually what happens, though. Normally, when an object responds to an event, that's the end of the line for the event. If the event goes through the entire responder chain and no object handles the event, the event is then discarded.

Let's take a more specific look at the responder chain. An event first gets delivered to the UIApplication object, which in turn passes it to the application's UIWindow. The UIWindow handles the event by selecting an initial responder. The initial responder is chosen as follows:

- In the case of a touch event, the UIWindow object determines the view that the user touched, and then offers the event to any gesture recognizers that are registered for that view or any view higher up in the view hierarchy. If any gesture recognizer handles the event, it goes no further. If not, the initial responder is the touched view and the event will be delivered to it.

- For an event generated by the user shaking the device (which we'll say more about in Chapter 20) or from a remote control device, the event is delivered to the first responder.

If the initial responder doesn't handle the event, it passes the event to its parent view, if there is one, or to the view controller if the view is the view controller's view. If the view controller doesn't handle the event, it continues up the responder chain through the view hierarchy of its parent view controller, if it has one.

If the event makes it all the way up through the view hierarchy without being handled by a view or a controller, the event is passed to the application's window. If the window doesn't handle the event, the UIApplication object will pass it to the application delegate, if the delegate is a subclass of UIResponder (which it normally is if you create your project from one of Apple's application templates). Finally, if the app delegate isn't a subclass of UIResponder or doesn't handle the event, then the event goes gently into the good night.

This process is important for a number of reasons. First, it controls the way gestures can be handled. Let's say a user is looking at a table and swipes a finger across a row of that table. What object handles that gesture? If the swipe is within a view or control that's a subview of the table view cell, that view or control will get a chance to respond. If it doesn't respond, the table view cell gets a chance. In an application like Mail, in which a swipe can be used to delete a message, the table view cell probably needs to look at that event to see if it contains a swipe gesture. Most table view cells don't respond to gestures, however. If they don't respond, the event proceeds up to the table view, and then up the rest of the responder chain until something responds to that event or it reaches the end of the line.

Forwarding an Event: Keeping the Responder Chain Alive

Let's consider that table view cell in the Mail application. We don't know the internal details of the Apple Mail application; however, let's assume that the table view cell handles the delete swipe and only the delete swipe. That table view cell must implement the methods related to receiving touch events (discussed shortly) so that it can check to see if that event could be interpreted as part of a swipe gesture. If the event matches a swipe that the table view is looking for, then the table view cell takes an action, and that's that; the event goes no further.

If the event doesn't match the table view cell's swipe gesture, the table view cell takes the responsibility for forwarding that event to the next object in the responder chain. If it doesn't do its forwarding job, the table and other objects up the chain will never get a chance to respond, and the application may not function as the user expects. That table view cell could prevent other views from recognizing a gesture.

Whenever you respond to a touch event, you need to keep in mind that your code doesn't work in a vacuum. If an object intercepts an event that it doesn't handle, it needs to pass it along manually. One way to do this is to call the same method on the next responder. We see an example of this in Listing 18-1.

Listing 18-1. Passing Along a Gesture to Be Handled Elsewhere

```
func respondToFictionalEvent(event: UIEvent) {
    if shouldHandleEvent(event) {
        handleEvent(event)
    } else {
        nextResponder().respondToFictionalEvent(event)
    }
}
```

Notice that we call the same method on the next responder. That's how to implement a good responder-chain process. Fortunately, most of the time, methods that respond to an event also consume the event. However, it's important to know that if that's not the case, you need to make sure the event is passed along to the next link in the responder chain.

The Multitouch Architecture

Now that we've talked a little about the responder chain, let's look at the process of handling touches. As we've indicated, touches are passed along the responder chain, embedded in events. This means that the code to handle any kind of interaction with the multitouch screen needs to be contained in an object in the responder chain. Generally, that means we can choose to either embed that code in a subclass of UIView or embed the code in a UIViewController. So, does this code belong in the view or in the view controller?

If the view needs to do something to itself based on the user's touches, the code probably belongs in the class that defines that view. For example, many control classes, such as UISwitch and UISlider, respond to touch-related events. A UISwitch might want to turn itself on or off based on a touch. The folks who created the UISwitch class embedded gesture-handling code in the class so the UISwitch can respond to a touch. Often, however, when the gesture being processed affects more than the object being touched, the gesture code really belongs in the relevant view controller class. For example, if the user makes a gesture touching one row that indicates that all rows should be deleted, the gesture should be handled by code in the view controller. The way you respond to touches and gestures in both situations is exactly the same, regardless of the class to which the code belongs.

The Four Touch Notification Methods

Four methods are used to notify a responder about touches. When the user first touches the screen, the system looks for a responder that has a method called touchesBegan(_:withEvent:). To find out when the user first begins a gesture or taps the screen, implement this method in your view or your view controller. An example of what that method might look like can be seen in Listing 18-2.

Listing 18-2. Discover When the Gesture or Tap Began

```swift
override func touchesBegan(touches: Set<UITouch>, withEvent event: UIEvent?) {
    if let touch = touches.first {
        let numTaps = touch.tapCount
        let numTouches = event?.allTouches()?.count
    }

    // Do something here
}
```

Each time a finger touches the screen for the first time, a new UITouch object is allocated to represent that finger and added to the set that is delivered with each UIEvent and can be retrieved by calling its allTouches() method. All future events that report activity for that same finger will contain *the same UITouch instance* in the allTouches() set (and it will also appear in the touches set if there is new activity to report for the corresponding finger) until that finger is removed from the screen. Thus, to track the activity of any given finger, you need to monitor its UITouch object.

You can determine the number of fingers currently pressed against the screen by getting a count of the objects returned by allTouches(). If the event reports a touch that is part of a series of taps by any given finger, you can get the tap count from the tapCount property of the UITouch object for that finger. If there's only one finger touching the screen, or if you don't care which finger you ask about, you can quickly get a UITouch object to query by using the first property of the Set structure. In the preceding example, a numTaps value of 2 tells you that the screen was tapped twice in quick succession by at least one finger. Similarly, a numTouches value of 2 tells you the user has two fingers touching the screen.

Not all of the objects in touches or the allTouches() set may be relevant to the view or view controller in which you've implemented this method. A table view cell, for example, probably doesn't care about touches that are in other rows or that are in the navigation bar. You can get the set of touches that fall within a particular view from the event using let myTouches = event?.touchesForView(self.view).

Every UITouch represents a different finger, and each finger is located at a different position on the screen. You can find out the position of a specific finger using the UITouch object. It will even translate the point into the view's local coordinate system using let point = touch.locationInView(self.view) // point is of type CGPoint.

You can get notified while the user is moving fingers across the screen by implementing touchesMoved(_:withEvent:). This method gets called multiple times during a long drag, and each time, you will get another set of touches and another event. In addition to being able to find out each finger's current position from the UITouch objects, you can also discover the previous location of that touch, which is the finger's position the last time either touchesMoved(_:withEvent:) or touchesBegan(_:withEvent:) was called.

When any of the user's fingers is removed from the screen, another method, touchesEnded(_:withEvent:), is invoked. When this method is called, you know that the user is finished with some interaction using the affected finger.

There's one final touch-related method that responders might implement: touchesCancelled(_:withEvent:). It is called if the user is in the middle of a sequence of operations when something happens to interrupt it, like the phone ringing. This is where you can do any cleanup you might need so you can start fresh with a new gesture. When this method is called, touchesEnded(_:withEvent:) will not be called for the current set of touches.

Creating the TouchExplorer Application

We're going to build a little application that will give you a better feel for when the four touch-related responder methods are called. In Xcode, create a new project using the Single View Application template. Enter **TouchExplorer** as the Product Name and select Universal from the Devices pop-up. TouchExplorer prints messages to the screen that indicate the touch and tap count every time a touch-related method is called. On devices that support 3D Touch, it will also show the force applied by the finger that caused the most recent touch event, as shown in Figure 18-1.

Figure 18-1. The TouchExplorer application

■ **Note**   Although the applications in this chapter will run on the simulator, you won't be able to see all the available multitouch or 3D Touch functionality unless you run them on a real iOS device. 3D Touch requires an iPhone 6s or iPhone 6s Plus.

We need four labels for this application: one to indicate which method was last called, another to report the current tap count, a third to report the number of touches and a fourth for the 3D Touch force value. Single-click ViewController.swift and add four outlets to the view controller class:

```
class ViewController: UIViewController {
    @IBOutlet var messageLabel: UILabel!
    @IBOutlet var tapsLabel: UILabel!
    @IBOutlet var touchesLabel: UILabel!
    @IBOutlet var forceLabel: UILabel!
```

Now select Main.storyboard to create the user interface. You'll see the usual empty view contained in all new projects of this kind. Drag a label onto the view, using the blue guidelines to place the label toward the upper-left corner of the view. Hold down the Option key and drag three more labels out from the original, spacing them one below the other. This leaves you with four labels (see Figure 18-1). Feel free to play with the fonts and colors if you're feeling a bit creative. When you're done, select the bottom label and use the Attributes Inspector to set its Lines property to 0, because we're going to use it to show more than one line of text.

Now we need to set the auto layout constraints for the labels. In the Document Outline, Control-drag from the first label to the main view and release the mouse. Hold down the Shift key and select Vertical Spacing to Top Layout Guide and Leading Space to Container Margin, and then click Return. Do the same for the other three labels. The next step is to connect the labels to their outlets. Control-drag from the View Controller icon to each of the four labels, connecting the top one to the messageLabel outlet, the second one to the tapsLabel outlet, the third one to the touchesLabel outlet and the bottom one to the forceLabel outlet. Finally, double-click each label and press the Delete key to get rid of its text.

Next, single-click either the background of the main view or the View icon in the Document Outline, and then bring up the Attributes Inspector (see Figure 18-2). In the Inspector, go to the View section and make sure that both User Interaction Enabled and Multiple Touch are checked. If Multiple Touch is not checked, your controller class's touch methods will always receive one and only one touch, no matter how many fingers are actually touching the phone's screen.

Figure 18-2. *In the View attributes, both User Interaction Enabled and Multiple Touch are checked*

When you're finished, switch back ViewController.swift and make the changes, as shown in Listing 18-3.

Listing 18-3. The ViewController.swift file to Support TouchExplorer

```swift
override func viewDidLoad() {
    super.viewDidLoad()
    // Do any additional setup after loading the view, typically from a nib.
}

private func updateLabelsFromTouches(_ touch: UITouch?, allTouches: Set<UITouch>?) {
    let numTaps = touch?.tapCount ?? 0
    let tapsMessage = "\(numTaps) taps detected"
    tapsLabel.text = tapsMessage

    let numTouches = allTouches?.count ?? 0
    let touchMsg = "\(numTouches) touches detected"
    touchesLabel.text = touchMsg

    if traitCollection.forceTouchCapability == .available {
        forceLabel.text = "Force: \(touch?.force ?? 0)\nMax force: \(touch?.
        maximumPossibleForce ?? 0)"
    } else {
        forceLabel.text = "3D Touch not available"
    }
}

override func touchesBegan(_ touches: Set<UITouch>, with event: UIEvent?) {
    messageLabel.text = "Touches Began"
    updateLabelsFromTouches(touches.first, allTouches: event?.allTouches())
}

override func touchesCancelled(_ touches: Set<UITouch>, with event: UIEvent?) {
    messageLabel.text = "Touches Cancelled"
    updateLabelsFromTouches(touches.first, allTouches: event?.allTouches())
}

override func touchesEnded(_ touches: Set<UITouch>, with event: UIEvent?) {
    messageLabel.text = "Touches Ended"
    updateLabelsFromTouches(touches.first, allTouches: event?.allTouches())
}

override func touchesMoved(_ touches: Set<UITouch>, with event: UIEvent?) {
    messageLabel.text = "Drag Detected"
    updateLabelsFromTouches(touches.first, allTouches: event?.allTouches())
}
```

In this controller class, we implement all four of the touch-related methods we discussed earlier. Each one sets messageLabel so the user can see when each method has been called. Next, all four of them call updateLabelsFromTouches() to update the other three labels. The updateLabelsFromTouches() method gets the tap count from the current touch, figures out the number of fingers touching the screen by looking at the count property of the set of touches that it receives (which is taken from the UIEvent object), and updates the labels with that information. It also obtains and displays force information. Let's take a close look at that part of the code:

```
if traitCollection.forceTouchCapability == .available {
    forceLabel.text = "Force: \(touch?.force ?? 0)\nMax force:
        \(touch?.maximumPossibleForce ?? 0)"
} else {
    forceLabel.text = "3D Touch not available"
}
```

3D Touch is not available on all devices, so the first line of code uses the forceTouchCapability property of the UITraitCollection class to check whether it is. Every view controller has a trait collection and here we use the trait collection of the application's only view controller to make the check. If 3D Touch is supported, we use the force property of UITouch to find out how hard the user is currently pressing on the screen and the maximumPossibleForce property to get the largest possible force value. If 3D touch is not available, we simply say so.

Build and run the application. If you're running in the simulator, try repeatedly clicking the screen to drive up the tap count. You should also try clicking and holding down the mouse button while dragging around the view to simulate a touch and drag. If you have a device that supports 3D Touch, try pressing with varying amounts of force to see the measurements that are reported.

You can emulate a two-finger pinch in the iOS simulator by holding down the Option key while you click with the mouse and drag. You can also simulate two-finger swipes by first holding down the Option key to simulate a pinch, moving the mouse so the two dots representing virtual fingers are next to each other, and then holding down the Shift key (while still holding down the Option key). Pressing the Shift key will lock the position of the two fingers relative to each other, enabling you to do swipes and other two-finger gestures. You won't be able to do gestures that require three or more fingers, but you can do most two-finger gestures on the simulator using combinations of the Option and Shift keys.

If you're able to run this program on a device, see how many touches you can get to register at the same time. Try dragging with one finger, followed by two fingers, and then three. Try double- and triple-tapping the screen, and see if you can get the tap count to go up by tapping with two fingers.

Play around with the TouchExplorer application until you feel comfortable with what's happening and with the way that the four touch methods work. When you're ready, continue on to see how to detect one of the most common gestures: the swipe.

Creating the Swipes Application

The application we're about to build does nothing more than detect swipes, both horizontal and vertical. If you swipe your finger across the screen from left to right, right to left, top to bottom, or bottom to top, the app will display a message across the top of the screen for a few seconds, informing you that a swipe was detected (see Figure 18-3).

Figure 18-3. The Swipes application detects both vertical and horizontal swipes

Using Touch Events to Detect Swipes

Detecting swipes is relatively easy. We'll define a minimum gesture length in pixels, which is how far the user needs to swipe before the gesture counts as a swipe. We'll also define a variance, which is how far from a straight line our user can veer and still have the gesture count as a horizontal or vertical swipe. A diagonal line generally won't count as a swipe, but one that's just a little off from horizontal or vertical will.

When the user touches the screen, we'll save the location of the first touch in a variable. We'll then check as the user's finger moves across the screen to see if it reaches a point where it has gone far enough and straight enough to count as a swipe. There's actually a built-in gesture recognizer that does exactly this, but we're going to use what we've learned about touch events to make one of our own. Let's build it. Create a new project in Xcode using the Single View Application template, set Devices to Universal, and name the project **Swipes**. Single-click ViewController.swift and add the following code to class:

```
class ViewController: UIViewController {
    @IBOutlet var label: UILabel!
    private var gestureStartPoint: CGPoint!
```

This code declares an outlet for our label and a variable to hold the first spot the user touches.

Select Main.storyboard to open it for editing. Make sure that the view controller's view is set so User Interaction Enabled and Multiple Touch are both checked using the Attributes Inspector, and drag a label from the library and drop it in the upper portion of the View window. Set the text alignment to center and

606

feel free to play with the other text attributes to make the label easier to read. In the Document Outline, Control-drag from the label to its parent view, release the mouse, hold down Shift and select Vertical Spacing to Top Layout Guide and Center Horizontally in Container, and then press Return. Control-drag from the View Controller icon to the label and connect it to the label outlet. Finally, double-click the label and delete its text. Now switch over to ViewController.swift and update it to that shown in Listing 18-4.

Listing 18-4. Updates to ViewController.swift File for the Touches App

```swift
class ViewController: UIViewController {
    @IBOutlet var label: UILabel!
    private var gestureStartPoint: CGPoint!
    private static let minimumGestureLength = Float(25.0)
    private static let maximumVariance = Float(5)

    override func viewDidLoad() {
        super.viewDidLoad()
        // Do any additional setup after loading the view, typically from a nib.
    }

    override func touchesBegan(_ touches: Set<UITouch>, with event: UIEvent?) {
        if let touch = touches.first {
            gestureStartPoint = touch.location(in: self.view)
        }
    }

    override func touchesMoved(_ touches: Set<UITouch>, with event: UIEvent?) {
        if let touch = touches.first, gestureStartPoint = self.gestureStartPoint {
            let currentPosition = touch.location(in: self.view)

            let deltaX = fabsf(Float(gestureStartPoint.x - currentPosition.x))
            let deltaY = fabsf(Float(gestureStartPoint.y - currentPosition.y))

            if deltaX >= ViewController.minimumGestureLength
                        && deltaY <= ViewController.maximumVariance {
                label.text = "Horizontal swipe detected"
                DispatchQueue.main.after(when: DispatchTime.now() + Double(Int64(2 * NSEC_
                PER_SEC)) / Double(NSEC_PER_SEC)) {
                    self.label.text = ""
                }
            } else if deltaY >= ViewController.minimumGestureLength
                        && deltaX <= ViewController.maximumVariance {
                label.text = "Vertical swipe detected"
                DispatchQueue.main.after(when: DispatchTime.now() + Double(Int64(2 * NSEC_
PER_SEC)) / Double(NSEC_PER_SEC)) {
                    self.label.text = ""
                }
            }
        }
    }
}
```

Let's start with the touchesBegan(_:withEvent:) method. All we do there is grab a touch from the touches set and store its touch point. We're primarily interested in single-finger swipes right now, so we don't worry about how many touches there are; we just grab the first one in the set:

```
if let touch = touches.first {
    gestureStartPoint = touch.location(in: self.view)
}
```

We're using the UITouch objects in the touches argument instead of the ones in the UIEvent because we're interested in tracking changes as they happen, not in the overall state of all of the active touches. In the next method, touchesMoved(_:withEvent:), we do the real work. First, we get the current position of the user's finger:

```
if let touch = touches.first, gestureStartPoint = self.gestureStartPoint {
    let currentPosition = touch.location(in: self.view)
```

Here, we're using a form of the if let statement that lets us check more than one condition—we're ensuring both that there is a current touch and that we have previously stored a gesture start point. In practice, both of these conditions should always be met, but the fact that the touches.first property, which we use both here and in the touchesBegan(_:withEvent:) method, returns an optional value means that we should make these checks to be sure that we don't crash our application by trying to unwrap a nil optional value in the event that something unexpected happens.

Next, we calculate how far the user's finger has moved both horizontally and vertically from its starting position. fabsf() is a function from the standard C math library that returns the absolute value of a float. This allows us to subtract one from the other without needing to worry about which is the higher value:

```
let deltaX = fabsf(Float(gestureStartPoint.x - currentPosition.x))
let deltaY = fabsf(Float(gestureStartPoint.y - currentPosition.y))
```

Once we have the two deltas, we check to see if the user has moved far enough in one direction without having moved too far in the other to constitute a swipe. If that's true, we set the label's text to indicate whether a horizontal or vertical swipe was detected. We also use the GCD DispatchQueue.main.after() function to erase the text after it has been on the screen for 2 seconds. That way, the user can practice multiple swipes without needing to worry whether the label is referring to an earlier attempt or the most recent one:

```
if deltaX >= ViewController.minimumGestureLength
            && deltaY <= ViewController.maximumVariance {
    label.text = "Horizontal swipe detected"
    DispatchQueue.main.after(when: DispatchTime.now() +
            Double(Int64(2 * NSEC_PER_SEC)) / Double(NSEC_PER_SEC)) {
        self.label.text = ""
    } else if deltaY >= ViewController.minimumGestureLength
            && deltaX <= ViewController.maximumVariance {
    label.text = "Vertical swipe detected"
    DispatchQueue.main.after(when: DispatchTime.now() +
            Double(Int64(2 * NSEC_PER_SEC)) / Double(NSEC_PER_SEC)) {
        self.label.text = ""
    }
}
```

Build and run the application. If you find yourself clicking and dragging with no visible results, be patient. Click and drag straight down or straight across until you get the hang of swiping.

Automatic Gesture Recognition

The procedure we just used for detecting a swipe wasn't too bad. All the complexity is in the touchesMoved(_:withEvent:) method, and even that wasn't all that complicated. But there's an even easier way to do this. iOS includes a class called UIGestureRecognizer, which eliminates the need for watching all the events to see how fingers are moving. You don't use UIGestureRecognizer directly, but instead create an instance of one of its subclasses, each of which is designed to look for a particular type of gesture, such as a swipe, pinch, double-tap, triple-tap, and so on. Let's see how to modify the Swipes app to use a gesture recognizer instead of our hand-rolled procedure. As always, you might want to make a copy of your Swipes project folder and start from there. In the example source code archive, you'll find the completed version of this application in the Swipes 2 folder.

Start by selecting ViewController.swift and deleting both the touchesBegan(_:withEvent:) and touchesMoved(_:withEvent:) methods because you won't need them and add a couple of new methods in their place:

```
func reportHorizontalSwipe(_ recognizer:UIGestureRecognizer) {
    label.text = "Horizontal swipe detected"
    DispatchQueue.main.after(when: DispatchTime.now() +
            Double(Int64(2 * NSEC_PER_SEC)) / Double(NSEC_PER_SEC)) {
        self.label.text = ""
    }
}

func reportVerticalSwipe(_ recognizer:UIGestureRecognizer) {
    label.text = "Vertical swipe detected"
        DispatchQueue.main.after(when: DispatchTime.now() +
            Double(Int64(2 * NSEC_PER_SEC)) / Double(NSEC_PER_SEC)) {
        self.label.text = ""
    }
}
```

These methods implement the actual functionality (if you can call it that) that's provided by the swipe gestures, just as the touchesMoved(_:withEvent:) did previously, except that there is no longer any code to detect the actual swipes. Now add the new code shown here to the viewDidLoad method:

```
super.viewDidLoad()
// Do any additional setup after loading the view, typically from a nib.

let vertical = UISwipeGestureRecognizer(target: self, action:
"reportVerticalSwipe:")
vertical.direction = [.up, .down]
view.addGestureRecognizer(vertical)

let horizontal = UISwipeGestureRecognizer(target: self,
        action: "reportHorizontalSwipe:")
horizontal.direction = [.left, .right]
view.addGestureRecognizer(horizontal)
```

All we're doing here is creating two gesture recognizers—one that will detect vertical movement and another to detect horizontal movement. When one of them recognizes its configured gesture, it will call either the reportVerticalSwipe() or the reportHorizontalSwipe() method and sets the label's text appropriately. To sanitize things even further, you can also delete the declaration of the gestureStartPoint property and the two constant values from ViewController.swift. Now build and run the application to try out the new gesture recognizers.

In terms of total lines of code, there's not much difference between these two approaches for a simple case like this. But the code that uses gesture recognizers is undeniably simpler to understand and easier to write. You don't need to give even a moment's thought to the issue of calculating a finger's movement over time because that's done for you by the UISwipeGestureRecognizer. And better yet, Apple's gesture recognition system is extendable, which means that if your application requires really complex gestures that aren't covered by any of Apple's recognizers, you can make your own, and keep the complex code (along the lines of what we saw earlier) tucked away in the recognizer class instead of polluting your view controller code. We'll build an example of just such a thing later in this chapter. Meanwhile, run the application and you'll see that it behaves just like the previous version.

Implementing Multiple Swipes

In the Swipes application, we worried about only single-finger swipes, so we just grabbed the first object in the touches set to figure out where the user's finger was during the swipe. This approach is fine if you're interested in only single-finger swipes, the most common type of swipe used. But what if you want to handle two- or three-finger swipes? In the earliest versions of this book, we dedicated about 50 lines of code, and a fair amount of explanation, to achieving this by tracking multiple UITouch instances across multiple touch events. Now that we have gesture recognizers, this is a solved problem. A UISwipeGestureRecognizer can be configured to recognize any number of simultaneous touches. By default, each instance expects a single finger, but you can configure it to look for any number of fingers pressing the screen at once. Each instance responds only to the exact number of touches you specify, so what we'll do is create a whole bunch of gesture recognizers in a loop.

Make another copy of your Swipes project folder to experiment with this—you'll find the completed version in the Swipes 3 folder of the example source code archive. Edit ViewController.swift and modify the viewDidLoad method, replacing it with the one shown here:

```
override func viewDidLoad() {
    super.viewDidLoad()
    // Do any additional setup after loading the view, typically from a nib.

    for touchCount in 0..<5 {
        let vertical = UISwipeGestureRecognizer(target: self,
            action: #selector(ViewController.reportVerticalSwipe(_:)))
        vertical.direction = [.up, .down]
        vertical.numberOfTouchesRequired = touchCount
        view.addGestureRecognizer(vertical)

        let horizontal = UISwipeGestureRecognizer(target: self,
            action: #selector(ViewController.reportHorizontalSwipe(_:)))
        horizontal.direction = [.left, .right]
        horizontal.numberOfTouchesRequired = touchCount
        view.addGestureRecognizer(horizontal)
    }
}
```

What we're doing here is adding 10 different gesture recognizers to the view—the first one recognizes a vertical swipe with one finger, the second a vertical swipe with two fingers, and so on. All of them call the reportVerticalSwipe() method when they recognize their gesture. The second set of recognizers handle horizontal swipes and call the `reportHorizontalSwipe()` method instead. Note that in a real application, you might want different numbers of fingers swiping across the screen to trigger different behaviors. You can easily do that using gesture recognizers, simply by having each of them call a different action method.

Now all we need to do is change the logging by adding a method that gives us a handy description of the number of touches, and then using that in the reporting methods, as shown here. Add this method toward the bottom of the `ViewController` class, just above the two swipe-reporting methods:

```
func descriptionForTouchCount(_ touchCount:Int) -> String {
    switch touchCount {
    case 1:
        return "Single"
    case 2:
        return "Double"
    case 3:
        return "Triple"
    case 4:
        return "Quadruple"
    case 5:
        return "Quintuple"
    default:
        return ""
    }
}
```

Next, modify the two swipe-reporting methods as shown:

```
func reportHorizontalSwipe(_ recognizer:UIGestureRecognizer) {
    label.text = "Horizontal swipe detected"
    let count = descriptionForTouchCount(recognizer.numberOfTouches())
    label.text = "\(count)-finger horizontal swipe detected"
    DispatchQueue.main.after(when: DispatchTime.now() +
            Double(Int64(2 * NSEC_PER_SEC)) / Double(NSEC_PER_SEC)) {
        self.label.text = ""
    }
}

func reportVerticalSwipe(_ recognizer:UIGestureRecognizer) {
    label.text = "Vertical swipe detected"
    let count = descriptionForTouchCount(recognizer.numberOfTouches())
    label.text = "\(count)-finger vertical swipe detected"
    DispatchQueue.main.after(when: DispatchTime.now() +
            Double(Int64(2 * NSEC_PER_SEC)) / Double(NSEC_PER_SEC)) {
        self.label.text = ""
    }
}
```

Build and run the app. You should be able to trigger double- and triple-swipes in both directions, yet still be able to trigger single-swipes. If you have small fingers, you might even be able to trigger a quadruple- or quintuple-swipe.

■ **Tip**   In the simulator, if you hold down the Option key, a pair of dots, representing a pair of fingers, will appear. Get them close together, and then hold down the Shift key. This will keep the dots in the same position relative to each other, allowing you to move the pair of fingers around the screen. Now click and drag down the screen to simulate a double-swipe.

With a multiple-finger swipe, one thing to be careful of is that your fingers aren't too close to each other. If two fingers are very close to each other, they may register as only a single touch. Because of this, you shouldn't rely on quadruple- or quintuple-swipes for any important gestures because many people will have fingers that are too big to do those swipes effectively. Also, on the iPad some four- and five-finger gestures are turned on by default at the system level for switching between apps and going to the home screen. These can be turned off in the Settings app, but you're probably better off just not using such gestures in your own apps.

Detecting Multiple Taps

In the TouchExplorer application, we printed the tap count to the screen, so you've already seen how easy it is to detect multiple taps. It's not quite as straightforward as it seems, however, because often you will want to take different actions based on the number of taps. If the user triple-taps, you get notified three separate times. You get a single-tap, a double-tap, and finally a triple-tap. If you want to do something on a double-tap but something completely different on a triple-tap, having three separate notifications could cause a problem, since you will first receive notification of a double-tap, and then a triple-tap. Unless you write your own clever code to take this into account, you'll wind up doing both actions. Fortunately, Apple anticipated this situation, and provided a mechanism to let multiple gesture recognizers work nicely together, even when they're faced with ambiguous inputs that could seemingly trigger any of them. The basic idea is that you place a restriction on a gesture recognizer, telling it to not trigger its associated method unless some other gesture recognizer fails to trigger its own method.

That seems a bit abstract, so let's make it real. Tap gestures are recognized by the UITapGestureRecognizer class. A tap recognizer can be configured to do its thing when a particular number of taps occur. Imagine that we have a view for which we want to define distinct actions that occur when the user taps once or double-taps. You might start off with something like the following:

```
let singleTap = UITapGestureRecognizer(target: self,
action: #selector(ViewController.singleTap))
singleTap.numberOfTapsRequired = 1
singleTap.numberOfTouchesRequired = 1
view.addGestureRecognizer(singleTap)

let doubleTap = UITapGestureRecognizer(target: self,
 action: #selector(ViewController.doubleTap))
doubleTap.numberOfTapsRequired = 2
doubleTap.numberOfTouchesRequired = 1
view.addGestureRecognizer(doubleTap)
```

The problem with this piece of code is that the two recognizers are unaware of each other, and they have no way of knowing that the user's actions may be better suited to another recognizer. If the user double-taps the view in the preceding code, the doDoubleTap() method will be called, but the doSingleMethod() will also be called—twice!—once for each tap.

The way around this is to create a failure requirement. We tell singleTap that it should trigger its action only if doubleTap doesn't recognize and respond to the user input by adding this single line:

```
singleTap.require(toFail: doubleTap)
```

This means that, when the user taps once, `singleTap` doesn't do its work immediately. Instead, `singleTap` waits until it knows that `doubleTap` has decided to stop paying attention to the current gesture (that is, the user didn't tap twice). We're going to build on this further with our next project.

In Xcode, create a new project with the Single View Application template. Call this new project Taps and use the Devices pop-up to choose Universal. This application will have four labels: one each that informs us when it has detected a single-tap, double-tap, triple-tap, and quadruple-tap (see Figure 18-4).

Figure 18-4. *The Taps application detects up to four sequential taps*

We need outlets for the four labels and we also need separate methods for each tap scenario to simulate what we would have in a real application. We'll also include a method for erasing the text fields. Open ViewController.swift and add the label outlets to the class:

```
class ViewController: UIViewController {
    @IBOutlet var singleLabel:UILabel!
    @IBOutlet var doubleLabel:UILabel!
    @IBOutlet var tripleLabel:UILabel!
    @IBOutlet var quadrupleLabel:UILabel!
```

Save the file and select Main.storyboard to edit the GUI. Once you're there, add four labels to the view from the library and arrange them one above the other. In the Attributes Inspector, set the text alignment for each label to Center. In the Document Outline, Control-drag from the top label to its parent view and release the mouse. Hold down Shift and select Vertical Spacing to Top Layout Guide and Center Horizontally in Container, and then press Return. Do the same for the other three labels to set their auto layout constraints. When you're finished, Control-drag from the View Controller icon to each label and connect each one to singleLabel, doubleLabel, tripleLabel, and quadrupleLabel, respectively. Finally, make sure you double-click each label and press the delete key to get rid of any text. Now select ViewController.swift and make the code changes shown in Listing 18-5.

Listing 18-5. The Taps App Changes to the ViewController.swift File

```swift
override func viewDidLoad() {
    super.viewDidLoad()
    // Do any additional setup after loading the view, typically from a nib.

    let singleTap = UITapGestureRecognizer(target: self,
            action: #selector(ViewController.singleTap))
    singleTap.numberOfTapsRequired = 1
    singleTap.numberOfTouchesRequired = 1
    view.addGestureRecognizer(singleTap)

    let doubleTap = UITapGestureRecognizer(target: self,
            action: #selector(ViewController.doubleTap))
    doubleTap.numberOfTapsRequired = 2
    doubleTap.numberOfTouchesRequired = 1
    view.addGestureRecognizer(doubleTap)
    singleTap.require(toFail: doubleTap)

    let tripleTap = UITapGestureRecognizer(target: self,
            action: #selector(ViewController.tripleTap))
    tripleTap.numberOfTapsRequired = 3
    tripleTap.numberOfTouchesRequired = 1
    view.addGestureRecognizer(tripleTap)
    doubleTap.require(toFail: tripleTap)

    let quadrupleTap = UITapGestureRecognizer(target: self,
            action: #selector(ViewController.quadrupleTap))
    quadrupleTap.numberOfTapsRequired = 4
    quadrupleTap.numberOfTouchesRequired = 1
    view.addGestureRecognizer(quadrupleTap)
    tripleTap.require(toFail: quadrupleTap)

}

func singleTap() {
    showText("Single Tap Detected", inLabel: singleLabel)
}

func doubleTap() {
    showText("Double Tap Detected", inLabel: doubleLabel)
}
```

```
func tripleTap() {
    showText("Triple Tap Detected", inLabel: tripleLabel)
}

func quadrupleTap() {
    showText("Quadruple Tap Detected", inLabel: quadrupleLabel)
}

private func showText(_ text: String, inLabel label: UILabel) {
    label.text = text
    DispatchQueue.main.after(when: DispatchTime.now() +
            Double(Int64(2 * NSEC_PER_SEC)) / Double(NSEC_PER_SEC)) {
        label.text = ""
    }
}
```

The four tap methods do nothing more in this application than set one of the four labels and use DispatchQueue.main.after() to erase that same label after 2 seconds. The interesting part of this is what occurs in the viewDidLoad method. We start off simply enough, by setting up a tap gesture recognizer and attaching it to our view:

```
let singleTap = UITapGestureRecognizer(target: self,
        action: #selector(ViewController.singleTap))
singleTap.numberOfTapsRequired = 1
singleTap.numberOfTouchesRequired = 1
view.addGestureRecognizer(singleTap)
```

Note that we set both the number of taps (touches in the same position, one after another) required to trigger the action and touches (number of fingers touching the screen at the same time) to 1. After that, we set another tap gesture recognizer to handle a double-tap:

```
let doubleTap = UITapGestureRecognizer(target: self,
        action: #selector(ViewController.doubleTap))
doubleTap.numberOfTapsRequired = 2
doubleTap.numberOfTouchesRequired = 1
view.addGestureRecognizer(doubleTap)
singleTap.require(toFail: doubleTap)
```

This is pretty similar to the previous code, right up until that last line, in which we give singleTap some additional context. We are effectively telling singleTap that it should trigger its action only in case some other gesture recognizer—in this case, doubleTap—decides that the current user input isn't what it's looking for.

Let's think about what this means. With those two tap gesture recognizers in place, a single tap in the view will immediately make singleTap think, "Hey, this looks like it's for me." At the same time, doubleTap will think, "Hey, this looks like it *might* be for me, but I'll need to wait for one more tap." Because singleTap is set to wait for doubleTap's "failure," it doesn't trigger its action method right away; instead, it waits to see what happens with doubleTap.

After that first tap, if another tap occurs immediately, doubleTap says, "Hey, that's mine all right," and it fires its action. At that point, singleTap will realize what happened and give up on that gesture. On the other hand, if a particular amount of time goes by (the amount of time that the system considers to be the maximum length of time between taps in a double-tap), doubleTap will give up, and singleTap will see the failure and finally trigger its event. The rest of the method goes on to define gesture recognizers for three and four taps, and at each point it configures one gesture to be dependent on the failure of the next:

```
    let tripleTap = UITapGestureRecognizer(target: self,
            action: #selector(ViewController.tripleTap))
    tripleTap.numberOfTapsRequired = 3
    tripleTap.numberOfTouchesRequired = 1
    view.addGestureRecognizer(tripleTap)
    doubleTap.require(toFail: tripleTap)

    let quadrupleTap = UITapGestureRecognizer(target: self,
            action: #selector(ViewController.quadrupleTap))
    quadrupleTap.numberOfTapsRequired = 4
    quadrupleTap.numberOfTouchesRequired = 1
    view.addGestureRecognizer(quadrupleTap)
    tripleTap.require(toFail: quadrupleTap)
```

Note that we don't need to explicitly configure every gesture to be dependent on the failure of each of the higher tap-numbered gestures. That multiple dependency comes about naturally as a result of the chain of failure established in our code. Since `singleTap` requires the failure of `doubleTap`, `doubleTap` requires the failure of `tripleTap`, and `tripleTap` requires the failure of `quadrupleTap`. By extension, `singleTap` requires that all of the others fail.

Build and run the app. Whether you single-, double-, triple-, or quadruple-tap, you should see only one label displayed at the end of the sequence. After about a second and a half, the label will clear itself and you can try again.

Detecting Pinch and Rotation Gestures

Another common gesture is the two-finger pinch. It's used in a number of applications (e.g., Mobile Safari, Mail, and Photos) to let you zoom in (if you pinch apart) or zoom out (if you pinch together). Detecting pinches is really easy, thanks to `UIPinchGestureRecognizer`. This one is referred to as a **continuous gesture recognizer** because it calls its action method over and over again during the pinch. While the gesture is underway, the recognizer goes through a number of states. When the gesture is recognized, the recognizer is in state `UIGestureRecognizerState.began` and its `scale` property is set to an initial value of 1.0; for the rest of the gesture, the state is `UIGestureRecognizerState.changed` and the `scale` value goes up and down, relative to how far the user's fingers move from the start. We're going to use the `scale` value to resize an image. Finally, the state changes to `UIGestureRecognizerState.ended`.

Another common gesture is the two-finger rotation. This is also a continuous gesture recognizer and is named `UIRotationGestureRecognizer`. It has a rotation property that is 0.0 by default when the gesture begins, and then changes from 0.0 to 2.0*PI as the user rotates her fingers. In the next example, we'll use both pinch and rotation gestures. Create a new project in Xcode, again using the Single View Application template, and call this one **PinchMe**. First, drag and drop the beautiful yosemite-meadows.png image from the 18 - Image folder in the example source code archive (or some other favorite photo of yours) into your project's Assets.xcassets. Now make the changes in Listing 18-6 to the ViewController.swift file.

Listing 18-6. Updated ViewController.swift File for the PinchMe App Modifications

```
class ViewController: UIViewController, UIGestureRecognizerDelegate {
    private var imageView:UIImageView!
    private var scale = CGFloat(1)
    private var previousScale = CGFloat(1)
    private var rotation = CGFloat(0)
    private var previousRotation = CGFloat(0)
```

```swift
override func viewDidLoad() {
    super.viewDidLoad()
    // Do any additional setup after loading the view, typically from a nib.

    let image = UIImage(named: "yosemite-meadows")
    imageView = UIImageView(image: image)
    imageView.isUserInteractionEnabled = true
    imageView.center = view.center
    view.addSubview(imageView)

    let pinchGesture = UIPinchGestureRecognizer(target: self,
            action: #selector(ViewController.doPinch(_:)))
    pinchGesture.delegate = self
    imageView.addGestureRecognizer(pinchGesture)

    let rotationGesture = UIRotationGestureRecognizer(target: self,
            action: #selector(ViewController.doRotate(_:)))
    rotationGesture.delegate = self
    imageView.addGestureRecognizer(rotationGesture)
}

func gestureRecognizer(_ gestureRecognizer: UIGestureRecognizer,
            shouldRecognizeSimultaneouslyWith
                otherGestureRecognizer: UIGestureRecognizer) -> Bool {
    return true
}

func transformImageView() {
    var t = CGAffineTransform(scaleX: scale * previousScale, y: scale * previousScale)
    t = t.rotate(rotation + previousRotation)
    imageView.transform = t
}

func doPinch(_ gesture:UIPinchGestureRecognizer) {
    scale = gesture.scale
    transformImageView()
    if gesture.state == .ended {
        previousScale = scale * previousScale
        scale = 1
    }
}

func doRotate(_ gesture:UIRotationGestureRecognizer) {
    rotation = gesture.rotation
    transformImageView()
    if gesture.state == .ended {
        previousRotation = rotation + previousRotation
        rotation = 0
    }
}
}
```

First, we define four instance variables for the current and previous scale and rotation. The previous values are the values from a previously triggered and ended gesture recognizer; we need to keep track of these values as well because the UIPinchGestureRecognizer for scaling and UIRotationGestureRecognizer for rotation will always start at the default positions of 1.0 scale and 0.0 rotation. Next, in viewDidLoad(), we begin by creating a UIImageView to pinch and rotate, load our Yosemite image into it, and center it in the main view. We must remember to enable user interaction on the image view because UIImageView is one of the few UIKit classes that have user interaction disabled by default.

```
let image = UIImage(named: "yosemite-meadows")
imageView = UIImageView(image: image)
imageView.isUserInteractionEnabled = true
imageView.center = view.center
view.addSubview(imageView)
```

Next, we set up a pinch gesture recognizer and a rotation gesture recognizer. We tell them to notify us when their gestures are recognized via the doPinch() and doRotation() methods, respectively. We tell both to use self as their delegate:

```
let pinchGesture = UIPinchGestureRecognizer(target: self,
        action: #selector(ViewController.doPinch(_:)))
pinchGesture.delegate = self
imageView.addGestureRecognizer(pinchGesture)

let rotationGesture = UIRotationGestureRecognizer(target: self,
        action: #selector(ViewController.doRotate(_:)))
rotationGesture.delegate = self
imageView.addGestureRecognizer(rotationGesture)
```

In the gestureRecognizer(_:shouldRecognizeSimultaneoslyWithGestureRecognizer:) method (which is the only method from the UIGestureRecognizerDelegate protocol that we need to implement) we always return true to allow our pinch and rotation gestures to work together; otherwise, the gesture recognizer that starts first would always block the other:

```
func gestureRecognizer(_ gestureRecognizer: UIGestureRecognizer,
            shouldRecognizeSimultaneouslyWith
                otherGestureRecognizer: UIGestureRecognizer) -> Bool {
    return true
}
```

Next, we implement a helper method for transforming the image view according to the current scaling and rotation from the gesture recognizers. Notice that we multiply the scale by the previous scale. We also add to the rotation with the previous rotation. This allows us to adjust for pinch and rotation that has been done previously when a new gesture starts from the default 1.0 scale and 0.0 rotation.

```swift
func transformImageView() {
    var t = CGAffineTransform(scaleX: scale * previousScale, y: scale * previousScale)
    t = t.rotate(rotation + previousRotation)
    imageView.transform = t
}
```

Finally we implement the action methods that take the input from the gesture recognizers, and update the transformation of the image view. In both doPinch() and doRotate(), we first extract the new scale or rotation values. Next, we update the transformation for the image view. And finally, if the gesture recognizer reports that its gesture has ended by having a state equal to UIGestureRecognizerState.Ended, we store the current correct scale or rotation values, and then reset the current scale or rotation values to the default 1.0 scale or 0.0 rotation:

```swift
func doPinch(_ gesture:UIPinchGestureRecognizer) {
    scale = gesture.scale
    transformImageView()
    if gesture.state == .ended {
        previousScale = scale * previousScale
        scale = 1
    }
}

func doRotate(_ gesture:UIRotationGestureRecognizer) {
    rotation = gesture.rotation
    transformImageView()
    if gesture.state == .ended {
        previousRotation = rotation + previousRotation
        rotation = 0
    }
}
```

And that's all there is to pinch and rotation detection. Build and run the app to give it a try. As you do some pinching and rotation, you'll see the image change in response (see Figure 18-5). If you're on the simulator, remember that you can simulate a pinch by holding down the Option key and clicking and dragging in the simulator window using your mouse.

Figure 18-5. *The PinchMe application detects the pinch and rotation gesture.*

Summary

You should now understand the mechanism iOS uses to tell your application about touches, taps, and gestures. You also learned how to detect the most commonly used iOS gestures. We also saw a couple of basic examples of the use of the new 3D Touch feature. There's quite a bit more to this than we were able to cover here—for the full details, refer to Apple's document on the subject, which you can find at https://developer.apple.com/library/ios/documentation/UserExperience/Conceptual/Adopting3DTouchOniPhone/.

The iOS user interface relies on gestures for much of its ease of use, so you'll want to have these techniques at the ready for most of your iOS development. In the next chapter we'll tell you how to figure out where in the world you are by using Core Location.

CHAPTER 19

■ ■ ■

Determining Location

Every iOS device has the ability to determine where in the world it is, using a framework called **Core Location**. iOS also includes the **Map Kit** framework, which lets you easily create a live interactive map that shows any locations you like, including, of course, the user's location. In this chapter, we'll work with both of these frameworks. Core Location can actually leverage three technologies to do this: GPS, cell ID location, and Wi-Fi Positioning Service (WPS). GPS provides the most accurate positioning of the three technologies, but it is not available on first-generation iPhones, iPod touches, or Wi-Fi-only iPads. In short, any device with at least a 3G data connection also contains a GPS unit. GPS reads microwave signals from multiple satellites to determine the current location.

■ **Note**   Apple uses a version of GPS called **Assisted GPS**, also known as A-GPS. A-GPS uses network resources to help improve the performance of stand-alone GPS. The basic idea is that the telephony provider deploys services on its network that mobile devices will automatically find and collect some data from. This allows a mobile device to determine its starting location much more quickly than if it were relying on the GPS satellites alone.

Cell ID location lookup gives a rough approximation of the current location based on the physical location of the cellular base station that the device is currently in contact with. Since each base station can cover a fairly large area, there is a fairly large margin of error here. Cell ID location lookup requires a cell radio connection, so it works only on the iPhone (all models, including the very first) and any iPad with a 3G data connection. The WPS option uses the media access control (MAC) addresses from nearby Wi-Fi access points to make a guess at your location by referencing a large database of known service providers and the areas they service, but can have a mile or more inaccuracy.

All three methods significantly drain the battery, so keep that in mind when using Core Location. Your application shouldn't poll for location any more often than is absolutely necessary. When using Core Location, you have the option of specifying a desired accuracy. By carefully specifying the absolute minimum accuracy level you need, you can prevent unnecessary battery drain. The technologies that Core Location depends on are hidden from your application. We don't tell Core Location whether to use GPS, triangulation, or WPS. We just tell it how accurate we would like it to be, and it will decide from the technologies available to it which is best for fulfilling our request.

The Location Manager

Apple provides a fairly easy to use Core Location API. The main class we'll work with is CLLocationManager, usually referred to as the location manager. To interact with Core Location, you need to create an instance of the location manager:

```
let locationManager = CLLocationManager()
```

© Molly Maskrey, Kim Topley, David Mark, Fredrik Olsson and Jeff Lamarche 2016
M. Maskrey et al., *Beginning iPhone Development with Swift 3*, DOI 10.1007/978-1-4842-2223-2_19

This creates an instance of the location manager, but it doesn't actually start polling for your location. You must create an object that conforms to the CLLocationManagerDelegate protocol and assign it as the location manager's delegate. The location manager will call delegate methods when location information becomes available or changes. The process of determining location may take some time—even a few seconds.

Setting the Desired Accuracy

After you set the delegate, you also want to set the desired accuracy. As mentioned, don't specify a degree of accuracy any greater than you absolutely need. If you're writing an application that just needs to know which state or country the phone is in, don't specify a high level of precision. Remember that the more accuracy you demand of Core Location, the more power you're likely to use. Also, keep in mind that there is no guarantee that you will get the level of accuracy you have requested. Listing 19-1 shows an example of setting the delegate and requesting a specific accuracy.

Listing 19-1. Setting the Delegate and Desired Accuracy

```
locationManager.delegate = self
locationManager.desiredAccuracy = kCLLocationAccuracyBest
```

The accuracy is set using a CLLocationAccuracy value, a type that's defined as a Double. The value is in meters, so if you specify a desiredAccuracy of 10, you're telling Core Location that you want it to try to determine the current location within 10 meters, if possible. Specifying kCLLocationAccuracyBest (as we did previously) or specifying kCLLocationAccuracyBestForNavigation (where it uses other sensor data as well) tells Core Location to use the most accurate method that's currently available. In addition, you can also use: kCLLocationAccuracyNearestTenMeters, kCLLocationAccuracyHundredMeters, kCLLocationAccuracyKilometer, and kCLLocationAccuracyThreeKilometers.

Setting the Distance Filter

By default, the location manager will notify the delegate of any detected change in the device's location. By specifying a distance filter, you are telling the location manager not to notify you of every change, but instead to notify you only when the location changes by more than a certain amount. Setting up a distance filter can reduce the amount of polling your application does. Distance filters are also set in meters. Specifying a distance filter of 1000 tells the location manager not to notify its delegate until the iPhone has moved at least 1,000 meters from its previously reported position as in locationManager.distanceFilter = 1000.

If you ever want to return the location manager to the default setting, which applies no filter, you can use the constant kCLDistanceFilterNone, like this:

```
locationManager.distanceFilter = kCLDistanceFilterNone.
```

Just as when specifying the desired accuracy, you should take care to avoid getting updates any more frequently than you really need them; otherwise, you waste battery power. A speedometer app that's calculating the user's velocity based on location changes will probably want to have updates as quickly as possible, but an app that's going to show the nearest fast-food restaurant can get by with a lot fewer updates.

Getting Permission to Use Location Services

Before your application can use location services, you need to get the user's permission to do so. Core Location offers several different services, some of which can be used when your application is in the background—in fact, you can even request to have your application launched when certain events happen while it is not running. Depending on your application's functionality, it may be enough to request permission to access location services only while the user is using your application, or it might need to always be able to use the service. When writing an application, you need to decide which type of permission you require and make the request before initiating the services that you need. You'll see how to do this in the course of creating the example application for this chapter.

Starting the Location Manager

When you're ready to start polling for location, and after you request from the user to access location services, you tell the location manager to start. It will go off and do its thing, and then call a delegate method when it has determined the current location. Until you tell it to stop, it will continue to call your delegate method whenever it senses a change that exceeds the current distance filter. Here's how you start the location manager:

```
locationManager.startUpdatingLocation()
```

Using the Location Manager Wisely

If you need to determine the current location only and you don't need continuous updates, you can use the requestLocation() method instead of startUpdatingLocation(). This method automatically stops location polling as soon as the user's position has been determined. On the other hand, if you need to poll, make sure you stop polling as soon as you possibly can. Remember that as long as you are getting updates from the location manager, you are putting a strain on the user's battery. To tell the location manager to stop sending updates to its delegate, call stopUpdatingLocation(), like this:

```
locationManager.stopUpdatingLocation()
```

It's not necessary to call this method if you use requestLocation() instead of startUpdatingLocation().

The Location Manager Delegate

The location manager delegate must conform to the CLLocationManagerDelegate protocol, which defines several methods, all of them optional. One of these methods is called by the location manager when the availability of user authorization to use location services changes, another when it has determined the current location or when it detects a change in location. Yet another method gets called when the location manager encounters an error. We'll implement all of these delegate methods in this chapter's project.

Getting Location Updates

When the location manager wants to inform its delegate of the current location, it calls the locationManager (_:didUpdateLocations:) method. This method takes two parameters:

- The first parameter references the location manager that called the method.

- The second parameter contains an array of CLLocation objects representing the current location of the device and perhaps a few previous locations. If several location updates occur in a short period of time, they may be reported all at once with a single call to this method. In any case, the most recent location is always the last item in this array.

Getting Latitude and Longitude Using CLLocation

Location information gets passed from the location manager using instances of the CLLocation class. This class provides seven properties that might be of interest to your application:

- coordinate
- horizontalAccuracy
- altitude
- verticalAccuracy
- floor
- timestamp
- description

The latitude and longitude are stored in a property called coordinate. To get the latitude and longitude in degrees, use the code in Listing 19-2.

Listing 19-2. Getting Latitude and Longitude

```
let latitude = theLocation.coordinate.latitude
let longitude = theLocation.coordinate.longitude
```

The latitude and longitude variables will be inferred to be of type CLLocationDegrees. The CLLocation object can also tell you how confident the location manager is in its latitude and longitude calculations. The horizontalAccuracy property describes the radius of a circle (in meters, like all Core Location measurements) with the coordinate as its center. The larger the value in horizontalAccuracy, the less certain Core Location is of the location. A very small radius indicates a high level of confidence in the determined location.

You can see a graphic representation of horizontalAccuracy in the Maps application, as shown in Figure 19-1. The circle shown in Maps uses horizontalAccuracy for its radius when it detects your location. The location manager thinks you are at the center of that circle. If you're not, you're almost certainly somewhere inside the circle. A negative value in horizontalAccuracy is an indication that you cannot rely on the values in coordinate for some reason.

Figure 19-1. *The Maps application uses Core Location to determine your current position. The outer circle is a visual representation of the horizontal accuracy.*

The `CLLocation` object also has a property called `altitude`, of type `CLLocationDistance`, that tells you how many meters above (or below) sea level you are:

```
let altitude = theLocation.altitude
```

Each `CLLocation` object maintains a property called `verticalAccuracy` that is an indication of how confident Core Location is in its determination of altitude. The value in altitude could be off by as many meters as the value in `verticalAccuracy`. If the `verticalAccuracy` value is negative, Core Location is telling you it could not determine a valid altitude.

The `floor` property gives the floor within the building in which the user is located. This value is only valid in buildings that are able to provide the information, so you should not rely on its availability.

`CLLocation` objects include a `timestamp` that tells when the location manager made the location determination.

In addition to these properties, `CLLocation` has a useful instance method that will let you determine the distance between two `CLLocation` objects. The method is called `distanceFromLocation()` and it returns a value of type `CLLocationDistance`, which is just a `Double`, so you can use it in arithmetic calculations, as you'll see in the application we're about to create. Here's how you use this method:

```
let distance = fromLocation.distanceFromLocation(toLocation)
```

The preceding line of code returns the distance between two `CLLocation` objects: `fromLocation` and `toLocation`. This `distance` value returned contains the result of a great-circle distance calculation that ignores the `altitude` property and calculates the distance as if both points were at sea level. For most purposes, a great-circle calculation provides more than sufficient information; however, if you do want to take altitude into account when calculating distances, you'll need to write your own code to do it.

■ **Note**   If you're not sure what's meant by *great-circle distance*, the idea is that the shortest distance between any two points on the earth's surface will be found along a path that would, if extended, go the entire way around the earth: a "great circle." The most obvious great circles are perhaps the ones you've seen on maps: the equator and the longitudinal lines. However, such a circle can be found for any two points on the surface of the earth. The calculation performed by `CLLocation` determines the distance between two points along such a route, taking the curvature of the earth into account. Without accounting for that curvature, you would end up with the length of a straight line connecting the two points, which isn't much use, since that line would invariably go straight through some amount of the earth.

Error Notifications

If Core Location needs to report an error to your application, it will call a delegate method named `locatio nManager(_:didFailWithError:)`. One possible cause of an error is that the user denied access to location services, in which case the method will be called with the error code `CLError.Denied`. Another commonly encountered error code supported by the location manager is `CLError.LocationUnknown`, which indicates that Core Location was unable to determine the location but that it will keep trying. While a `CLError. LocationUnknown` error indicates a problem that may be temporary, `CLError.Denied` and other errors may indicate that your application will not be able to access Core Location any time during the remainder of the current session.

■ **Note**   The simulator has no way to determine your current location, but you can choose one (such as Apple's HQ, which is the default) or set your own, from the simulator's Debug ➤ Location menu.

Creating the WhereAmI Application

Let's build a small application to detect your device's current location and the total distance traveled while the program has been running. You can see what the first version of our application will look like in Figure 19-2.

Figure 19-2. The WhereAmI application in action

In Xcode, create a new project using the Single View Application template and call it **WhereAmI**. When the project window opens, select ViewController.swift, and make the following changes:

```
import UIKit
```

```
import CoreLocation
import MapKit

class ViewController: UIViewController, CLLocationManagerDelegate {
```

First, notice that we've imported the Core Location framework. Core Location is not part of either UIKit or Foundation, so we need to import it manually. Next, we conform this class to the CLLocationManagerDelegate method, so that we can receive location information from the location manager. Now add these property declarations:

```
private let locationManager = CLLocationManager()
private var previousPoint: CLLocation?
private var totalMovementDistance = CLLocationDistance(0)

@IBOutlet var latitudeLabel: UILabel!
@IBOutlet var longitudeLabel: UILabel!
@IBOutlet var horizontalAccuracyLabel: UILabel!
@IBOutlet var altitudeLabel: UILabel!
@IBOutlet var verticalAccuracyLabel: UILabel!
@IBOutlet var distanceTraveledLabel: UILabel!
@IBOutlet var mapView:MKMapView!
```

The locationManager property holds the reference to the CLLocationManager instance that we'll be using. The previousPoint property will keep track of the location from the last update we received from the location manager. This way, each time the user moves far enough to trigger an update, we'll be able to add the latest movement distance to our running total, which we'll keep in the totalMovementDistance property. The remaining properties are outlets that will be used to update labels on the user interface.

Now select Main.storyboard and let's start creating the user interface. First, expand the view controller hierarchy in the Document Outline, select the View item, and in the Attributes Inspector, change its background color to light gray. Next, drag a UIView from the object library, drop it onto the existing view, and then position and size it so that it covers the bottom part of the Main View. Make sure that the bottom, left, and right sides of the view exactly match those of the gray view. You are aiming to create something like the arrangement shown in Figure 19-2, where the view that you just dropped is the one at the bottom of the figure with the white background.

In the Document Outline, select the view that you just added, Control-drag from it to its parent view and release the mouse. In the pop-up menu that appears, hold down the Shift key and click Leading Space to Container Margin, Trailing Space to Container Margin, and Vertical Spacing to Bottom Layout Guide. This pins the view in place, but does not yet set its height. To fix that, with the view still selected in the Document Outline, click the Pin button. In the pop-up, select the Height check box, set the height to **166**, set Update Frames to Items of New Constraint, and then press Add 1 Constraint to set the height. That should do the job.

Next, we'll create the rightmost column of labels shown in Figure 19-2. Drag a label from the object library and drop it a little way below the top of the white view. Resize it to a width of about **80** points and move it so that it is close to the right edge of the view. Option-drag a copy of this label downward five times to create a stack of labels, as shown in Figure 19-2. Now let's fix the labels' sizes and positions relative to their parent view.

Starting with the topmost label in the Document Outline, Control-drag from the label to its parent view. Release the mouse. Hold down the Shift key, select Top Space to Container and Trailing Space to Container, and then press Return. To set the label's size, click the Pin button to open the Add New Constraints pop-up menu, click the Width and Height check boxes to select them, enter **80** as the width and **21** as the height (if they are not already set), and click Add 2 Constraints. You have now fixed the size and position of the top label. Repeat the same procedure for the other five labels.

Next, we'll add the second column of labels. Drag a label from the object library and place it to the left of the topmost label, leaving a small horizontal gap between them. Drag the left side of the label so that it almost reaches the left edge of the white view, and then in the Attributes Inspector, set the Alignment so that the label text is right-aligned. Make five copies of this label by Option-dragging downward, aligning each of them with the corresponding label on the right, to make the arrangement in Figure 19-3.

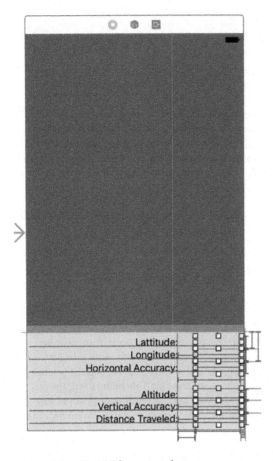

Figure 19-3. *Our UI layout goal*

Select the top label in the left column and Control-drag from its left side to the left side of the white view. Release the mouse and, in the context menu, select Leading Space to Container. Next, Control-drag from the same label to the matching label in the right-hand column. Release the mouse to open the context menu, hold down the Shift key, select Horizontal Spacing and Baseline, and press Return. Do the same for the other five labels in the left column. Finally, select the View Controller icon in the Document Outline, click the Resolve Auto Layout Issues button, and select Update Frames, if it's enabled.

We are almost there. We now need to connect the labels in the right column to the outlets in the view controller. Control-drag from the yellow view controller icon in the Document Outline to the top label in the right column and release the mouse. In the pop-up that appears, select latitudeLabel. Control-drag from the view controller icon to the second label to connect it to the longitudeLabel outlet, to the third label to connect it to horizontalAccuracyLabel, to the fourth to connect it to altitudeLabel, to the fifth to connect it to verticalAccuracyLabel, and to the bottom label to connect it to the distanceTraveledLabel outlet. You have now connected all six outlets.

Finally, clear the text from all of the labels in the right column, and change the text of the labels in the left column to match that shown in Figure 19-3; the top label's text should be Latitude:, the next one down should be Longitude:, and so on.

Now let's write the code to display some useful information in all those labels. Select ViewController. swift and insert the following lines in viewDidLoad() to configure the location manager:

```
override func viewDidLoad() {
    super.viewDidLoad()
    // Do any additional setup after loading the view, typically from a nib.
    locationManager.delegate = self
    locationManager.desiredAccuracy = kCLLocationAccuracyBest
    locationManager.requestWhenInUseAuthorization()
```

We assign our controller class as the location manager's delegate, set the desired accuracy to the best available, and then request permission to use the location service while the user is using our application. This is sufficient authorization for the purposes of this example. To use some of the more advanced features of Core Location, which are beyond the scope of this book, you will probably need to request permission to use Core Location at any time by calling the requestAlwaysAuthorization() method instead.

■ **Note**   In this simple example, the request for authorization is made as the application starts up, but Apple recommends that, in a real application, you should delay making the request until you actually need to use location services. The reason for this is that the user is more likely to agree if it's obvious why you need access to the device's location, based on operation that has been requested, than if an application, probably one that the user has just installed, requests permission as soon as it launches.

The first time this application runs, iOS will display an alert asking the user whether your application should be allowed to use your location. You need to supply a short piece of text that iOS will include in the alert pop-up, explaining why your application needs to know the user's location. Open the Info.plist file and add the text you'd like to have displayed under the key NSLocationWhenInUseUsageDescription (if you need to request permission to use location services even when the application is not actively being used, the text should be added under the key NSLocationWhenInUseUsageDescription instead. For the purposes of this example, use something like "This application needs to know your location to update your position on a map".

■ **Caution**   In some earlier versions of iOS, supplying text to qualify the permission request was optional. Beginning with iOS 8, it became mandatory. If you don't supply any text, the permission request will not be made.

If you run the application now, you'll see that iOS uses your text in the permission request, as shown in Figure 19-4. If the prompt does not appear, make sure that you have spelled the name of the key in Info.plist properly. Because we haven't completed our app yet at this point in time, you won't see the map yet in the background. But, Figure 19-4 gives you an idea of where we are headed.

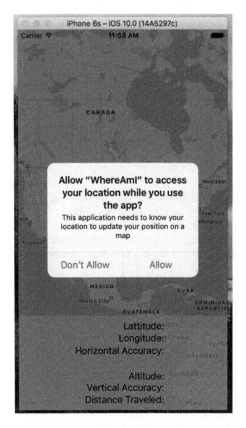

Figure 19-4. *Prompting the user for permission to use location services*

This prompt appears only once in the lifetime of the application. Whether or not the user allows your application to use location services, this request will never be made again, no matter how many times the application is run. That's not to say that the user can't change his mind about this, of course. We'll say more about that in the upcoming "Changing Location Service Permissions" section. As far as testing is concerned, rerunning the application from Xcode has no effect on the user's saved response—to get a clean state for testing, you have to delete the application from the simulator or device. If you do that, iOS will prompt for permission again when you reinstall and relaunch the application. For now, reply "Allow" to the prompt and let's continue writing our application.

You probably noticed that the viewDidLoad() method did not call the location manager's startUpdatingLocation() method immediately after calling requestWhenInUseAuthorization(). There is, in fact, no point in doing so, because the authorization process does not take place immediately. At some point after viewDidLoad() returns, the location manager delegate's locationManager(_:didChangeAuthor izationStatus:) method will be called with the application's authorization status. This may be the result of the user's reply to the permission request pop-up, or it may be the saved authorization state from when the application last executed. Either way, this method is an ideal place to start listening for location updates or request the user's location, assuming you are authorized to. Add the following implementation of this method to the *ViewController.swift* file:

```
func locationManager(_ manager: CLLocationManager,
                didChangeAuthorization status: CLAuthorizationStatus) {
    print("Authorization status changed to \(status.rawValue)")
    switch status {
    case .authorizedAlways, .authorizedWhenInUse:
        locationManager.startUpdatingLocation()

    default:
        locationManager.stopUpdatingLocation()
    }
}
```

This code starts by listening for location updates if authorization was granted, and stops listening if it was not. Since we don't start listening unless we have authorization, what's the point of calling stopUpdatingLocation() if we didn't get permission? That's a good question. The reason this code is required is because the user can give your application permission to use Core Location and then later revoke it. In that case, we need to stop listening for updates. For more on this, see "Changing Location Service Permissions" later in this chapter.

If your application tries to use location services when it doesn't have permission to do so, or if an error occurs at any time, the location manager calls its delegate's locationManager(_:didFailWithError:) method. Let's add an implementation of that method to the view controller:

```
func locationManager(_ manager: CLLocationManager,
                didFailWithError error: NSError) {
    let errorType = error.code == CLError.denied.rawValue
                    ? "Access Denied": "Error \(error.code)"
    let alertController = UIAlertController(title: "Location Manager Error",
                          message: errorType, preferredStyle: .alert)
    let okAction = UIAlertAction(title: "OK", style: .cancel,
                          handler: { action in })
    alertController.addAction(okAction)
    present(alertController, animated: true,
                          completion: nil)
}
```

For the purposes of this example, when an error occurs, we just alert the user. In a real application, you would use a more meaningful error message and clean up the application state as required.

Using Location Manager Updates

Now that we've dealt with getting permission to use the user's location, let's do something with that information. Insert this implementation (see Listing 19-3), of the delegate's locationManager(_:didUpdateL ocations:) method in ViewController.swift.

Listing 19-3. Our didUpateLocations Location Manager Delegate Method

```
func locationManager(_ manager: CLLocationManager, didUpdateLocations
                        locations: [CLLocation]) {
    if let newLocation = locations.last {
        let latitudeString = String(format: "%g\u{00B0}",
                        newLocation.coordinate.latitude)
```

```
latitudeLabel.text = latitudeString

let longitudeString = String(format: "%g\u{00B0}",
                newLocation.coordinate.longitude)
longitudeLabel.text = longitudeString

let horizontalAccuracyString = String(format:"%gm",
                newLocation.horizontalAccuracy)
horizontalAccuracyLabel.text = horizontalAccuracyString

let altitudeString = String(format:"%gm", newLocation.altitude)
altitudeLabel.text = altitudeString

let verticalAccuracyString = String(format:"%gm",
                newLocation.verticalAccuracy)
verticalAccuracyLabel.text = verticalAccuracyString

if newLocation.horizontalAccuracy < 0 {
    // invalid accuracy
    return
}

if newLocation.horizontalAccuracy > 100 ||
        newLocation.verticalAccuracy > 50 {
    // accuracy radius is so large, we don't want to use it
    return
}

if previousPoint == nil {
    totalMovementDistance = 0
} else {
    print("movement distance: " +
        "\(newLocation.distance(from: previousPoint!))")
    totalMovementDistance +=
        newLocation.distance(from: previousPoint!)
}
previousPoint = newLocation

let distanceString = String(format:"%gm", totalMovementDistance)
distanceTraveledLabel.text = distanceString
    }
}
```

The first thing we do in the delegate method is to update the first five labels in the second column of Figure 19-3 with values from the CLLocation objects passed in the locations argument. The array could contain more than one location, but we always use the last entry, which represents the most recent information.

■ **Note**   Both the longitude and latitude are displayed in formatting strings containing the cryptic-looking \u{00B0}. This is the hexadecimal value of the Unicode representation of the degree symbol (°). It's never a good idea to put anything other than ASCII characters directly in a source code file, but including the hex value in a string is just fine, and that's what we've done here.

Next, we check the accuracy of the values that the location manager gives us. High accuracy values indicate that the location manager isn't quite sure about the location, while negative accuracy values indicate that the location is actually invalid. Some devices do not have the hardware required to determine vertical position. On these devices, and on the simulator, the verticalAccuracy property will always be –1, so we don't exclude position reports that have this value. The accuracy values are in meters and indicate the radius of a circle from the location we're given, meaning that the true location could be anywhere in that circle. Our code checks to see whether these values are acceptably accurate; if not, it simply returns from this method rather than doing anything more with garbage data:

```
if newLocation.horizontalAccuracy < 0 {
    // invalid accuracy
    return
}

if newLocation.horizontalAccuracy > 100 ||
        newLocation.verticalAccuracy > 50 {
    // accuracy radius is so large, we don't want to use it
    return
}
```

Next, we check whether previousPoint is nil. If it is, then this update is the first valid one we've gotten from the location manager, so we zero out the distanceFromStart property. Otherwise, we add the latest location's distance from the previous point to the total distance. In either case, we update previousPoint to contain the current location:

```
if previousPoint == nil {
    totalMovementDistance = 0
} else {
    print("movement distance: " +
        "\(newLocation.distance(from: previousPoint!))")
    totalMovementDistance +=
        newLocation.distance(from: previousPoint!)
}
previousPoint = newLocation
```

After that, we populate the final label with the total distance that we've traveled from the start point. While this application runs, if the user moves far enough for the location manager to detect the change, the Distance Traveled: field will be continually updated with the distance the user has moved since the application started:

```
let distanceString = String(format:"%gm", totalMovementDistance)
distanceTraveledLabel.text = distanceString
```

And there you have it. Core Location is fairly straightforward and easy to use. Compile and run the application, and then try it. If you have the ability to run the application on your iPhone or iPad, try going for a drive, having someone else doing the driving, with the application running and watch the values change as you move around.

Visualizing Your Movement on a Map

What we've done so far is pretty interesting, but wouldn't it be nice if we could visualize our travel on a map? Fortunately, iOS includes the Map Kit framework to help us out here. Map Kit utilizes the same back-end services that Apple's Maps app uses, which means it's fairly robust and improving all the time. It contains a view class that presents a map, which responds to user gestures just as you'd expect of any modern mapping app. This view also lets us insert annotations for any locations we want to show up on our map, which by default show up as "pins" that can be touched to reveal some more info. We're going to extend our WhereAmI app to display the user's starting position and current position on a map.

Select ViewController.swift and add the following line to import the Map Kit framework:

```
import UIKit
import CoreLocation
import MapKit
```

Now add a new property declaration for the Map View that will display the user's location:

Now select Main.storyboard to edit the view. Drag a Map View from the object library and drop it onto the top half of the user interface. Resize the Map View so that it covers the whole screen, including the view that we added earlier and all of its labels, and then choose Editor ➤ Arrange ➤ Send to Back to move the Map View behind the other view.

■ **Tip**   If the Send to Back option is not enabled, you can get the same effect by dragging the Map View in the Document Outline upward, so that it appears before the view that contains the labels in its parent's child list.

In the Document Outline, Control-drag from the Map View to its parent view and, in the context menu, hold down the Shift key and select Leading Space to Container Margin, Trailing Space to Container Margin, Vertical Spacing to Top Layout Guide, and Vertical Spacing to Bottom Layout Guide, and then press the Return key.

The Map View is now locked in place, but the bottom part of it is obscured. We can fix that by making the view at the bottom partly transparent. To do that, select it in the Document Outline, open the Attributes Inspector, click the Background color editor, and, in the pop-up that appears, choose Other... to open a color chooser. Select a white background and move the Opacity slider to about 70%. Finally, Control-drag from the view controller icon in the Document Outline to the Map View and select mapView in the pop-up that appears to connect the map to its outlet.

Now that these preliminaries are in place, it's time to write a little code that will make the map do some work for us. Before dealing with the code required in the view controller, we need to set up a sort of model class to represent our starting point. MKMapView is built as the View part of an MVC (Model-View-Controller) architecture. It works best if we have distinct classes to represent markers on the map. We can pass model objects off to the map view and it will query them for coordinates, a title, and so on, using a protocol defined in the Map Kit framework.

Press ⌘N to bring up the new file assistant, and in the iOS Source section, choose Cocoa Touch Class. Name the class Place and make it a subclass of NSObject. Open Place.swift and modify it as shown next. You need to import the Map Kit framework, specify a protocol that the new class conforms to, and specify the properties as shown in Listing 19-4.

Listing 19-4. Our New Place Class in the Place.swift File

```swift
import UIKit
import MapKit

class Place: NSObject, MKAnnotation {
    let title: String?
    let subtitle: String?
    var coordinate: CLLocationCoordinate2D

    init(title:String, subtitle:String, coordinate:CLLocationCoordinate2D) {
        self.title = title
        self.subtitle = subtitle
        self.coordinate = coordinate
    }
}
```

This is a fairly "dumb" class that acts solely as a holder for these properties. In a real-world example, you may have real model classes that need to be shown on a map as an annotation, and the MKAnnotation protocol lets you add this capability to any class of your own without messing up any existing class hierarchies. Select ViewController.swift and add the two bold lines to the locationManager(_:didChangeAut horizationStatus:) method:

```swift
func locationManager(_ manager: CLLocationManager,
                didChangeAuthorization status: CLAuthorizationStatus) {
    print("Authorization status changed to \(status.rawValue)")
    switch status {
    case .authorizedAlways, .authorizedWhenInUse:
        locationManager.startUpdatingLocation()
        mapView.showsUserLocation = true

    default:
        locationManager.stopUpdatingLocation()
        mapView.showsUserLocation = false
    }
}
```

The Map View's showsUserLocation property does just what you probably imagine: it saves us the hassle of manually moving a marker around as the user moves by automatically drawing one for us. It uses Core Location to get the user's location and it works only if your application is authorized for that; so we enable the property when we are told that we have permission to use Core Location and then disable it again if we lose permission.

Now let's revisit the `locationManager(_:didUpdateLocations:)` method. We've already got some code in there that notices the first valid location data we receive and establishes our start point. We're also going to allocate a new instance of our `Place` class. We set its properties, giving it a location. We also add a title and subtitle that we want to appear when a marker for this location is displayed. Finally, we pass this object off to the map view. We also create an instance of `MKCoordinateRegion`, a `struct` included in Map Kit that lets us tell the view which section of the map we want it to display. `MKCoordinateRegion` uses our new location's coordinates and a pair of distances in meters (100, 100) that specify how wide and tall the displayed map portion should be. We pass this off to the map view as well, telling it to animate the change. All of this is done by adding the bold lines shown here:

```
if previousPoint == nil {
    totalMovementDistance = 0
    let start = Place(title:"Start Point",
              subtitle:"This is where we started",
              coordinate:newLocation.coordinate)
    mapView.addAnnotation(start)
    let region = MKCoordinateRegionMakeWithDistance(newLocation.coordinate,
                 100, 100)
     mapView.setRegion(region, animated: true)
    } else {
        print("movement distance: " +
          "\(newLocation.distance(from: previousPoint!))")
        totalMovementDistance +=
        newLocation.distance(from: previousPoint!)
}
```

So now we've told the map view that we have an annotation (i.e., a visible placemark) that we want the user to see. But how should it be displayed? Well, the map view figures out what sort of view to display for each annotation by asking its delegate. In a more complex app, that would work for us. But in this example we haven't made ourselves a delegate, simply because it's not necessary for our simple use case. Unlike `UITableView`, which requires its data source to supply cells for display, `MKMapView` has a different strategy: if it's not provided with annotation views by a delegate, it simply displays a default sort of view represented by a red "pin" on the map that reveals some more information when touched.

There's one final thing you need to do—enable your application to use Map Kit. To do this, select the project in the Project Navigator and then select the WhereAmI target. At the top of editor area, select Capabilities, locate the Maps section, and move the selector switch on the right from OFF to ON. Now build and run your app, and you'll see the map view load. As soon as it gets valid position data, you'll see it scroll to the right location, drop a pin at your starting point, and mark your current location with a glowing blue dot (see Figure 19-5). Not bad for a few dozen lines of code.

Figure 19-5. The red pin marks our starting location, and the blue dot shows how far we've gotten—in this case, no distance at all

---

■ **Tip**   If you are using a real device and the map does not zoom to show your current position, it's because Core Location can't figure out where you are to within 100 meters. You might be able to help it out by enabling Wi-Fi, which can sometimes improve Core Location's accuracy.

Changing Location Service Permissions

When your application runs for the first time, you hope the user will give it permission to use location services. Whether you get permission or not, you can't assume that nothing changes. The user can grant or revoke location permission via the Settings app. You can test this on the simulator. Launch the app and grant yourself permission to use Core Location (if you've previously denied permission, you'll need to remove and reinstall the app first). You should see your location on the map. Now go to the Settings app and choose Privacy ➤ Location Services. At the top of the screen is a switch that turns location services on or off. Turn the switch to OFF and go back to your application. You'll see that the map no longer shows your position. That's because the location manager called the `locationManager(_:didChangeAuthorizationStatus:)` method with authorization code `CLAuthorizationStatus.denied`, in response to which the application stops receiving position updates and tells Map Kit to stop tracking the user's position. Now go back to the Settings app, re-enable Core Location in Locations Services, and come back to your application; you'll find that it's tracking your position again.

Switching Location Services off is not the only way for the user to change your app's ability to use Core Location. Go back to the Settings app. Below the switch that enables Location Services, you'll see a list of all the apps that are using it, including WhereAmI, as shown on the left in Figure 19-6. Clicking the application name takes you to another page where you can allow or deny access to your application, which you can see on the right in Figure 19-6. At the moment, the application can use location services while the user is using the app. If you click Never, that permission is revoked, as you can prove by returning to the application again. This demonstrates that it's important to code the application so that it can detect and respond properly to changes in its authorization status.

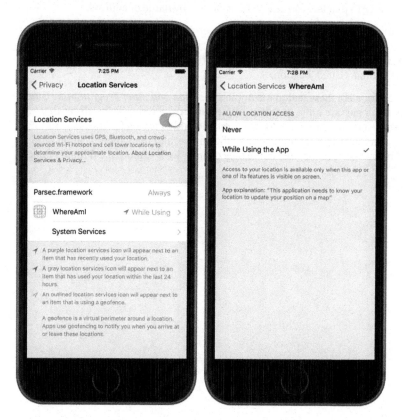

Figure 19-6. *Changing Core Location access permission for the WhereAmI app*

Summary

That's the end of our introduction to Core Location and Map Kit. There is quite a lot more to be discovered about both of these frameworks. Here are just a few of the highlights:

- Instead of closely tracking the user's location using the startUpdatingLocation() method, applications that need less positional accuracy and/or less frequent updates, such as Weather apps, can use the Significant Location Updates service. You should use this service if at all possible, because it can significantly reduce power consumption.

- On devices that have a magnetometer, Core Location can report the user's heading. If the device also has a GPS, it can report the direction in which the user is moving.

- Core Location can report when the user enters or leaves application-defined geographical regions (defined as a circle of a given radius and center) or when the application is in the vicinity of an iBeacon.

- You can convert between the coordinates reported by Core Location and a user-friendly placemark object and vice versa, using the Geocoding service. In addition to this, Map Kit includes an API that lets you search for locations by name or address.

- Core Location monitors the user's movement and can determine when the user stops for a period of time at a location. When this happens, the user is assumed to be "visiting" that location. Your application can receive notification when the user arrives at and departs from a visited location.

The best source of information for all of these features is Apple's *Location and Maps Programming Guide*.

Although the underlying technologies are quite complex, Apple has provided simple interfaces that hide most of the complexity, making it quite easy to add location-related and mapping features to your applications so that you can tell where the users are, notice when they move, and mark their location (and any other locations) on a map. And speaking of moving, in the next chapter we'll explore the iPhone's built-in accelerometer.

CHAPTER 20

■ ■ ■

Device Orientation and Motion

The iPhone, iPad, and iPod touch all include a built-in accelerometer—the tiny device that lets iOS know how the device is being held and if it's being moved. iOS uses the accelerometer to handle autorotation, and many games use it as a control mechanism. The accelerometer can also be used to detect shakes and other sudden movement. This capability was extended even further with the introduction of the iPhone 4, which was the first iPhone to include a built-in gyroscope to let developers determine the angle at which the device is positioned around each axis. The gyro and accelerometer are now standard on all new iPads and iPod touches. In this chapter, we'll explore using the Core Motion framework to access the gyro and accelerometer values in your application.

Accelerometer Physics

An **accelerometer** measures both acceleration and gravity by sensing the amount of inertial force in a given direction. The accelerometer inside your iOS device is a three-axis component. This means that it is capable of detecting either movement or the pull of gravity in three-dimensional space. In other words, you can use the accelerometer to discover not only how the device is currently being held (as autorotation does), but also to learn if it's laying on a table and even whether it's face down or face up. Accelerometers give measurements in g-forces (**g** for gravity), so a value of 1.0 returned by the accelerometer means that 1g is sensed in a particular direction, as in these examples:

- If the device is being held still with no movement, there will be approximately 1 g of force exerted on it by the pull of the earth.

- If the device is being held perfectly upright, in portrait orientation, it will detect and report about 1 g of force exerted on its y axis.

- If the device is being held at an angle, that 1 g of force will be distributed along different axes depending on how it is being held. When held at a 45-degree angle, the 1 g of force will be split roughly equally between two of the axes.

Sudden movement can be detected by looking for accelerometer values considerably larger than 1 g. In normal usage, the accelerometer does not detect significantly more than 1 g on any axis. If you shake, drop, or throw your device, the accelerometer will detect a greater amount of force on one or more axes.

Figure 20-1 shows a graphic representation of the three axes used by the accelerometer. Notice that the accelerometer uses the more standard convention for the y coordinate, with increases in y indicating upward force, which is the opposite of Quartz 2D's coordinate system (discussed in Chapter 16). When you are using the accelerometer as a control mechanism with Quartz 2D, you need to translate the y coordinate. When working with Sprite Kit, which is more likely when you are using the accelerometer to control animation, no translation is required.

© Molly Maskrey, Kim Topley, David Mark, Fredrik Olsson and Jeff Lamarche 2016
M. Maskrey et al., *Beginning iPhone Development with Swift 3*, DOI 10.1007/978-1-4842-2223-2_20

Figure 20-1. *The iPhone accelerometer's axes in three dimensions. The front view of an iPhone on the left shows the x and y axes. The side view on the right shows the z axis*

Rotation Detection Using the Gyroscope

I mentioned earlier that all current devices include a gyroscope sensor, allowing you to read values describing the device's rotation around its axes. If the difference between the gyroscope and the accelerometer seems unclear, consider an iPhone lying flat on a table. If you begin to turn the phone around while it's lying flat, the accelerometer values won't change. That's because the forces bent on moving the phone—in this case, just the force of gravity pulling straight down the z axis—aren't changing. (In reality, things are a bit fuzzier than that, and the action of your hand bumping the phone will surely trigger a small amount of accelerometer action.) During that same movement, however, the device's rotation values will change—particularly the z-axis rotation value. Turning the device clockwise will generate a negative value, and turning it counterclockwise gives a positive value. Stop turning, and the z-axis rotation value will go back to zero. Rather than registering an absolute rotation value, the gyroscope tells you about changes to the device's rotation as they happen. You'll see how this works in this chapter's first example.

Core Motion and the Motion Manager

We'll access accelerometer and gyroscope values using the Core Motion framework. This framework provides, among other things, the CMMotionManager class, which acts as a gateway for all the values describing how the device is being moved by its user. An application creates an instance of CMMotionManager and then puts it to use in one of two modes:

- It can execute some code for you whenever motion occurs.

- It can hang on to a perpetually updated structure that lets you access the latest values at any time.

The latter method provides an ideal solution for games and other highly interactive applications that need to be able to poll the device's current state during each pass through the game loop. I'll show you how to implement both approaches. Note that the CMMotionManager class isn't actually a singleton, but your application should treat it like one and you should create only one of these per app. So, if you need to access the motion manager from several places in your app, you should probably create it in your application delegate and provide access to it from there.

Besides the `CMMotionManager` class, Core Motion also provides a few other classes, such as `CMAccelerometerData` and `CMGyroData`, which are simple containers through which your application can access raw accelerometer and gyroscope information; and `CMDeviceMotion`, a class that combines accelerometer and gyroscope measurements together with attitude information—that is, whether the device is lying flat, tilting upward or to the left, and so on. We'll be using the `CMDeviceMotion` class in the examples in this chapter.

Creating the MotionMonitor Application

I mentioned that the motion manager can operate in a mode where it executes some code for you each time the motion data changes. Most other Cocoa Touch classes offer this sort of functionality by letting you connect to a delegate that gets a message when the time comes, but Core Motion does things a little differently. Instead of using a set of delegate methods to let us know what happens, `CMMotionManager` lets you pass in a closure to execute whenever motion occurs. We've already used closures a couple of times in this book, and now you're going to see another application of this technique.

Use Xcode to create a new Single View Application project named MotionMonitor. This will be a simple app that reads both accelerometer data, gyroscope data (if available), and attitude information, and then displays the information on the screen.

■ **Note**   The applications in this chapter do not function on the simulator because the simulator has no accelerometer.

Now select the ViewController.swift file and make the following changes:

```
class ViewController: UIViewController {
    @IBOutlet var gyroscopeLabel: UILabel!
    @IBOutlet var accelerometerLabel: UILabel!
    @IBOutlet var attitudeLabel: UILabel!
```

This provides us with outlets to three labels where we'll display the information. Nothing much needs to be explained here, so just go ahead and save your changes. Next, open Main.storyboard in Interface Builder. Now drag out a `Label` from the library into the view. Resize the label to make it run from the left side of the screen to the right, resize it to be about one-third the height of the entire view, and then align the top of the label to the top blue guideline. Now open the Attributes Inspector and change the `Lines` field from 1 to 0. The `Lines` attribute is used to specify the number of lines of text that may appear in the label, and it provides a hard upper limit. If you set it to 0, no limit is applied, and the label can contain as many lines as you like.

Next, drag a second label from the library and drop it directly below the first one. Align its top with the bottom of the first label and align its sides with the left and right edges of the screen. Resize it to be about the same height as the first label. You don't need to be too exact with this since we will be using auto layout to control the final height of the labels. Drag out a third label, placing it with its top edge along the bottom edge of the second label, and then resize it so that its bottom edge is along the bottom edge of the screen, and align its sides to the left and right edges of the screen. Set the `Lines` attribute for both labels to 0.

Now let's fix the positions and sizes of the three labels. In the Document Overview, Control-drag from the top label to its parent view and release the mouse. In the pop-up menu, hold down the Shift key and select Leading Space to Container Margin, Vertical Spacing to Top Layout Guide, and Trailing Space to Container Margin, and then press Return. Control-drag from the second label to the parent view. In the pop-up menu, hold down Shift and select Leading Space to Container Margin and Trailing Space to Container Margin, and press Return. Control-drag from the third label to Main View, and this time, holding down Shift, select Leading Space to Container Margin, Vertical Spacing to Bottom Layout Guide, and Trailing Space to Container Margin.

Now that all three labels are pinned to the edges of their parent view, let's link them to each other. Control-drag from the second label to the first label and select Vertical Spacing from the pop-up menu. Control-drag from the second label to the third label and do the same. Finally, we need to ensure that the labels have the same height. To do this, hold down the Shift key and click all three labels so that they are all selected. Click the Pin button. In the pop-up, click the Equal Heights check box and press Add 2 Constraints. Click the Resolve Auto Layout Issues button and then click Update All Frames in View Controller. If this item is not available, select the View Controller icon in the Document Outline and try again.

That completes the layout; now let's connect the labels to their outlets. Control-drag from the view controller icon in the Document Outline the top label, release the mouse and select gyroscopeLabel from the pop-up menu to connect the label to its outlet. Do the same with the second label, connecting it to accelerometerLabel and the third label, which should be linked to attitudeLabel. Finally, double-click each of the labels and delete the existing text. This simple GUI is complete, so save your work and get ready for some coding.

Next, select ViewController.swift. Now comes the interesting part. Add the code in Listing 20-1 to the ViewController.swift file.

Listing 20-1. Add the Following Code to the ViewController.swift File

```
private let motionManager = CMMotionManager()
private let queue = OperationQueue()

override func viewDidLoad() {
    super.viewDidLoad()
    // Do any additional setup after loading the view, typically from a nib.

    if motionManager.isDeviceMotionAvailable {
        motionManager.deviceMotionUpdateInterval = 0.1
        motionManager.startDeviceMotionUpdates(to: queue) {
                (motion:CMDeviceMotion?, error:NSError?) -> Void in
            if let motion = motion {
                let rotationRate = motion.rotationRate
                let gravity = motion.gravity
                let userAcc = motion.userAcceleration
                let attitude = motion.attitude

                let gyroscopeText =
                    String(format: "Rotation Rate:\n-----------------\n" +
                                "x: %+.2f\ny: %+.2f\nz: %+.2f\n",
                        rotationRate.x, rotationRate.y, rotationRate.z)
                let acceleratorText =
                    String(format: "Acceleration:\n---------------\n" +
                                "Gravity x: %+.2f\t\tUser x: %+.2f\n" +
                                "Gravity y: %+.2f\t\tUser y: %+.2f\n" +
                                "Gravity z: %+.2f\t\tUser z: %+.2f\n",
                        gravity.x, userAcc.x, gravity.y,
                        userAcc.y, gravity.z,userAcc.z)
                let attitudeText =
                    String(format: "Attitude:\n----------\n" +
                                "Roll: %+.2f\nPitch: %+.2f\nYaw: %+.2f\n",
                        attitude.roll, attitude.pitch, attitude.yaw)

                DispatchQueue.main.async {
                    self.gyroscopeLabel.text = gyroscopeText
                    self.accelerometerLabel.text = acceleratorText
```

```
                    self.attitudeLabel.text = attitudeText
                }
            }
        }
    }
}
```

First, we import the Core Motion framework and add two additional properties to the class:

```
import UIKit
import CoreMotion

class ViewController: UIViewController {
    @IBOutlet var gyroscopeLabel: UILabel!
    @IBOutlet var accelerometerLabel: UILabel!
    @IBOutlet var attitudeLabel: UILabel!
    private let motionManager = CMMotionManager()
    private let queue = OperationQueue()
```

This code first creates an instance of CMMotionManager, which we'll use to monitor motion events. The code then creates an operation queue, which is simply a container for a work that needs to be done.

▪ **Caution** The motion manager wants to have a queue in which it will put the bits of work to be done, as specified by the closure you will give it, each time an event occurs. It would be tempting to use the system's default queue for this purpose, but the documentation for CMMotionManager explicitly warns not to do this. The concern is that the default queue could end up chock-full of these events and have a hard time processing other crucial system events as a result.

Next, in the viewDidLoad method, we add the code to request device motion updates and update the labels with the gyroscope, accelerometer, and attitude readings as we get them. We first check to make sure the device actually has the required equipment to provide motion information. All handheld iOS devices released so far do, but it's worth checking in case some future device doesn't. Next, we set the time interval we want between updates, specified in seconds. Here, we're asking for a tenth of a second. Note that setting this doesn't guarantee that we'll receive updates at precisely that speed. In fact, that setting is really a cap, specifying the best rate the motion manager will be allowed to give us. In reality, it may update less frequently than that:

```
    if motionManager.isDeviceMotionAvailable {
        motionManager.deviceMotionUpdateInterval = 0.1
```

Next, we tell the motion manager to start reporting device motion updates. We pass in the closure that defines the work that will be done each time an update occurs and the queue where the closure will be queued for execution. In this case, the closure receives a CMDeviceMotion object that contains the most recent motion data and possibly an NSError object if an error occurs while acquiring the data:

```
    motionManager.startDeviceMotionUpdates(to: queue) {
        (motion:CMDeviceMotion?, error:NSError?) -> Void in
```

What follows is the closure itself. It creates strings based on the current motion values and pushes them into the labels. We can't do that directly here because UIKit classes like UILabel usually work well only when accessed from the main thread. Due to the way this code will be executed, from within an NSOperationQueue,

we simply don't know the specific thread in which we'll be executing. So, we use the `DispatchQueue.main.`
`async` function to pass control to the main thread before setting the labels' `text` properties.

The gyroscope values are accessed through the `rotationRate` property of the `CMDeviceMotion` object that
was passed into the closure. The `rotationRate` property is of type `RotationRate`, which is just a simple `struct`
containing three `Float` values that represent the rotation rates around the x, y, and z axes. The accelerometer
data is a little more complex, since Core Motion reports two different values—the acceleration due to gravity
and any additional acceleration caused by forces applied by the user. You get these values from the `gravity`
and `userAcceleration` properties, which are both of type `CMAcceleration`. `CMAcceleration` is another
simple `struct` that holds the accelerations along the x, y, and z axes. Finally, the device attitude is reported in
the `attitude` property, which is of type `CMAttitude`. We'll discuss this further when we run the application.

Before trying out the application, there is one more thing to do. We are going to be moving and rotating
the device in various ways to see how the values in the `CMDeviceMotion` structure correlate to what's
happening to the device. While we're doing this, we don't want autorotation to kick in. To prevent this, select
the project in the Project Navigator, select the MotionMonitor target, and then the General tab. In the Device
Orientation section under Deployment Info, select Portrait and make sure that the other three orientations
are not selected. This locks the application to Portrait orientation only. Now build and run your app on
whatever iOS device you have, and then try it, as shown in Figure 20-2.

Figure 20-2. *MotionMonitor running on an iPhone. Unfortunately, you'll get no useful information if you run
this app in the simulator*

As you tilt your device around in different ways, you'll see how the rotation rate, accelerometer, and attitude values adjust to each new position and will hold steady as long as you hold the device steady. Whenever the device is standing still, no matter which orientation it is in, the rotation values will hover around zero. As you rotate the device, you'll see that the rotation values change, depending on how you turn it around its various axes. The values will always move back to zero when you stop moving the device. We'll look more closely at all of the results shortly.

Proactive Motion Access

You've seen how to access motion data by passing CMMotionManager closures to be called as motion occurs. This kind of event-driven motion handling can work well enough for the average Cocoa app, but sometimes it doesn't quite fit an application's particular needs. Interactive games, for example, typically have a perpetually running loop that processes user input, updates the state of the game, and redraws the screen. In such a case, the event-driven approach isn't such a good fit, since you would need to implement an object that waits for motion events, remembers the latest positions from each sensor as they're reported, and is ready to report the data back to the main game loop when necessary. Fortunately, CMMotionManager has a built-in solution. Instead of passing in closures, we can just tell it to activate the sensors using the startDeviceMotionUpdates() method. Once we do so, we can simply read the values any time we want, directly from the motion manager.

Let's change our MotionMonitor app to use this approach, just so you can see how it works. Start by making a copy of your MotionMonitor project folder or compressing it as we did in earlier examples.

■ **Note** You'll find a completed version of this project in the MonitorMotion2 folder in the example source code.

Close the open Xcode project and open the one from the new copy instead, heading straight to ViewController.swift. The first step is to remove the queue property and add a new property, a pointer to an NSTimer that will trigger all our display updates:

```
class ViewController: UIViewController {
    @IBOutlet var gyroscopeLabel: UILabel!
    @IBOutlet var accelerometerLabel: UILabel!
    @IBOutlet var attitudeLabel: UILabel!
    private let motionManager = CMMotionManager()
    private var updateTimer: Timer!
```

Next, delete the viewDidLoad() method because we are not going to need it. We'll use a timer to collect motion data directly from the motion manager every tenth of a second instead of having it delivered to a closure. We want our timer—and the motion manager itself—to be active only while the application's view is actually being displayed. That way, we keep the usage of our main game loop to a bare minimum. We can accomplish this by implementing the viewWillAppear() and viewDidDisappear() methods, as shown in Listing 20-2.

Listing 20-2. Our viewWillAppear and viewDidDisappear Methods for Proactive Motion Access

```
override func viewWillAppear(_ animated: Bool) {
    super.viewWillAppear(animated)
    if motionManager.isDeviceMotionAvailable {
        motionManager.deviceMotionUpdateInterval = 0.1
        motionManager.startDeviceMotionUpdates()
        updateTimer =
            Timer.scheduledTimer(timeInterval: 0.1, target: self,
                    selector: #selector(ViewController.updateDisplay), userInfo: nil,
                    repeats: true)
```

```
        }
    }

    override func viewDidDisappear(_ animated: Bool) {
        super.viewDidDisappear(animated)
        if motionManager.isDeviceMotionAvailable {
            motionManager.stopDeviceMotionUpdates()
            updateTimer.invalidate()
            updateTimer = nil
        }
    }
}
```

The code in `viewWillAppear()` calls the motion manager's `startDeviceMotionUpdates()` method to start it off device motion information, and then creates a new timer and schedules it to fire once every tenth of a second, calling the `updateDisplay()` method, which we haven't created yet. Add the method in Listing 20-3 just below `viewDidDisappear()`.

Listing 20-3. The updateDisplay Method Goes in the ViewController.swift File

```
func updateDisplay() {
    if let motion = motionManager.deviceMotion {
        let rotationRate = motion.rotationRate
        let gravity = motion.gravity
        let userAcc = motion.userAcceleration
        let attitude = motion.attitude

        let gyroscopeText =
            String(format: "Rotation Rate:\n----------------\n" +
                        "x: %+.2f\ny: %+.2f\nz: %+.2f\n",
                    rotationRate.x, rotationRate.y, rotationRate.z)
        let acceleratorText =
            String(format: "Acceleration:\n--------------\n" +
                        "Gravity x: %+.2f\t\tUser x: %+.2f\n" +
                        "Gravity y: %+.2f\t\tUser y: %+.2f\n" +
                        "Gravity z: %+.2f\t\tUser z: %+.2f\n",
                    gravity.x, userAcc.x, gravity.y,
                    userAcc.y, gravity.z,userAcc.z)
        let attitudeText =
            String(format: "Attitude:\n----------\n" +
                        "Roll: %+.2f\nPitch: %+.2f\nYaw: %+.2f\n",
                    attitude.roll, attitude.pitch, attitude.yaw)

        DispatchQueue.main.async {
            self.gyroscopeLabel.text = gyroscopeText
            self.accelerometerLabel.text = acceleratorText
            self.attitudeLabel.text = attitudeText
        }
    }
}
```

This is a copy of the code from the closure in the previous version of this example, except that the `CMDeviceMotion` object is obtained directly from the motion manager. Notice the `if let` expression that ensures that the `CMDeviceMotion` value returned by the motion manager is not `nil`; this is required because the timer may fire before the motion manager has acquired its first data sample. Build and run the app on your device, and you should see that it behaves exactly like the first version. Now you've seen two ways of accessing motion data. Use whichever suits your application best.

Gyroscope and Attitude Results

The gyroscope measures the rate at which the device is rotating about the x, y, and z axes. Refer to Figure 20-1 to see how the axes relate to the body of the device. First, lay the device flat on a table. While it's not moving, all three rotation rates will be close to zero and you'll see that the roll, pitch, and yaw values are also close to zero. Now gently rotate the device clockwise. As you do, you'll see that the rotation rate around the z axis becomes negative. The faster you rotate the device, the larger the absolute value of the rotation rate will be.

When you stop rotating, the rotation rate will return to zero, but the yaw does not. The yaw represents the angle through which the device has been rotated about the z axis from its initial rest position. If you rotate the device clockwise, the yaw will decrease through negative values until the device is 180° from its rest position, when its value will be around –3. If you continue to rotate the device clockwise, the yaw will jump to a value slightly larger than +3 and then decrease to zero as you rotate it back to its initial position. If you start by rotating counterclockwise, the same thing happens, except that the yaw is initially positive. The yaw angle is actually measured in radians, not degrees. A rotation of 180° is the same as a rotation by π radians, which is why the maximum yaw value is about 3 (since π is a little larger than 3.14).

With the device flat on the table again, hold the top edge and rotate it upward, leaving the base on the table. This is a rotation around the x axis, so you'll see the x rotation rate increase through positive values until you hold the device steady, at which point it returns to zero. Now look at the pitch value. It has increased by an amount that depends on the angle through which you have lifted the top edge of the device. If you lift the device all the way to the vertical, the pitch value will be around 1.5. Like yaw, pitch is measured in radians, so when the device is vertical, it has rotated through 90°, or $\pi/2$ radians, which is a little over 1.5. If you lay the device flat again and repeat—but this time lift the bottom edge and leave the top on the table, you are performing a counterclockwise rotation about the x axis and you'll see a negative rotation rate and a negative pitch.

Finally, with the device flat on the table again, lift its left edge, leaving the right edge on the table. This is a rotation about the y axis and you'll see this reflect in the y-axis rotation rate. You can get the total rotation angle at any point from the roll value. It will be about 1.5 (actually $\pi/2$) radians when the device is standing upright on its right edge and it will increase all the way to π radians if you turn it on its face; although, of course, you'll need a glass table to be able to see this.

In summary, use the rotation rates to see how fast the device is rotating about each axis and the yaw, pitch, and roll values to get its current total rotation about these axes, relative to its starting orientation.

Accelerometer Results

I mentioned earlier that the iPhone's accelerometer detects acceleration along three axes; it provides this information using two `CMAcceleration` structs. Each `CMAcceleration` has an x, y, and z field, each of which holds a floating-point value. A value of 0 means that the accelerometer detects no movement on that particular axis. A positive or negative value indicates force in one direction. For example, a negative value for y indicates that a downward pull is sensed, which is probably an indication that the phone is being held upright in portrait orientation. A positive value for y indicates some force is being exerted in the opposite direction, which could mean the phone is being held upside down or that the phone is being moved in a downward direction. The `CMDeviceMotion` object separately reports the acceleration along each axis due to gravity and any additional forces caused by the user.

For example, if you hold the device flat, you'll see that gravity value is close to –1 along the z axis and the user acceleration components are all close to zero. Now if you quickly raise the device, keeping it level, you'll see that the gravity values remain about the same, but there is positive user acceleration along the z axis. For some applications, it is useful to have separate gravity and user acceleration values, while for others, you need the total acceleration, which you can get by adding together the components of the `gravity` and `userAcceleration` properties of the `CMDeviceMotion` object.

Keeping the diagram in Figure 20-1 in mind, let's look at some accelerometer results in Figure 20-3. This figure shows the reported acceleration due to gravity while the device is in a given attitude and not moving. Note that in real life you will almost never get values this precise, as the accelerometer is sensitive enough to sense even tiny amounts of motion, and you will usually pick up at least some tiny amount of force on all three axes. This is real-world physics, not high-school physics.

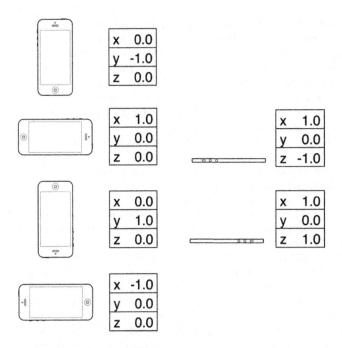

Figure 20-3. *Idealized gravity acceleration values for different device orientations*

Probably the most common usage of the accelerometer in third-party applications is as a controller for games. We'll create a program that uses the accelerometer for input a little later in the chapter, but first we'll look at another common accelerometer use: detecting shakes.

Detecting Shakes

Like a gesture, a shake can be used as a form of input to your application. For example, the drawing program GLPaint, which is one of Apple's iOS sample code projects, lets users erase drawings by shaking their iOS device, sort of like an Etch A Sketch. Detecting shakes is relatively trivial. All it requires is checking for an absolute value of user acceleration on one of the axes that is greater than a set threshold. During normal usage, it's not uncommon for one of the three axes to register values up to around 1.3g, but getting values much higher than that generally requires intentional force. The accelerometer seems to be unable to register values higher than around 2.3g (at least in our experience), so you might not want to set your threshold any higher than that.

To detect a shake, you could check for an absolute value greater than 1.5 for a slight shake and 2.0 for a strong shake, by adding code like this to the motion manager closure in the MotionMonitor example:

```
let userAcc = motion.userAcceleration
if fabsf(Float(userAcc.x)) > 2.0
        || fabsf(Float(userAcc.y)) > 2.0
        || fabsf(Float(userAcc.z)) > 2.0 {
    // Do something here…
}
```

This code would detect any movement on any axis that exceeded two g-forces.

Baked-In Shaking

There's actually another, much simpler way to check for shakes—one that's baked right into the responder chain. Similar to back in Chapter 18 where we implemented methods like touchesBegan(_:withEvent:) to get touches, iOS also provides three similar responder methods for detecting motion:

- When motion begins, the motionBegan(_:withEvent:) method is called on the first responder and then on through the responder chain, as discussed in Chapter 18.

- When the motion ends, the motionEnded(_:withEvent:) method is called.

- If the phone rings, or some other interrupting action happens during the shake, the motionCancelled(_:withEvent:) method is called.

The first argument to each of these methods is an event subtype, one of which is UIEventSubtype. motionShake. This means that you can actually detect a shake without using CMMotionManager directly. All you need to do is override the appropriate motion-sensing methods in your view or view controller, and they will be called automatically when the user shakes the phone. Unless you specifically need more control over the shake gesture, you should use the baked-in motion detection rather than the manual method described previously. However, I thought we would show you the basics of the manual method in case you ever need more control.

The Shake and Break Application

For this project we'll write an application that detects shakes, and then makes your phone look and sound as if it broke as a result of the shake. When you launch the application, the program will display a picture that looks like the iPhone home screen shown in Figure 20-4. Shake the phone hard enough, though, and your poor phone will make a sound that you never want to hear coming out of a consumer electronics device. What's more, your screen will look like the one shown in Figure 20-5. Don't worry. You can reset the iPhone to its previously pristine state by touching the screen.

Figure 20-4. *The ShakeAndBreak application looks innocuous enough*

Figure 20-5. *Shake it and it will simulate a broken iPhone screen*

Create a new project in Xcode using the Single View Application template. Make sure that the device type is set to iPhone—unlike most of the other examples in this book, this one only works on iPhone because the images are of the correct size for an iPhone 6/6s screen (and they should scale reasonably well if you have an iPhone 6/6s Plus) . Of course, it's easy to extend this project to iPad if you create additional images. Call the new project ShakeAndBreak. In the Images and Sounds folder of the example source code, we've provided the two images and the sound file you need for this application. Select Assets.xcassets in the Project Navigator and drag the images Home.png and BrokenHome.png into it. Drag glass.wav into the Project Navigator.

Now let's start creating our view controller. We're going to need to create an outlet to point to an image view so that we can change the displayed image. Single-click ViewController.swift and add the following property to it:

```
class ViewController: UIViewController {
    @IBOutlet var imageView: UIImageView!
```

Save the file. Now select Main.storyboard to edit the file in Interface Builder. Drag an Image View over from the library to the view in the layout area and resize it so that it fills its parent view. In the Document Overview, Control-drag from the Image View to its parent View, hold down Shift, and in the context menu, select Leading Space to Container Margin, Trailing Space to Container Margin, Vertical Spacing to Top Layout Guide, and Vertical Spacing to Bottom Layout Guide, and press Return to lock the size and position of the image view. Finally, Control-drag from the View Controller icon to the image view and select the imageView outlet, and then save the storyboard.

Next, go back to the ViewController.swift file. We're going to add some additional properties for both of the images we're going to display, to track whether we're showing the broken image. We're also adding an audio player object that we'll use to play our breaking glass sound. The following bold lines go near the top of the file:

```
import UIKit
import AVFoundation

class ViewController: UIViewController {
    @IBOutlet var imageView: UIImageView!
    private var fixed: UIImage!
    private var broken: UIImage!
    private var brokenScreenShowing = false
    private var crashPlayer: AVAudioPlayer?
```

Add the following code to the viewDidLoad() method:

```
        if let url = url = Bundle(for: type(of: self)).url(forResource:"glass",
withExtension:"wav"){
            do {
                crashPlayer = try AVAudioPlayer(contentsOf: url, fileTypeHint:
AVFileTypeWAVE)
            } catch let error as NSError {
                print("Audio error! \(error.localizedDescription)")
            }
        }

        fixed = UIImage(named: "Home")
        broken = UIImage(named: "HomeBroken")
        imageView.image = fixed
```

At this point, we've initialized the url variable to point to our sound file and initialized an instance of AVAudioPlayer, a class that will simply play the sound. Then we loaded both images we need to use and put the first one in place. Next, add the following new method:

```
override func motionEnded(_ motion: UIEventSubtype, with event: UIEvent?) {
    if !brokenScreenShowing && motion == .motionShake {
        imageView.image = broken;
        crashPlayer?.play()
        brokenScreenShowing = true;
    }
}
```

This overrides the UIResponder motionEnded(_:withEvent:) method, which is called whenever a shake happens. After checking to make sure the broken screen isn't already showing and that the event we're looking at really is a shake event, the method shows the broken image and plays our shattering noise.

The last method is one you should already be familiar with by now. It's called when the screen is touched. All we need to do in that method is set the image back to the unbroken screen and set brokenScreenShowing back to false:

```
override func touchesBegan(_ touches: Set<UITouch>, with event: UIEvent?) {
    imageView.image = fixed
    brokenScreenShowing = false
}
```

Build and run the application, and try shaking your device. For those of you who don't have the ability to run this application on your iOS device, you can still give this a try. The simulator does not simulate the accelerometer hardware, but it does include a menu item that simulates the shake event, so this will work with the simulator, too. Go have some fun with it. When you're finished, we'll see how to use the accelerometer as a controller for games and other programs.

Accelerometer As a Directional Controller

Instead of using buttons to control the movement of a character or object in a game, developers often use an accelerometer to accomplish this task. In a car-racing game, for example, twisting the iOS device like a steering wheel might steer your car, while tipping it forward might accelerate, and tipping it back might activate the brakes. Exactly how you use the accelerometer as a controller will vary greatly, depending on the specific mechanics of the game. In the simplest cases, you might just take the value from one of the axes, multiply it by a number, and add that to one of the coordinates of the controlled objects. In more complex games where physics are modeled more realistically, you would need to make adjustments to the velocity of the controlled object based on the values returned from the accelerometer.

The one tricky aspect of using the accelerometer as a controller is that the delegate method is not guaranteed to call back at the interval you specify. If you tell the motion manager to read the accelerometer 60 times a second, all that you can say for sure is that it won't update more than 60 times a second. You're not guaranteed to get 60 evenly spaced updates every second. So, if you're doing animation based on input from the accelerometer, you must keep track of the time that passes between updates and factor that into your equations to determine how far objects have moved.

The Ball Application

For our next project, we're going to move a sprite around the iPhone's screen by tilting the phone. This is a very simple example of using the accelerometer to receive input. We'll use Quartz 2D to handle our animation.

▪ **Note**   As a general rule, when you're working with games and other programs that need smooth animation, you'll probably want to use Sprite Kit, OpenGL ES or Metal. We're using Quartz 2D in this application for the sake of simplicity and to reduce the amount of code that's unrelated to using the accelerometer.

In this application, as you tilt your iPhone, the marble will roll around as if it were on the surface of a table, as shown in Figure 20-6. Tip it to the left, and the ball will roll to the left. Tip it farther, and it will move faster. Tip it back, and it will slow down, and then start going in the other direction.

Figure 20-6.   *The Ball application lets you roll a marble around the screen*

In Xcode, create a new project using the Single View Application template. Set the device type to Universal and call the project Ball. In the Images and Sounds folder in the example source code, you'll find an image called ball.png. Using the Project Navigator, drag ball.png into Assets.xcassets.

Next, select the Ball project in the Project Navigator followed by the General tab of the Ball target. In the Device Orientation section under Deployment Info, select Portrait and deselect all of the other check boxes, as you did for the MotionMonitor application earlier in this chapter. This disables the default interface orientation changes; we want to roll our ball and not change interface orientation as we move our device around.

Now single-click the Ball folder and select File ➤ New ➤ File.... Select Cocoa Touch Class from the iOS Source section, and click Next. Make the new class a subclass of UIView and name it BallView, and then click Create. We'll get back to editing this class a little later. Select Main.storyboard to edit the file in Interface Builder. Single-click the View icon in the Document Outline and use the identity inspector to change the view's class from UIView to BallView. Next, switch to the Attributes Inspector and change the view's Background to Light Gray Color. Finally, save the storyboard.

Now it's time to edit ViewController.swift. Add the lines in Listing 20-4 to the top of the file.

Listing 20-4. Modify the ViewController.swift and the viewDidLoad Method As Shown

```
import UIKit
import CoreMotion

class ViewController: UIViewController {
    private static let updateInterval = 1.0/60.0
    private let motionManager = CMMotionManager()
    private let queue = OperationQueue()

    override func viewDidLoad() {
        super.viewDidLoad()
        // Do any additional setup after loading the view, typically from a nib.

        motionManager.startDeviceMotionUpdates(to: queue) {
                (motionData: CMDeviceMotion?, error: NSError?) -> Void in
            let ballView = self.view as! BallView
            ballView.acceleration = motionData!.gravity
            DispatchQueue.main.async {
                ballView.update()
            }
        }
    }
}
```

■ **Note** After entering this code, you will see errors as a result of BallView not being complete. We're doing the bulk of our work in the BallView class.

The viewDidLoad() method here is similar to some of what we've done elsewhere in this chapter. The main difference is that we are using a much higher update interval of 60 times per second. In the closure where we tell the motion manager to execute when there are accelerometer updates to report, we pass the acceleration object along to our view. We then call a method named update, which updates the position of the ball in the view based on acceleration and the amount of time that has passed since the last update. Since that closure can be executed on any thread, and the methods belonging to UIKit objects (including UIView) can be safely used only from the main thread, we once again force the update method to be called in the main thread.

Writing the Ball View

Select BallView.swift. Here, we'll need to import the Core Motion framework and add the property that our controller will use to pass along an acceleration value and five other properties that we'll use in the class implementation:

```
import UIKit
import CoreMotion

class BallView: UIView {
    var acceleration = CMAcceleration(x: 0, y: 0, z: 0)
    private let image = UIImage(named : "ball")!
    private var currentPoint : CGPoint = CGPoint.zero
    private var ballXVelocity = 0.0
    private var ballYVelocity = 0.0
    private var lastUpdateTime = Date()
```

Let's look at the properties and talk about what we're doing with each of them. The `acceleration` property will hold the most recent acceleration values, which the controller gets from a device motion update. Next is a `UIImage` that points to the sprite that we'll be moving around the screen:

```
private let image = UIImage(named : "ball")!
```

The `currentPoint` property will hold the current position of the ball. We'll use this value, together with its previous value (which Swift gives us for free) so that we can build an update rectangle that encompasses both the new and old positions of the ball, so that it is drawn at the new spot and erased at the old one:

```
private var currentPoint : CGPoint = CGPoint.zero
```

We also have two variables to keep track of the ball's current velocity in two dimensions. Although this isn't going to be a very complex simulation, we do want the ball to move in a manner similar to a real ball. We'll calculate the ball movement in the next section. We'll get acceleration from the accelerometer and keep track of velocity on two axes with these variables.

```
private var ballXVelocity = 0.0
private var ballYVelocity = 0.0
```

Finally, the `lastUpdateTime` property is set each time we update the ball's position. We'll use it to calculate speed changes based on the time between updates and the ball's acceleration.

Now let's write the code to draw and move the ball around the screen. First, add the methods shown in Listing 20-5 to the BallView.swift file.

Listing 20-5. Add init Methods for the BallView Class

```
override init(frame: CGRect) {
    super.init(frame: frame)
    commonInit()
}

required init?(coder aDecoder: NSCoder) {
    super.init(coder: aDecoder)
    commonInit()
}
```

```
private func commonInit() -> Void {
    currentPoint = CGPoint(x: (bounds.size.width / 2.0) +
                                (image.size.width / 2.0),
                           y: (bounds.size.height / 2.0) +
                                (image.size.height / 2.0))
}
```

Both the init?(coder:) and the init(frame:) methods call our commonInit() method. Our view that is created in a storyboard file will be initialized with the initWithCoder() method. We call the commonInit() method from both initializer methods so that our view class can safely be created both from code and from a nib file. This is a nice thing to do for any view class that may be reused, such as this fancy ball rolling view. Now uncomment the commented-out drawRect: method and give it this simple implementation to draw the ball image at currentPoint:

```
override func draw(_ rect: CGRect) {
    // Drawing code
    image.draw(at: currentPoint)
}
```

Next, add our update() method to the end of the class, as shown in Listing 20-6.

Listing 20-6. The BallClass Update Method

```
func update() -> Void {
    let now = Date()
    let secondsSinceLastDraw = now.timeIntervalSince(lastUpdateTime)
    ballXVelocity =
            ballXVelocity + (acceleration.x * secondsSinceLastDraw)
    ballYVelocity =
            ballYVelocity - (acceleration.y * secondsSinceLastDraw)

    let xDelta = secondsSinceLastDraw * ballXVelocity * 500
    let yDelta = secondsSinceLastDraw * ballYVelocity * 500
    currentPoint = CGPoint(x: currentPoint.x + CGFloat(xDelta),
    y: currentPoint.y + CGFloat(yDelta))
    lastUpdateTime = now
}
```

Finally, add the property observer in Listing 20-7 to the currentPoint property.

Listing 20-7. The currentProperty Observer

```
var currentPoint : CGPoint = CGPoint.zero {
    didSet {
        var newX = currentPoint.x
        var newY = currentPoint.y
        if newX < 0 {
            newX = 0
            ballXVelocity = 0
        } else if newX > bounds.size.width - image.size.width {
            newX = bounds.size.width - image.size.width
            ballXVelocity = 0
        }
```

```
        if newY < 0 {
            newY = 0
            ballYVelocity = 0
        } else if newY > bounds.size.height - image.size.height {
            newY = bounds.size.height - image.size.height
            ballYVelocity = 0
        }
        currentPoint = CGPoint(x: newX, y: newY)

        let currentRect = CGRect(x: newX, y: newY,
                                    width: newX + image.size.width,
                                    height: newY + image.size.height)
        let prevRect = CGRect(x: oldValue.x, y: oldValue.y,
                                width: oldValue.x + image.size.width,
                                height: oldValue.y + image.size.height)
        setNeedsDisplay(currentRect.union(prevRect))
    }
}
```

Calculating Ball Movement

Our drawRect() method couldn't be much simpler. We just draw the ball image at the position stored in currentPoint. The property observer for currentPoint is another story, however. When a new position is set (from the update() method, which you'll see shortly), we need to check whether the ball has hit the edges of the screen and, if so, stop its motion along either the x or y axis. We do that by implementing a property observer from which we can access the new value of the property and modify it without causing the property observer to be called again (which would be infinite recursion).

The first thing we do is get the current x and y coordinates of the ball and do a boundary check. If either the x or y position of the ball is less than 0 or greater than the width or height of the screen (accounting for the width and height of the image), then the acceleration in that direction is stopped and we change the ball's coordinate so that it appears at the edge of the screen:

```
        var newX = currentPoint.x
        var newY = currentPoint.y
        if newX < 0 {
            newX = 0
            ballXVelocity = 0
        } else if newX > bounds.size.width - image.size.width {
            newX = bounds.size.width - image.size.width
            ballXVelocity = 0
        }
        if newY < 0 {
            newY = 0
            ballYVelocity = 0
        } else if newY > bounds.size.height - image.size.height {
            newY = bounds.size.height - image.size.height
            ballYVelocity = 0
        }
```

■ **Tip**   Do you want to make the ball bounce off the walls more naturally, instead of just stopping? It's easy enough to do. Just change the two lines in setCurrentPoint: that currently read ballXVelocity = 0 to **ballXVelocity = -(ballXVelocity / 2.0)**. And change the two lines that currently read ballYVelocity = 0 to **ballYVelocity = -(ballYVelocity / 2.0)**. With these changes, instead of killing the ball's velocity, we reduce it in half and set it to the inverse. Now the ball has half the velocity in the opposite direction.

Throughout this code, we keep the ball's coordinates in local variables called newX, newY. Once we've modified its position, if necessary, we use these values to create and store the updated value back in the property:

```
currentPoint = CGPoint(x: newX, y: newY)
```

After that, we calculate two CGRects based on the size of the image. One rectangle encompasses the area where the new image will be drawn, and the other encompasses the area where it was last drawn. We calculate the second of these rectangles using the previous value of the ball's location, which Swift stores for us in a constant variable called oldValue. We'll use these two rectangles to ensure that the old ball is erased at the same time the new one is drawn:

```
let currentRect = CGRect(x: newX, y: newY,
                         width: newX + image.size.width,
                         height: newY + image.size.height)
let prevRect = CGRect(x: oldValue.x, y: oldValue.y,
                      width: oldValue.x + image.size.width,
                      height: oldValue.y + image.size.height)
```

Finally, we create a new rectangle that is the union of the two rectangles we just calculated and feed that to setNeedsDisplay(currentRect:) to indicate the part of our view that needs to be redrawn:

```
setNeedsDisplay(currentRect.union(prevRect))
```

The last substantive method in our class is update(), which is used to figure out the correct new location of the ball. This method is called from the accelerometer method of its controller class after it feeds the view the new acceleration object. First, we calculate how long it has been since the last time this method was called. The NSDate instance returned by Date() represents the current time. By asking it for the time interval since lastUpdateTime, we get a number representing the number of seconds between now and the last time this method was called:

```
let now = Date()
let secondsSinceLastDraw = now.timeIntervalSince(lastUpdateTime)
```

Next, we calculate the new velocity in both directions by adding the current acceleration to the current velocity. We multiply acceleration by secondsSinceLastDraw so that our acceleration is consistent across time. Tipping the phone at the same angle will always cause the same amount of acceleration:

```
ballXVelocity =
        ballXVelocity + (acceleration.x * secondsSinceLastDraw)
ballYVelocity =
        ballYVelocity - (acceleration.y * secondsSinceLastDraw)
```

After that, we figure out the actual change in pixels since the last time the method was called based on the velocity. The product of velocity and elapsed time is multiplied by 500 to create movement that looks natural. If we didn't multiply it by some value, the acceleration would be extraordinarily slow, as if the ball were stuck in molasses:

```
let xDelta = secondsSinceLastDraw * ballXVelocity * 500
let yDelta = secondsSinceLastDraw * ballYVelocity * 500
```

Once we know the change in pixels, we create a new point by adding the current location to the calculated acceleration and assign that to currentPoint:

```
currentPoint = CGPoint(x: currentPoint.x + CGFloat(xDelta),
                       y: currentPoint.y + CGFloat(yDelta))
```

That ends our calculations, so all that's left is to update lastUpdateTime with the current time:

```
lastUpdateTime = now
```

Now build and run the app. If all went well, the application will launch, and you should be able to control the movement of the ball by tilting the phone. When the ball gets to an edge of the screen, it should stop. Tip the phone back the other way, and it should start rolling in the other direction.

Summary

Well, we've certainly seen some interesting things in this chapter with physics and the iOS accelerometer and gyroscope. We created a prank app to "break" a phone and we saw the basics of using the accelerometer as a control device. The possibilities for applications with the accelerometer and gyro are wide and varied. In the next section we're going to get into using another bit of iOS hardware: the built-in camera.

CHAPTER 21

■ ■ ■

Using the Camera and Accessing Photos

It should come as no surprise that the iPhone, iPad, and iPod touch contain a built-in camera with the Photos application to help you manage the pictures and videos you've taken (see Figure 21-1). What you may not know is that your programs can use the built-in camera to take pictures. Your applications can also allow the user to select from among and view the media already stored on the device. We'll look at both of these abilities in this chapter.

Figure 21-1. *In this chapter, we'll explore accessing the iPhone camera and photo library in our own application*

© Molly Maskrey, Kim Topley, David Mark, Fredrik Olsson and Jeff Lamarche 2016
M. Maskrey et al., *Beginning iPhone Development with Swift 3*, DOI 10.1007/978-1-4842-2223-2_21

Using the Image Picker and UIImagePickerController

Because of the way iOS applications are sandboxed, ordinarily they can't get access to photographs or other data that live outside their own sandboxes. Fortunately, both the camera and the media library are made available to your application by way of an image picker.

Using the Image Picker Controller

As the name implies, an image picker provides the mechanism allowing you to select an image from a specified source. When this class first appeared in iOS, it was used only for images. Nowadays, you can use it to capture video as well. Typically, an image picker uses a list of images and/or videos as its source, as shown in Figure 21-2 (left side). You can, however, specify that the picker use the camera as its source, as shown in Figure 21-2 (right side).

Figure 21-2. *An image picker presents users with a list of their pictures (left), allowing one to be moved and scaled (right) after selection*

We implement the image picker interface using a controller class called `UIImagePickerController` We create an instance of this class, specify a delegate, specify its image source and whether you want the user to pick an image or a video, and then present it. The image picker takes control of the device allowing the user to select a picture or video from the existing media library. Or, the user can take a new picture or video with the camera. Once the user makes a selection, we can give her an opportunity to do some basic editing, such as scaling or cropping an image, or trimming away a bit of a video clip. All of that behavior gets implemented by the `UIImagePickerController`, so our effort becomes minimized.

Assuming the user doesn't press Cancel, the image or video that the user either captures or selects from the library passes to your delegate. Regardless of whether the user selects a media file or cancels, your delegate becomes responsible for dismissing the `UIImagePickerController` so that the user can return to your application.

Creating a `UIImagePickerController` is extremely straightforward. You just create an instance the way you would with most classes. There is one catch, however: not every iOS device has a camera, so before you create an instance of `UIImagePickerController`, you need to check to see whether the device your app is currently running on supports the image source you want to use. For example, before letting the user take a picture with the camera, you should make sure the program is running on a device that has a camera. You can check that by using a class method on `UIImagePickerController`, like this:

```
if UIImagePickerController.isSourceTypeAvailable(.Camera) {
```

In this example, we're passing `UIImagePickerControllerSourceType.Camera` to indicate that we want to let the user take a picture or shoot a video using the built-in camera. The method `isSourceTypeAvailable()` returns `true` if the specified source is currently available. We can specify two other values in addition to `UIImagePickerControllerSourceType.camera`:

- `UIImagePickerControllerSourceType.PhotoLibrary` specifies that the user should pick an image or video from the existing media library. That image will be returned to your delegate.

- `UIImagePickerControllerSourceType.SavedPhotosAlbum` specifies that the user will select the image from the library of existing photographs, but that the selection will be limited to the camera roll. This option will run on a device without a camera, where it is less useful but still allows you to select any screenshots you have taken.

After making sure that the device your program is running on supports the image source you want to use, launching the image picker is shown in Listing 21-1.

Listing 21-1. Launching the Image Picker from Inside a View Controller

```
let picker = UIImagePickerController()
picker.delegate = self
picker.sourceType = UIImagePickerControllerSourceType.camera
picker.cameraDevice = UIImagePickerControllerCameraDevice.front
self.present (picker, animated:true, completion: nil)
```

■ **Tip**   On a device that has more than one camera, you can select which one to use by setting the `cameraDevice` property to `UIImagePickerControllerCameraDevice.front` or `UIImagePickerControllerCameraDevice.rear`. To find out whether a front or rear camera is available, use the same constants with the `isCameraDeviceAvailable()` method.

After we have created and configured the UIImagePickerController, we use a method that our class inherited from UIView called self.present(_:animated:completion:) to present the image picker to the user, called as a method of the view controller, which we refer to here using self.

Implementing the Image Picker Controller Delegate

To find out when the user has finished using the image picker, you need to implement the UIImagePickerControllerDelegate protocol. This protocol defines two methods: imagePickerController (_:didFinishPickingMediaWithInfo:) and imagePickerControllerDidCancel().

The imagePickerController(_:didFinishPickingMediaWithInfo:) method gets called when the user has successfully captured a photo or video, or selected an item from the media library. The first argument is a pointer to the UIImagePickerController that you created earlier. The second argument returns a dictionary that contains the chosen photo or the URL of the chosen video, as well as optional editing information if you enabled editing in the image picker controller (and if the user actually did some editing). That dictionary contains the original, unedited image stored under the key UIImagePickerControllerOriginalImage. Listing 21-2 shows an example of a delegate method that retrieves the original image.

Listing 21-2. Delegate Method for Retrieving an Image

```
func imagePickerController(picker: UIImagePickerController,
                      didFinishPickingMediaWithInfo info: [String : AnyObject]) {
    let selectedImage: UIImage? =
        info[UIImagePickerControllerEditedImage] as? UIImage
    let originalImage: UIImage? =
        info[UIImagePickerControllerOriginalImage] as? UIImage

    // do something with selectedImage and originalImage

    picker.dismiss(animated: true, completion:nil)
}
```

The editingInfo dictionary will also tell you which portion of the entire image was chosen during editing by way of an NSValue object stored under the key UIImagePickerControllerCropRect. You can convert this NSValue instance into a CGRect, as shown in Listing 21-3.

Listing 21-3. Converting an NSValue into a CGRect

```
let cropValue:NSValue? = info[UIImagePickerControllerCropRect] as? NSValue
let cropRect:CGRect? = cropValue?.cgRectValue()
```

After this conversion, cropRect specifies the portion of the original image selected during the editing process. If you do not need this information, just ignore it.

■ **Caution**   If the image returned to your delegate comes from the camera, that image will not be stored in the photo library automatically. It is your application's responsibility to save the image, if necessary.

The other delegate method, imagePickerControllerDidCancel(), gets called if the user decides to cancel the process without capturing or selecting any media. When the image picker calls this delegate method, it's just notifying you that the user is finished with the picker and didn't choose anything.

Both of the methods in the UIImagePickerControllerDelegate protocol are marked as optional, but they really aren't, and here is why: modal views like the image picker must be told to dismiss themselves. As a result, even if you don't need to take any application-specific actions when the user cancels an image picker, you still need to dismiss the picker. At a bare minimum, your imagePickerControllerDidCancel() method will need to look like this for your program to function correctly:

```
func imagePickerControllerDidCancel(picker: UIImagePickerController) {
    picker.dismiss(true, completion:nil)
}
```

In this chapter, we're going to build an application that lets the user take a picture or shoot some video with the camera. Or, the user can select something from the photo library, and then display the selection on the screen, as shown in Figure 21-3. If the user is on a device without a camera, we will hide the New Photo or Video button and allow selection only from the photo library.

Figure 21-3. *Our Camera application in action*

Creating the Camera Interface

Create a new project in Xcode using the Single View Application template, naming the application **Camera**. The first order of business is to add a couple of outlets to this application's view controller. We need one to point to the image view so that we can update it with the image returned from the image picker. We'll also need an outlet to point to the New Photo or Video button so that we can hide the button if the device doesn't have a camera. We also need two action methods: one for the New Photo or Video button and one that lets the user select an existing picture from the photo library.

```
class ViewController: UIViewController, UIImagePickerControllerDelegate,
                                        UINavigationControllerDelegate {
    @IBOutlet var imageView: UIImageView!
    @IBOutlet var takePictureButton: UIButton!
```

The first thing you might notice is that we've actually conformed our class to two different protocols: UIImagePickerControllerDelegate and UINavigationControllerDelegate. Because UIImagePickerController is a subclass of UINavigationController, we must conform our class to both of these protocols. The methods in UINavigationControllerDelegate are optional. We don't need either of them to use the image picker; however, we do need to conform to the protocol, or the compiler will give us an error later on.

The other thing you might notice is that, while we added a property of type UIImageView for displaying a chosen image, we didn't add anything similar for displaying a chosen video. UIKit doesn't include any publicly available class like UIImageView that works for showing video content, so we'll have to show video using another technique instead. When we get to that point, we will use an instance of AVPlayerViewController, grabbing its view property and inserting it into our view hierarchy. This is a highly unusual way of using any view controller, but it's actually an Apple-approved technique to show video inside a view hierarchy.

We're also going to add two action methods that we want to connect our buttons to. For now, we'll just create empty implementations so that Interface Builder can see them. We'll fill in the actual code later:

```
@IBAction func shootPictureOrVideo(sender: UIButton) {
}

@IBAction func selectExistingPictureOrVideo(sender: UIButton) {
}
```

The layout we're going to build for this application is very simple—just an image view and two buttons. The finished layout is shown in Figure 21-4. Use this as a guide as you work.

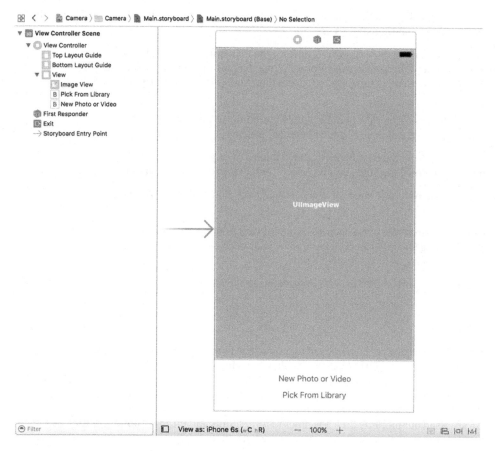

Figure 21-4. *The storyboard layout for our Camera application*

Drag two Buttons from the library and drop them onto the view in the storyboard. Place them one above the other, aligning the bottom button with the bottom blue guideline. Double-click the top button and give it a title of New Photo or Video. Now double-click the bottom button and give it a title of Pick from Library. Next, drag an Image View from the library and place it above the buttons. Expand the image view to take up the entire space of the view above the buttons, as shown earlier in Figure 21-3. In the Attributes Inspector, change the image view's background to black and set its Mode to Aspect Fit, which will cause it to resize images so that they fit within its bounds, but maintain their original aspect ratio.

Now Control-drag from the View Controller icon to the image view and select the imageView outlet. Drag again from View Controller to the New Photo or Video button and select the takePictureButton outlet. Next, select the New Photo or Video button and bring up the connections inspector. Drag from the Touch Up Inside event to View Controller icon, and then select the shootPictureOrVideo: action. Now click the Pick from Library button, drag from the Touch Up Inside event in the connections inspector to the View Controller icon, and select the selectExistingPictureOrVideo: action.

The final step, as usual, is to add auto layout constraints. Start by expanding the view controller in the Document Outline and then add constraints as follows:

1. In the Document Outline, Control-drag from the Pick from Library button to its parent view, and then release the mouse. When the pop-up appears, hold down Shift and select Center Horizontally in Container and Vertical Spacing to Bottom Layout Guide.

2. Control-drag from the New Photo or Video button to the Pick from Library button, release the mouse, and select Vertical Spacing.

3. Control-drag from the New Photo or Video button to its parent view, release the mouse, hold down the Shift key, and select Center Horizontally in Container.

4. Control-drag from New Photo or Video to the image view and select Vertical Spacing.

5. Control-drag from the image view to its parent view and use the Shift key to select Leading Space to Container Margin, Trailing Space to Container Margin, and Vertical Spacing to Top Layout Guide.

All of the layout constraints should now be in place, so save your changes.

Privacy Options

Because we're planning on using the camera, and that bit of hardware is protected by iOS, we'll have to ask the user's permission to do so. Similarly, because we plan on taking video, we'll want to have access to the microphone... unless we're only interested in silent movies. And we'll also want to access the photo library. Fortunately, iOS handles much of this for us as long as we properly request what we need. To do so requires adding a couple of lines to the Info.plist file.

Since we've accessed our property list a few times before, simply add the three bottom entries as shown in Figure 21-5. The text in the rightmost column is what will be displayed to the user as additional information about the request to use a specific resource. As such, it helps to be clear and succinct.

Item 0	String	array
▶ Supported interface orientations ⬍	Array	(3 items)
▶ Supported interface orientations (i... ⬍	Array	(4 items)
Privacy - Camera Usage Description ⬍	String	My App Would Like to access the camera
Privacy - Microphone Usage Desc... ⬍	String	My App would also like to use the mic
Privacy - Photo Library Usage Des... ⬍	String	My App would like to look at your pictures

Figure 21-5. *Add the privacy options for the camera and microphone to the Info.plist file*

When the app needs to access one of the three resources, the user is presented a message like that shown in Figure 21-6.

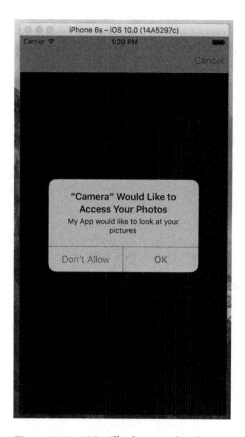

Figure 21-6. *iOS will take care of making requests to the user, but you'll want to make it clear as to why your app is needing a specific resource.*

Implementing the Camera View Controller

Select ViewController.swift, where we have some more changes to make. Since we're going to allow users to optionally capture a video, we need a property for an AVPlayerViewController instance. Two more properties keep track of the last selected image and video, along with a string to determine whether a video or image was the last thing chosen. We also need to import a few additional frameworks to make this all work. Add the bold lines shown here:

```
import UIKit
import AVKit
import AVFoundation
import MobileCoreServices

class ViewController: UIViewController, UIImagePickerControllerDelegate,
                                        UINavigationControllerDelegate {
```

```
@IBOutlet var imageView: UIImageView!
@IBOutlet var takePictureButton: UIButton!
var avPlayerViewController: AVPlayerViewController!
var image: UIImage?
var movieURL: URL?
var lastChosenMediaType: String?
```

Now let's enhance the viewDidLoad() method, hiding the New Photo or Video button if the device we're running on does not have a camera. We also implement the viewDidAppear() method, having it call the updateDisplay() method, which we'll implement soon. First, change the viewDidLoad and viewDidAppear methods as shown in Listing 21-4 in ViewController.swift file.

Listing 21-4. Updated viewDidLoad and viewDidAppear Methods

```
override func viewDidLoad() {
    super.viewDidLoad()
    // Do any additional setup after loading the view, typically from a nib.

    if !UIImagePickerController.isSourceTypeAvailable(
        UIImagePickerControllerSourceType.camera) {
        takePictureButton.isHidden = true
    }
}

override func viewDidAppear(_ animated: Bool) {
    super.viewDidAppear(animated)
    updateDisplay()
}
```

It's important to understand the distinction between the viewDidLoad() and viewDidAppear() methods. The former is called only when the view has just been loaded into memory. The latter is called every time the view is displayed, which happens both at launch and whenever we return to our controller after showing another full-screen view, such as the image picker.

Next up are three utility methods, the first of which is the updateDisplay() method. It is called from the viewDidAppear() method, which is called both when the view is first created and again after the user picks an image or video and dismisses the image picker. Because of this dual usage, it needs to make a few checks to see what's what and set up the GUI accordingly. Add the code in Listing 21-5 toward the bottom of the ViewController.swift file.

Listing 21-5. The updateDisplay Method

```
func updateDisplay() {
    if let mediaType = lastChosenMediaType {
        if mediaType == kUTTypeImage as NSString {
            imageView.image = image!
            imageView.isHidden = false
            if avPlayerViewController != nil {
                avPlayerViewController!.view.isHidden = true
            }
        } else if mediaType == kUTTypeMovie as NSString {
            if avPlayerViewController == nil {
                avPlayerViewController = AVPlayerViewController()
                let avPlayerView = avPlayerViewController!.view
```

```
            avPlayerView?.frame = imageView.frame
            avPlayerView?.clipsToBounds = true
            view.addSubview(avPlayerView!)
            setAVPlayerViewLayoutConstraints()
        }

        if let url = movieURL {
            imageView.isHidden = true
            avPlayerViewController.player = AVPlayer(url: url)
            avPlayerViewController!.view.isHidden = false
            avPlayerViewController!.player!.play()
        }
    }
  }
}
```

This method shows the correct view based on the type of media that the user selected—the image view for a photograph and the AV player for a movie. The image view is always present, but the AV player is created and added to the user interface only when the user picks a movie for the first time. Each time a movie is chosen, we create an AVPlayer instance initialized with the movie file's URL and attach it to the AVPlayerViewController via its player property, and then use the player's play() method to start playback.

When we add the AV player, we need to ensure that it occupies the same space as the image view and we need to add layout constraints that ensure that remains the case even if the device is rotated. Here's the code that adds the layout constraints, as shown in Listing 21-6.

Listing 21-6. Setting the AV Player's Layout Constraints in the ViewController.swift File

```
func setAVPlayerViewLayoutConstraints() {
    let avPlayerView = avPlayerViewController!.view
    avPlayerView?.translatesAutoresizingMaskIntoConstraints = false
    let views = ["avPlayerView": avPlayerView!,
                 "takePictureButton": takePictureButton!]
    view.addConstraints(NSLayoutConstraint.constraints(
                withVisualFormat: "H:|[avPlayerView]|", options: .alignAllLeft,
                metrics:nil, views:views))
    view.addConstraints(NSLayoutConstraint.constraints(
                withVisualFormat: "V:|[avPlayerView]-0-[takePictureButton]",
                options: .alignAllLeft, metrics:nil, views:views))
}
```

The horizontal constraints tie the movie player to the left and right sides of the main view, and the vertical constraints link it to the top of the main view and the top of the New Photo or Video button.

The final utility method, pickMediaFromSource(), is the one that both of our action methods call. This method is pretty simple. It just creates and configures an image picker, using the passed-in sourceType to determine whether to bring up the camera or the media library. We do so by adding the code in Listing 21-7 to the bottom of the ViewController.swift file.

Listing 21-7. The pickMediaFromSource Method in the ViewController.swift File

```
func pickMediaFromSource(_ sourceType:UIImagePickerControllerSourceType) {
    let mediaTypes =
        UIImagePickerController.availableMediaTypes(for: sourceType)!
    if UIImagePickerController.isSourceTypeAvailable(sourceType)
```

```
                    && mediaTypes.count > 0 {
        let picker = UIImagePickerController()
        picker.mediaTypes = mediaTypes
        picker.delegate = self
        picker.allowsEditing = true
        picker.sourceType = sourceType
        present(picker, animated: true, completion: nil)
    } else {
        let alertController = UIAlertController(title:"Error accessing media",
                    message: "Unsupported media source.",
                    preferredStyle: UIAlertControllerStyle.alert)
        let okAction = UIAlertAction(title: "OK",
                    style: UIAlertActionStyle.cancel, handler: nil)
                    alertController.addAction(okAction)
        present(alertController, animated: true, completion: nil)
    }
}
```

Next, implement the action methods that are linked to the buttons:

```
@IBAction func shootPictureOrVideo(_ sender: UIButton) {
    pickMediaFromSource(UIImagePickerControllerSourceType.camera)
}
```

```
@IBAction func selectExistingPictureOrVideo(_ sender: UIButton) {
    pickMediaFromSource(UIImagePickerControllerSourceType.photoLibrary)
}
```

Each of these simply calls out to the pickMediaFromSource() method, passing in a constant defined by UIImagePickerController to specify where the picture or video should come from.

Now it's finally time to implement the delegate methods for the picker view, as shown in Listing 21-8.

Listing 21-8. Our Picker View's Delegate Methods

```
func imagePickerController(_ picker: UIImagePickerController,
                didFinishPickingMediaWithInfo info: [String : AnyObject]) {
    lastChosenMediaType = info[UIImagePickerControllerMediaType] as? String
    if let mediaType = lastChosenMediaType {
        if mediaType == kUTTypeImage as NSString {
            image = info[UIImagePickerControllerEditedImage] as? UIImage
        } else if mediaType == kUTTypeMovie as NSString {
            movieURL = info[UIImagePickerControllerMediaURL] as? URL
        }
    }
    picker.dismiss(animated: true, completion: nil)
}
```

```
func imagePickerControllerDidCancel(_ picker: UIImagePickerController) {
    picker.dismiss(animated: true, completion:nil)
}
```

The first delegate method uses the values passed in the info dictionary to check whether a picture or video was chosen, makes note of the selection, and then dismisses the modal image picker. If the image is larger than the available space on the screen, it will be resized by the image view when it's displayed, because we set the image view's content mode to Aspect Fit when we created it. The second delegate method is called when the user cancels the image picking process and just dismisses the image picker.

That's all you need to do. Compile and run the app. If you're running on the simulator, you won't have the option to take a new picture, but will only be able to choose from the photo library—as if you had any photos in your simulator's photo library! If you have the opportunity to run the application on a real device, go ahead and try it. You should be able to take a new picture or movie, and zoom in and out of the picture using the pinch gestures. The first time the app needs to access the user's photos on iOS, the user will be asked to allow this access; this is a privacy feature that was added back in iOS 6 to make sure that apps aren't sneakily grabbing photos without users' consent.

After choosing or taking a photo, if you zoom in and pan around before hitting the Use Photo button, the cropped image will be the one returned to the application in the delegate method.

Summary

Believe it or not, that's all there is to letting your users take pictures with the camera so that the pictures can be used by your application. You can even let the user do a small amount of editing on that image if you so choose.

In the next chapter, we're going to look at reaching a larger audience for your iOS applications by making them oh-so-easy to translate into other languages.

CHAPTER 22

■ ■ ■

Translating Apps Using Localization

At the time of this writing, you'll find iOS devices available in about half the world's countries, with that number continuing to increase over time (see Figure 22-1). Available on every continent except Antarctica, the iPad and iPod touch continue to sell all over the world and are nearly as ubiquitous as the iPhone. If you plan on releasing applications through the App Store, think about more than just people in your own country who speak your own language. Fortunately, iOS provides a robust **localization** architecture letting you easily translate your application (or have it translated by others) into, not only multiple languages, but even into multiple dialects of the same language. Providing different terminology to English speakers in the United Kingdom as opposed to the United States no longer represents a problem.

Figure 22-1. With iOS devices available in over half the world, developing for multiple languages puts your app in a more favorable position to be the success you want it to be

Localization presents minimal issues if you've written your code correctly whereas retrofitting an existing application to support localization increases the amount of work needed to get it right. In this chapter, I'll show you how to write your code so it is easy to localize, and then we'll go about localizing a sample application.

© Molly Maskrey, Kim Topley, David Mark, Fredrik Olsson and Jeff Lamarche 2016
M. Maskrey et al., *Beginning iPhone Development with Swift 3*, DOI 10.1007/978-1-4842-2223-2_22

Localization Architecture

When an application that has not been configured for localization executes, all of its text gets presented in the developer's own language, also known as the **development base language**. When developers decide to localize their applications, they create a subdirectory in their application bundle for each supported language. Each language's subdirectory contains a subset of the application's resources that were translated into that language. Each subdirectory is called a **localization project**, or **localization folder**. Localization folder names always end with the .lproj extension.

In the iOS Settings application, the user has the ability to set the device's preferred language and region format. For example, if the user's language is English, available regions might be the United States, Australia, and Hong Kong—all regions where English is spoken.

When a localized application needs to load a resource—such as an image, property list, or nib—the application checks the user's language and region, and then looks for a localization folder that matches that setting. If it finds one, it loads the localized version of the resource instead of the base version. For users who select French as their iOS language and Switzerland as their region, the application will look first for a localization folder named fr-CH.lproj. The first two letters of the folder name are the ISO country code that represents the French language. The two letters following the hyphen are the ISO code that represents Switzerland.

If the application cannot find a match using the two-letter code, it will look for a match using the language's three-letter ISO code. In our example, if the application is unable to find a folder named fr-CH.lproj, it looks for a folder named fre-CH or fra-CH.

All languages have at least one three-letter code. Some have two three-letter codes: one for the English spelling of the language and another for the native spelling. Some languages have only two-letter codes but when a language has both a two-letter code and a three-letter code, the two-letter code is preferred.

■ **Note**   You can find a list of the current ISO country codes on the ISO web site www.iso.org/iso/country_codes.htm. Both the two- and three-letter codes are part of the ISO 3166 standard.

If the application cannot find a folder with an exact match, it looks for a localization folder in the application bundle matching just the language code without the region code. So, staying with French, the application next looks for a localization folder called fr.lproj. If it doesn't find a language folder with that name, it will look for fre.lproj and then fra.lproj. If none of those are found, it checks for French.lproj. The last construct exists to support legacy Mac OS X applications; generally speaking, you should avoid it.

If the application doesn't find a matching folder for either the language/region combination or just the language, it uses the resources from the development base language. If it does find an appropriate localization folder, it then always looks there first for any resources that it needs. If you load a UIImage using imageNamed(), for example, the application will look first for an image with the specified name in the localization folder. If it finds one, it will use that image. If it doesn't, it falls back to the base language resource.

If an application has more than one localization folder that matches—for example, a folder called fr-CH.lproj and one called fr.lproj—it searches first in the more specific match, fr-CH.lproj, if the user has selected Swiss French as their preferred language. If it doesn't find the resource there, it looks in fr.lproj. This gives you the ability to provide resources common to all speakers of a language in one folder, localizing only those resources impacted by differences in dialect or geographic region.

You should choose to localize only those resources affected by language or country. For example, if an image in your application has no words and its meaning is universal, there's no need to localize that image.

Strings Files

What do you do about string literals and string constants in your source code? Consider the source code from Chapter 19, as shown in Listing 22-1.

Listing 22-1. Example of String Literals and Constants

```
let alertController = UIAlertController(title: "Location Manager Error",
                                        message: errorType, preferredStyle: .alert)
let okAction = UIAlertAction(title: "OK", style: .cancel,
                             handler: nil)
alertController.addAction(okAction)
self.presentViewController(alertController, animated: true,
                           completion: nil)
```

If you've gone through the effort of localizing your application for a particular audience, you certainly don't want to be presenting alerts written in the development base language. The answer is to store these strings in special text files called **strings files**.

The Strings File

Strings files are nothing more than Unicode text files that contain a list of string pairs, each identified by a comment. Listing 22-2 shows an example of what a strings file might look like in your application.

Listing 22-2. Example Strings File

```
/* Used to ask the user his/her first name */
"LABEL_FIRST_NAME" = "First Name";

/* Used to get the user's last name */
"LABEL_LAST_NAME" = "Last Name";

/* Used to ask the user's birth date */
"LABEL_BIRTHDAY" = "Birthday";
```

The values between the /* and the */ characters are comments for the translator. They are not used in the application; you could skip adding them, although they are a good idea. The comments give context, showing how a particular string is being used in the application. You'll notice that each line is in two parts, separated by an equals sign. The string on the left side of the equal sign acts as a key, and it will always contain the same value, regardless of language. The value on the right side of the equal sign is the one that is translated to the local language. So, the preceding strings file, localized into French, might look like Listing 22-3.

Listing 22-3. A French Version of the Strings File

```
/* Used to ask the user his/her first name */
"LABEL_FIRST_NAME " = "Prénom";

/* Used to get the user's last name */
"LABEL_LAST_NAME" = "Nom de famille";

/* Used to ask the user's birth date */
"LABEL_BIRTHDAY" = "Anniversaire";
```

The Localized String Function

At run time, you'll get the localized versions of the strings that you need by using the NSLocalizedString() function. Once your source code is final and ready for localization, Xcode searches all your code files for occurrences of this function, pulls out all the unique strings and embeds them into a file that you send to a translator, or you can add the translations yourself. Once that's completed, you'll have Xcode import the updated file and use its content to create the localized string files for the languages for which you have provided translations. Let's see how the first part of this process works. First, here's a traditional string declaration: let myString = "First Name".

To make this string localizable:

```
let myString = NSLocalizedString("LABEL_FIRST_NAME",
                    comment: "Used to ask the user his/her first name")
```

The NSLocalizedString() macro takes five parameters, but three of them have defaults, good enough in most cases, so usually you only need to provide two:

- The first parameter is a key that will be used to look for the localized string. If there is no localization that contains text for the key, the application will use the key itself as the localized text.

- The second parameter is used as a comment to explain how the text is being used. The comment will appear in the file sent to the translator and in the localized strings file after import.

NSLocalizedString() searches in the application bundle within the appropriate localization folder for a strings file named Localizable.strings. If it does not find the file, it returns its first parameter, which is the key for the text that was required. If NSLocalizedString() finds the strings file, it searches the file for a line that matches its first parameter. In the preceding example, NSLocalizedString() will search the strings file for the string "LABEL_FIRST_NAME". If it doesn't find a match in the localization folder that matches the user's language settings, it will then look for a strings file in the base language and use the value there. If there is no strings file, it will just use the first parameter you passed to the NSLocalizedString() function.

You could use the base language text as the key for the NSLocalizedString() function because it returns the key if no matching localized text can be found. This would make the preceding example look like:

```
let myString = NSLocalizedString("First Name",
                    comment: "Used to ask the user his/her first name")
```

We don't recommend this approach for two reasons. First, you most likely won't come up with the perfect keys on the first attempt, having to go back and change them in in the strings files, a cumbersome and error-prone effort, still ending up with keys that do not match what is used in the app. The second reason is that, by clearly using uppercase keys, you can immediately notice if you have forgotten to localize any text when you run the app just by looking at it.

Now that you have an idea of how the localization architecture and the strings file work, let's take a look at localization in action.

Creating the LocalizeMe App

We'll create a small application that displays the user's current **locale**. A locale (an instance of NSLocale) represents both the user's language and region. The system uses the locale to determine which language to use when interacting with the user, as well as how to display dates, currency, and time information, among other things. After creating the application, we'll localize it into other languages, learning how to localize storyboard files, strings files, images, and even the application's display name.

Figure 22-2 depicts what our app will look like showing the name across the top that comes from the user's locale. The ordinals down the left side of the view are static labels, and their values will be set by localizing the storyboard file. The words down the right side, and the flag image at the bottom of the screen, will all be chosen in our app's code at run time based on the user's preferred language.

Figure 22-2. *The LocalizeMe application shown with two different language settings*

Create a new project in Xcode using the Single View Application template and call it LocalizeMe. If you look in the folder 22 - Images in the example source code, you'll find a pair of images named flag_usa.png and flag_france.png. In Xcode, select the Assets.xcassets item, and then drag both flag_usa.png and flag_france.png into it. Now let's add some label outlets to the project's view controller. We need to create one outlet for the label across the top of the view, another for the image view that will show a flag, and an outlet collection for all the words down the right-hand side (see Figure 22-2). Select ViewController.swift and make the following changes:

```
class ViewController: UIViewController {
    @IBOutlet var localeLabel : UILabel!
    @IBOutlet var flagImageView : UIImageView!
    @IBOutlet var labels : [UILabel]!
```

Select Main.storyboard to edit the GUI in Interface Builder. Drag a label from the library, dropping it at the top of the main view, aligned with the top blue guideline. Resize the label so that it takes the entire width of the view, from the left margin guideline to the right margin guideline. With the label selected, open the Attributes Inspector. Look for the Font control and click the small T icon it contains to bring up a small font-selection pop-up. Click the Style selector and change it to Bold to make the title label stand out a bit from the rest. Next, use the Attributes Inspector to set the text alignment to centered. You can also use the font selector to make the font size larger if you wish. As long as Autoshrink is set to Minimum Font Size in the object Attributes Inspector, the text will be resized if it gets too long to fit. With your label in place, Control-drag from the View Controller icon in the Document Outline (or the one in the storyboard) to this new label, and then select the localeLabel outlet.

Next, drag five more labels from the library and put them against the left margin using the blue guideline, one above the other (again, see Figure 22-2). Double-click the top one and change its text from Label to First. Repeat this procedure with the other four labels, changing the text to the words Second, Third, Fourth, and Fifth. Make sure that all five labels are aligned to the left margin guideline.

Drag another five labels from the library, this time placing them against the right margin. Change the text alignment using the object Attributes Inspector so that they are right-aligned. Control-drag from View Controller to each of the five new labels, connecting each one to the labels outlet collection, and making sure to connect them in the right order from top to bottom.

Drag an Image View from the library over to the bottom part of the view, so that it touches the bottom and left blue guidelines. In the Attributes Inspector, select flag_usa for the view's Image attribute and resize the image horizontally to stretch from blue guideline to blue guideline, and vertically so that it is about a third of the height of the user interface. In the Attributes Inspector, change the Mode attribute from its current value to Aspect Fit. Not all flags have the same aspect ratio, and we want to make sure the localized versions of the image look right. Selecting this option will cause the image view to resize any images that it displays so they fit, but it will also maintain the correct aspect ratio (height to width). Now Control-drag from the view controller to this image view and select the flagImageView outlet.

To complete the user interface, we need to set the auto layout constraints. Starting with the label at the top, Control-drag from it to its parent view in the Document Outline, press the Shift key, select Leading Space to Container Margin, Trailing Space to Container Margin, and Vertical Spacing to Top Layout Guide, and press Return.

Next, we'll fix the positions of each of the five rows of labels. Control-drag from the label with the text First to its parent view in the Document Outline, select both Leading Space to Container Margin and Vertical Spacing to Top Layout Guide, and press Return. Control-drag from the label to the label on the same row to its right and select Baseline, and then Control-drag from the label on the right to its parent view in the Document Outline and select Trailing Space to Container Margin.

We've now positioned the top row of labels. Let's do exactly the same thing for the other four rows. Next, select all of the five labels on the right by holding down the Shift key while clicking them with the mouse, and then Editor ➤ Size to Fit Content. Finally, clear the text from all of these labels because we will be setting it from our code.

To fix the position and size of the flag, Control-drag from the flag label to its parent view in the Document Outline, select Leading Space to Container Margin, Trailing Space to Container Margin, and Vertical Spacing to Bottom Layout Guide, and press Return. With the flag label still selected, click the Pin button, check the Height check box in the pop-up, and press Add 1 Constraint. You have now added all of the auto layout constraints that we need.

Save your storyboard, and then switch to ViewController.swift and add the code from Listing 22-4 to the viewDidLoad() method.

Listing 22-4. Modify the viewDidLoad Method As Shown

```
override func viewDidLoad() {
    super.viewDidLoad()
    // Do any additional setup after loading the view, typically from a nib.
    let locale = Locale.current
    let currentLangID = Locale.preferredLanguages[0]
    let displayLang = locale.displayName(forKey: Locale.Key.languageCode, value:
currentLangID)
    let capitalized = displayLang?.capitalized(with: locale)
    localeLabel.text = capitalized

    labels[0].text = NSLocalizedString("LABEL_ONE", comment: "The number 1")
    labels[1].text = NSLocalizedString("LABEL_TWO", comment: "The number 2")
    labels[2].text = NSLocalizedString("LABEL_THREE", comment: "The number 3")
    labels[3].text = NSLocalizedString("LABEL_FOUR", comment: "The number 4")
```

```
labels[4].text = NSLocalizedString("LABEL_FIVE", comment: "The number 5")

let flagFile = NSLocalizedString("FLAG_FILE", comment: "Name of the flag")
flagImageView.image = UIImage(named: flagFile)
}
```

The first thing we do in this code is get an NSLocale instance (remembering that the new version of Xcode and Swift supports much more user-friendly names such as Locale though technically, it's still an NSLocale) that represents the user's current locale. This instance tells us both the user's language and region preferences, as set in the device's Settings application:

```
let locale = Locale.current
```

Next, we grab the user's preferred language. This gives us a two-character code, such as "en" or "fr", or a string like "fr_CH" for a regional language variant:

```
let currentLangID = Locale.preferredLanguages[0]
```

The next line of code might need a bit of explanation:

```
let displayLang = locale.displayName(forKey: Locale.Key.languageCode, value: currentLangID)
```

NSLocale works somewhat like a dictionary. It can give you a whole bunch of information about the current user's locale, including the name of the currency and the expected date format. You can find a complete list of the information that you can retrieve in the NSLocale API reference. Here, we're using a method called displayName(forKey value:) to retrieve the actual name of the chosen language, translated into the language of the current locale itself. The purpose of this method is to return the value of the item we've requested in a specific language.

The display name for the French language, for example, is *français* in French, but French in English. This method gives you the ability to retrieve data about any locale, so that it can be displayed appropriately for all users. In this case, we want the display name of the user's preferred language in the language currently being used, which is why we pass currentLangID as the second argument. This string is a two-letter language code, similar to the one we used earlier to create our language projects. For an English speaker, it would be en; and for a French speaker, it would be fr.

The name we get back from this call is going to be something like "English" or "français"—and it will only be capitalized if language names are always capitalized in the user's preferred language. That's the case in English, but not so in French. We want the name capitalized for displaying as a title, however. Fortunately, NSString has methods for capitalizing strings, including one that will capitalize a string according to the rules of a given locale! Let's use that to turn *français* into *Français*:

```
let capitalized = displayLang?.capitalized(with: locale)
```

Here, we are using the fact that the Objective-C class NSString and Swift's String are transparently bridged to call the capitalizedStringWithLocale() method of NSString on our String instance. Once we have the display name, we use it to set the top label in the view:

```
localeLabel.text = capitalized
```

Next, we set the five other labels to the numbers 1 through 5, spelled out in our development base language. We use the NSLocalizedString() function to get the text for these labels, passing it the key and a comment indicating what each word is. You can just pass an empty string for the comment if the words are obvious, as they are here; however, any string you pass in the second argument will be turned into a comment in the strings file, so you can use this comment to communicate with the person doing your translations:

```
labels[0].text = NSLocalizedString("LABEL_ONE", comment: "The number 1")
labels[1].text = NSLocalizedString("LABEL_TWO", comment: "The number 2")
labels[2].text = NSLocalizedString("LABEL_THREE", comment: "The number 3")
labels[3].text = NSLocalizedString("LABEL_FOUR", comment: "The number 4")
labels[4].text = NSLocalizedString("LABEL_FIVE", comment: "The number 5")
```

Finally, we do another string lookup to find the name of the flag image to use and populate our image view with the named image:

```
let flagFile = NSLocalizedString("FLAG_FILE", comment: "Name of the flag")
flagImageView.image = UIImage(named: flagFile)
```

Build and run the application and it should appear similar to Figure 22-3 providing your base language is English.

Figure 22-3. *The language running under the authors' base language. The application is set up for localization, but it is not yet localized*

Because we used the NSLocalizedString() function instead of static strings, we are now ready for localization. However, we are not localized yet, as is glaringly obvious from the uppercase labels in the right column and the lack of a flag image at the bottom. If you use the Settings application on the simulator or on your iOS device to change to another language or region, the results look essentially the same, except for the label at the top of the view, as shown in Figure 22-4. If you're not sure how to change the language, hold off for now and we'll get to that shortly.

Figure 22-4. The nonlocalized application running on an iPhone and set to use the French language

Localizing the Project

Now let's localize the project. In the Xcode Project Navigator, single-click LocalizeMe, click the LocalizeMe project (not one of the targets) in the editing area, and then select the Info tab for the project. Look for the Localizations section in the Info tab. You'll see that it shows one localization, which is for your development language—in my case, that's English. This localization is usually referred to as the base localization and it's added automatically when Xcode creates a project. We want to add French, so click the plus (+) button at the bottom of the Localizations section and select French (fr) from the pop-up list that appears (see Figure 22-5).

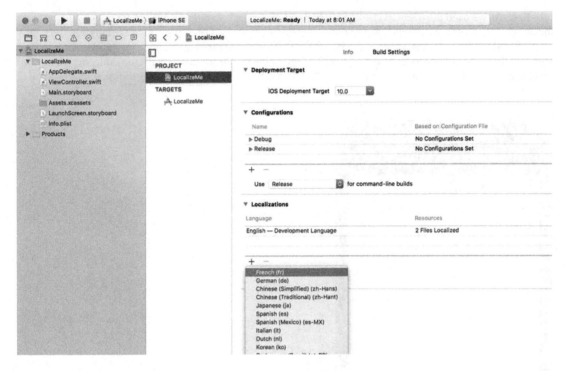

Figure 22-5. *The project info settings showing localizations and other information*

Next, you will be asked to choose all existing localizable files that you want to localize and which existing localization you want the new French localization to start from (see Figure 22-6). Sometimes when you add a new language, it is advantageous to start with the files for the new language based on those of another one for which you already have a localization; for example, to create a Swiss French localization in a project that's already been translated into French (as we will, later in this chapter), you would almost certainly prefer to use the existing French localization as the start point instead of your base language. You would do this by selecting French as the Reference Language when you add the Swiss French localization. Right now, though, there are only two files to be localized and one choice of starting point language (your base language), so just leave everything as it is and click Finish.

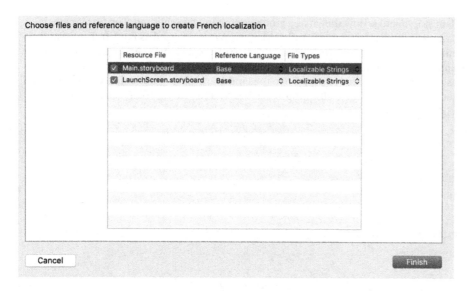

Figure 22-6. *Choosing the files for localization*

Now that you've added a French localization, take a look at the Project Navigator. Notice that the Main. storyboard and Launch.storyboard files now have a disclosure triangle next to them, as if they were a group or folder. Expand them and take a look, as shown in Figure 22-7.

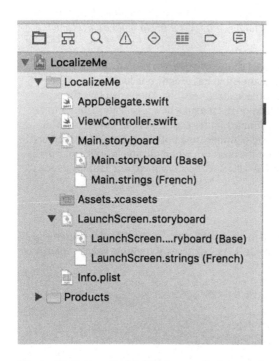

Figure 22-7. *Localizable files have a disclosure triangle and a child value for each language or region you add*

In our project, Main.storyboard is now shown as a group containing two children. The first is called Main.Storyboard and tagged as Base; the second is called Main.strings and tagged as French. The Base version was created automatically when you created the project, and it represents your development base language. The same applies to the LaunchScreen.storyboard file. These files actually live in two different folders: one called Base.lproj and one called fr.lproj. Go to the Finder and open the LocalizeMe folder within your LocalizeMe project folder. In addition to all your project files, you should see folders named Base.lproj and fr.lproj, as shown in Figure 22-8.

Figure 22-8. *From the outset, our Xcode project included a Base language project folder (Base.lproj). When we chose to make a file localizable, Xcode created a language folder (fr.lproj) for the language we selected.*

Note that the Base.lproj folder was there all along, with its copies of Main.storyboard and LaunchScreen.storyboard inside it. When Xcode finds a resource that has exactly one localized version, it displays it as a single item. As soon as a file has two or more localized versions, Xcode displays them as a group. When you asked Xcode to create the French localization, it created a new localization folder in your project called fr.lproj and placed in it strings files that contain values extracted from Base.lproj/Main.storyboard and Base.lproj/LaunchScreen.storyboard. Instead of duplicating both files, Xcode just extracts every text string from them and creates strings files ready for localization. When the app is built and run, the values in the localized strings files get pulled in to replace the values in the storyboard and launch screen.

Localizing the Storyboard

In the Xcode Project Navigator, select Main.strings (French) to open the French strings file, the contents of which will be injected into the storyboard shown to French speakers. You'll see something like the following text:

```
/* Class = "UILabel"; text = "Fifth"; ObjectID = "5tN-O9-txB"; */
"5tN-O9-txB.text" = "Fifth";

/* Class = "UILabel"; text = "Third"; ObjectID = "GO5-hd-zou"; */
"GO5-hd-zou.text" = "Third";

/* Class = "UILabel"; text = "Second"; ObjectID = "NCJ-hT-XgS"; */
"NCJ-hT-XgS.text" = "Second";
```

```
/* Class = "UILabel"; text = "Fourth"; ObjectID = "Z6w-b0-U06"; */
"Z6w-b0-U06.text" = "Fourth";

/* Class = "UILabel"; text = "First"; ObjectID = "kS9-Wx-xgy"; */
"kS9-Wx-xgy.text" = "First";

/* Class = "UILabel"; text = "Label"; ObjectID = "yGf-tY-SVz"; */
"yGf-tY-SVz.text" = "Label";
```

Each of the pairs of lines represents a string that was found in the storyboard. The comment tells you the class of the object that contained the string, the original string itself, and a unique identifier for each object (which will probably be different in your copy of this file). The line after the comment is where you actually want to add the translated string on the right-hand side of the equals sign. You'll see that some of these are ordinals such as First; those come from the labels on the left of Figure 22-4, all of which were given names in the storyboard. The entry with the name Label is for the title label, which we set programmatically, so you don't need to localize it.

Prior to iOS 8, the usual practice was to localize the storyboard by directly editing this file. With iOS 8, you can still do that if you choose, but if you plan to use a professional translator, it's likely to be more convenient to have them translate the storyboard text and the strings in your code at the same time. For that reason, Apple has made it possible to collect all of the strings that need to be translated into one file per language that you can send to your translator. If you plan to use that approach, you would leave the storyboard strings file alone and proceed to the next step, which is described in the next section. It's still possible to modify the storyboard strings file and, if you do so, those changes would not be lost should you need to have your translator make changes or localize additional text. So, just on this occasion, let's localize the storyboard strings in the old-fashioned way. To do so, locate the text for the First, Second, Third, Fourth, and Fifth labels, and then change the string to the right of the equal sign to Premier, Deuxième, Troisième, Quatrième, and Cinquième, respectively (similar to):

```
/* Class = "UILabel"; text = "Fifth"; ObjectID = "5tN-O9-txB"; */
"5tN-O9-txB.text" = "Cinquième";

/* Class = "UILabel"; text = "Third"; ObjectID = "GO5-hd-zou"; */
"GO5-hd-zou.text" = "Troisième";

/* Class = "UILabel"; text = "Second"; ObjectID = "NCJ-hT-XgS"; */
"NCJ-hT-XgS.text" = "Deuxième";

/* Class = "UILabel"; text = "Fourth"; ObjectID = "Z6w-b0-U06"; */
"Z6w-b0-U06.text" = "Quatrième";

/* Class = "UILabel"; text = "First"; ObjectID = "kS9-Wx-xgy"; */
"kS9-Wx-xgy.text" = "Premier";

/* Class = "UILabel"; text = "Label"; ObjectID = "yGf-tY-SVz"; */
"yGf-tY-SVz.text" = "Label";
```

Finally, save the file. Our storyboard is now localized in French. There are three ways to see the effects of this localization on your application—you can preview it in Xcode, use a customized scheme to launch it, or change the active language on the simulator or a real device. Let's look at these options in turn, starting with getting a preview.

Using the Assistant Editor to Preview Localizations

Select Main.storyboard in the Project Navigator and open the Assistant Editor. In the Assistant Editor's jump bar, select Preview ➤ Main.storyboard and you'll see the application as it appears in the base development language, as shown on the left in Figure 22-9.

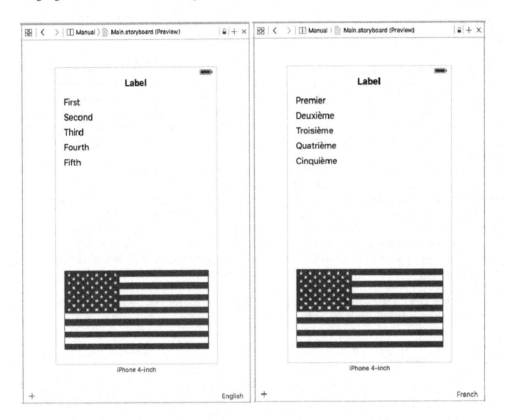

Figure 22-9. *Previewing the application in the base language and in French*

At the bottom right of the Assistant Editor, you'll see that the current language (English) is displayed. Click here to open a pop-up that lists all of the localizations in your project and select French. The preview updates to show how the application appears to a French user, as shown on the right in Figure 22-9, except that the flag is not correct. That's because the preview considers only what's in the localized version of the storyboard, whereas we are actually setting the flag image in code. If you're using code to install localized resources, you'll need to choose one of the other options to get an accurate view.

Using a Custom Scheme to Change Language and Region Settings

Creating a customized scheme gives you a quick way to see a localized version of your application running on the simulator or on a real device. Unlike preview, this options lets you see localizations made in code as well as in the storyboard. Start by clicking on the left side of the Scheme selector in Xcode—you'll find it in the top bar, next to the Run and Stop buttons. Currently, the selector should be displaying the text LocalizeMe, which is the name of the current Scheme, and the currently selected device or simulator. When you click LocalizeMe, Xcode opens a pop-up with several options. Choose Manage Schemes... to open the Scheme dialog, as shown in Figure 22-10.

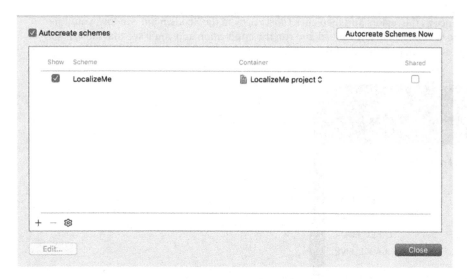

Figure 22-10. *The Scheme dialog lets you view, add, and remove schemes*

Currently, there is only one scheme. Click the + icon below the scheme list to open another window that allows you to choose a name for your new scheme. Call it `LocalizeMe_fr` and press OK. Back in the Scheme dialog, select your newly created scheme and click Edit... to open the Scheme editor (see Figure 22-11).

Figure 22-11. *The Scheme editor, with French selected as the Application Language and France as the Application Region*

Make sure that Run is selected in the left column, and then turn your attention to the Application Language and Application Region selectors in main body of the editor. Here, you can choose the language and region to be used when the application is launched with your custom scheme. Choose French as the language and France as the region, and then click Close. Back in the Xcode main window, you'll see that your new scheme is now selected. Go ahead and run the application and you'll see that the French localization is active, as shown in Figure 22-12.

Figure 22-12. *Viewing the current state of the application in French*

As you can see, the flag is missing. Of course, that's because we're installing the flag image in code and we haven't completed the French localization yet. To revert to the base language view, just switch back to the original LocalizeMe scheme and run the application again.

Switching the Language and Region Settings on a Device or Simulator

The final way to see how the application looks in a different language or with different regional settings is to switch those settings in the simulator or on your device. This takes a little more time than either of the other two options, so it's probably better to do this only at the end of the testing cycle, when you are pretty sure that everything works. Here's how to make French the primary language for your device (or simulator).

Go to the Settings application, select the General row, and then select the row labeled Language and Region. From here, you'll be able to change your language and region preferences, as shown in Figure 22-13.

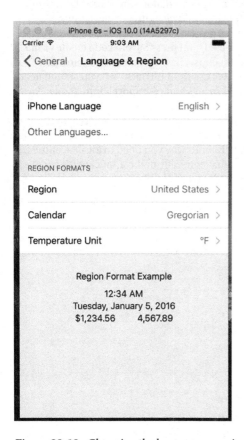

Figure 22-13. *Changing the language or region setting*

Tap iPhone Language to reveal the list of languages into which iOS has been localized, and then find and select the entry for French (which appears in French, as *Français*). You can also change the Region to France for complete authenticity, although that's not necessary for this example since we're not using numbers, dates or times in our code. Press Done and then confirm that you want the device language to be changed. This will cause the device to do a partial reboot, which will take a few seconds. Now run the app again and you'll see once again that the labels on the left side are showing the localized French text (see Figure 22-12). However, as before, the flag is missing and right-hand column of text is still wrong. We'll take care of those in the next section.

Generating and Localizing a Strings File

In Figure 22-12, the words on the right side of the view are still in SHOUT_ALL_CAPS style because we haven't translated them yet; what you are seeing are the keys that NSLocalizedString() is using to look for the localized texts. In order to localize those, we need to first extract the key and comment strings from the code. Fortunately, Xcode makes it easy to extract the text that needs to be localized from your project and put it all in a separate file for each language. Let's see how that works.

In the Project Navigator, select your project. In the editor, select either the project or one of its targets. Now choose Editor ➤ Export for Localization... from the menu. This opens a dialog where you choose which languages you want to localize and where the files for each language should be written. Select a suitable location for the file (for example, in a new folder called XLIFF in the project's root directory), ensure that the check boxes for Existing Translations and French are both selected, and press Save. Xcode creates a file called fr.xliff in a folder called LocalizeMe inside the folder that you chose. If you plan to use a third-party service to translate your application's text, it's likely that they can work with XLIFF files—all you should need to do is send them this file, have them update it with the translated strings and re-import it into Xcode. For now, though, we are going to do the translation ourselves.

Open the fr.xliff file. You'll see that it contains a lot of XML. It breaks down into three different sections that contain the strings from the storyboard, the strings that Xcode found in your source code, and a number of localizable values from your application's Info.plist file. We'll talk about why you need to localize entries from Info.plist later in the chapter. For now, let's translate the text that comes from the application's code. Look through the file and you'll find that text embedded in some XML that looks like this:

```
<file original="LocalizeMe/Localizable.strings" source-language="en" datatype="plaintext"
target-language="fr">
    <header>
      <tool tool-id="com.apple.dt.xcode" tool-name="Xcode" tool-version="n.n.n" build-
num="nnnnn"/>
    </header>
    <body>
      <trans-unit id="FLAG_FILE">
        <source>FLAG_FILE</source>
        <note>Name of the flag</note>
      </trans-unit>
      <trans-unit id="LABEL_FIVE">
        <source>LABEL_FIVE</source>
        <note>The number 5</note>
      </trans-unit>
      <trans-unit id="LABEL_FOUR">
        <source>LABEL_FOUR</source>
        <note>The number 4</note>
      </trans-unit>
      <trans-unit id="LABEL_ONE">
        <source>LABEL_ONE</source>
        <note>The number 1</note>
      </trans-unit>
      <trans-unit id="LABEL_THREE">
        <source>LABEL_THREE</source>
        <note>The number 3</note>
      </trans-unit>
      <trans-unit id="LABEL_TWO">
        <source>LABEL_TWO</source>
        <note>The number 2</note>
```

```
        </trans-unit>
      </body>
  </file>
```

Notice that the `<file>` element has a `target-language` attribute that gives the language into which the text needs to be translated, and that there is a nested `<trans-unit>` element for each string that needs to be translated. Each of them contains a `<source>` element with the original text and a `<note>` element that contains the comment from the `NSLocalizedString()` call in the source code. Professional translators have software tools that present the information in this file and allow them to enter the translations. We, on the other hand, are going to do it manually by adding `<target>` elements containing the French text, like this:

```
<file original="LocalizeMe/Localizable.strings" source-language="en" datatype="plaintext"
target-language="fr">
    <header>
      <tool tool-id="com.apple.dt.xcode" tool-name="Xcode" tool-version="n.n.n" build-
num="nnnnn"/>
    </header>
    <body>
      <trans-unit id="FLAG_FILE">
        <source>FLAG_FILE</source>
        <note>Name of the flag</note>
        <target>flag_france</target>
      </trans-unit>
      <trans-unit id="LABEL_FIVE">
        <source>LABEL_FIVE</source>
        <note>The number 5</note>
        <target>Cinq</target>
      </trans-unit>
      <trans-unit id="LABEL_FOUR">
        <source>LABEL_FOUR</source>
        <note>The number 4</note>
        <target>Quatre</target>
      </trans-unit>
      <trans-unit id="LABEL_ONE">
        <source>LABEL_ONE</source>
        <note>The number 1</note>
        <target>Un</target>
      </trans-unit>
      <trans-unit id="LABEL_THREE">
        <source>LABEL_THREE</source>
        <note>The number 3</note>
        <target>Trois</target>
      </trans-unit>
      <trans-unit id="LABEL_TWO">
        <source>LABEL_TWO</source>
        <note>The number 2</note>
        <target>Deux</target>
      </trans-unit>
    </body>
  </file>
```

If you haven't already translated the storyboard strings, you can do that too. You'll find them in a separate block of <trans-unit> elements, which are easy to find because of the comments that include the links to the labels from which the text came. On the other hand, if you have done the translations already, you'll find that Xcode included them in the XLIFF file, like this:

```
<trans-unit id="GO5-hd-zou.text">
    <source>Third</source>
    <target>Troisième</target>
    <note>Class = "UILabel"; text = "Third"; ObjectID = "GO5-hd-zou";</note>
</trans-unit>
<trans-unit id="NCJ-hT-XgS.text">
    <source>Second</source>
    <target>Deuxième</target>
    <note>Class = "UILabel"; text = "Second"; ObjectID = "NCJ-hT-XgS";</note>
</trans-unit>
```

Save your translations. The next step is to import the results back into Xcode. Make sure that the project is selected in the Project Navigator. Then, choose Editor ➤ Import Localizations in the menu bar, navigate to your file, and open it. Xcode will show you a list of keys that have been translated and their translations. Press Import to complete the import process. If you look at the Project Navigator, you'll see that two files have been added—InfoPlist.strings and Localizable.strings. Open Localizable.strings and you'll see that it contains the French translations of the strings that Xcode extracted from ViewController.swift:

```
/* Name of the flag */
"FLAG_FILE" = "flag_france";

/* The number 5 */
"LABEL_FIVE" = "Cinq";

/* The number 4 */
"LABEL_FOUR" = "Quatre";

/* The number 1 */
"LABEL_ONE" = "Un";

/* The number 3 */
"LABEL_THREE" = "Trois";

/* The number 2 */
"LABEL_TWO" = "Deux";
```

Now, build and run the app with French as the active language. You should see the labels on the right-hand side translated into French and at the bottom of the screen, you should now see the French flag, as shown in Figure 22-14.

Figure 22-14. *Our properly localized app, for French, including the correct flag*

So are we done yet? Not quite. Rerun the app with English as the active language. You'll see the unlocalized version of the app shown in Figure 22-3. To make the app work in English, we have to localize it for English. To do that, select the Project in the Project Navigator and then select Editor ➤ Export for Localization… from the menu to export strings for localization again; but this time, choose Development Language Only and then press Save. This creates a file called en.xliff, where we'll add the localizations for English. Edit the file and make the following changes:

```
<file original="LocalizeMe/Localizable.strings" source-language="en" datatype="plaintext">
  <header>
    <tool tool-id="com.apple.dt.xcode" tool-name="Xcode" tool-version="n.n.n" build-
num="nnnnn"/>
  </header>
  <body>
    <trans-unit id="FLAG_FILE">
```

```
        <source>FLAG_FILE</source>
        <note>Name of the flag</note>
        <target>flag_usa</target>
      </trans-unit>
      <trans-unit id="LABEL_FIVE">
        <source>LABEL_FIVE</source>
        <note>The number 5</note>
        <target>Five</target>
      </trans-unit>
      <trans-unit id="LABEL_FOUR">
        <source>LABEL_FOUR</source>
        <note>The number 4</note>
        <target>Four</target>
      </trans-unit>
      <trans-unit id="LABEL_ONE">
        <source>LABEL_ONE</source>
        <note>The number 1</note>
        <target>One</target>
      </trans-unit>
      <trans-unit id="LABEL_THREE">
        <source>LABEL_THREE</source>
        <note>The number 3</note>
        <target>Three</target>
      </trans-unit>
      <trans-unit id="LABEL_TWO">
        <source>LABEL_TWO</source>
        <note>The number 2</note>
        <target>Two</target>
      </trans-unit>
    </body>
  </file>
```

Import these changes back into Xcode using Editor ➤ Import Localizations.

Xcode creates a folder called en.lproj and adds to it files called InfoPlist.strings, Localizable.strings, and Main.strings that contain the English localization. What you have added is the reference to the image file for the flag and the text to replace the keys used in the NSLocalizedString() function calls in the code. Now if you run the app with English as your selected language, you'll see the correct English text and the US flag.

The requirement to provide the flag image file name and the text strings for the base localization arises because we chose not to use localized text as the keys when calling NSLocalizedString(). Had we done something like this, the English text would appear in the user interface for any language for which there is no localization, even if we didn't provide a base localization:

```
labels[0].text = NSLocalizedString("One", comment: "The number 1")
labels[1].text = NSLocalizedString("Two", comment: "The number 2")
labels[2].text = NSLocalizedString("Three", comment: "The number 3")
labels[3].text = NSLocalizedString("Four", comment: "The number 4")
labels[4].text = NSLocalizedString("Five", comment: "The number 5")
let flagFile = NSLocalizedString("flag_usa", comment: "Name of the flag")
```

While this is perfectly legal, the downside is that if you need to change any of the English text strings, you are also changing the key used to look up the strings for all of the other languages, so you will need to manually update all of the localized .strings files so that they use the new key.

Localizing the App Display Name

We want to explore one final piece of localization that is commonly used: localizing the app name that's visible on the home screen and elsewhere. Apple does this for several of the built-in apps, and you might want to do so, as well. The app name used for display is stored in your app's Info.plist file, which you'll find in the Project Navigator. Select this file for editing, and you'll see that one of the items it contains, Bundle name, is currently set to ${PRODUCT_NAME}. In the syntax used by Info.plist files, anything starting with a dollar sign is subject to variable substitution. In this case, it means that when Xcode compiles the app, the value of this item will be replaced with the name of the product in this Xcode project, which is the name of the app itself. This is where we want to do some localization, replacing ${PRODUCT_NAME} with the localized name for each language. However, as it turns out, this doesn't quite work out as simply as you might expect.

The Info.plist file is sort of a special case, and it isn't meant to be localized. Instead, if you want to localize the content of Info.plist, you need to make localized versions of a file named InfoPlist.strings. Before you can do that, you need to create a Base version of that file. If you followed the steps in the previous section to localize the app, you'll already have English and French versions of this file that are empty. If you don't have these files, you can add one, as follows:

1. Select File ➤ New ➤ File.... In the iOS section, choose Resource and then Strings File (see Figure 22-15). Press Next, name the file InfoPlist.strings, assign it to the Supporting Files group in the LocalizeMe project, and create it.

2. Select the new file and, in the File Inspector, press Localize. In the dialog box that appears, have the file moved to the English localization. Back in the File Inspector, check the check box for French under Localizations. You should now see copies of this file for both French and English in the Project Navigator.

Figure 22-15. *The Strings File option under the iOS Resource file type selection*

We need to add a line to each localized copy of this file to define the display name for the app. In the Info.plist file, we were shown the display name associated with a dictionary key called **Bundle name**; however, that's not the real key name. It's merely an Xcode nicety, trying to give us a friendlier and readable name. The real name is CFBundleName, which you can verify by selecting Info.plist, right-clicking anywhere in the view, and then selecting Show Raw Keys/Values. This shows you the true names of the keys in use. So, select the English localization of InfoPlist.strings and either add or modify the following line:

```
"CFBundleName" = "Localize Me";
```

This key may already exist if you followed the localization steps for English, because it's inserted as part of the process of importing an XLIFF file. In fact, another way to localize your app's name is to add the translation to the XLIFF file in the same way as we did for the other texts that we needed to translate—just look for the entry for CFBundleName and add a <trans> element with the translated name. Similarly, select the French localization of the InfoPlist.strings file and edit it to give the app a proper French name:

```
"CFBundleName" = "Localisez Moi";
```

Build and run the app, and then go back to the launch screen. And of course, switch the device or simulator you're using to French if it's currently running in English. You should see the localized name just underneath the app's icon, but sometimes it may not appear immediately. iOS seems to cache this information when a new app is added, but it doesn't necessarily change it when an existing app is replaced by a new version—at least not when Xcode is doing the replacing. So, if you're running in French and you don't see the new name—don't worry. Just delete the app from the launch screen, go back to Xcode, and then build and run the app again.

■ **Warning** You won't see the localized app name if you are running the application with a custom scheme. The only way to see it is to switch the device or simulator language to French.

Now our application is fully localized for both French and English.

Adding Another Localization

To wrap up, we're going to add another localization to our application. This time, we'll localize it to Swiss French, which is a regional variation of French with language code **fr-CH.**

The basic principle is the same as before—in fact, now that you have done this once, it should go much faster this time. Start by selecting the project in the Project Navigator, and then select the project itself in the editor, followed by the Info tab. In the Localizations section, press + to add a new language. You won't see Swiss French in the menu, so scroll down and select Other. This opens a submenu with a very large number of languages to choose from—fortunately, they are in alphabetical order. If you scroll down, you will eventually find French (Switzerland), so select it. In the dialog that appears (which looks like Figure 22-6), change the Reference Language for all of the listed files to French, so that Xcode uses your existing French translations as the basis for the Swiss French localization, and then click Finish. Now if you look at the Project Navigator, you'll see that you have Swiss French versions of the storyboard, localizable strings, and InfoPlist.strings files. To demonstrate that this localization is distinct from the French one, open the Swiss French version of InfoPlist.strings and change the bundle name to this:

```
"CFBundleName" = "Swiss Localisez Moi";
```

Now build and run the application. Switch to the Settings application and go to Language & Region. You probably won't find Swiss French in the list of iPhone Languages. Instead, click Add Language... and scroll down (or search) until you find French (Switzerland); and then select it and press Done. This will bring up an action sheet in which you will be asked if you prefer Swiss French or your current language. Select Swiss French and let iOS reset itself. Go to the home screen and you should now see that our application is called **Swiss Localisez Moi** (in fact, you may not see the whole name, because it's too long, but you get the point). If you open the application, you'll see that the text is all in French. Unfortunately, the flag is also the French flag, not the Swiss one. By now, you should be able to figure out how to fix this by editing the Swiss localization files. So as an exercise, try downloading a Swiss flag image from the Internet and see if you can make it appear in the Swiss version of the application.

Summary

To maximize sales of your iOS application, you'll probably want to localize it as much as possible. Fortunately, the iOS localization architecture makes easy work of supporting multiple languages, and even multiple dialects of the same language, within your application. As you saw in this chapter, nearly any type of file that you add to your application can be localized.

Even if you don't plan on localizing your application, you should get in the habit of using NSLocalizedString() instead of just using static strings in your code. With the Xcode IDE's Code Sense feature, the difference in typing time is negligible. And, should you ever want to translate your application, your life will be much, much easier. Going back late in the project to find all text strings that should be localized is a boring and error-prone process, which you can avoid with a little effort in advance.

Book Summary

The programming language and frameworks we've worked within this book are the end result of more than 25 years of evolution. And Apple engineers are feverishly working round the clock, thinking of that next, cool, new thing. The iOS platform has just begun to blossom. There is so much more to come. By making it through this book, you've built yourself a sturdy foundation. You have a solid knowledge of Swift, Cocoa Touch, and the tools that bring these technologies together to create incredible new iPhone, iPod touch, and iPad applications. You understand the iOS software architecture—the design patterns that make Cocoa Touch sing. In short, you're ready to chart your own course. Good Luck.

APPENDIX A

■ ■ ■

An Introduction to Swift

Until recently, writing an iPhone or iPad application meant working with Objective-C. Because of its unusual syntax, Objective-C is one of the most polarizing of programming languages—people tend to love it or hate it. At the World Wide Developer Conference in 2014, Apple changed all that by unveiling an alternative—a new language called **Swift**. Swift's syntax is designed to be easily recognizable to programmers who are used to some of the more popular object-oriented programming languages like C++ and Java, therefore making it easier for them to start writing applications for iOS (and for Macs, since Swift is also fully supported as a development language on macOS). This appendix covers the parts of Swift that you'll need to know in order to understand the example code in this book. We assume that you already have some programming experience and that you know what variables, functions, methods, and classes are. This appendix is neither a reference nor an exhaustive guide to the language—for that, there are numerous other resources, some of which are listed in Chapter 1.

Swift Basics

One of the most useful new features introduced in Xcode 6 alongside Swift is the **playground**. As the name suggests, a playground is a place where you can go to play with code without having to create an environment in which to run it—just open a playground, type in some code, and see the results. Playgrounds are a great place to prototype something new and they are also an ideal place to start learning a new language, so we're going to use them throughout this appendix.

Let's begin by creating a new playground. Start Xcode and go to File ➤ New ➤ Playground.... In the dialog that opens, choose a name for your playground (something like SwiftBasics) and make sure that the Platform is iOS, and then press Next. Choose the folder in which your playground will be saved and then press Create. Xcode creates the playground and opens it in a new window, as shown in Figure A-1. As you read through the examples in this appendix, feel free to experiment by adding code of your own to the playground or by modifying the examples to see what happens.

© Molly Maskrey, Kim Topley, David Mark, Fredrik Olsson and Jeff Lamarche 2016
M. Maskrey et al., *Beginning iPhone Development with Swift 3*, DOI 10.1007/978-1-4842-2223-2_23

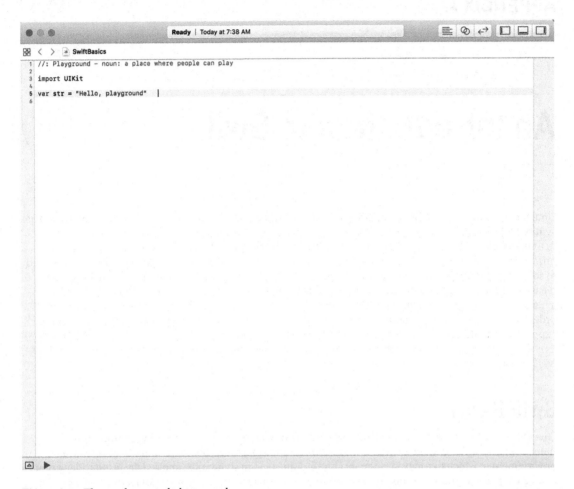

Figure A-1. *The newly created playground*

Playgrounds, Comments, Variables, and Constants

Let's take a moment to look at what we've got in our playground. It's divided into two areas—code is on the left and results appear on the right. As you type code, the Swift compiler compiles and executes it, and shows you the result almost immediately. The code in Figure A-1 declares a new variable called str and initializes it with the string "Hello, playground". You can see this string in the results column on the right. Try changing the value and notice that the result updates to match as soon as you stop typing.

The code on line 1 in Figure A-1 is a comment. Anything following the character sequence // up to the end of the line is ignored by the compiler. Here, the comment occupies the whole line, but that's not the only option. We could add a comment to the end of a line of code too:

```
var str = "Hello, playground"    // my comment for this line
```

To write a comment that's longer than one line, start it with /* and end it with */, like this:

```
/*
 This is a comment that occupies
```

```
More than one line.
*/
```

There are various different ways to write a multiline comment. Some people like to make it clear that a line is part of a comment by starting each line with a * character:

```
/*
 * This is a comment that occupies
 * More than one line.
 */
```

Other people like to write single-line comments like this:

```
/* This is another way to write a single-line comment. */
```

The import statement on line 3 of Figure A-1 makes Apple's UIKit framework available for use in the playground:

```
import UIKit
```

IOS includes many frameworks, some of which you'll read about in this book. UIKit is the user interface framework, which we'll be using in all of our code examples. Another framework that you'll frequently make use of is Foundation, which contains classes that provide basic functionality like date and time handling, collections, file management, networking, and much more. To get access to this framework, you need to import it, like this:

```
import Foundation
```

However, UIKit automatically imports Foundation, so any playground that imports UIKit gets access to Foundation for free, without having to add an explicit import for it.

Line 5 is the first (and only) line of executable code in this playground:

```
var str = "Hello, playground"
```

The var keyword declares a new variable with a given name. Here, the variable is called str, which is appropriate because it's a string. Swift is very liberal with variable names: you can use almost any character you like in the name, with the exception of the first character, which is somewhat restricted. You can find the precise rules in Apple's documentation at https://developer.apple.com/library/ios/documentation/Swift/Conceptual/Swift_Programming_Language.

Following the declaration of the variable comes an expression that assigns its initial value. You don't have to initialize a variable when you declare it, but you must do so before you use it (i.e., before you execute any code that reads its value). However, if you choose to assign a value, then Swift can infer the variable's type, saving you the trouble of stating it explicitly. In this example, Swift infers that str is a string variable, because it was initialized with a string literal. If you choose not to provide an initializer (perhaps because there is no fixed initial value), you must declare the variable's type by appending it to the name and separated from it by a colon, like this:

```
var str2: String          // an uninitialized variable
```

Try changing the code on line 5 of the playground to this:

```
var str: String
str = "Hello, playground"
```

This is completely equivalent to the original code, but now you've had to explicitly state that str is a string variable (String is the Swift type that represents a string). In most cases, it's easier to combine the declaration and initialization, and allow the compiler to infer the variable's type.

Here's another example that makes use of Swift's type inference feature:

```
var count = 2
```

Here, the compiler infers that the count variable is an integer. Its actual type is Int (we'll cover the numeric types that Swift provides in the next section). How can you be sure that this is the case? Easy. Let Swift tell you. Type the preceding code into the playground, hover the mouse over count, and hold down the ⌥ (Option) key. The cursor changes to a question mark. Now click the mouse and Swift shows you the type that it's inferred for the variable in a pop-up, as shown in Figure A-2.

Figure A-2. *Getting the inferred type of a variable*

The fact that you haven't explicitly declared the type of a variable doesn't mean that it doesn't have one, or that you can play fast and loose with it. Swift assigns a type when the variable is declared and then you have to stick with that type. Unlike dynamic languages like JavaScript, you can't change the type of a variable simply by assigning a new value to it. Try doing this:

```
var count = 2
count = "Two"
```

Attempting to assign a string value to an integer variable is an error; you'll see a red marker in the margin on the left of the playground. Click it, and Swift displays a message explaining the problem (see Figure A-3).

```
19
20   var count = 2
 21  count = "Two"                                           ⊙ Cannot assign value of type 'String' to type 'Int'
22
```

Figure A-3. *Swift is not a dynamic language. You can't change the type of a variable*

If you've programmed before, you may notice that we aren't bothering to add semicolons at the end of our statements. That's one of the many nice little features of Swift: it's almost never necessary to end a statement with a semicolon. If you're used to writing in C, C++, Objective-C, or Java, that will probably feel a bit strange at first, but after a while, you'll get used to it. Of course, you *can* type the semicolon if you want to, but most likely you'll wind up not doing so. The only time you must use a semicolon is if you want to write two statements on the same line. This code is not valid:

```
var count = 2 count = 3
```

Add a semicolon, and the compiler is happy again:

```
var count = 2; count = 3
```

As the preceding line of code shows, you can change the value of a variable. That's why it's called a **variable**, after all. What if you just want to give a name to a fixed value? In other words, you want to create a constant and give it a name? For that, Swift provides the let statement which is just like var, except that you must provide an initial value:

```
let pi = 3.14159265
```

As with variables, Swift can infer the type of the constant (or you can explicitly state it if you want to), but you can't reassign the value of a constant, which is, of course, the point of making it constant:

```
pi = 42        // Error - Cannot assign to value: 'pi' is a 'let' constant
```

Naturally, you can initialize the value of a variable from a constant:

```
let pi = 3.14159265
var value = pi
```

As you've seen, Swift prints the results of executable statements to the right of the corresponding code. You can also create output using the print() function from the Swift standard library. For example, try this:

```
print("Hello, world")
```

The string "Hello, world" followed by a newline character appears in the playground output area, as usual, but you can also make it appear inline with the code. To do that, hover the mouse over the results area, and you'll see a couple of circular controls appear. Click the control on the right and the result appears right below the print() statement, as shown in Figure A-4. Also notice at the bottom is the debug area where the output also appears. You can open or close the debug area using the triangle disclosure button to the left of the bottom of the playground.

Figure A-4. *Viewing output inline with the code and in the debug area*

If you don't want the newline to be automatically appended to the string, you can get rid of it or replace it with another string by using a slightly different version of print() that takes an additional argument. Try this:

```
print("Hello, world", terminator: "")
```

This code replaces the newline with an empty string and if you check in the results area, you'll see that the newline is no longer there.

■ **Tip** print() is a function from the Swift standard library. You'll find documentation for the library at
https://developer.apple.com/library/ios/documentation/General/

Reference/SwiftStandardLibraryReference. Another way to see what's in the standard library is to add the line import Swift to your playground, and then hold down the ⌘ (Cmd) key and click the word Swift. The playground switches to a listing of the content of the standard library. There's a lot of information here, and you'll need to know a lot more about Swift to understand all of it, but it's worth looking it over to get a feel for what's available.

Predefined Types, Operators, and Control Statements

Swift comes with a set of basic, predefined types. In later sections, you'll see that you can add to these by defining your own classes, structures, and enumerations. You can even add functionality to an existing type by creating an extension of that type. Swift also has operators and control statements that will no doubt be familiar to you from other languages. Let's start with a quick overview of the basic types.

Numeric Types

Swift has four basic numeric types—Int, Uint, Float, and Double—and a collection of more specialized integer types. The full set of integer types, together with their sizes (in bits) and the ranges of values that they can represent, is listed in Table A-1.

Int and its derivatives are signed values, whereas the types related to UInt are unsigned. The default type for integer values (i.e., the type that's inferred when you write something like var count = 3) is Int and this is the recommended type to use, unless you have a specific reason to use one of the others.

Table A-1. *Integer Types*

Type	Size in Bits	Maximum Value	Minimum Value
Int	32 or 64	As Int32 or Int64	As Int32 or Int64
UInt	32 or 64	As UInt32 or UInt64	0
Int64	64	9,223,372,036,854,775,807	–9,223,372,036,854,775,808
UInt64	64	18,446,744,073,709,551,615	0
Int32	32	2,147,483,647	–2,147,483,648
UInt32	32	4,294,967,295	0
Int16	16	32767	–32768
Uint16	16	65535	0
Int8	8	127	–128
UInt8	8	255	0

As you can see from the table, the range of values that Int and UInt can represent depends on the platform. On 32-bit systems (e.g., some iPads and all iPhones before the iPhone 4s, and the iPhone 5c), these are both 32-bit values, whereas on 64-bit systems, they are 64 bits wide. If you need a value that's definitely 32-bit or definitely 64-bit, then use Int32 or Int64 instead. The Int8 and UInt8 types can be used to represent bytes.

You can discover the maximum and minimum values for each of these types programmatically by using their max and min properties. For example, try entering these lines into your playground (without the comments, which show the results):

```
print(Int8.max)     // 127
print(Int8.min)     //  -128
print(Int32.max)    // 2,147,483,647
print(Int32.min )   // -2,147,483,648
print(UInt32.max)   // 4,294,967,295
```

Integer literals can be written in decimal, hexadecimal, binary, or octal number bases. Try out these examples:

```
let decimal = 123      // Value is 123
let octal = 0o77       // Octal 77 = decimal 63
let hex = 0x1234       // Hex 1234 = decimal 4660
let binary = 0b1010    // Binary 1010 = decimal 10
```

The prefix 0o indicates octal, 0x indicates hexadecimal, and 0b indicates binary. For readability, you can also use an underscore character (_) anywhere to separate number groups:

```
let v = -1_234         // Same as -1234
let w = 12_34_56    // Same as 123456
```

Notice that you don't have to stick with the normal rule of grouping by units of three digits.

The Float and Double types are respectively 32-bit and 64-bit floating-point numbers. You assign a value to a floating-point variable by using a floating-point literal. Swift infers a type of Double, unless otherwise specified:

```
let a = 1.23            // This is inferred to be a Double
let b: Float = 1.23     // Forced to be Float
```

You can also use exponential (or scientific) notation, which is convenient for large numbers:

```
let c = 1.23e2          // Evaluated as 123.0
let d = 1.23e-1         // Evaluated as 0.123
let e = 1.23E-1         // Same as 1.23e-1
```

By their nature, floating-point numbers are not completely precise. One reason for this is that fractional values cannot be accurately represented in binary floating-point form. You can see this if you enter the following into the playground (where, as before, the comment shows the result):

```
let f: Float = 0.123456789123      // 0.1234568
let g: Double = 0.123456789123     // 0.123456789123
```

You can see that the Float representation of this value is less accurate than the Double representation. If you make the fractional part longer, you'll exceed the precision of the Double format as well:

```
let g: Double = 0.12345678912345678   // 0.1234567891234568
```

Floating-point numbers also lose precision when their value is large:

```
let f: Float = 123456789123456       // Inaccurate: 1.234568e+14
let g: Double = 123456789123456      // Accurate: 123,456,789,123,456.0
let h: Double = 123456789123456789   // Inaccurate: 1.234567891234568e+17
```

Unlike other languages, Swift does not provide implicit type conversion when you assign a variable (or expression) of one numeric type to a variable of another numeric type. For example, this code does not compile, as shown in Figure A-5.

```
let a = 123
let b = 0.456
let c = a + b
```

Variable a is of type Int and b is a Double. Swift could convert the Int to a Double and perform the addition, but it does not. You have to perform the conversion yourself:

```
let a = 123
let b = 0.456
let c = Double(a) + b
```

The expression Double(a) invokes an initializer of the Double type with an integer argument. The numeric types all provide initializers that let you perform conversions of this kind.

```
48  let a = 123
49  let b = 0.456
50  let c = a + b        ⓘ Binary operator '+' cannot be applied to operands of type 'Int' and 'Double'
51
52
53
```

Figure A-5. Swift does not allow you to combine variables of different types

Another example that arises frequently involves the CGFloat type. CGFloat is a floating-point type defined by the Core Graphics framework. It's used to represent coordinates and sizes, among other things. Depending on whether your application is running on a 32-bit or 64-bit platform, it's equivalent either to Float or Double. To perform operations that involve a mix of CGFloats and other types, you need to explicitly convert one to the other. For example, the following code adds a Double and a CGFloat, producing a CGFloat result by converting the Double to CGFloat:

On 32-bit platforms, CGFloat is less precise than Double, so this operation may lose information, but that's inevitable if you need a value of type CGFloat. If you need a result of type Double, you can convert the CGFloat to Double without losing accuracy:

```
let a: CGFloat = 123
let b: Double = 456
let c = Double(a) + b      // Result is of type Double
```

It's important to note that Swift allows you to mix numeric types when all of the values concerned are literals. For example:

```
1 + 0.5      // Evaluated as 1.5
```

You'll find all of the usual binary arithmetic operators in Swift. You can use them to combine numbers of the same type and you can apply them to numbers of different types if you explicitly convert one of the operands, as you have just seen. Table A-2 lists the arithmetic operators that are available. Operators are listed in decreasing order of precedence.

The arithmetic operations +, -, *, /, and % detect overflow. If you want overflow to be ignored, use &+, &-, &*, &/, or &% instead. For example, enter this code into the playground:

Table A-2. *Predefined Binary Arithmetic Operators*

OPERATOR	MEANING
<<	**Bitwise left shift**
>>	**Bitwise right shift**
, &	**Multiplication**
/, &/	**Division**
%, &%	**Remainder**
&	**Bitwise AND**
+, &+	**Addition**
-, &-	**Subtraction**
|	**Bitwise OR**
^	**Bitwise XOR**

```
let a = Int.max
let b = 1
let c = Int.max + b
```

We're adding 1 to the largest representable integer value, which will trigger overflow. In the playground, you'll see an error message for the line containing the assignment to the variable c but if you execute this same code in an application, it would crash. To allow the operation to proceed ignoring the overflow, use &+ instead:

```
let a = Int.max
let b = 1
let c = a &+ b
```

The << and >> operators perform a left and right shift of the left operand by the amount specified by their right operand. This is equivalent to multiplication and division by a power of two. For example:

```
let a = 4
let b = a << 2   // Result is 16
let c = b >> 1   // Result is 8
```

When the left operand is negative, the sign of the result is preserved:

```
let a = -4
let b = a << 2   // Result is -16
let c = b >> 1   // Result is -8
```

The &, |, and ^ operations perform bitwise AND, OR, and XOR operations on their operands. This is not to be confused with the operators && and ||, which are logical operators that give a Boolean result (see the "Booleans" section later in this appendix). Here are some examples:

```
let a = 7        // Value 0b111
let b = 3        // Value 0b011
let c = a & b    // Result is 0b011 = 3

let a = 7        // Value 0b111
let b = 3        // Value 0b011
let c = a | b    // Result is 0b111 = 7

let a = 7        // Value 0b111
let b = 3        // Value 0b011
let c = a ^ b    // Result is 0b100 = 4
```

There are also compound variants of these operators that perform the operation followed by an assignment, with the target of the assignment acting as the left operand of the operation. For example:

```
var a = 10
a += 20          // Shorthand for a = a + 20, result = 30

var b = 7
b &= 3           // Shorthand for b = b & 3, result = 3
```

■ **Note** In Swift 3, the unary operators ++ and -- are no longer available. You'll need to use a format to replace something like "a++" with "a += 1". This also means you'll need to be aware, when converting code with these unary types, to the order of the operator (i.e., ++a vs. a++ and so on).

The ~ unary operator performs bitwise inversion of the bits of its integer operand:

```
let a = 0b1001
let b = ~a
```

The result of this operation in 32-bits is 0b11111111111111111111111111110110, which is the same as –10.

Strings

A string, represented by the String type, is a sequence of Unicode characters. The fact that Swift uses Unicode in strings makes it possible to build applications that support many different character sets without requiring special code. However, it has some complications, some of which are mentioned here. For a full discussion on the implications of the use of Unicode, refer to *The Swift Programming Language*, which you'll find on Apple's Developer web site at the URL shown earlier, or in iBooks.

A string literal is a sequence of characters enclosed in double quotes, like this example that you've already seen:

```
let str = "Hello, playground"
```

If you need to include a " character in a string, escape it with a \ character, like this:

```
let quoted = "Contains \"quotes\""      // Contains "quotes"
```

To get a \, escape it with another \:

```
let backslash = "\\"      // Result is \
```

Any Unicode character can be embedded in a string by giving its hexadecimal representation (or **code point**), surrounded by \u{}. For example, the @ symbol has code point 0x40, so the following example shows two ways to represent @ in a Swift string:

```
let atSigns = "@\u{40}"      // Result is @@
```

Certain characters have special escape representations. For example, \n and \t represent the new line and tab characters, respectively:

```
let specialChars = "Line1\nLine2\tTabbed"
```

Strings have the useful ability to interpolate expressions enclosed in the escape sequence \(). For example:

```
print("The value of pi is \(M_PI)")   // Prints "The value of pi is 3.14159265358979\n"
```

This code interpolates the value of the predefined constant M_PI into the string and then prints the result. The interpolated value can also be an expression, and there can be more than one of them:

```
// This code prints: "Area of a circle of radius 3.0 is 28.2743338823081\n"
let r = 3.0
print("Area of a circle of radius \(r) is \(M_PI * r * r)")
```

The + operator can be used to concatenate strings. This is the only way to combine strings that you want to split over more than one line of a source code file:

```
let s = "That's one small step for man, " +
        "one giant leap for mankind"
print(s)   // "That's one small step for man, one giant leap for mankind\n"
```

You can compare two strings using the == and != operators (see the "Booleans" section), which effectively perform a character-by-character comparison of their operands. For example:

```
let s1 = "String one"
let s2 = "String two"
let s3 = "String " + "one"
s1 == s2    // false: strings are not the same
s1 != s2    // true: strings are different
s1 == s3    // true: strings contain the same characters.
```

The seemingly simple task of getting the length of a string is complicated by the fact that strings are composed of Unicode characters, because not every Unicode character is represented by a single code point. We're going to skip a detailed discussion of this subject here, but there are two things to be aware of. First, if you want to get an accurate count of the number of characters in a string, which works under all circumstances, use the string's characters property and then get its length:

```
s3.characters.count    // 10
```

If you know that the string only contains characters that are represented by a single Unicode code point, you can use get a count of a UTF-16 view of the string instead, which may be faster under some circumstances:

```
s3.utf16.count       // 10
```

The String type itself provides quite a few useful string operations, which you'll find documented in the Swift library reference cited earlier in this appendix. You can also make use of the fact that Swift automatically bridges the String type to the NSString class in the Foundation framework, which means that methods defined by NSString can be used as if they were also defined on String itself.

The Character type can be used to hold a single character from a string. This allows iteration over the individual characters of a string via its characters property:

```
let s = "Hello"
for c in s.characters {
    print(c)
}
```

The body of the for loop in this example (the syntax of which is discussed later) is executed once for each character in the string, with the character assigned to the variable c, which is inferred to be of type Character. In the playground, you can't directly see the result of this loop in the results column—only that it was executed five times. Instead, click the leftmost of the two controls that appear when you hover over the result in the results column (the one that looks like an eye) to get a pop-up, and then right-click the pop-up and select Value History from the menu that appears to see all of the characters, as shown in Figure A-6. At the time of writing at least, clicking on any scrollbar that appears with the results does not work—you have to use the up/down arrows on the keyboard to scroll.

Figure A-6. *Value History pop-up*

■ **Tip**   If you don't see the results column, hover the mouse over the right edge until you see the column-width drag bar, and then use it to widen the width of the results panel.

You can create and initialize a `Character` in the same way as a `String`, but you need to explicitly state the type to avoid the inference of `String`, and the initializer must consist of exactly one character:

```
let c: Character = "s"
```

There's not much you can do with `Characters` other than compare them with other `Characters`. You can't append them to each other and you can't directly add them to `Strings`. You have to use the `append()` method of `String` instead:

```
let c: Character = "s"
var s = "Book"  // "var" because we want to modify it
s += c              // Error - illegal
s.append(c)      // "Books"
```

Strings in Swift are not immutable, but they are **value objects**, which means that whenever you assign a string to a variable or use one as a function argument or return value, the string is copied. Modifications made to the copy do not affect the original:

```
var s1 = "Book"
var s2 = s1          // s2 is now a copy of s1
s2 += "s"            // Appends to s2; s1 is unchanged
s1                   // "Book"
s2                   // "Books"
```

■ **Note**   For the sake of efficiency, the actual copy of a string's content does not happen immediately upon assignment. In the preceding example, the strings `s1` and `s2` share the same copy of their character content after the assignment `s1 = s2`, until the statement `s2 += "s"` is executed. At this point, a copy of the shared content is made and installed in `s2` before the character `"s"` is appended to it. All of this happens automatically.

Booleans

Booleans are represented by the `Bool` type, with possible values of `true` or `false`:

```
var b = true            // Inferred type is Bool
var b1: Bool
b1 = false
```

Swift has the usual set of comparison operators (`==`, `!=`, `>`, `<`, `>=`, `<=`) that return a Bool value when applied to numeric values:

```
var a = 100
var b = 200
var c = a

a == c      // true
a == b      // false
a != b      // true
a > b       // false
a < b       // true
a >= c      // true
```

Incidentally, these operators can also be applied to strings:

```
let a = "AB"
let b = "C"
let c = "CA"
let d = "AB"
a == b      // false - strings have different content
a == d      // true - strings have the same content
a != c      // true - strings have different content
a > b       // false: uses sorting order
a < c        // true: both start with C, but string c is longer than a
```

You can negate a Boolean value with the unary `!` operator:

```
var a = 100
var b = 200
a == b            // false
!(a == b)         // !false == true
```

Boolean expressions can be combined using the `==`, `!=`, `&&`, and `||` operators. The `&&` and `||` operators are short-circuiting, which means that they evaluate their second operand only if the result is not determined by the value of the first operand. Specifically, the second operand of a `||` operator does not need to be evaluated if the first is `true`, and the second operand of `&&` is not evaluated if the first is `false`:

```
var a = 100
var b = 200
var c = 300

a < b && c > b    // true; both expression are evaluated
a < b || c > b     // true: second expression is not evaluated
a > b && c > b    // false: second expression is not evaluated
```

Enumerations

Enumerations let you give meaningful names to the values of types where that set of values is fixed and known in advance. To define an enumeration, you give it a name and list all of the possible values as cases:

```
enum DaysOfWeek {
    case Sunday, Monday, Tuesday, Wednesday,
         Thursday, Friday, Saturday
}
```

You can also define each case separately:

```
enum DaysOfWeek {
    case Sunday
    case Monday
    case Tuesday
    case Wednesday
    case Thursday
    case Friday
    case Saturday
}
```

To refer to an enumeration value, use the enumeration name and the case name, separated by a period:

```
var day = DaysOfWeek.Sunday     // "day" is inferred to be of type "DaysOfWeek"
```

When the context is clear, you can omit the enumeration name. In the following example, the compiler already knows that the variable day is of type DaysOfWeek, so there is no need to explicitly say so when assigning to it:

```
day = .Friday     // Note that the "." Is required
```

In Swift, you can also give an associated value to an enumeration case. Try this example in your playground:

```
enum Status {
    case OK
    case ERROR(String)
}

let status = Status.OK
let failed = Status.ERROR("That does not compute")
```

Here, the ERROR case has an associated value—a string that describes the error. You can recover the associated value in a switch statement, as you'll see in upcoming "Control Statements" section.

In some cases, it is useful to map each enumeration cases to value, referred to as a **raw value**. To do this, specify the type of the value along with the enumeration name, and then assign individual values to each case as it is defined. Here's a variant of the DaysOfWeek enum that assigns an integer value to each case:

```
enum DaysOfWeek : Int {
    case Sunday = 0
    case Monday
```

```
    case Tuesday
    case Wednesday
    case Thursday
    case Friday
    case Saturday
}
```

Raw values can be strings or any of the numeric types. When the raw value type is an integer, you don't need to assign an explicit value to each case; unassigned values are inferred by adding 1 to the previous raw value. In the preceding example, Sunday was assigned the raw value 0, and as a result, Monday is automatically given the raw value 1, Tuesday is assigned the raw value 2, and so on. You can override the automatic assignment of values, as long as each case has a unique value:

```
enum DaysOfWeek : Int {
    case Sunday = 0
    case Monday              // 1
    case Tuesday             // 2
    case Wednesday           // 3
    case Thursday            // 4
    case Friday = 20         // 20
    case Saturday            // 21
}
```

You can get the raw value for a case by accessing its rawValue property:

```
var day = DaysOfWeek.Saturday
let rawValue = day.rawValue            // 21. DaysOfWeek.Saturday.rawValue is also valid
```

Here's another example, using String as the raw value type:

```
enum ResultType : String {
    case SUCCESS = "Success"
    case WARNING = "Warning"
    case ERROR = "Error"
}
let s = ResultType.WARNING.rawValue    // s = "Warning"
```

Given a raw value, you can construct the corresponding case value by passing it to an initializer:

```
let result = ResultType(rawValue: "Error")
```

In this example, the type of the result variable is not ResultType, but ResultType?, an example of an **optional**. Since it's possible to pass an invalid raw value to the initializer, there has to be some way to indicate that there is no valid case with that value. Swift does this by returning the special value nil; but nil cannot be assigned to an ordinary variable, only to an optional. Optional types are indicated by a trailing ? and you need to be careful when manipulating them. We will discuss optionals in more detail later.

In Objective-C, it is common to use an enumeration as a way to define a bit mask. Each individual enumeration value is a mask containing one bit, and it's usually possible to combine values by ORing two or more enumeration cases together. You'll see an example of this in Chapter 14, where we look at the methods of the NSFileManager class in the Foundation framework that let you locate well-known directories, such as your application's Documents directory. One of the arguments that these methods require specifies the domain or domains in which the search is to be performed. In Objective-C, the possible domains are defined by an enumeration that looks like this:

```
enum {
    NSUserDomainMask = 1,
    NSLocalDomainMask = 2,
    NSNetworkDomainMask = 4,
    NSSystemDomainMask = 8,
    NSAllDomainsMask = 0x0ffff,
};
typedef NSUInteger NSSearchPathDomainMask;
```

As you can see, the individual values are all powers of two, which allows them to be combined by ORing while still allowing the original values to be recovered.

Arrays, Ranges, and Dictionaries

Swift provides three basic collection types (arrays, dictionaries, and sets) and a range syntax that provides a convenient way to represent a (possibly large) range of values. Ranges are particularly useful when accessing arrays.

Arrays and Ranges

Swift supports the creation of an array of values using the syntax [type], where type is the type of the array value. The following code creates and initializes an array of integers and an array of strings:

```
var integers = [1, 2, 3]
var days = ["Sunday", "Monday", "Tuesday", "Wednesday",
                    "Thursday", "Friday", "Saturday"]
```

You can, of course, separate the declaration and initialization of an array, as long as it's initialized before it is used. This requires explicit specification of the array type:

```
var integers: [Int]         // [Int] means "ar
ray of Ints"
integers = [1, 2, 3]
```

Use [] to initialize an empty array:

```
var empty: [String] = []
```

To access the elements of an array, use a numeric subscript as an index. The first element of the array has index 0:

```
integers[0]         // 1
integers[2]         // 3
days[3]             // "Wednesday"
```

Use the same syntax to assign a new value to an element of the array:

```
integers[0] = 4                         // [4, 2, 3]
days[3] = "WEDNESDAY"           // Replaces "Wednesday" with "WEDNESDAY"
```

To extract or modify part of an array, use the Swift **range syntax**. This can result in a change in the number of elements in the array:

```
var integers = [1, 2, 3]
integers[1..<3]                  // Get elements 1 and 2 as an array. Result is [2, 3]
integers[1..<3] = [4]            // Replace elements 1 and 2 with [4]. Result is [1, 4]

integers = [1, 2, 3]
integers[0...1] = [5, 4]      // Replace elements 0 and 1 with [5, 4]. Result is [5, 4, 3]
```

■ **Note** If you view this in the results column you won't see the correct answer; you'll need to expand the result as we showed earlier or view it in the debug panel at the bottom.

The range syntax a..<b means all the values from a to b, excluding b; so 1..<5 is the same as 1, 2, 3, 4. The syntax a...b (note that there are three consecutive periods) includes b in the range, so that 1...5 means 1, 2, 3, 4, 5. The range a..<a is always empty, whereas the range a...a contains exactly one element (a itself). The value of b must be greater than or equal to the value of a, and there is an implicit increment of 1.

To get the number of elements in an array, use its count property:

```
var integers = [1, 2, 3]
integers.count                   // 3
integers[1..<3] = [4]
integers.count                   // 2
```

To add an element to an array, use the append() method or the insert(_:atIndex:) method:

```
var integers = [1, 2, 3]
integers.append(4)               // Result is [1, 2, 3, 4]
integers.insert(-1, atIndex: 0)  // Result is [-1, 1, 2, 3, 4]
```

You can also use the + operator to concatenate two arrays and the += operator to add one array to another:

```
var integers = [1, 2, 3]
let a = integers + [4, 5] // a = [1, 2, 3, 4, 5]; integers array unchanged
integers += [4, 5]              // Now integers = [1, 2, 3, 4, 5]
```

Use the remove(), removeSubrange(), and removeAll() methods to remove all or some of the elements of an array:

```
var days = ["Sunday", "Monday", "Tuesday", "Wednesday",
            "Thursday", "Friday", "Saturday"]

days.remove(at: 3)         // Removes "Wednesday" and returns it to the caller
days.removeSubrange(0..<4)                  // Leaves ["Friday", "Saturday"]
days.removeAll(keepingCapacity: false)     // Leaves an empty array
```

The keepingCapacity argument passed to removeAll() indicates whether the space allocated for the array's elements should be kept (value true) or released (value false).

You can iterate over a whole array or over a part of an array using the `for` statement, which is discussed in the "Control Statements" section.

If an array is created using a `let` statement, neither it nor its contents can be modified in any way:

```
let integers = [1, 2, 3]       // Constant array
integers = [4, 5, 6]           // Error: cannot replace the array
integers[0] = 2                // Error: cannot reassign elements
integers.removeAll(keepingCapacity: false)  // Error: cannot modify content
```

Like strings, arrays are value objects, so assigning them or passing them to or from functions creates a copy:

```
var integers = [1, 2, 3]
var integersCopy = integers    // Creates a copy of "integers"
integersCopy[0] = 4            // Does not change "integers"
integers                       // [1, 2, 3]
integersCopy                   // [4, 2, 3]
```

You can use the `contains()` method to find out whether an array contains a given element:

```
let integers = [1, 2, 3]
integers.contains(2)      // true
integers.contains(4)      // false
```

To get the index of an element in an array, use the `index(of: )` method:

```
let integers = [1, 2, 3]
integers.index(of: 3)          // Result is 2
```

If the element is not found in the array, the result is `nil`:

```
let integers = [1, 2, 3]
integers.index(of: 5)          // Result is nil
```

Dictionaries

You can create a **dictionary**, a data structure mapping instances of a key to a corresponding value, using a syntax that is similar to that used for an array. You'll sometimes see dictionaries referred to as maps. The following code creates a dictionary in which the keys are strings and the values are integers:

```
var dict = ["Red": 0,
            "Green": 1,
            "Blue": 2]
```

The formal type of this dictionary is [String: Int]. You may also see this referred to as Dictionary<String, Int>, using **generics** syntax, which we're not going to cover in this appendix. Similarly, you may see an array of type [Int] referred to as Array<Int>.

If you don't use an initializer, you need to explicitly state the type of the dictionary when you declare it:

```
var dict: [String: Int]
dict = ["Red": 0, "Green": 1,  "Blue": 2]
```

To get the value of a dictionary entry given its key, use subscript notation, like this:

```
let value = dict["Red"]  // Result is 0, the value mapped to the key "Red"
```

You can modify a dictionary in much the same way as you modify an array:

```
dict["Yellow"] = 3     // Adds a new value with key Yellow
dict["Red"] = 4        // Updates the value with key Red
```

To remove an element from the dictionary, use the removeValue(forKey:) method; to remove all values, use removeAll():

```
var dict = ["Red": 0, "Green": 1,  "Blue": 2]
dict.removeValue(forKey: "Red")    // Removes value with key "Red"
dict.removeAll()                   // Empties the dictionary
```

Dictionaries created using the let statement cannot be modified:

```
let fixedDict = ["Red": 0,  "Green": 1, "Blue": 2]
fixedDict["Yellow"] = 3               // Illegal
fixedDict["Red"] = 4                  // Illegal
fixedDict = ["Blue", 7]               // Illegal
fixedDict.removeValue(forKey:"Red")   // Illegal
```

You can iterate over the keys of a dictionary using the for statement, as you'll see in the "Control Statements" section. To get the number of key-value pairs in dictionary, use the count property:

```
var dict = ["Red": 0, "Green": 1, "Blue": 2]
dict.count      // 3
```

Like arrays, dictionaries are value types and are copied on assignment or when passed to and from functions. Modifications to the copy do not affect the original:

```
var dict = ["Red": 0, "Green": 1, "Blue": 2]
var dictCopy = dict
dictCopy["Red"] = 4    // Does not affect "dict"
dict                   // "Red":0, "Green": 1, "Blue": 2
dictCopy               // "Red":4, "Green": 1, "Blue": 2
```

Sets

The third and final Swift collection type is Set. A Set is a collection of elements that has no defined ordering and in which each element can appear only once. Adding another instance of an element that is already present does not change the content of the set. In most other respects, a set is much like an array.

The syntax for initializing a set is the same as that used for arrays. To disambiguate, you need to explicitly state that you are creating a Set. Here are two (equivalent) ways to do that:

```
let s1 = Set([1, 2, 3])
let s2: Set<Int> = [1, 2, 3]
```

The contains() method returns a Bool that indicates whether a set contains a given element and the count property holds the number of elements in the set:

```
s1.contains(1)    // true
s2.contains(4)    // false
s1.count          // 3
```

As you'll see later, you can enumerate the elements of a set using a for loop.

To add an element to or remove an element from a set, use the insert() and remove() methods:

```
var s1 = Set([1, 2, 3])    // [2, 3, 1] (note that order does not matter in a set)
s1.insert(4)               // [2, 3, 1, 4]
s1.remove(1)               // [2, 3, 4]
s1.removeAll()             // [] (empty set)
```

NSArray, NSDictionary, and NSSet

The Foundation framework has Objective-C classes that represent arrays, dictionaries and sets—NSArray, NSDictionary and NSSet. The relationship between these classes and their Swift counterparts is similar to that between NSString and String: in general, you can treat a Swift array as an NSArray, a Swift dictionary as an NSDictionary and a Swift set as an NSSet. As an example, suppose you had an NSString like this:

```
let s: NSString = "Red,Green,Blue"
```

Suppose also that you want to separate this into three separate parts, each containing one color name, NSString has a method called components(separatedBy:) that will do exactly what you want (and so does String, but we have an NSString in this case, not a String). This method takes the separator string as an argument and returns an NSArray containing the individual components:

```
let s: NSString = "Red,Green,Blue"
let components = s.components(separatedBy: ",")// Calls the NSString method
components        // ["Red", "Green", "Blue"]
```

Even though this method returns an NSArray, Swift is clever enough to map it to the corresponding Swift collection—an array of Strings—so the inferred type of components is [String], not [NSString]. You can confirm this by hovering the mouse over the variable name and clicking while holding down the ⌥ (Option) key.

You can directly create NSDictionary, NSSet and NSArray instances in Swift code. For example:

```
let d = NSDictionary()
```

The inferred type of the variable d is, of course, NSDictionary. You can explicitly cast an NSDictionary (whether you created it or obtained it from a method in the Foundation framework or another framework) to the Swift Dictionary type using the as keyword (which we'll say more about later):

```
let e = d as Dictionary
```

Now if you ⌥-click the name e, you'll see that Swift infers a type of Dictionary<NSObject, AnyObject> for this variable, which is another way of saying its type is [NSObject: AnyObject]. What are these key and value types and where did they come from? An NSDictionary created in the preceding Swift code is type-free: the compiler does not know the types of the keys and values that might be added to it (the same applies to NSSet and NSArray). The compiler has no choice but to infer a couple of general types: NSObject is the base class for all Foundation objects and AnyObject is a Swift protocol (discussed later) that corresponds to any Swift class type—the type signature [NSObject: AnyObject] says "I have almost no idea what this dictionary contains." When you retrieve elements from an NSDictionary or an NSArray in Swift, you usually have to use the as! operator (more on this later) to cast them explicitly to the correct types, or cast the NSDictionary itself to the type that you know it must be. For example, if you know that an NSDictionary instance maps strings to strings, you can do this:

```
let d = NSDictionary()
let e = d as! [String: String]
```

Here, we cast the NSDictionary to [String: String]. This code works even if the dictionary actually contains NSStrings instead of Strings, because Swift automatically maps between String and NSString. Beware, though: if the NSDictionary key and value types are not both what you claim they are, your application will crash. You may have noticed that in this example we performed the cast using as! instead of as. I'll explain the difference between these two operators shortly.

There is a safer way to handle all of this that involves optionals, which is the subject of the next section.

Optionals

Let's go back to an example that we used in the previous section on dictionaries:

```
var dict: [String: Int]
dict = ["Red": 0, "Green": 1,  "Blue": 2]
let value = dict["Red"]
```

Although the values in this dictionary are all of type Int, the inferred type for value is not Int, but Int?—an **optional integer**. The ? signals the optional nature of the type. What does *optional* mean and why is it being used here? To answer that, think about what should happen if you access the dictionary with a key for which there is no value:

```
let yellowValue = dict["Yellow"]
```

What value should be assigned to yellowValue? Most languages address this by having a distinguished value that means, by convention, "no value." In Objective-C, this value is referred to as nil (which is really just a redefinition of 0); in C and C++ it's NULL (again, a redefinition of 0); and in Java it's null. The problem with this is that it can be dangerous to use a nil (or equivalent) value. In Java, for example, using a null reference causes an exception; in C and C++, the application is likely to crash. What's worse, there's no way to know from its declaration whether a variable might contain a null (or nil or NULL) value. Swift solves this problem in a neat way: it has a nil value, but a variable (or constant) can only be set to nil if it's declared as an optional, or its type is inferred to be optional. As a result, you can tell immediately whether a variable or constant could be nil by examining its type: if it's not optional, it can't be nil. Further to that, Swift requires you to take that into account explicitly whenever you use the value.

Let's look at some examples to make this clearer. Suppose we define a variable called color, like this:

```
var color = "Red"
```

Because of the way it's defined, the inferred type is String, which is not optional. Therefore, it's illegal to attempt to assign nil to this variable:

```
color = nil   // Illegal: color is not an optional type.
```

Because of this, we know for sure that we don't need to worry about color having a nil value, ever. It also means that we can't use this variable to hold a value returned from a dictionary, even if we know that value will not be nil:

```
let dict = [0: "Red", 1: "Green", 2: "Blue"]
color = dict[0]!    // Illegal: value of dict[0] is optional string, color is not optional.
```

To make this assignment legal, we have to change the type of color from String to optional String:

```
let dict = [0: "Red", 1: "Green", 2: "Blue"]
var color: String?     // "String?" means optional String
color = dict[0]        // Legal
print(color)           // What does this print?
```

How do we make use of the value assigned to the color variable? Enter the preceding code into the playground and you'll see that what's printed is not "Red" but Optional("Red"). The dictionary access doesn't return the actual value; it returns the value "wrapped" as an optional. To get the string value, we need to "unwrap" the optional using the ! operator, like this:

```
let actualColor = color!    // "color!" means unwrap the optional
```

The inferred type of actualColor is String and the value that gets assigned to it is "Red". It follows from this that whenever you retrieve a value from a dictionary, it's going to be of optional type, and you have to unwrap it to get the value that you want. But remember, we said that nil references are dangerous; in Swift that translates as unwrapping optionals can be dangerous. Change your playground code to this:

```
let dict = [0: "Red", 1: "Green", 2: "Blue"]
let color = dict[4]
let actualColor = color!
```

Swift correctly infers that the type of color is String?, but when you unwrap the result of the dictionary access to assign the value to actualColor, you get an error. In the playground, this error is just reported to you; in an application, it would cause a crash. Why did this happen? Well, there is no entry in the dictionary with key 4, so the color variable was assigned the value nil. If you try to unwrap nil, you crash. You're probably thinking that this is no improvement on what happens in other languages, but that's not true. First, the fact that color is of optional type tells you that you must expect that it could be nil—and the converse (which is equally valuable). And second, Swift gives you a way to handle the case where the optional value is nil. In fact, it gives you several ways.

The first thing you can do is check whether you got nil from the dictionary access and only unwrap the value if you didn't:

```
if color != nil {
    let actualColor = color!
}
```

This construction is so common that Swift has shorthand for it. Here's the second way to handle optional unwrapping:

```
if let actualColor = color {
    // Executed only if color was not nil
    print(actualColor)
}
```

The code block associated with the if statement is executed only if color is not nil, and the unwrapped value is assigned to the constant actualColor. You can even make actualColor a variable by changing let to var:

```
if var actualColor = color {
    // Executed only if color was not nil. actualColor can be modified
    print(actualColor)
}
```

In these examples, we defined the new variable actualColor to receive the unwrapped value, which requires us to give it a new name. Sometimes, it can seem artificial to have to use a different name for what it really the same thing and, in fact, it isn't necessary—we can actually give the new variable the same name as the optional variable that's being unwrapped, like this:

```
if var color = color {
    // Executed only if the value of the original color variable was not nil
    print(color)      // Refers to the new variable, holding the unwrapped value
}
```

It's important to realize that the new color variable is not related to the existing one and, indeed, it has a different type (String instead of String?). In the body of the if statement, the name color refers to the new, unwrapped variable, not the original one.

```
let dict = [0: "Red", 1: "Green", 2: "Blue"]
let color = dict[0]
if var color = color {
    // Executed only if color was not nil
    print(color)                            // "Red"
    color = "Green"                         // Reassigns the local variable
}                                           // New color variable is now out of scope
color                                       // Refers to the original value: "Red"
```

How about if we want to use a default value for a key that's not present in the dictionary? Swift gives you a convenient way to do that too. Here's the third way to handle optional unwrapping:

```
let dict = [0: "Red", 1: "Green", 2: "Blue"]
let color = dict[4]
let actualColor = color ?? "Blue"
```

The ?? operator (called the **coalescing operator**) unwraps its left operand, if it's not nil, and returns its value; otherwise, it returns its second operand. In this case, since color is nil, actualColor would be assigned the value "Blue". Of course, you can contract the preceding code into two statements to make it slightly easier to read:

```
let dict = [0: "Red", 1: "Green", 2: "Blue"]
let actualColor = dict[4] ?? "Blue"
```

Dictionaries are not the only context in which optionals are used. If you look through the Swift API documentation, you'll see plenty of methods that return optional values. It's even possible for a type initializer to return an optional value. We've already seen an example of this; if you try to initialize an instance of an enumeration using an invalid raw value, the result is nil:

```
enum ResultType : String {
    case SUCCESS = "Success"
    case WARNING = "Warning"
    case ERROR = "Error"
}
```

```
let result = ResultType(rawValue: "Invalid")
```

The inferred type of result is ResultType?, and in this case, its value would be nil because there is no enumeration case that has the raw value "Invalid".

You've learned that you have to be careful when unwrapping optionals, but sometimes that can be both inconvenient and unnecessary. As you'll see as you try out the examples in this book, it's common to define a variable in a class that cannot be given a useful value while the class itself is being initialized, but which you know will have a valid value before your code needs to use it. In cases like that, you could define the variable as optional and unwrap it every time you use it. That keeps the compiler happy, but it means that you have to keep adding ! operators everywhere, or wrap the access in an if let construction, even though you know that the unwrapping will always succeed.

Fortunately, Swift lets you sidestep this. All you have to do is tell Swift that you want it to automatically unwrap the optional whenever you access it. Here's how you would do that in our dictionary example:

```
let dict = [0: "Red", 1: "Green", 2: "Blue"]

var color: String!      // Notice the !
color = dict[0]         // Assigns Optional("Red")
print(color)            // Automatically unwraps the optional
```

The key to this code is that the color variable was declared to be of type String!, not String?. Variables declared this way are called **implicitly unwrapped optionals**. The ! tells Swift that you want it to assume that the variable will always have a non-nil value whenever you use it, and to go ahead and unwrap it. That means you can write print(color) instead of print(color!). Although we're not saving much here, if you had to access the result more than once, you would end up typing fewer characters by using this feature.

Beware, however. You've now told Swift that color will never be nil. If it turns out that it is nil when you try to use it, Swift will unwrap it and your application will crash.

We can use optionals to address another issue that came up while discussing dictionaries: how to handle values obtained from an NSDictionary. Let's set the problem up by creating a Foundation dictionary with some initial values:

```
let d = NSDictionary(objects: ["Red", "Green", "Blue"], forKeys: [0 as NSCopying, 1 as
NSCopying, 2 as NSCopying])
```

This code initializes an NSDictionary with a mapping from Ints to Strings. In reality, of course, you wouldn't create an NSDictionary and cast it like this; you would just create a Swift dictionary. But suppose you got the dictionary from a call to a Foundation method—perhaps it was populated from the content of a file. As long as the dictionary really does map Ints to Strings, this code works fine and you can access its content in the usual way:

```
let color = d[1]     // Gets an optional, wrapping "Green"
```

Note, however, that Swift doesn't really know the type of the value that it got from the dictionary; it infers AnyObject?, which is an optional wrapping some kind of object. You can do better by explicitly casting the result to the correct type:

```
let color = d[1] as! String
```

But what if you got the type of the dictionary wrong? Maybe what you've actually got is a [Int: Int]. To see what happens, change the types of the keys in the first line from numbers to strings, like this:

```
let d = NSDictionary(objects: [ 0, 1, 2], forKeys: [0 as NSCopying, 1 as NSCopying, 2 as
NSCopying])
let value = d[1] as! String
```

This code crashes when casting the value obtained from the dictionary to String. That's a little drastic. We really want to be able to detect this condition and take some corrective action instead of crashing. We can do that by using the as? operator instead of as. The as? operator returns an optional: if its first operand is not of the type given by its second operand, it returns nil instead of crashing. So now we can do something like this:

```
let d = NSDictionary(objects: [ 0, 1, 2], forKeys: [0 as NSCopying, 1 as NSCopying, 2 as
NSCopying])
if let value = d[1] as? String {  // as? returns nil if d is not of type String?
    print("OK")                         // As expected - use value as normal
} else {
    print("Incorrect types")     // Executed if d is not of type [Int: String]
}
```

There is another way to achieve the same effect. You can use the is keyword to check whether the dictionary is of the expected type before using it:

```
if d is [Int: String] {    // Evaluate to true if d maps Ints to Strings
    print("Is [Int: String]")
} else {
    print("Incorrect types")
}
```

You've probably noticed that we have been using both the as and as! operators when casting. What's the difference? Roughly speaking, you use as when the cast is guaranteed to work and as! when it's not—the ! expresses the fact that you are forcing the compiler to accept code that it would otherwise report an error for, such as when downcasting. Here's an example of a safe cast, where we can use as:

```
let s = "Fred"
let n = s as NSString
```

The inferred type of s is String and we're trying to cast it to NSString. Swift performs this bridging operation automatically, so we can use as in this case. Similarly, any upcast can be done with the as operator:

```
let label = UILabel()
let view = label as UIView
```

Here, label is of type UILabel, a UIKit class that represents a label, which is a user interface component that displays text. Every UIKit user interface component is a subclass of UIView, so we can freely upcast the label to its base class UIView with the as operator. The converse, however, is not true:

```
let view: UIView = UILabel()
let label = view as! UILabel    // Downcast requires !
```

This time, we created a UILabel but we assigned it to a variable of type UIView. To cast this variable back to the type UILabel, we need to use the as! operator, because there is no guarantee that a variable of type UIView refers to a UILabel—it could be referencing another type of UIKit component, such as a UIButton. Here's another example that you have already seen:

```
let d = NSDictionary(objects: ["Red", "Green", "Blue"], forKeys: [0 as NSCopying, 1 as
NSCopying, 2 as NSCopying])
let color = d[1] as! String
```

As you saw earlier, when you recover a value from an NSDictionary, its type is inferred to be AnyObject?, which could refer to any Swift object type. To cast the value to String, you need to use the as! operator.

That's enough about optionals for now. We'll have more to say about this topic when we discuss calling methods in the upcoming "Properties" and "Methods" sections.

Control Statements

You've seen Swift's data types and how you can initialize them and perform operations on them. Now let's look at Swift's control statements. Swift supports all of the control statements you find in most other languages and adds some interesting new features to some of them.

The if Statement

Swift's if statement works just like it does in most other languages: you test a Boolean condition and execute some code only if it evaluates to true. You can optionally include an else block that executes if the condition is false. For example:

```
let random = arc4random_uniform(10)
if random < 5 {
    print("Hi")
} else {
    print("Ho")
}
```

The arc4random_uniform() function returns a random integer between 0 (inclusive) and its argument value (exclusive), so in this case any integer from 0 to 9. We test the returned value and print "Hi" if it's less than 5, but print "Ho" if it's not. Notice that Swift does not require you to put the test condition in parentheses, so either of these will work:

```
if random < 5 {  // Parentheses not required
}
if (random < 5) { // But can be used
}
```

By contrast to other languages, the code to be executed *must* be enclosed in braces, even if it's only a single line. That means that this code is not valid in Swift:

```
if random < 5
    print("Hi")         // Invalid: must be in braces
else
    print("Ho")         // Invalid: must be in braces
```

Swift also has the ternary operator ?:, which may be familiar to you and which you probably either love or hate. This operator evaluates the Boolean expression before the ? and executes either the statement between the ? and the : if the result is true, or the statement after the : if the result is false. We can use it to write the preceding code like this:

```swift
let random = arc4random_uniform(10)
random < 5 ? print("Hi") : print("Ho")
```

In this case, we can shorten the code even more by observing that all we're doing is printing one string or the other, and write this instead:

```swift
let random = arc4random_uniform(10)
print(random < 5 ? "Hi" : "Ho")
```

Depending on your point of view, that's either much clearer than the code we started with, or it's impossible to read.

You've already seen that there is a special form of the if statement that simplifies the handling of optionals:

```swift
let dict = [0: "Red", 1: "Green", 2: "Blue"]
let color = dict[0]
if let color = color {
    // Executed only if color was not nil
    print(color)                              // "Red"
}
```

You can actually unwrap more than one optional in a single if let or if var statement:

```swift
let dict = [0: "Red", 1: "Green", 2: "Blue", 3: "Green", 4: "Yellow"]
let color1 = dict[Int(arc4random_uniform(6))]
let color2 = dict[Int(arc4random_uniform(6))]
if let color1 = color1, color2 = color2 {
    // Executed only if both colors were not nil
    print("color1: \(color1), color2: \(color2)")
}
```

This code generates a pair of random keys in the range 0 through 5 and uses them to get color strings from the dictionary. Since there is no entry with key 5, it's possible that either (or both) of the values that we get are nil. The compound if let statement lets you safely unwrap both values and executes its body only if both were not nil. You can also include a test condition by adding a where clause:

```swift
let dict = [0: "Red", 1: "Green", 2: "Blue", 3: "Green", 4: "Yellow"]
let color1 = dict[Int(arc4random_uniform(6))]
let color2 = dict[Int(arc4random_uniform(6))]
if let color1 = color1, color2 = color2 where color1 == color2 {
    // Executed only if both colors were the same
    print("color1: \(color1), color2: \(color2)")
}
```

You can even include a test before unwrapping the optionals:

```swift
let dict = [0: "Red", 1: "Green", 2: "Blue", 3: "Green", 4: "Yellow"]
let color1 = dict[Int(arc4random_uniform(6))]
let color2 = dict[Int(arc4random_uniform(6))]
if dict.count > 3, let color1 = color1, color2 = color2 where color1 == color2 {
    print("color1: \(color1), color2: \(color2)")
}
```

730

The for Statement

Swift used to contain two variants of the for statement. The first, very much like the one that will be familiar to anybody who has worked with a C-based language, has been deprecated in Swift 3 and is no longer valid:

```
for var i = 0; i < 10; i += 1 {
    print(i)
}
```

The current acceptable form allows you to iterate over a sequence of values, such as a range or a collection. This code produces the same result as the for loop shown earlier:

```
for i in 0..<10 {
    print(i)
}
```

Notice that you don't need to use var to introduce the variable when using this form. You can create and iterate over a more general range by using the stride() method. Here's an example that prints the even integers from 10 down to 0, inclusively:

```
for i in stride(from: 10, through: 0, by: -2) {
    print(i)
}
```

Looping over the elements of an array is very simple and the intent of the code is more obvious than it would be with an indexed loop:

```
let strings = ["A", "B", "C"]
for string in strings {
    print(string)
}
```

The same construction also works for sets, although the iteration order is undefined since sets do not provide any ordering:

```
let strings = Set<String>(["A", "B", "C"])
for string in strings {
    print(string)
}
```

You can iterate over the keys of a dictionary by using its keys property. As with sets, the iteration order is undefined:

```
let d = [ 0: "Red", 1: "Green", 2: "Blue"]
for key in d.keys {
    print("\(key) -> \(d[key])")
}
```

You can do the same thing more directly by iterating the dictionary as a set of key-value pairs:

```
for (key, value) in d {
    print("\(key) -> \(value)")
}
```

Each key-value pair is returned as **tuple** with two elements, where the name key is linked to the first element of the tuple and the name value to the second. Refer to the *Swift Programming Language* book for further discussion of tuples.

The repeat and while Statements

The repeat and while statements are the same as the do and while statements in C, C++, Java, and Objective-C. They both execute a body of code until a condition is met; the difference being that the while statement tests the condition before each pass of the loop, whereas repeat tests it at the end of each pass:

```
var i = 10
while i > 0 {
    print(i)
    i -= 1
}

var j = 10
repeat {
    print(j)
    j -= 1
} while j > 0
```

The switch Statement

The Swift switch statement is very powerful. We don't have space here to talk about all of its features, but you should definitely read about it in more detail in Apple's *Swift Programming Language* book. We'll illustrate just the most important features with a few examples.

You can use the switch statement to select a code path based on one of several possible values of a variable or expression. For example, this code prints something different based on the value of the value variable:

```
let value = 11
switch value {
case 2, 3, 5, 7, 11, 13, 17, 19:
    print("Count is prime and less than 20")

case 20...30:
    print("Count is between 20 and 30")

default:
    print("Greater than 30")
}
```

There are several points to note about this code. First, a case can have multiple possible values, separated by commas. The case is executed if the switch expression has any of the listed values. Second, the case value can be a range. In fact, the switch statement is capable of some very powerful pattern matching, the details of which are covered in Apple's documentation. Third, control does not pass from one case into another, as it does in most other languages. That means that the preceding example will execute only one case and print only once; it is not necessary to include a break statement between cases in a switch. If you really want to continue execution from one case into the following case, you can do so by adding a fallthrough statement at the end of the first case.

The case list must be exhaustive: if the `default` case had not been included in the preceding code, the compiler would have flagged an error. Furthermore, every case must have at least one line of executable code. That means that the following code is not legal (and is also misleading):

```
switch (value) {
case 2:
case 3:  // Illegal - previous case is empty.
    print("Value is 2 or 3")
default:
    print("Value is neither 2 nor 3")
}
```

The correct way to write that code is to include both 2 and 3 in the same case:

```
switch (value) {
case 2, 3:   // Correct: catches value 2 and value 3
    print("Value is 2 or 3")
default:
    print("Value is neither 2 nor 3")
}
```

Alternatively, you can use `fallthrough`:

```
switch (value) {
case 2: fallthrough
case 3:  // Illegal - previous case is empty.
    print("Value is 2 or 3")
default:
    print("Value is neither 2 nor 3")
}
```

The `switch` expression does not have to be numeric. Here's an example that switches based on the value of a string:

```
let s = "Hello"
switch s {
case "Hello":
    print("Hello to you, too")

case "Goodbye":
    print("See you tomorrow")

default:
    print("I don't understand")
}
```

The next example uses the `Status` enumeration that we defined earlier and shows how to get access to the associated value of an enumeration case that has one:

```
enum Status {
    case OK
    case ERROR(String)
```

```
}
let result = Status.ERROR("Network connection rejected")
switch (result) {
case .OK:
    print("Success!")

case .ERROR(let message):
    print("Ooops: \(message)")
}
```

Since the compiler knows that the type of the switch expression is Status, there is no need to fully qualify the case values; we can say case .OK instead of case Status.OK. The compiler also knows that the enumeration only has two possible values, and since both of those values are listed as cases, there is no need to add a default case. Notice the form of the .ERROR case; the .ERROR(let message) causes the compiler to extract the associated value of the ERROR and assign it to a constant called message, which is valid only in the scope of the case itself. If the enumeration has more than one associated value, you can get all of the values by including one let statement for each, separated by commas.

Functions and Closures

Unlike many other languages, Swift uses a keyword (func) to denote a function. To define a function, you need to give its name, its argument list, and its return type. This function calculates and returns the area of a rectangle given the lengths of its sides:

```
func areaOfRectangle(width: Double, height: Double) -> Double {
    return width * height
}
```

The function arguments are enclosed in parentheses, separated by commas, and written in the same way as variable declarations—that is, name followed by type. Unlike variable declarations, though, specifying the type of an argument is not optional. If the function has no arguments, the parentheses must be empty:

```
func hello() {
    print("Hello, world")
}
```

If the function returns a value, the type of that value must be given, preceded by the symbol ->. In this case, the arguments are both Doubles, as is the return value. If the function doesn't return anything, you can either omit the return type (as shown in the definition of the preceding hello() function), or you can write it as -> Void. Here's a function that either does nothing or prints its argument, depending on the value of the debug variable, and returns nothing:

```
let debug = true    // Enables debugging
func debugPrint(value: Double) {
    if debug {
        print(value)
    }
}
```

The definition of this function could also be written slightly more verbosely, like this:

```
func debugPrint(value: Double) -> Void {  // "-> Void" is optional
```

To invoke a function, refer to it by name and supply the appropriate arguments:

```
let area = areaOfRectangle(width: 20, height: 10)
```

Prior to Swift 3, it was acceptable to omit the name of the first argument as in:

```
let area = areaOfRectangle(20, height: 10)   // no longer valid in Swift 3
```

Another feature of Swift is that function arguments can have two names—an **external** name (the name that's used by the function's caller) and an **internal** name (the name that's used in the body of the function). It's always optional to supply an external name. If you don't supply one, the external name is taken to be the same as the internal one. Here's another way to write the areaOfRectangle() function, this time with both external and internal argument names:

```
func areaOfRectangle(width w: Double, height h: Double) -> Double {
    return w * h
}
```

When you specify both an external and an internal argument name, the external name comes first; if you only supply one argument name, then it is the internal argument name and there is no external name. Notice that the body of the code uses the internal argument names (w and h), not the external names (width and height). So why would you want to use external argument names? This feature is partly motivated by the naming conventions used for Objective-C methods, which need to be mapped by the compiler so that they can be called from Swift. We'll say more about that when we examine Swift classes later in this appendix. In this example, the only benefit of adding external names is that if they exist, the caller is required to supply them when invoking the function, which makes the code more readable:

```
let area = areaOfRectangle(width: 20, height: 10)   // Now "width" and "height" are
mandatory
```

You can provide a default value for a function argument by including it in the argument list. The following function breaks an input string into components separated by the given delimiter, and defaults the delimiter to a space if it's not given:

```
func separateWords(str: String, delimiter: String = " ") -> [String] {
    return str.components(separatedBy: delimiter)
}
```

You can call this function without supplying an explicit delimiter, in which case a single space is used as the delimiter:

```
let result = separateWords(str:"One small step")
print(result)    // [One, small, step]
```

Swift automatically supplies an external name for an argument with a default value, making it the same as the internal name (although you can override this by supplying your own external name). That means that the argument name must be used if its value is not defaulted:

```
let result = separateWords(str: "One. Two. Three", delimiter: ". ")  // "delimiter" is
required
print(result)     // [One, Two, Three]
```

If you really don't want to force the user to include the argument name, you can write the external name as _, although this is not recommended because it reduces readability:

```
func separateWords(str: String, _ delimiter: String = " ") -> [String] {
    return str.components(separatedBy: delimiter)
}
let result = separateWords(str: "One. Two. Three", ". ")  // "delimiter" is required
print(result)     // [One, Two, Three]
```

You can use this to change the areaOfRectangle() function so that neither argument name needs to be supplied:

```
func areaOfRectangle(_ w: Double, _ h: Double) -> Double {
    return w * h
}
let area = areaOfRectangle(20, 10)
```

Notice that it is necessary to precede the first argument with an _ if you want to use an unnamed argument first.

```
func areaOfRectangle(_ w: Double, _ h: Double) -> Double {
    return w * h
}
```

In Swift, functions are types, so you can create a variable of function type, assign a reference to a function to it, and use that variable to call the function. Similarly, you can pass a function as an argument to another function or return a function from a function.

To declare a function variable, you specify the function's signature as the type of the variable. The signature consists of the function's argument types in parentheses (unless there is just one argument, when the parentheses can be omitted), followed by ->, followed by the return type. The following code creates a variable that can hold a reference to a function that performs an unspecified operation on a Double and returns another Double:

```
var operation: (Double) -> Double
```

For one function arguments, previous versions of Swift allowed omitting the parentheses, but this is no longer valid:

```
var operation: Double -> Double                        // No Longer valid in Swift 3
```

You can write functions that operate on a Double and assign any of those functions to the variable. For example:

```
func doubleMe(number: Double) -> Double {
    return 2 * number
}
operation = doubleMe
```

Now you can invoke the function using the function variable, supplying the argument as if you were directly calling the function:

```
operation(2)     // Result is 4
```

You can make the `operation` variable refer to a different function and perform a different operation using the same call expression:

```
func quadrupleMe(number: Double) -> Double {
    return 4 * number
}
operation = quadrupleMe
operation(2)     // Result is 8
```

The ability to pass functions around in this way is very powerful. There are several Swift methods that accept function arguments. One of them is the `sorted()` method, which sorts an ordered collection based on an ordering provided by a function that's passed as its argument. The ordering function is required to accept two arguments, which are elements of the collection being sorted, and return the `Bool` value `true` if the first argument is less than the second and `false` otherwise. Here's an example of such a function that compares two `Int`s:

```
func compareInts(_ first: Int, _ second: Int) -> Bool {
    return first < second
}
```

Now you can create an array of `Int`s and use `sort()` and the `compareInts()` function to sort them. To do so, pass the `compareInts()` function an argument to `sort()`, like this:

```
var values = [12, 3, 5, -4, 16, 18]
let sortedValues = values.sorted(isOrderedBefore: compareInts)
sortedValues     // Result:  [-4, 3, 5, 12, 16, 18]
```

The `sorted()` function returns a sorted copy of the array. There's a similar method called `sort ()` that sorts the original collection in ascending order.

```
var values = [12, 3, 5, -4, 16, 18]
values.sort(compareInts)
values     // Result:  [-4, 3, 5, 12, 16, 18]
```

Swift takes this one step further by allowing you to write the comparison function right in the argument list of the `sorted()` call. This means you don't have to separately define a function and give it a name that's not otherwise used. Here's how you would sort the `values` array using that technique:

```
var values = [12, 3, 5, -4, 16, 18]
let sortedValues = values.sorted(isOrderedBefore: {(first: Int, second: Int) -> Bool in
    return first < second
})
```

This probably looks ridiculously complex at first, so let's break it down. The comparison function must be enclosed in braces. After that, the first part of the definition is just its argument list and its return type, followed by the keyword `in`, which separates the arguments and return type from the function body:

737

```
{(first: Int, second: Int) -> Bool in
```

Next, we have the body of the function, which is the same as the original code from the `compareInts()` function, followed by the closing brace and the parenthesis that closes the argument list of the `sorted()` method:

```
    return first < second
})
```

There's a name for this kind of anonymous function that's written in-place: it's called a **closure**. Once you're used to how it works, you'll probably find yourself making a lot of use of closures. Other languages also support this capability such as in Python where it would be called a **lambda**.

If a closure is the final argument of a function, Swift lets you clean the syntax up a bit by taking it outside the function's argument list, like this:

```
let sortedValues = values.sorted() {    // The closure is now outside the parentheses
        (first: Int, second: Int) -> Bool in
                return first < second
    }
```

That's still quite a lot of code. Fortunately, we can clean it up a little more. Swift can infer that the closure requires two `Int` arguments and must return a `Bool`. It knows this because of the way in which the `sort()` method is defined in the standard library. Because of this, we can omit the argument types, the parentheses around the argument names, and the return type, leaving us with just this:

```
let sortedValues = values.sorted() {
    first, second in    // Swift infers the argument types and return type!
    return first < second
}
```

That's much better. But we can take it one step further by omitting the argument names too. Swift knows there are two arguments, and if you don't name them, it calls them $0 and $1 (and $2, $3, etc., if there were more). That lets you reduce our closure to just one line of code:

```
let sortedValues = values.sorted() { return $0 < $1 }
```

That's not quite the end. Swift also lets you drop the `return` keyword. So finally we get to this:

```
let sortedValues = values.sorted() { $0 < $1 }
```

We think you'll agree, that's a lot more expressive than what we started with. Or at least it is once you're used to reading the somewhat terse syntax. Experiment with this in the playground, try out some variations, and see what works and what doesn't.

If you're wondering why closures are called closures, it's because they "close over" variables that are in their scope when they are created. That means that they can read and even write those variables. It's difficult to appreciate how useful this is without the correct context. You'll see examples in the rest of the book that illustrate the point. For now, let's just demonstrate that we can write a closure that uses a value that's defined outside of that closure. Take a look at the following code:

```
func getInterestCalculator(rate: Double) -> (Double, Int) -> Double {
    let calculator = {
```

```
        (amount: Double, years: Int) -> Double in rate * amount * Double(years)
    }
    return calculator
}
```

The function signature tells us that the getInterestCalculator() function requires an argument of type Double and returns a function. The returned function requires two arguments—a Double and an Int—and it returns a Double.

What we're actually doing here is passing an interest rate to the getInterestCalculator() function and it's going to return to us a function that will calculate simple interest at that given rate.

Inside the getInterestCalculator() function, we create a closure and assign it to the calculator variable:

```
let calculator = {
        (amount: Double, years: Int) -> Double in rate * amount * Double(years)
    }
```

As you can see, the closure function requires the amount as a Double, and the period over which interest will be calculated in years as an Int. The most important point to notice is that the body of the closure uses the rate argument that was passed to the getInterestCalculator() function. Finally, the closure is returned to the caller of getInterestCalculator().

Now let's write some code that calls this function and uses the function that it returns:

```
let calculator = getInterestCalculator(rate: 0.05)
calculator(100.0, 2)    // Result is 10: interest at 5% on $100 over 2 years.
```

The returned function is assigned to the calculator constant and then it's invoked to compute the interest on $100 over two years, at an interest rate of 5%. So what's so interesting about this? Well, think about what is happening here. The returned closure is referencing the value of the rate argument of the getInterestCalculator() function, but it's doing so after that function has returned. How is that possible? It works because the closure **captures** the function argument by referencing it. When a variable is captured by a closure as the closure is being created, a copy of its value is taken and that copy is used when the closure is executed. That's how the interest rate value that was passed as an argument to getInterestCalculator() is made available to the closure after the argument itself no longer exists.

Error Handling

If you scan through the Xcode documentation page for the NSString class, you'll come across several methods declarations that include a throws clause, like this one:

```
init(contentsOfFile path: String, encoding enc: UInt) throws
```

Whenever you see a throws clause, it means that the method reports an error that you can choose to ignore or to handle by catching it. We'll first of all see how we might ignore it, and then we'll look at how to catch and handle the error. Let's try to ignore it by just pretending the throws clause is not there:

```
let s = String(contentsOfFile: "XX", encoding: String.Encoding.utf8)
```

If you type that into the playground, you'll see the error "Call can throw but is not marked with 'try'". To make the compiler accept this call, we have to add a try clause. There are three variants of try, two of which allow you to ignore the error and a third that is used when you intend to catch it. Let's continue to ignore the potential error:

```
let s = try? String(contentsOfFile: "XX", encoding: String.Encoding.utf8)
```

That gets rid of the compilation error. Now the playground executes the statement and shows the result nil. When you use try?, you're converting the return type of the method that you're calling into an optional. Since this method is actually an initializer for the String class (which String actually gets from NSString), the return type is converted to String?, and that is the inferred type of the variable s. In this case, the value is nil because the file "XX" doesn't actually exist.

We can use a try? clause in an if statement to do something only if the file exists and its content was successfully loaded:

```
if let s = try? String(contentsOfFile: "XX", encoding: String.Encoding.utf8) {
    print("Content loaded")
} else {
    print("Failed to load contents of file")
}
```

If you're sure that the file that you are trying to read exists and its content can be read, you can replace try? with try!, like this:

```
let s = try! String(contentsOfFile: "XX", encoding: String.Encoding.utf8)
```

Although this is legal syntax, it's not good practice because your application would crash if anything went wrong—you can see that by trying this statement in the playground.

Catching Errors

You've seen that if you use try? as part of an if let statement, you can find out whether the operation completed correctly and you can take some different action if it wasn't. The try? statement implicitly tells you that an error occurred by returning a nil value, but there is no way to find out what that error was. To do that, you have to use the try statement and wrap it in a do-catch block, like this:

```
do {
    let s = try String(contentsOfFile: "XX", encoding: String.Encoding.utf8)
    print("Loaded content \(s)")
} catch {
    print(error)
}
```

The statements inside the do block are executed to completion or until one of them throws an error, at which point control transfers to the catch block. The init(contentsOfFile:encoding:) initializer throws a value of type NSError, which is the Foundation framework's generic error type. Inside the catch block, you can get the value of the error from the error variable, as shown in the preceding example.

Throwing an Error

Any function or method can throw an error, provided that it declares that it does so by including a throws clause in its definition. The thrown value can be any type that adopts the ErrorType protocol, as NSError does—in fact, if you check the inferred type of the error variable in the preceding example, you'll find that it is ErrorType. Errors thrown by methods in the Foundation framework (and other Apple frameworks) are of type NSError, but you are free to define custom error types in your own code. It's common to use an enumeration for this purpose, because it can conveniently represent one or more error cases and even include additional information about the error.

As an example, let's write a function that calculates the length of the third side of a triangle given the lengths of the other two sides and the angle between them. We're going to insist that the values of the arguments that correspond to the lengths of the sides must both be positive and the angle must be between 0 and π radians. Let's start by writing the function without any error checking:

```swift
func calcThirdSide(_ side1: Double, side2: Double, angle: Double) -> Double {
    return sqrt(side1 * side1 + side2 * side2 - 2 * side1 * side2 * cos(angle))
}
```

We're using the cosine rule to calculate the length of the third side. To check that the implementation is correct, let's try it out on a right-angled triangle with sides of length 3 and 4:

```swift
let side3 = calcThirdSide(3, side2: 4, angle: M_PI/2)
print(side3)
```

Pythagoras's theorem tells us that the length of the third side in this case should be 5, and that's the result you'll see in the playground if you run this code. Now let's start adding error checking. We have two different types of condition that we need to check—the lengths of the sides and the value of the angle. This is a natural fit for an enumeration, so let's define one:

```swift
enum TriangleError : ErrorProtocol {
    case SideInvalid(reason: String)
    case AngleInvalid(reason: String)
}
```

Since we're going to throw instances of this enumeration, it is required to conform to ErrorProtocol. We defined cases for each of the types of error that we'll check to provide an error message, so both cases have an associated string value.

Before we can add error checking to our function, we have to tell the compiler that it might throw an error. To do that, we add the throws keyword to the function definition. This keyword must be placed after the function's argument list and before its return type (if it has one):

```swift
func calcThirdSide(_ side1: Double, side2: Double, angle: Double) throws  -> Double {
    return sqrt(side1 * side1 + side2 * side2 - 2 * side1 * side2 * cos(angle))
}
```

As soon as you add the throws keyword, the compiler starts complaining that the function call is not made in a try statement. Let's fix that by adding some code to catch the error:

```swift
do {
    let side3 = try calcThirdSide( 3, side2: 4, angle: M_PI/2)
    print(side3)
} catch {
    print(error)
}
```

Now we can start adding error checks to the calcThirdSide(side1:side2:angle:) function. Modify the function definition to:

```swift
func calcThirdSide(_ side1: Double, side2: Double, angle: Double) throws  -> Double {
    if side1 <= 0 {
```

```
            throw TriangleError.SideInvalid(reason: "Side 1 must be >= 0, not \(side1)")
    }
    return sqrt(side1 * side1 + side2 * side2 - 2 * side1 * side2 * cos(angle))
}
```

The if statement tests whether the value of the side1 argument is zero or negative and, if so, uses the throw keyword to throw an instance of our TriangleError enumeration with an appropriate message. To test whether this works, change the value of the side1 argument in the test code from 3 to -1:

```
let side3 = try calcThirdSide(-1, side2: 4, angle: M_PI/2)
```

You should see the text SideInvalid("Side 1 must be >= 0, not -1.0") in the playground's results area, indicating that the correct error was thrown and caught.

Now let's add the other three error checks to the calcThirdSide(side1:side2:angle:) function:

```
func calcThirdSide(_ side1: Double, side2: Double, angle: Double) throws -> Double {
    if side1 <= 0 {
        throw TriangleError.SideInvalid(reason: "Side 1 must be >= 0, not \(side1)")
    }

    if side2 <= 0 {
        throw TriangleError.SideInvalid(reason: "Side 2 must be >= 0, not \(side2)")
    }

    if angle < 0 {
        throw TriangleError.AngleInvalid(reason: "Angle must be >= 0, not \(angle)")
    }

    if angle >= M_PI {
        throw TriangleError.AngleInvalid(reason: "Angle must be <= π, not \(angle)")
    }

    return sqrt(side1 * side1 + side2 * side2 - 2 * side1 * side2 * cos(angle))
}
```

Experiment with the arguments passed to the calcThirdSide(side1:side2:angle:) function to verify that these checks work.

The guard Statement

It's quite common to have argument checking code like this at the start of a function. Swift gives you another way to express these error tests—you can use the guard statement instead of an if statement. Here's how you would rewrite the calcThirdSide(side1:side2:angle:) function to use guard instead of if:

```
func calcThirdSide(_ side1: Double, side2: Double, angle: Double) throws  -> Double {
    guard side1 > 0 else {
        throw TriangleError.SideInvalid(reason: "Side 1 must be >= 0, not \(side1)")
    }

    guard side2 > 0 else {
        throw TriangleError.SideInvalid(reason: "Side 2 must be >= 0, not \(side2)")
    }
```

```
    guard angle >= 0 else {
        throw TriangleError.AngleInvalid(reason: "Angle must be >= 0, not \(angle)")
    }

    guard angle < M_PI else {
        throw TriangleError.AngleInvalid(reason: "Angle must be <= π, not \(angle)")
    }

    return sqrt(side1 * side1 + side2 * side2 - 2 * side1 * side2 * cos(angle))
}
```

The body of the guard statement must be preceded by the keyword else and is executed only if the tested condition is not met. You can think of the meaning of guard as "unless this condition is met, execute the statement body". Because of that, the sense of test must be the opposite of what would be tested by an if statement—for example, the condition tested by the first if statement was side1 <=0, whereas the condition for the equivalent guard statement is side1 > 0. This might seem strange at first, but once you get used to it, you'll see that the guard version of the code is clearer, because we're stating the conditions that need to be met in order for execution to proceed, not the inverse condition.

The general form of the guard statement is:

```
guard expression else {
    // Guard body statements
    // Transfer of control outside the scope containing the guard
}

// Control must not reach here if the guard body was executed
```

The guard body can include as many separate statements as required, provided that one condition is met—at the end of the statement body, control must transfer outside the immediate scope of the guard statement. In the preceding example, the guard statement is in the scope of the calcThirdSide(side1:s ide2:angle:) function, so control must be transferred out of that function at the end of the guard block. Here, we achieve that by throwing an error, but we could also return from the function. If the guard block is contained in a for statement, the immediate scope is the for statement and you can use either a continue statement or a break statement to meet the requirements of the guard statement. The same applies to repeat and while statements. If you allow the flow of control to continue from the end of the guard block into the statements that follow it, you will get a compiler error.

More on Error Catching

So far, we've used a single, generic catch block to capture and print any error that's thrown from the calcT hirdSide(side1:side2:angle:) function. More generally, a do-catch statement can have multiple catch blocks and each catch block can have an expression that is matched against the error that is thrown to select the block that should be executed. If none of the catch block expressions match the error, then the block without an expression is used; if there is no such block, the error is thrown to the caller of the function or method containing the do-catch statement, and that function or method must declare that this may happen by including a throws clause in its definition. Let's look at some examples.

Change the do-catch block in the playground as follows:

```
do {
    let side3 = try calcThirdSide( -1, side2: 4, angle: M_PI/2)
    print(side3)
```

```
} catch let e as TriangleError {
    print(e)
}
```

Here, we've added an expression to the catch block that causes it to catch only errors that are of type TriangleError. The error itself is assigned to the variable e, which is in scope only in the catch block. Since the calcThirdSide(side1:side2:angle:) function only throws errors of this type, we don't need any further catch blocks. If we wanted to handle specific types of error differently, we simply add more cases. Here's an example:

```
do {
    let side3 = try calcThirdSide( -1, side2: 4, angle: M_PI/2)
    print(side3)
} catch TriangleError.SideInvalid(let reason) {
    print("Caught invalid side: \(reason)")
} catch {
    print("Caught \(error)")
}
```

The first catch block handles the SideInvalid case and assigns the error message from the enumeration value to the variable reason so that it can be used in the body of the catch block. The second catch block has no expression, so it captures any error that's not handled by earlier blocks. In this case, that corresponds to the AngleInvalid case. When a catch-all block like this last one is present, it must be the final catch block, so this is invalid:

```
do {
    let side3 = try calcThirdSide(-1, side2: 4, angle: M_PI/2)
    print(side3)
} catch {   // Invalid - this must be the last catch block
    print("Caught: \(error)")
} catch TriangleError.SideInvalid(let reason) {
    print("Caught invalid side: \(reason)")
}
```

To handle each case individually, just give each one its own catch block:

```
do {
    let side3 = try calcThirdSide(-1, side2: 4, angle: -M_PI/2)
    print(side3)
} catch TriangleError.AngleInvalid(let reason) {
    print("Caught invalid angle: \(reason)")
} catch TriangleError.SideInvalid(let reason) {
    print("Caught invalid side: \(reason)")
}
```

Since we have explicitly handled both of the possible errors that the calcThirdSide(side1:side2:angle:) function may throw, there is no need to add a catch-all catch block.

Classes and Structures

Swift provides two different ways to create custom types—classes and structures. Both may contain properties, initializers, and methods. A **property** is a variable defined within the body of a class or structure; a **method** is a function defined in a class or structure; and an **initializer** is a special type of method that is used to establish the initial state of a class or structure instance while it's being created.

Structures

Here's an example of a structure that represents a circle with a given radius:

```
struct CircleStruct {
    var radius: Double

    func getArea() -> Double {
        return M_PI * radius * radius
    }

    func getCircumference() -> Double {
        return 2 * M_PI * radius
    }
}
```

The circle has one property that holds its radius and two methods that return its area and circumference.

Swift automatically creates an initializer for a structure that assigns values to its properties using the initializer's arguments. Here's how you would use that initializer to create an instance of `CircleStruct`:

```
var circleStruct = CircleStruct(radius: 10)
```

The synthesized initializer for a structure has one argument for each property. The argument names are the same as the property names and they appear in the order that the properties are defined in the structure itself. Notice that the argument names are required when using the initializer, because the initializer arguments have both external and internal names.

Once you have created a structure instance, you can directly read and modify the properties using the property name. This code reads the radius of the circle and then doubles it:

```
var circleStruct = CircleStruct(radius: 10)
let r = circleStruct.radius        // Reads the radius property - result = 10
circleStruct.radius = 2 * r        // Doubles the radius.
```

Structures are value objects, so the following code creates a copy of the original `CircleStruct` object and assigns it to the `newCircleStruct` variable. Changes made to the `radius` property using the `newCircleStruct` variable do not affect the original, and vice versa:

```
var newCircleStruct = circleStruct    // Copies the structure
newCircleStruct.radius = 32            // Affects only the copy
newCircleStruct.radius                 // New value: 32
circleStruct.radius                    // Old value: 20
```

If you assign a structure to a constant using a `let` statement, all of its properties become read-only:

```
let constantCircleStruct = CircleStruct(radius: 5)
constantCircleStruct.radius = 10    // Invalid: constantCircleStruct is constant
```

Swift requires that all properties of a structure (or class) be initialized before the initializer finishes execution. You can choose to set property values in the initializer itself or as part of the property definition. Here's a slightly different implementation of the CircleStruct structure that initializes the radius to a default value of 1 when it's defined:

```
struct CircleStruct {
    var radius: Double = 1

    init() {
    }

    init(radius: Double) {
        self.radius = radius
    }

    func getArea() -> Double {
        return M_PI * radius * radius
    }

    func getCircumference() -> Double {
        return 2 * M_PI * radius
    }
}
```

Notice that the structure now has two initializers (initializers are always called `init`): one that takes no arguments and another that takes the radius as its argument. The first initializer lets you create an instance of the structure using the default radius set by the definition of the `radius` property:

```
let circleStructDefault = CircleStruct()
circleStructDefault.radius    // Result is 1
```

The second initializer assigns its argument to the `radius` property:

```
init(radius: Double) {
    self.radius = radius
}
```

Before we added the zero-argument initializer, we didn't need to write this one because Swift created it for us; but it does not do that if you add initializers of your own. Notice that the assignment to the property uses the form `self.radius`. The `self` variable represents the instance of the structure that's being initialized. In method calls, it represents the instance on which the method was invoked. Usually, you don't need to qualify the property access with `self`, but in this case we need to do so because the initializer argument has the same name as the property.

As noted, by default, Swift requires you to use the initializer argument name when creating a structure instance (as you'll soon see, the same applies to classes). When you define your own initializer, you can opt out of this by using _ as an external argument name, as shown by the following modification to the second CircleStruct initializer:

```swift
init(_ radius: Double) {
    self.radius = radius
}
```

With this change, you must use the initializer like this:

```swift
var circleStruct = CircleStruct(10)    // Argument name must be omitted
```

The implementations of the getArea() and getCircumference() methods don't introduce anything new; they just perform a simple calculation using the value of the radius property. Notice that here we don't use self when reading the property value, although we could. This version of the getArea() method is equivalent to the one shown previously:

```swift
func getArea() -> Double {
    return M_PI * self.radius * self.radius  // Explicit use of "self" - not recommended
}
```

You invoke these methods just like any other function, except that an instance of the structure is required:

```swift
let circleStructDefault = CircleStruct()
circleStructDefault.getArea()            // Returns the area
circleStructDefault.getCircumference()   // Returns the circumference
```

Classes

Creating a class is syntactically very similar to creating a structure, but there are a few differences to be aware of. Here's an implementation of a circle as a class:

```swift
class CircleClass {
    var radius: Double = 1

    init() {
    }

    init(radius: Double) {
        self.radius = radius
    }

    func getArea() -> Double {
        return M_PI * radius * radius
    }

    func getCircumference() -> Double {
        return 2 * M_PI * radius
    }
}
```

The only syntactic difference between this and the structure version is the keyword class instead of struct, but there are some differences in the way that Swift handles class and structure initializers:

- Swift does not create an initializer that sets the initial values of the properties of a class. Instead, it creates an empty init() initializer.

- As with structures, if you add initializers of your own, you no longer get the free init() initializer.

In the case of CircleClass, the presence of the init(radius: Double) initializer means that Swift would not generate the init() version, so we had to add it ourselves.

You can use either initializer to create a CircleClass instance, depending on whether you want to set the radius:

```
var circleClassDefault = CircleClass()       // Sets the default radius
circleClassDefault.radius                     // Result is 1
var circleClass = CircleClass(radius: 10)     // Explicitly set the radius
circleClass.radius                            // Result is 10
```

Classes are not value objects, so assigning a class instance to a variable or passing one to a function does not create a copy, as the following code demonstrates:

```
var newCircleClass = circleClass     // Does not copy
newCircleClass.radius = 32           // Only one copy, so this change is visible…
newCircleClass.radius                // …through both references. Result is 32
circleClass.radius                   // Result is 32
```

Properties

The radius property of our circle is called a **stored property**, because the value is stored with the class or structure. It's also possible to have **computed properties**, which don't have storage of their own. Instead, you calculate the value of the property every time it's read. The area and circumference of a circle could be regarded as properties, so we could reasonably reimplement them as computed properties. Here's how you would do that for CircleClass (the implementation would be the same for CircleStruct):

```
class CircleClass {
    var radius: Double = 1
    var area: Double {
        return M_PI * radius * radius
    }

    var circumference: Double {
        return 2 * M_PI * radius
    }

    init() {
    }

    init(radius: Double) {
        self.radius = radius
    }
}
```

The syntax is very simple: you state the property name and its type (which is mandatory for a computed property), followed by a code block containing the code required to calculate the property value. With area and circumference as properties, we can get their values with slightly fewer keystrokes than when using a method:

```
let circleClass = CircleClass(radius: 10)
circleClass.area
circleClass.circumference
```

We are actually using a shortcut in the implementation of these properties; the full form of the area property, for example, would be:

```
var area: Double {
    get {
        return M_PI * radius * radius
    }
}
```

The difference is the get keyword and the additional set of braces around the code that calculates the property value. Since area is a read-only property, we haven't implemented a setter, so Swift allows us to omit this extra boilerplate.

It's perfectly possible to regard area as a settable property. If a new area is set, we can calculate and store the corresponding radius—and similarly for circumference. To make a property settable, you need to add a set block, and put back the get boilerplate if you omitted it. Here's how you would implement the setters for area and circumference:

```
var area: Double {
    get {
        return M_PI * radius * radius
    }

    set {
        radius = sqrt(newValue/M_PI)
    }
}

var circumference: Double {
    get {
        return 2 * M_PI * radius
    }

    set {
        radius = newValue/(2 * M_PI)
    }
}
```

In the implementation of the setter, you get the value that's being set from a variable called newValue. If you don't like that name, you can choose one of your own by declaring it after the set keyword:

```
set (value) {
    radius = value/(2 * M_PI)
}
```

Now that these properties are settable, we can use them to find out the radius for a given circumference or area:

```
circleClass.area = 314
circleClass.radius          // Radius for area 314 is 9.997
circleClass.circumference = 100
circleClass.radius          // Radius for circumference 100 is 15.915
```

Swift supports adding code to observe changes to a stored (but not computed) property. To do so, you add a willSet or didSet block (or both) to the property definition. These blocks are called whenever the property value is being set, even if the new and old values are the same, except when the property is being initialized. The willSet block is called before the new value is assigned to the property and didSet is called after the assignment. A typical use for a property observer is to ensure that the property can only be assigned valid values. Here's how you would modify the radius property in CircleClass to make sure that only non-negative values can be assigned:

```
class CircleClass {
    var radius: Double = 1 {
        didSet {
            if (radius < 0) {
                radius = oldValue
            }
        }
    }
}
```

When the didSet block is called, the new value has already been stored in the radius property. If it's negative, we set it back to the previous value, which we can get from the oldValue variable. As with property setter blocks, you can change the name of this variable if you want to. Setting the property value from within the didSet block does not cause the property observer blocks to be invoked again. With this change, an attempt to set a negative radius is ignored:

```
circleClass.radius = 10     // Valid: radius set to 10
circleClass.radius          // Result: 10.0
circleClass.radius = -1     // Invalid - trapped by didSet block
circleClass.radius          // Result: 10.0
```

Methods

As you have seen, classes and structures can both have methods. Methods behave just like functions, except that they have access to an implicitly defined value called self that refers to the instance of the class or structure on which the method was invoked. Methods defined on a class can change the value of its properties, but by default, structure methods cannot. Let's see how this works adding a new method to CircleClass called adjustRadiusByAmount(_:times:), which adjusts the circle's radius by a given amount a specified number of times. Here's the method definition:

```
func adjustRadiusByAmount(amount: Double, times: Int = 1) {
    radius += amount * Double(times)
}
```

With this definition, you call this method as follows:

```
var circleClass = CircleClass(radius: 10)
circleClass.radius                          // Result: 10
circleClass.adjustRadiusByAmount(5, times: 3)
circleClass.radius                          // Result = 10 + 3 * 5 = 25
circleClass.adjustRadiusByAmount(5)     // "times" is defaulted to 1
circleClass.radius                          // Result = 30
```

Now try to add the same method to the CircleStruct structure:

```
struct CircleStruct {
    var radius: Double = 1

    init() {
    }

    init(radius: Double) {
        self.radius = radius
    }

    func getArea() -> Double {
        return M_PI * radius * radius
    }

    func getCircumference() -> Double {
        return 2 * M_PI * radius
    }

    func adjustRadiusByAmount(amount: Double, times: Int = 1) {
        radius += amount * Double(times)
    }
}
```

Unfortunately, this does not compile. By default, structure methods cannot mutate the structure's state. This is because you are encouraged to make value objects immutable, if possible. If you really want to add a mutating method like this one, you have to add the mutating keyword to its definition:

```
mutating func adjustRadiusBy(amount: Double, times: Int = 1) {
    radius += amount * Double(times)
}
```

Optional Chaining

How do you call a method or access a property of an optional? You first have to unwrap the optional. You need to be very careful when doing this because, as you already know, unwrapping an optional that is nil causes your application to crash. Suppose we have the following variable and we want to get the radius of whatever circle it's pointing at:

```
var optionalCircle: CircleClass?
```

Since the value of `optionalCircle` could be `nil` (and, in this case, it is), we can't just do this:

```
optionalCircle!.radius        // CRASH!
```

Instead, we need to check whether `optionalCircle` is `nil` before unwrapping it, like this:

```
if optionalCircle != nil {
    optionalCircle!.radius
}
```

This is safe, but it's really too much code. There's a better way, which is called **optional chaining**. Instead of using ! to unwrap the optional, you use ?. Using optional chaining, you can go back to writing just one line of code:

```
var optionalCircle: CircleClass?
var radius = optionalCircle?.radius
```

When optional chaining is in use, the property access occurs only if `optionalCircle` is not `nil`, and since there may be no value to assign to the `radius` variable, Swift infers its type as `Double?` instead of `Double`. It's common to use this technique in conjunction with the `if let` construction, like this:

```
var optionalCircle: CircleClass?
if let radius = optionalCircle?.radius {
    print("radius = \(radius)")
}
```

The real value of this comes if you have objects embedded in other objects, where the references to the embedded objects are optionals. To follow the chain of objects to the value that you want, you would have had to make a `nil` check for each reference. With optional chaining, you can let Swift do the hard work for you by using an expression like this:

```
outerObject?.innerObject?.property
```

Optional chaining also works for method calls:

```
var optionalCircle: CircleClass?
optionalCircle?.adjustRadiusByAmount(5, times: 3)
```

The method call happens only if `optionalCircle` is not `nil`; if it is `nil`, the call is skipped.

Subclassing and Inheritance

So we've got a fairly useful class that represents a circle. What if we wanted to add something new to it? For example, let's say we want to add a color property. Well, we would just add the property to the existing class definition and we're done. But what if we don't own the `CircleClass` class? Maybe it's part of a third-party framework. We can't modify the source code. In many cases like this, we might be able to add an **extension** to the class. Extensions let you add functionality to any class—even classes that you don't own, and sometimes that's the right thing to do. In this case, though, it's not the right thing because we want to add a stored property. Instead, we'll extend the class by creating a **subclass**. Subclasses inherit the properties and methods of the class from which they are derived (their **base class**). If what the subclass provides isn't quite right, you can override its behavior, keeping what you want and changing what you need to (subject, of course, to the base class being properly designed).

In this section, we're going to extend `CircleClass` and create `ColoredCircleClass`. `ColoredCircleClass` will have the same features as `CircleClass`—it will still have the radius, area, and circumference properties—and it will have a new color property. Before we get started on that, let's add a few more things to `CircleClass` so that you can see how to override them in a derived class.

Clear everything from your playground and enter the following modified definition of `CircleClass`:

```swift
class CircleClass {
    var radius: Double = 1 {
        didSet {
            if (radius < 0) {
                radius = oldValue
            }
        }
    }
    var area: Double {
        get {
            return M_PI * radius * radius
        }

        set {
            radius = sqrt(newValue/M_PI)
        }
    }

    var circumference: Double {
        get {
            return 2 * M_PI * radius
        }

        set {
            radius = newValue/(2 * M_PI)
        }
    }

    var description: String {
        return "Circle of radius \(radius)"
    }

    required init() {
    }

    init(radius: Double) {
        self.radius = radius
    }

    func adjustRadiusByAmount(amount: Double, times: Int = 1) {
        radius += amount * Double(times)
    }

    func reset() {
        radius = 1;
    }
}
```

First, we added a computed `description` property that just returns a description of the class in string form. It's a computed property because we want the return value to contain the current radius, which can change. In our `ColoredCircleClass`, we'll want to add the circle's color to this description and, as you'll see, we'll do so by overriding the version of the property.

Next, we added the keyword `required` to the initializer with no arguments. It's very useful to have an initializer like this one that sets every property to a default value. The designer of this class thought it was so useful that he wanted to ensure that any subclass that's created from it also provides such an initializer. Adding `required` to the initializer achieves that because the Swift compiler will ensure that subclasses also implement an `init()` initializer; furthermore, it will ensure that it's also marked as required so that subclasses of the subclass have the same obligation. In `ColoredCircleClass`, we'll set a default `color` in our version of this initializer.

Finally, we added a `reset()` method that reverts the radius property to its default value. We'll need to override this in our subclass to also reset the circle's new `color` property.

We know what we have to do. Let's do it. As you read through what follows, add the new code to your playground. As you go along, you will encounter errors and warnings; don't worry about those because we'll fix them as we go along.

First, we need to create our subclass and tell the Swift compiler that its base class is `CircleClass`. Here's how we do that:

```
class ColoredCircleClass : CircleClass {
}
```

This is the normal way to start a class definition, which tells Swift that `ColoredCircleClass` has `CircleClass` as its base class. Any class can have exactly one base class, which must be declared in this way. As you'll see soon, it can also claim conformance to one or more `protocols`, which would also be listed here.

Next, we add the new stored property:

```
class ColoredCircleClass : CircleClass {
    var color: UIColor = UIColor.black
}
```

The type of our property is `UIColor`—a class from the UIKit framework that represents a color. We've initialized the property to a `UIColor` instance that represents black. Next, let's override the `description` property to add our color to the returned string. Here's how we do that:

```
class ColoredCircleClass : CircleClass {
    var color: UIColor = UIColor.black

    override var description: String {
        return super.description + ", color \(color)"
    }
}
```

The first thing to notice is the `override` keyword, which tells the compiler that we are aware that there is already a definition of a `description` property in the base class and we are intentionally overriding it. In some languages, it's very easy to accidentally create a method or a property of the same name as something in the base class without realizing it. That can lead to bugs that are hard to find.

The new implementation of this property first calls the base class version using the expression `super.description`. The keyword `super` tells the compiler that we want to reference the description property of our super class (the one from which we are derived), not our own. Having done that, it then adds a string representation of our color property. The result will be that the description will include both the radius (from the super class) and the color (from this class).

Moving on, we need to add the required override of the init() initializer. Here it is:

```
required init() {
    super.init()
}
```

Every initializer is required to ensure that all the properties of its own class are initialized, and then ensure that its base class does the same. We only have the color property, and it is initialized at the point of declaration. So all we have to do is give the base class an opportunity to initialize its own state, which we do by calling super.init(). If we had any other properties that we needed to initialize, the compiler requires us to set them before calling super.init(). Also, note the required keyword, which is necessary because the base class init() is marked as required.

■ **Note** We said earlier that marking the base class init() initializer as required makes it mandatory for any subclass to implement the same initializer. Up to this point, our ColoredCircleClass did not have an explicit init() initializer, yet there was no error. Why? The reason is that since ColoredCircleClass has no other initializers, the compiler created the init() initializer for us, which satisfies the base class requirement.

Next, we need an initializer that sets nondefault radius and color values. Add the following code to the class:

```
init(radius: Double, color: UIColor) {
    self.color = color
    super.init(radius: radius)
}
```

We first set the value of our Color property from the initializer argument, and then we pass the radius value to the initializer of the base class. That's all we need to do.

The last thing we need to do is override the reset() method to reset the color property to black. By now, you should be familiar with what's required:

```
override func reset() {
    super.reset()
    color = UIColor.black
}
```

As before, the override key tells the compiler that we are overriding a method from the base class (by the way, if we mistyped the name and called it, say, "resets", the compiler would complain that there is no such method in the base class; that's another benefit we get from the override keyword). The rest of this method follows the pattern you've seen before; do your part of the work—and delegate to the base class to do its part using the super keyword to invoke the base class method. Here, it doesn't matter whether we do our part first, or call the base class method first—in other words, this version would also work:

```
override func reset() {
    color = UIColor.black
    super.reset()
}
```

That's it. Let's try out the default initializer:

```
var coloredCircle = ColoredCircleClass()
coloredCircle.radius            // Result: 1
coloredCircle.color             // Result: black
coloredCircle.description
        // Result: "Circle of radius 1.0, color UIDeviceWhiteColorSpace 0 1"
```

Now let's try out the other initializer:

```
coloredCircle = ColoredCircleClass(radius: 20, color: UIColor.red())
coloredCircle.radius     // Result: 20
coloredCircle.color      // Result: red
coloredCircle.description
// Result: "Circle of radius 20.0, color UIDeviceRGBColorSpace 1 0 0 1"
```

Subclassing is a very useful technique. Every example that you see in this book will use at least one subclass! It's worth taking the time to review the "Initialization" and "Inheritance" sections in Apple's *Swift Programming Language* book. There are a lot of subtle details that we didn't have time to cover here.

Protocols

A **protocol** is the declaration of a group of methods, initializers, and properties to which a class, structure, or enumeration can conform by providing implementations of them. As you'll see throughout this book, protocols are frequently used to define objects known as **delegates**, which provide hooks that allow you to customize the behavior of framework classes, react to events, and so forth.

Here's the definition of a protocol called Resizable:

```
protocol Resizable {
    var width: Float { get set }
    var height: Float { get set }

    init(width: Float, height: Float)
    func resizeBy( wFactor: Float, hFactor: Float) -> Void
}
```

The Resizable protocol requires any type that claims conformance to it to provide the two properties, one initializer, and one function that it declares. Notice that the protocol itself does not define anything; it simply dictates what a conforming type must do. Here's a class called Rectangle that conforms to the Resizable protocol:

```
class Rectangle : Resizable, CustomStringConvertible {
    var width: Float
    var height: Float
    var description: String {
        return "Rectangle, width \(width), height \(height)"
    }

    required init(width: Float, height: Float) {
        self.width = width
        self.height = height
    }
```

```
    func resizeBy( wFactor: Float, hFactor: Float) -> Void {
        width *= wFactor
        height *= hFactor
    }
}
```

A type declares that it conforms to a protocol by including the protocol name after the name of its base class, if any, in its declaration. This class conforms to both the Resizable protocol and the CustomStringConvertible protocol, which is defined in the Swift standard library.

As you can see, the class provides the actual implementation of the features required by the Resizable protocol. If a protocol requires the implementation of an initializer, then that initializer must be marked as required, as shown here. Instances of types that conform to a protocol can be assigned to variables of the protocol's type, like this:

```
let r: Resizable = Rectangle(width: 10, height: 20)
```

Conformance to the CustomStringConvertible protocol requires the type to provide a String property called description, which is used when a human-readable representation of the type is required. In particular, this property is used when an instance of the conforming type is passed as an argument to the print() function:

```
let rect = Rectangle(width: 10, height: 20)
print(rect)    // Prints "Rectangle, width 10.0, height 20.0"
```

Extensions

Extensions are a powerful feature that Swift shares with Objective-C. An extension allows you to add functionality to any class, structure, or enumeration, including those in the standard Swift library or the system frameworks. The syntax of an extension definition is similar to that of classes and structures. The extension is introduced by the keyword extension followed by the name of the extended type and then the extensions themselves. You can add computed (but not stored) properties, methods, initializers, nested types, and protocol conformance to the extended type.

In Chapter 16, we use an extension to add a method to the UIColor class (from the UIKit framework) that returns a random color. Here's how the extension is defined:

```
extension UIColor {
    class func randomColor() -> UIColor {
        let red = CGFloat(Double((arc4random() % 256))/255)
        let green = CGFloat(Double(arc4random() % 256)/255)
        let blue = CGFloat(Double(arc4random() % 256)/255)
        return UIColor(red: red, green: green, blue: blue, alpha:1.0)
    }
}
```

And here's how it's used:

```
let randomColor = UIColor.randomColor()
```

Summary

So now you've had a tour of the most important features of Swift. What you've seen here is by no means everything there is to know. We've left out quite a lot (and simplified some of the rest) and you should read the official documentation (or one of the books listed in Chapter 1) to expand your knowledge, when you have the time. In the meantime, turn back to Chapter 3 (or where you left off in the main part of this book) and start writing your first iOS application with Swift.

Index

Get the eBook for only $4.99!

Why limit yourself?

Now you can take the weightless companion with you wherever you go and access your content on your PC, phone, tablet, or reader.

Since you've purchased this print book, we are happy to offer you the eBook for just $4.99.

Convenient and fully searchable, the PDF version enables you to easily find and copy code—or perform examples by quickly toggling between instructions and applications.

To learn more, go to http://www.apress.com/us/shop/companion or contact support@apress.com.

CPSIA information can be obtained
at www.ICGtesting.com
Printed in the USA
LVOW04s1551020617
536736LV00004B/223/P